LEONARD AND VIRGINIA WOOLF
AS PUBLISHERS:
THE HOGARTH PRESS, 1917–41

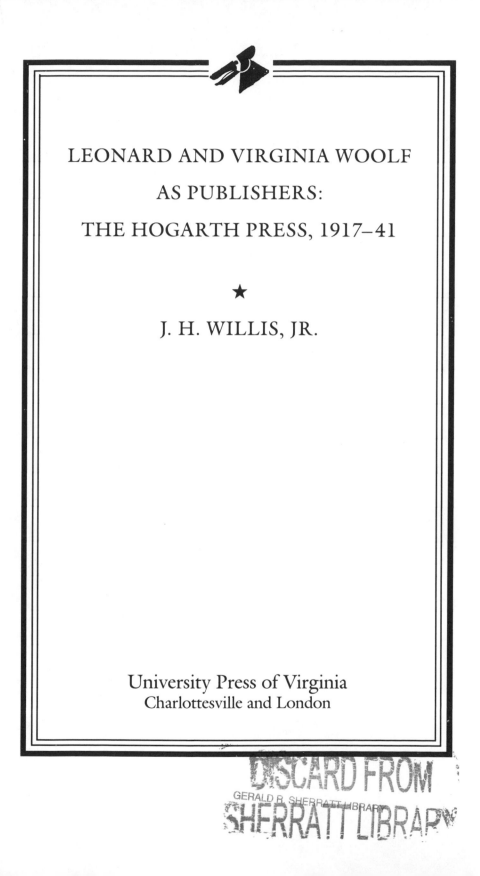

LEONARD AND VIRGINIA WOOLF

AS PUBLISHERS:

THE HOGARTH PRESS, 1917–41

★

J. H. WILLIS, JR.

University Press of Virginia
Charlottesville and London

THE UNIVERSITY PRESS OF VIRGINIA
Copyright © 1992 by the Rector and Visitors
of the University of Virginia

First published 1992

Library of Congress Cataloging-in-Publication Data
Willis, J. H. (John H.), 1929–
   Leonard and Virginia Woolf as publishers : the Hogarth Press,
1917–41 / J. H. Willis, Jr.
      p.   cm.
   Includes bibliographical references and index.
   ISBN 0-8139-1361-6
   1. Hogarth Press—History.   2. Woolf, Virginia, 1882–1941—
Knowledge—Publishers and publishing.   3. Woolf, Leonard,
1880–1969—Knowledge—Publishers and publishing.   4. Publishers and
publishing—England—History—20th century.   5. Woolf, Virginia,
1882–1941—Knowledge—Printing.   6. Woolf, Leonard, 1880–1969—
Knowledge—Printing.   7. Private presses—England—History—20th
century.   8. Printing—England—History—20th century.
Z232.H73W54   1992
070.5'09421—dc20   91-41505
                                                            CIP

Printed in the United States of America

To *Anne*
and to
John, Tom, and Susan

CONTENTS

ILLUSTRATIONS

★

following page 168

PREFACE

F irst with a handpress, then with a treadle-operated press, then
with commercial printers, the writers Leonard and Virginia
Woolf became publishers. They began as amateur printers seeking diversion from the demands of their work and became professionals who earned an important part of their income through the
business. They founded the Hogarth Press in 1917, in the midst of war,
and saw it through a depression and into a second world war. After Virginia committed suicide in 1941, the press went on under Leonard's direction with his partner John Lehmann; and it continues today as part of a
larger publishing corporation years after the dissolution of the partnership in 1946 and Leonard's death in 1969. But with Virginia's suicide and
the grinding on of the war, the press took a different shape and responded
to different times.

What interests me is the nature of the Hogarth Press between 1917
and 1941, how it came into being, how it survived and prospered under
the Woolfs' guidance with the help of John Lehmann and various assistants, what it published, how it related to other publishers. My narrative
tells of a small but individualistic and dynamic publishing enterprise and
describes the critical and commercial success of some of the 474 titles the
Woolfs published between the wars.

This history of the Hogarth Press is about the Woolfs and Bloomsbury, about Virginia as a writer and partner in publishing, and about
Leonard as a writer and managing director of the press. It chronicles one
of the most notable achievements of Bloomsbury. But the history of the
press is also about Freud, Chekhov, Tolstoy, Rilke, Keynes, H. G. Wells,
Vita Sackville-West, T. S. Eliot, Christopher Isherwood, and many of the
other authors who published their books and pamphlets with the press.

The very diversity and heterogeneity of the Hogarth Press writers and their publications characterize the broad interests of the press's author-publishers, Virginia and Leonard Woolf. With the exception of publications on political and social subjects, mostly attributable to Leonard, and the poetry and prose of the young 1930s writers, mostly attributable to John Lehmann, the press offerings do not reveal a clear or consistent plan of development. The Woolfs and their assistants cultivated Bloomsbury friends as authors, and Leonard would solicit manuscripts on political subjects from Fabian Society or Labour party associates, but the Woolfs cannot be said to have shaped their publications deliberately to any predetermined aesthetic or ideological end. They, as most publishers of the time, were guided largely by what manuscripts came to them.

Nor can much of a case be made, I think, for the influence of one line of books or pamphlets, say the political, on another line, say the poetry or fiction. Did the psychoanalytical books and pamphlets, for example, influence the availability or number of manuscripts and the subsequent publication by Hogarth of poetry, fiction, international affairs, literary criticism? I think not. Freudianism as an intellectual movement affected both literature and social and political thought between the wars, and the Hogarth Press was the sole publisher in England of Freudian works in translation. But the Freudian influence is a story well told by others and beyond the scope of this history. Nevertheless, I hope that this account of the Hogarth Press, broadening out from the Woolfs and Bloomsbury, will add new information to the intellectual and social history of England between the wars.

I have generally followed chronology in this history of the Hogarth Press, dividing the period from 1917 to 1941 into five phases of development and thus into five chapters: 1917–23, the first years at Hogarth House, Richmond; 1924–30, the great development of the press after the Woolfs moved into Tavistock Square, Bloomsbury; 1931–32, the period of John Lehmann's first association with the press as a manager; 1933–37, the politically active thirties; and 1938–41, the period of John Lehmann's partnership at the press with Leonard, concluding with Virginia's suicide during the early war years.

For a more thorough examination of certain types of press publications, I have interrupted the chronology of the press's development three times with separate chapters on the Russian translations in the early 1920s, on the political, social, and international publications of the 1920s and 1930s, and on the publication of Freud's work and the International Psycho-Analytical Library in the 1920s and 1930s. And I have begun the history with a chapter devoted to the beginnings of the press with the Woolfs' handprinting and concluded it with a chapter examining the press as a business.

Narrating the historical development of the press, I have seldom called attention to the enormous differences between the publishing enterprise in England between the wars and that same enterprise today. So it seems to me worth suggesting to readers that they notice in the following pages the intimate personal relations in the Hogarth Press business, the small scale of operations, the pressruns of a few thousand copies, the marginal profits, the correspondence written and sometimes returned with an answer the same day, the swift passage from manuscript to published book often in a matter of weeks or a month or two at most. In the midst of present-day publishing giants and the obliterating tide of so many books, readers and publishers may look at the operation of the Hogarth Press with amusement, perhaps with disbelief, possibly with nostalgia. Most of all, I hope readers will look with admiration at what Leonard and Virginia Woolf achieved as publishers in the context of their times and will see the Hogarth Press as a brilliant addition to their accomplishments as writers and intellectuals.

The problem I faced at the outset over ten years ago was the apparent absence of records. There were papers, letters, diaries aplenty by the Woolfs, an embarrassment of riches on Bloomsbury, and a few documents relevant to the Hogarth Press, but no detailed publisher's records. Nigel Nicolson, writer and editor of Virginia Woolf's letters, generously interested himself in my project, encouraged me, and introduced me to Mrs. Norah Smallwood, then Director of Chatto & Windus and the Hogarth Press. She, in turn, led me to the dark, cluttered storage and packing room at the press offices in William IV Street, presided over by Les Booth, mail clerk and book packer extraordinaire. With his help I uncovered thirty-two file boxes of Hogarth Press records containing over six hundred separate files on press authors and their books. Covered with a thick layer of grime, the boxes had not been opened in over twenty years and had been overlooked by previous writers on the Woolfs and their press. The yellowing contents of these boxes provided me with the basic data necessary for a full-length analysis of the press. They reside now, tidy, catalogued, and available to everyone, in the library of the University of Reading.

Other sources and consultants were indispensable to me in researching this history. The late George Spater kindly allowed me to work in his private collection of press publications, the most complete in existence. The Woolf papers at the University of Sussex Library, especially the early account book, the papers at the Berg Collection in New York, and the collections at the University of Texas provided essential information. And most important of all, J. Howard Woolmer's *Checklist of the Hogarth Press,* in its first and then revised editions, gave me meticulously accurate bibliographical information without which this history would have been unthinkable. And, as every writer on the Woolfs must be, I am deeply indebted to the excellent editorial work of Anne Olivier Bell on Virginia Woolf's diaries and of Nigel Nicolson on Virginia's letters. During the time I have worked on this history of the press, the number of articles and books on the Woolfs and Bloomsbury has run on unabated, and I have tried to take account of the new information and insights as each became available. Certainly, I am grateful for all those who have written on the Woolfs.

Support for the research and writing of this history have come from a number of sources, but most importantly from the National Endowment for the Humanities, which provided both a Summer Grant and a Faculty Fellowship, and from the College of William and Mary, which provided two Summer Research Grants and a Semester Research Assignment.

For permission to quote from unpublished letters and records, I wish to thank: The Harry Ransom Humanities Research Center, the University of Texas at Austin for the Leonard Woolf papers and the John Lehmann papers; the Manuscripts Section of the University of Sussex Library for the Monks House Papers and the Leonard Woolf Papers; Chatto & Windus-the Hogarth Press for the Press records; Jill Balcon and the Peters Fraser & Dunlop Group Ltd. for C. Day-Lewis; the Provost and Scholars of King's College, Cambridge, for E. M. Forster; S.

Yorke for Henry Green; Elizabeth Friedman for Laura Riding Jackson; Mrs. Richard Kennedy for Richard Kennedy; Miles Huddleston for John Lehmann; Sir Rupert Hart-Davis for William Plomer; Janet Adam Smith for Michael Roberts; Nigel Nicolson for Vita Sackville-West; the Society of Authors on behalf of the Bernard Shaw Estate for Bernard Shaw; Stephen Spender; Ian Douglas Stone for D. T. Stone; Trekkie Parsons for Leonard Woolf.

I am grateful for the kindness and professional assistance of the manuscript and special collections librarians who provided access to the primary sources of my research. They are Elizabeth Inglis of the University of Sussex Library, Michael Bott of the University of Reading Library, Leila Ludeking of Washington State University Library, Cathy Henderson of the Humanities Research Center, University of Texas–Austin, the late Lola Szladits of the Berg Collection, New York Public Library, and P. J. Croft of King's College Library, Cambridge University.

I owe a debt of gratitude to the William and Mary librarians who assisted me in many ways, especially to Carol Linton, our Interlibrary Loan Librarian, and to our reference librarians Hope Yelich, Nolan Yelich, Bettina Manzo, Carol McAllister, and Del Moore.

I am especially grateful to Nigel Nicolson, Stephen Spender, J. Howard Woolmer, George Spater, and Hermione Lee, who read sections of this history and generously shared their expert knowledge with me to improve my text. And I am grateful to those present and former faculty colleagues who have read portions of the manuscript and made helpful suggestions: Tom Heacox, especially, and Kathy Hill, Alex Kallos, and Jim McCord.

During the years of this work in progress, I have benefited from the labors of graduate research assistants Celeste Goodrich, David Rose, Lee Canter, Eugenia Cook, Michael Hawks, Ben Madison, Melissa Edeburn, Kim Babcock, Katie Calvano, and Ashley King. I want to thank them for their help.

I also want to thank our departmental secretary Martha Smith for assistance with correspondence related to this project and to editorial assistant David Morrill for help with computer programming. I am grateful to secretary Kim Sands Thomas, who began transcribing the manuscript. Most especially I am grateful for the patience, perseverance, outstanding skill, and unfailing cheerfulness of Bonnie Chandler, who prepared this manuscript and saw it through its many stages of revision. I could not have completed this work without her.

Above all, I owe more than I can tell to the humor, encouragement, and love of my wife Anne, who has supported me in this project and read so many of my words, and to our children John, Tom, and Susan, who have also provided spirited and loving support.

ABBREVIATIONS

AAR   Author's Accounts (Reading), Hogarth Press account book in the University of Reading Library.

ABR   Account Book (Reading), Hogarth Press account book in the University of Reading Library, continuing the first account book at Sussex.

ABS   Account Book (Sussex), the first Hogarth Press account book, in the University of Sussex Library.

Beginning   Leonard Woolf, *Beginning Again: An Autobiography of the Years 1911 to 1918* (New York: Harcourt, Brace & World, 1964).

Checklist   J. Howard Woolmer, *A Checklist of the Hogarth Press, 1917–1946* (Revere, Pa.: Woolmer/Brotherson, 1986).

Diary   Virginia Woolf, *The Diary of Virginia Woolf,* ed. Anne Olivier Bell, 4 vols. (New York: Harcourt Brace Jovanovich, 1977–84).

Downhill   Leonard Woolf, *Downhill All the Way: An Autobiography of the Years 1919 to 1939* (New York: Harcourt, Brace & World, 1967).

Growing   Leonard Woolf, *Growing: An Autobiography of the Years 1904–1911* (New York: Harcourt, Brace & World, 1961).

HP   Hogarth Press files, University of Reading Library.

Journey   Leonard Woolf, *The Journey Not the Arrival Matters: An Autobiography of the Years 1939 to 1969* (London: Hogarth Press, 1969).

Letters   Virginia Woolf, *The Letters of Virginia Woolf,* ed. Nigel Nicolson and Joanne Trautmann, 6 vols. (New York: Harcourt Brace Jovanovich, 1975–80).

LWP   Leonard Woolf Papers, University of Sussex Library.

MHP   Monks House Papers of Virginia and Leonard Woolf, University of Sussex Library.

MSR   Monthly Sales (Reading), Hogarth Press account book in the University of Reading Library.

Sowing   Leonard Woolf, *Sowing: An Autobiography of the Years 1880–1904* (London: Hogarth Press, 1960).

LEONARD AND VIRGINIA WOOLF
AS PUBLISHERS:
THE HOGARTH PRESS, 1917–41

CHAPTER ONE

★

THE HANDPRESS

On her thirty-third birthday in 1915, a frosty, brisk, and cheerful January 25, as Virginia Woolf recorded it in her diary, she was surprised by Leonard's birthday gifts: a green purse, a first edition of *The Abbot* by Sir Walter Scott, a trip uptown to see the war films at the Picture Palace (they left without seeing them after waiting an hour and a half), and a treat at Buszard's Tea Rooms in Oxford Street. "Sitting at tea," she wrote, "we decided three things: in the first place to take Hogarth, if we can get it; in the second, to buy a Printing press; in the third, to buy a Bull dog, probably called John" (*Diary* 1:28). Leonard gave her a packet of sweets for the train ride home to 17 The Green, Richmond. There is no further mention of John the bulldog, but the Woolfs soon bought Hogarth House in Richmond, and they purchased a handpress two years later, thereby combining house and new hobby into the Hogarth Press. The realization of the birthday vows significantly changed their lives.

Hogarth House, built by Lord Suffield in 1720 and divided into two houses in the nineteenth century, was beautiful; as Leonard Woolf described it, "every room except one was perfectly proportioned and panelled; there was quite a good garden" (*Beginning* 171). In this comfortable house the Woolfs found a more permanent home after temporary residences in their first two years of marriage. The move on March 25, however, was complicated and darkened by Virginia's bout of mental illness which had begun in mid-February. Leonard moved alone, Virginia then under the care of nurses in a nursing home, and she did not spend a night in the new house until April. Only in June did she begin to recover, to enjoy the house, garden, and nearby parks. The Woolfs found Hogarth

House a pleasant and convenient place in which to live and work. It was close enough to the city for business, pleasure, and friends and to easy rail connections south to their weekend and summer place in Sussex, first Asheham House and then Monks House in Rodmell. It was just far enough removed from Bloomsbury to provide some sense of peace and protection from the more exciting, yet potentially disturbing, social stimulus of their many friends.

Between Hogarth House and Sussex during nine years, the Woolfs established their married lives and began the first phase of their careers. Leonard was increasingly active in Fabian Society affairs with the Webbs and the Labour party; he wrote numerous articles, reviews, and essays; served as editor of the International Section of the *Contemporary Review* (1919–20); became literary editor of the *Nation and Athenaeum* (1923); and published five pamphlets and five books including the collection of his fiction, *Stories of the East* (1921). Virginia, during this period, wrote and published over two hundred reviews or articles, two separately published stories, and four books, including her first three novels, *The Voyage Out* (1915), *Night and Day* (1919), and *Jacob's Room* (1922). In addition to their enormous personal productivity during these years, the Woolfs established the Hogarth Press and developed it from a hobby into a thriving publishing venture.

From the time the Woolfs purchased their first handpress in March 1917 until March 1924 when they moved to London's Tavistock Square, Leonard and Virginia Woolf hand set and printed eighteen books and published eighteen others using commercial printers, for a total of thirty-six titles.[1] When the Woolfs moved into Bloomsbury, they did so partly because of their desire to be closer to work and friends and partly to provide more room for the rapidly expanding press and its staff. The Hogarth Press by then had become a small publishing house. From Richmond to Tavistock Square, and through a subsequent move to Mecklenburgh Square in 1939, the Woolfs and the Hogarth Press were never separated, always living under the same roof with their creation. Some of the manuscripts were read and evaluated at Asheham House or Monks House in Rodmell, Sussex, so that the work of the press often continued in the country even though the editorial offices, staff assistants, and press itself were in London. Only an act of war, the disastrous bombing of

Mecklenburgh Square in September 1940, caused the Woolfs finally to sever their physical bond with the press. The large treadle press they then had was put in storage in Rodmell, and John Lehmann, Leonard's partner at the time, moved the editorial and staff operations to the temporary shelter of the Garden City Press at Letchworth.

Amateur printers and their private presses are inclined to begin and sustain their printing on the kitchen table or a workbench in any available attic, basement, or garage, but the Woolfs appear unique in using their drawing room for a start. It is also unusual to find a private press growing into a small publishing house with staff and managers still working in the same premises occupied by the proprietors. Neither Leonard nor Virginia seems to have considered any other arrangement. Almost their first criterion when house hunting in 1924 and 1939 was to find a residence large enough to accommodate the press operations. Convenience and economy were certainly important, but so too, one suspects, was their personal need to remain close to their creation. John Lehmann says flatly that he discovered in the early 1930s "that both the Woolfs, but in particular Leonard, had an emotional attitude towards the Press; as if it were the child their marriage had never produced."[2] Dream child or not, the press was always for Leonard a very personal achievement from which he and Virginia could not long be physically separated, and in his old age he rather glumly predicted that the press "as an entity" would surely die with him and be buried in his grave (*Journey* 123). His words proved a premature obituary, for the Hogarth Press continues today as a publisher under the compatible direction of the Chatto & Windus group, although its existence as a personal entity of the Woolfs ceased well before Leonard's death in 1969.

Neither Virginia nor Leonard could possibly have foreseen in 1915 over tea at Buszard's or in 1917 in their drawing room that the amusing and exciting pastime they were beginning would so complicate and enrich their lives for the next twenty-five years and more. Their reasons for buying a handpress in the first place seem simple enough; their motives for continuing to print and publish were more complex. Leonard explained in his autobiography the need they felt in 1915–17 to find some sort of engaging relief from their strenuous literary, journalistic, and political activities. Even the change to criticism or review writing from the

arduous struggles over her early fiction gave Virginia some moderate relief, some refreshing change of pace; but it was not enough.

Leonard moved from committee work to writing long reports for
the Fabian Society, to writing his first books on international politics and
economics. He was deeply involved in all these projects with Sidney and
Beatrice Webb, formidable and indefatigable founder-directors of the Fabian Society, and the strain of this relationship was felt by Virginia. In
February 1915, on the eve of her breakdown, she seems to have viewed the
purchase of a press as a means of extracting Leonard from the clutches of
the Webbs. "We're both so excited that we can talk and think of nothing
else," she wrote, "and I think there's a chance of damaging the Webb
influence irretrievably, (which is my ambition in life)" (*Letters* 2:59). The
Webbs, she thought, had "their claws fixed in his entrails" (ibid., 68).

The Woolfs' weekend amusements were simple and necessarily fru-
gal, a bus trip up the river from Richmond, a walk in Hampton Court,
Kingston, or Kew Gardens, tea, perhaps a treat or two, and home. What
both of them needed was a pastime more refreshing and stimulating than
a weekend stroll. "The difficulty with Virginia," as Leonard recounted,
"was to find any play sufficiently absorbing" (*Beginning* 233). They discussed printing as a possibility which interested them both. "It struck
me," he continued, "that it would be a good thing if Virginia had a manual occupation of this kind which, in say the afternoons, would take her
mind completely off her work."

Virginia seems to have tried something of the sort early in 1914, as
she recuperated from a suicidal bout of mental illness, by asking to type
Lytton Strachey's manuscripts. She spent the afternoons typing Strachey's *Ermyntrude and Esmeralda,* the erotic, comic epistolary exchanges between two Victorian girls about bowwows and pouting pussies. All the
more reason for Leonard to think of a press as therapy for Virginia, after
her second major mental illness in 1915. But how characteristic and representative it is of these two products of the Victorian era to find a recreation requiring hard work which produced a useful product. Printing was
earnest, skilled play. Printing required dedication. It was undeniably manual, until it became pedal with a treadle platen machine. It was messy and
inky, and thoroughly satisfying to body and mind. Not everyone could

do it, and something of value was produced which could be shared with friends.

Before the pleasures of typing *Ermyntrude* or printing in the drawing room, Virginia's youthful recreations were appropriate to a late nineteenth-century, upper-middle-class girlhood, as enriched or modified by the presence of her father, Leslie Stephen, eminent Victorian man of letters. There were the expected exercises in female accomplishments— drawing, dancing, music, and even riding—but neither Virginia nor her sister Vanessa were particularly apt pupils. Vanessa, of course, showed early promise in drawing, but Virginia found little pleasure in any of these genteel recreations. More pleasing to her were the bathing during the summers at St. Ives, lawn bowling, and family cricket (Virginia was the "demon bowler"); there were long walks with Father, the prodigious pedestrian, Alpine climber, and instigator of twenty-mile Sunday tramps; there was, passionately for a few years, "bug" hunting for moths and butterflies with brother Thoby and Vanessa; there was the juvenile family newspaper the *Hyde Park Gate News* to which, appropriately, Virginia was a precocious contributor. Curiously, there was no printing, even though small tabletop handpresses had become popular amusements in many Victorian households, and ladies were encouraged to print in the bou-doir.[3] Virginia and Vanessa did have a short fling with a "silver point press" in 1905 which produced "little reddy brown" reproductions of their drawings or prints (*Letters* 2:173–74). But most significantly among Virginia's recreations, there was bookbinding.

Virginia began binding books sometime in 1901 when she was nineteen. It was both the latest of her youthful recreations and the only one requiring some of the materials, craft, manual skill, and visual creativity of Vanessa's art. For Virginia, adoring, dependent, and yet competitive with and sometimes envious of her older sister, bookbinding must have been a particularly satisfying occupation as it approximated Vanessa's activity. Both girls received instruction in their art—Virginia from Miss Power, Vanessa from Mr. Cope's School of Art and, by 1902, the Academy Schools. Vanessa had her studio, and Virginia had her equivalent—the old nursery at the top of the stairs which she furnished with her high-standing desk, bookcases, worktables, and bright blue curtains. Virginia often wrote standing up, which seems patterned after Vanessa's stance at her easel. Both sisters took their activities seriously, but Virginia's book-binding was more of a hobby or recreation than Vanessa's art. "What Books have you got?" she wrote Thoby in May 1902. "I am really rather a good binder" (*Letters* 1:52).

Virginia could share her excitement and bookbinding skills with her beloved older cousin Emma Vaughan. She wrote to Emma in 1902: "Do come to lunch—then we can begin directly afterwards. . . . I have been making endless experiments and almost smelt my room out this after-noon trying to do gold lettering. Tomorrow I shall experiment with gold on cloth. I believe there is an immense field for this kind of thing. There seem ever so many ways of making covers—of leather—linen—silk—parchment—vellum—japanese paper, etc. etc. etc. which the ordinary lidders never think of" (*Letters* 1:56). Virginia's exuberant experimenta-tion with materials, including Japanese paper, foreshadowed one of the characteristics of the early Hogarth Press books. Printed and often bound by Leonard and Virginia, the books had special papers as covers—many hand-painted or mottled by Vanessa or Roger Fry or imported from Eu-rope. Virginia's experiments early in 1903 also went beyond materials to technique for, as she wrote to Thoby, "I have invented a new way of bookbinding, which takes half the time, is just as strong etc. etc. etc." (ibid., 67).

In addition to her lessons from Miss Powers and her workshop ex-periments shared with Emma Vaughan, Virginia may have learned some of her techniques from a textbook by Douglas Cockerell, one of the great bookbinders of the late nineteenth and early twentieth centuries. After working in the famed Doves Bindary, Cockerell became an instructor in art binding at the London Central School for Arts and Crafts in 1900 and published his influential *Bookbinding and the Care of Books* a year later. The Woolfs had a copy of it in their collection.[4]

Virginia's bookbinding coincided with the development of the arts and crafts movement from the 1890s to the early 1900s. Whatever interest in bookbinding she owed to an awareness of the crafts movement or to Cockerell's text, Virginia was no disciple of William Morris and his Kelmscott Press. The Stephen household, for all its easy familiarity with George Meredith, Thomas Hardy, Henry James, John Morley, F. M.

Maitland, and other Victorian men of letters, apparently took little notice of Morris. It was characteristic of Virginia's generation to reject Victorian style. As she wrote from a house she was visiting with her family in April 1902: "This place where we are staying is a *sham* country cottage—all white paint and Morris patterns, and green wood furniture. I can't bear the washy-artistic style and I long for something honestly ugly" (*Letters* 1:50).

Many of the books Virginia bound or re-covered, before the Hogarth Press books, are in the Woolf collection at Washington State University. They show the skill she had developed and her taste in materials. None of the re-covered books are expensively or elaborately designed. Interesting in this regard are the volumes of Leslie Stephen's edition of Edward Arber's *English Garner* (1877–83), a seven-volume anthology of poetry and prose, mostly Elizabethan. Virginia re-covered volumes 3–7 of the well-used set, using such materials as blue wrappers, "semi-limp morocco leather," stiff blue paper, and red cloth. On the spine of volume 4, she stamped in gilt a monogram heart enclosing the initial "V."[5] She rejected the high art style for the practical and workmanlike binding, which agrees with her professional approach to books.

For all their dependence on books, neither Leslie Stephen nor his daughter Virginia were collectors or bibliophiles to any marked degree. The library at Hyde Park Gate, as Virginia Woolf recalled, was large, unexpurgated, and always available to her at fifteen. It was a working library more than a collection of valuable or rare editions, and Leslie Stephen with self-deprecating humor called the books "mangy and worthless."[6] But there were loved and prized volumes in Virginia's own library, aesthetically pleasing if not of rare value. For example, there was the birthday gift from her father in 1897, when she was fifteen, of John Lockhart's *Life of Sir Walter Scott*—"ten most exquisite little volumes, half bound in purple leather, with gilt scrolls and twirls and thistles everywhere, and a most artistic blue and brown mottling on their other parts."[7] She delighted in her "beloved leather backed books standing up so handsome in their shelves," as she wrote Madge Vaughan in 1904 (*Letters* 1:167). There was Clive Bell's Christmas present in 1908 of Byron. "Then I saw the margins," she wrote, "and the binding, and the print. The magnificence was overwhelming" (ibid., 376).

At least from her nineteenth year, therefore, Virginia had an appreciative and practical knowledge of bookbinding to add to her love of books, newly printed or leather bound. Above all, she appreciated books as a formidable reader, writer, and professional literary journalist. Only a very few of the hundreds of titles mentioned in her letters and diaries are described as objects, and these are usually gift books. Collecting books, conversing with sellers of old books, reading for hours in a library, writing at a stand-up desk, or hand binding books in a converted nursery with white walls and blue curtains doesn't lead inexorably to a handpress and a publishing venture at age thirty-three, but these experiences must have predisposed Virginia Woolf to the idea of a press and partly determined what sort of printing and binding she would do with Leonard.

Leonard Woolf was also a prodigious reader and lover of books. At Trinity College, Cambridge, he was a serious-minded member of the Apostles, the intellectually rarefied society of undergraduates including Lytton Strachey and John Maynard Keynes. Books, conversations about them, and occasional weekend reading parties absorbed the young Woolf. When he went down from Cambridge, sailing out to Ceylon in 1904 as a cadet in the Ceylon Civil Service, he took with him his clothes, a fox terrier, and some of his prized books—the Oxford University Press miniature edition of Shakespeare, a four-volume set of Milton given to him by Desmond MacCarthy, and "ninety large volumes of the beautiful eighteenth century edition of Voltaire printed in the Baskerville type."[8]

In the course of their lives, the Woolfs amassed thousands of books. They were energetic consumers of books, readers with vast interests, professional reviewers and editors. They enjoyed fine books, but they were not meticulous bibliophiles concerned with the beautiful and rare. George Spater vividly described the Monks House collection: "From the collector's point of view the Woolfs, like Dr. Johnson, were singularly careless about most of their books, which were allowed to accumulate dust, spider webs and defunct spiders. . . . Books were everywhere; some on shelves, some on floors; the whole house was a mass of reading material—perhaps some 5,000 to 6,000 volumes—collected by two of the most sensitive and intelligent people of our era."[9]

So it would seem that the Woolfs' early experience with books, their reading, collecting, criticizing, and reviewing, shaped their later approach to printing and publishing. The experience of relatives and friends—their private printing of pamphlets and poems and the development of Roger Fry's Omega Workshops—also may have stimulated the Woolfs to purchase a press in 1915.

To the amusement of Virginia, Thoby Stephen, while he was a Cambridge undergraduate in 1904, wrote a pamphlet attacking the practice of compulsory chapel and, in the customary way at the time, had it privately printed and circulated among friends. Even more amusing to Virginia was *Euphrosyne,* a volume of poetry anonymously arranged by Clive Bell and privately printed in 1905 containing poems by the melancholy but "ever youthful poets," as she called them: Lytton Strachey, Leonard Woolf, Clive Bell, Saxon Sydney-Turner, Walter Lamb, and others (*Letters* 1:202). These somewhat haphazard and youthful publications gave way to the later efforts of the Woolfs and their Bloomsbury friends, who, in addition to their frequent contributions to journals, sought established publishing houses for their longer works.

By 1915, when the Woolfs made their birthday resolutions, the Bloomsbury friends had published a number of significant works through established publishers. But they were often writing or editing shorter pieces—poems, stories, essays—which were not easily placed with the larger commercial publishers and for which they turned to private presses or small, quality commercial presses. One of the major reasons for starting the Hogarth Press, as Leonard Woolf recalled, was to print and publish small books and pamphlets "which would have little or no chance of being published by ordinary publishers" (*Beginning* 236). Roger Fry, for example, had published his edition of Albrecht Dürer's *Record of Journeys to Venice and the Low Countries* (1913) with D. B. Updike's distinguished Merrymount Press of Boston. Clive Bell had his thirteen poems in *Ad Familiares* (1917) privately printed by Francis Meynell's Pelican Press.

It is not surprising then to find Virginia Woolf writing to Lady Robert Cecil in 1916: "We are thinking of starting a printing press, for all our friends stories. Don't you think its a good idea?" (*Letters* 2:120). And she wrote to David Garnett in July 1917 after he had admired "The Mark on the Wall," "Anyhow its very amusing to try with these short things, and the greatest mercy to be able to do what one likes—no editors, or publishers, and only people to read who more or less like that sort of thing" (ibid., 167). To escape from the unpleasant pressures of publishers and to write and print for one's friends were thus two of the powerful justifications for beginning and continuing the Hogarth Press.

The first press book was the Woolfs' *Two Stories* (1917), followed by Katherine Mansfield's *Prelude* (1918). During the first five years of its history, the press published works written either by the Woolfs or their friends. Gorky's *Reminiscences of Tolstoi* (1920) and his *Reminiscences of Tchekov* (1921) were the only exceptions. Bloomsbury authors predominate on the Hogarth list until the late 1920s, long after the Woolfs had turned to commercial printers to produce the majority of their books and pamphlets.

Roger Fry's creation and operation of the Omega Workshops from 1913 to 1919 must also be considered a formative influence on the Woolfs' interest in printing. Fry finally had seized the opportunity in 1913 to assist young artists in their long-contemplated revolution in tastes, to help them transform what Fry saw as the excrescences of Victorian ugliness into new designs—fresh, modern, and pleasurable. At the same time Fry believed that young artists needed a means of support while they developed their own art, carried on the good fight, and battled the outraged Philistines for survival and recognition. The "missionary side" to the Omega, as Quentin Bell has written, was to supply first aid to the terrible railway accident of Victorian decoration.[10] Through their carpets, pottery, fabrics, and their exuberantly decorated screens, wallpapers, and painted furniture, the Omega artists were to supply iodine and bandages to a wounded public, leaving the major surgery for later. But the first aid, added Bell, was fun.

Whatever inspiration Roger Fry may have taken from William Morris and his workshop, the Omega was quite unlike its predecessor. Fry's interests were not those of the highly skilled craftsman, and through the six-year saga of the Omega's uncertain fortunes, Fry maintained in all the workshop productions an air of the playful and improvisational. If the dyes and paint ran occasionally, if a chair came unglued, or some of the tables and trays warped, there was no worry. The freshness, the vigor of bold designs and bright colors, not the polish of craftsmanship, were important. Anyone could try his hand at anything. Vanessa Bell, Duncan

Grant, Wyndham Lewis, and others splashed about in fine style; Bell and Grant designed entire interiors; Fry, Bell, and Grant learned to throw pots, Fry becoming an inventive potter overnight. Some of the designs were also left to professional craftsmen for execution.

Although Omega artists were almost exclusively concerned with the decorative arts, Fry was not. As Denys Sutton has pointed out, it was typical that Fry, with his enormous range of interests and energy, would apply himself to publishing.[11] The four books the Omega published under Fry's direction were neither significant for the operation of the workshop nor particularly important as books, but they are of interest here because three of them were produced at the very time Leonard and Virginia Woolf were seriously planning to purchase a press. The books were A. Clutton-Brock's *Simpson's Choice* (1915), P. J. Jouve's *Men of Europe* (1915), R. C. Trevelyan's *Lucretius on Death* (1917), and Fry's *Original Woodcuts by Various Artists* (1918). The first three are thin books of poetry. *Original Woodcuts,* the last of the Omega books, was assembled by Fry and contained prints by Vanessa Bell, Fry, Duncan Grant, McKnight Kauffer (the American artist who later designed one of the wolf's-head devices for the Hogarth Press), Roald Kristian (who illustrated two Omega books), and Edward Wolfe. Virginia thought the book "very magnificent but fearfully expensive" (*Letters* 2:296).

The Omega books were generally large (11 by 8 inches) and hand-some, although thin, running to no more than sixteen pages.[12] They were printed on thick cream paper in large type with heavy black inking, the wide margins cleanly setting off the text. The initial capital letters were strikingly large. The woodcuts by Roald Kristian used as illustrations and decorations in *Simpson's Choice* and *Men of Europe* were printed with generous margins. The initial capitals and the small woodcut designs by Kristian at the beginning and end of *Men of Europe* were printed in dark red ink, making a handsome contrast to the black type and cream paper. Although Roger Fry's consistent policy at the Omega Workshop was for anonymity of the artist, he did provide the compositor's and printer's names in two of the books. *Simpson's Choice* states that it was "Printed under the direction of J. H. Mason," and *Men of Europe* that it was "Printed by Richard Madley, under the direction of the Omega Work-shops, Ltd."

It would have been entirely in character for Fry to have acquired a press, taught himself how to print, and then to have printed the Omega books himself. Instead, he turned to professionals for help. His choice of J. H. Mason to direct the printing of *Simpson's Choice* was understandable. Mason, one of the outstanding compositors, typographers, and printers of a generation of fine printers, originally had worked for Cobden-Sanderson at the Doves Press. The five-volume edition of the Bible (1903–5) hand set by Mason and printed at the Doves is a recognized masterpiece of modern printing. Mason left the Doves Press in 1909 to teach printing at the London Central School of Arts and Crafts, and he was there when Fry had him supervise *Simpson's Choice*. There appears to be no evidence to indicate Mason's setting or direction of other Omega books, but the style of *Simpson's Choice* pervades the other two books of poems.

Richard Madley, acknowledged as the printer of *Men of Europe*, seems to have printed all four Omega books with his "ordinary commercial type." Fry might have turned to the Doves Press to print the first two Omega Books or to an outstanding commercial firm which specialized in fine printing such as the Chiswick or Curwen presses yet he chose instead a capable but not distinguished professional. In this choice of Madley, Fry followed his pattern of having some of the Omega designs in furniture or carpets executed by ordinary professional craftsmen. It was also to be the practice of the Woolfs and the Hogarth Press when they went beyond the limits of their own hand printing. After the 150 copies of the hand-printed edition of *Kew Gardens* quickly sold out in June 1919, the Woolfs sought Richard Madley to reprint the volume for them. It was their first commercially printed book.

The example of Roger Fry's Omega Workshops was before the Woolfs as they made their birthday resolution in 1915 and bought their first press in 1917. Leonard and Virginia may have shared Fry's belief in the need to improve taste and may have been influenced by his spirit of adventure, his enthusiastic sense that artists could, even should, have some firsthand experience with crafts. Like Fry, they would partly conceive the press as a way to help their friends. And certainly the Woolfs could have learned from the example of Fry's Omega books, which were published for pleasure, contained the short work of friends, and were carefully handset, but were printed by a commercial printer. The books were illustrated with woodcuts from Omega artists and wrapped in paper covers. The first Hogarth press productions would be largely in that spirit and style, yet with notable differences.

The two years' delay from the moment in Buszard's Tea Rooms on 25 January 1915 until the moment on 23 March 1917 when Leonard and Virginia Woolf walked into the Excelsior Printing Supply Co. on Farrington Street and purchased a small handpress was occasioned by Virginia's mental illness in the spring and summer of 1915, their frustrated attempts to learn printing, and the low ebb of their finances. Leonard Woolf remembered that late in 1916 they decided to learn how to print and went to the St. Bride's School of Printing on Bride Lane, off Fleet Street. They learned only "that the social engine and machinery made it impossible to teach the art of printing to two middle-aged, middle-class persons" (*Beginning* 233); the school was restricted to trade union apprentices whose number was carefully controlled. The same was true of the London Central School of Arts and Crafts.[13] They might have tried one of the polytechnic schools, but probably without luck. Novelist Anthony Powell, for example, recalled going several evenings a week to the Holborn Polytechnic in Southhampton Row to study printing around 1926–27—he was working at Duckworth and trying to learn more about publishing—but the trade unions restricted the amount of instruction "to what might easily be picked up, with a little experience and common sense, while handling books in their nascent state."[14] He was able only to lay out a title page and set it up in Caslon Old Face for the inspection of his instructors.

Finances were another problem. "Presses only cost £17.17," Virginia Woolf wrote to Margaret Llewelyn Davies in February 1915, "and can be worked easily" (*Letters* 2:59). But the money was not easily obtained. By October 1916 the Woolfs hoped to use an income tax refund to buy the press. "I hope we shall get our press now," Virginia wrote to Vanessa, "as we've just heard that they [Inland Revenue] are soon sending our money" (ibid., 124). As always in such matters, the actual refund in December 1916 was less than expected—£15 instead of £35—and, Virginia wrote Vanessa, "as the press costs £20, and we are rather hard up just now, I'm afraid we shall have to wait to buy it until March, unless we can raise some money on The Vanity Fair page [an attempt to sell some inherited Thackeray manuscripts]" (ibid., 128). "My fear," Virginia added, from wifely experience, "is that the £15 will be used for house expenses, and the hope of the press disappear." The actual cost of the press when they purchased it from the Excelsior Co. was £19.5.5, including some Caslon Old Face type and "all the necessary implements and materials" (*Beginning* 234). Leonard later recalled that the press was probably a model called "The Eclipse."[15] With it came a sixteen-page pamphlet which, the sympathetic man at Excelsior assured the Woolfs, would tell them all they needed to know about printing. It was not necessary, he said, to attend a printing school.

The press, pamphlet, type, and a few accessories were delivered to Hogarth House on Tuesday, April 24, 1917. "We unpacked it," wrote Virginia to Vanessa, "with enormous excitement, finally with Nelly's help, carried it into the drawing room, set it on its stand—and discovered that it was smashed in half!" (*Letters* 2:150). The shop had to replace a part, but in the meantime there was the type to sort out and store properly. "The work of ages, especially when you mix the h's with the n's, as I did yesterday," added Virginia. The joys and treats of these preliminaries proved so absorbing that Virginia thought "real printing will devour one's entire life." The Excelsior man had been right, however; Leonard recalled that with the pamphlet's help "we found that we could pretty soon set the type, lock it up in the chase, ink the rollers, and machine a fairly legible page" (*Beginning* 234). By May 2 Virginia wrote to Margaret Llewelyn Davies that they had set up a one-page notice announcing the first publication of the press but could not yet print it because of the broken part. Amusingly, Virginia recounted how Leonard had "heaved a terrific sigh" after two hours of typesetting and said: "'I wish to God we'd never bought the cursed thing!' To my relief, though not surprise, he added 'Because I shall never do anything else.' You can't think how exciting, soothing, ennobling and satisfying it is" (*Letters* 2:151).

Leonard's search for play fascinating enough to take their minds off work was over. They were both intrigued, both snared by the pleasures and demands of the new pastime. Later, printing would become work, and they would grow to hate the restrictions it imposed on their lives. They would contemplate selling the press and closing out the business, but they never did. Printing and publishing had become a part of them. Their lives were forever changed.

The laboriously hand-set notice read, in part:

THE HOGARTH PRESS

It is proposed to issue shortly a pamphlet containing two short stories by Leonard Woolf and Virginia Woolf, (price, including postage 1/2).

If you desire a copy to be sent to you, please fill up the form below and send it with a P. O. to L. S. Woolf at the above address before June

A limited edition only will be issued.[16]

The inking and impression were uneven, "above" was divided at the end of the line as "ab-ove," the spacing was inconsistent (too much leading between words, especially in the second sentence) or not enough (none after the commas). A period at the end of the second sentence was omitted. The notice was mailed to their friends and probably to a list of the Omega Workshop supporters; Virginia had asked Roger Fry for such a list as early as 1916 (*Letters* 2:115).

The notice and word of mouth through Bloomsbury got the job done; the Woolfs were in business. And business it was from the very beginning, which is surprising. Most small, private presses, especially those operated by complete beginners like the Woolfs, commence with greeting cards, announcements, letterheads, labels, perhaps a one- or two-page setting of a favorite poem, possibly some bit of foolery to amuse one's friends. Productions are given away, not sold. Leonard always maintained that he and Virginia operated the press as a hobby, not as a business to make money, until around 1920 when they began to consider seriously becoming professional publishers. But from the start, the Woolfs were more ambitious, obviously more literary, and more business-like than other beginners.

The affairs of the press reveal Leonard's business instincts. Absorbing play the press might be for Virginia and even for Leonard, but it must also be operated on sound principles. Leonard's autobiographies are full of careful notations of expenditures, income, profits, and overhead. Forty-six years later he could write with considerable pride that the first publication cost £3.7 to produce, including 12s.6d. for paper, 10s. for covers, and 15s. for woodcuts by Carrington; that the receipts were £10.8, and the net profit was £7.1.[17] It is astonishing that a first publication could not only pay for itself but produce a tidy profit (over one-third of the cost of the printing press). After that the Hogarth Press was never in the red, although an individual title might not pay for itself.

Leonard Woolf's operation of the press, with his passion for details, his meticulous accounting for every penny, his obvious relish for the minute particulars of all expenditures from stamps and glue to fonts of type, above all his canny budgeting and pricing, surely is as much a distinguishing characteristic of Hogarth as the presence of a great novelist with composing stick in hand, Virginia Woolf inky and determined. Leonard Woolf would become a man of affairs, drawn to the challenging enterprises of government and politics, to committee work, to journalism, editing, and writing on social and political topics. He had been, by all accounts, a highly successful civil servant in Ceylon for seven years (1904–11) and fully discovered there his managerial abilities. Given his highly developed sense of duty and responsibility, his work ethic, and the absence in 1917 of anything comparable to his Ceylonese experiences, it is probable that the business operation of the press filled a need for Leonard even more compelling than Virginia's need for manual recreation.

The first publication of the press was *Two Stories,* combining Leonard's "Three Jews" with Virginia's "The Mark on the Wall" and illustrated with four small woodcuts by Dora Carrington. It came to thirty-four pages and sold for 1s.6d., four pence more than the flyer had indicated. *Two Stories* was an ambitious beginning for two neophytes with a small handpress. It was prose, to begin with, more type to set per page than poetry and requiring greater care with word spacing, and it was fairly long. With their first handpress the Woolfs could only set two pages at a time, machining one before distributing the type. The process was long and tedious for a thirty-four-page book. The inclusion of woodcuts presented special problems. Undaunted and excited, Leonard and Virginia began setting "Three Jews" early in May 1917. By May 22 Virginia wrote to Vanessa that they had just started printing Leonard's story, with Virginia so absorbed in printing that she had not yet written her own story. Sixty orders had been received.

They were halfway through Leonard's story by June 8 and looking for colored papers for the wrappers. The printing, wrote Virginia, "gets ever so much quicker, and the fascination is something extreme" (*Letters* 2:159). Carrington's woodcuts were not yet completed by July 3, but ten days later they were in hand and printed. "We like the wood cuts immensely," wrote Virginia to Carrington, adding that they made the book more interesting (ibid., 162). She especially liked the servant girl with plates (for "Three Jews") and the snail (for "The Mark on the Wall"). They had struggled to print the woodcuts, she wrote. The margins had marked occasionally, and they had chopped away at the block with a chisel. The rollers had scraped and there were smudges. But, Virginia said, they were pleased with the results. Shortly afterwards, probably around the middle of July, they covered the book with a variety of wrappers including Japanese grass paper and paper-backed cloth in a red-and-white geometrical design, printed the title, and sent the volume off to the subscribers. It had taken about two and a half months to produce *Two Stories*.

Friends responded favorably to both the content and the printing. Lytton Strachey thought the production was cheering.[18] He couldn't have believed it possible. His only criticism was that there did not appear to be sufficient ink. The problem is a familiar one to all beginning printers. There were a few other problems, a typographical error for example ("*country Housse,*" p. 25), but the most notable evidence of the Woolfs' inexperience was in the printing of the third woodcut (p. 19). It was printed at an angle, the upper left corner an eighth of an inch higher than the upper right corner, suggesting insufficient furniture or a loosely locked chase.[19] Leonard also recognized that the "backing" was sometimes wrong. He had not realized, he wrote in his autobiography, that "a page on one side of the sheet must be printed so that it falls exactly on the back of the page on the other side of the sheet" (*Beginning* 235). But on the whole the production was a good one; the demy octavo pages were well set with attractive margins (1 inch on top and 2 sides, 2 inches at the bottom, with a 2 3/4-inch top margin on the first page); and Carrington's four woodcuts, especially the large one of a snail at the end of "The Mark," added visual interest.

The edition virtually sold out in three months, ninety-one buyers accounting for 134 copies. Some of the Woolfs' relatives and friends bought multiple copies. Leonard's mother, for example, took two copies,

Lady Ottoline Morrell three copies, Roger Fry five copies (four of which were to be displayed and sold at the Omega Workshops), and Saxon Sydney-Turner six copies. The big buyer was Violet Dickinson, Virginia Woolf's once-dearest friend. Dickinson, perhaps with a view to distributing the book among her friends, first purchased five copies in advance of publication (May 15) and then four more copies (July 25, 27) after publication, in spite of a price hike. Virginia had written to Violet on July 21, glad that she had liked the stories: "It is tremendous fun doing it, and we are now in treaty for a much larger press, and mean to take it up seriously and produce novels with it. And we are even getting an apprentice! We are nearly at an end of our copies, and have raised the price from 1/6 to 2/–If you want 4 in spite of the price, we will send them to you. It has been quite a success" (*Letters* 2:165–66). Shrewd and tough-minded of Leonard and Virginia to raise the price for the last twenty-seven copies, and loyal of Dickinson, Fry, and twelve others to pay it.

There were no complimentary copies. Even Carrington paid, the first to buy at the increased price, so that as illustrator for the volume she made a profit of only thirteen shillings. Among the buyers who were not close friends or members of Bloomsbury were John Drinkwater, Mrs. George Bernard Shaw, William Rothenstein, Michael Sadler, and Katherine Mansfield, who bought two copies at the original price. Rothenstein, an artist himself, wrote that the woodcuts were very attractive. Enclosing his two shillings, he added that the handprinting gave the book a more human quality.[20]

Even before the publication date of *Two Stories,* Leonard and Virginia envisioned expansion, a tribute to their energy, enthusiasm, optimism, and, probably, Leonard's business sense. To Vanessa, Virginia had written in June about another income tax return "which we mean to spend on a press (I need hardly say) which will print 8 pages at a time, and then we shall be very professional" (*Letters* 2:159). And in her letter of July 13 to Carrington about the woodcuts and the surgical operation with the chisel, Virginia had added that they were "in treaty" for a press costing £100, which was "specially good at printing pictures, and we see that we must make a practice of always having pictures" (ibid., 162). She mentioned Alix Sargant-Florence as a possible assistant. Treaty or not, the Woolfs were unable to complete arrangements for buying a new press, even though, as she wrote to Vanessa, "the head of a great printing school" in London was consulted and agreed to watch out for sales of presses (ibid., 168). It was not until the autumn of 1921 that they finally purchased a secondhand Minerva platen machine, treadle operated (ibid., 487). In the meantime they hand printed eight more books on the small press and used commercial presses for several others. And Alix, it turned out, was somewhat of a disappointment.

James Strachey, Lytton's brother, had introduced Alix Sargant-Florence to the Woolfs in the summer of 1916, and a year later they considered her as an apprentice to help with the press. By the time she came to them on October 16, 1917, they were setting Katherine Mansfield's story *Prelude*. "We started printing in earnest after lunch," Virginia wrote, "& Alix came punctually; was instructed, & left on her high stool while we took the air with Tinker [the dog]" (*Diary* 1:60). When they returned, Virginia noted, "Alix solemnly and slowly explained that she was bored, & also worried by her 2 hours composing, & wished to give it up." Virginia, like Leonard, had little patience with slowness and solemnity of any sort, and she attributed Alix's reaction to two hours of work at the press to a "morbid scrutiny of values," even to "crass laziness." With some acerbity Woolf concluded her entry by commenting that "the idea weighed upon her, & I assured her there was no need for it to weigh."

So the first assistant was in and out in two hours. Alix was to remain a friend and associate of the Woolfs, helping Leonard research his book *Empire and Commerce in Africa* (1918). Eventually, after a long campaign on her part, she married James Strachey (in 1920), became a psychoanalyst with him, and a skilled translator of psychoanalytic literature. Over the years the Woolfs had more than ten assistants and one apprentice, but the relationships were sometimes turbulent and difficult, marked on both sides by misunderstandings. Unlike Alix, however, the others lasted longer and sometimes enjoyed the labors of typesetting and printing. Almost immediately after Alix Sargant-Florence's departure, the Woolfs found Barbara Hiles, one of the young "crop heads," as Virginia called the short-haired, spirited, and unconventional young women who became part of the newer Bloomsbury groupings. She started taking her first lessons in printing from Leonard on November 21, 1917; the Woolfs were already printing the first pages of *Prelude* (*Letters* 2:196).

From *Two Stories* in 1917 to Dorothy Wellesley's poem *Jupiter and the Nun* in 1932, Leonard and Virginia with their periodic assistants hand set and printed thirty-four volumes. Most of these books were fairly short (sixteen to thirty-two pages) and were poetry (twenty-six books of poetry, seven of prose, one of woodcuts). The Woolfs hand printed at least one volume a year during those sixteen years, with the single exception of 1929; they reached a peak in 1923 with five hand-set and printed books.[21] In 1922, for the first time, the number of books printed by commercial printers for the Hogarth Press exceeded the number of hand-printed books. After 1926, when the affairs of the press and their own writing absorbed their energies, the Woolfs customarily hand printed only one volume a year. Inevitably in such an undertaking, the literary quality of the publications varied considerably. Some of the writers and their works were undistinguished then and totally forgotten now, but among the books hand printed by the Woolfs were works by Katherine Mansfield, T. S. Eliot, E. M. Forster, Robert Graves, Herbert Read, John Crowe Ransom, Edwin Muir, and Virginia herself. Of these, four or five works claim attention today as significant publications and as interesting examples of the Woolfs' early hand printing: Mansfield's *Prelude* (1918), Eliot's *Poems* (1919) and *The Waste Land* (1923), and Virginia Woolf's "The Mark on the Wall" (1917) and *Kew Gardens* (1919).

The Woolfs had met Katherine Mansfield and her future husband J. Middleton Murry through Lytton Strachey sometime late in 1916 (*Diary* 1:43). The friendship developed, primarily between Virginia and Katherine, and by January or February 1917 the two couples were having dinner together. Katherine Mansfield by 1917 had achieved some recognition as a short-story writer. Although she had collected thirteen of her early stories and published them as *In a German Pension* (1911), she had published little else of significance. She came to see the stories as immature and would never reprint them. Katherine Mansfield's modest literary success at the time and her complex personality both attracted and repelled Virginia Woolf, causing her moments of professional jealousy as well as moments of sympathetic and generous understanding. The relationship which developed between the two talented and sensitive women proved many-sided, tension-filled, and occasionally sustaining and illuminating. When Mansfield died of tuberculosis in 1923, Woolf would feel the loss keenly.[22]

As they did with all their literary friends, the Woolfs soon approached Mansfield for a story to print on their press. "I am going to see Katherine Mansfield," Virginia wrote to Vanessa Bell in late April 1917, "to get a story from her, perhaps" (*Letters* 2:150). By July 26 Woolf confirmed to Bell, "At present we've promised to do Katherine Mansfield's story" (ibid., 168). The story was a thoroughly revised version of *The Aloe,* an uncompleted long work begun in 1915; it marked a significant change in Mansfield's subject matter as she turned back to her New Zealand childhood experiences, the source of her best work. Her compression and modification of the story into *Prelude* demonstrate impressively Mansfield's artistic development, although it occurred at a time of physical and emotional stress. "My Story," she wrote to Woolf in August, "I have sent to the typist who lets me have it back on Thursday. I couldn't cope with the bloody copying: I've been so 'ill.' Rheumatiz plus ghastly depression PLUS fury."[23]

"When I look at my copy of *Prelude* today," wrote Leonard Woolf in 1964, "I am astonished at our courage and energy in attempting it and producing it only a year after we had started to teach ourselves to print" (*Beginning* 237). In spite of the Woolfs' greater experience and efficiency with the handpress, it took them nine months to set and print *Prelude.* For one reason, at sixty-eight pages it was over twice the length of *Two Stories,* and for another, they printed twice as many copies (300). There were other factors. There was the time off from printing devoted to the continuing search for a larger press (they expected one to be delivered momentarily between November and January after a £10 deposit). There were the apprenticeships of Alix Sargant-Florence and Barbara Hiles; broken rollers which had to be replaced; and the sudden battlefield death of Leonard's younger brother Cecil and the decision in March to interrupt progress on *Prelude* to print, posthumously, a slim volume of Cecil's poems.

Upon their return from a late summer vacation at Asheham in Sussex, the Woolfs began setting type for *Prelude,* and on October 9, 1917, Virginia Woolf recorded: "We took a proof of the first page of K. M.'s story, *The Prelude*. It looks very nice, set solid in the new type" (*Diary* 1:56). (The Woolfs were frequently in error over the title, using the definite article as in Wordsworth's poem.) Katherine Mansfield was pleased with the arrangements. As she wrote to Dorothy Brett on October 11: "I threw my darling to the wolves and they ate it and served me up so much praise in such a golden bowl that I couldn't help feeling gratified. I did not think they would like it at all and I am still astounded that they do."[24]

The new type that so solidly set Mansfield's darling was the result of the Woolfs' decision to expand the capabilities of the press. To the original 10-point type, Leonard had added five pounds of 24-point Caslon Old Face titling type on May 21 (for 18s.) and then a font of 12-point type with cabinet in late July (for £11.6), just before they left for Asheham (ABS 89). On the day they took the first page proof, they received the generous windfall of Emma Vaughan's old bookbinding equipment, apparently dating back to 1902 when she and Virginia shared an interest in "lidding." The "masses" of equipment from Emma included a nipping press (Virginia called it a "Kipping" press) and, more importantly, a cutting press (*Letters* 2:186). The Woolfs were then able to bind the press publications in boards if they wished. Leonard added a paper-cutting machine to the equipment in November (for £3.3). Except for minor purchases—extra type, some additional furniture, an engraved plate for the door (October 1919)—there were no significant additions to the press equipment until they bought the Minerva press in 1921 (ABS 89).

Printing *Prelude* began in earnest on November 13 when the Woolfs got their new paper ("soft & yellow tinted") and printed off 300 copies of the first page. Barbara Hiles came a week later and at first was more hindrance than help. "We had Barbara here for 3 days, with disastrous results, for when we looked at her work, it was so full of faults we had to take it down. I should have expected, not much intelligence, but the quickness & accuracy of a good needlewoman. This was annoying" (*Diary* 1:83). Leonard spent another day in "futile misery" trying to print one of Barbara's set pages from a chase which she had not locked up properly. And the exuberant Barbara was constantly bursting into Virginia's room asking for help. "The infliction of our apprentice," lamented Virginia (ibid., 90). But the good-natured, practical, talkative, and ever-willing apprentice was doing her best, three days a week, in return for lunch, tea, bus fare, and a share in any profits. Soon things got better, Hiles became more skilled, and Virginia's nerves eased. It was rather typical of the Woolfs to be impatient with their helper's first inept bumblings over typesetting and printing, forgetting their own sometimes calamitous confusions at the beginning. Leonard, always quick and adroit himself, an exacting perfectionist, was usually less tolerant of mistakes than Virginia.

By January 12 the Woolfs had printed the first eighteen pages, and on January 18 Virginia noted that she and Leonard had worked for three days "so as to have 8 pages set up to print at McDermotts" (*Diary* 1:109). In his autobiography Leonard recalled seeking help in 1917 from Mc-Dermott the printer, whose small commercial printing business, the Prospect Press, was in Richmond near Hogarth House. In printing some page proofs of *Two Stories* the previous year, Woolf had noticed that none of the letters printed black enough; "there were tiny white dots everywhere" (*Beginning* 238). McDermott had explained that the chase wasn't "on its feet"; that is, the type was not all perfectly flat when Woolf had locked up the chase, and so it did not print evenly. McDermott became a friend and consultant to the Woolfs in their printing while they lived in Richmond, and it was he who had attempted to obtain a larger press for Hogarth. Now it was the generous McDermott who offered Woolf the use of chases that could print four pages at a time. Virginia and Barbara would set type, and Leonard would lock up four pages and then carry the chases to the Prompt Press where McDermott would let Leonard machine them himself on the treadle platen press. Although Leonard remembered that *Prelude* was entirely machined at McDermott's, the diaries and letters of Virginia indicate that the first eighteen or so pages were probably hand printed at Hogarth House and the rest printed by Leonard at the Prompt Press.

In the midst of printing *Prelude* at McDermott's, the Woolfs decided suddenly in March to print the poems of Cecil Woolf, Leonard's brother who had been killed in Bourlon Wood, France, on November 29, 1917. On December 2 they had received news of his death. The terrible irony was that the same German shell which had killed Cecil also had wounded Philip, the youngest brother. Philip was long hospitalized in Fishmonger's Hall. While convalescing, he brought the Woolfs some of Cecil's poems, and they agreed to print them on their handpress. The press became a therapy for Philip. He helped set type several times. The Woolfs seem to have completed printing in the first week of April soon after returning to London from their Easter visit to Asheham. The thin, nineteen-page edition of the poems of C. N. Sidney Woolf, with plain, white paper wrappers, is the rarest of Hogarth Press publications. Only five copies are known to exist.[25] The poems were obviously a family gesture, a few copies printed, none to be sold. Philip, in dedicating the volume to Cecil, "the dearest and bravest brother that a man was ever loved by," stated that "some of these poems, revised and re-published, might have appeared one day in a volume under both our names."[26] Virginia with characteristic clear sight and lack of sentiment noted of the poems, "They're not good; they show the Woolf tendency to denunciation, without the vigour of my particular Woolf" (*Diary* 1:124).

So it was that Katherine Mansfield's *Prelude*, originally intended to be the second press publication, was actually the third by the time it was published in July. Virginia and Katherine had a slight estrangement during the printing of *Prelude* but were quickly back on good terms. On May 12 Mansfield wrote to Dorothy Brett: "I saw Virginia on Thursday. She was very nice. She's the only one of them that I shall ever see. . . . My poor dear Prelude is still piping away in their little cage and not out yet. I read some pages of it & scarcely knew it again. It all seems so once upon a time."[27] There was only the minor difficulty of Katherine's desire to use a print of a woman's head by her friend the Scottish artist J. D. Fergusson to illustrate the story. The design, wrote Virginia to Lady Ottoline Morrell on May 24, "makes our gorges rise, to such an extent that we can hardly bring ourselves to print it" (*Letters* 2:244). Mansfield was not pleased. The Woolfs would dislike Fergusson's designs, wouldn't they? she wrote to Murry. "Its their press. I suppose they'd better not use them. . . . To Hell with other people's presses." She would have Virginia send Murry a proof of the cover, and added; "I don't want Roger Fly [Fry] on it, at any rate. (That 'Fly' seems to me awfully funny. It must be the sun on my brain.)" The same day, May 29, Katherine had written more diplomatically to Virginia, conceding the issue. "Its of course for you and Leonard to use em or not and as you don't like them—why theres an end on't. But the blue paper with just the title on it would be nice: I hope you use that."[28] They did, and they also printed a few copies with Fergusson's woman for Mansfield and Murry. "I take it for granted," Virginia wrote to Clive Bell, "that you would prefer K. M. without the bold black woodcuts of Mr Fergusson. We are printing some plain" (*Letters* 2:246).

Virginia set the last words of the story on June 24, and on July 2 she began folding and stapling the pages. Finally, on July 10, she recorded: "We have sent off our first copies this evening, after spending the afternoon in glueing & covering. They surprised us when done by their professional look—the stiff blue cover pleases us particularly. I must read the book through after dinner, partly to find possible faults, but also to make up my mind how much I like it as literature" (*Diary* 1:165). Before publication, Woolf had touted *Prelude* to Violet Dickinson as "much the best thing [Mansfield's] done yet" (*Letters* 2:248). Then, as she recorded two days after reading the finished book, she made up her mind: "I myself find a kind of beauty about the story; a little vapourish I admit, & freely watered with some of her cheap realities; but it has the living power, the detached existence of a work of art" (*Diary* 1:167).

The sales of *Prelude* were slow, only sixty-seven prepublication copies through subscribers and a total of eighty-four copies by November 8, 1918. Four years after publication, the sales finally totaled 236 copies (ABS 101, 137). Most of the initial buyers were the same friends, family, or acquaintances who had bought *Two Stories*. Aldous Huxley was one of the newcomers. The most interesting aspect of the sales, however, was that the Woolfs traveled the book in a modest way, selling one or two copies to several bookstores and book clubs. James Bain, the bookseller who bought *Two Stories,* took several copies, but token copies also were sold to the Chelsea Book Club, the Times Book Club, Mudies, W. H. Smith & Sons, Simpkin Marshall, and Birrell & Garnett's Bookshop. To boost the sales of *Prelude* and other books in the summer of 1920, the Woolfs took out their first advertisements in the *Times, Nation, Manchester Guardian,* and *New Statesman.* By the time *Prelude* was sold out around 1923, the press had made a net profit of £17.16.11 and Katherine Mansfield had been paid £5.18.5.

Katherine Mansfield had sent *Prelude* to the Woolfs in the autumn of 1917 at a time when she was living in London with her own studio in Chelsea while Murry worked at the War Office. Following a bout of pleurisy in November, she traveled first to Bandol, France, then to Paris in March 1918, and finally back to London in April where she and Murry were married in May. Increasingly ill from tuberculosis while in France, Mansfield nevertheless wrote two new stories "Je ne parle pas français" and "Bliss." Thus she was out of England during most of the setting and printing of *Prelude* but back in the country with two new stories by the time of its publication. Katherine published "Bliss" in the August 1918 issue of the *English Review.* After she read it, Virginia threw it down, exclaiming, "She's done for!" (*Diary* 1:179). She thought the story poorly conceived, thin in content, and badly written. Murry about this time, probably inspired by the Woolfs, bought a handpress and with his brother Richard's help established the short-lived Heron Press at his home in Hempstead. There during the remainder of 1918 the Murrys printed one hundred copies of "Je ne parle pas français," covered it during January 1919, and later issued the thirty-page booklet at 10s.6d., considerably above the Hogarth Press price of 3s.6d. for *Prelude*. They issued only about sixty copies.[29]

Ill again during the spring and summer of 1919, Katherine Mansfield planned to return to the Mediterranean for her health. Virginia, writing to Janet Case in late July 1919, noted Katherine's intention to go to San Remo, adding, "She has written several stories which we think of printing" (*Letters* 2:379). But Mansfield did not give the stories to the Hogarth Press. Instead, while abroad, Murry arranged with Constable in February 1920 to print them, and they were published as *Bliss and Other Stories* the following December. The brief publishing relationship with the Woolfs was over, and the Hogarth Press for the first time had lost an author to an established and larger publishing house. Leonard Woolf, new to publishing, had not yet learned the publisher's common practice of contracting a new author's next two or three books, and so Mansfield was under no contractual obligation to submit her second book to the Hogarth Press.

In April 1918, as the Woolfs completed printing Cecil Woolf's poems and returned to the task of machining *Prelude* at the Prompt Press, Harriet Shaw Weaver, at the suggestion of Roger Fry, wrote to ask if the Hogarth Press would consider publishing James Joyce's new novel *Ulysses*. They met her on April 18 for Sunday tea, Virginia finding the publisher and editor of the *Egoist* "inalterably modest judicious & decorous," with the table manners of a "well bred hen" but "incompetent from the business point of view" (*Diary* 1:140). She wondered how so proper a woman had come in contact with Joyce. Harriet Weaver left the uncompleted manuscript in a brown paper parcel for the Woolfs to consider.

The Woolfs read the first four chapters of *Ulysses* ("Telemachus," "Nestor," "Proteus," and "Calypso"), then being serialized in the American *Little Review* published by Margaret Anderson and Jane Heap. Virginia Woolf did not like it; the directness of language and incident made her blush, she wrote to Nick Bagenal (*Letters* 2:231). Although Joyce's stream of consciousness was interesting as an experiment, she thought he had little of significance to say, and reference to the bodily functions became boring. "First there's a dog that p's," she wrote to Lytton Strachey in April 1918, "then there's a man that forths, and one can be monotonous even on that subject" (ibid., 234). Later, she would grow to dislike *Ulysses* more vehemently. Reading the published book in 1922, she was "amused, stimulated, charmed interested" through the first three chapters, only to be "puzzled, bored, irritated, & disillusioned as by a queasy undergraduate scratching his pimples" by the end of chapter six ("Hades") (*Diary* 2:188–89). It was an "illiterate, underbred book" by a "self-taught working man." She could not understand "great Tom" Eliot's praise of *Ulysses* as comparable to *War and Peace*. With time, Virginia Woolf would temper, but never abandon, her feelings about Joyce's masterpiece.

Aside from the Woolfs' distaste for the text, *Ulysses* proved impossible for the Hogarth Press to undertake. It was immensely long and difficult textually, far beyond the capabilities of Virginia's typesetting and Leonard's machining, even on McDermott's press. Furthermore, the commercial printers Leonard consulted refused to take it on the grounds of obscenity. He recalled in his autobiography sending the "remarkable piece of dynamite" to R. & R. Clark of Edinburgh and to Clay, both respectable printers, who rejected the book instantly, declaring that prosecution would certainly follow publication (*Beginning* 247). Virginia Woolf wrote diplomatically to Harriet Weaver on May 17, a month after their meeting, rejecting *Ulysses* because "the length is an insuperable difficulty to us"; she estimated that a 300-page book would take them at least two years to produce (*Letters* 2:242). She made no mention of her own repulsion or the difficulties with printers.

The rejection of the *Ulysses* manuscript was the first for the Woolfs. There were to be other rejections inevitably, but none so famous as this. *Ulysses* was finally published in France for Joyce in 1922 through the good offices of Sylvia Beach and the courageous French printer Darantière in

Dijon. The patient French printers labored through five sets of proofs, all spattered with Joyce's endless corrections and revisions, devoting nearly 2,000 hours to revising the proofs. No wonder that Jack Dalton counted at least 2,000 textual errors in the Darantière printing.[30] How impossible a task *Ulysses* would have been for them, the Woolfs could never have imagined. In 1932, on the eve of the precedent-shattering publication of *Ulysses* in America by Random House, Joyce approached an interested T. S. Eliot to arrange publication in England, preferably with Faber & Faber. Eliot finally had to abandon the project of publishing a complete, unexpurgated edition of *Ulysses* for fear of prosecution. Not until 1936 would the novel be published in England, by John Lane.

T. S. Eliot was Harriet Weaver's assistant editor on the *Egoist* at the time she brought *Ulysses* to the Woolfs. There has been some confusion over when Eliot met the Woolfs. Clive Bell believed he introduced Eliot to the Woolfs in 1916, and Leonard thought it was in 1916 or 1917.[31] But by mid-October 1918 Leonard Woolf wrote formally to Mr. Eliot, on a tip from Roger Fry, inquiring about Eliot's poems for the Hogarth Press.[32] He and Virginia had liked *Prufrock,* wrote Leonard, and wondered if Eliot would care to have them consider his poems for the press. The letter sounds as if they had not met. Whether or not it happened earlier, the Woolfs and Eliot certainly got together on November 15, 1918, Virginia noting, as if seeing Eliot for the first time, that he was "a polished, cultivated, elaborate young American" who beneath the surface was "very intellectual, intolerant, with strong views of his own, & a poetic creed" (*Diary* 1:218). Eliot showed them three or four poems and discussed his poetic theories with them. So began a long friendship with the immediate result that, as Virginia wrote to Vanessa on November 26, "Eliot has sent us some of his poems which we are going to print as soon as Kew Gardens is done" (*Letters* 2:299). They began to set the poems on January 22 and finished printing on March 19, 1919. Leonard Woolf had purchased 8s.6d. worth of Greek type needed for the epigraph to "Sweeney" and two words in "Mr. Eliot's Service." Eliot, when he saw the first page proofs, thought they were admirable, and Virginia believed the finished product was "our best work so far by a long way, owing to the quality of the ink."[33]

Shortly after accepting Eliot's poems, Virginia Woolf recorded that she brought home in her bag, "with a view to printing," Middleton Murry's poem "A Fable for Critics" (*Diary* 1:223). It was retitled *The Critic in Judgment or Belshazzar of Baronscourt,* hand set by the Woolfs and machined by both Leonard Woolf and McDermott, and published in May 1919 with Virginia's *Kew Gardens* and Eliot's *Poems.* All three productions were carried on simultaneously, the setting and machining of *Kew Gardens* having begun before the other two, with a view to offering an attractive press package of three small volumes at once.

They made an odd trio: Eliot's Sweeney and Virginia's snail were daring, modernist, memorable, prototypical of their best work; and Murry's Belshazzar was old-fashioned, talky, thoroughly forgettable. Reading the poems together, Virginia Woolf found Murry hard to read "from reasons the opposite of those that make Eliot hard to read" (*Diary* 1:223). As she amusingly explained to Violet Dickinson, "Mr Eliot is an American of the highest culture, so that his writing is almost unintelligible; Middleton Murry edits the Athenaeum, and is also very obscure" (*Letters* 2:355).

Leonard Woolf maintained that Eliot's *Poems* was the sort of short work "which commercial publishers could not or would not publish," like Virginia Woolf's *Kew Gardens* (*Downhill* 66). To Ian Parsons in March 1966, Woolf wrote that "when we published *Poems,* Tom was practically unknown and so he was in 1923 when we published *Waste Land.* A few people, like ourselves, thought him a very good poet, but the general view was that he was unintelligible and ridiculous" (LWP). Woolf cited sales figures to prove his point, but he seems to have exaggerated his risk in publishing Eliot's *Poems.* Woolf was no doubt right about the large publishing houses, but there were a number of publishers who frequently issued small volumes of poetry that could not hope to make money—Blackwell of Oxford, for example, or Chatto & Windus, Benn, Heinemann, Grant Richards, Cape, or Constable. Most publishers, in fact, published poetry as a matter of pride or commitment to literature, although the market was small and the returns were negligible. Furthermore, Eliot was not "practically unknown" in London by 1919. Granted that most patrons of Mudies would never have heard of Eliot, in the world of poetry, criticism, and literary journalism, in the circles, that is, of Bloomsbury, Garsington, the Poetry Bookshop, the *New Statesman, Art and*

Letters, and the *Athenaeum,* Eliot was not only known but fast becoming an established figure. For a poet-critic-editor these circles were the ones that mattered.

The seven poems that Eliot brought to Leonard and Virginia Woolf in November 1918 and that they set and printed from January to March 1919 were a mixture of styles and themes showing Eliot in transition. In order of appearance in *Poems* they were: "Sweeney among the Nightingales," "The Hippopotamus," "Mr. Eliot's Sunday Morning Service," "Whispers of Immortality," "Le spectateur," "Mélange adultère de tout," and "Lune de miel." All seven of the poems had appeared previously in the *Little Review,* four in July 1917 and three in September 1918. The Hogarth Press text of the poems is interesting chiefly because the epigraphs for "Sweeney" and "Hippopotamus" were altered or omitted in later editions and because of a word change in a later version of "Whispers"[34]: the Hogarth Press text of "Whispers of Immortality" carried the line "sleek and sinuous jaguar," which was changed to the more evocative "sleek Brazilian jaguar" in Knopf's edition of *Poems* (1920) and all subsequent editions.

Approximately two hundred copies of *Poems* were printed and sold for 2s.6d. It was issued first with the same patterned paper cover as *Two Stories* but later in blue-black marbled paper prepared by Roger Fry, the first of several such marbled covers for the press.[35] Within a year the issue had virtually sold out (180 copies sold immediately, plus 12 presentation or review copies) (ABS 108). The Woolfs were more successful this time with booksellers. They sold eight copies to Bain, ten copies to Hatchard, seventeen copies to Simpkin Marshall, and twenty-four copies to Harold Monro's Poetry Bookshop. Bain the bookseller supplied the answer. Writing to Vanessa, Virginia described her visit to Bain "with our bag of books." " 'Mrs. Woolf,' he said, 'so long as you print things yourself I can guarantee you an immediate sale and high prices; but when you have books printed for you, its a very different matter.' 'But you see, Mr. Bain,' I said, 'my taste is very bad.' 'It's not a question of taste, Madam,' he replied; 'It's the personal touch'" (*Letters* 2:378). When Leonard Woolf closed out the account on August 3, 1920, he had paid £4.17.4 to Eliot and £9.6.10 ½ to the press as profit.

Virginia Woolf's *Kew Gardens,* issued with the Eliot and Murry books, included two woodcuts by Vanessa Bell. Gradually, the Woolfs were involving their Bloomsbury friends in different aspects of their printing—first Carrington for woodcuts, then Roger Fry and Duncan Grant for wrappers, and, most importantly, Vanessa Bell for woodcuts. The contributions of Bell to the press publications included woodcuts, paper wrappers, complete page designs and layouts with decorations (as in the third edition of *Kew Gardens*), and many jacket designs. It was also Bell who designed the wolf's-head printer's device used by the press on all its publications for many years.

Vanessa Bell's participation was artistically important to the press, but more personally to Virginia Woolf. Virginia's direct relationship with Vanessa about her artwork, the letters and consultations with Vanessa over paper, layout, printing, and design, provided Virginia with an additional means of binding herself to her sister. It became a way of sharing their creative lives in addition to Virginia's frequent involvement with Vanessa's domestic world of servants and children.

From the very beginning Virginia seems to have desired Vanessa's help with *Kew Gardens*. In an exchange of letters during late June and July 1918 Virginia sent the story, with her usual self-doubts, and asked Vanessa first to design a title page and then some woodcuts. The results pleased Virginia; one of the sample drawings seemed to capture perfectly the mood of the story, although she professed to doubt that her story was good enough to print. *Kew Gardens* was set up, beginning on November 7, 1918, and Virginia immediately sent Vanessa a page proof of a print, asking her to design another smaller one. "I think the book will be a great success," she wrote to Vanessa, "owing to you: and my vision comes out much as I had it, so I suppose, in spite of everything, God made our brains upon the same lines, only leaving out two or three pieces in mine" (*Letters* 2:289).

Virginia's letters to Vanessa in November and December 1918 trace the difficulties the Woolfs had with the choice of paper and suitable marble covers (Roger Fry's papers were too expensive, thought Virginia) and their problems with printing the woodcuts to Vanessa's satisfaction. "I see," wrote Virginia to Vanessa on December 9, "we shan't print the wood cuts nearly as well as Roger's man [Richard Madley who printed the Omega books]; but apparently one ought to use a special ink" (*Letters*

2:303). Printing was complete by December 17, and the Woolfs began negotiating with McDermott to print J. Middleton Murry's poems at £4.10 for 200 copies, the Woolfs supplying the paper and the cover (*Diary* 1:229). Murry's *Critic in Judgment* was actually the first contracted commercial printing done for the Hogarth Press, although Leonard maintained in his autobiography that the reprint of *Kew Gardens* was the first. Virginia probably set the type and Leonard locked up the pages in the chases for McDermott to machine himself. But McDermott, the Woolfs thought, botched the printing (ibid., 257).

Shortly after the three works of Woolf, Eliot, and Murry were published, Virginia had an upsetting argument with Vanessa over the printing of *Kew Gardens*. Virginia recorded on June 9, 1919: "But Nessa & I quarrelled as nearly as we ever do quarrel now over the get up of Kew Gardens, both type and woodcuts; & she firmly refused to illustrate any more stories of mine under those conditions, & went so far as to doubt the value of the Hogarth Press altogether. An ordinary printer would do better in her opinion. This both stung & chilled me" (*Diary* 1:279). The sting healed, but the Woolfs only once more would attempt to print woodcuts by Vanessa as illustrations for the poems and stories they hand set and printed. They had McDermott set and print Vanessa's woodcuts for Virginia's *Night and Day* two years later in March 1921 and were much dismayed by his poor job. They themselves printed an entire book of Roger Fry's woodcuts in December 1921, and then they printed Clive Bell's *Legend of Monte della Sibella* (1923) with two woodcuts by Duncan Grant and two by Vanessa. Both books were printed after they had obtained the Minerva treadle platen press in October 1921.

Regardless of Vanessa Bell's critical assessment of its visual limitations, *Kew Gardens* sold well. At first the Woolfs were discouraged by the sales. A favorable review in the *Times Literary Supplement,* however, changed their fortunes. "We came back [from Asheham]," wrote Virginia to Vanessa on June 4, "to find ourselves flooded with orders for Kew" (*Letters* 2:364). The press account book shows orders totaling 107 copies for June 3, including 12 copies requested by Mudies (ABS III). As Virginia recorded, she and Leonard found "the hall table stacked, littered, with orders . . . they strewed the sofa, & we opened them intermittently through dinner, & quarrelled . . . because we were both excited, & opposite tides of excitement coursed in us, & they were blown to waves by the critical blast of Charleston" (*Diary* 1:280). Vanessa's sharp criticism from Charleston probably caused the Woolfs to seek her help with an immediate reprint of *Kew Gardens*. They asked Vanessa if she would supervise a 500-copy reprint by Richard Madley. They wanted her to work with Madley on the title page and on the placement and printing of the woodcuts. It was a small victory for Virginia to report that Madley had agreed with her placement of the woodcuts and the spacing between title and first paragraph in the hand-printed edition.

Before Vanessa could get to London, however, Madley had set the story and threatened to charge extra for any delays, so the Woolfs had him print the volume. It was then that Madley cut all the covers crooked, requiring extra cutting and trimming by Virginia with a penknife and prompting her satisfying comment to Vanessa that "a professional printer isn't necessarily infallible as you seem to think" (*Letters* 2:369).

The first edition of *Kew Gardens* of 150 copies quickly sold out, bringing a profit of £14.10 to the press and requiring Madley's reprint of 500 copies. By November 1920 a total of 620 copies had been sold, virtually exhausting the reprint (ABS 128). Years later, in 1927, the Woolfs issued a new edition of *Kew Gardens,* with elaborate page designs by Vanessa which encircled or bordered the text. Herbert Reiach of Hammersmith, highly skilled printers and engravers, printed the volume. At the time the Woolfs had Richard Madley reprint *Kew Gardens,* they had the Pelican Press of Francis Meynell reprint "The Mark on the Wall," Virginia's part of *Two Stories.* Unfortunately the printers could not include Carrington's woodcuts without delay and increased cost. The separate edition of *The Mark on the Wall* corrected the typos and incorporated Virginia's slight editorial changes.

Leonard Woolf, assessing the development both of Virginia's writing and of the press in his autobiography, thought that the first edition of *Kew Gardens* "had great importance for us, for its immediate success was the first of many unforeseen happenings which led us, unintentionally and often reluctantly, to turn the Hogarth Press into a commercial publishing business" (*Downhill* 59). *Kew Gardens* was the last work of fiction by Virginia that the Woolfs hand set and printed. Not until 1930 did they hand print another of Virginia's works, a small essay *On Being Ill.*

To possible critics of the slightly botched printing of *On Being Ill,* Virginia composed a tongue-in-cheek form letter which she never sent. Such a charming disclaimer could well serve as a summing up of the Woolfs' hand printing over the years. Beginning "Dear Madam," Virginia agreed that "the colour is uneven, the letters not always clear, the spacing inaccurate, and the word 'campion' should read 'companion'" (*Letters* 4:260). Her defense was that she and Leonard were amateur printers without formal training, who fit in their hobby amid busy lives. But, she added, the volume was already worth more than it cost because of over-subscription, so that although "we have not satisfied your taste, we hope that we have not robbed your purse."

After their peak year of 1923 when they printed five books, including Eliot's *Waste Land,* the Woolfs maintained an easier schedule of one to three titles a year. The books they printed, like the first volumes, were generally plain, workmanlike printings. They were completely in keeping with the Woolfs' attitude toward books—practical, no nonsense about fine printing, the content more important than style, the standard Caslon Old Face giving a clean readable text. They did not experiment with other typefaces.

Their typesetting skill was tested at least twice, however. T. S. Eliot's *Waste Land* (1923) required adroit spacing, and *Paris* (1920) by Hope Mirrlees was self-consciously modern in its typographical configuration, one line running vertically down the page. Eliot appreciated the Woolfs' efforts in printing his work and thought that its appearance was better than the American edition by Boni and Liveright in 1922 (MHP).

Twice in 1923 the Woolfs set and printed volumes of superior quality. The care with which they designed, printed, and covered Clive Bell's *Legend of Monte della Sibilla* and Herbert Read's *Mutations of the Phoenix* mark them as beautiful books. Both books were printed on heavy stock, Read's on watermarked paper, with attention to wide margins and strongly contrasting capital letters. Bell's book contains four handsome illustrations (including the one on the cover) by Duncan Grant and Vanessa Bell, well printed on the semigloss paper, and Read's book was beautifully covered with deep red and black marbled paper and a blue spine. The books are evidence of the Woolfs' accomplishments as fine printers when they wished to extend themselves.

Late in his life in 1968 Leonard Woolf enjoyed a brief correspondence with a professional compositor and small jobbing printer who, having read Woolf's account of his hand printing in *Downhill All the Way,* wrote in praise of the achievement. Leonard sent the printer, D. T. Stone of Bristol, a copy of one of the 1924 Hogarth Press hand-set books for his inspection, either Theodora Bosanquet's *Henry James at Work* or John Crowe Ransom's *Grace after Meat.* Stone's evaluation must have pleased Woolf mightily. "As I have some pride in my craft," wrote Stone, "I often see examples of printing performed by people with no industrial training and it is usually quite easy to recognize the typographical errors, the bad spacing, inadequate margins, over-inking and under-inking, etc. However, and I hope this doesn't sound patronizing, the book you have sent me is quite professional. Assuming I had known nothing of the history of its production and it had come into my possession I would not have guessed that the type had been hand-set and the pages printed on a platen" (MHP).

Among Hogarth Press books, however, the only volume that is truly distinguished by its fine printing is one the Woolfs had little to do with—the translation of Rilke's *Duino Elegies* by Vita and Edward Sackville-West and printed in Germany by Count Harry Kessler at his Cranach Press in 1931. The book is an excellent example of the best printing of the day, the colophon reading like an international Who's Who of printing: Kessler planned the format; Eric Gill designed the initials and cut them on wood; Edward Johnson designed the italic type, which was cut by E. Prince and G. T. Friend; Kessler and Max Goertz supervised the typesetting and printing; Walter Tanz and Hans Schulze served as compositors; and Willi Laste operated the press (*Checklist* 96). The book was printed on handsome watermarked Maillol-Kessler paper. A limited edition of 230 numbered copies was printed and signed by the translators, plus 8 numbered copies of a special edition printed on vellum with hand-gilded initials. The regular edition sold for three guineas (£3.3). The Woolfs distributed the book under the Hogarth label as a courtesy to the Sackville-Wests. It would be hard to imagine a book more unlike in every way the typical Hogarth Press book. The quality of Kessler's printing emphasizes through contrast with the Woolfs' hand-printed or commercially printed books how far the Hogarth Press was outside the movement of fine printing.

By the time Leonard and Virginia Woolf realized their two-year dream, received their income tax return, and bought their handpress in 1917, private presses and fine commercial printing had been the vogue in England for over twenty-five years, ever since the revival begun by William Morris and Emory Walker in the late 1880s. However one defines a private press, it is useful to an understanding of the Hogarth Press to include it with other small presses, strictly private or not, as is the practice of such authorities as Will Ransom and Roderick Cave. Although the first wave was over when the Woolfs entered the private press world, many independent and fine presses were established about the same time as Hogarth, and there was a great fund of talent and skill among the typographers, printers, and designers who had developed their careers since Morris. Moreover, the St. Bride's Institute with its printing and typographical library long had been established, and so too the London Central School of Arts and Crafts, which taught fine printing and bookbinding. From January to November 1913 nine issues of the influential journal *Imprint* had appeared devoted to improving printing. The future great typographer and printer Stanley Morison was on the staff.

All the more interesting, then, that the Woolfs did not pursue the path of the other presses into fine printing. Whether they lacked the visual sense of style, the artist's and designer's eye for materials and spatial relationships necessary for fine printing and book design, or whether they lacked the skill, or the time and interest to develop it, or the money, the Woolfs produced books plainly printed, in various dimensions, with attractive but inexpensive wrappers. Leonard Woolf in his autobiography recalled with pride the chilly reception the Hogarth Press books received from booksellers in the early 1920s because of their unorthodox sizes and bindings (*Downhill* 75).

The Woolfs deliberately rejected fine printing. "We did not want the Press to become one of those (admirable in their way) 'private' or semi-private Presses," recalled Woolf in his autobiography, "the object of which is finely produced books, books which are not meant to be read, but to be looked at" (*Downhill* 79). He and Virginia were interested in the contents, in "what the author had to say and how he said it," not in the form. They wanted Hogarth Press books to look "nice," he added, but neither of them was interested in fine printing or binding. As a result, the Woolfs rejected the offers of James Whitall, "a cultured American," to manage the press for them in 1922 because they feared his bookish culture would lead Hogarth into the paths of the Kelmscott or Nonesuch presses (ibid., 79). He and Virginia, Leonard added, had a particular dislike of "the refinement and preciosity which are too often a kind of fungoid growth which culture breeds upon art and literature." Americans often had it, he thought.

The first great development in the revival of printing since Morris was largely over by 1914 when the European war broke out. Many of the fine presses expired during the war years, and few new presses were established. In Europe, Count Harry Kessler founded his Cranach Press in Weimar in 1913 on the eve of the war, but he had to wait until after the armistice to begin his true work. Francis Meynell started his small private Romney Street Press in 1915, much as the Woolfs wanted to that year, but he discontinued it in 1918 after printing only two books.

The next year, 1916, however, Meynell founded the Pelican Press, which was to prove a distinct commercial and printing success. Under the joint direction of Meynell and Stanley Morison, the Pelican Press established a reputation for fine commercial printing distinguished by its use of fleurons, a wide variety of excellent typefaces, and distinctive composition. By 1920 it was printing for many businesses, such as Rolls Royce and the Midland Bank, as well as for the publishers Chatto & Windus, Jonathan Cape, Basil Blackwell, Longmans Green, Ernest Benn, and Sidgwick & Jackson. Quite understandably, Leonard and Virginia turned to the Pelican Press as one of their first printers for the separate edition of *The Mark on the Wall* (1919). The Pelican Press printed two other books for Hogarth, Gorky's *Tolstoi* (1920) and Logan Pearsall Smith's *Stories from the Old Testament* (1920), before the Woolfs decided to find less expensive printing.

Aside from Francis Meynell's Pelican Press and Hilary Pepler's small handpress, the St. Dominic's Press of Sussex, the Hogarth Press was virtually alone as a new small press when the Woolfs established it in 1917. The Beaumont Press, founded by Cyril Beaumont, was the only other press established in 1917. It had a distinguished history of fine printing (original works by Drinkwater, De la Mare, D. H. Lawrence, Aldington, and Blunden), but it ceased publishing in 1931 after issuing only twenty-six books. The year 1917 was clearly a bad time to start anything. Leonard

Woolf, looking back at the war years in his autobiography, saw them as "the most horrible period of my life," worse even than the years of the Second World War. "The horror of the years 1914 to 1918," he wrote, "was that nothing seemed to happen, month after month and year after year, except the pitiless, useless slaughter in France" (*Beginning* 197). It is evidence of the Woolfs' courage and their serious need to be diverted that they launched the press during these years.

After the Hogarth Press, the deluge. The postwar years of the 1920s proved to be the second great flowering of presses and publishers in a rich variety from the very small to the large, from the most strictly private to the highest-quality commercial. In the ten-year period between 1919, when John Rodker established the Ovid Press (printing T. S. Eliot's *Ara Vos Prec*), and 1929, when the small Aquila Press and Mandrake Press were established, between twenty-five and thirty new presses were set up, several of these in France by expatriate American and English writers. There must have been countless other abortive efforts to establish presses, now all but forgotten, like those of J. Middleton Murry and his brother (the Heron Press, 1919), Ralph Partridge with Lytton Strachey (the Tidmarsh Press, c. 1922–23), Evelyn Waugh and Alastair Graham (1924), or Stephen Spender (he handprinted forty-five copies of Auden's *Poems,* 1929). No wonder that in 1919 when the painter Simon Bussy and his wife Dorothy sought the Woolfs' advice on private presses (they intended to establish one in France), it seemed to Virginia Woolf, as she wrote to Janet Case, that "everyone is setting up private presses now" (*Letters* 2:379). The growing success of the Hogarth Press must have been an encouraging example.

The postwar presses established when the Hogarth Press was becoming a small publishing house highlight the distinct nature of the Woolfs' press. At least three major presses established in the 1920s overshadowed all the others in quality of printing and, in their way, rank with the best of the prewar presses: the Golden Cockerel (1920) by Harold Taylor and, later, Robert Gibbings; the Gregynog (1922) in Wales by the sisters Gwendolyn and Margaret Davies with the direction of R. A. Maynard; and the Nonesuch (1923) by Francis Meynell, his wife Vera, and David Garnett.

Aside from a few slim volumes of short stories and poems by such contemporaries as A. E. Coppard, Richard Hughes, and Peter Quennell, the Golden Cockerel Press followed the pattern of most fine private presses by reprinting selections of past masters beloved by the printers. The Golden Cockerel presented large slices of Sir Thomas Browne, Swift, and the Bible, with fillips of Burns, Browning, Chaucer, and Sterne among others. The Gregynog Press, perhaps the most elegant and perfectionist of the postwar presses, on a level with the Doves Press, was as exclusively concerned with Welsh writing as the Dun Emer (later the Cuala) Press of the Yeats sisters was with Irish writing. The Gregynog printed beautiful and expensive volumes of George Herbert, Edward Vaughan, Edward Thomas, Walter Davies, and the Welsh Bible.

The Meynells' Nonesuch Press proved more publisher than press, using for its printing such fine printers as the Kynoch, Pelican, and Oxford University presses. Francis Meynell, having left the Pelican Press to start the Nonesuch, set out, he remembered, "to be a new kind of publisher-designer, an architect of books rather than a builder, seeking . . . the services . . . of the best printing houses, papermakers, binders." The first one hundred Nonesuch books, he recalled, employed twenty-six different typefaces and nineteen different printers.[36] The press was distinguished by the beautifully designed and printed editions of standard works of English literature, particularly those of such seventeenth-century writers as Marvell, Donne, Burton, Walton, Herbert, Vaughan, and Milton. The volumes were handsomely priced, also. When David Garnett, as Nonesuch partner and bookseller, wrote to Virginia Woolf in 1923 about the new Nonesuch edition of Congreve (complete in four volumes, edited by Rev. Montague Summers, and costing three guineas), she wrote back: "Lytton advises me that the Congreve is more for people of wealth than for hungry students like myself, (which of course is a nasty one for the Nonesuchers) so, with a thousand thanks for your offer, I won't spend my £3/3 on that, but lay it out, I swear, upon other books" (*Letters* 3:73). The Hogarth Press and its owners were not in the same market as the Nonesuch, and were glad of it.

To the three great presses of the 1920s can be added several interesting if smaller ones among the twenty-five or thirty presses established between the wars: the Favil Press (1920), a commercial printing firm which also printed fine limited editions, including works by the Sitwells;

the Fanfrolico Press (begun in Australia in 1922 and moved to Bloomsbury in 1926); the Fleuron (1923), founded by Oliver Simon and Stanley
Morison to publish the influential *Fleuron,* a journal of typography and
printing, but which also published books including a series on modern
British artists such as Mark Gertler and Duncan Grant; the Cresset Press
(1927); and the Scholartis Press (1927) of Eric Partridge.

During this time a number of publications, like the *Fleuron,* provided scholarly and practical information on all aspects of fine printing
and publishing, from type design, layout, printing, and binding to editing, distribution, and sales. There were Stanley Morison's monumental
Four Centuries of Fine Printing (1914) and Oliver Simon's *Printing To-Day*
(1928), a survey of postwar typography. The Woolfs had a copy of Simon's
book and three issues of the *Fleuron* in their library, together with such
works as Norman Paley's *New Methods of Reproductions of Books and Manuscripts* (1928), Alfred Johnson's *One Hundred Title Pages* (1928), and Gerard Meynell's *Pages from Books* (1927).[37] They were well aware of modern
developments and historic precedents but chose to ignore most of them.

In Europe, mostly Paris, American and English expatriates established a remarkable number of small presses during the 1920s. Among
them were Sylvia Beach's Shakespeare and Company (1922–29), which
published Joyce's *Ulysses;* Robert McAlmon's Contact Editions (1922–31);
William Bird's Three Mountains Press (1923–26); Harry and Caresse
Crosby's Black Sun Press (1925–36); Edward Titus's Black Maniken Press
(1926–32); and Nancy Cunard's Hours Press (1928–31).[38] And there was
the Seizin Press (1928–37) of Robert Graves and Laura Riding, established first in London and then moved to Majorca in 1930. Nancy Cunard, Robert Graves, and Laura Riding had all been published previously
by the Hogarth Press. It is likely that they conceived the idea of their own
presses from their experience with the Woolfs.

Nancy Cunard, like Simon and Dorothy Bussy, apparently sought
the advice of the Woolfs about printing. As she recalled in a memoir:
"Leonard and Virginia Woolf of the Hogarth Press (she had hand-set my
long poem, *Parallax,* herself, published by them in 1925) wrote: 'Your
hands will always be covered with ink.' Once I had begun, I noticed,
laughing, how that was no deterrent, nor even true; plain petrol washes
off all that good-smelling printer's ink as well as it cleans type."[39] Leonard

Woolf, when questioned years later about giving Cunard discouraging advice, answered that "we knew Nancy and were very fond of her," but he did not remember discouraging her from printing and doubted that he gave her any such advice.[40] Cunard, with her usual slapdash energy and enthusiasm, established her press with Louis Aragon at Réanville, near Paris, under the somewhat puzzled tutelage of professional printer Maurice Levy. The Hours Press, first in Réanville and later in Paris, printed and published twenty-four volumes in its four-year existence, including works by George Moore, Richard Aldington, Arthur Symons, Norman Douglas, Robert Graves, Laura Riding, Samuel Beckett (his poem *Whoroscope*), Ezra Pound (*XXX Cantos*), and Roy Campbell.

The Seizin Press, established by Laura Riding and Robert Graves, was more narrowly focused than the Hours Press and was illuminated by the linguistic and moral idealism of Riding and Graves. Like the Woolfs, they were more concerned with content than with form. They established adequate standards of presswork but rejected fine printing. Unlike the Woolfs, however, Riding and Graves printed more of their own work than that of their friends. In its seven-year existence, the Seizin Press published only eighteen books.[41] The Hogarth Press in its first seven years published thirty-three books.

The English and American presses in Europe were by nature avant-garde, experimental, sometimes eccentric, and always expressive of the publishers' personal interests. Expatriates themselves, the publishers printed and published the work of other expatriates, exploiting the freedom an adopted country gave them from the critical or moral dictates of a conservative, unenlightened readership at home. They were unworried by the need for commercial success. Their presses averaged a life span of from four to seven years and published on the average four books a year. The Hogarth Press, distinctive among most of the small presses in England, printed modern writers and stayed afloat. Whether or not the Hogarth Press directly helped to spawn the Hours Press, the Seizin Press, or any other of the smaller presses of the 1920s, it was the first press of its kind during the war and provided young writers and would-be printers with an example for their own enterprises.

The international economic depression of the late 1920s and early 1930s, like the First World War, acted against presses and publishers. Not many of the 1920s presses endured through the next decade, whether in London or in Paris, and only a few new presses began in the 1930s. Jack Kahane's Obelisk Press (1930–39) in Paris was one of them. It is further evidence of the unique character of the Hogarth Press, the shrewd management of Leonard, and the artistic presence of Virginia that their press survived and flourished during more than two decades of fierce competition and economic disaster. It is well to remember when assessing the achievement of the Hogarth Press that the established commercial publishing houses and presses, the newer fine presses, and the avant-garde private presses were all competing for reprints of classics or for the work of new writers.

The Woolfs, during the period 1917 to 1941 covered by this history, built a solid publishing business by printing only original work, not reprints of classics, and by diversifying beyond fiction and poetry into translations, politics, economics, history, psychoanalysis, art criticism, and memoirs. The Woolfs published what interested them, kept their prices down, and made the book designs attractive but not elaborate.

CHAPTER TWO

★

BEGINNINGS, 1917–23

S tarting the Hogarth Press gave the Woolfs the pleasure of print-ing their own work. For them this meant fiction, and they be-gan in fine style with *Two Stories*—Leonard's "Three Jews" and Virginia's "The Mark on the Wall." At the time, mid-July 1917, both were published novelists, Leonard with *The Village in the Jungle* (1913) and *The Wise Virgins* (1914) and Virginia with *The Voyage Out* (1915). They were also active literary journalists. Virginia had many reviews and essays to her credit, and Leonard already had written and edited two works for the Fabians and the Women's Co-operative movement.

Neither Virginia's essays nor Leonard's tracts were suitable for friends or for Omega Workshop customers, however, and novels were clearly too long to hand print. They were not writing poetry. So short fiction it was, for "Publication No. 1," turned out at Hogarth House, Richmond, with the somewhat uneven inking and the slightly skewed woodcut by Carrington. Moreover, the fiction they printed could be ex-hilaratingly free from editorial restraints, could be, in fact, experimental. If Leonard did not experiment with his ironic yet traditional and anec-dotal tale of the Jewish widower and the gravedigger, Virginia made full use of her freedom in "The Mark on the Wall," her first important break with conventional realism.

"I daresay one ought to invent a completely new form," Virginia wrote to David Garnett the week after *Two Stories* was mailed out to buy-ers (*Letters* 2:167). She had just described traditional novels as "frightfully clumsy and overpowering" and then added: "Any how its very amusing to try with these short things, and the greatest mercy to be able to do what one likes—no editors, or publishers, and only people to read who more or less like that sort of thing." Their new friend S. S. Koteliansky, she wrote, had warned them against writing for a small public, but, she concluded, "I dont like writing for my half brother George." She must have meant her other half brother, Gerald Duckworth, director of the publishing firm Duckworth & Co., publisher of her first novel. After one more novel for Duckworth, *Night and Day* (1919), Virginia Woolf would publish all of her subsequent writing under the Hogarth Press imprint: seven more novels (including *Between the Acts* published four months after her death), one collection of short stories, two biographies, and eight volumes of wide-ranging essays.

What began as a recreation became a necessity. Virginia Woolf's genius surely would have survived in some form under any publisher, but it developed as it did in the novels and essays because she was free from editorial pressures, real or imagined, and needed to please only herself, an editor severe enough for all seasons.

Virginia Stephen had begun her first novel as *Melymbrosia* in the autumn of 1907, and Virginia Woolf had published it as *The Voyage Out* in 1915. Unlike her later novels, the first one evolved slowly in more or less public fashion, Virginia discussing its progress with her sister Vanessa, with Clive Bell and others, seeking advice, showing the manuscript. She had eight chapters finished by April 1911 after several revisions, reworked it once again, and read portions of it to Leonard Woolf in March 1912.

Miss Stephen became Mrs. Woolf in May 1912, finally finished her manuscript in February 1913, and, in a pattern which she would repeat to the end of her life, gave her husband Leonard the book to read before sending it to Duckworth. What Clive Bell had once provided in 1908–9, Leonard now provided more fully—unqualified admiration for Virginia's writing combined with perceptive criticism and reassurance. Virginia would wait anxiously for the responses of Lytton Strachey and E. M. Forster, her most-respected and slightly feared Bloomsbury critics, but she came to depend most fully on Leonard's reading. The fact that Leonard had praised *Voyage Out* as "extraordinarily good" when she read portions of it to him in March 1912 encouraged her and helped her to accept his marriage proposal two months later (*Beginning* 81).

It was a novelists' honeymoon. Leonard and Virginia Woolf at the beginning of it in the rainy August of 1912 tramped the Quantocks and sat by the fire of a Somerset inn reading novels "like tigers." As Virginia reported to Janet Case, "Now that we've done our own its great fun to read other people's" (*Letters* 2:4). She had completed a draft of *The Voyage Out* and Leonard a draft of *The Village in the Jungle* just before the wedding, but only Leonard's book neared completion. After the honeymoon Leonard sent off his novel to Edward Arnold, who published it in February 1913. Virginia, who had already labored on *The Voyage Out* for five years, began an extensive redrafting of it which would not be complete until February, the month of Leonard's publication. Before Duckworth & Co. could publish Virginia's novel, her bouts of severe mental illness intervened, delaying publication until March 1915. By that time Leonard's *Village in the Jungle* had gone through two reprints, and he had published his second novel, *The Wise Virgins,* in 1914.

Virginia Woolf's experience during the completion, acceptance, and publication of *The Voyage Out,* while more terrible than with any of her other books, foreshadowed later reactions. When Leonard read the completed manuscript of *The Voyage Out* in early March 1913, he was uneasy about Virginia's increasing headaches, nervousness, and sleeplessness. He took the book to Gerald Duckworth on March 9. Edward Garnett, the publisher's reader, wrote what Leonard Woolf recalled "an extremely appreciative" report on the book, and Duckworth accepted it for publication on April 12 (*Beginning* 87).

The editorial decision took only one month, but the interval was agony for Virginia. The relief provided by acceptance was only temporary, however, as she faced the perils of publication. Virginia's sleeplessness and depression grew during the spring and summer, delusions occurred in August, followed by a resistance to food. She attempted suicide on September 9 by taking 100 grains of veronal and nearly died. *The Voyage Out,* probably planned as an autumn release, was postponed because of her illness. Not until a year later, in October and November 1914, did she seem sufficiently recovered for the publication process to start once more. The novel appeared on March 26, 1915, two years after its submission to Duckworth, but with almost perverse timing and terrible irony. Virginia Woolf was once again submerged by her mental illness, unable to appreciate either her first publication or her new home in Hogarth House.

Virginia Woolf's reactions to her novels as they were completed and proceeded to publication followed a pattern of varying intensity. As she finished the first draft and drove herself to rewrite each novel, her periodic headaches, tension, and sleeplessness increased in duration and severity. The strain at this stage was both emotional and physical. Obsessively absorbed in her creation, she struggled to achieve the mastery of her vision, to refine the cadences and colors of her language. Then came a tension-filled period as she awaited the verdict from Leonard, her first reader. She seems to have gone about with held breath, tense, distracted, tight with nervous anticipation. A favorable reply from Leonard produced a flood of relief, an almost audible gasp of air. Then with the release, Virginia generated new self-doubts that she gradually tempered with an increasingly objective view of the work. The final stage was apt to be most severe, occurring as the book went to press and was released to the public. At this point her dread of failure, her sense of having muddled her original concept and reduced it to gibberish or dullness, was coupled with her terror of exposure to an uncomprehending general public.

Such fears were never realized, however. From the beginning of her writing career to the end, Virginia Woolf showed a toughness of intellect and spirit and a self-conviction which belied her fears. She knew what she was doing. Her anxieties were in the abstract; she was little affected intellectually or artistically by actual criticism. When rejection came with increasingly sexist overtones from offended and entrenched male critics, her anger or her cool wit and irony replaced depression and worry. Even under the savage mockery of Wyndham Lewis's anti-Bloomsbury blasts in the 1920s and 1930s, or Prince Mirsky's unexpected Marxist assault in 1935, or Q. D. Leavis's personalized and angry attack on *Three Guineas* in 1938, when public derision might have confirmed her in her darkest fears, she turned aside the criticism with her own mockery. "Oh I've had such a drubbing and a scourging from the Cambridge ladies," she wrote to Ethel Smyth about Mrs. Leavis's review of *Three Guineas* (entitled "Caterpillars of the Commonwealth Unite"). "I'm a disgrace to my sex: and a caterpillar on the community," she added. "I thought I should raise their hackles—poor old strumpets" (*Letters* 6:271).

In spite of Virginia Woolf's essential resilience in the face of hostile criticism, her fears when completing and publishing a work of fiction were vivid enough. In order to minimize these anxieties, she began the practice, after her first novel, of never showing a work to a reader while writing it. Another way to lessen the pressures on herself was to eliminate the worry over the middleman, the masculine editor or publisher's reader who decided the fate of her creation. But only in 1922, when the Hogarth Press was sturdy enough to bear the weight of a novel, could she dispense with the judgment of Duckworth or his reader.

Gerald Duckworth was a logical choice as publisher for Virginia Woolf's first two novels, although she distrusted and despised both her half brothers, later accusing Gerald of fondling her when she was six and George of more continuous sexual abuse during her adolescence.[1] Her heightened anxiety over her first novel may have come from the fear of a renewed exposure of her intimate self through her fiction to the man who had abused her as a child. Gerald Duckworth had founded his firm in 1898 when he was twenty-eight and Virginia sixteen. By 1913, when Virginia was ready to submit *The Voyage Out* to a publisher, Duckworth & Co. was a small, well-established house. With the services of Edward Garnett as reader, it had published Henry James, Joseph Conrad, John Galsworthy, Edward Thomas, and Ford Madox Hueffer (later Ford Madox Ford). Edward Garnett, the husband of Constance, the redoubtable Russian translator, and father of David, a young member of Bloomsbury, was himself a man of letters—playwright, poet, novelist, anthologist—a perceptive and discerning critic, and sage counsel to such writers as Conrad, Galsworthy, and W. H. Hudson. It would be hard to imagine a more formidable masculine bastion of Edwardian and Georgian literary values than Duckworth & Co. at the time.

Virginia Woolf was fortunate, however, in having Edward Garnett as her reader, for Gerald Duckworth was more businessman than man of letters. The modest success of the firm was due largely to the shrewd judgment of Garnett and the good management of partner Thomas Balston. Virginia had no illusions about her half brother's talents. As she wrote to Violet Dickinson in May 1913, "Gerald has accepted my book (I don't think he got through it) and I'm now correcting proofs" (*Letters* 2:28). When she submitted her second novel, *Night and Day* (1919), Virginia wrote to Janet Case, "I was even a little pleased this morning to be accepted by Gerald Duckworth—who doesn't know a book from a bee-hive" (ibid., 354). Novelist Anthony Powell, who joined Duckworth & Co. in 1926–27 as an unpaid apprentice, realized that Gerald was not much interested in books. He saw that the small firm was by then "staunchly anti-avant garde" and out of touch with literary fashion, especially with Bloomsbury.[2] When the Woolfs bought the rights to *The Voyage Out* and *Night and Day* from Duckworth, to reissue them in 1929 and 1930 under the Hogarth Press, Powell commented that there was "a sense of relief probably felt on both sides at this rearrangement."

Virginia Woolf had conceived the idea for her second novel, *Night and Day,* as early as the summer of 1916, but she did not begin drafting it until sometime between January and July 1917. A year later, by March 12, 1918, she had completed over 100,000 words; the next week she worried that her novel was "destined to be pawed & snored over" by Gerald (*Diary* 1:127, 129). Woolf had interrupted the early stages of her novel during the summer of 1917 to write and print "The Mark on the Wall," and she interrupted herself again the following summer of 1918 to write and print *Kew Gardens*. Both short works were exploratory, free from the restrictions of the conventional form she was employing in the novel, and tied directly to the serious recreation of providing the Hogarth Press with stories and poems of "suitable length and interest."

It occurred to the Woolfs while hand printing Virginia's *Kew Gardens* in November 1918 that they might expand operations by offering their friends more than one volume at a time. As Virginia wrote to Vanessa, "we think of getting 2 or 3 little books ready before we send out, so as to give people something at once" (*Letters* 2:297). Eliot sent them his *Poems* in late November, and they soon had Murry's *Critic in Judgment,* both of which they set and printed early in 1919. With three books in hand, the Woolfs began to conceive of a subscription plan in March to encourage sales. Leonard shrewdly adapted subscription publishing, designed to underwrite the cost of expensively printed limited editions or multivolumed specialized trade publications, to suit his need for a small amount of working capital and a list of regular buyers.

Leonard created two subscription categories: A subscribers, who deposited £1 and received all publications, and B subscribers, who ordered and paid for only those publications they desired. Clive Bell, for example, who had been among the first to order *Two Stories* and *Prelude,* paying a total of five shillings for them, immediately became an A subscriber, sent in his £1 deposit on May 6, received the three publications in return (costing seven shillings total), and carried a balance on the Hogarth books of thirteen shillings (ABS 113).

Between May 6, 1919, when the subscription scheme began, and October 1920, there were thirty-four A subscribers and fifteen B subscribers. Gradually the number increased. Subscribers were mostly Bloomsbury members, but there were some interesting friends such as H. G. Wells, Rebecca West, Hugh Walpole, Edward Garnett, and James Bain the bookseller. Wallace Stevens wrote in from America and became a subscriber on September 23, 1920. There were three more A subscribers and two more B subscribers in 1921, fifteen more A and twenty-two more B in 1922, and three more A and four more B in 1923. Six subscribers changed categories. When Leonard Woolf abandoned the scheme, the subscribers numbered fifty-two A and forty-six B.[3] With such small numbers, far below the actual number of volumes sold for each publication, the subscription scheme was useful less for its financial support than for its success in spreading the Hogarth Press name before a larger audience than that of Bloomsbury.

The subscription scheme promoted the Hogarth Press at a crucial time in its development. When the Woolfs solicited their first subscribers, they had not yet advertised in the press, nor had they traveled the bookstores. In late May 1919 they undertook the latter task, going around to the London bookstores at the suggestion of Logan Pearsall Smith.

In 1919 the Woolfs also turned to commercial printers for the first time: McDermott's Prompt Press for Murry's *Critic in Judgment,* Richard Madley for the immediate second impression of Virginia's *Kew Gardens* after its astonishing over-the-weekend success, and Francis Meynell's Pelican Press for the separate edition of Virginia's *Mark on the Wall.* After these productions, the Woolfs used commercial printers with increasing frequency. Appropriately, the first recognition of the press as publisher came in the 1919 volume of *The English Catalogue of Books* (published in 1920). One of the authoritative annual compilations of books published in England, it listed Murry's *Critic in Judgment* and Virginia Woolf's *Kew Gardens* and *Mark on the Wall,* all printed by professionals, but not Eliot's

Poems, hand printed by the Woolfs. The 1920 edition of *The English Cat-alogue of Books* listed the Hogarth Press for the first time in the directory of publishers, and all books published by the press, hand printed or not, appeared from this time on in the annual editions. The Hogarth Press was becoming recognized by the publishing and bookselling fraternity.

The Hogarth Press finally turned the corner from private press to small publishing house in 1920 when Leonard Woolf decided to publish S. S. Koteliansky's translation of Maxim Gorky's *Reminiscences of Tolstoi,* the first of Hogarth's Russian translations. He used a commercial printer from the beginning; it was the first time Woolf had contracted with a printer (Meynell's Pelican Press) for the entire book production. He ordered 1,250 copies printed for the July 7, 1920, publication date, by far his largest pressrun up to this time, in shrewd anticipation of hefty sales. When the orders poured in, the Woolfs had their first commercial success and had to reprint in early January 1921.

When E. M. Forster brought his *Story of a Siren* to the Woolfs in March 1920, he became the first member of Bloomsbury to have a work published by the Hogarth Press. Lytton Strachey had nicknamed him the "Taupe," or mole, at Cambridge, as Leonard Woolf reported in his autobiography, not only because of a slight physical similarity "but principally because he seemed intellectually and emotionally to travel unseen underground and every now and again pop up unexpectedly with some subtle observations or delicate quip which somehow or other he had found in the depths of the earth or of his own soul" (*Sowing* 172). Forster's relationship with the Woolfs and their press was very much of this sort, with Forster popping up unexpectedly, but always welcome, with observations and quips and sometimes with manuscripts. Over a period of twenty years, from 1920 to 1940, Forster published seven books or pamphlets with the Hogarth Press. None of these were major works, but two of them, *The Story of the Siren* (1920) and *What I Believe* (1939), rank with the best of his stories and essays. The seven works mark Forster as the only Bloomsbury member to sustain a publishing connection with the Woolfs.

Forster's position within Bloomsbury, like his unfolding friendship with Leonard and Virginia Woolf, seems to have mirrored his press relationship—long-lived but mostly peripheral. Although Leonard Woolf listed Forster among the twelve members of "Old Bloomsbury," Leon

Edel did not include him in his study of the original nine members of Bloomsbury in *A House of Lions* because Forster's life did not become intimately involved with the others. Forster more often than not was absent from the lion house. He and Leonard were nearly the same age and died within a year of each other, Forster entered Cambridge two years ahead of Woolf, and they were both members of the Apostles. When Woolf went off to Ceylon in 1904, Forster wrote a farewell letter characteristically truthful and oblique, declaring that he liked Leonard better than he knew him (*Sowing* 172). Their friendship grew when Woolf returned to England. Before Forster left for India in 1912, Woolf helped teach him how to ride. They kept up sporadic contact during the war years while Forster served with the Red Cross in Alexandria (1915–19), and then in the early 1920s Forster and the Woolfs became more intimate.

Forster had not published a book in nine years when he brought *The Story of the Siren* to the Woolfs in March 1920. Behind him were three early novels—*Where Angels Fear to Tread* (1905), *The Longest Journey* (1907), *A Room with a View* (1908)—and his artistic breakthrough, *Howard's End* (1910). After he had published *A Room with a View,* Forster offered his publisher Edward Arnold a collection of short stories in lieu of his next novel, which was not yet finished (*Howard's End*). Arnold rejected the manuscript on the grounds that stories did not sell.[4] After publishing *Howard's End* with Arnold, Forster again tried to place the stories. Finally, Sidgwick & Jackson accepted six of the ten stories he had submitted and published them as *The Celestial Omnibus* (1911). The six stories, including the title story, as well as "The Other Side of the Hedge" and his most famous early effort, "The Story of a Panic" (written in 1902), had been published in various magazines between 1904 and 1909.[5] *The Story of the Siren* dates from the same period, but it had never been published, and it may have been one of the four stories rejected by Sidgwick & Jackson.

The Hogarth Press had come into existence while Forster acted as a Red Cross searcher in Alexandria; but by the time Leonard and Virginia had hand printed his story in June 1920, they had published only nine titles. *The Story of the Siren,* issued in 500 copies to the subscribers in July, appeared with Gorky's *Reminiscences of Tolstoi.* While not matching the unusual success of the *Tolstoi,* Forster's story sold well, 325 copies purchased in the first six months and the printing nearly sold out by March 1922, one year after Forster gave the manuscript to the Woolfs (ABS 133–34). Leonard Woolf paid Forster £20 for the story in three installments: £10 on March 3, 1920 (presumably when the manuscript was delivered), £5 on December 30, 1920, and £5 on July 7, 1921 (the anniversary of publication). The press had realized a modest profit of £6.3 when the account was finally closed in November 1925.

After the long pull of completing her second novel, *Night and Day,* which Duckworth published in October 1919, Virginia Woolf turned once again to writing short, impressionistic pieces, a refreshing therapy made possible for her by the press. She wrote seven stories after "The Mark on the Wall" and *Kew Gardens* and published them together as her next book, *Monday or Tuesday,* early in March 1921. They were "A Haunted House," "A Society," "Monday or Tuesday," "An Unwritten Novel," "The String Quartet," "Blue and Green," and "Solid Objects." McDermott's Prompt Press printed the stories for the Hogarth Press, and did it badly. The book was "an odious object," Virginia Woolf complained to Violet Dickinson, and left "black stains wherever it touches" (*Letters* 2:466).

Bloomsbury friends responded enthusiastically to the stories of *Monday or Tuesday.* Lytton Strachey remarked that he thought the "String Quartet" marvelous. Roger Fry commented that she was "on the track of real discoveries, & certainly not a fake." She noted that the book had broken all records for sales. Then came a note of resignation. "And I'm not nearly as pleased as I was depressed; & yet in a state of security; fate cannot touch me; the reviewers may snap; & sales decrease" (*Diary* 2:109). She had overcome her great fear of being "dismissed as negligible." A day later she noted her "complete absence of jealousy" as Lytton Strachey's *Queen Victoria* was published; its appearance overshadowed that of *Monday or Tuesday.* Woolf's hard-won equanimity toward an admired competitor's success was sorely tested when she learned on April 15 that *Queen Victoria* had sold 5,000 copies in a week; she recorded that *Monday or Tuesday* had sold only 300 copies (ibid., 110). On April 17 she noted with resignation that "sales & reviews flag, & I much doubt if M. & T. will sell 500, or cover expenses" (ibid., 111).

It may be surprising to see that Virginia Woolf was interested in sales figures, contrary to the popular image of her as a writer concerned exclusively with her own art, spurning popular success. But she had an ambitious, uncompromising, and competitive side. When coupled with her desire to see the Hogarth Press flourish, this side of her expressed itself in volume counts. Low sales figures temporarily demoralized her, but high sales figures made her slightly uneasy because they smacked of commercialism. The Woolfs did not establish the Hogarth Press for large profits. When the receipts rolled in for her *Orlando* in 1928, Virginia Woolf's reaction to a best-seller was surprise and amused self-detachment.

Virginia's mention of the 300 copies sold by April 15, 1921, and a Simpkin & Marshall order for 50 more copies raise interesting but unanswerable questions about the sale of *Monday and Tuesday*. Contrary to her claims to be breaking sales records, the Hogarth Press account book (Sussex) records a far different balance sheet, showing that sales were slow to begin and never increased beyond a trickle. *Monday and Tuesday,* published in March 1921, had sold a total of only 81 copies by the end of April 1921, and there is no record of an additional order for 50 copies.[6] Sales dwindled to 15 copies sold in May, spurted up to 100 copies in June, 61 copies in July, dropped to 30 copies in August, and peaked at 104 copies in September 1921. After that it was downhill. At the end of the first year, April 1922, the book had sold a total of 503 copies, showing a deficit to the press of £8.3.9. During the next two years, the book averaged 70 copies per year. When Leonard Woolf closed out the account at the end of March 1924, *Monday or Tuesday* in three years had sold only 643 copies and made a slim profit of £11.17.10.[7] Virginia, as author, was awarded approximately one-fifth of the third year's profit, amounting to £2.16.5. With such modest returns, the press and its authors just managed to stay afloat during its first five years of existence.

The discrepancies between Virginia Woolf's diary entries and the press account book must result from some misunderstanding or misinformation. Ralph Partridge, their new assistant, may have given her incorrect sales figures through error, although the differences seem too great for miscalculation. It is possible that Leonard or Ralph may have deceived Virginia about the sales to boost her spirits. But her spirits seem not to have needed boosting at the time. It is possible but highly unlikely that Leonard recorded some sales figures in another account book which is now lost. It is true that the monthly sales (Reading) account book shows 511 copies of *Monday or Tuesday* sold in the first six months, but this figure seems to have been calculated years later and does not correspond to either the first account book (Sussex) or its continuation, the account book (Reading).[8] Virginia Woolf sometimes cheerfully and knowingly exaggerated facts for the sake of a good story, but she never deceived herself in her diary. There seems to be no good explanation for the differences between her diary and the account books.

With the joys of success from Gorky's *Tolstoi* came burdens. In the early summer of 1920, the Woolfs had been flooded with manuscripts from Bloomsbury friends as they labored to handprint Forster's *Story of the Siren*. "The Hogarth Press is growing like a beanstalk," Virginia Woolf wrote to Violet Dickinson in July 1920, "and we think we must set up a shop and keep a clerk" (*Letters* 2:434). The Birrell and Garnett Bookshop, owned and operated by two Bloomsbury friends, had opened in 1919 and may have inspired the Woolfs to talk about having a shop. It would not be the last of such imagined enterprises for the Woolfs (Virginia liked the idea of opening a "tea shop, book shop, gallery in Bond Street" in 1921, and they thought about buying out Birrell and Garnett in 1927), but nothing ever came of these dreams.[9] It is hard to imagine Virginia, with her ink-stained fingers and hand-rolled shag cigarettes, as proprietress of a Bond Street book boutique, or Leonard in the back room, aproned amid packing boxes and teapots.

Bookshops must have been in the air in that summer of 1919, when everyone was luxuriating in the first year of peace. Logan Pearsall Smith, self-appointed adviser to the Woolfs on the press operation, introduced them to Arundell del Re on the eve of his opening the Chelsea Book Club, which he would stock with finely printed books and modern art. He had been an associate of Harold Monro at his Poetry Bookshop. Unimpressed by del Re's aestheticism, his "weakness and paleness" as Virginia wrote, the Woolfs had been interested, nevertheless, in his proposal to stock Hogarth Press books, keep the accounts, and run the business side of things in exchange for printing lessons (*Diary* 1:290). The Woolfs eventually rejected his offer, as they would decide against setting up a shop with a clerk the next summer of 1920. But Leonard, in early August 1920, busy with the success of Gorky and exhausted by printing Forster's story (fourteen pages of prose in 500 copies), was "on the verge of destruction," as Virginia observed (ibid., 2:55). "As a hobby," she wrote, "The Hogarth Press is clearly too lively & lusty to be carried on in this private way any longer. Moreover, the business part of it can't be shared, owing to my incompetence. The future, therefore, needs consideration." The Woolfs had used the part-time volunteer printing apprentices Alix Sargant-Florence and Barbara Hiles in 1917–18, but they had never had an assistant to help with both the printing and publishing. Relief came in the form of Ralph Partridge, friend of Lytton Strachey and recent Oxford graduate. By becoming the first paid press assistant, Partridge would help move the press irrevocably into the public ranks of publishing. The Woolfs would never go back to private practice.

Leonard Woolf originally conceived of offering Partridge a share in the press and, as Virginia noted, "baiting this perhaps minute tidbit with the plumper morsel of secretaryship to L" (*Diary* 2:56). And then the entrepreneurial Leonard went further, wrote Virginia, as he thought "why not install Partridge at Suffield, & buy a complete printing outfit? Why not? Run a shop there too, perhaps." As plans simmered in Leonard's mind, Virginia wrote to Roger Fry three days later about their turmoil. "We now think," she wrote, "of setting up a proper printing plant and doing all production ourselves—that is with a manager" (*Letters* 2:439). The alternative, she thought, would be to end the press, "as we can't go on with it as we've been doing." In the end, they abandoned the idea of the plant and the shop and agreed to take on Partridge as an assistant for £100 per year and 50 percent of the net profits (*Downhill* 72). He came two or three days a week and earned slightly more than £56 in 1920 and £125 in 1921.

When the Woolfs had set up their handpress at Hogarth House in April 1917 and begun to write short fiction, Leonard Woolf had seemed on his way to a successful career as a fiction writer. Actually, he had written his last novel and was turning his formidable energy and journalistic skill to those political subjects which would engage him to the end of his life. Woolf's first story, "Three Jews" (1917), and the three stories he would publish with the press as *Stories of the East* (1921) now seem diversions, serious enough for hand printing but not to be placed on a level with his two novels, *The Village in the Jungle* (1913) and *The Wise Virgins*

(1914) or with his Fabian Society and Labour party books. Yet Woolf had displayed a novelist's talent in his first two books, and his Eastern stories confirmed his skills as a narrative writer.

Leonard Woolf abandoned the novel form after his second try, probably for a variety of reasons. The most obvious was the low return on his invested labor. He had earned only £42 from *The Village in the Jungle* and £20 from *The Wise Virgins* at a time when he needed to increase his income to support himself and Virginia. There was a more substantial and reliable livelihood to be earned from editing, journalism, and political writing, which quickly absorbed most of his creative energies. Then, too, there must have been his realization that Virginia's art far outstripped his own, that he could not possibly follow her lead as she evolved the novel beyond his modest capabilities with traditional form. The short story offered Woolf a less demanding genre than the time-consuming novel, and he must have approached it as a serious diversion, first with "Three Jews" and then with *Stories of the East* (1921).

Woolf's Eastern stories, three in number, owe their subject matter to his seven years' stay in Ceylon and their method to Conrad and Kipling. The last story, "The Two Brahmans," a short, amusing Kiplingesque tale approaching the fable, is the slightest of offerings, tracing the consequences of breaking caste among Tamils in a large northern village. Of more craft and consequence are Woolf's two longer stories, "A Tale Told by Moonlight" and "Pearls and Swine."

The setting, narrative technique, subject matter, and pervasive irony of "A Tale Told by Moonlight" show how well Woolf knew Conrad's *Heart of Darkness*. Woolf places his five representative characters—the unnamed narrator, the novelist and host Alderton, the poet Pemberton, the critic Smith, and the man-of-the-world storyteller Jessop—not on the cruising yawl *Nellie* at dusk in the Thames estuary pointing seaward, but on the banks of a river coursing out to sea, under the trees in the moonlight. The framed story, like Conrad's, permits Woolf to introduce a topic commented on superficially by the characters (in this case, the sentimental, fictional treatment of love) and then to have it exposed by the storyteller's sardonic account of a "real" experience. Jessop resembles Marlow as narrator in his ironic asides, but the tale he tells lacks the dark reverberations of Conrad's moral probings.

Leonard Woolf's second story, "Pearls and Swine," follows much the same Conradian pattern of the frame story and echoes the horrors of Marlow's experiences with Kurtz at the Inner Station. Woolf's five characters in search of enlightenment sit around the fire in the smoking room of a Torquay resort hotel while a colonel, a stockjobber, and an archdeacon blather self-righteously about the white man's burden in the East. They know nothing, of course, blindly prejudiced against the "natives" and chauvinistically proud to be members of the superior race. The anonymous narrator (fifteen years in the East) chafes at the conversation until the fifth character, an Anglo-Indian (thirty years in India), exposes their smug ignorance with his story of a pearl fishery in India. The vivid details of the fishery camp, somewhat altered from Woolf's own experience in northern Ceylon, provide the substance of the Anglo-Indian's story.[10]

Leonard Woolf's *Stories of the East,* skillfully written, ironic narratives in a familiar genre, reveals character amid exotic surroundings. The stories emphasize the severe testing ground of the East and point to the harsh realities of an existence unknown to those who stay at home. As such, Woolf's stories subtly provided evidence of his own virtues as an administrator and survivor.

It is possible but unprovable without more evidence that Leonard Woolf wrote one or more of his Eastern stories earlier than his publication of them in 1921 would indicate. George Spater and Ian Parsons, knowledgeable about Woolf's life, imply as much.[11] There is an undated manuscript copy of "A Tale Told by Moonlight" in the Woolf papers at the University of Sussex library, together with fragments of other stories. There is no indication of when these manuscripts were written, but they might have been drafted when he was in Ceylon or soon after he returned to England. E. M. Forster wrote to Leonard Woolf in May 1912 and referred to a draft of a story similar, if not identical, to "Pearls and Swine." Forster liked the story Woolf had sent him, he wrote, and suggested that Woolf send it to the *English Review.*[12]

Although the Woolfs had made the important step toward becoming a publishing house with the July 1920 publication of Gorky's *Reminiscences of Tolstoi* (printed by the Pelican Press), they were still doing most of the printing and binding themselves. With *Stories of the East,* the Woolfs hand set the book themselves but paid McDermott £5.11.6 to machine it and 16s.6d. to bind it (ABS 139). Dora Carrington, who had designed the woodcuts for *Two Stories,* and who had recently married Ralph Partridge, provided an attractive woodcut for the cover; it showed an irrelevant but fiercely prowling tiger framed by palm trees, floating flowers, and pineapples. They printed it in red ink on buff-colored stock and paid Carrington one guinea for her work. *Stories of the East* was published April 1921 in 300 copies and very nearly sold out. At the end of the first year, the Hogarth Press had sold over 230 copies, to realize a profit of £6.11.5 (ABS 140). When Leonard Woolf closed out the account in January 1924, *Stories of the East* had sold 267 copies. Of the six books published by Hogarth in 1921, Leonard's stories outsold all but Gorky's second book, *The Note-Books of Tchekhov* and Virginia's *Monday or Tuesday,* and in the scale of the press operations it was a successful venture.

The commercial potential of Leonard Woolf's stories was not lost on Henry Holt (no relation to the distinguished American publisher by that name), an American agent of stereotypical brashness and breezy familiarity. He wrote to Woolf in April 1922, one year after publication, to see if he could take "Pearls and Swine" for the American market at a 15 percent agent's fee. Woolf agreed and thus began an amazing and hilarious correspondence lasting for three months as Holt chivied Woolf to write more stories (LWP). "Pearls and Swine," it developed, needed altering for American consumption. Holt was in correspondence with his "Magazine Specialist" Anne Watkins in New York, who thought that, although Woolf's realism was "so great as to be terrific," the story presented problems for the American market. "But holy, suffering cats!" added Watkins, "how Woolf can write."

What Woolf thought about such praise is not recorded. When he demurred about altering "Pearls and Swine" and refused to write other stories for Holt and Watkins to peddle in America, Holt unleashed his awful powers of persuasion. He knew that Woolf could make "a big name" for himself if he would only try. "I may never again have the patience to bully a man into making several thousand a year," wrote Holt encouragingly, "so for the last time, *do think it over.*" Four days later, Holt importuned again in italics: "If I were *you* I wouldn't *dare* go to bed tonight without gritting my teeth and saying I'd do it if it killed me." Getting no response from the shamefully recalcitrant Woolf, Holt wrote back two days later proposing a meeting with him to show him how to write short stories, adding, "But you've got to, if I have to drag you through it by the scruff of your neck and bellow at you." When even this offer, guaranteed to bring shy authors out of their mouse holes, failed with Woolf, Holt tried one last inducement. He sent along a plot outline for Woolf to turn into a story. The correspondence mercifully ended at this point. Woolf was left with the letters and a confirmation of Bloomsbury's general dislike of Americans.

As usual, Virginia Woolf had begun her next book before the previous one reached the reviewers' desks. When *Monday or Tuesday* appeared in early March 1921, Woolf had been working on *Jacob's Room* for over a year. She had started the novel in April 1920 and was writing steadily on it in September 1920. According to Leonard Woolf, the possibility of expanding the press so that they could publish Virginia's novels occurred to them at this time, at the beginning of *Jacob's Room,* when Virginia was "filled with horror and misery" at the thought of submitting her new experimental novel to Duckworth (*Downhill* 68). The week before *Monday or Tuesday* was published in March, Virginia struggled with her novel, trying to write the important scene of Mrs. Flanders in the orchard. As she noted, "If I were at Rodmell I should have thought it all out walking on the flats. I should be in writing trim" (*Diary* 2:94). But the affairs of London intruded, and she could not settle down. She worked on the draft only to be stopped by a two months' illness from June to August.

At Monks House in Sussex for the summer, Virginia Woolf suffered from headaches and sleeplessness through August but mended by September and returning to Hogarth House in October, pushed on to complete *Jacob's Room* by November 4, 1921. She calculated that her third novel had taken approximately one year of writing time, "allowing for 6 months interval due to Monday or Tuesday & illness" (*Diary* 2:141). Virginia did not immediately set to work revising the manuscript but rather turned to the essays for a projected book, provisionally titled "Reading," which she had conceived the previous May. It would become *The Common Reader,* her first major collection of critical essays. By June 11, 1922, she had revised *Jacob* and submitted it to the typist for transcription. After one final editing, she gave the novel to Leonard to read for the first time on Sunday, July 23. Not until the following Wednesday did she record his response to her new method: "He thinks it my best work. But his first remark was that it was amazingly well written. We argued about it. He calls it a work of genius; he thinks it unlike any other novel; he says that the people are ghosts; he says it is very strange: I have no philosophy of life he says; my people are puppets, moved hither & thither by fate. He doesn't agree that fate works in this way" (ibid., 186). In spite of his criticism, Leonard pleased her by judging the book "very interesting, & beautiful, & without lapse . . . & quite intelligible." She felt confident, she added, that finally, at forty, she had found a way "to say something in my own voice." On the strength of that, she believed she could "go ahead without praise."

The doldrums set in with her proofreading, as she entered a period of uncertainty and depression before publication. "The thing now reads thin & pointless," she wrote in early September, "& I expect to be told that I've written a graceful fantasy, without much bearing upon real life" (*Diary* 2:199). Advance copies of *Jacob's Room* went off in the mail to Bloomsbury friends several weeks before the publication scheduled for Friday, October 27, 1922.

"As for my views about the success of Jacob, what are they?" (*Diary* 2:208). Pondering the problem in her diary two weeks before publication, Virginia Woolf estimated cautiously that it would sell 500 copies at the start and then eventually reach 800 copies by June. For the first time, the sales figures for a novel meant more to Virginia than her professional pride; they pointed to the very well-being of the Hogarth Press. The trial run had been *Monday or Tuesday,* the first moderately long work of hers published by the Hogarth Press. But a collection of stories running to 90 pages is a far different risk and enterprise than a full-length novel of 290 pages.

Jacob's Room was an important milepost for the press in several ways. It was the Woolf's longest book published to date, it was the first novel, and it was one of the first books to be printed by R. & R. Clark of Edinburgh, thus initiating a long and fruitful association between publisher and printer. Virginia's sister, Vanessa Bell, designed her first dust wrapper for the press, which was printed in cinnamon and black. Most important, *Jacob's Room* marked Virginia's complete break from Duckworth into the freedom of self-editing and self-publishing. There had been no problem with the Hogarth printing the stories in *Monday or Tuesday*, but the Woolfs had to seek and gain permission from Gerald Duckworth to end Virginia's contract when it came to her new novel. Gerald agreed, although Virginia thought him "a little cross" (*Diary* 2:205).

Leonard, with Virginia's somewhat nervous support, moved boldly to order a second printing of 1,000 copies of *Jacob's Room* within a few weeks of publication, thereby sacrificing, as Virginia noted in a letter to Ka Arnold-Foster, "a certain profit for a possible greater [one]" (*Letters* 2:580). In addition to the uncertain public reception of her experimental novel, there was the distraction of the general election in 1922, which threatened all book sales. "Publishing one's own books," added Virginia to Ka, "is very nervous work, and we don't know how this is going."

Once again there is a puzzling discrepancy between Virginia's statements in her diary of "how this is going" and the data in the Hogarth Press account book (Sussex). For example, the account book shows only 29 copies sold ten days before publication, a total of 50 copies sold by October 29 (not 650), and 79 copies (not 850) sold by the end of November (ABS 171–72). The second printing of 1,000 copies, ordered on November 1, was paid for on January 3 (costing £56.14), when the account book records only 133 copies sold of the first impression. And so it went, slowly. The break-even point of about 1,000 copies was not reached until April 1923. Leonard closed the account on March 17, 1924, with a total of 1,413 copies sold for a press profit of £42.4.6 and a payment "To author" of a modest £14.1.5.

To Virginia Woolf went more than the trifle of fourteen pounds from the Hogarth Press; the publisher had bestowed upon the author of *Jacob's Room* an artistic freedom and a degree of self-determination she prized above all else. The completion and publication of the novel led Virginia, as Leonard observed in his autobiography, to "a period of great fertility" (*Downhill* 61). Approaching the height of her powers in 1922–23 with optimism and energy, Virginia Woolf began increasingly to take an aggressive public stance in her essays, denouncing Victorian and Edwardian fiction and formulating her own aesthetic.

Virginia Woolf's "Mr. Bennett and Mrs. Brown," one of her best-known literary essays, developed partly in defiant response to Arnold Bennett's criticism of *Jacob's Room* in *Cassell's Weekly* (March 1923). She replied to Bennett by turning the tables on him in "Mr. Bennett and Mrs. Brown," which Leonard published in the literary pages of the *Nation and Athenaeum* (December 1923). Later Virginia would refine this first angry reply, rewrite it extensively, and further develop the imaginary character of old Mrs. Brown in the railway carriage. She would read the revised essay on May 1924 to the Heretics undergraduate literary society at Cambridge and then publish it as "Character in Fiction" in the July issue of Eliot's *Criterion*. She would reissue it as the first of the new Hogarth Press Essays series in October 1924 as *Mr. Bennett and Mrs. Brown*.

Between the arrival of Ralph Partridge as assistant at Hogarth in August 1920 and his unhappy departure two and a half years later in March 1923, there were several events worth remembering, such as the purchase and installation of the Minerva platen printing press in November 1921, the fifth anniversary of the press in the summer of 1922, the publication of Virginia Woolf's *Jacob's Room* in October 1922, and, shortly after Partridge left, the appointment of Leonard to the literary editorship of the *Nation and Athenaeum* in April 1923, and the publication of T. S. Eliot's *Waste Land* in September 1923. As the Woolfs slowly expanded the operation of the press, going from four titles a year in 1920 to six a year in 1921 and 1922 and eleven in 1923, they found the presence of Partridge at first helpful and then unsettling. The pattern would become a familiar one with subsequent assistants.

All went smoothly at first, but by the time the Minerva press arrived and was finally installed in the basement larder-cum-printing room, Partridge's mannerisms had begun to grate. "Ralph is very obstinate and crude," wrote Virginia Woolf to her sister in November 1921 (*Letters* 2:492). "He and Leonard argue incessantly; and then appeal to me, and I have been thinking about something else." Virginia would often find herself thrust as mediator between the perfectionist, demanding, sometimes inflexible Leonard and the young assistant of the moment, inevitably less adroit and dedicated than his mentor. By December, Partridge was sleeping at Hogarth House during the week and laboring in the basement, doing much of the machining of the hand-printed Hogarth books. Sometimes he left the press and the type uncleaned, sticky with ink, and then Leonard would become "white with rage." Such a moment in February 1922 focused the Woolfs' dissatisfaction with their assistant, leading Virginia to summarize in her diary that Partridge was "lazy, undependable, now industrious, now slack, unadventurous, all corroded by Lytton, can't praise, yet has no view of his own" (*Diary* 2:160). The Woolfs wondered if they should continue the association, and Virginia began to suspect "that the work is not possible for an educated & vigorous young man." Perhaps a woman drudge would be more satisfactory, she thought.

Before the relations with Partridge turned for the worse in the summer, the Woolfs celebrated the fifth anniversary of the Hogarth Press in May 1922. Virginia Woolf wrote Violet Dickinson that they were becoming "rather full blown and important" and "a circular to this effect" would soon be mailed to her (*Letters* 2:528). "It is our 5th birthday this month," she added, "and we have published 19 books." Although the first Hogarth Press book had been published in July 1917, the Woolfs chose May as the anniversary month because then it was that they had begun setting and printing *Two Stories*. Furthermore, spring, not summer, coincided with the publishing season and was a propitious time for a flyer extolling their five-year-old and its products. The Hogarth anniversary publication, running to two pages of text and two pages of listings of future, recent, and past books, began with a surprisingly hard sell and ended with a plea for more A and B subscribers. Containing the Woolfs' credo, some self-congratulatory assessments, and a promise of future expansion, the flyer is an important document in Hogarth Press history.

After an opening statement about the anniversary year and the nineteen books published to date, the circular explained:

> Of these [the nineteen publications] not one, we are glad to state, has failed to justify, even in a pecuniary sense, the faith we put in it. In each case both author and Press have found themselves in pocket and not out of pocket by their venture. When we remind you of the aims which we had in view in starting the Press, you will agree, we think, that these results are highly encouraging.
>
> We aimed in the first place at producing works of genuine merit which, for reasons well known and difficult to gainsay, could scarcely hope to secure publication through ordinary channels. In the second place we were resolved to produce no book merely with a view to pecuniary profit. We meant to satisfy ourselves to the best of our ability that the work had literary or artistic merit before we undertook to produce it. [LWP]

Leonard, for he probably wrote the statement, then emphasized the commercial success of the nineteen volumes—four out of print, one in a third impression, three in a second impression, less than twenty copies in stock of four others, and *Two Stories,* published at 1s.6d., now worth 25s. in secondhand bookshops.

Particularly interesting here is the Woolfs' emphasis on "in pocket" matters, a subtle mixture of self-assertion and salesmanship wherein they quietly boasted of their business acumen in running a tight and profitable operation in spite of altruistic aims, while at the same time they cleverly reassured skeptics and future subscribers that the press was a solid enterprise worthy of their investment. Of equal interest is the statement of purpose in founding and operating the press, expressed in retrospect with a clarity and conviction not immediately evident in 1917 when recreation and therapy were at least part of the reasons for printing in the drawing room. One can see in such a statement the enormous pride and satisfaction Leonard and Virginia Woolf obtained from the operation of the press.

The anniversary circular continued by pointing to the future with an expanded staff and an improved "plant" (the Minerva press). The Woolfs' intention was "to proceed more boldly in the future" with more and longer books. They would continue to feature young, unknown writers, to publish Russian translations (Andreyev and Dostoyevsky were listed for the future), and to publish "reproductions from the works of living painters" (a project which produced only one volume, on Duncan Grant in 1924). They would not reprint the classics, nor would they embellish their books with fine and costly printing. Rather, they would concentrate on the reading ease and decent appearance of the books, to be sold at inexpensive prices. At the end of the statement came the appeal for new subscribers to help them gauge the size of a printing in order to avoid prepublication sellouts and delayed reprintings.

As a promotional piece, the fifth-anniversary flyer boosted sales and brought in a spurt of new subscribers, fifteen A and twenty-two B paying customers. Taken together with the newspaper ads Leonard Woolf was beginning to use more frequently, the visits to London booksellers, the list of press books in print run at the back of each new volume, and the regular mailing of review copies to reviewers, the flyer was part of Leonard's increased effort to expand and promote the offerings of the press. In September 1920 Bernard Shaw had written to Leonard about Fabian politics, adding in a postscript: "Does that Hogarth Press publish any catalogues or season's lists? They seem to print some nice books; but I hear of them only by accident" (MHP). G. B. S. might have solved his problem and helped the press by becoming a subscriber and receiving notice of each book published, but he did not. The press first issued the traditional publisher's seasonal lists in 1923, no doubt in response to the success of the flyer. The first annual catalogue did not appear until 1928, however.

In the meantime, nothing seemed to improve the gradually deteriorating relationship between Partridge and the Woolfs. Into this increasing muddle of cross-purposes and misunderstandings stepped Roger Fry and the young American James Whitall, son of Logan Pearsall Smith's cousin John. Fry, with Smith's support, proposed Whitall as a partner-manager for the Woolfs, causing them once more, as Virginia wrote, to confront the question of Partridge's "lumpiness, grumpiness, slovenliness, & stupidity versus his niceness, strength, fundamental amiability & connections" (*Diary* 2:189). To further complicate matters, he had become nearly as proprietary of the Hogarth Press as Leonard and repeatedly refused to leave.

Through August and September 1922 the Woolfs in intense conversations with Partridge, Strachey, Carrington, Fry, and other members of Bloomsbury explored one solution after another, including making Whitall a partner and keeping Partridge as printer. They particularly objected to what they saw as Partridges's "fixed determination to make a permanent hobby out of what's a profession to us" (*Diary* 2:211). The story, recorded in Virginia Woolf's diary and letters, assumes epic proportions and then grows tedious, but it illustrates once more the complex emotional tangles between members of Bloomsbury, and it shows with what tenacity the Woolfs, especially Leonard, clung to the fifth-anniversary vision of the press.

When the Woolfs met Whitall in late October, Virginia thought him "a greyhound looking nervous American, serious, matter of fact, forced to make money" (*Diary* 2:210). She distrusted the "American element" in him, and later the Woolfs would think of him the way they had considered Arundell del Re, as an aesthete bent on fine printing and deluxe editions.

Logan Pearsall Smith, never at a loss for suggestions, proposed a well-meaning arrangement with the publisher Constable & Co. To this Partridge reacted almost hysterically, accusing the Woolfs of willingness to sell out their prize possession to the highest bidder and implying that Virginia might welcome such a merger for the benefit of her own sales and publicity. Virginia penned a scorching letter to Partridge putting him in his place. Her blood boiled, she wrote, at his assumption that she and Leonard could be "bamboozled with a bargain which would destroy the character of the press for the sake of money or pride or convenience; and that you must protect its rights" (*Letters* 2:583). They had, after all, created the press, given it an identity, and if he thought he knew better than the Woolfs what was good for it, he was "a donkey." The conflict with Partridge soon cooled off, but the exchange reveals Virginia Woolf as passionately protective of the identity and survival of the press as Leonard. She would not always be so ferocious a defender.

Soon a more intriguing offer than Constable's surfaced. James Whitall, now a reader for Heinemann, informed the Woolfs of Heinemann's offer of a merger in November 1922. The Woolfs met the managing director, Charles Evans, at his office to learn the details of the "flattering" offer: the Woolfs to give the "brains & blood" and Heinemann to take over "sales & ledgers."[13] Fearing exploitation, the Woolfs rejected this first serious corporate proposal and decided, as Virginia noted, "for freedom & a fight with great private glee" (*Diary* 2:215).

James Whitall's version of his Hogarth affair differed markedly from the Woolfs'. Writing in his memoir *English Years* (1935), Whitall remembered being taken to Hogarth House by Logan Pearsall Smith, charmed by Virginia, and immediately offered £150 a year to work at the press. Three days later, he rejected their offer ("long daily journeys in the underground railway and eight hours of hard work for three pounds a week"), and decided instead to continue his perilous existence translating French literature.[14] He made no mention of Fry, Partridge, or Heinemann or of several meetings with the Woolfs. Among other curious aspects of Whitall's account is the improbable spectacle of Leonard Woolf offering him a job at £150 per year at their first meeting.

So the first crisis of the press was over, Constable, Heinemann, and Whitall were out, Partridge was still in, and the Woolfs had stumbled on their next assistant, Marjorie Thompson Joad, in the midst of their discussion with Whitall at the 1917 Club. The Woolfs were immediately attracted to her. One of those "shabby, loose, cropheaded, small faced bright eyed young women" at the club, she had presented herself to them as a possible assistant (*Diary* 2:213). To Partridge's dismay, they soon offered her a joint position to begin after the first of the year. Partridge, Carrington, and Strachey were then busy hatching their would-be Tidmarsh Press. Although Partridge would hang on doggedly until March 1923, his usefulness at the Hogarth Press was over.

Soon after the beginning of the year, Marjorie Joad began work at the press and quickly proved herself more consistent and reliable an assistant than the erratic Partridge. Production reached a new high in 1923 as the Woolfs published eleven books, five of them hand set and printed on the Minerva platen machine. One of these was E. M. Forster's account of Alexandria, *Pharos and Pharillon.*

Waiting for the belated publication of his *Alexandria: A History and a Guide,* based on his four years in Egypt with the Red Cross, Forster had conceived a book collecting his articles on Egyptian history, culture, and local curiosities published both in the *Egyptian Mail,* usually under the ironic pseudonym of "Pharos," and in the *Athenaeum.* The new book's title, *Pharos and Pharillon,* refers to the ancient Greek lighthouse, Pharos, which was replaced by an obscure and temporary modern one, the Pharillon. Under this rubric, Forster collected his pieces on ancient Alexandria and counterpointed them with his modern impressions. The Woolfs agreed to Forster's proposal to publish the book, received his manuscript in June 1922, and labored through a printing on the Minerva platen press of the eighty-page book by early May 1923, in an edition of 900 copies (HP 93).

The year 1923 was the Woolfs' most active year for printing as they published four other self-printed books (all poetry, including Eliot's *Waste Land*). The plans for all this activity prompted Forster to worry about the press finances in a letter to Leonard Woolf in January and to argue mildly against expanding the offerings, believing that any relaxation of the Woolfs' "high-browedness" might have bad effects (HP 93). Later, on May 28, as he sent in the one-page "Conclusion" to his book and a list of people he wanted to receive advance copies, Forster included one of his typically wry notes: "Dear Leonard, I think that the reasons against my writing for you are sufficiently good. I am sorry that I should be famous and fastidious at the same moment, but it is not a coincidence that is likely to recur" (HP 93).

The first edition of Forster's book sold better than his story of the Siren. Over 600 copies were sold in four months, the rate of sale so vigorous that Woolf ordered a second impression of 1,000 copies to be printed by R. & R. Clark in June. The first edition nearly sold out in eleven months. After paying Forster a £25 advance for the book and covering all other expenses including 11s.6d. for some Greek type, the press realized a profit of £44.11.11 on the first edition, a large amount for the Woolfs at the time (ABS 169–70).

Leonard Woolf's business sense prevailed over Forster's well-intentioned advice, and the Woolfs expanded carefully, ensuring the press's continuing prosperity. But the labor was almost too much, even with the willing and hardworking Joad. Virginia Woolf frequently complained in her letters and diary of having "to spend hours standing at the box of type with Margery, to wonder what its all for" (*Diary* 2:250). Or, as she wrote to Barbara Bagenol in July, "the Press is worse than 6 children at breast simultaneously" (*Letters* 3:55). She and Leonard lived apart, she wryly noted, she in the printing room and he in the basement, meeting only at meals and then so cross they could not talk.

Out of their hectic printing in 1923, however, came two of the Woolfs' most beautifully printed and bound books, Clive Bell's *Legend of Monte della Sibilla* and Herbert Read's *Mutations of the Phoenix,* and one of the Hogarth Press's greatest books, T. S. Eliot's *Waste Land.* The exhilarating toil of so much printing seems to have burned them out, for never again would they print five volumes in one year. Their work had produced 219 pages of text in the five volumes, published in over 2,200 copies. In 1924 they dropped to two self-printed volumes, came back up to four volumes in 1925, and soon settled on one or two a year until they ceased their own printing in 1932.

The first six books Leonard and Virginia Woolf had published at the Hogarth Press between 1917 and 1920 (not counting Cecil Woolf's *Poems*) were their *Two Stories,* Mansfield's *Prelude,* Eliot's *Poems,* Murry's *Critic in Judgment,* Virginia Woolf's *Kew Gardens,* and a separate edition of *The*

Mark on the Wall. The four volumes of prose and two of poetry represented slightly different aspects of literary modernism, suggesting the future direction the press might take; in neither the poetry nor the fiction it published over the twenty-four-year period covered by this history, however, would the Hogarth Press prove to be as modernist as its beginnings. Eliot's determinedly new *Poems* (1919) was issued simultaneously with Murry's old-fashioned *Critic in Judgment* (1919), and although the press published Eliot's *Waste Land,* the archetypal modernist poem, in 1923, it would go on to publish more traditional poems than innovative ones. Most of the Hogarth poets published one, perhaps two, slim volumes of poetry and disappeared from view. The Hogarth Press poetry list was not as interesting as the fiction list.

Three times during the interwar period, however, the press issued volumes of poetry that were of contemporary interest: first, in the early and mid-1920s with works by Eliot, Herbert Read, Robert Graves, Laura Riding, Conrad Aiken, and John Crowe Ransom; second, in the early 1930s with volumes by C. Day-Lewis and the anthologies *New Signatures* and *New Country* edited by Michael Roberts; and third, at the end of the decade in 1939–40 with the anthology series *Poets of Tomorrow.* The two periods in the 1930s when the press published contemporary poetry coincided with John Lehmann's presence as assistant and partner. He gave a sense of direction and modernity to the poetry list at an interesting time in the press history.

The Woolfs had little interest in shaping a distinctive list of poetry and seem to have been content to publish what they liked from the manuscripts that came their way. In 1928 Dorothy Wellesley helped finance and direct the Hogarth Living Poets series, which for five years gave a name if not a consistent quality to the volumes published. T. S. Eliot at Faber & Faber, in contrast, was developing at the same time one of the most distinguished lines of poetry in the twentieth century. It no doubt helps to have an active poet behind the publisher's desk to attract other poets; neither Leonard nor Virginia wrote poetry for publication, and there were more artists and essayists than bards in Bloomsbury. Only John Lehmann, a poet and friend of poets, gave the Hogarth Press poetry list the attention it deserved.

Dorothy Wellesley once commented cattily about the Woolfs that "poetry was not in any way their *specialité de la maison;* like many other brilliant persons, they imagined that if you were clever you therefore understood poetry—a strange but common error." [15] No doubt prose was the Woolfs' métier; but Leonard wrote poems as a young man and became a literary editor who read and reviewed poetry, and Virginia, whose prose sometimes approached poetry, read poems with passion and wrote about them in reviews and essays.

The most important poet for the Woolfs, as a friend and as a published writer, was T. S. Eliot. His first Hogarth volume, *Poems* (1919), issued in May in about 250 copies, sold out in August 1920 after a slow start. Eliot and the press turned a small profit. During the year the Woolfs' friendship with Eliot had also prospered, and soon he had become "Dear Tom" rather than "Mr. Eliot." In September 1920 Eliot spent the first of several weekends at Monks House, beginning the process, always slow for him, of unbending into intimacy. After tea on Sunday, they talked about his poetry, and Virginia noted that she had "taxed him with wilfully concealing his transitions" (*Diary* 2:67). Eliot replied that "explanation [was] unnecessary" and diluted the facts. Furthermore, he said that he was interested in people and believed his strength was for caricature.

Although the Eliot-Woolf relationship developed well in 1919–20, Eliot turned to other publishers for his next two books: John Rodker and his Ovid Press for *Ara Vos Prec* (February 1920) and Methuen for *The Sacred Wood* (November 1920). There was every justification for Eliot's choice of an established publishing house for his essays in *The Sacred Wood*. The book ran to 155 pages with seventeen essays compiled from those he had published in the *Athenaeum, Egoist,* and *Art and Letters.* At the time, the Woolfs were hand setting and printing all the original editions of their books. A prose book the length of *Sacred Wood* would have been beyond their typesetting and printing capabilities in 1919–20. Eliot's choice of John Rodker's one-man private press for *Ara Vos Prec,* however, was more personal.

Eliot may have given the book to Rodker as a gesture of friendship to an American compatriot, fellow poet, and beginning printer. Rodker's poems had been published in the early issues of *Poetry* (1914–17) along with Eliot's and Pound's. Allowing Rodker to print the book was typical of Eliot's generosity and his casual approach to the sale of his poetry. There was no money to be made in poetry, unlike prose, and so Eliot may have felt it little mattered who among his friends printed the poems. At the time, Leonard Woolf had not yet instituted the standard publisher's agreement binding an author to submit his next two or three books to the same publisher. Arrangements between the Woolfs and their writers at this time were informal, and Eliot was presumably free to take his writing to any publisher. Then, too, the timing was such that Rodker must have been setting the poems during the summer and early autumn 1919 when the Hogarth Press edition of *Poems* was barely on the market. Eliot had written to Rodker in May to give him permission to print his poems and added that he would send along a copy of the Hogarth Press volume for him to use.[16] Eliot may have felt it was too soon to burden the Woolfs with another poetry volume.

Ara Vos Prec was Rodker's first book. The printing was completed December 10, 1919 (only six months after the issue of *Poems*), but it was not published until early February 1920. It makes an interesting contrast to the Hogarth Press books. *Ara Vos Prec* contained all of Eliot's poems since *Prufrock,* including those in the Hogarth Press *Poems,* and added the previously unpublished poem "Gerontion." The volume was issued in 264 copies; 30 copies were signed by Eliot and priced at 25s., and the remainder were priced at 15s.[17] Presentation copies were printed on Japanese vellum and bound in pigskin with gold lettering; one went to the American patron John Quinn. It was a typical private press edition, contrasting in printing and cost with the Egoist Press *Prufrock* (500 copies at 1s.) and the Hogarth Press *Poems* (200 copies at 2s.6d.). *Ara Vos Prec* failed to sell out, even after Harold Monro bought out all copies of the book and reduced the price in his Poetry Bookshop. The sales of the Hogarth Press *Poems* were superior, and so was the printing.

Although the loss of *Ara Vos Prec* for the Hograth Press was unfortunate, the Woolfs were more than compensated when Eliot brought them his next work. "It was not until the end of 1922," wrote Leonard Woolf in his autobiography, "that Tom gave us *The Waste Land* to read; we agreed to publish it; printed it ourselves and published it on September 12, 1923" (*Beginning* 245). So with characteristic brevity and understatement, Leonard summed up one of the major publishing events of the twentieth century in England. There was, of course, more to it than that. In March 1922 Eliot had first told Virginia Woolf about "a poem of 40 pages" which he would give them to print (*Diary* 2:171). He was pleased, she recorded, and thought it his best work. It was not until June 18, however, that they heard the poem. As Virginia noted: "Eliot dined last Sunday & read his poem. He sang it & chanted it rhythmed it. It has great beauty & force of phrase: symmetry; & tensity. What connects it together, I'm not so sure. But he read till he had to rush . . . & discussion thus was curtailed. One was left, however, with some strong emotion. The Waste Land, it is called; & Mary Hutch [Hutchinson], who has heard it more quietly, interprets it to be Tom's autobiography—a melancholy one" (ibid., 178). Eliot published his poem in the first issue of the *Criterion* (October 1922), the periodical funded by Lady Rothermere for him to edit. Then the *Dial* in America published "The Waste Land" in its November 1922 issue. It would win the *Dial* prize of $2,000 for the best poem published that year.

Eliot published the poem in the *Criterion* and *Dial* without the famous notes, which he added when *The Waste Land* was first published in book form by Boni and Liveright of New York on December 12, 1922. Eliot later explained the "bogus scholarship" of the notes as an attempt to provide enough pages for the publisher to round out the book. It seems likely, however, that Roger Fry encouraged Eliot to provide notes to the poem, for they were actually prepared before the *Dial* publication.[18] Boni and Liveright published *The Waste Land* in a first impression of 1,000 copies, followed early in 1923 by a second impression of 1,000 copies (incorrectly called a "Second Edition").[19] Consequently, by the time the Woolfs began to set type for the poem early in 1923, it had been through two publications in periodicals and two impressions in book form. It was creating a considerable stir in literary circles on both sides of the Atlantic. Virginia Woolf set the poem herself, working apparently from the *Criterion* printing, with the notes taken from the Boni and Liveright edition.[20]

Leonard Woolf printed the text, but not without a few familiar mishaps. "We've had a desperate afternoon printing," Virginia wrote to Barbara Bagenal in June, "and I'm more in need of the love of my friends than you are. All the 14 pt quads have been dissed [distributed] into the

12 pt boxes! Proof taking has been made impossible; and Eliots poem delayed a whole week" (*Letters* 3:50). By July 18 Virginia could write triumphantly: "I have just finished setting up the whole of Mr. Eliots poem with my own hands: You see how my hand trembles" (ibid., 56). It had been one of the most typographically challenging of the Hogarth books. Printing was not completed until later, due to the Woolfs' August sojourn at Monks House. The Hogarth Press edition of *The Waste Land* was finally published on September 12, 1923, nine months after the Boni and Liveright edition. It was issued in 460 copies with blue marbled boards probably prepared by Vanessa Bell. Eliot was delighted with the appearance of the volume when he received his copy. Writing to Virginia, Eliot praised the Woolfs' setting of his poem, which he thought superior to the Boni and Liveright edition, and recognized that the job must have caused them much trouble (MHP).

The Woolfs in their printing of *The Waste Land* did better by Eliot than John Rodker, but there were errors. Three of the mistakes seem to have been corrected by Eliot himself in the presentation copies, but several others remained.[21] A few typos in a handprinted book may be the despair of printers, but they become the delight of friends, bibliographers, and collectors. The Hogarth Press edition of *The Waste Land* is now a valuable property. In 1923, however, the sales were not sensational. According to Leonard Woolf's account book, the press had sold only 47 copies by subscription before publication and 189 copies by December 4. In the first three months of 1924, *The Waste Land* sold an additional 141 copies, bringing the total to 330 copies sold by March 31, 1924 (six and a half months after publication) (ABS 183). Eliot earned £7.5 on these copies (25 percent of the profits), and the press earned £21.16.6. The edition did not sell out until early 1925.

Sometime in June 1924 there seems to have occurred a typical Bloomsbury misunderstanding between the Woolfs and the Eliots over *The Waste Land*. Vivienne Eliot's letter to Leonard on June 27 reassured him that they had not thought the Woolfs had said anything critical of the poem (TWP). She went on to say that neither she nor Tom had ever questioned the sales figures of the Hogarth Press, knowing that poetry could not pay.

Publishing Eliot's *Poems* and *The Waste Land* was an act of friendship by the Woolfs as well as a shrewd publishing decision. The rewards to both parties were far greater than the small royalties. Eliot's English career thereby was assisted, the audience for his poetry expanded, and the Hogarth Press's reputation as a modernist press grew. Leonard, thinking back about his role in Eliot's life, wrote, "I helped him to become an Englishman by becoming one of his statutory sponsors, and I am, I think legitimately, proud that I not only printed and published *The Waste Land* but had a hand in converting its author from an American to an English poet" (*Sowing* 52). But, he added, he played no part in converting Eliot to Anglicanism.

"The literary establishment . . . [thought] *Waste Land* absurd," wrote Leonard Woolf to Ian Parsons in 1966, "but it had an immediate success with the young."[22] After 1925 he and Virginia would be deluged by imitations in the Eliot manner. They would reject all but a few.

After Eliot's *Poems,* but before *The Waste Land,* the Woolfs published several volumes of now-forgotten poetry. One was *Paris: A Poem* (1920) by Hope Mirrlees, fellow student at Newnham College, Cambridge, with Virginia's sister-in-law Karen Stephen and later a close friend of Eliot's. Mirrlees wrote in the current modernist vein. Her poem in tone, imagery, and discontinuity seems indebted to Eliot's early poems and anticipatory of *The Waste Land.* Less interesting but typical of the more conventional neo-Georgian poetry published by the press, were volumes by the Canadian war poet Frank Prewett (*Poems,* 1921), Ruth Manning-Sanders (*Karn,* 1922), and Fredegond Shove, Virginia Woolf's cousin (*Daybreak,* 1922).

Many of the poets published by the Woolfs in the twenties had roots in Cambridge. They were inspired by the Georgian poets and moved in and out of Bloomsbury. Five of the early Hogarth Press poets, Prewett, Shove, R. C. Trevelyan, Robert Graves, and Vita Sackville-West, had been published in Edward Marsh's periodic collections of *Georgian Poetry* (five volumes from 1911 to 1922). By the time the Woolfs began to publish poetry in 1919, the original prewar vigor of the Georgians, their anti-Victorian realism, wit, humor, and rural values, had degenerated into pallid escapist verse, tiresome and repetitive. After reading the last of Marsh's collections, Virginia wrote that she was "bored to death with apple trees and acorns" (*Letters* 2:602). The best of the Hogarth Press

Georgians, Robert Graves and Vita Sackville-West, never fit comfortably in the later volumes.

Although no first-generation member of Bloomsbury became a serious poet, in spite of the undergraduate exercises of several of the young men, Clive Bell flirted intermittently with the Muse. The Woolfs hand printed two volumes of his poetry. In early 1921, as Virginia noted, Clive Bell proposed that the Woolfs should "bring out his private poems" (*Diary* 2:96). They agreed, and Bell assembled the thirteen poems from his earlier *Ad Familiares* (privately published in 1917), added four new poems, and wrote an introduction in which he said he accepted "with joy an offer by the Hogarth Press to publish a complete edition of my poems—seventeen in number."[23] The Woolfs hand printed *Poems* and published it on December 1, 1921. One of the new poems was "To Lopokova Dancing," dated 1918, about the time John Maynard Keynes and Bloomsbury first met Lydia Lopokova and seven years before Keynes married her. *Poems* sold 163 copies in four months and 243 copies by March 1923 for a very small profit to Bell of slightly over £2 and to the press of £5.17.5 (ABS 149).

If *Poems* contained Clive Bell's familiar and dated poems (from 1909 to 1921), more old than new, his last Hogarth Press volume had more to show and tell. *The Legend of Monte della Sibilla* (1923), subtitled *Le paradis de la Reine Sibille,* is a rollicking amorality tale of wine, women, and song in twenty-five pages, illustrated by Vanessa Bell and Duncan Grant. The volume beautifully captures the earthy playfulness of Charleston, the farmhouse—studio in Sussex where Vanessa and Clive Bell and Duncan Grant lived and worked. More than any other book published by the Hogarth Press, *The Legend of Monte della Sibilla* points up the contrast between the painters' Bloomsbury of Vanessa and Duncan and the highly serious writers' Bloomsbury of Virginia and Leonard. It was not the sort of book to be conceived by the Woolfs, but they willingly labored to produce it.

Vanessa designed the dust jacket, showing a heavy-bodied Sibyl, looking like a recumbent nature deity, against a background of mountains, clouds, lakes, and sailboat. Duncan's frontispiece more appropriately epitomized the spirit of Clive's poem: two amorous and unblushing lovers embracing under a tree, he clothed in boots and feathered hat, she plump and three-quarters naked, with hat and one shoe off and dress down below her Rubenesque belly. Vanessa chastely provided a decoration of pitcher and bowl with fruit at the top of the first page, and Duncan another wonderfully buxom nude asprawl on the last page, one shoe and a mandolin with flowers completing the design.

The successful union of text with handsome pen-and-ink drawings shows what Charleston and Hogarth House could accomplish when working together. The visual components in *The Legend of Monte della Sibilla,* especially Duncan Grant's frontispiece, did more than flesh out the words, they transformed a spirited but lightweight bauble into a more richly satisfying jewel of a book. Only Vanessa's designs and decorations for the Woolfs' separate edition of Virginia's *Kew Gardens* would surpass in excellence the production of Sibyl's legend as created by Clive, depicted by Vanessa and Duncan, set by Virginia, printed by Leonard, and published by the Hogarth Press in 1923. The combination helped sell the book. Within the first four months, sales totaled 184 copies, only £6 under the break-even point (ABS 179). By June 1926, two and a half years after publication, it had sold 311 copies and earned a profit.

Herbert Read and Robert Graves, the two other poets published for the first time by the Hogarth Press in 1923, had war experience in common and earlier volumes of war poems to their credit. Read's *Mutations of the Phoenix,* so beautifully printed by the Woolfs, marked a change in his poetic development toward long, discursive, philosophical poems, less imagistic than his previous volumes. Robert Graves developed differently.

"Figure," wrote Virginia Woolf in April 1925, "a bolt eyed, blue shirted shockheaded hatless man in a blue overcoat standing goggling at the door at 4:30, on Friday" (*Diary* 3:13). She thought him some alarming young contributor to the *Nation* and whisked him to the basement staff rooms of the Hogarth Press, where he announced "I'm Graves." Everyone stared at him, Virginia wrote, for "he appeared to have been rushing through the air at 60 miles an hour & to have alighted temporarily." Reassured, Virginia took Graves upstairs and made tea and conversation until 7:15 when she and Leonard eased him out so they could go see Shaw's *Caesar and Cleopatra* at the Kingsway Theatre. Virginia thought him "all emphasis protestation and pose," looking slightly like Shelley; "still," she added, "he is a nice ingenuous rattle headed young man." His talk had been about his feminist wife Nancy, daughter of the painter William Nicholson, his children, his house, and their way of life. He was proud of his sensibility, but "No," wrote Virginia, "I don't think he'll write great poetry: but what will you?" (ibid., 14).

At the time, and in contrast to Virginia Woolf's impressions, Robert Graves was thirty years old, a psychologically scarred veteran of the First World War, the father of four children, the author of twelve published books (nine poetry, three prose). He had published sixteen reviews and articles and four poems in Leonard Woolf's literary pages of the *Nation and Athenaeum*. Graves wrote constantly in his struggle to support his family. Two volumes of his poetry had already been published by the Hogarth Press by the time he appeared on the Woolfs' doorstep: *The Feather Bed* (1923) and *Mock Beggar Hall* (1924). The press would publish one more volume of his poetry (*The Marmosite's Miscellany*, 1925) and three books of criticism (1925, 1926, 1927). Based on what she knew of his two press books, Virginia Woolf might have been right in her prediction that he would not write great poetry, but neither she nor Graves could have foreseen the arrival from America of Laura Riding in nine months' time. Riding's involvement in his life and career would change him in a remarkable way. The Woolfs presided over a relatively uninteresting period of Graves's development as a poet.

In *The Feather Bed* Graves presented the monologue of a young man fatigued in mind and body "and under the stress of an abnormal conflict," as an "Introductory Letter" to John Crowe Ransom described him.[24] Graves's young man carries on an internal debate over the nature of love, sexuality, and the religious calling of nuns and priests. It is less daring today than when Graves sent it to Ransom, half expecting "the honest Burgesses of Nashville, Tenn.," to be as scandalized as they had been over Ransom's *Poems about God* (1918).

William Nicholson, the artist father-in-law of Graves, provided a handsome cover design of spaced feathers, and the Woolfs published the twenty-eight-page volume in 250 copies in July 1923. In spite of, or because of, the untypical nature of Graves's poem, it sold well for poetry. Eight months after publication *The Feather Bed* had sold 235 copies, bringing a payment to Graves of £6.8.9 and a profit to the press of £19.6.1 (ABS 177). Graves reportedly was disappointed that the Hogarth Press did not later issue a cheap edition to make the most of the interest in the poem.[25]

In the spring of 1923, Leonard Woolf made a major career change and began what would be a seven-year stint as the literary editor of the *Nation and Athenaeum,* his first regularly salaried position in journalism. Marjorie Joad had been discovered in the nick of time to ease his managerial burdens with the press as he found himself engaged several times a week with new editorial responsibilities. Then in September the Woolfs met George ("Dadie") Rylands, a young, handsome Cambridge poet, who soon declared his desire to join the Woolfs at Hogarth as an assistant. By October, Virginia noted: "This young man with hair like the husk of corn, says he wishes to devote his life to the Hogarth Press, & is writing a letter to that effect to Leonard. This will begin in June" (*Diary* 2:271).

With the prospect of another live-in assistant, the expanding business of the press, and her own desire for the daily stimulation of London as she composed the street scenes of *Mrs. Dalloway,* her next novel, Virginia began serious house hunting in Bloomsbury in November. She discovered 52 Tavistock Square in early January 1924 and signed a ten-year lease. It is interesting that Virginia, not Leonard the businessman, inevitably handled the gritty matters of house hunting and lease signing for their various moves. She sometimes enjoyed feigning unworldliness. As she gaily wrote to Jacques Raverat in July 1923 about Leonard's mastery of their affairs, "Poor devil, I make him pay for his unfortunate mistake in being born a Jew by discharging the whole business of life" (*Letters* 3:58). Leonard's management induced in her a sense of "the unreality of matter" which she found "highly congenial and comfortable." But she was better at some kinds of business affairs than she liked to admit.

The Woolfs moved into their renovated rooms in Tavistock Square in mid-March, beginning an important new phase of their lives and developing the press beyond their expectations in the fifth-anniversary flyer. As she noted the Tavistock Square lease signing in her diary, Virginia gratefully acknowledged the importance of Hogarth House. It had given her stability and calm during her periods of illness in the midst of the war years. "Moreover," she wrote, "nowhere else could we have started the Hogarth Press, whose very awkward beginning had rise in this very room, on this very green carpet. Here that strange offspring grew & throve; it ousted us from the dining room, which is now a dusty coffin; & crept all over the house" (*Diary* 2:283). Virginia's analogies of the dining room as womb/tomb and the press as a growing child vibrate with emotional intensity.

CHAPTER THREE

★

RUSSIAN TRANSLATIONS

W e are publishing Gorki," wrote Virginia Woolf in her diary, "& perhaps this marks some step over a precipice— I don't know" (*Diary* 2:34). When the Hogarth Press published a translation of Maxim Gorky's *Reminiscences of Tolstoi* in July 1920, the book quickly sold 1,000 copies, requiring a reprint of another 1,000. It was the Woolfs' first truly commercial undertaking. "The success of Gorky's book," wrote Leonard Woolf in his autobiography, "was really the turning point for the future of the Press and for our future" (*Downhill* 67).

Precipice or turning point, *Reminiscences of Tolstoi* marked the transition of the Hogarth Press from handpress to small publishing house. If Gorky's book proved to the Woolfs that they could successfully expand their publishing, it also demonstrated that the cultural and aesthetic satisfactions of translations could be combined with commercial success. It is one thing to operate a small handpress, publishing the untried works of one's friends; it is another to publish translations of recognized or suspected masters. Responsibilities and obligations are different; the one is a private act of friendship and faith, the other a public act of greater consequence, a commitment, however modest, to European literary culture. The Woolfs, from their first published translation, were no longer operating merely an exciting coterie press. They had become a small-scale international publisher. The horizons of Hogarth had dramatically expanded.

In the three years after the appearance of *Reminiscences of Tolstoi,* the Hogarth Press published seven more translations from Russian literature, all but one brought to the Woolfs by the earnest émigré S. S. Koteliansky.

They included works by Chekhov, Dostoevsky, Andreyev, and Bunin. Later in the 1930s there were translations of Italo Svevo, Joyce's friend, and of the great German poet Rilke. In all, the Hogarth Press published twenty-nine translations during the interwar period, some of them of considerable literary and historical significance. Taken together, the Russian, German, and Italian translations were remarkable achievements for the Woolfs and their press.

Leonard and Virginia Woolf, like other upper middle-class English intellectuals, knew Continental languages, although they were not fluent in them. Leonard, true to his generation, had received a classical education in Latin and Greek and then acquired other languages mostly through travel. He was unique in Bloomsbury for his mastery of Ceylonese dialects learned during his seven civil service years, 1904–11. Virginia, following the educational pattern of her brothers at a distance, had been tutored at home in Latin and Greek by Walter Pater's sister Clara. French, however, was the language most thoroughly acquired by the Woolfs and their friends through study, through reading classical and modern French writers, and through frequent, almost yearly travel in France. Mastery varied. The Woolfs read French more easily than they wrote or spoke it.

French was so well known by the Woolfs and their Bloomsbury friends that they formed a policy of not publishing French translations, making only four exceptions over the years. Virginia thus wrote Dorothy Bussy in 1924 expressing a desire to see a translation of Gide, probably of *La porte étroite* (*Straight Is the Gate*), but explaining that "it is hardly possible to make translations from the French pay," for "our sort of public reads French, or pretends that it does, and the printing costs leave very little chance of covering expenses" (*Letters* 3:144). As she noted in her *New Republic* article "On Not Knowing French" (1929), "Every second Englishman reads French, and many speak it, and some write it."[1] It seems likely that this intellectual snobbery toward French translations caused the Hogarth Press to miss the opportunity to be the English publisher of Gide. Bussy, beginning with her translation of *Straight Is the Gate* (1924), translated virtually all of Gide and published her translations with Alfred Knopf. She might have chosen her friends the Woolfs as publishers had they been more receptive.

However, the Woolfs were under no misapprehension about translations from other languages; they were swept up in the enthusiasm for Russian literature which pervaded England in the 1920s. English interest in Russian literature did not begin to develop until after the Crimean War (1854–56). It was marked by fits and starts, shaped by fluctuating international relations and the sporadic appearance of translations based on inferior French translations. In the 1860s and 1870s both England and America experienced an intense awareness of Russian culture and literature. To translations of Turgenev were added those of Tolstoy, Gogol, Chekhov, and Dostoyevsky. In the early 1900s English readers became passionately interested in the novels of Tolstoy and Dostoyevsky. As Royal Gettmann has observed: "The vogue of Russian fiction in England and America . . . , especially from 1910 through the postwar period, was so great that only a few reminders are necessary to recall the enthusiasm evoked by Tolstoy, Dostoyevsky and Chekhov. The feeling was current that the Russians had exalted the novel as a literary form and that they had unveiled a new and precious vision of life."[2] Moreover, the literary vogue for Russian fiction was not an isolated phenomenon but part of a larger interest in Russian culture spurred by imports of brilliant Russian music, art, ballet, and, later, film.

Hardly a year passed between 1912 and 1922 without a new translation of the Russians, published by a variety of publishers and translators. The popularity of Tolstoy and Chekhov continued to grow during this time, but Dostoyevsky soon became a cult figure. Helen Muchnic has said that the Dostoyevsky cult from 1912 to 1921 "was a complex intellectual phenomenon, composed partly of wartime sympathies, partly of mysticism, partly of a new interest in abnormal psychology and in the revelations of psychological analysis, partly of an absorbed concern with artistic experimentation."[3] Lytton Strachey, for one, became an early enthusiast by reading *The Idiot, Crime and Punishment,* and *The Possessed* in French translations. Leonard and Virginia Woolf were caught up in the Dostoyevskian fervor also, for they began reading some of Constance Garnett's translations as soon as they appeared. Other Bloomsbury friends were equally enamored with Russian language, literature, and ballet. Maynard Keynes met Russian ballerina Lydia Lopokova in 1918 when she was dancing with Leonide Massine in Diaghilev's company, the Ballet Russe, and married her in 1925. Russian language and literature, more than the ballet, however, fascinated literary Bloomsbury.

Leonard and Virginia Woolf soon began learning Russian with future Hogarth translations in mind. Shortly after they began their hand printing in the dining room in Richmond, they met the remarkable Russian expatriate S. S. Koteliansky. During this time Virginia reviewed nine volumes of Russian translations. Her extended analysis of Russian writers and the problems of translations appeared in her article "The Russian Point of View," first published in 1919 and then in *The Common Reader* (1925). Thereafter, when she wrote at length about fiction in her two major essays "Modern Fiction" (1925) and "Phases of Fiction" (1929), she drew heavily on her knowledge of the Russian novelists, often using them as standards of excellence against which she measured English writers.

Leonard and Virginia Woolf seem to have met Koteliansky in the summer of 1917, probably through J. Middleton Murry and Katherine Mansfield. "Kot," as he was called by everyone, had been in England for six years working at the Russian Law Bureau, translating legal documents. A Russian Jew born in a village near Kiev in 1892, his liberal political views had brought him in conflict with the authorities. After a university education and law training, he emigrated to England. Through an English barrister, Kot came to know Murry and Mansfield and, in 1914, D. H. Lawrence. Soon he knew Mark Gertler, Aldous Huxley, and most of the Bloomsbury circle. Over the years his greatest involvement was with the Murrys and Lawrences, in emotional and exhausting entanglements. For a short period around 1923 he became business manager of Murry's *Adelphi*. Kot was no writer, but he had a knack for translation and a resourcefulness in finding untranslated Russian works that he brought to the Woolfs, the Murrys, and Lawrence for refining into better English than his own. Middleton Murry was the first of Kot's collaborators, working with him on three translations in 1915–16. Unique and eccentric, Kot played out his lively but minor role in English letters during the 1920s and 1930s.

Writing Kot's obituary in 1955, Leonard Woolf called him a remarkable man, a Jew of the Trotsky type with thick upstanding hair and piercing eyes. "When he shook hands with you," Woolf wrote, "you felt that all the smaller bones in your hand must certainly have been permanently crushed to a fine powder. The handshake was merely an unconscious part of Kot's passionate intensity and integrity."[4] Kot was "not a comfortable man," thought Woolf, "but neither was Elijah or Isaiah," having "the same qualities of steely, repressed, purged passion." Among his minor accomplishments, Kot could howl like a dog so convincingly that all the dogs in Russell Square or Tavistock Square would howl in reply. But his major accomplishment was as a translator. Kot's method, described by Woolf, was to write out a rough translation in "his own strange English," leaving spaces between the lines for his collaborator's version. "Kot's English . . . was usually very strange, but it was also so vivid and individual that I was often tempted to leave it untouched. For instance, he wrote: 'She came into the room carrying in her arms a peeled-off little dog,' and on another occasion: 'she wore a haggish look.' . . . One only learned to the full Kot's iron integrity and intensity only by collaborating with him in a Russian translation" (*Beginning* 248). After reworking Kot's English into the King's, Leonard would go over the translation with Kot word for word. Kot's strong mind and sensitive feeling for language, for the nuances of meaning, continued Woolf, meant that he "would pass no sentence until he was absolutely convinced that it gave the exact shade of meaning and feeling of the original, and we would sometimes be a quarter of an hour arguing over a single word." To prepare for such strenuous exercises, both Leonard and Virginia Woolf studied Russian with Kot.

The Woolfs learned enough Russian to work cooperatively and creatively with Kot on seven Hogarth translations—Leonard on four, Virginia on three. The combination of the Woolfs' rudimentary Russian but polished English prose and Kot's scrupulous Russian and vivid "English" produced excellent translations superior to all but those of gifted, fluent translators like Aylmer Maude and Constance Garnett. Virginia denied having been a true translator of the Russians, however; "I scarcely like to claim that I 'translated' the Russian books credited to me," she wrote in 1932. "I merely revised the English of a version made by S. Koteliansky" (*Letters* 5:91).

Reading translations of the great Russian writers, Virginia Woolf thought, was like viewing them stripped of their clothes by an earthquake or a railway accident. She knew how embarrassingly bare they could be and wrote tellingly about the difficulty English readers had of relying "blindly and implicitly" on translators in her article "The Russian Point of View" (1919). "When you have changed every word in a sentence from Russian to English," wrote Virginia, and "have thereby altered the sense a little, the sound, weight, and accent of the words in relation to each other completely, nothing remains except a crude and coarsened version of the sense."[5] The wrecked Russians had lost not only their clothes, she added, but "something subtler and more important—their manners, the idiosyncrasies of their characters." Yet the power, the intensity, and the humanity of the Russians were amazingly undiminished. Virginia Woolf's assessment of the difficulties of Russian translation carries with it the vivid truth of a novelist and stylist aware of the writer's perpetual language barriers and the pressing need to translate experience and vision into print.

When the Woolfs published Gorky's *Reminiscences of Tolstoi* in July 1920, English interest in the Russians was so well established that the Hogarth Press could count on a solid readership. Leonard Woolf's judgment of the market and the quality of the book was unerring. Tolstoy's major works had been available in several translations for at least twenty years. There had been the twenty-two-volume series translated by Nathan Dole and published by Scribner's from 1899 to 1912. Constance Garnett's two-volume set of *War and Peace* and *The Death of Ivan Ilyitch and Other Stories* had been published by Heinemann in 1911 and 1915. And there were others. The uncertainty of some of these translations and the haphazard appearance of major and minor works would lead Aylmer Maude and his wife Louise to launch their great centenary edition of *The Works of Leo Tolstoy* in twenty-one volumes published by Oxford University Press (1928–37). In addition to a superb translation, the Maudes supplied extensive biographical, historical, and critical material.

What Koteliansky brought to the Woolfs was not primary works of Tolstoy but rather peripheral material—biographical, anecdotal, and personal—illuminating the life and mind of the great Russian. Only one of the four Tolstoy books introduced to the Hogarth Press by Kot was by Tolstoy—his *Love Letters* (1923). One book was Countess Sophie Tolstoy's *Autobiography* (1922), and two were by friends of Tolstoy: Gorky's *Reminiscences* (1920) and A. B. Goldenweizer's *Talks with Tolstoi* (1923). Later, in 1936, Ruth Fry, Roger Fry's youngest sister, brought Tolstoy's essay

On Socialism to the Woolfs. It was the last work written by Tolstoy, a few weeks before his death in November 1910. The Hogarth Press contribution to Tolstoyana, therefore, provided an expansion of the English understanding of Tolstoy's personality and ideas, supplying vivid personal testimony to an audience already fascinated by the complexities and contradictions of the man and his writing.

The first Hogarth Press Tolstoy book was Gorky's account of his visits with Tolstoy in 1901–2. Kot seems to have had some relationship with Gorky, although it is not clear that they ever met. No payments were made to Gorky for the translation rights, which must have belonged to Kot, for the translations were labeled "authorized." As Gorky stated in his short preface to the volume, "These fragmentary notes were written by me during the period when I lived in Oleise and Leo Nikolaevich at Gaspra in the Crimea."[6] Tolstoy was recovering from malaria at Countess Panin's sumptuous villa at Gaspra, chaffing against his luxurious comforts and seeing a number of writers and intellectuals including Gorky and Chekhov. It was, as Helen Muchnic has called it, a "little drama of Russian letters at the turn of the century," and the meetings among the three writers epitomized the enormous intellectual and social changes that were astir.[7]

When Kot brought the *Reminiscences* to the Woolfs, Gorky had just published them in Russia. The book is a fascinating mixture of Tolstoy and Gorky. The first half of the volume consists of thirty-six vignettes of Tolstoy that reproduce his conversation. Gorky controlled the apparently random and fragmentary pronouncements of Tolstoy through arrangement and juxtaposition. Some of the entries were Gorky's clear-eyed description of the old man, revealing the observer as well as the observed and gradually building an impressive portrait of the great sage and writer. Occasionally Gorky provided quick insights, as when he noted of Tolstoy's vanity that he seemed to be "conceited and intolerant like a Volga preacher."[8] The second half of Gorky's *Reminiscences* consists of a long unfinished and undelivered letter to a friend of Gorky's prompted by the news of Tolstoy's departure from Yasnaya Polyana and his death in the railway stationmaster's house at Astapovo.

For Leonard Woolf, the translation of Gorky was a memorable experience. "I do not think," he wrote, "that I have ever got more aesthetic pleasure from anything than from doing that translation" (*Downhill* 67). He saw it as "one of the most remarkable biographical pieces ever written," capturing the immensely great and complex Tolstoy in all his dimensions. And, he added, "the writing is beautiful; every word and every sentence are perfect, and there is not one superfluous word or sentence in the book. I got immense pleasure from trying to translate this ravishing Russian into adequate English."

Shortly after publication, Virginia Woolf wrote to Violet Dickinson that "the Tolstoy, in spite of our being the publisher, seems to me splendid; and we've just sold it to America which of course tempts us to set forth on fresh enterprises" (*Letters* 2:434). The sale of the American rights to Gorky's *Reminiscences* to the Curtis Brown agency brought the Hogarth Press £90, which Leonard split with Kot (ABS 135). The original edition of 1,250 copies sold well, and the press had a second impression printed by the Pelican Press on January 8, 1921. Previously, the *London Mercury* had paid the press £15 for the right to publish portions of the book. For the first time in its three-year history, the Hogarth Press generated revenue well beyond expenses. The fresh enterprises that the Woolfs envisioned included an expanded list of books, more translations, and the use of commercial printers.

The income for both Kot and the press from Gorky's *Tolstoi* was welcome but not overwhelming. Leonard paid Kot a half share of all the revenue (including that from the sale of the American rights) through the first printing and then scaled his share to one quarter. By 1924 when the second impression sold out, Leonard had paid Kot £77.18.9. Kot brought six more translations to the Woolfs.

The press's next Tolstoy book after Gorky's *Reminiscences* was *The Autobiography of Countess Sophie Tolstoi*. The first biographies of Tolstoy by Biryakov, Bienstock, and Maude were written during Tolstoy's lifetime and were partly edited by Tolstoy or his wife. The biographers wrote conscientiously but with some restraint about the tensions and strains between husband and wife. In Russia such fanatic Tolstoyans as Chertkov and Tolstoy's daughter Alexandra were seldom restrained in their public adoration of Tolstoy and their vilification of Sophie. The violent crises of 1909 and 1910 that precipitated Tolstoy's final estrangement from the countess, his departure from Yasnaya Polyana, and his death in Astapovo had yet to occur when the early biographies were written. After his death, a number of more personal documents began to appear. Tolstoy's son Ilya published his *Reminiscences of Tolstoy* in an English translation in 1914. Biryakov edited and published in 1917 Tolstoy's *Journal intime* (1895—1910), first in French and later in English translation.

The Hogarth Press translation of Countess Tolstoy's autobiography in 1922, therefore, was the first appearance in English of her version of her tumultuous life with Tolstoy. She had been dead less than three years. Not until six years later would the countess's diaries be published in English translation by Alexander Werth: in 1928, the *Diary* of 1860—91, and in 1929, the *Later Diary* of 1891—97. Finally, in 1936, the Maudes published a translation of Countess Sophie's last diary of 1910. Although the diaries have assumed a greater documentary importance than the autobiography, it remains an interesting work. It was her first published attempt at self-justification.

The autobiography was begun in 1913 at the invitation of S. A. Vengerov, a professor of Russian literature, who was interested in information about Tolstoy's life at Yasnaya Polyana during the writing of *War and Peace* and *Anna Karenina*. Countess Tolstoy tried to supply Vengerov with the information he desired, but her writing was shaped by her need to defend herself and her life with Tolstoy against the rumors and criticism then circulating. Less than sixty pages long, the autobiography traces Countess Tolstoy's life from birth in 1844 to the time of writing in 1913, with major emphasis on her intensely happy early married years with Tolstoy and the later years of estrangement and bitterness. The self-portrait that emerges is one of an intelligent, devoted, self-sacrificing young mother (she was eighteen years old when married and bore thirteen children, nursing ten of them herself), absorbed in the genius of her puzzling but loving husband until the intervention of Chertkov and the other fanatic Tolstoyans.

To Countess Tolstoy's autobiography, Koteliansky and Leonard Woolf added in the Hogarth Press volume a preface by Vasilii Spiridonov and five brief appendixes containing biographies by Vengerov and Strakhov, copies of Tolstoy's two wills (of 1895 and 1910), and Tolstoy's own versions of his going away as recounted in a letter to his daughter Alexandra. As Kot and Leonard wrote in their note to the autobiography, the importance of the book, amid the "immense literature" in Russia about the Tolstoys, "lies in the fact that in it Countess Sophie Andreevna Tolstoi herself states her own case in full."[9] They reminded the reader, however, that the countess presented only one side of the story. By ending the volume with Tolstoy's own views, Koteliansky and Woolf skillfully suggested the complexities and irreconcilable differences between husband and wife.

In contrast to the accounts of Tolstoy's tumultuous marriage, the *Love Letters of Tolstoi* (1923) recorded a happier time in his life (1856–57) when the twenty-eight-year-old writer corresponded with Valeria Arsenev. They were engaged but did not marry. Countess Tolstoy had not permitted Biryakov to use the letters in his biography of Tolstoy but allowed him to publish them after her death. The letters, edited by Biryakov along with his study of the autobiographical elements in Tolstoy's work, became another significant Hogarth Press addition to Tolstoyana. It seems appropriate that Virginia Woolf, herself a formidable letter writer, worked on the translation with Kot.

A. B. Goldenweizer's *Talks with Tolstoi* (1923) provided extensive observations of the writer.[10] From his introduction to Tolstoy in 1896, when he was twenty years old and Tolstoy was sixty-eight, until Tolstoy's death in 1910, Goldenweizer was frequently with the writer at Yasnaya Polyana or accompanying him on his travels. He was at Gaspra in the Crimea and provided brief glimpses of the Tolstoy-Chekhov-Gorky meeting. Goldenweizer seems almost to have been a member of the Tolstoy household, playing the piano or reading to Tolstoy, somewhat in the position of court musician and confidant. But unlike Gorky's passionate, probing, at times lyrical, impressions of Tolstoy, Goldenweizer's *Talks* are unadorned, flat reports.

The title of *Talks* is rather misleading, therefore, because it suggests an interchange between Goldenweizer and Tolstoy. Goldenweizer, as note taker, merely reported a one-way conversation: Tolstoy on life, on art, on women, on politics, on modern writers, on God. Tolstoy was, as Maude, Goldenweizer, and others have indicated, an often patient and generous listener, but the effect of both Gorky's and Goldenweizer's books is to emphasize Tolstoy as a talker, teacher, and sage. He is viewed from the outside by the respectful Goldenweizer, who made little effort to plumb the depths of Tolstoy's inner life.

Although the Hogarth Press published only one part of Goldenweizer's two-volume diary, their version gave a representative sense of Tolstoy's character and mind as observed over a thirteen-year period by the self-effacing Goldenweizer. Running to 182 pages, *Talks* was the largest of the press's Tolstoy books. It was, thought Virginia Woolf writing to Barbara Bagenal in June 1923, "a very amazing book" (*Letters* 3:52). Seventeen years later, she would record in her diary her impression of rereading Goldenweizer at breakfast. Tolstoy's words, she wrote, had "always the same reality—like touching an exposed electric wire" (*Diary* 5:273).

In spite of the public's exhilarating response to Gorky's *Reminiscences,* the other three Tolstoy books published by the Woolfs were commercial disappointments. Countess Tolstoy's *Autobiography* fared better than the other two. Published in a standard edition of 1,000 copies, the *Autobiography* generated serial rights from *John O'London's Weekly* of £82.13.9, American rights of £150, and Swedish rights of £10. The income from these publishing rights saved the book. Sales up to June 1923, one year after publication, totaled only 585 copies. At the end of March 1923 the press had realized a profit of £76.3.2 (ABS 160–61). Tolstoy's *Love Letters* brought £20 in serial rights from *John O'London's* but failed to sell in America. At the end of March 1924, almost a year after publication, the *Love Letters* had sold only 342 copies, with a resulting loss to the press of £46.11.4. Leonard Woolf, in addition to splitting the income from the publication rights with Kot, as usual, had also paid Biryakov £30 for his scholarly contribution to the volume (ABS 173). Goldenweizer's *Talks* produced serial rights of £21.19 from *Cassell's Weekly* but also did not sell to America. Sales were extremely poor. By the end of March 1924, nearly a year after publication, the book had sold only 269 copies. The press suffered a loss of £39.14.2 (ABS 181).

All this was puzzling, given the remarkable fate of Gorky's *Tolstoy,* and no doubt vexing to Woolf, who rightly prided himself on correctly judging his market and anticipating costs. "Our list grows more & more distinguished, but why is there no boom in Tolstoi?" pondered Virginia Woolf on June 23, 1922, shortly after the publication of Countess Tolstoy's

Autobiography (*Diary* 2:178). It had sold only sixty-three copies at the time. There seems to have been a sharp downturn in the Tolstoy market, a falling off of readers' interest after the deluge of Tolstoy books; yet the other Hogarth Press Russian books in the early 1920s struggled also. Bunin's *Gentleman from San Francisco* (1922) eventually produced a small profit, but neither it nor Dostoyevsky's *Stavrogin's Confession* (1922) nor Andreyev's *The Dark* (1923) was as successful as Gorky's *Tolstoi*.

The second book S. S. Koteliansky brought to the Woolfs after Gorky's *Tolstoi* was a three-in-one volume containing Chekhov's *Note-Books*, a collection of his themes and thoughts, and a reminiscence of Chekhov by Gorky. It was published by the Hogarth Press in 1921 as *The Note-Books of Anton Tchekhov Together with Reminiscences of Tchekhov by Maxim Gorky*. It was translated by Kot and Leonard Woolf. Just as they seemed to have caught the Tolstoy interest at its peak with Gorky's book, Kot and the Woolfs were timely with the Chekhov book.

A few of Chekhov's stories and plays had appeared in translation, mostly in America, as early as 1908 and 1912. Kot with J. Middleton Murry had translated a volume of stories in 1915. But it was not until the indefatigable Constance Garnett began her translations in 1916 that the vast range of Chekhov's work became available in reliable English versions, eight years after his death. Garnett eventually published thirteen volumes of the stories (1916–22) and a two-volume edition of the plays (1923–24) with Chatto & Windus. In 1920 she published a translation of Chekhov's *Letters*. The Hogarth Press 1921 edition of Chekhov's *Note-Books* with Gorky's *Reminiscences,* therefore, came at a time when ten of Garnett's volumes of the stories and her volume of letters had just appeared. Unlike Tolstoy, Chekhov had no biographers either in Russian or English until long after his death. Constance Garnett's *Letters* was the first book to provide Chekhov readers with a glimpse into the writer's life, and so the Hogarth Press *Note-Books* with Gorky's inimitable recollections provided an important and fascinating view of the Russian.

Chekhov's notebooks, as Kot and Leonard Woolf explained in their note to the volume, were written from 1892 to 1904 and contained the ideas, quotations, one-liners, bare plot outlines, comic names for characters, and overheard conversations which were the raw material for Chekhov's writing. Part Russian jokebook, part collection of Joycean-like epiphanies, part commonplace book, the volume revealed in every line the brooding, sad, sardonic humor of Chekhov. Some themes recur—the ambitions and pretentions of social climbers, the vulgarity of the middle class, the failures of love and marriage, the stupidity of officials and intellectuals.

The second part of the Hogarth Press edition is entitled "Themes, Thoughts, Notes, and Fragments." It might be a title for the *Note-Books* as well, but Kot and Leonard explained that the writings were found with that label among Chekhov's papers, in a special cover. The entries are more of the same. Gorky's *Reminiscences* of Chekhov, which forms the last section of the book, is similar to his Tolstoy, although shorter and more fragmentary. Again the observant, sympathetic Gorky recorded the writer's conversations with strangers and disciples. After Tolstoy's tempestuous personality, Chekhov's gentleness and irony were captured by Gorky in an autumnal mood.

The *Note-Books* sold well, the only translation published by the Hogarth Press in the early 1920s to approach the success of Gorky's *Tolstoi*. J. C. Squire's *London Mercury* paid £15 for the serial rights in January 1921, before publication, and the American rights were sold to B. W. Heubsch in May for £150. Woolf divided these profits with Kot, as before. Within the first year of publication, the *Note-Books* sold 634 copies, for a profit to the press of £80.16 (ABS 142). When Woolf closed out the account in April 1924, three years after publication, the book had sold 732 copies and generated £92.03.8 in profits for the press (ABS 160). Sales, after the first year, had been a mere trickle, but the *Note-Books* did more than pay for itself; it helped the press overcome the losses from the Tolstoy books.

Ivan Bunin was fifty-two years old, already an honored and distinguished Russian émigré writer who had been living in France for two years, when the Hogarth Press published *The Gentleman from San Francisco and Other Stories* in 1922. He had won the Pushkin Prize in 1903 and had been elected in 1909 to the Russian Academy as one of the twelve honorary academicians. Despite his reputation in Russia as a brilliant writer and poet in the mode of classical Russian realism derived from Turgenev and Tolstoy, Bunin was virtually unknown at this time among Western readers. Only a half-dozen poems and one story had been translated into English and published in the *Russian Review* (1916) and the

Proceedings of the Anglo-Russian Literary Society (1918). It was the Hogarth Press, therefore, which effectively introduced Bunin to English readers through *The Gentleman from San Francisco,* eleven years before he won the Nobel Prize in 1933. The press went on to publish two other Bunin books: *The Well of Days* (1933) and *Grammar of Love* (1935). Bunin was an important literary find for Koteliansky and the Woolfs, and one of the few living authors they published in translation.

The Gentleman from San Francisco was a volume composed of four stories written by Bunin in his most prolific period of 1912–18, before the Revolution and his exile: "The Gentleman from San Francisco," "Gentle Breathing," "Kasimir Stanislavovitch," and "Son." Koteliansky's translation of the title story had previously been revised by D. H. Lawrence and published in the January 1922 issue of the *Dial.* Leonard Woolf acted as cotranslator with Kot for the remaining three stories.

D. H. Lawrence, to whom Kot sent "The Gentleman from San Francisco" for re-Englishing, was the fourth of his friends to help with his translations. Leonard and Virginia Woolf were unique among Kot's collaborators in knowing some Russian; they were able to work with Kot on one side and with the original Russian text on the other. Lawrence, without Russian, was also without Kot. He received the story by mail in June 1921 while he and Frieda were traveling in Germany. It seems appropriate that this story of a rich American's travels abroad and his ironic death in Italy should have been worked on by Lawrence as he restlessly traveled through Germany and Austria on the global course that would take him eventually to San Francisco and thence to Taos, New Mexico. The progress of Lawrence's work with Bunin's story can be traced in his letters to Kot.

"Send the two stories along and I will have a shot at them now immediately," wrote Lawrence to Kot from Baden-Baden on June 9, 1921. "Then you can offer them if you like to Woolf," added Lawrence, "& if that is no go, we will make Curtis Brown do something with them (if you like): & Mountsier in America." So Lawrence expected two Bunin stories from Kot for his polishing job and planned from the outset to send them either to the Woolfs' Hogarth Press, which had already published two of Kot's translations, or to his own English and American literary agents. "The Gentleman from San Francisco" reached Lawrence

on June 15, and the next day he responded to Kot: "Have read the *Gent.*—
& in spite of its lugubriousness, grin with joy. Was Bunin one of the
Gorky-Capri crowd?—or only a visitor? But it is screamingly good of
Naples & Capri: so comically like the reality: only just a trifle too earnest
about it. I will soon get it written over: don't think your text needs much
altering. I love a 'little carved peeled-off dog'—it is too good to alter." [11]

Lawrence sent his rewritten version of "Gentleman" to his typist,
who soon forwarded it to Scofield Thayer of the *Dial.* The story was
accepted in late September 1921, and Lawrence received half payment of
£12 from Kot in December. Lawrence, insisting on his minor role in the
translation, was annoyed with Kot's generosity ("I *wish* you would let it
be ¼ for me") and testy to find himself listed as cotranslator when he
received the published story. "They are impudent people," Lawrence
wrote about the *Dial* editors to Kot; "I have told them not to put my
name." [12] Ironically, Lawrence's name was unintentionally left off the title
page of the Hogarth Press edition, and an errata slip had to be pasted in
crediting him as a cotranslator with Kot.

"What a pretty cover Bunin has," wrote Lawrence when he received
his copy of the Hogarth Press volume in Australia. Leonard Woolf, too,
was pleased by the printing and binding of the volume. He and Virginia
had carefully designed the book and bound it in blue, green, and yellow
paper obtained from Czechoslovakia. Lawrence thought that the tales
were not very good, with the exception of "Gentleman," which "is much
the best." [13]

"The Gentleman from San Francisco" has always been popular with
critics and readers. Critics have been almost unanimous in praising Bunin's merciless story of the doomed American millionaire's search for culture in Italy, his sudden death by stroke at Capri, and the hasty, callous
treatment of his corpse as it is finally shipped home in a soda-water crate,
placed in the dark bottom of the opulent cruise ship *Atlantis,* the very
ship which had carried him expensively and alive to Europe. Western
readers instantly recognized the repellent American nouveau riche traveler and understood the savage ironies involved with his family's loss of
status upon his death. Even with its echoes of Chekhov and Tolstoy, Bunin's story is more Western than Russian, and this aspect, as well as its
stylistic brilliance, served to spread Bunin's reputation among English-

speaking readers. The story was a fortunate choice to lead off the Hogarth Press volume.

D. H. Lawrence's somewhat giddy response to "Gentleman" may have been caused partly by Kot's translation about the dog, so unusual that it stuck in Leonard Woolf's mind for forty-one years (*Beginning* 248). In spite of Lawrence's avowal that the description was "too good to alter," he apparently modified it before sending it to the *Dial*. There the passage read: "The Gentleman from San Francisco, wearing for his part a silk hat and grey spats over patent-leather shoes, kept eyeing the famous beauty who stood near him, a tall, wonderful figure, blonde, with her eyes painted according to the latest Parisian fashion, holding on a silver chain a tiny, cringing, peeled-off little dog, to which she was addressing herself all the time."[14] Although he does not mention doing so, Leonard Woolf may have further edited the description, for the Hogarth Press edition described the bounteous blonde "holding on a silver chain a tiny, cringing, hairless little dog." So with a sad metamorphosis, but no doubt in the interest of accuracy, the dog had changed from "carved peeled-off" to "cringing peeled-off," and finally to "cringing hairless."[15]

Published in May 1922, *The Gentleman from San Francisco and Other Stories* proved only a modest commercial success. Woolf had printed about 1,000 copies, but only 387 were sold in the first eight months, and by the end of February 1924, sales had totaled 693 copies. Including the press share of the sale of the American rights to *Dial* and Thomas Seltzer, there was a loss of £2.17.4 to Hogarth in the first year but a profit by February 1924 of £10.16.4 after payments to Kot and Lawrence (ABS 158). The sales would continue slowly for years. In 1934 Leonard took advantage of Bunin's Nobel Prize and reprinted *The Gentleman from San Francisco* in 1,200 copies (*Checklist*). In such a marginal business, every shilling counted, and Woolf's strict accounting angered Koteliansky. The exchange of letters between Kot and Woolf reveals both men and provides an engaging look into Hogarth Press affairs in its fifth year of operation.

Koteliansky had written to Woolf in December 1922 asking to be paid $50 from Seltzer's $100 American rights payment (expected in January) and requesting that Woolf direct the American agent Mountsier (who handled the account with *Dial* and Seltzer) to remit $25 to Lawrence directly as his share (HP 38). This action would have left the Hogarth Press with a $25 share of the original $100. Woolf had received only slightly more than £10 from Seltzer as an advance, but he carefully sent Kot a check for £8.1.6, "as you thought that you and Lawrence ought to get 75% of it." Woolf stated that he was thus willing to divide the advance, because they had no formal agreement, but that in the future they should establish a definite understanding. As Woolf wrote: "Ordinarily publishers take as much as 50% of American copyrights and payments, when they sell them on behalf of authors. Hitherto, when Virginia or I have done the translation with you, we have simply taken our half share, as translator, and credited it to the Press and the Press itself has taken nothing as publisher. But if we are not translators, it means of course that the Press gets absolutely nothing—as in this case of Bunin—and since we now have people beside ourselves interested in the press as a business, we obviously cannot do this" (HP 38).

Kot failed to understand Woolf's explanation or to accept his version of their relationship, and several heated letters were exchanged. At the end, Kot replied with feeling: "Now I don't know whether you intended your refusal to instruct Mountsier to pay Lawrence his share out of the next instalment as a personal insult to me; and also whether you meant it as an insult to tell me that you were generous to me. If you want to insult me there is no need doing it in a round about way: we could put an end to our relations, if you want it in a straight-forward way, without any need at all to insult each other" (HP 38). Kot then proceeded to detail his understanding of their relationship, adding, "Is it generous to claim a bigger part than 25% of your share on that book?" There is no record of Woolf's response, but a resolution must have been achieved. Kot and Woolf remained friends. The Hogarth Press published two more of Kot's translations in 1923, but the cotranslator in each case was Virginia, not Leonard.

Another Russian writer published by the Woolfs was Leonid Andreyev. "Leonid was talented by nature," wrote Gorky in his "Reminiscences of Leonid Andreyev," "organically talented; his intuition was astonishingly keen. In all that touched on the dark side of life, the contradictions in the human soul, the rumblings in the domain of the instincts, he had eerie powers of divination."[16] The "dark side of life" was Andreyev's obsession, and it touched a responding chord in his readers' minds.

As Marc Slonim has written, "His tales and plays between 1907 and 1912 were received by thousands of readers as an expression of their own despondence."[17] Andreyev's popularity in Russia was sudden and immense, reaching a peak around 1908, and as quickly extinguished after the Revolution. He died at forty-eight, in 1919, an embittered foe of the Bolsheviks, alone and ill, self-exiled in Finland, severed from such old literary friends as Gorky.

It was in 1908, at the height of his fame, that Andreyev's works began to appear in English translation. The first volumes were collections of short stories (*Silence and Other Stories,* 1910; *The Little Angel and Other Stories,* 1915), soon followed by the regular publication of his plays (*Anathema,* 1910; *The Sorrows of Belgium,* 1915; *The Life of Man,* 1915). By 1924, when publishing interest in Andreyev seems to have expired, nearly as many of his plays as volumes of his short stories had been published, evenly distributed among American and English firms of a wide variety, from the *Dial* to Macmillan in the United States and from Duckworth to the Hogarth Press in England. *The Dark,* published by the Hogarth Press in 1923, was a German import for the Woolfs, translated into English by L. A. Magnus and K. Walter and printed in Weimar by Kietsch & Bruckner. How the Woolfs came to publish it is not clear. The press played no role of any importance in the development of Andreyev's literary reputation in England, and the novel was not a critical success; nevertheless, it has claimed some attention.

Written in 1907, *The Dark* (or *Darkness,* to use its more familiar title) mirrored Andreyev's pessimistic, despondent mood at a time of personal and political crises—the death of his first wife and the failure of the liberal movement in the years of reaction to the October revolution of 1905. The arrogant terrorist and revolutionary Alexis in *The Dark* is jolted by the prostitute Liuba's challenge, "What right have you to be fine when I am so common."[18] Confronted by Liuba's probing questions, Alexis realizes the futility of his heroic ideals in an evil world and sees with shattering clarity the meaninglessness of his moral suppositions.

The topicality of Andreyev's *Dark,* its pessimistic view of man so appropriate to the Russian mood of 1907, was no less appropriate to some aspects of the English and European mood of 1922–23 when the Hogarth Press published the story. Four years after the trauma of the world war,

1922 was the year the press published Bunin's darkly ironic *The Gentleman from San Francisco,* Dostoyevsky's *Stravrogin's Confession,* Freud's *Beyond the Pleasure Principle,* and Virginia Woolf's *Jacob's Room.* And in 1923, the year of *The Dark,* the Hogarth Press published T. S. Eliot's *Waste Land,* a work which provided an entire postwar generation with the images, tone, and attitudes of ironic disillusionment and despair.

The cultlike popularity of Dostoyevsky during the decade 1912–21 in England coincided with war and postwar experiences and with Freudian studies of the dark compulsions of the mind. The fires of enthusiasm for Dostoyevsky were unquestionably fueled by the excellent translations of Constance Garnett. Beginning in 1912 with her translation of *The Brothers Karamazov,* Garnett with her publisher Heinemann had produced a volume a year of Dostoyevsky translations, sometimes two volumes a year, until the twelve-volume collection was complete in 1920—seven novels and five volumes of shorter fiction. The Garnett translations were soon the standards in English.

Gradually there appeared published collections of letters, hitherto unpublished fragments of writing, and biographical-critical studies. When the Woolfs published *Stavrogin's Confession* in 1922, two publications of personal writings had come out (*Letters of Dostoevsky to His Family and Friends,* translated by Ethel Mayne from a German version, published by Chatto & Windus, 1914, and *Pages from the Journals of an Author,* translated by Koteliansky and John Middleton Murry, published by Maunsel and Co., 1916). Three biographical and critical studies, by Middleton Murry (1916), E. A. Soloviev (1916), and J. Lavrin (1920), had been published. These last three studies reflected the enthusiasms of the time and the scanty information available about Dostoyevsky.

The Hogarth Press publication of *Stavrogin's Confession* (1922) ushered in the second phase of Dostoyevsky enthusiasm, a period of ten to fifteen years marked by the publication of autobiographical and biographical materials providing revelations that led to the first complete biography, by E. H. Carr, in 1931. Avrahm Yarmolinsky's massive biography followed in 1934. During this second phase beginning in 1922, Aimée Dostoyevsky's sensational and highly unreliable biographical study of her father was published, followed nine months later by *Stavrogin's Confession,* then by Kot's and Murry's translation of more Dostoyevsky letters and reminiscences in 1923. "All this material that revealed Dostoyevsky the man," wrote Helen Muchnic, "tended to qualify admiration of Dostoevsky the author; when the one was shown as all too human, it was difficult to continue thinking the other divine."[19]

While Leonard Woolf worked with Koteliansky on Countess Tolstoy's autobiography, Virginia collaborated with him on the Dostoyevsky book. In the meantime, the first issue of T. S. Eliot's *Criterion* was to be published in October 1922, and Eliot requested some Russian translations. The Woolfs sent him portions of the Dostoyevsky material, which Eliot accepted. The Virginia Woolf–Koteliansky translation "Plan of the Novel 'The Life of a Great Sinner' " appeared in the first issue of October 1922 where it kept company with Eliot's *Waste Land* and Valery Larbaud's pioneering explanation of Joyce's *Ulysses*. Dostoyevsky's plan for his novel was included with *Stavrogin's Confession* in the Hogarth Press volume when it was published in October 1922.

In their "Translator's Note," Virginia and Kot explained the source and contents of the volume. "The Russian Government has recently published a small paper-covered book containing *Stavrogin's Confession*, unpublished chapters of Dostoevsky's novel *The Possessed*, and Dostoevsky's plan or sketch of a novel which he never actually wrote but which he called *The Life of a Great Sinner*."[20] The Woolfs included three articles on Dostoyevsky in the volume and a translation of the government's account of the discovery of a store of Dostoyevsky materials. With suitable but ponderous drama, the Soviet Government's "Note" recounted how "on November 12, 1921, in the presence of A. V. Lunacharsky, Commissar of Education, and M. N. Pokrovsky, Assistant Commissar of Education, in the Central Archive Department of the Russian Socialist Federative Soviet Republic there was opened a white tin case numbered 5038 from the State Archives containing F. M. Dostoevsky's papers."[21] What the commissars discovered when they opened the case was not so monumental as the opening of the famous tomb in Luxor one year later, but it was interesting enough. Inside were assorted letters, documents, and several notebooks containing Dostoyevsky's notes, plans, and materials for *Crime and Punishment, The Idiot*, and *The Possessed*. In addition, there were the proof sheets of several chapters excluded from the published version of *The Possessed*. The Russian government had published the contents of the notebooks early in 1922, and Koteliansky had moved with considerable speed to obtain a copy and prepare a rough translation by late March when Virginia Woolf began to work with it. English readers of *Stavrogin's Confession* were thus able to read the revelations less than a year after the opening of the tin case in Moscow.

Dostoyevsky had been persuaded by his publisher to omit the chapters from *The Possessed* when it appeared (1871–72) because of their sensational account of Stavrogin's coldly evil rape of a young girl and her subsequent suicide. As Strakhov had written to Tolstoy in 1883, in a letter translated by Kot and published in Eliot's *Criterion,* "One scene from Stavrogin (rape, etc.) Katkov refused to publish, but Dostoyevsky had read it here to many persons."[22] The scenes were thought not only morally offensive but graphic to the point of pornography or obscenity. English readers in 1922 were probably less easily offended, although the reviewer for the *Saturday Review* thought the confession a "crude statement of horrors far exceeding in turpitude the crime of Rashkolnikoff" and maintained that it was "difficult in decent language to hint at the nature of the offence."[23]

The Hogarth Press edition of *Stavrogin's Confession* provided both general and specialized readers of Dostoyevsky with materials for further study. Significant though the volume was for Dostoyevsky studies, however, it did not sell any better than the later Tolstoy translations. Leonard Woolf had 1,000 copies printed by R. & R. Clark of Edinburgh in October 1922, but only 557 copies were eventually sold by February 1924. The book produced over £129 in income, but costs were greater (ABS 166). Woolf's accounting, after Koteliansky's customary payments, showed a loss to the press of 1s.4d. Virginia Woolf, as cotranslator, received no payment.

In 1947 a photo-offset reprint of *Stavrogin's Confession* was published by Lear Publishers of New York, the only reprint of the Hogarth Press edition in either England or America. The reprint is a hybrid, containing the Koteliansky-Woolf translation of the confession but omitting the plan for the "Great Sinner." Included, however, is an article by Sigmund Freud, "Dostoevsky and Parricide." Written in 1928 by Freud as an introduction to one of the supplementary volumes of the complete German edition of Dostoyevsky's works, the article has nothing to do with *The*

Possessed or the "Great Sinner," but everything to do with Freud's view of Dostoyevsky's life.

If Leonard and Virginia Woolf in 1923 had decided to end the Hogarth Press with their move into London from Hogarth House to Tavistock Square and to give over the complex frustrations and pleasure of hand printing and publishing for the less life-complicating endeavors of writing and journalism, their press might still be remembered as an interesting semiprivate endeavor with thirty-three titles to its credit in seven years. In the last four years before the London move, from 1920 through 1923 when the press had evolved into a true publishing house, the Woolfs had published twenty-seven titles, of which eight, nearly one-third, were Russian translations. A retrospective evaluation of those four years must single out Virginia Woolf's *Monday or Tuesday* (1921) and *Jacob's Room* (1922), T. S. Eliot's *Waste Land* (1923), and the eight Russian translations.

Put in such a context, the Russian translations loom large in number and importance, overshadowing all other titles except those of Woolf and Eliot. Following their timely interests in the Russians and using to their advantage the offerings of S. S. Koteliansky, the Woolfs had made Hogarth an important, if small-scale, publisher of Russian letters in the immediate postwar, postrevolutionary period. Such an international tone to the press would be amplified by Leonard Woolf in the first years at Tavistock Square when he took on the Freudian books of the International Psycho-Analytical Library and when he expanded into works on antiimperialism, disarmament, and peace.

Fired by the successes of their press and their own writing, the Woolfs put Richmond behind them and moved energetically into the literary, political, and publishing life of London to begin the most productive period of their lives. The Russian translations undoubtedly had helped point the way for the press. Leonard and Virginia Woolf would not turn back.

CHAPTER FOUR

★

MATURITY, 1924–30

The Woolfs and their press moved into 52 Tavistock Square over March 13 and 14, 1924, and for the first time in their writing and publishing careers they could enjoy something approaching adequate space for both activities. The ground and first floors were occupied by the solicitors Dollman & Pritchard who came with the building as tenants, the upper two floors became the Woolfs' home, decorated by Vanessa Bell and Duncan Grant, and the basement housed the Hogarth Press in a series of rooms once used as kitchen, scullery, and pantry. The Woolfs converted these rooms into offices, a shop for booksellers' representatives, a printing room, and storage space. A long, dark passage connected these rooms with a large, skylighted back room, once used for billiards, which became Virginia Woolf's "Studio." Quentin Bell has described it vividly: "It had also to serve as a storeroom and repository for Hogarth Press publications, and here, among the heaped-up parcels of books and piles of paper, in conditions of dirt and disorder, surrounded by what the Stracheys called "filth packets"—accumulations of old pen nibs, paper-clips, buttons and fluff, empty ink bottles and unemptied ashtrays, used envelopes and galley proofs—Virginia could be found in the morning, seated beside the gas fire in an old arm chair, the stuffing of which emerged in disembowelled confusion upon the floor, a board of three-ply on her lap, writing and re-writing her books."[1] Leonard and Virginia Woolf, their press, and a series of partners and assistants would live and work in these facilities for fifteen years. Virginia's greatest novels and literary essays would be written here or at Monks House.

With the new space, the exhilaration of living in London again, and the work going well, the Woolfs expanded the press offerings dramatically in 1924, one of the most important years in the history of the press. Virginia, busy writing *Mrs. Dalloway* (completed in October 1924 but not published until 1925), had no novel for the year, but she published her frequently revised important polemic *Mr. Bennett and Mrs. Brown* as an essay, her first separately published criticism. The press broke new ground in fiction, however, with its first three novels written by authors other than Virginia Woolf: F. M. Mayor's *Rector's Daughter* and Coralie Hobson's *In Our Town,* both published in May, and Vita Sackville-West's *Seducers in Ecuador,* published in October.

Few of the forty writers of fiction published by the Woolfs between 1917 and 1941 were complete strangers. Typically a Hogarth Press novelist was someone with a Cambridge connection who published one novel, showing a promise which was not fulfilled by subsequent publications. Only a handful published more than one book with the press. Notable exceptions were E. M. Forster, Vita Sackville-West, and William Plomer. Virginia and Leonard Woolf inclined to be generous toward beginning novelists, and especially those with a Cambridge-Bloomsbury background.

Flora Macdonald Mayor brought *The Rector's Daughter* to the Woolfs in February 1924. She was fifty-two, unmarried, and in ill health (she would die eight years later), the daughter of a Cambridge clergyman and scholar (a professor of classics and moral philosophy at King's College, University of London) and herself an early student at Newnham College in 1892. Her brother, R. J. G. ("Robin") Mayor, was an Apostle and a former fellow of King's College, Cambridge. Virginia Woolf had known Robin Mayor's wife in 1912 before their marriage. With such impeccable Cambridge connections, F. M. Mayor also brought considerable talent and some experience. She had written and published pseudonymously in 1901 a collection of children's stories after leaving Newnham and then published a short novel in 1913 with a preface by John Masefield, *The Third Miss Symons.* It received respectful critical recognition at the time and has been republished as a Virago Modern Classic. Unlike most other press authors from Cambridge, Mayor was not a first-time novelist, and her mastery of form and style shone through.

The Rector's Daughter presents a deeply moving and quietly rendered portrait of the saintly spinster, Mary Jocelyn, trapped in a life of genteel impoverishment, where love is seen (in the minister Mr. Herbert), barely grasped, and then lost forever. Canon Jocelyn, the severe and self-occupied old Cambridge clergyman scholar, rector of Dedmayne, barely acknowledges Mary's presence. Mary, after her father's death, joins her Aunt Lothe and her friends Dora and Ella Redland, clergyman's daughters also, in a classic cycle of good works and quiet martyrdom. She dies of influenza in middle age.

Leonard Woolf agreed to publish *The Rector's Daughter* on a commission basis. Under this arrangement, the press printed and distributed the book, receiving for its services a lump-sum payment for costs and a 10 percent commission from Mayor on each copy sold (HP 277). She owned the printed book as property in a reversal of the usual publishing arrangement. Although Woolf would occasionally act as publisher for a private printing, as with Harold Nicolson's biographical essay *Jeanne de Henaut* (fifty-five copies paid for and mailed to friends by Nicolson in 1925) or the Sackville-Wests' translation of Rilke (printed in Germany and published in 1931 on commission by Hogarth), this was the first and only time that he entered into a commission agreement with a novelist. He must have done so out of inexperience and uncertainty about the novel's commercial success and in fear of the risks he ran with such a long work by a relatively unknown author.

F. M. Mayor's novel printed up at 347 pages, considerably longer than Virginia Woolf's *Jacob's Room* (290 pages) or Sackville-West's novella *Seducers in Ecuador* (74 pages). Leonard Woolf need not have worried. Mayor's novel succeeded immediately and sold out the first printing of 1,000 copies, requiring a second impression in November, six months after publication. She easily recovered her initial investment of £155.14.4 and the press earned some royalties (HP 277). In 1927, three years after publication, the novel continued to sell, earning £46.2 for the year (MSR). But as Stanley Unwin pointed out in his authoritative study of the trade, *The Truth about Publishing* (1926), most established publishers seldom engaged in commissioned work because their publishing overhead costs could never be met by the small royalty paid by the author.[2] Although Woolf did not lose money on Mayor's novel, he did not make much, and its surprising success must have cured him of timidity. He never again took a novel on commission but returned to the standard publishing practice of either accepting a manuscript at risk on a royalty agreement or rejecting it outright.

The remarkable qualities of *The Rector's Daughter* have attracted many readers over the years, as shown by the continued popularity of the Penguin Modern Classics edition, reprinted three times since 1973. Virginia Woolf praised the book when it appeared but skewered the author with several of her unforgettably malicious epithets, writing to Pernel Strachey (principal of Newnham College) in 1924: "She has the profile of a gorilla and once acted Ophelia. . . . Where ordinary women have hair, she has a brown sea weed—Lytton once had tea with her, and she hated us all, until I wrote to her in praise of her novel, when she whipped round the other way, and now steps the world (it is said) like a stallion in the sun" (*Letters* 3:126). Woolf might have been more sympathetic to a woman writer trying to establish a room of her own through her feminist novel. She would address such issues with understanding and her own feminist books, *A Room of One's Own* (1929) and *Three Guineas* (1938). *The Rector's Daughter* was followed five years later by *The Squire's Daughter* (1929), in spite of its title no sequel, which F. M. Mayor chose to publish with Constable. It has been republished as a Virago Modern Classic.

Although Coralie Hobson's novel failed to sell and has been lost to time, Vita Sackville-West's *Seducers in Ecuador,* the third of the Hogarth Press novels of 1924, did much better and inaugurated a seventeen-year personal and professional relationship of great importance between Sackville-West and the Woolfs. As a novelist Vita Sackville-West wrote romantic melodramas that she produced rapidly, often at the rate of one per year. She came to care sufficiently about her craft, however, to break out of the formula, to write more deliberately, and to include contemporary concerns. The change in Sackville-West's style and subject matter occurred when she became a Hogarth Press author at the age of thirty-two. She developed as a novelist and a professional writer—biographer, travel writer, critic, and essayist—under the influence of Virginia Woolf and the Hogarth Press. Their relationship, flowering into friendship and love, interpenetrated both their lives. It warmed Virginia into a new, intensely emotional experience and led to her writing *Orlando,* as it strengthened and developed Vita's critical faculties, inspiring her to write her two best-selling novels, *The Edwardians* (1930) and *All Passion Spent* (1931).

When the two writers met in December 1922 through Clive Bell's introduction, Vita Sackville-West had already published two volumes of poetry, two novels, and a collection of stories, not counting her first two privately published books before she was married. She had written in 1918−19 but not yet published a third novel, *Challenge,* so closely patterned on her tempestuous love affair with Violet Trefusis that the families had discouraged publication. Within months of meeting Virginia Woolf, however, she published *Challenge* in America and brought out *Grey Wethers,* her last novel in the old romantic style. As she wrote to Woolf five years later, "Yes, my dear Virginia: I was at a crossways just about the time I first met you," and she drew a picture of a signpost at an intersection labeled "Bad novels" and "Good poetry." "It is quite true," Vita wrote, "that you have had infinitely more influence on me intellectually than anyone, and for this alone I love you. I feel my muscles hardening."[3] Virginia Woolf responded by giving more advice, commenting that "I think there are odder, deeper, more angular thoughts in your mind than you have yet let come out" (*Letters* 3:321).

The earliest evidence of Sackville-West's more angular thoughts appeared in *Seducers in Ecuador* (1924), a novella of seventy-four pages. As was her custom, Virginia Woolf had sought a manuscript from Sackville-West once their friendship developed. The Woolfs were anxious to keep Dadie Rylands, their new assistant, busy with new books, and they liked the idea of adding a Sackville-West novel to their autumn list. She agreed to their request, writing most of *Seducers* between July 8 and 21 when the Nicolsons were walking in the Italian Dolomites. Vita finished it in time to give it to Virginia on Saturday, September 13, the first night she stayed at Monks House. She made an impression. Virginia recorded Vita's entrance, driving through Rodmell in her "large new blue Austin car," arriving "dressed in ringed yellow jersey, & large hat, & [with] a dressing case all full of silver & night gowns wrapped in tissue" (*Diary* 2:313). She seemed to Virginia "like an over ripe grape in features, mustached, pouting," as she strode on "fine legs, in a well cut skirt." With her "good sense & simplicity" Sackville-West pleased both the Woolfs, and Virginia thought that they might develop a lasting friendship.

Virginia Woolf read the manuscript of *Seducers* on Sunday after Vita returned home to Long Barn and sent it off to the printer on Monday. The story interested her, Virginia noted, partly because "I see my own face in it, its true" (*Diary* 1:313). But she also thought that Vita had "shed that old verbiage, & come to terms with some sort of glimmer of art." Virginia admired Vita's production of a 20,000-word manuscript in a fortnight while being a "mother, wife, great lady, hostess." Such energy caused Virginia to question her own vigor as she worked to complete *Mrs. Dalloway*. To Vita, Virginia wrote on Monday morning that she thought *Seducers* "could be tightened up, and aimed straighter," but she liked its texture, "the sense of all the fine things you have dropped in to it" (*Letters* 3:131). She was certain that Vita had done "something more interesting . . . than you've yet done."

What is more interesting about *Seducers in Ecuador* than her previous novels is the way Vita Sackville-West saves the story from melodrama by undercutting it with irony. The plot, nothing to do with either seducers or Ecuador, is economically developed but perilously borders on the sensational and implausible: three comparative strangers on a rich man's yacht sailing the Mediterranean and Aegean seas, an impulsive marriage between two of them, a storm at sea, the rich man's story of a terminal disease and a request for euthanasia, the eventual mercy killing, a surprising inheritance, a trial for murder, and the hanging of the well-intentioned euthanist.

When the Woolfs sent *Seducers in Ecuador* off to the printer, they sent it to R. & R. Clark, by then the established printer for Virginia Woolf's books, who thus became the printer for Sackville-West's novels. The novel was published in November 1924 with books by T. S. Eliot (*Homage to John Dryden*), Roger Fry, John Crowe Ransom, and Sigmund Freud (the first two volumes of his *Collected Papers*). Leonard Woolf issued *Seducers* in an edition of 1,500 copies, 600 bound at publication and the remaining 900 copies bound by the first week in November, in anticipation of strong sales. Virginia reported to Vita an order for 25 copies from America and sales-to-date of 899 copies by December 26, 1924 (*Letters* 3:151). Sales were helped by Edwin Muir's enthusiastic review in the *Nation and Athenaeum,* calling *Seducers* a "fantastic psychological study" which contained "involuntary symbolism."[4] By January 1926 the novel had sold over 1,200 copies (*Checklist* 29).

Leonard and Virginia Woolf thus began their first publishing year in

London at Tavistock Square in excellent fashion by issuing three novels, a flurry of fiction which might have suggested to the observer that the Hogarth Press would continue to expand along its already established lines of traditional literary genres. But in this important year of 1924, Leonard Woolf changed the direction of the press dramatically, publishing Norman Leys's *Kenya* in October, the first of a swelling tide of books and pamphlets on political, social, and economic subjects. And most importantly, Leonard began his association with Dr. Ernest Jones and the Institute of Psycho-Analysis as he and Virginia contracted to publish Freud's *Collected Papers* and the other publications of the International Psycho-Analytical Library (IPL). The Hogarth Press published the first two volumes of Freud's *Papers* this year and began to distribute the six previously published volumes of the IPL. The press publications on political and psychoanalytical subjects are examined in chapters 6 and 8.

In 1924 the Woolfs also started their first series, the Hogarth Essays, by publishing four pamphlets: Virginia Woolf's *Mr. Bennett and Mrs. Brown* (October); Roger Fry's *The Artist and Psycho-Analysis* (November), a thorough and knowledgeable defense of the artist against Freud's reductive theories; Theodora Bosanquet's *Henry James at Work* (November); and T. S. Eliot's *Homage to John Dryden* (November).

Leonard Woolf published Eliot's *Homage to John Dryden* in 2,000 copies, twice the number printed for the previous three titles in the series. Eliot had published *The Sacred Wood* with Methuen in 1920, his first collection of some seventeen essays and reviews. Many of them had appeared previously in journals, including the now-famous "Tradition and the Individual Talent," "The Possibility of a Poetic Drama," and "Hamlet and His Problems." His Hogarth Press volume honoring John Dryden and others was only his second collection of essays and extended the ideas he had developed in *The Sacred Wood*.

For his Hogarth Press pamphlet, Eliot collected an essay and two reviews. He had published his appreciative essay "Andrew Marvell" in the March 21, 1921, issue of *TLS*. In June he had reviewed Mark Van Doren's book on John Dryden, and then in October, he wrote "The Metaphysical Poets" for the *TLS* as a review of H. J. C. Grierson's landmark collection of seventeenth-century metaphysical poetry. Brought together in the Hogarth Press pamphlet and thus given increased visibility, the review on

Dryden and the essay on Marvell became fixtures in the Eliot canon, and the review "The Metaphysical Poets," with Eliot's well-known dictum on the dissociation of sensibility, had a pervasive influence on twentieth-century poetry and criticism. Eliot rewrote literary history to suit his needs and taught several generations the value of densely conceited verse as a way of uniting thought and feeling.

With the advantage of hindsight, we can see that Virginia Woolf's essay number one and Eliot's essay number four in the Hogarth series were two of the most significant statements by the early modernists in the refashioning of attitudes toward fiction and poetry. They have become minor classics, their terminology passing into the vocabulary of criticism.

The Woolfs hand printed Theodora Bosanquet's essay on Henry James, the only one they would ever print themselves in the series, and contracted with two printers for the other three titles. Vanessa Bell's bold jacket design added to the attractive format, and the series became uniform in size and appearance the next year in 1925 when Neill & Co. in Edinburgh took over the printing on a regular basis. The Hogarth Essays on a wide range of subjects—literature, art, politics, law, history, feminism, music—ran through two series and thirty-five titles before expiring in 1928 and giving way to two new press series, the Lectures on Literature and the Living Poets. The Essays proved successful in England and abroad in France, and may even have found a market in Japan. Edmund Blunden wrote to Leonard Woolf from Tokyo in September 1925 to report that the Essays, which he had not yet seen, "seem to be exactly the stimulating and up-to-date sort of discussions that the Japanese undergraduates want" (LWP). The overtly educational nature of the series was prominent from the start. The Essays underscore the instructional, at times ideological, aspects of Leonard Woolf's Bloomsbury, his and Virginia's passion to shape opinion, to teach.

A series in a standardized format with uniform page size, binding, and cover, and sometimes with controlled word count offers several business advantages as well as the intellectual ones to a publisher. Large publishers have several series going at a time, and if some of these are short-lived, a few reach the status of classics such as Dent's Everyman's Library, which listed 750 titles in 1924, or the St. Martin's Library of Chatto &

Windus, which listed over 125 titles, or the Traveller's Library launched by Jonathan Cape in 1926. And there were smaller series, similar to those of the Hogarth Press, such as Constable's Makers of Nineteenth Century (8 titles in 1936), Duckworth's Great Lives (57 titles in 1936), or Chatto & Windus's Life and Art in Photographs (10 titles in 1936). Leonard Woolf's venture into series publication with the Hogarth Essays thus marked an important step toward the diversity characteristic of established publishers. Both the IPL publications and the Uniform Editions of Virginia Woolf's novels begun in 1929 constitute less obvious series.

By 1941 the Hogarth Press had published thirteen series (not including the IPL or the Uniform Editions) totaling 162 titles. Three of the series were extensive: the Essays (35 titles, 1924–28), the Living Poets (29 titles, 1928–37), and the Day to Day Pamphlets (41 titles, 1930–39). Two were moderately so, the Lectures on Literature (16 titles, 1927–34) and the Letters (12 titles, 1931–33), but others died aborning: the Stories (2 titles in 1927), the Biographies through the Eyes of Contemporaries (2 titles, 1934–35), and the World-Makers and World-Shakers (4 titles in 1937). Three of the series were begun courageously by John Lehmann under wartime conditions: the Six-Penny Pamphlets (5 titles, 1939), the Poets of Tomorrow (3 titles, 1939–41), and the New Hogarth Library (6 titles, 1940–41). But what would have been their first series ran afoul of another publisher's series and folded after one title in 1924.

In January 1923 Leonard Woolf had conceived the idea of "a series of books illustrating the work of modern artists," as he described it to the Peacock Publicity Service, writing to obtain estimates for thirty halftone reproductions of photos on art paper (HP 133). He may have seen the Duckworth series Masters of Painting (six titles in 1924, each with thirty-two photogravure illustrations) which featured old masters but included one volume on Rossetti. Woolf's series would have served as a natural bridge between the Post impressionist easel painters of Bloomsbury (Vanessa Bell, Roger Fry, Duncan Grant), the art critics (Fry and Clive Bell), and the literary publishers of the Hogarth Press. Not until July, however, had Leonard Woolf formulated his idea clearly enough to approach Roger Fry, proposing that Fry edit a Living Painters series. He suggested that the first volume be on Duncan Grant, have twenty-four plates, and carry an introduction by Fry (HP 133). But Duncan Grant, it turned out, had been approached by the publisher Ernest Benn to be a part of Benn's series Contemporary British Artists, and he was torn between the two publishers.

Leonard Woolf, after a year's deliberation and negotiation, part of it with Victor Gollancz, then a director of Benn's, decided to proceed with the Duncan Grant volume. Fry's edited volume *Duncan Grant* was published in February 1924 with nine pages of introduction and twenty-four plates. The half title read *Living Painters—Duncan Grant,* but the series began and ended with this one volume. Whether Leonard Woolf decided that a Living Painters Series was not worth the effort and time, or whether he realized that the ground was well covered by other publishers, he made no other attempt to publish art books on the Charleston painters or any others.

With their first series underway in the autumn of 1924, the Woolfs continued to publish fiction and poetry. They had published a second volume of poetry, *Mock Beggar Hall,* for the "bolt eyed, blue shirted" Robert Graves in May and then, through him, a volume by the fast-developing American poet John Crowe Ransom, *Grace after Meat,* in October 1924. Graves learned about Ransom, his magazine the *Fugitive,* and his group through a Rhodes scholar at Oxford in 1921, read Ransom's *Poems about God* (1919), and initiated a correspondence with the American in 1922. Soon Graves proposed to find an English publisher for *Poems about God,* but Ransom had already moved beyond the manner of those youthful poems and suggested that Graves consider some of his more recent poems. In August 1922 Ransom sent Graves a poetry manuscript provisionally entitled "Philomela," which included forty-six poems in over a hundred pages, made up of more than half the poems from *Poems about God* and some of his "later stuff."[5] Pleased with Graves's attention and judgment and eager to have the volume published in England after Henry Holt had rejected it in America, Ransom gave Graves editorial license to select and edit the poems. The result would be *Grace after Meat,* hand printed by the Woolfs and published in November 1924.

The forty-six-poem manuscript Graves received from Ransom needed pruning. Graves eventually whittled the collection down to twenty poems, only eight of which were from Ransom's first publication. They agreed on every choice except "Grace" and the book's title. In the meantime Graves was busy scouting publishers. Not until November 1923 did Ransom learn from Graves that the Woolfs would publish his book. "I am overjoyed," he wrote to Graves, "to hear about my election to British publicity through Hogarth Press."[6] *Grace after Meat* (1924) as finally printed by the Woolfs carried Robert Graves's title, his introduction, and his selection and arrangement of the poems.[7] In his enthusiastic introduction, Graves provided a brief biography of Ransom, whom he had never met, and then explained the genesis of the volume. Graves hoped that the book published in England would gain Ransom some attention in America, where he was virtually unknown.

Robert Graves thus aided John Crowe Ransom abroad and at home, although Ransom's milestone volume *Chills and Fever* (containing such famous poems as "Bells for John Whiteside's Daughter," "Miss Euphemia," "Emily Hardcastle," and "Captain Carpenter") was published in America by Knopf in November, just before the Hogarth Press volume. Whatever English audience Ransom gained from Graves's efforts, he did not publish again in England. Only 139 copies of the volume had sold fourteen months after publication (*Checklist* 28). The Woolfs were peripheral to the entire event, Robert Graves acting as agent and editor for an interesting moment in Anglo-American publishing history.

In the midst of their first busy summer of publishing from Tavistock Square, the Woolfs expanded their staff as they expanded their list of publications. Dadie Rylands joined Marjorie Joad at the press in July 1924 for what proved to be a congenial but short-lived tenure. Before his arrival, Virginia Woolf had contemplated Ryland's employment "with a little alarm," as she noted, because it meant a serious commitment to publishing. "It seems to me the beginning of ten years of very hard work," she wrote, "because, for one thing, I should hate failure, & not to fail, we must keep on pressing forward, thinking, planning, imagining, letter writing" (*Diary* 2:304). She misjudged the length of Rylands's tenure, for he left Hogarth six months later in December to take up a fellowship at Cambridge and pursued a distinguished academic career; but she was right about the need to keep planning and pressing forward. Virginia's competitive spirit and her determination not to fail shine out here, but she does not sound enthusiastic. Leonard, more the entrepreneur, enjoyed the challenge and found the need for careful expansion stimulating.

Few publishers survive beyond their first seven years, noted Stanley Unwin, unless the founder has successful management experience at a prior firm or unless he obtains additional capital to carry on the business.[8] Woolf had neither past publishing experience nor additional funding as he moved the Hogarth Press through its crucial seventh year in 1924, beating Unwin's odds by his own shrewd management and cautious expansion.

In the six crowded years of Hogarth Press development from 1924 to 1930, the Woolfs and their press published a number of distinguished books and its first international best-seller; but the period belonged to Virginia Woolf, who rose splendidly to the height of her career and dominated the Hogarth Press list. She began by publishing the *Common Reader* in April 1925, her first book since *Jacob's Room* three years earlier and her first collection of critical essays. *Mrs. Dalloway* appeared three weeks later in May, making 1925 one of the most remarkable years in Virginia Woolf's career, with two major works in different genres. In 1927 the Hogarth Press published *To the Lighthouse* and the third edition of *Kew Gardens* with Vanessa Bell's page decorations. Then came *Orlando* the next year in 1928, and Virginia Woolf's feminist credo *A Room of One's Own* in 1929. In four remarkable years, no doubt stimulated in part by the extraordinary freedom of being her own publisher, Virginia Woolf re-created the informal critical essay and achieved mastery of it and wrote two of her most important novels, each one daringly innovative and experimental, and a popular and commercially successful novel, *Orlando,* which forever changed the material fortunes of the Woolfs.

Shortly after the publication of her Hogarth Essay, *Mr. Bennett and Mrs. Brown,* Virginia Woolf assembled twenty-four of her articles previously published in journals, revised many of them, wrote a lead essay, and published them on May 14 as *The Common Reader* (1925). It was slow to catch on with the critics. Eight days after publication, Virginia had seen no reviews, "all signs which point to a dull chill depressing reception; & complete failure," she noted (*Diary* 3:15). Then she read "2 columns sober & sensible praise—neither one thing nor the other" in the *TLS,* before a strongly favorable and welcome review by Hugh I'Anson Fausset in the *Manchester Guardian* (ibid., 17, 18). He thought her criticism showed brilliance and profundity. When the *Observer* praised the book, sales began to pick up. By mid-June, Lytton Strachey had called it divine and a classic, and Virginia worried that it had been overpraised (ibid., 32, 33). Sales took off and never slowed.

Leonard Woolf put *The Common Reader* into a second impression of 1,000 copies in November 1925 and into a Uniform Edition of 3,200 copies in September 1929. The latter sold over 1,200 copies in the first six months (MSR). Virginia, in refashioning the informal, critical essay to her own unique perspective, had taught a new generation how to read, how to become uncommon readers. Her first *Common Reader* and its sequel, *The Common Reader: Second Series* (1932) have endured as popular and influential nonfiction publications.

As was her practice, Virginia Woolf overlapped her writing, beginning a new work while finishing the ongoing one. She found the scheme of alternating essay writing with fiction an especially productive method of work. So in August 1922, as she began to write and rewrite the essays of *The Common Reader,* she started to write a story which became "Mrs. Dalloway in Bond Street" when she published it the next year in *Dial.* By October 1922 she noted, "Mrs. Dalloway has branched into a book; & I adumbrate here a study of insanity & suicide; the world seen by the sane & the insane side by side" (*Diary* 2:207). In November she planned the "aeroplane chapter." By the following June 1923, she was calling the book "the Hours" and noting in her diary that writing it was "going to be the devil of a struggle . . . so queer & so masterful" was the design (ibid., 249).

The struggle to realize her design can be traced in Virginia Woolf's diaries over the next sixteen months. At times she thought her writing was "sheer weak dribble," but then she would swing the other way and view it with excitement. In mid-October 1923 she was drafting the mad scene in Regent's Park, writing slowly at the rate of fifty words a morning; in April 1924 she wrote her "Dr Chapter"; in August she struggled with the death of Septimus, the "low ebb" of her book, grateful to be busy with the Hogarth Press, which kept her from brooding and gave her "something solid to fall back on" (*Diary* 2:308). And then in mid-October 1924 she entered the "astounding fact" that she had finished the novel the previous week by writing the last words, "For there she was" (ibid., 316). She thought that the book was a feat, "finished without break from illness, wh. is an exception; & written really, in one year."

With the draft of *Mrs. Dalloway* completed, Virginia Woolf plunged into the rewriting on November 1 and rushed to have it retyped by Christmas so Leonard could read it over the holidays at Monks House. The revisions had been the "dullest part," the "most depressing & exacting," she noted on January 6, 1925, but Leonard had read it with enthusiasm. He thought it her best, "but then has he not *got* to think so?" she wondered (*Diary* 3:4). Leonard considered that it had more continuity than *Jacob's Room,* and she agreed. And so off went the typescript to R. & R. Clark, who promised proofs in another week. *Mrs. Dalloway* was ready for the spring publishing season, coming out on May 14, 1925, in 2,000 copies just a few weeks after *The Common Reader.*

The reviews when they came were mixed, and so was Bloomsbury's reaction. E. M. Forster praised *Mrs. Dalloway* and Virginia, gallantly kissing her hand and telling her the novel was better than *Jacob's Room* and he was very pleased; but Vita Sackville-West was doubtful; and Lytton Strachey, admiring *The Common Reader* more, thought the novel was a flawed stone (*Diary* 3:24, 25, 32). Readers bought the book, however, and the sales were brisk. By June 18, one month after publication, Virginia noted that 1,250 copies had been sold, which seems on target with the total of 1,990 copies recorded sold by January 1926 in one of the Sussex account books (*Checklist* 38). Leonard issued a second impression of 1,000 copies in November 1925.

Forster, having published his masterpiece, *A Passage to India,* with Edward Arnold in 1924, reentered the Woolfs' professional lives briefly in 1925 with two short Hogarth Press publications: an edition with introduction and notes of Mrs. Eliza Fay's *Original Letters from India (1779 – 1815)* and an essay, *Anonymity: An Enquiry.* Forster had discovered Mrs. Fay's letters during his second trip to India (1921–22) and had included excerpts from her letters about Egypt in his Hogarth Press *Pharos and Pharillon* (1923). His introduction to her complete letters expressed his admiration for her plucky character and her lively, if sometimes ungrammatical, prose.

After Eliza's letters, Forster offered his essay on literary art and the writer to the Hogarth Press, and Leonard Woolf published it in December 1925 as number twelve in his two-year-old Hogarth Essays series. *Anonymity: An Enquiry* was less an inquiry than a statement of deeply felt beliefs about the autonomy and depersonalized character of literary work, and as such it resembled a lecture, hortatory at times. Forster may have given an early version of it in February 1924 at the Working Men's College where he lectured so diligently for many years. He published the completed essay first in the *Atlantic Monthly* (November 1925) and then revised it slightly for Edgell Rickword's *Calendar of Modern Letters* (November 1925) and the Hogarth Press.

After Leonard Woolf had taken the Hogarth Press into new publishing ventures in 1924—the first political and psychoanalytical books, the first series—he and Virginia expanded the Hogarth list rapidly in 1925. From sixteen published titles in 1924, they increased to twenty-eight in 1925, many of them in the literary genres. The Hogarth Press published nine volumes of poetry in 1925, more than double the number in 1924, and more than it ever would again issue in a single year. Although the Woolfs published mostly conventional and neo-Georgian poetry with a Cambridge flavor during the year, volumes such as those by their new assistant Dadie Rylands (*Russet and Taffeta*), by R. C. Trevelyan (*Poems and Fables*), and H. E. Palmer (*Songs of Salvation, Sin, and Satire*), they also published three volumes of more than passing interest by Nancy Cunard, Conrad Aiken, and Edwin Muir.

Robert Graves, in his Hogarth Essay *Contemporary Techniques of Poetry* (1925), published in July, divided modern poets wittily into three parties, mixing political satire with shrewd literary criticism. Conservatives (sterile traditionalists) and Liberals (Georgian poets) took the brunt of Graves's satire, but he admired the Left, with its malcontents, revolutionaries, and rowdies. In the Left he put the best poets of his generation, as he saw them: T. S. Eliot, the three Sitwells, Isaac Rosenberg, Siegfried Sassoon, Aldous Huxley, Edgell Rickword, Gertrude Stein, and Nancy Cunard.

Leonard Woolf remembered that it was around 1920 when he first met Nancy Cunard, the dashing rebellious, iconoclastic daughter of Emerald, Lady Cunard, one of London's great hostesses. As he wrote to Hugh Ford, Woolf recalled that "she seemed to drift in and out, in and out of one's room and one's life," always unchanged and enchanting. He had a great affection for her, he said, but one tinged with apprehension at her "air of vulnerability" beneath her surface gaiety.[9] Virginia Woolf described Nancy Cunard in 1924 as "the little anxious flibbertigibbet with the startled honest eyes, & all the green stones hung about her" (*Diary* 2:320). Nancy Cunard is remembered today as a glittering personality of the 1920s, but she was also a talented poet, a printer and publisher with her French-based Hours Press (1928–31), a daring and crusading editor in the 1930s (her huge anthology *Negro* in 1934 was one of the first collections of black literature published), and a political activist for Republican Spain. She assisted the Resistance in France during the Second World War, edited *Poems for France* (1944), and wrote two lively books of reminiscences about her literary friends Norman Douglas (1954) and George Moore (1956). Images of Nancy Cunard remain: the character of Iris March in Michael Arlen's best-seller *The Green Hat* (1925); Lady Tantamount in Huxley's *Point Counter Point* (1928); the angular, delicate pencil drawings by Wyndham Lewis; the memorable 1930s photograph by Cecil Beaton.

When Leonard and Virginia Woolf hand printed and published her long poem *Parallax* in 1925, Nancy Cunard had published seven poems in the first issue of the annual collection *Wheels* (1916), edited by the Sitwells, a few more poems in periodicals, and two books of poetry: *Outlaws* (1921) and *Sublunary* (1923). She published one more volume of poetry, *Poems (Two) 1925*, at the Aquila Press in 1930 and then stopped publishing her poems. Most of her energies after 1925 were devoted to her press, her political causes, her editing, and to her growing literary journalism. The Hogarth Press volume, therefore, assumes an importance in her life and art, representing her fullest development as a poet.

Parallax is long (nearly 600 lines), on a large scale (encompassing several seasonal orbits and geographical shifts from London to Paris, from the English countryside to the French), and complex (rhythmical and tonal variations from free to rhymed verse in several voices, meditative, ironic, exalted). There are echoes of Eliot throughout, but *Parallax* is less derivative than Cunard's earlier poems. True to its title (which may have been suggested by Virginia Woolf), *Parallax* is largely about sight, the apparent displacement caused by differing viewpoints that must be reconciled (*Diary* 2:320). The stark line drawings of city and country by Eugene McCown for the Hogarth Press's cover of *Parallax* show splendidly the skewed perspectives of the poem. *Parallax* sold 263 copies by August 1926 and was out of print a few years later (*Checklist* 31).

The second interesting poet published by the Hogarth Press in 1925 was Edwin Muir, a far more important poet-to-be than Cunard. T. S. Eliot wrote forty years later that Edwin Muir "will remain among the poets who have added glory to the English language."[10] He confessed, however, that he had paid little attention to Muir's poetry when he was young because he had developed in a different direction from Muir. It was not until the 1940s that Muir wrote the mature poems upon which his reputation, and Eliot's appraisal, rests. Of modern times but not a modernist, Muir wrote mythic and metaphysical poems that defy easy classification. Leonard Woolf considered Muir a natural poet. He did not merely write poetry, Woolf observed; "the sap of poetry was in his bones and veins, in his heart and brain" (*Downhill* 131).

Leonard Woolf in his autobiography thus looked back over forty years "with great pleasure and some sadness," remembering how he and Virginia had printed Muir's *First Poems* in 1925 "with our own hands and he was the kind of author and they were the kind of poems for whom and which we wanted the Press to exist." The next year he and Virginia published Muir's second volume of poetry, *Chorus of the Newly Dead,* less successful than the first volume and, as Leonard accurately noted, "not a book which in 1926 an ordinary publisher would have looked at." Leonard got the books confused as to printing, however. He and Virginia had hand printed *Chorus of the Newly Dead,* and Neill & Co. had printed *First Poems.* The Woolfs also published a collection of Muir's essays, a short novel, and a work of criticism during the three years 1925 to 1928.

Edwin Muir came to the Hogarth Press through the *Nation and Athenaeum.* Leonard Woolf recounted in his autobiography how, as literary editor, he had seen a poem of Muir's, invited him to send more, and soon published several of them. "Childhood," the first of Muir's poems Woolf published in the *Nation and Athenaeum,* became the lead-off poem in *First Poems* (1925) when the Hogarth Press published it two years later. The poetry led to regular reviewing by Muir in the periodical and a long friendship with Woolf. In 1926 Muir would collect nine of his judicious and perceptive *Nation and Athenaeum* articles and publish them with the Hogarth Press as *Transition: Essays on Contemporary Literature.*

The volume of his first poems Muir assembled for the Hogarth Press in 1925 divided into two sections: "Poems," containing eighteen lyrics, beginning with "Childhood" and moving chronologically and geographically from the Orkneys of Muir's boyhood to the Prague and Salzburg of his adulthood, and "Ballads," containing six poems worked unevenly in the ballad meter of iambic tetrameter and trimeter lines, two of them ("Ballad of the Monk" and "Ballad of the Flood") in Scots dialect. Of the eighteen poems in the first section, Muir had published five in the *Nation and Athenaeum,* two in the *Dial,* and one in the *Observer,* so that he had tried out in public nearly half of the poems he presented in the Hogarth Press volume. The best poems in the volume, such as "Childhood," "Horses," "October at Hellbrünn," and "Autumn in Prague," carry the mythic, hauntingly portentous quality of dreams and foreshadow his later poems.

Conrad Aiken, the American poet and critic, the third interesting poet the Woolfs published in 1925, had been a classmate of T. S. Eliot at Harvard and a frequent associate of Eliot's in London and Paris. While Eliot took up permanent residence in England, Aiken worked in the literary establishment of London only fitfully, moving back and forth across the Atlantic, living for periods in England but finding permanent roots only in America.

In late 1922 Aiken with his family moved to England for three years, before he returned to America in 1926. He not only developed into a consistently fine reviewer and critic of literature during this period but also matured as a poet. By 1925, when the Hogarth Press published his *Senlin: A Biography,* Aiken had become an established and respected poet. Prolific always, Conrad Aiken never had difficulty publishing his poetry. But his productivity could be a disadvantage. The almost yearly publication of yet another long poem about self-searching poet-dreamers with curiously echoing names—Senlin, Forslin, Festus, Punch—dulled readers' perceptions and drove critics to admiring but superficial comments about his poetry. The books were slow to sell.

With Aiken's later rearrangement and editing of these early books, critics have seen more clearly the patterns and organization he intended. In 1949 he edited and regrouped five of the early volumes, added an unpublished section ("Changing Mind") he had composed in England at the time of the Hogarth Press edition of *Senlin: A Biography,* and titled the compilation *The Divine Pilgrim.* The poems, placed in sequence according to their date of composition, were "Charnel Rose," "Forslin," "House of Dust," "Senlin," "Festus," and "Changing Mind." Aiken wrote in his notes to *The Divine Pilgrim* that *Senlin* had been "considerably revised for the Hogarth Press edition in 1925, [and] has now been revised again, in some instances back to the original."[11] Thus Aiken had reissued the poem in England through the Hogarth Press as *Senlin: A Biography* (1925) in a shortened version from the original that he had published in 1918 in America and offered his English readers the key to an unassembled sequence of poems.

There are no existing Hogarth Press files on Conrad Aiken and his *Senlin*, no references to him in Virginia Woolf's letters or diaries, no remaining correspondence with Leonard Woolf that I have found. But Aiken would have known about the Woolfs and their press by reputation, or certainly from T. S. Eliot since both of them were equally at home in literary London. Aiken began to review for Leonard Woolf's literary pages of the *Nation and Athenaeum* almost as soon as he was settled in London, becoming an active contributor with eight reviews and three poems ("Exile," "The Road," and "Memory") in that publication between July 14, 1923, and July 25, 1925, on the eve of his return to America.[12] (By contrast, Aiken contributed only five reviews and one poem to Eliot's *Criterion* during this time.) So Aiken, like Muir and many other Hogarth Press authors, first were reviewers for Leonard in the *Nation and Athenaeum* before joining the Hogarth list. J. Howard Woolmer points out in his *Checklist* that the number of copies Leonard Woolf had printed of the book and the name of the printer are unknown, but one press account book shows 143 copies sold by January 28, 1926, six months after publication (*Checklist* 29). Although Aiken's *Senlin* did not pay for itself, the Hogarth Press publication of it in England made available a work significant in itself and important to a future understanding of Aiken's other meditative poems. And Vita Sackville-West, for one, saw its significance, calling it in her *Nation and Athenaeum* review of August 1, 1925, a "fine, moving, and important piece of work," full of beauty.

Leonard Woolf, busy writing and editing the literary pages of the *Nation and Athenaeum* in 1925, on the lookout for new writers like Muir and Aiken to lure to Hogarth, began to be a press author himself. His first nonfiction Hogarth publication was a seriocomic, political beast fable, *Fear and Politics: A Debate at the Zoo,* issued as number seven of the Hogarth Essays series in July. From this time on, Leonard, like Virginia, would publish his books and pamphlets with Hogarth, reflecting his confidence in the strength and growing diversification of the press. To give additional variety and distinction to his developing list of political and international titles, Leonard published two works by Maynard Keynes in 1925 (*The Economic Consequences of Mr. Churchill* and *A Short View of Russia*) and began a series of pamphlets aimed at schoolchildren by Kathleen Innes (*The Story of the League of Nations Told for Young People*). The next year Leonard Woolf followed these by publishing another Keynes pamphlet (*The End of Laissez-Faire*) and another one by Innes, but the Hogarth Press list of books on international subjects in 1926 was distinguished by Noel-Baker's landmark book *Disarmament.* These and others on similar subjects are discussed in chapter six.

As the books and pamphlets on political subjects grew in number and importance, the Woolfs continued to publish more volumes of poetry, fiction, and literary criticism in 1926 than in any other areas. A significant event was the publication of another book in 1926 by Robert Graves. He published a pamphlet on poetry and brought with him Laura Riding. Graves met Laura Riding Gottschalk in 1926 after he had published his first Hogarth Press essay on modern poetry. By July 1926 their literary partnership had been established after Graves, his wife Nancy, the children, and Riding had returned to London following his six-month stint as an English professor at the University of Cairo. Graves's second Hogarth pamphlet published then, *Another Future of Poetry* (1926), continued his defense of modern poetry, but with references to Riding, including frequent quotations from her work. Graves argued for "poetic relativism," wherein traditional methods and modernist's methods could coexist without self-contradiction. After this pamphlet, almost every book Graves wrote for the next thirteen years, whether criticism or poetry, would show the influence of Laura Riding. His last Hogarth Press essay, *Impenetrability or the Proper Habit of English* (1927), carried the Riding message.

Appropriately Laura Riding published her first two books of poems with the Hogarth Press. Riding had been associated briefly with John Crowe Ransom, Allen Tate, and the Fugitives in the early 1920s, publish-

ing poems in the *Fugitive* and the *Sewanee Review.* Through his association with Ransom, Graves saw copies of the former periodical with
Riding's poems, including her boldly innovative, prizewinning "The
Quids" (February 1924). He wrote to invite her to England for a collaboration. She accepted and changed both their lives and careers in consequence.

Laura Riding's *The Close Chapelet,* published under her married
name of Gottschalk by the Woolfs in October 1926, contained thirty-four
poems, including "The Quids." She had published ten of the poems before collecting them in the volume, and they represented her best work
to date. In her poems Riding searched for the resolution between such
traditional polarities as sensation and thought, pleasure and austerity,
beauty and truth, diversity and unity. The poems "Simple Line," "Truth
and Time," and "Mortal" show Riding's attempted balance, but she was
already moving perceptively in the direction of her later poetry where
thought, austerity, truth, and unity would dominate the dichotomies.
"The Quids," punning on kids, slang for the English pound, and the
Latin for *what,* playfully stressed the variety of the world, which is unified
in the parental "Monoton." Riding's coolly rational insistence on the primacy of each word in a poem foreshadowed her later poetry as well as
her eventual abandonment of poetry for the study of linguistics and the
philosophy of language.

The second and last book that Laura Riding published with the
Woolfs proved less interesting and enduring than the poems of her first
volume, but its printing caused a skirmish at the press and revealed the
character of both author and publisher. *Voltaire: A Biographical Fantasy*
(1927) with a preface, marginal notes, and twelve sections (each with an
"Argument" and an "Epilogue") seemed at first a relatively easy book to
hand set and print when Leonard Woolf accepted it in July 1926. Agreeing
to print it in their spare time, Leonard could not guarantee when he and
Virginia would finish it, but he estimated sometime before Christmas
(HP 377). Laura Riding was pleased with the arrangement and requested
that the volume be dedicated to her husband, Louis Gottschalk. Woolf
wrote again to "Miss Laura Gottschalk" in October to confess that he
had miscalculated the space needed for her marginal notes and could not
now print them with the text. It was not a happy beginning.

Woolf began sending page proofs to Riding in late November, but not until July 1927, a full year after he had accepted her manuscript, did he send her a complete set of proofs. When he had not received her corrected proofs by late August, he let her know his displeasure, addressing her as Miss Laura Riding (she had recently dropped her married name after her divorce) (HP 377). She bristled that she had never received the proofs and added that she wanted Gottschalk put in parenthesis on the title page. At this, Leonard Woolf's irascible fussiness over details and his determination to be right led him to cite the evidence of his letter book and an expenditure for a one-and-a-half pence stamp on July 23. He fumed that the delay was not Hogarth's, implied that she was at fault over the proofs, and grumbled that "since we began printing your book, we have printed nothing else at all." He had expunged "Gottschalk" from the title page and admitted that "it looks ugly, but that [in] any case was inevitable."

Leonard Woolf had not reckoned with the redoubtable Riding. Her dander up, Riding blasted back at the implication that she was a liar. She granted that he may have sent the proofs, but she had never received them. The delays were not her fault, nor had she ever complained before. She observed that the taste of the book had gone horrid for both of them, but most to her. Later, Riding commented that a parenthesis around Gottschalk would have made less mess than ruling out the name. She was right. *Voltaire,* when it finally appeared in November 1927, carried a heavy black double-ruled overprinting, blocking out Gottschalk on the title page. It is the ugliest title page among all the Hogarth Press books. Since the expunging occurred in page proofs, the Woolfs could have reset the page, or, as Riding requested, they could have inserted a space and added a parenthesis. The blackened name was an unpleasant gesture from a stubborn Woolf who determined to waste no more time and effort on the job.

The episode and its aftermath soured everyone's taste. Virginia Woolf's latent dislike of Laura Riding can be traced through several references in her letters and diary as she seems almost deliberately to have misunderstood her name. First it was "Robert Graves, Mrs. R. [Riding], and Nancy Gottshalk," confusing Nancy Graves with Riding and misspelling the name (*Letters* 3:226). Later it was the irreverent "Gottstalk" whose *Voltaire* she disliked even as she hand printed it (*Diary* 3:136). In 1931, two years after Graves had separated from his wife Nancy, and Riding and Graves had gone to Mallorca, Virginia Woolf's opinion of Riding's feminism and her poetry surfaced in letters to Ethel Smythe. When Riding protested aggressively about hostile reviews of her book in *Time and Tide,* Woolf called her a "shallow egotistical cock crowing creature" whose vanity would hurt the feminist cause (*Letters* 4:328). She expanded on this three days later by referring to Riding as one "whom I despise for writing perpetually to explain her own cause when reviewers say what is true—that she is a damned bad poet" (ibid., 329).

Virginia Woolf might have been more sympathetic to the struggles of feminist Riding to defend herself against hostile male critics, but for Virginia the style was the woman. She disapproved of heated public arguments and displays of what she saw as ego and pride. With her lack of sympathy for modernist poetry, Virginia Woolf misjudged Riding's poems. At the present, Riding's poetry and criticism together with her feminism have undergone a serious reevaluation, reclaiming her from near oblivion and bringing her out from under the shadow of Robert Graves.

After Leonard Woolf's exchanges with Laura Riding over *Voltaire,* a reconciliation was effected when Riding wrote from Mallorca in December 1929 to ask for reprint permissions. Having left England for good, she wished to thank him for publishing her two books. "I remember now grumbling about *Voltaire* and that you grumbled too (I think over the title page)," she wrote. She added that she knew Virginia Woolf did not like her work or that it infuriated her, and she did not like Woolf's but realized that it "had to be" (LWP). Leonard replied graciously that neither of them had been infuriated by her work, "but I am glad to think that now there is no ill feeling and it is good of you to write as you do" (LWP).

Another formidable lady of the avant-garde, Edith Sitwell, had added her voice to the press the previous year, and had brought to the Woolfs in 1926 the most remarkable iconoclastic modernist of all, Gertrude Stein. Virginia Woolf had neither understood nor liked Edith Sitwell's poems from *Façade* (1922) when she had attended the famous reading in 1923 at the Aeolian Hall, Sitwell speaking through a megaphone in time to William Walton's music. Yet when she dined with the aristocratic Edith and her two brothers, Osbert and Sacheverell, in 1925 she found her not severe and rigid but "very kind . . . & timid, & admiring & easy & poor, & I liked her more than admired or was frightened of her" (*Diary* 3:24). Sitwell, it developed, was eager to write for the press.

Edith Sitwell's Hogarth Essay *Poetry and Criticism* (1925) appeared in October, three months after Robert Graves's Hogarth Essay *Contemporary Techniques of Poetry*. She quoted his words, joined him in an attack on the Georgians and other bloodless traditionalists, and vigorously defended the modernists. She quoted her own poem "Aubade" as example and proceeded through a line-by-line explication to show how "a poem which many people pretended was incapable of an explanation" was actually "extremely simple and quite explainable."[13] Moreover, she argued in her essay, the modern poet stylized and abstracted language the way such modern painters and composers as Picasso, Matisse, Modigliani, and Stravinsky formed abstract patterns in their work.

This pantheon of artists reshaping and retexturing the modern world led Sitwell to her next example of Gertrude Stein, the American in Paris famous for her patronage of Picasso and other painters. For Sitwell, prose writer Gertrude Stein reworked language the way the poets did, "bringing back life to our language" by breaking down "predestined groups of words."[14] She thought that Stein examined their texture and built them "into new and vital shapes." From Edith Sitwell's relationship with Virginia Woolf and the Hogarth Press and from her admiration of Stein came Gertrude Stein's *Composition as Explanation* (1926). But before the Woolfs accepted Stein's composition, they had rejected an earlier offering.

Edith Sitwell met Gertrude Stein in Paris during the autumn of 1924 and began actively to champion her cause in England. When she gave the Woolfs her manuscript of *Poetry and Criticism* in August 1925, she also sent them Stein's *Making of Americans,* recently printed for Robert McAlmon's Contact Editions Press in Paris by Maurice Darantière, the printer of Joyce's *Ulysses*. Virginia Woolf noted in a letter to Vita Sackville-West that she was "weighed down by innumerable manuscripts," including Sitwell's and "the whole of Gertrude Stein, which I flutter with the tips of my little fingers, but don't open" (*Letters* 3:198). She thought Stein's "dodge" was to repeat a word "100 times over in different connections, until at last you feel the force of it." A month later, in September 1925, Virginia Woolf wrote to Roger Fry that she and Leonard were "lying crushed under an immense manuscript of Gertrude Stein's" which she could not "brisk" herself up to deal with (ibid., 209). She could not decide whether Stein's "contortions [were] genuine and fruitful" or only the "spasms" suffered by every prose writer of English. In spite of Sitwell's encouragement, the Woolfs rejected the 928-page *The Making of Americans,* apparently convinced that it had more spasms than genuine fruitfulness. Edith Sitwell, writing to Stein on January 1, 1926, thought it "miserably disappointing, Virginia Woolf not taking the book," but she assured Stein that "a great writer like yourself is absolutely bound to win through." [15]

During the spring Edith Sitwell encouraged Stein to accept invitations to lecture at the Cambridge and Oxford literary societies, and then she organized Stein's visit in June. Virginia Woolf met Stein at the Sitwells' introductory party on June 1, 1926, and wrote in her diary that the American was much like Roger Fry's sister Joan, "but more massive; in blue-sprinkled brocade, rather formidable" (*Diary* 3:89). To Vanessa, Virginia reported that Stein, "a resolute old lady," was "stuck about with jewels like a drowned mermaiden" and "inflicted great damage on all the youth" by contradicting them (*Letters* 3:269). Sitwell, Stein, and company were soon off to Cambridge, where Stein read her "Composition as Explanation" at Trinity College on June 4 and then to Oxford, where she read it again at Christ Church College on June 7. The Woolfs did not attend.

The two lectures were an outstanding success for Stein. She startled but captivated two large university audiences and then retired to Paris, as she noted in her *Autobiography of Alice B. Toklas,* having "had enough of glory and excitement" for the moment.[16] Leonard Woolf, apparently hearing the news from those who had attended her presentation, wrote to Stein immediately saying that he and Virginia "should very much like" to publish her lecture if she would allow them to consider it.[17] She agreed, and her *Composition as Explanation* appeared in November 1926 as the first number in the second series of the Hogarth Essays.

Gertrude Stein's lecture reading at Cambridge and Oxford consisted of "Composition as Explanation" followed by four examples of her writing to illustrate her techniques: "Preciosilla," "A Saint in Seven," "Sitwell Edith Sitwell" (Stein celebrating her English admirer and hostess), and "Jean Cocteau." Stein previously had stressed elaboration or example in her work and had avoided a discussion of her meaning. "An Elucidation," written in 1923, was not published until 1934 (as part of *Portraits and Prayers*) and, in spite of the title, provided more examples than rationale. *Composition as Explanation,* therefore, was her first attempt to survey what she had written previously (*Tender Buttons,* 1914, and *The Making of Americans,* 1925) and to explain herself to a public. Her explanation of composition is one of Stein's most important discourses on the philosophical and linguistic concepts underlying her writing. Many of her later pronouncements, such as those in *Lectures in America* (1935) and *Narration* (1935), echo the ideas of *Composition as Explanation.*

Leonard Woolf printed about 1,000 copies of Gertrude Stein's pamphlet. Exact figures are not available. It sold briskly at first, 508 copies being purchased in the first six months, and slowly thereafter, reaching a total of 574 copies in the first year (MSR). Stein's popularity and influence in the 1920s and 1930s waxed and then waned, affected by what were considered her eccentricities and excesses. With time and the present reassessment of modernism and women writers, Gertrude Stein's importance as an innovator has been freshly appreciated. It is to the Woolfs' credit that they published so radical a statement as Stein's, one in such contrast to their own more conservative literary tastes.

The Woolfs could not count on a large market for such pronouncements as Gertrude Stein's, but travel writing targeted a much larger and more traditional readership. Although E. M. Forster's *Pharos and Pharillon* (1923), Roger Fry's *Sampler of Castile* (1923), and Maynard Keynes's *Short View of Russia* (1925) might be considered Hogarth Press entries into the popular field of travel writing, none of them is exclusively about journeys to exotic places. The 1920s, most notably with D. H. Lawrence's personalized and polemical books on Italy, Sardinia, and Mexico, began a period of nearly two decades of remarkable English travel writing between the world wars. Among Hogarth Press authors, Vita Sackville-West distinguished herself and the press with two excellent accounts of her travels to Persia, *Passenger to Teheran* (1926) and *Twelve Days* (1928), where her diplomat husband Harold Nicolson was serving in the British

Embassy in Teheran. Sackville-West had not previously attempted sustained narrative and descriptive prose, but she handled them with all the dash and confidence she displayed in driving her blue Austin. The two travel books contain some of her best writing, the exotic landscape and people of Persia, the ironies and unexpected events of travel in a remote country, and the strict chronology of events all provided her with a form and substance almost as rich as fiction, but in a genre more restricted and disciplined.

The fiction offerings of the press for 1925–26 were few (only six titles out of fifty-eight published during the two years) and undistinguished, with the obvious exception of Virginia Woolf's *Mrs. Dalloway* (1925). It was as if the powerful field force of a Woolf novel repelled all lesser fictional charges. The press offerings in the genre, seldom strong, seem particularly weak in any year in which one of Virginia's novels appeared. But in 1926 the Woolfs published a provocative, although uneven, first novel by William Plomer and so brought into the Hogarth Press ranks a young novelist-poet who would for six years and eight books be one of their most loyal and productive authors.

When the twenty-one-year-old William Plomer announced himself to the Woolfs in June 1924, writing from Entumeni, Zululand, South Africa, he declared his interest in them and the Hogarth Press "because I suspect you are nearer the heart of things than any other publisher in London" (HP 351). He was neither an "A Subscriber" nor a "B Subscriber" to the press publications because of poverty, not indifference. His green ink was all he had, not a mark of cleverness. Young and poor, he confessed, he was writing a novel which he hoped the Woolfs would let him submit when finished in a year or two; "careful workmanship is a duty," he added fervently.

Young, unpublished writers may thus introduce themselves self-consciously to their mentors and future publishers, but rarely in green ink from a remote trading post in the Native Reserve in Zululand, one heart of South African darkness. Plomer's awareness of the Hogarth Press confirms both his astute knowledge of literary London (he had submitted poems to Harold Monro as early as 1922) and the spreading recognition of the Woolfs and their press. Leonard Woolf was particularly receptive to anticolonial writing. He had written extensively on the abuses of colonialism in Africa and at the moment when Plomer's letter arrived was seeing Norman Leys's *Kenya* through the press. Plomer's novel *Turbott Wolfe*, like *Kenya*, proved something of a racial and political bombshell.

Far earlier than he had predicted, Plomer sent his manuscript to the Woolfs on December 21, 1924, and along with it provided a "balance sheet" on himself as a developing novelist. He listed among his assets his high standards and his youth; one might add his refreshingly guileless enthusiasm. He listed his deficits as his lack of leisure and his difficult working conditions. "I write without silence, light, peace, air, or ease," and, he admitted, without much modesty or reticence (HP 351). Leonard Woolf replied by February 1925 that he had received the manuscript of *Turbott Wolfe* and read enough of it to find it very interesting; however, he wanted to read it carefully and he wanted his wife, who was ill at the moment, to read it before they reached a decision on whether to publish. Leonard's comment underscores Virginia's essential role as a reader of fiction manuscripts. Leonard always sought her judgment before accepting or rejecting fiction for publication. Virginia had been ill for two weeks with influenza at the time and was correcting the proofs for *Mrs. Dalloway*. Leonard, meanwhile, worried about the autobiographical elements in Plomer's manuscript and the possibility of libel. Three months later, with Virginia recovered, *The Common Reader* published, and *Mrs Dalloway* in the hands of R. & R. Clark to be released in two weeks, Leonard wrote to Plomer the welcome news that Virginia had read and approved the novel and they would like to publish it in the autumn.[18] Leonard continued to be alarmed by the dangers of libel, however, and he urged Plomer to make manuscript changes to avoid legal action. Woolf then offered the young author 33⅓ percent of any profits but no advance, as he anticipated losing money on a first novel.

Over the next two months, Plomer edited his manuscript according to the suggestions of the Woolfs and the American publisher, Donald Brace, who read the novel in manuscript. The London–South Africa mail run seems to have taken about four weeks, too long a delay for Woolf to see the book run through the press for the autumn 1925 list, which was already loaded with twelve books. When Hogarth Press finally issued *Turbott Wolfe* in March 1926, it was only the eighth novel to be published by the Woolfs.

William Plomer had written *Turbott Wolfe* "with a hard pencil on thin paper," between the ages of nineteen and twenty-one, as he recalled in his autobiography, sending it to the Hogarth Press with "the false confidence of inexperience and a kind of youthful priggishness."[19] Looking back with the experience of his mature writing and his years as a publisher's reader for Jonathan Cape, Plomer saw clearly the youthful flaws in *Turbott Wolfe,* becoming his own most incisive critic. The book was a "violent ejaculation," poorly constructed with absurd plot, episodic development, and poorly drawn characters, the whole being "crude and immature."

Public reception of the novel, especially in South Africa, was an outraged cry of garbage and pornography, delighting Plomer and ensuring the book a succès de scandale. The three or four English reviewers who praised the book, such as the South African poet Roy Campbell, saw the novel as a fresh and bold onslaught against the political and racial corruption of the South African government. By attacking the stupidity and prejudice of white rule and by writing openly of interracial love, Plomer hit the raw nerves of his society. The Hogarth Press edition, published in 1,000 copies in March 1926, sold 663 copies in the first six months and returned a modest profit in the first year of £9.14.4 (MSR).

To his friend and younger contemporary Laurens van der Post, Plomer's *Turbott Wolfe* was "a book of revelations." Recounting the effect of the novel in South Africa in his lengthy introduction to a 1985 Oxford University Press reprint, van der Post praised it as "a pioneering achievement of courage and originality as great as any in our history." He concluded that Plomer had "changed the course of our imagination in South Africa."[20] *Turbott Wolfe* remains an important cultural document. Oxford put the reprint in its Twentieth Century Classic series.

Virginia Woolf had begun thinking about her next novel, *To the Lighthouse,* as *Mrs. Dalloway* was published in May 1925. After beginning it optimistically in that summer, however, she suffered a physical and emotional collapse on August 19 and for five months thereafter experienced unstable health. Not until January 1926 could she return to writing *To the Lighthouse.* In March she worked on the dinner scene, and by April she had finished part one. By May 25 she had finished the experimental, intermediate part two, "Time Passes."

During June and July, as she struggled to transmute her memories of her mother and father into the fictional portraits of Mr. and Mrs. Ramsay, Virginia Woolf began to assemble material for a book of photographs by her great-aunt Julia Margaret Cameron. One of the early, talented amateur photographers, Julia Cameron took pictures of the great (Tennyson, Browning, Carlyle, Jowett), of the unknown (postmen, servant girls, delivery men), and often of children and members of the family. She is particularly remembered today for her evocative portraits of Virginia Woolf's mother Julia, then married to her first husband, Herbert Duckworth. Virginia, preparing to write an introduction to the book of twenty-four photographic plates, asked her sister Vanessa if she had any of Julia Cameron's letters. She pointedly did not want to ask her half brother George Duckworth for help. The project must have affected Virginia at a level too deeply personal for her to contemplate involving her despised half brother. The Hogarth Press published great-aunt Julia's pictures with introduction by Virginia Woolf and Roger Fry as *Victorian Photographs of Famous Men and Fair Women* in October 1926. The title might almost have applied to Woolf's novel.

As if to underscore the perils of delving into the past, Virginia Woolf experienced another severe bout of depression in late summer and early autumn, unsettling her and interrupting the completion of the novel. Writing in her diary on Saturday, July 31, at Monks House, Woolf summed up her condition under the heading "My own Brain," giving a "whole nervous breakdown in miniature," from a state of exhaustion on Tuesday when everything was "insipid; tasteless, colourless," to Thursday when she had "no pleasure in life whatsoever," finally to Saturday when things became "much clearer & lighter" and she desired to read poetry again (*Diary* 3:103). She quickly regained her zest for writing and pushed on to complete the first draft of *To the Lighthouse* on September 16, only to plunge back into depression. Eight years later, in 1934, she would recall that "after Lighthouse I was I remember nearer suicide, seriously, than since 1913" (ibid., 4:253).

After her serious, almost suicidal depression in late September, Virginia Woolf recovered her equilibrium and enthusiasm for work in the autumn and launched into the crucial rewriting of *To the Lighthouse*. By late November she was reworking six pages a day. She completed the final version on January 14, 1927, after approximately one year's writing time, in spite of her bouts of depression and headaches, and assessed her work with considerable satisfaction: "It is a hard muscular book, which at this age proves that I have something in me." Leonard called it a masterpiece, a "psychological poem," when he read the manuscript (*Diary* 3:123). For Virginia, the most moving tribute came from Vanessa, who wrote that "in the first part of the book you have given a portrait of mother which is more like her to me than anything I could ever have conceived as possible. It is almost painful to have her so raised from the dead" (*Letters* 3:572). The relief at being finished was tempered, however, by the labor of proofreading and the anxieties before publication scheduled for May 5, 1927.

The signs were good. Advance sales totaled over 1,600 copies, more than twice the number for *Mrs. Dalloway.* Virginia's mood at the time expressed itself in her gaily ironic joke with Vita Sackville-West. When Vita returned from her second trip to Persia, she found a copy of *To the Lighthouse* waiting for her, inscribed by Virginia, "In my opinion the best novel I have ever written" (*Letters* 3:372). It was a bound dummy copy, with blank pages. Leonard Woolf, anticipating both an artistic and a commercial success for *The Lighthouse,* ordered 3,000 copies printed by R. & R. Clark (a thousand more than *Mrs. Dalloway*) and quickly ordered another 1,000 copies in a second impression. The novel outsold her previous fiction. The American publisher of Hogarth Press books, Harcourt Brace, printed 4,000 copies initially (almost twice the number of copies for *Mrs. Dalloway*). American readers had begun to take notice of Woolf's novels.

After the drain of a major novel, Virginia Woolf's practice was to refresh herself with the less stressful creation of short stories or criticism. Unusual for her had been the extended labor of two serious novels back to back, *Mrs. Dalloway* followed by *To the Lighthouse,* but now she romped through the exhilarating pleasures of *Orlando,* a valentine to Vita Sackville-West and her beloved Knole. In March, before the *Lighthouse* was published, Virginia had conceived a "fantasy" to be called "The Jessamy Brides" about "two women, poor, solitary at the top of a house" (*Diary* 3:131). It is hard to imagine Vita and Virginia alone in an attic. Nothing came of it directly, but later in October, Virginia marked the true beginning of the novel: "a biography beginning in the year 1500 & continuing to the present day, called Orlando: Vita; only with a change about from one sex to another" (ibid., 161).

It took Virginia Woolf, writing at lightning speed, only five months to cover four hundred years in the transsexual escapades of Orlando: Vita at Knole and elsewhere. She finished the book on March 17, 1928. Part of the fun then came with supplying pictures of Orlando, including one posed by her niece, Angelica Bell, and writing the list of acknowledgments, a great inside joke for Bloomsbury. Vita, dazzled and bewitched when she read the novel, was moved to write to Virginia, "Darling, I don't know and scarcely even like to write it, so overwhelmed am I, how you could have hung so splendid a garment on so poor a peg" (*Letters* 3:574). Leonard Woolf shrewdly anticipated the potential sales and ordered over 5,000 copies printed for publication on October 11, 1928. It sold so well and so quickly that he immediately ordered a second impression of 3,000 copies and a third impression of another 3,000 in January 1929 (*Checklist* 69). Harcourt Brace issued its first edition in over 6,000 copies (HP 567).

The popular and commercial success of *Orlando* both in England and America, coming as it did after the solid return of *To the Lighthouse*, meant that the Woolfs became financially secure and prosperous. Leonard, with the sales in mind, called the publication of *Orlando* "the turning-point in Virginia's career as a successful novelist" (*Downhill* 143). They purchased their first real luxury, a Singer car, in July 1927, and from then on the Woolfs took increasing pleasure in travel and material comforts. "After 1928," wrote Leonard Woolf as he summed up his yearly income in his autobiography, "we were always well off" (ibid., 145). The combined annual income of the Woolfs after *Orlando* was from two to six times as great as it had been in 1924. They were never prodigal, however, and enjoyed their new prosperity with characteristic sobriety.

Although *To the Lighthouse* never produced the income of *Orlando*, it did fetch Woolf the literary prize Femina Vie Heureuse, much to her amazement. The presentation of the £40 prize by Hugh Walpole on behalf of the Institut Français on May 2, 1928, both amused and flustered Woolf, unused to such public praise and scrutiny. "My dog show prize," she bantered with her nephew Julian Bell (*Letters* 3:491) and recorded that "the prize was an affair of dull stupid horror: a function; not alarming; stupefying" (*Diary* 3:183).

The years of Virginia Woolf's greatest artistic and commercial success, 1927 and 1928, were also the peak years for the Hogarth Press, when the Woolfs published more titles than they ever would again. From a total of thirty titles in 1926, the press jumped to thirty-eight titles in 1927 and then back to thirty-six titles in 1928. The large production in these years partly stemmed from the new series, the Stories, the Merttens Lectures on War and Peace (later subsumed under the Day to Day Pamphlets), and the Lectures on Literature begun in 1927 and the Living Poets begun in 1928. As a result, 1928 proved to be the most diverse year in Hogarth Press history, with books or pamphlets published in virtually every category. In addition to poetry and fiction, there were works on politics, society, economics, disarmament, feminism, education, literary criticism, travel, memoirs, biography, and psychoanalysis. (For a year-by-year account of the publications by category, see Appendix A.)

Such diversity confirms Leonard Woolf's development of the Hogarth Press from a small, private press into a general publisher. The very heterogeneity of the press offerings argues against any conclusion that the Woolfs shaped their list with deliberate intention or that the books and pamphlets in one area such as fiction or poetry were influenced by those published in another area such as politics or psychoanalysis. Only in the broad field of political and social subject matter did Leonard Woolf exercise his particular interests to develop the press publications, but here as well as in other areas he aimed at diversity.

Freud's *The Ego and the Id,* published by the press in January in the International Psycho-Analytical Library, started off 1927 and carried companion volumes by the Freudians Sandor Ferenczi and Karl Abraham. Leonard Woolf published his second satirical pamphlet with the press, *Hunting the Highbrow,* in March and then in May collected twenty-six of his reviews and articles, many of them published in the literary pages of the *Nation and Athenaeum* and released them with the straightforward but inelegant title of *Essays on Literature, History, Politics, etc.* Woolf followed his essay writing and editing with a more ambitious project which began in the pages of the *Nation and Athenaeum* and was published by Hogarth in September as *Books and the Public*.

This time when the Woolfs and their press were most productive was a period of important activity in the ranks of publishers and booksellers. Stanley Unwin, the director of George Allen & Unwin, responded to the times by publishing a definitive analysis of the industry in *The Truth about Publishing* (1926), a frank revelation of the particulars of book production. Leonard Woolf, using his literary pages of the *Nation and Athenaeum*, followed Unwin's lead by coordinating a series of eleven wide-ranging articles on the book trade during the four months from February to May 1927. The public forum provided by Woolf became a valuable one for members of the book trade who responded to the *Nation and Athenaeum*'s invitation.

Three topics loomed large in the articles: the increasing cost of books, their overproduction, and the reluctance of readers to buy books. Contributors having their say on these topics included Hubert Henderson, Maynard Keynes, Michael Sadleir, Basil Blackwell, Stanley Unwin, and Woolf himself. Of particular interest was Maynard Keynes's "Are Books Too Dear?" (March 12, 1927), a closely argued economic analysis of production costs which managed to cover all three topics in convincing form. He reasoned that "publishing is a *gambling* business, kept alive by occasional windfalls," and that under "the normal circulation of the typical good book" (less than 3,000 copies sold) "it is uneconomic, and indeed impossible if author and publisher are to gain a living wage, to reduce the price of books."[21] In his article "On Advertising Books" (March 19), Leonard Woolf had his say about one of his pet peeves, the high cost and relative inefficiency of advertising. Stanley Unwin had addressed the subject in his book, and Woolf echoed the wisdom of the day, but with his usual journalistic flair.[22]

Leonard Woolf's visibility in the series of *Nation and Athenaeum* articles was appropriate to his dual roles of literary editor and publisher, but unusual for him nevertheless. Woolf preferred to remain on the sidelines of the business, fostering one of his self-images as the small-time amateur among the giant professionals. He might lecture about publishing to his Hogarth Press staff, his authors, or fellow members of Bloomsbury, but he usually avoided public expression of opinion on the subject and never played an active part in such increasingly important trade organizations as the Publishers Association, the Society of Bookmen, and the National Book Council. Only late in life, in his abundantly anecdotal and frank autobiography, did Woolf discuss in detail his experiences as publisher. But even then, he was almost completely silent about the book trade, seldom mentioning a fellow publisher by name, as if the Hogarth Press had existed separate and untouched by the sweeping changes in English publishing between the wars.

In addition to books on domestic affairs, Leonard Woolf added several titles in 1927 to his growing list of works on international affairs, including Noel-Baker's pamphlet *Disarmament and the Coolidge Conferences* and Lord Olivier's book *The Anatomy of African Misery,* an analysis of the suppression and economic exploitation of South African blacks by the white minority ruling class. With coincidental timing, William Plomer sent in his second book to the press, a collection of stories entitled *I Speak of Africa.*

By the time *Turbott Wolfe* had appeared in 1926, Plomer was living and working with Roy Campbell to bring out their iconoclastic and short-lived magazine *Voorslag* (whiplash) where Plomer's long story "Ula Masondo" first appeared. He and Campbell, as Plomer wrote to Leonard Woolf in May 1926, were attacking the "vast mass of crawling filthiness called South Africa" and probably would be jailed or deported. He concluded: "It is a lovely country, it is my own county, and I know it and love it, and I know the nobility of the natives and their unsurpassable human qualities, but the whites are unspeakable. I am a white South African myself, and a man doesn't go against his countrymen without reason" (HP 351). Typical of young Plomer to emphasize his African heritage for an African book, as he would absorb and represent Japanese culture for his Japanese books, and do the same later for his English books, but in fact Plomer's family was transplanted from England. Both parents were English born and bred, and although Plomer was born in Petersburg in North Transvaal, he had spent some of his most formative school years in England during World War I, first at Beechmont near Seven Oaks and then at Rugby.

When he sent the Woolfs his second manuscript in November 1926, the restless Plomer was in Osaka, Japan, transforming himself into an Anglo-Japanese. He had not been jailed or forcibly exiled from South Africa after *Turbott Wolfe,* as he had hoped. Instead, Plomer had accepted the sudden invitation of Japanese merchant Captain Mori to sail on his ship to Japan with his friend Laurens van der Post. The three novellas, seven short stories, and two puppet plays comprising *I Speak of Africa* (1927) marked an end to his African work, as he wrote to Woolf in November 1926, and was the fruit of two years' hard writing (HP 343). The stories stemmed from the *Voorslag* experience with Roy Campbell at Umdoni Park. Only "Ula Masonda" became well known.

A tale of moral disintegration, the story traces the decline and fall of Masondo from stereotypical noble savage, barefooted and red-blanketed in his tribal village, to corrupted miner in Goldenville, flashily and cheaply dressed in tight-fitting brown suit and high-heeled shoes. Tragic and inevitable, Masondo's fall from grace parallels his absorption of Western decadence. Although the plot is predictable, Masondo and the varied African landscape are undeniably alive. The pattern of Masondo's degradation through contact with white industrialized society became the model for other South African writers. Frequently anthologized, "Ula Masondo" appeared most notably in the 1937 edition of the *Faber Book of Modern Stories,* edited by the Anglo-Irish novelist Elizabeth Bowen, friend of both Plomer and Virginia Woolf.

Only one other work of fiction published by the Hogarth Press in 1927, the year of *To the Lighthouse,* deserves mentioning: Edwin Muir's *Marionette.* Muir had more success with poetry, criticism, and translation than with fiction, but he wrote three novels over a period of five years, beginning with *The Marionette* (1927), which the Hogarth Press published. The first novel, a reflection of Muir's stay in Salzburg in 1923, had been written in St. Tropez during the Muirs' second trip to Europe in 1926. It features the strangely poetic yet darkly obsessive inner life of a fourteen-year-old mentally handicapped boy, Hans, and his widowed father, Martin Scheffer. Muir's fiction borders on allegory. He called it, in a letter to his American publisher B. W. Huebsch, "less a novel than a sort of metaphysical or symbolical tragedy."[23] The tragedy takes form through Hans's compulsive and self-destructive identification with the dolls he collects, especially with a facsimile of Gretchen, the beautiful marionette in Herr Hoffman's famous puppet-theater production of *Faust*. Muir's portrait of Hans owes something to his own childhood with its rich, sometimes fearful, fantasies and something to the theories of child development and psychology espoused by the progressive educator A. S. Neill at whose school in Europe Muir's wife Willa had taught.

The last book Edwin Muir published with the Hogarth Press, *The Structure of the Novel* (1928), brought him recognition as an important critic and success through a large readership in England and America. The Hogarth Press edition, published in the Lectures series, began with 2,250 copies and went through three impressions. Structure meant plot to Muir as he examined such nineteenth-century novelists as Dickens, Thackeray, Scott, Austen, and Hardy. In spite of Muir's overreliance on plot as a measure of fiction, *The Structure of the Novel* remains readable and interesting today and holds its own with such classics as Percy Lubbock's *Craft of Fiction* (1921) and E. M. Forster's *Aspects of the Novel* (1927), to which Muir referred.

With this major critical work, Muir abandoned regular reviewing and devoted himself to translating German literature with his wife Willa. The Hogarth Press, in its association with Muir, had published his best work to date in poetry, fiction, and literary criticism. Only the translations of the Muirs escaped the Woolfs; Martin Secker and then Gollancz published these. The Woolfs and their press had helped Muir become an established and important writer. Muir turned to other publishers for his work after 1928, especially to T. S. Eliot's Faber & Faber for his poetry, but he renewed his relationship with the Hogarth Press in 1954 when it published his *Autobiography*.

Although Muir's *Structure of the Novel* outshone other works of literary criticism in 1928, three other critical pamphlets published by the press that year are still remembered, Harold Nicolson's *Development of English Biography*, Herbert Read's *Phases of English Poetry*, and Clive Bell's *Proust*. Harold Nicolson, at the suggestion of Leonard Woolf, wrote his 158-page analysis of biography for Woolf's Lectures on Literature series. The pamphlet was instantly popular, has been reprinted several times, and continues to find readers. Leonard, as he wrote to Herbert Read, thought Nicolson's work was "nearest in form" to the lecture format he had in mind than any other work in the series.[24]

Herbert Read, after publishing *Mutations of the Phoenix* (1923) and *In Retreat* (1925), had been lured away from the Hogarth Press by T. S. Eliot to publish his first major critical work, *Reason and Romanticism* (1926), and his *Collected Poems* (1926) with Eliot's firm of Faber & Gwyer. The Woolfs had not been pleased. Read returned to the fold momentarily in 1928, however, to publish his pamphlet in the Hogarth Lectures on Literature series. It is the shortest of his books of literary criticism, tracing types of poets and poetry from the anonymous ballad writer through the humanist, religious, and romantic to the modern poet. His reading of poetic modernism stresses the importance of Wordsworth as precursor, true to the developing ideas that were fully expressed in his *Wordsworth*, published two years later. *Phases of English Poetry*, designed to fit Leonard Woolf's lecture format for the intelligent student, proved a solid general guide to poetry. Printed in 2,000 copies, it became successful enough to warrant an edition in Braille for the National Library for the Blind in 1931, and Read revised it with the addition of two new chapters for publication by New Directions 1951.

Clive Bell, Virginia Woolf's brother-in-law, was an enthusiastic reader of Proust, helping to introduce him to Bloomsbury in the early 1920s when most members began reading him in French.[25] His *Proust*, the third well-remembered critical work published by Hogarth in 1928, was the most thorough examination of the French novelist's work by a member of Bloomsbury, providing an intelligent and useful commentary on the novels of *A la recherche du temps perdu*. It was also one of the earliest guides in English to Proust's complex work. Leonard Woolf had 1,200 copies of the eighty-nine-page booklet published in November and soon ordered a second impression. Bell's *Proust* proved almost as successful in the simultaneous American edition; Donald Brace reported that the volume, selling in America at $1.15 a copy, had sold 821 copies during the six months ending June 30, 1929 (HP 17).

Adding to the diversity of press offerings in 1928, Leonard Woolf published his major study of imperialistic exploitation, *Imperialism and Civilization*, the culmination of years of writing on this subject. And Viscountess Rhondda published her feminist tract *Leisured Women*. It was the first pamphlet on women since Willa Muir's *Women: An Enquiry* (1925); it was the eleventh title in the Hogarth Essays, second series, and the thirtieth title overall since the Woolfs had begun this successful venture in 1924. Although the Hogarth Stories series folded in 1928 after the initial two publications, the series of Merttens Lectures on War and Peace, in its second year, continued to feature one "lecture" a year through 1936. The Woolfs and their series were doing very well and were about to launch an important new series under an interesting financial arrangement. The Merttens was being subsidized marginally by the Peace Committee of the Society of Friends, but in 1928 the Woolfs began the Living Poets series completely funded by Dorothy Wellesley. It was the Woolfs' first and only venture into such a fully subsidized series.

"Dottie is going to spend £200 a year on poetry: to edit a series of books of unsaleable poetry," noted Virginia Woolf on September 20, 1927 (*Diary* 3:157). Dorothy Wellesley had decided to underwrite a Hogarth Press series rather than a Poetry Bookshop enterprise with Harold Monro. Nine days after Virginia's diary entry, Leonard wrote to Dorothy with a formal proposal for her to be editor of a series which would publish contemporary poetry.

Leonard and Virginia Woolf had met Lady Gerald Wellesley in 1924 through Vita Sackville-West. After their introduction, the Woolfs saw Dorothy Wellesley with increasing frequency, Virginia forming an uneasy friendship with her and becoming jealous of Dorothy's increasing intimacy with Vita. "Choose between us," she wrote to Vita. "Dottie if your taste inclines that way . . . but not the two of us in one cocktail" (*Letters* 4:36). Leonard was frequently annoyed with Wellesley's affectation or silliness, as he saw it. "We drove home at 40 miles an hour," Virginia wrote to Vita about their visit to Dorothy's home in 1928; "[Leonard] was so furious with her vanity, conceit, egotism, vulgarity; ill-breeding, violent temper, etc." (ibid., 3:530). Nevertheless, Leonard liked Dorothy's poetry, and he and Virginia published three volumes of it and an anthology which she edited as she financed and supervised the Hogarth Living Poets series from 1928 until 1932, thereby helping to shape the Hogarth poetry list during the peak years of press development.

Before the arrival of Dorothy Wellesley in 1927–28, the Woolfs had published thirty-six volumes of poetry after their first two volumes in 1919 (Eliot's *Poems* and Murry's *Critic in Judgment*). Twelve of these volumes, exactly one-third, had been written by seven poets of present or future stature—Eliot, Graves, Riding, Read, Ransom, Aiken, and Muir. They formed a distinguished minority among lesser lights with Cambridge or Bloomsbury connections and Georgian inspiration.

There were twenty such poets, most of whom published one volume of graceful but highly perishable lyrics on rural subjects or a volume or two of donnish verse dense with classical allusions or self-conscious wit. To list them is to show how charitable the Woolfs were to struggling poets if they had a Cambridge or Bloomsbury pedigree and how tolerant or uncritical they were of mediocrity. Among the poets were Frank Prew-ett (*Poems*, 1921), a Canadian war veteran, friend of Sassoon, Graves, Marsh, and Lady Ottoline Morrell; Fredegond Shove (*Daybreak*, 1922), daughter of F. W. Maitland, the Cambridge historian and biographer of Leslie Stephen, and the wife of Gerald Shove, fellow of King's College; Ruth Manning-Sanders (*Karn*, 1922, and *Martha Wish-You-Ill*, 1926), writer of children's stories and friend of Katherine Foster, Cambridge friend of Virginia Woolf; G. H. Luce (*Poems*, 1924), former Apostle and friend of Keynes and a teacher of English at the University of Rangoon; Ferenc Békassy (*Adriatic and Other Poems*, 1925), Hungarian aristocrat, former Apostle at King's College, friend of Keynes, and killed in the First World War; and F. L. (Peter) Lucas (*Time and Memory*, 1929), former Apostle, classical scholar and fellow of King's College whose unsuccessful novel *The River Flows* (1926) was also published by the Woolfs. Three poets of this group—H. E. Palmer, R. C. Trevelyan, and George ("Dadie") Rylands—were more prolific and more seriously committed as poets than the others and are examplars of these Cambridge-Bloomsbury writers.

H. E. Palmer had published three volumes of poetry over a five-year period when Leonard Woolf began to accept his poems for the *Nation and Athenaeum* in December 1923. During Woolf's seven years as literary editor, he printed ten of Palmer's poems, and the Hogarth Press pub-lished two volumes of his poetry (*Songs of Salvation, Sin, and Satire*, 1925, and *The Armed Muse*, 1930) and a pageant play (*The Judgment of François Villon*, 1927). Palmer's seven-year association with Leonard Woolf as edi-tor and publisher did little to change the traditional nature of his poetry, and his several appearances on the Hogarth list reflect the conservative nature of most of the press's poetry. Palmer, undeterred by changing tastes and world events, continued on his way with eleven more volumes of poetry with other publishers through 1949.

R. C. Trevelyan, member of a distinguished Victorian family and brother of the Cambridge historian G. M. Trevelyan, had been an Apostle at Trinity College, a friend of the Woolfs for years, and by the 1920s was a classical scholar, a translator (Sophocles, Aeschylus, Lucretius, Theocritus), and a poet. He would eventually publish over twenty volumes of poetry.

Leonard Woolf published an occasional poem of Trevelyan's in the pages of the *Nation and Athenaeum,* but he did more through the Hogarth Press, bonding their Cambridge connections with eight volumes of Trevelyan's poems and plays between 1925 and 1942. With so many slim volumes to his credit Trevelyan was the most published, if not the most distinguished, poet among the Hogarth writers. From his inclusion in the first volume of Edward Marsh's *Georgian Poetry, 1911–12,* to his later poems, Trevelyan remained a Georgian poet in spirit, determinedly traditional and classical in taste and craft, opposed to modern influences. Trevelyan published his poetry with a variety of publishers (Longmans, Green; Allen & Unwin; Macmillan), but beginning in the mid-twenties he began a run of nearly a volume a year with Hogarth, the books rolling off the presses with mind-numbing regularity: *Poems and Fables* (1925), *The Deluge and Other Poems* (1926), *Meleager* (1927), *Cheiron* (1928), *Three Plays* (1931), *Rimeless Numbers* (1932), *Beelzebub and Other Poems* (1935), and *The Aftermath* (dated 1941 but published in 1942).

George ("Dadie") Rylands as an undergraduate moved in the Cambridge Apostle circuit of young men who caught the attention of Maynard Keynes and Lytton Strachey. He became the Woolfs' short-term but beloved assistant from July to December 1924 and then returned to Cambridge where he became a fellow of King's College in 1927. The Woolfs published two volumes of Rylands's poetry, *Russet and Taffeta* (1925), peopled by Perditas and Corydons, and *Poems* (1931) about Chloe and Flora amid the flowers and hay-scented farmlands. The Woolfs also published his fellowship dissertation, *Words and Poetry* (1928). For all their skillful lyricism, Rylands's *Poems* are like pressed flowers, nosegays colorless and dry, preserved from change. Only one year older than William Plomer and two years older than Christopher Isherwood, Rylands wrote not of his generation but of a generation before the First World War.

The Hogarth Press arrangement for a Living Poets series with Dorothy Wellesley in 1928 did not immediately change the nature of the press poetry listings but gave promise of better things to come. The Woolfs could suggest poetry to Wellesley that she might consider for publication, and she in turn could suggest poetry to the Woolfs that they would publish unless they were "positively against it" (HP 176). A work could not be published unless both parties approved.

The business arrangements were designed to honor Dorothy's willingness to risk a maximum of £200 a year on the series. Leonard in September 1927 outlined how the arrangement might work with a fictitious and humorously titled volume of poetry, "Moonlight Fancies" by an imaginary Guinivere Jakes, running to sixty-four pages and costing £45 to manufacture (HP 176). If the press priced the book at 4s.6d. net and sold 50 copies, Leonard calculated, then Dorothy could expect to lose £37.10. Leonard, in this primer on publishing, spelled out in detail for Dorothy what her losses might be with increments up to 350 copies sold (a loss of £1.10). As a conclusion, Leonard provided the production costs and sales revenues for two actual but unnamed volumes of poetry the press had published. From Leonard's details they can be identified as Barrington Gates's *Poems* (1925), which lost £41.19.1 for the press, and R. C. Trevelyan's *Meleager* (1927), which lost £30.12.8.

If Leonard Woolf's figures held true, Dorothy Wellesley could expect to publish four or five volumes of poetry annually in the series for her £200 yearly subsidy of manufacturing costs. That projection governed their editorial decisions as Leonard and Dorothy published four volumes of poetry in 1928, the first year of the series. Leonard was, as usual, right on target. Dorothy's *Matrix* (1928), for example, cost £30 to produce, sold only sixty-two copies, and required her to pay a balance of £22.13.11, whereas *Roan Stallion* (1928) by Robinson Jeffers cost over £61 to produce, sold fifty copies, and required a subsidy from Dorothy of £47.19.2 to balance the account.[26] In 1929, the second year of the series, the press issued eight titles, perhaps rashly, and consequently cut back to five titles in 1930 and 1931, before closing out the series with two titles as Dorothy's patronage came to an end in 1932. Leonard continued the Living Poets in a second series for five years without the support of Wellesley beginning in 1933, but he issued only one title a year under the imprint and limited the press to one or two other volumes of poetry during that period. The Hogarth Press, without Wellesley's support or John Lehmann's presence, virtually abandoned the publication of poetry between 1932 and 1938.

The first three Hogarth Living Poets titles in 1928 were Frances Cornford's *Different Days,* R. Fitzurse's *It Was Not Jones,* and Dorothy Wellesley's *Matrix.* The first volume appropriately exemplified the best of the Cambridge-Georgian poetry by a poet more talented than either Rylands or Trevelyan. Born into a branch of the large Darwin family in Cambridge (her grandfather was Charles Darwin), Frances Cornford grew up and spent her life in the university town, was a contemporary and close friend of Rupert Brooke, married a classics fellow of Trinity College, bore five children (including the poet John Cornfield, killed in the Spanish civil war), and published seven volumes of poetry and a play. Most of Cornford's thirty brief poems in *Different Days,* especially those such as "Lincolnshire Remembered," "Cambridgeshire," "Ancestors," "The Garden near the Sea," and "On the Downs," look back on peaceful and sustaining visions of the English landscape. Others, such as "A Glimpse" and "The Title Page," provide nostalgic views of Cambridge academic life seen from the woman's perspective, but apparently without the feminist's sense of anger or exclusion. Her quietly lyrical volume was a safe choice with which to start the new series for readers accustomed to the classically restricted voices of the other Hogarth Press poets.

As sponsor and editor of the Living Poets series, Dorothy Wellesley, like Virginia Woolf, could publish what she wished of her own work without fear of rejection by a publisher's reader. She was neither as talented a writer nor as scrupulous a self-critic as Virginia, and the poems she published of her own did not add luster to the series.

Matrix, a long, repetitive, allegorical meditation on the notion that "the mind is a womb," traces the conception, gestation, birth, maturation, decline, and death of the mind-soul of Man. The terse, flat lines, 447 of them in twenty-one sections, seldom rise to any lyrical intensity, nor do they provide a clear argument. Wellesley's poetic aspirations in *Matrix* exceeded her grasp. Only sixty-two copies of the poem were sold in the first year, fewer than any other of the series publications (MSR). Virginia, when asked by Dorothy Wellesley to read the poem and tell her what she thought of it, wrote to Clive Bell, "as you see, nothing very much to the point" (*Letters* 3:453). Three months earlier Dorothy had loaned Virginia some of her poems to read, as Virginia noted, "which I promptly throw down the W.C." (*Diary* 3:162).

Dorothy Wellesley's next offering to the press and the Living Poets series, *Deserted Houses* (1930), ran to eighty pages, over twice the length of *Matrix*. Virginia reported to Vita Sackville-West in August 1930 that Leonard thought it "good of its kind," and although she had not read it herself, she thought Dorothy deserved "some credit for keeping her head up, and writing about cats and rocks this time instead of the birth of man" (*Letters* 4:198). But Leonard had a hundred fewer copies printed than for *Matrix,* anticipating losses. It sold only 115 copies in the first six months (MSR).

Several of the most interesting volumes of poetry in the period 1928–30 had little to do with Dorothy Wellesley or with Cambridge connections, but rather came from South Africa or America. William Plomer, on the move, sent in his third book to the Hogarth Press, his first of poetry. In spite of the pedantic and tentative title, Plomer's *Notes for Poems* (1928) provided no notes. The title may have been an ironic wink at Eliot's notes for *The Waste Land* or a wry admission that some of the poems were five-finger exercises. Whatever he intended to suggest by the title, Plomer wrote poems of two types. There were mocking, satirical verses tightly rhymed and often outrageously punned. And there were reflective, descriptive poems, deeply felt, about the South African landscape and its black inhabitants. The better poems in the volume were of the second sort, characterized by "A Basuto Coming of Age," "The Death of a Zulu," and "Ula Masondo's Dream." In such poems, Plomer captured the South African landscape in intense images, the veld seen by an artist's eye for color and contrast, but he also sympathetically projected himself into the puberty rites and death watches of the black culture.

Under the exotic surface of Plomer's South African poems lay an undeniable Englishness of voice and form which allowed them to blend easily with those of other Hogarth Press authors. Not so with the few American poets the press published, which makes their presence on the Hogarth list all the more surprising. Leonard and Virginia Woolf had little tolerance for Americans, distrusting them as either parvenus or as overly refined Jamesian aesthetes. They avoided both types but came to forgive T. S. Eliot his distressing American characteristics when they developed a firm friendship with "Great Tom."

As publishers, the Woolfs took no interest in American authors and little interest in the American market. Virginia published stories and articles in American journals, including *Vogue,* but she did so because they paid well. Leonard placed many Hogarth books with American publishers, especially with Harcourt Brace, having developed a respectful relationship with Donald Brace over the years, but he did little to expand his contacts or his knowledge of American writers and publishers. Unlike Jonathan Cape, for example, who made yearly trips to New York to discover new writers, Leonard Woolf never considered traveling to the States on business. Virginia turned down several offers to lecture in America and one expense-paid trip to write articles in 1926 for the New York *Herald-Tribune* when she learned that the hotel bills were not included (*Letters* 3:320). When the Woolfs traveled, they went to the Continent.

Nevertheless, more by circumstance than by design, the Woolfs and their press published the poetry of seven Americans. First there was T. S. Eliot with volumes in 1919 and 1923, then John Crowe Ransom in 1924, Conrad Aiken in 1925, and Laura Riding in 1926 and 1927. Later, in 1932, the Hogarth Press published five poems by Richard Eberhart in the *New Signatures* collection, but he was included as one of the Cambridge poets. Two other Americans, Robinson Jeffers in 1928, 1929, and 1930 and Edwin Arlington Robinson in 1930, became Hogarth poets by other means.

Leonard Woolf learned about Robinson Jeffers in April 1928 when the Curtis Brown literary agency sent him a copy of *Roan Stallion, Tamar, and Other Poems* for possible English publication. The American firm Boni & Liveright had published the volume in 1925 in 1,200 copies and had reprinted it four times when Curtis Brown sent it to the Hogarth Press.[27] The timing was propitious. The Woolfs had just started the Living Poets series with Dorothy Wellesley's patronage and were about to bring out the first three volumes as a package in May.

Leonard Woolf sent off the volume with other manuscripts for Wellesley to consider. She soon responded, rejecting a play by Yeats's friend T. Sturge Moore but pondering Jeffers's book. She liked the poetry, thought it interesting but uneven, but was willing to publish it in the series if Leonard thought she would not lose more than £20 on it (HP 176). When he reassured her, she agreed to publish, concluding, "I certainly think he has merit enough." Leonard Woolf then negotiated with Curtis Brown to purchase 520 sheets at forty cents a sheet from Boni & Liveright and sent a sample off to Neill & Co. to have a new title page printed with the Hogarth Press imprint (HP 203).

A slight hitch developed. Leonard Woolf had put the Living Poets series into the crown octavo size (7½ by 5 inches), a standard book size used in the Uniform Edition of Virginia's novels. The Boni & Liveright sheets of Jeffers's book were 8½ by 5%16 inches (a variant of medium octavo) and could not be cut down to the crown octavo without spoiling the margins. Neill & Co. trimmed what they could, but the resulting size (8 by 5½ inches) made the American import stand out on all sides from the other volumes in the series (HP 203). The Hogarth Press published the large, 254-page volume in October 1928 and sold it for 7s.6d., the usual price for a novel but three shillings more than that of the other volumes in the Living Poets series.

Roan Stallion, Tamar, and Other Poems was the fourth volume of poetry Jeffers had published in America but only the second by an established publishing house. His books had not sold, and reviewers had ignored the poetry. *Tamar and Other Poems* (1924, published by P. G. Boyle) finally caught on when James Rorty and Mark Van Doren gave favorable reviews almost a year after publication. The belated critical attention and blooming sales caught the eye of Boni & Liveright, which offered to reprint the volume. Instead, Jeffers added nineteen new poems to the twenty-two in *Tamar* and had Boni & Liveright publish the revised volume in November 1925.

The new poems Jeffers added to the old to make *Roan Stallion, Tamar, and Other Poems* brought him fame and controversy and ushered in an important phase of his career. "Roan Stallion" became one of Jeffers's most admired and popular narratives, a mythic and tragic story of a part-Indian heroine and her passionate attachment to a godlike stallion. To the new volume, Jeffers added his long verse drama on Orestes and Electra, "The Tower beyond Tragedy." Amid the new short poems in the volume, "Shine, Perishing Republic" became one of Jeffers's most frequently reprinted poems.

American critics praised or disagreed about Jeffers, but the book sold well before Curtis Brown engaged the Woolfs and Dorothy Wellesley to introduce Jeffers to the English public. The brooding, tragic vision, the sensational subject matter of California and Greece, the heightened rhetoric of Jeffers's poems, however, did not travel well. Big Sur made no stir in Bloomsbury. In spite of a generally favorable review in the *Nation and Athenaeum,* the Hogarth Press edition did not fare well. It sold only sixty-seven copies in the first six months and a total of eighty-one copies by the end of the first year (MSR). Leonard Woolf's purchase of 500 sheets proved overly optimistic, and Dorothy Wellesley lost more than her estimated £20. When Leonard Woolf later sent him two copies of the press edition, Jeffers replied in February 1929 that he had not known about the publication in England but that he was pleased with the binding and appearance of the volume (HP 201). He was sorry it had not sold well but was not surprised.

The next two books by Jeffers in America, *The Women at Point Sur* (1927) and *Poems* (1928), failed to stir into life, but *Cawdor and Other Poems* (1928) got the attention of critics and readers. The publisher, Horace Liveright, issued it in 1,900 copies and reprinted it three times before the Hogarth Press published it in England in 1929. The arrangement was the same as before. Curtis Brown acted as a go-between, offering Leonard Woolf 520 sheets at forty cents a sheet (HP 201). Woolf's reaction was not the same, however, and led to a heated exchange of letters and a dramatic telegram.

Leonard Woolf objected to Liveright's charging the same sheet rate for the shorter *Cawdor* (160 pages) that he charged for the larger *Roan Stallion* (254 pages). Woolf could not price the book at more than six shillings, he calculated. He refused to pay the old rate and proposed, instead, to buy 400 sheets at thirty cents a sheet. A month later, in June 1929, Liveright responded through Curtis Brown, setting Leonard straight: "Cawdor is a great poem, Robinson Jeffers is in the minds of the best critics, over here, America's greatest living poet, possibly the greatest since Whitman" (HP 201). If the press did not want the sheets at the price quoted, he wanted Curtis Brown to call off the deal. Liveright believed he could place the book with another English publisher.

Leonard wrote to Dorothy Wellesley explaining that she might lose up to £40 or £50 if they paid Liveright's asking price and the book sold only 100 copies. "I feel there is something in Jeffers," wrote Woolf, "but it is monstrous to ask the same for 160 pages as 254" (HP 201). Two days later, Wellesley telegrammed Woolf, "Please cable American we publish and be dammed." Publish they did in another oversized edition of 520 copies at six shillings each, on October 10, 1928. It performed only slightly better than the previous book, selling 84 copies in the first six months and a total of 91 copies at the end of the first year (MSR). In addition to a few memorable short poems such as "Hurt Hawks" and "Tor House" (commemorating Jeffers's hand-built granite-bouldered house at Big Sur), *Cawdor and Other Poems* featured in the title poem another of Jeffers's long, tragic narratives.

In the summer and autumn of 1929, Jeffers and his wife Una made a rare trip outside of California to Ireland and England and eventually met the Woolfs, their English publishers, in London. The visit was arranged by Ella Winter, wife of the journalist Lincoln Steffens and a neighbor of Jeffers in Carmel. As Virginia wrote to Gerald Brenan: "Miss Winter has asked us to ask Mr Robinson Jeffers to tea because he is only in London for a week and will return to a cave in California and write immortal poetry forever. Mr Jeffers is a genius so one must see him" (*Letters* 4:96). Leonard formalized the invitation by letter, and tea at Tavistock Square was served at 4:30 on Monday, October 7.[28] Virginia, busy recording her struggle with writing *The Waves,* gave only a note in her diary to the meeting, but the two taciturn and skeptical men must have hit it off because Leonard invited Jeffers back. Unfortunately a second visit could not be arranged, but Leonard wrote to Jeffers on January 3, 1930, that "perhaps if some day we come to America and California, you may allow us to visit you."[29] Lovers of Cornwall, the Woolfs might have appreciated Big Sur, but they never found the time to make the journey.

Perhaps as a result of the friendly meeting with Jeffers in October, Woolf accepted without demurral Curtis Brown's offer in November of sheets for *Dear Judas and Other Poems.* But the cautious Woolf agreed to only 312 sheets at forty cents each (HP 202). Hogarth Press published the book a year after the initial offer as the fifteenth title in the Living Poets series, in November 1930. It sold sixty-two copies in the first six months and only four more copies in the next six months, for a first-year total of sixty-six copies (MSR).

Jeffers's popularity peaked at home in the late 1920s and early 1930s when a few critics unblushingly compared him to Whitman, but Jeffers failed to excite the English public. Humbert Woolf, criticizing *Dear Judas* in the *Observer,* thought that it was because Jeffers wrote at inordinate length and in so loose a form that it was questionable whether he wrote poetry at all.[30] The dark, negative philosophy of Jeffers, coupled with his obsessively tragic subjects, may have further discouraged English readers. The three books of Jeffers, all published in Dorothy Wellesley's series, lost her money, but there must have been some satisfaction in having published the best of the genius from the California cave. Sales continued to trickle in over the years. When the Hogarth Press was offered the sheets of *Selected Poems* in 1938 by Random House, John Lehmann totaled the accounts of the three books over the ten-year period and recommended to Woolf that they decline the offer.[31] The *Roan Stallion* had sold 181 copies, *Cawdor* 132 copies, and *Dear Judas* 109 copies.

The second American poet making an unusual and unremunerative appearance on the Hogarth Press list at this time was Edwin Arlington Robinson. When Robinson had ventured from his New England fastness to old England in the summer of 1923 for his one excursion abroad, he did not meet Leonard and Virginia Woolf. It was too early for him and for them. In 1923 the Woolfs still lived at Hogarth House, Richmond, and spent that summer at Monks House where Virginia worked on the first version of *Mrs. Dalloway.* They remained aloof from literary London. Seven years later the Hogarth Press would publish Robinson's *Cavender's House* (1930). The intensely reserved Robinson, who avoided New York's literary swirl, had little to avoid in London. He was virtually unknown in England. He lacked no recognition in America, however. By the time of his English summer, Robinson had achieved a considerable degree of popularity and fame at home.

The wide American success of Robinson's *Collected Poems* in 1921 and 1922 caught the attention of Cecil Palmer, who purchased sheets from Robinson's publisher Macmillan and published the *Collected Poems* in England in 1922.[32] Palmer repeated with *Roman Bartholow* and *The Man Who*

Died Twice, but Robinson failed to gain an audience in England. Victor Gollancz bought sheets from Macmillan for *Tristram,* which he published in 1928 after the volume had won the Pulitzer Prize in America and been issued by the Literary Guild in an edition of 12,000 copies. It sold 57,000 copies in America in the ·first year.[33] But again, Robinson's success in America failed to spark an English audience.

Alert to Robinson's poetry, Dorothy Wellesley wrote to Leonard Woolf in May 1929 suggesting he make an offer to Curtis Brown for *Cavender's House* when it appeared (HP 176). Woolf did and obtained the book for the Living Poets series. Although the page size (8 by 5½ inches) and the wide margins of the Macmillan edition could have been adapted with a little trimming to the Living Poets format (7½ by 5 inches), Woolf chose not to buy sheets but to have Neill & Co. reset the volume. The press published it in April 1930 in an edition of 400 copies, one year to the month after the American edition. The Hogarth Press's *Cavender's House* was the only completely English publication of Robinson's work during his lifetime. He published seven more books of poetry before his death in 1935, but no English publisher thought them interesting enough to reprint.

Robinson's *Cavender,* a hundred pages of blank verse, owes something to Browning's "My Last Duchess" among other dramatic monologues and, as several critics have shown, something to Meredith's *Egoist.* There are echoes of tragedy from the Greeks to Ibsen. But none of this seems to have registered with English readers. James Thornton, reviewing *Cavender's House* in the *Nation and Athenaeum,* criticized Robinson's obsession with self-analysis, which led, he thought, to a joyless subversion of traditional moral values.[34] Robinson had his admirers in England, such as John Drinkwater, but not enough of them to sell books. The Hogarth Press edition of *Cavender's House* sold only seventy-four copies in the first six months and very few thereafter (MSR). English readers can be pardoned for not responding positively to Robinson in 1930. The far more appreciative American readers turned away in disappointment from *Cavender* after the passions and tragedies of *Tristam.* Robinson's popularity waned further with successive long poems. Frost, Eliot, Pound, Stevens, and Yeats dominated the poetry of the time, and the Auden generation was about to be born. Only in the late 1960s did a reawakening of critical interest in Robinson lead to reevaluations of his late poems, finding them less conventional than once thought and thereby indirectly justifying the commitment of Macmillan and Hogarth. *Cavender's House,* as now read, figures significantly in Robinson's canon, a worthy example of his increasingly subtle exploration of the multileveled self with attendant moral ambiguities.

The first three years of the Hogarth Living Poets series are now notable more for the publication of books by Robinson Jeffers and Edwin Arlington Robinson than for volumes by Dorothy Wellesley, R. Fitzurse, Ida Graves, or F. L. Lucas. But the series began to broaden out ambitiously in 1929–31 with four anthologies and with a first volume by C. Day-Lewis (*Transitional Poem,* 1929), a poet of major stature in the 1930s. His poetry is discussed in the next chapter.

It must have been one of Leonard Woolf's aims to use the Living Poets series to correct a serious imbalance in favor of Oxford's undergraduates. Blackwell had for years published an annual anthology of Oxford undergraduate verse, but no established publisher had espoused the Cambridge poets. In addition to all of their older Cambridge associations, Leonard and Virginia had more recent connections through Dadie Rylands and Julian Bell, Virginia's nephew. An annual anthology of Cambridge undergraduate poetry was congenial to the Woolfs, although it only lasted two years. But these were the years of a remarkably talented group of students.

Cambridge Poetry 1929, edited by Christopher Saltmarshe, John Davenport, and Basil Wright, contained poems by such future celebrities as Julian Bell, Ronald Bottrall, J. Bronowski, Richard Eberhardt, William Empson, John Lehmann, Michael Redgrave, and Hugh Sykes. The sequel, *Cambridge Poetry 1930,* edited by Davenport, Sykes, and Redgrave, had several repeat appearances and added Malcolm Lowry, among others. The next year, the press published a third Cambridge collection, *An Anthology of Cambridge Women's Verse* (1931). A fourth anthology, the *Broadcast Anthology of Modern Poetry* (1930), edited by Dorothy Wellesley, contained poems from such well-knowns as Edmund Blunden, Rupert Brooke, Roy Campbell, John Drinkwater, T. S. Eliot, Robert Graves, James Joyce, D. H. Lawrence, Wilfred Owen, Siegfried Sassoon, and Edith Sitwell, as well as from the ladies behind the anthology, Dorothy Wellesley and Vita Sackville-West. It proved the most commercially successful of the anthologies, selling 1,047 copies in the first six months (MSR).

Vita Sackville-West and William Plomer, two of Hogarth's most productive authors, also contributed volumes of poetry to the Living Poets series in 1929. Sackville-West published *King's Daughter,* a lightly disguised collection of romantic lesbian costume-piece narratives and lyrics set in the seventeenth century. It was her first volume of poetry since becoming a Hogarth Press author; and if it did not add luster to the press series, it at least sold well and turned a profit—730 copies sold in the first six months (MSR).

William Plomer had sent in his fourth book to the press from Japan in 1928, an 80,000-word manuscript collection of stories, *Paper Houses,* representing his two-and-a-half-year sojourn among the Japanese. The Woolfs published it in February 1929, and in April the peripatetic Plomer arrived in London and dined with them. In mid-May he sent Leonard his fifth book, a collection of forty-one poems written in Japan to be published as *The Family Tree* in October. Leonard thought the poems were "a great advance on the previous volume," but he objected to Plomer's rhyming "lichen" with "rich in" (HP 341). The self-confident Plomer proceeded to lecture Leonard Woolf about English usage, stating he preferred the sound "litchen" to "liken," that many educated people pronounced the word that way, and that "language must be allowed to grow and not become fixed" (HP 341). Leonard, probably amused, allowed Plomer to grow and not become fixed, deferring to the twenty-six-year-old's staunchly held opinions. Plomer's volume appeared in October as number ten in the series.

Although the Hogarth Press published more than twice as many volumes of poetry than of fiction in the last three years of the 1920s (twenty-five volumes of poetry, twelve volumes of fiction), the period 1928–30 belonged to the fiction writers, with two best-sellers (Woolf's *Orlando* and Sackville-West's *Edwardians*), a popular mystery (Kitchin's *Death of My Aunt*), and two collections of stories in translation by the Italian master Italo Svevo (*The Hoax* and *The Nice Old Man and the Pretty Girl and Other Stories*).

Whatever the uncertain fortunes of their poets, domestic or imported, the Woolfs were profitably engaged in their own writing and the development of the press in 1929. Virginia Woolf at this time was between novels, busy with journalism and nonfiction and marshaling her forces for the long struggle with one of her most ambitious and experimental fictions to come, *The Waves* (1931). In addition to her usual book reviews and literary essays, slowly reduced in number after 1928, Woolf published one short story in 1928, "Slater's Pins Have No Points" ("a nice little story about Sapphism, for the Americans," she called it [*Letters* 3:397]), and three monographs, *Street Haunting* (1930), *On Being Ill* (1930), and *Beau Brummel* (1930). But it was *A Room of One's Own,* published in October 1929, which caused the most immediate sensation and the most lasting effect. It sold over 12,000 copies in England and over 10,000 copies in America in the first six months and was reprinted several times. *Orlando* (1928) had presented the gay and witty adventures of a transsexual hero-heroine through several centuries, the timeless, wealthy possessor of many rooms. In *A Room of One's Own,* Woolf focused on the need to free all Orlandos from the paralyzing behavior forced on them by sexual stereotypes.

Now, in 1929, with the undeniable commercial success and critical importance of Virginia's writing, it seemed to the Woolfs a propitious moment to reprint her early books in a uniform or trade edition. They first had to obtain publishing rights from Gerald Duckworth, who had published *The Voyage Out* in 1915 and *Night and Day* in 1919. In the interval, George Doran had published American editions of the novels in 1920. For Doran's edition of *The Voyage Out,* Woolf had revised her novel substantially, making important changes in the sixteenth chapter. Then Duckworth reissued both novels in 1920, purchasing sheets from Doran with Woolf's revisions for *The Voyage Out* but reprinting from its own text of *Night and Day.* Duckworth issued another impression of *The Voyage Out* in 1927, this time purchasing sheets of the Doran edition from Harcourt Brace, which had bought the American rights in 1926.

So it was that when the Hogarth Press purchased the publishing rights to Woolf's first two novels from Duckworth in February 1929, it also obtained extra sheets and unsold copies of both novels. In the early spring of 1929, the Woolfs reissued the novels as "Third Impressions" with the Hogarth Press imprint, using the Duckworth sheets (the Doran-

Harcourt Brace sheets for *The Voyage Out*). In September, however, the Woolfs began their Uniform Editions by a photo-offset reprint of *The Voyage Out*, using the text of the Duckworth first edition, not the revised text of the Doran edition. Curiously, the text so carefully reworked by Woolf was never reprinted by the Hogarth Press, even though some copies of it had been distributed as the "Third Impression."[35]

For subsequent Uniform Editions, the Hogarth Press reprinted in small crown octavo by photo-offset from the first edition of each book, bound the volumes in jade-green cloth boards lettered in gold on the spine, and priced them at 5s. Only the dust wrappers of the volumes varied. The first Uniform Editions, appearing September 26, 1929, in one batch, were *The Voyage Out, Jacob's Room, The Common Reader,* and *Mrs. Dalloway.* The Woolfs chose not to reissue *Kew, Mark on the Wall,* or the stories of *Monday or Tuesday,* which may indicate either their sense that a Uniform Edition of the stories would not sell or that the works were too slight to be given such prominence. Nor did they reprint the monographs—short works like *Mr. Bennett and Mrs. Brown* or *On Being Ill*—in the Uniform Edition.

To the Lighthouse was issued in a Uniform Edition in February 1930, followed by *Night and Day* and *A Room of One's Own* in November 1930. It was the sixth printing of *A Room,* and the Woolfs thereby established the customary practice of putting each successive book of Virginia's into the cheaper Uniform Edition after several reprintings of the first edition. *Orlando,* perhaps because of the large number of copies printed in the first three impressions and its price of 9s. (to cover the cost of the photographs), did not go into the 5s. Uniform Edition until October 1933. It appeared at the same time that *The Waves* was published in this format.

Leonard Woolf had taken quiet pleasure in the unconventional form and content of the early hand-printed press books, somewhat the bane of booksellers. The commercially produced books, however, conformed to accepted printing practices and so appeared in a variety of standard sizes from the large royal octavo down through the demy and crown octavos. The Uniform Editions in small crown octavo volumes, therefore, marked one more stage in the evolution of the Hogarth Press into a commercial publishing house. The decision to issue Virginia Woolf's books in an inexpensive standard trade edition meant to the press greater ease of production, lower reprinting costs, and certain marketing advantages in the attractive, uniform volumes.

But the reissue of Virginia Woolf's books suggests something more significant than sound publishing practices. To put a living novelist's works into a standard edition is to make a claim for the permanence and importance of the writer's work, to establish a canon, to suggest the classic. All the more interesting and revealing is such a development when the novelist is in mid-career, forty-seven years old, and a partner in the publishing firm. By their editorial decision, the Woolfs seem to have declared publicly the commercial value of Virginia's novels and their claim to artistic greatness. They were confirmed in their judgment not only by sales but by the eagerness of both Chatto & Windus and Faber & Faber to reprint the novels in 1931.

After a six-year hiatus since *Seducers in Ecuador*, Vita Sackville-West returned to fiction with the best-selling *The Edwardians* in 1930. David Higham, literary agent for the Curtis Brown agency, took credit for suggesting the idea to Sackville-West. He had approached her with the suggestion of "a novel set in the Edwardian period she obviously knew so well," he recalled in his memoirs, adding that "Heinemann would commission it." [36] Sackville-West, while taking to the idea, insisted that the Hogarth Press publish the novel. Leonard Woolf heard of the Higham-Heinemann plan through Virginia and wrote to Vita in April 1929 offering to publish her novel (HP 416). He proposed 15 percent royalties on the first 3,000 copies, 20 percent on the remainder, and an advance of £200, better terms than she had previously enjoyed with her first Hogarth novel, *Seducers*. Vita was pleased. She had been horrified, she wrote to Leonard on April 30, to learn that Higham had offered the "as yet unwritten, and indeed unconceived, novel" to Heinemann. She would prefer to publish with Hogarth, she concluded, "if you really think that the resources of the Press would not be strained by the very liberal offer which you have made me" (HP 416). Her asterisk at the bottom of the letter explained about the "unwritten novel": "No longer. I started it this morning. It is about Edwardian society."

Ten months later in early March 1930 she had finished the book, informed the Woolfs, and sent her manuscript to the press offices in Tavistock Square. Sackville-West was always a disciplined and rapid writer, but ten months, even for her, was a short time for a long novel. "We found your MS waiting us," wrote Leonard upon the Woolfs' return from the country on March 9, "and, of course, Virginia pounced on it and I have had no chance. She approves so violently that I shall send it off to the printer and read it in proof to save time."[37] Leonard, delighted to have a large, potentially popular work of fiction for the spring list, rushed the novel through production and had it ready for publication on May 29, 1930. The press offerings that spring had been thin, only one other novel, Alice Ritchie's *Occupied Territory,* two volumes of poetry, and four short prose studies. Vita's novel was the big book that year for the press.

What Vita Sackville-West wrote in *The Edwardians* was for her something old and something new, a combination which proved a commercial if not a critical success. Old was her theme of the great house and the passing of its ancient English traditions. New was the satire. Sackville-West took aim at empty social conventions, the elaborate sexual charades of weekends in country houses, the banality of power and privilege. In 1930 satire was abroad with ravening maw in the novels of Aldous Huxley and Evelyn Waugh. But Vita Sackville-West was no satirist at heart; she cared too deeply for the traditions of houses like Knole to treat them satirically, although she disliked the excesses and affectations of society. The novel, as a result, proves to be an uncomfortable alliance between romance and satire.

Although one reviewer thought that the dialogue creaked, there was nothing creaky about the sales of *The Edwardians.* Selections by the Book Society for the May offering meant an immediate commitment of 9,000 copies to the society, with an option for a further 500 copies in the next three weeks (HP 416). Provincial booksellers, however, still new to the possibilities of book-of-the-month clubs, proved resistant to change, as the Woolfs learned when they traveled the Hogarth list with *The Edwardians* in early May. The booksellers were rude, wrote Virginia to Vita from Cornwall, and "violently against the Book Society and say it is ruining them" (*Letters* 4:165).

Leonard Woolf had ordered 18,000 copies printed at first, to include the Book Society's 9,000 copies, and had a second impression of 8,000 copies printed two days later (the book was selling 1,000 copies a day, at 7s.6d. per copy). By the first week in June, Virginia exuberantly wrote to

Quentin Bell that "Vita's book is such a best seller that Leonard and I are hauling in money like Pilchards from a net" (*Letters* 4:176). To Molly MacCarthy she could boast that "after the Edwardians . . . we can manage a best seller as well as Heinemann, and with far greater distinction" (ibid., 177). Leonard, always touchy about his ability to compete against larger publishing houses, was mightily pleased with his success in marketing *The Edwardians*. By the middle of September, he ordered a third impression of 3,000 copies, and a year later he put the book into a cheap edition (selling at 3s.6d.) with a printing of 3,000 copies.

By late summer Vita learned that the novel had been chosen by the American Literary Guild as book selection for September 1930, bringing her £5,000 in the transaction. Five years later Allen Lane sought *The Edwardians* in August 1935 for his new paperback series of Penguin Books then published by the Bodley Head Press. He had published his first ten titles and wished to include Sackville-West's novel in his second list of ten titles. Lane offered 30s. per 1,000 copies bound, with an advance of £40; the Woolfs and Sackville-West agreed, and everyone profited (HP 416). Between July 1, 1936, when *The Edwardians* became a Penguin, and December 31, 1939, the novel sold a remarkable 87,654 paperback copies, resulting in payments to the Hogarth Press of £131.18.9.

Although not in the same profit-making league as Vita Sackville-West's novel, C. H. B. Kitchin's crime novel of 1929 proved a big and surprising commercial success for the Woolfs. "Like most people," wrote Leonard Woolf in the *New Statesman and Nation* in 1927, "I am unable to resist the attractions of a detective story." [38] In spite of Leonard's avowed admiration for detective stories—he frequently reported on crime novels and notable criminal trials in the *Nation and Athenaeum*—the Hogarth Press avoided popular genres and would never have published thrillers or mysteries merely for the sake of the market. Kitchin's *Death of My Aunt* (1929), however, came about as an unexpected development of his fiction after he had already published two novels with the Hogarth Press.

After going down from Exeter College, Oxford, Kitchin served in the First World War and in 1924 was called to the bar, Lincoln's Inn, where he joined his friend Philip Ritchie in the chambers of C. P. Sanger, old acquaintance of Lytton Strachey and Leonard Woolf. Philip Ritchie, at the time an intimate friend of Lytton Strachey, moved in and out of the Bloomsbury circuit. Kitchin met the Woolfs and other lights of Bloomsbury through Ritchie. He confessed to Strachey's biographer Michael Holroyd that he was then a "tiresome mixture of shyness and conceit," uncomfortable with the others but on good terms with Virginia Woolf, who seemed protective and who sponsored his first two novels at the Hogarth Press.[39] He doubted that any other publisher would have taken the books.

Kitchin's Hogarth Press novels *Streamers Waving* (1925) and *Mr. Balcony* (1927) owed much to the satire of Aldous Huxley, but there were disturbing undercurrents of cruelty and heartless gaiety. *Mr. Balcony* had the added elements of the mystery and the thriller, with a touch of Conrad's *Heart of Darkness*. Neither novel appealed to sufficient readers to avoid losing money for the press. The Woolfs must have been surprised, therefore, when Kitchin delivered his third novel to them in 1929, a murder mystery with an engaging hero. *Death of My Aunt* made money and made Kitchin's reputation.

Much of the book follows the familiar English crime conventions of a country-house poisoning, a large and divided family, a proposed change in a will, a suspicious servant, and a stolid, literal-minded police inspector. What makes *Death of My Aunt* interesting is the narrative by Malcolm Warren, a somewhat successful broker (Kitchin had abandoned the bar for the stock exchange), who must solve the murder to clear himself from suspicion and to save his rough-cut, bumbling Uncle Hannibal who has been arrested for the crime. The plot twists and turns satisfactorily, and Warren struggles at considerable risk to piece together the clues.

While not as innovative as the brilliantly conceived Agatha Christie novel *The Murder of Roger Ackroyd* (1926), in which the narrator Dr. Sheppard was the murderer, Kitchin's crime novel helped establish a subgenre of the species. Jacques Barzun and Wendell Taylor, in their authoritative *Catalogue of Crime* (1971), cited *Death of My Aunt* as a classic model of a first-person narrative detective and praised it for its clear ratiocination, its effective unadorned prose, and its driving narration.[40] Readers responded, then and now, ensuring its popularity through several reprintings. It earned a profit of £103.19.8 the first year and £175.4.7 the second year (MSR). *Death of My Aunt* became one of Allen Lane's Penguin paperbacks in 1938, and Hamish Hamilton reissued it in 1968 in his mystery series as A Fingerprint Book. It continues to circulate through the public libraries.

Busy as they were with the publication of poetry and fiction in the late 1920s, the Woolfs returned briefly to translations, a genre which had occupied them so conspicuously in the first eight years of Hogarth's existence. By 1929, when the Woolfs published the work of Italo Svevo, they had issued eleven titles of translation, all but two of them (Charles Mauron's *Nature of Beauty in Art and Literature* and Fridtjof Nansen's *Adventure and Other Papers,* both in 1927) from the Russian texts brought to them by Koteliansky. Svevo was for the Woolfs an important development after several years of virtual inactivity in the field of translation.

The Italian novelist Ettore Schmitz, whose pen name Italo Svevo meant "Italian of Swabia," was hardly known in England when he was killed at age sixty-seven in an automobile accident in September 1928 near Trieste. Four months later, in January 1929, Beryl de Zoete brought Svevo to the attention of English readers in the literary pages of the *Nation and Athenaeum* through a critical essay. Some months later, in October 1929, just over a year after Svevo's death, the Hogarth Press published *The Hoax,* a long short story of Svevo's translated by Zoete. It was his first work to appear in English. The Hogarth Press followed this by publishing in November 1930 Svevo's collection *The Nice Old Man and the Pretty Girl and Other Stories,* translated by L. Collison-Morley. Earlier, in March 1930, Svevo's acknowledged masterpiece, *The Confessions of Zeno* (more accurately the "conscience" or "consciousness" of Zeno, from the Italian *La coscienza di Zeno*), had been translated by Beryl de Zoete and published in London and New York by Putnam. What English and American readers first read of Svevo's work through the translations of Zoete and the Hogarth Press was the last chapter in a strange publishing history which had begun in 1907 when James Joyce gave English lessons to the wealthy Triestine industrialist Ettore Schmitz and his wife, only to discover that Schmitz was a published, although forgotten, novelist. Joyce's praise of Svevo as a neglected novelist, his admiration of passages in *Senilita* (1889), fired Svevo into writing again after long dormancy.[41] Svevo broke his twenty-five years' silence by publishing *La coscienza di Zeno* in 1923, only to receive once more critical disapproval in Italy for his style and his use of Triestine vocabulary. Joyce's energetic defense and promotion of Svevo's work in Paris led to the translation of *Zeno* into French by P. H. Michel, published in 1927 by the NRF.

Beryl de Zoete, the companion of orientalist and Chinese translator Arthur Waley, discovered Svevo for the Woolfs. When she wrote to Leonard Woolf years later in 1957 requesting a spare copy of *The Hoax,* she recounted how she had first encountered Svevo in 1928 by reading the French translation of *Zeno.* She remembered returning to her hotel and thinking how readable the novel was (HP 479). She was in Italy in the summer of 1928 when Svevo was killed and immediately bought all of his available books. Her interest led to the article in the *Nation and Athenaeum* which introduced Svevo to English readers.

When Zoete submitted her translation of *The Hoax* to the Hogarth Press in February 1929, Leonard Woolf responded quickly that he liked the work and wished to publish it as a small book. He asked her to write an introduction similar to the *Nation and Athenaeum* article. She complied with a short biographical introduction, and the press published the book on October 24, 1929, printing 1,000 copies. The volume did not fare well, selling only 497 copies in the first six months (MSR). What royalties there were Leonard Woolf divided between Berryl de Zoete and Signora Livia Schmitz-Svevo, the writer's widow who had recently altered her name to reflect her husband's growing literary reputation.

The Hogarth Press published a second volume of Svevo's one year later. Signora Schmitz-Svevo had contracted with Hogarth to publish a collection of stories in English translation which became *The Nice Old Man and the Pretty Girl and Other Stories.* The collection had appeared posthumously in Italy in 1929, containing the title story and four others: "Vino generoso" ("Generous Wine"), "Una burla riuscita" ("The Hoax"), "La madre" ("The Mother"), and "Il vecchione" ("The Old, Old Man"). Svevo's widow hoped that Beryle de Zoete would translate the stories because, as she wrote to Leonard Woolf in January 1930, they were a continuation of the novel *Zeno* which Zoete had translated (HP 480). The title story, "The Nice Old Man," was an unfinished fragment of a novel intended by Svevo to be a sequel to *Zeno.* But Zoete declined the offer, writing to Woolf from Morocco in June 1930 that while a few of the stories amused her, she believed the others were unsuccessful. Leonard Woolf then suggested Collison-Morley, who had reviewed Italian literature for Leonard in the *Nation and Athenaeum,* to Signora Schmitz-Svevo as a translator, and the arrangements were completed. Svevo's *The Nice Old Man and the Pretty Girl and Other Stories* appeared in November 1930, but in spite of the intriguing title and Svevo's European reputation, it sold less well than *The Hoax.* Only 259 copies were purchased in the first six months (MSR).

Both translators were adept enough to allow the important qualities of Svevo to come through. "Svevo," as the critic Brian Maloney has written, "is a major novelist in the mainstream of the European tradition."[42] He added that "in a world in which irrationalism and anti-intellectualism are endemic diseases, Svevo's intelligent irony speaks with the voice of health." The Hogarth Press helped to advance Svevo's reputation as an important writer and helped to broadcast that voice of intelligent irony. It was, in some ways, the voice of Bloomsbury itself.

By the end of 1930, the Hogarth Press had been in operation for thirteen years, had moved once, and had published 240 titles of great diversity. It had achieved considerable artistic and financial success. The world in which Leonard and Virginia had boldly begun their hand printing had emerged from a world war and cascaded through the exuberant twenties. There were changes in the Hogarth Press to match the times, especially during the period 1924–30. Not only was this time marked by the expansion of press offerings and by the impressive productivity of the writer-publishers directing it but also by the comings and goings of a numerous cast of supporting characters. No fewer than seven assistants, managers, and assorted spear-carriers moved through the basement rooms of the Hogarth Press in six years. First there was Marjorie Joad, who had replaced Ralph Partridge. Then Dadie Rylands entranced in July 1924 and exited in December. He enriched the Woolfs' lives but complicated Joad's before being replaced by Angus Davidson. Virginia Woolf recorded the fourteen days of "a long press revolution—Dadie going Marjorie going, Marjorie staying, Angus Davidson coming . . . but achieved only at the cost of 40 million words" (*Diary* 2:323). Davidson, an uncertain performer in the company, remained on stage for three years (1924–27).

In early 1925 Marjorie Joad, ill with pneumonia, left Hogarth, eventually to go to Heinemann, and was replaced by Bernadette Murphy, who proved as brief a candle as Rylands—in and out in six months (February to July 1925). The solid Mrs. Cartwright replaced Murphy and became office manager, providing important continuity for five years (1925–30), the longest run of any manager. To aid Mrs. Cartwright as file clerk, typist, and secretary, the press first hired Winifred Holtby for a spell (1927–28) and then Peggy Belsher (1928–35), "a brisk girl," as Virginia Woolf described her, "who says very tart things, but is already Mrs. C's right hand" (*Letters* 3:467). She seems to have served the longest tenure of all press employees. After Angus Davidson left in 1927, the young, irreverent Richard Kennedy joined the firm for two years (1928–30). He became an admirer of Miss Belsher and Virginia Woolf but an accident-prone understudy of Leonard.

The increase of salaried personnel to two assistants in 1924 began a practice by the Woolfs which lasted through John Lehmann's first association with the Hogarth Press (1931–32). With the appearance of Dadie Rylands, an Apostle and scholar from King's College, Cambridge, Marjorie Joad became office manager. Rylands seemed destined for eventual partnership with Leonard Woolf, and a pattern became established. The Partridge-Rylands line of bright young university men (all but Partridge were from Cambridge) developed through Davidson, almost included Francis Birrell, and culminated with John Lehmann. Richard Kennedy, at sixteen a fail-out from Marlborough School, might be considered an abortive and somewhat comic subspecies of the line. The Marjorie Joad line of capable women office managers extended through Bernadette Murphy to Mrs. Cartwright and later to Margaret West in the 1930s. These managing ladies were assisted in turn by Miss Belsher and her line of successors.

"For my own part, I could never see Dadie as a permanent partner," Virginia Woolf confided to her diary in December 1924, "Dadie in his silver grey suit, pink shirts, with his powdered pink & white face . . . his love of praise. Angus, however, after 3 days, already seems to me permanent & dependable" (*Diary* 2:323). But Angus Davidson, in his turn, would be found wanting. Three years later in February 1927, Virginia noted the "flat talk" Leonard had with Angus. "L. says he doesn't 'manage.' Angus refuses to budge an inch. He can't see the point of it . . . doesn't want to leave. . . . But I'm persuaded we need . . . a fanatic at the moment; not this quiet easygoing gentlemanliness" (ibid., 3:128). Eight months later in October, after a heated argument with Davidson, Leonard dismissed him, then reinstated him. There followed another "painful interview" in December, and Davidson resigned in the midst of Leonard's renewed determination to dismiss him.

At the time of Davidson's departure, the Woolfs had invited Francis Birrell to join the press. "We think of Francis Birrell as partner," Virginia Woolf noted, "shall ask him tomorrow; & broach the Hogarth Miscellany" (*Diary* 3:167). A critic and reviewer contributing frequently to Woolf's literary pages of the *Nation and Athenaeum,* Birrell had partnered the Birrell & Garnett bookshop with David Garnett. It had become a Bloomsbury satellite. Apparently the "Hogarth Miscellany" or "Annual" was intended to be a house journal, perhaps on the order of Jonathan Cape's *Now and Then* (first issued in 1921), which developed a considerable reputation among subscribers.[43] Nothing came of it, however, as Birrell, describing himself as a "piece work man" who preferred reviewing and loathed the bookshop business, declined the Woolfs' offer (LWP). But he offered to help if they ever began to publish the "Hogarth Miscellany." Francis Birrell may have been lucky and perceptive enough to have avoided the inevitable complications of working for Leonard Woolf.

Part of the problem Leonard Woolf had with the young men he hired as potential partners was self-generated. He found it nearly impossible to share authority. His own complex personality shaped his management style and affected his choice of assistants. Highly intelligent, sensitive, poets, and writers, the young men before Lehmann were generally indecisive, unambitious, and unworldly. They were not interested in business and were unsullied by the slightest taint of practical experience. They drifted into the Hogarth Press, struggled to learn printing, had trouble with accounts, adored Virginia, tolerated but quarreled with Leonard, and departed generally wiser but less happy than when they entered. In a sense, they never should have been hired. Ill equipped as they were for any business, they nevertheless became devoted to the press and worked at it in their fashion for minimal pay under cramped and somewhat shabby conditions.

The development of the Hogarth Press might have been different if

Leonard Woolf, following customary business practices, had advertised for an assistant and found one in the trade. At one point in their deliberations with Angus Davidson in June 1926, the Woolfs briefly considered replacing him with a man who had twelve years' experience with the publisher Edward Arnold, but they deferred to Davidson's charm and his promise to mend his ways (*Letters* 3:274). It was as close as they came to an assistant with publishing experience. A young man with such experience and ambition, however, might not have been attracted to the position with its marginal salary, cluttered basement offices, and firm-minded director.

From the first the press was a shoestring operation, and it might have been immediately obvious to a shrewd and knowledgeable observer that Leonard Woolf preferred it that way. "I was determined not to treat publishing as a means of making a living," Woolf confessed in his autobiography, "and I was determined not to become a full-time publisher." Moreover, he admitted that he had tried "to get the best of two contradictory worlds" by "asking these brilliant young men to perform an impossible feat, namely to publish best-sellers with the greatest professional efficiency for an amateur publisher in a basement kitchen." Woolf was enormously proud of his efficiency, his iron resolve learned in Ceylon to answer every letter the day it was received, to account daily for every penny spent, to calculate exactly the cost of each publication, and to anticipate correctly the need for reprinting or rebinding so that the press was never out of stock. "This was the result," he wrote, "of meticulous daily, sometime hourly, supervision, checking, organization" (*Downhill* 170).

With the comfortable and forgiving self-knowledge of an old man, Leonard Woolf could look back at himself in his autobiography and admit his personal shortcomings. Ceylon had formed him as a man of affairs, and it was in Ceylon that he got the reputation, not undeserved he thought, of being "a strict and ruthless civil servant," of being "too severe and too opinionated" (*Growing* 109). He became obsessed with work, exalting it to a mania of perfection, indulging a "dangerous passion" for efficiency. No doubt Woolf in his forties and fifties, presiding over affairs in the basement rooms of Tavistock Square, had matured considerably beyond the imperious and zealous young czar of the Ceylonese kachcheris in his mid-twenties, but his attitude toward work, coupled with his stubborn pride in always being right, characterized Woolf's style as a manager throughout his life. Memorable and typical was the furious argument Woolf had with Angus Davidson one morning. To Woolf's charge that he was late to work, Davidson replied that he was on time. Woolf produced his watch to prove his point; Davidson countered with his watch which showed a difference of two minutes. The controversy became so fierce, and both men so adamant, that Woolf insisted they go out to a public clock in Russell Square to settle the argument. They trooped out, resolved the issue, but hardly spoke to each other the rest of the day.[44]

The sometimes comic side of all this has been wonderfully described by Richard Kennedy in *A Boy at the Hogarth Press* (1972). Although cast as a contemporary diary and series of letters to a friend, the book was put together and illustrated by Kennedy over forty years after the events. Kennedy was sixteen and recently sent down from preparatory school when his uncle George, a distinguished architect and acquaintance of Leonard Woolf, proposed him for a Hogarth Press assistant in February 1928. Woolf agreed to take young Kennedy for a year beginning in late April as an unpaid assistant. He was to keep regular office hours (9:15–5:00), to have two months' vacation a year, and "to do any of the work that the rest of the staff do" (LWP). They would reconsider the arrangement at the end of the year.

Richard Kennedy accepted Woolf's offer and plunged into life below stairs at the Hogarth. Kennedy's line drawings and foldout map of the basement rooms add much to the text of his book. Particularly vivid are the drawing of Virginia Woolf rolling shag tobacco cigarettes amid a Bloomsbury gathering and the one of the infamous shelf, so confidently constructed by Kennedy, collapsing in a shower of leaflets upon Leonard Woolf and Lord Olivier. Virginia Woolf at the time had mentioned in a letter to Vanessa Bell that "Kennedy says he is going to put up a shelf, as he knows a man who sells wood wholesale, and he is very fond of putting up shelves" (*Letters* 3:495). She added that he was "a nice simple-minded boy." In spite of, or perhaps because of, Kennedy's high-spirited misadventures, Leonard Woolf kept him on for a second year, paid him a minimal wage, and once took him ice-skating in Richmond Park.

After two years at the press, Kennedy determined to seek his fortune in more congenial pursuits and left the Woolfs in September 1930 to pursue a certificate in journalism at University College. Kennedy went on to a successful career as a book illustrator, chiefly of children's books. Before he left the Hogarth Press, Kennedy had designed two dust jackets, a pictorial design for Kitchin's *Death of My Aunt* (1929) and a geometrical design used on over twenty titles. When Leonard Woolf published *Growing* in 1961, Kennedy wrote expressing nostalgia and admiration. "Nobody took your rages at the Hogarth Press very seriously," he wrote to Leonard, "as it was so easy to flannel round you. . . . I mean you could not easily be deceived but it was possible to switch planes to that of the heart rather than the head" (LWP). The warmer side of Woolf's personality comes through in this letter and helps soften the image of the formidable director of Hogarth affairs.

"Meanwhile Leonard left the Nation," Virginia Woolf wrote to Hugh Walpole in March 1930, "and we are now supporting ourselves entirely by the Hogarth Press, which when I remember how we bought £5 worth of type and knelt on the drawing room floor ten years ago setting up little stories and running out of quads . . . makes my breast burst with pride" (*Letters* 4:152). Inaccuracies of fact never troubled Virginia; being true to the spirit was more important in such vivid anecdotes. No matter that her income in 1930 was nearly three times more than the press profits, or that she and Leonard had started it thirteen years before, or that they had paid more than £12.4 for extra type.[45] The subjective truth was that she and Leonard not only took justifiable pride in the press but had come to depend on it. When Leonard left the *Nation and Athenaeum,* he soon began more congenial journalism as cofounder and coeditor of the *Political Quarterly.* He was never out of work as Virginia implied. But the Woolfs needed the press, and they worked at sustaining it by traveling the books themselves for a week in the West Country in May, with little success. "No one reads, no one wants books, the booksellers say, and they keep us hanging about," Virginia reported to Ethel Smyth (*Letters* 4:163).

In August, Virginia had fainted in the garden at Monks House, her "brush with death" a result of heat and nervous exhaustion (*Diary* 3:315). Richard Kennedy left the press in September for his journalism course, and the press staff was down to Mrs. Cartwright, Miss Belsher, and the Woolfs, all laboring to publish twenty-nine books for the year. No wonder that in October the Woolfs resented the "incessant drudgery" of the press and decided to end it as a publishing house. In the future, they thought, they would only publish Virginia's novels, Leonard's books, and the poetry of the Living Poets series, which they could hand print. The income from the press was less important to the overworked Woolfs than their time. "But what's money if you sell freedom?" Virginia asked herself. "And what's the point of publishing these innocuous novels & pamphlets that are neither good nor bad" (ibid., 327). Their spirits soon revived, however, the press continued unchecked, and the Woolfs set about once more to find a suitable young man to assist Leonard as manager and partner. They found John Lehmann in 1931.

Leonard Woolf, c. 1933. (Reprinted by permission from Quentin Bell, *Virginia Woolf: A Biography*, 2 vols. [London: Hogarth Press, 1972])

Virginia Woolf and John Lehmann at Monks House, c. 1931. (Reprinted by permission from Quentin Bell, *Virginia Woolf: A Biography,* 2 vols. [London: Hogarth Press, 1972])

Hogarth Press devices, designed (*left*) by Vanessa Bell and (*right*) by E. McKnight Kauffer

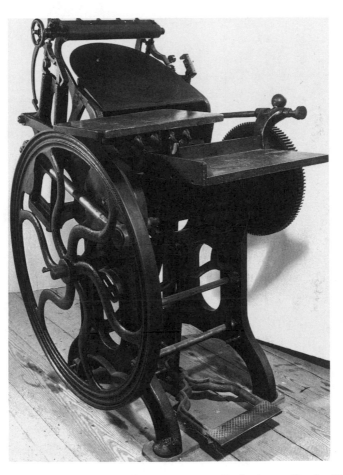

The Woolfs' treadle-operated press, now at Sissinghurst Castle, Kent. (Courtesy of Nigel Nicolson)

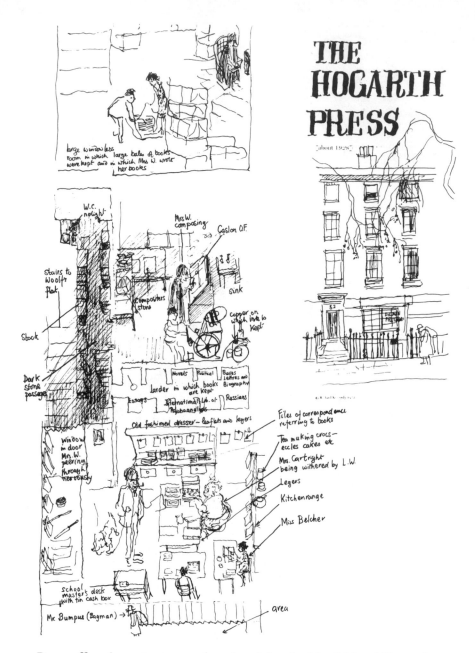

Press offices in 1928 as remembered and sketched by Richard Kennedy.
(Courtesy of Mrs. Kennedy)

One of the first Hogarth Press ads, July 1920

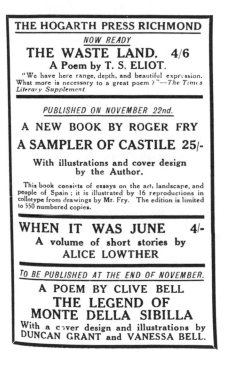

Ad announcing T. S. Eliot's *Waste Land,* November 1923

Full-page ad using Kauffer's device, October 1931

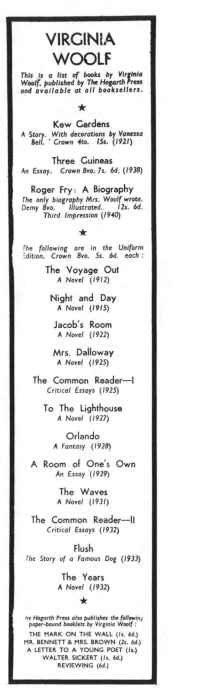
First ad after Virginia Woolf's death, April 1941

Cover design by Carrington for Leonard's *Stories of the East,* 1921. (Courtesy of Leonard and Virginia Woolf Library, Washington State University)

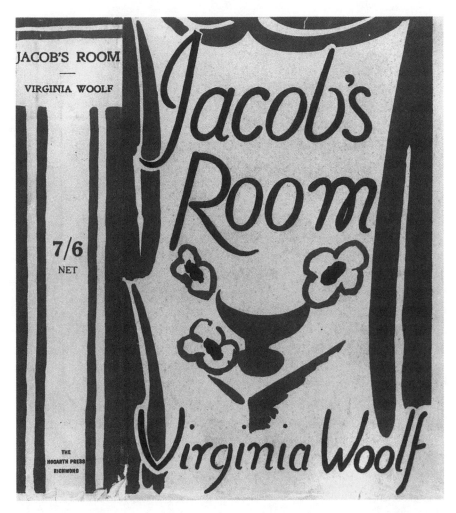

Vanessa Bell's jacket design for Virginia's *Jacob's Room,* 1922 (Courtesy of Leonard and Virginia Woolf Library, Washington State University)

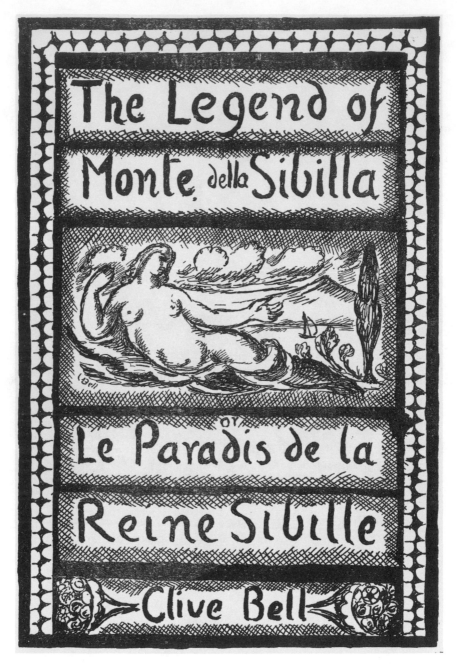

Vanessa Bell's cover design for Clive Bell's *Legend of Monte della Sibilla*, 1923. (Courtesy of Leonard and Virginia Woolf Library, Washington State University)

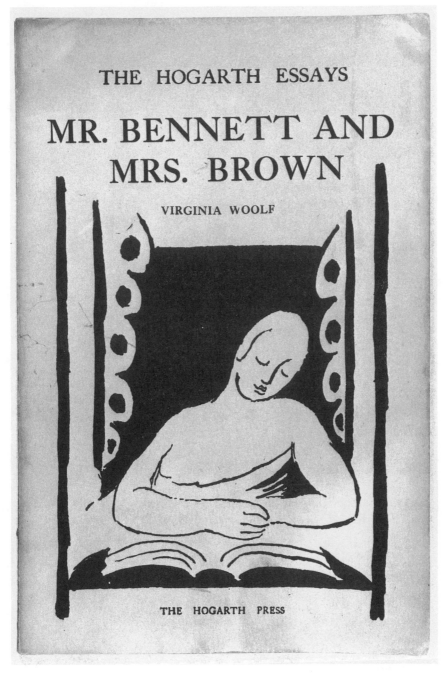

THE HOGARTH ESSAYS

MR. BENNETT AND MRS. BROWN

VIRGINIA WOOLF

THE HOGARTH PRESS

Vanessa Bell's cover design for Virginia's *Mr. Bennett and Mrs. Brown,* 1924.
(Courtesy of Leonard and Virginia Woolf Library, Washington State
University)

Richard Kennedy's jacket design for C. H. B. Kitchin's *Death of My Aunt,*
1929. (Courtesy of Leonard and Virginia Woolf Library, Washington State
University)

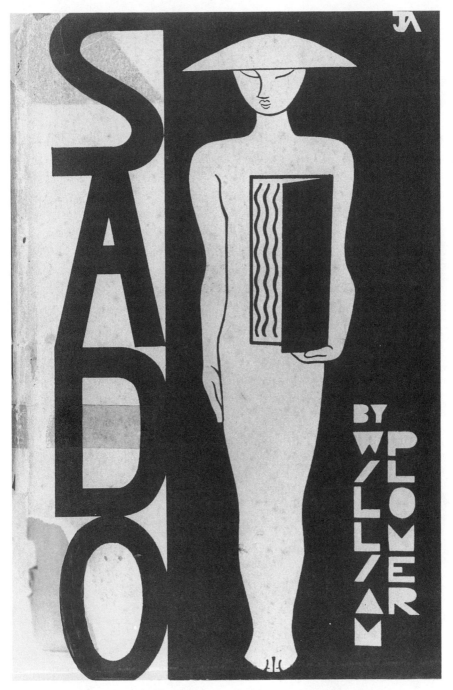

John Armstrong's jacket design for William Plomer's *Sado*, 1931. (Courtesy of Leonard and Virginia Woolf Library, Washington State University)

Vanessa Bell's jacket design for Virginia's *Three Guineas,* 1938. (Courtesy of Leonard and Virginia Woolf Library, Washington State University)

CHAPTER FIVE

★

JOHN LEHMANN, 1931–32

John Lehmann came to the Hogarth Press with impeccable qualifications. Fresh out of Trinity College, Cambridge, Lehmann was a close friend of Virginia Woolf's nephew Julian Bell, a close friend of Dadie Rylands, a neo-Georgian nature poet whose first volume had been recommended to the Woolfs by Rylands, and a handsome and cultivated young man with an interest in printing. He had not the slightest experience in business. He adored Virginia Woolf. When Leonard Woolf accepted Lehmann's *Garden Revisited and Other Poems* in December 1930 for the Living Poets series, he acknowledged Lehmann's interest in joining the press and proposed a meeting in January.[1] After the meeting Virginia Woolf recorded that "Lehmann may do: a tight aquiline boy, pink, with the adorable curls of youth; yes, but persistent, sharp" (*Diary* 4:6). He kept asking questions about his pay and prerogatives. "Not much atmosphere," thought Virginia, "save perhaps that his eyes are imaginative." They asked Lehmann for an investment of £5,000 to form a partnership.

Not only in his persistently sharp questions was Lehmann different from his predecessors but in his willingness to buy into the press as partner. The original idea was for the Woolfs to sell three-quarters of their interest in the press, retaining a one-quarter interest, and to allow Lehmann to run the business. Furthermore, the astute Lehmann sought advice from his friends about the Woolfs, particularly from Julian Bell, as he negotiated with his family solicitors. From Bell he learned that Leonard could be "rather interfering and overbearing, also obstinate and argumentative," and that Dadie Rylands had hated the job, which, added Bell, "by all accounts is distinctly a difficult and heavy one."[2] But Lehmann could not raise sufficient funds to buy into the partnership, and so, in spite of Bell's friendly warnings, he finally agreed to be a manager, not a partner. Woolf first proposed a contract with a one-year probationary period, during the first six months of which Lehmann would be paid at the rate of £100 per year and at the rate of £250 per year for the last six months.[3] At the end of the first year, Lehmann would be paid an annual salary of £250 plus 10 percent of the press profits. He was to have a six-week holiday each year. His working hours were to be from 9:15 A.M. to 5:00 P.M. This proposal was renegotiated by Woolf and Lehmann into a contract whereby the probationary period was shortened to eight months, to terminate on September 30, 1931, with the first six months' salary fixed at the rate of £100 per year, then increased to the rate of £150 per year plus 10 percent profits until March 31, 1932. At that time the contract called for Lehmann to go on an annual salary of £250 per year plus 10 percent of the profits. He had the option of buying into a partnership after March 31, 1933. Before exercising this option, however, John Lehmann would call it quits eighteen months later, in August 1932, to seek the headier pleasures of Germany where his friend Christopher Isherwood had established himself.

Much about Lehmann's eighteen months at the Hogarth Press followed the pattern set by Partridge, Rylands, and Davidson: initial delight and stumbling success, gradual tension and occasional conflicts with Leonard, mediation by Virginia, growing disagreements leading to emotion-filled "talks," resolution, and then departure with hurt feelings, with eventual reconciliation and resumption of friendship some months later. But Lehmann's tenure also differed considerably from those of the others. He proved to be a more energetic and resourceful manager than his predecessors, tirelessly attempting to expand the press offerings. Gifted with excellent literary judgment, Lehmann demonstrated a flair for entrepreneurial business which might have balanced nicely the more cautious and detail-obsessed Woolf had they been able to work more harmoniously together. Nevertheless, during his first residency in the basement offices at Tavistock Square, Lehmann made several important contributions to the press.

John Lehmann reported to work on January 21, 1931, and found several books in production that would be published in February and

March. Among them, two collections of poetry, two novels, and a translation are worth noting. The Living Poets series continued in February 1931 with three collections: *Fifty Poems* by Lord Derwent; *An Anthology of Cambridge Women's Verse*, compiled by Margaret Thomas, containing verse by eight poets from Girton College and six poets from Newnham College; and *A Collection of Poems* by Joan Adeney Easdale. The Cambridge women's anthology was a goodwill gesture by the Woolfs to balance their previous two collections of men's verse, but the quality was disappointing. It seems not to have been a good year at Cambridge for women poets. Only Kathleen Raine (Girton College) from among them would fulfill the expectations of such a volume by becoming an established writer. Joan Easdale's collection, "Written between the ages of 14 and 17," as it was subtitled, must have confounded Lehmann, a committed poet.

"The girl poet is my discovery," wrote Virginia Woolf to Hugh Walpole in April after publishing Easdale's *Collection of Poems (Written between the Ages of 14 and 17)*; "she sent me piles of dirty copy books written in a scrawl without any spelling; but I was taken aback to find, as I thought some real merit" (*Letters* 4:311). She could not be sure how far the poetry would go: "It may be a kind of infantile phosphorescence; and she is a country flapper, living in Kent, and might be from behind a counter." Very odd, she thought. Odd indeed were the seventy poems collected by Joan Easdale and published by the press, and amusing and puzzling the tangled relationship that developed between the Woolfs and the Easdales, Joan and her mother, over the years as the Hogarth Press published two more of Joan's books.

From her notation in January 1930 that she was "pondering the early works of Miss Easedale" (*Diary* 3:281), and getting the name wrong, to her last mention of Joan in a letter in September 1940, Virginia's diary entries and letters trace a ten-year often comic, involvement with the Easedales. One month before publishing the first book, Virginia and Leonard went to see Joan "act in a play in a shed in the garden," and six months later they went to Bumpus's bookshop to hear her sing her poems set to music by her composer brother (*Letters* 4:272, 347). Although Bloomsbury frequently amused itself with amateur theatricals and performances with parts for children—Virginia's comedy *Freshwater* (1923, 1935) is a famous example—the presence of the Woolfs in shed or bookshop attending to Joan's productions defies expectation. By September 1931 the relationship had progressed so that the Woolfs and Easdales exchanged invitations to tea, both visits memorable and recorded in Virginia's letter to Vita Sackville-West in September (Joan "looks like a chocolate box flapper . . . [who] talks like one . . . and yet produces those strange poems") and in Mrs. Easdale's autobiography *Middle Age, 1885–1932* (1935).[4]

By 1935 the twenty-one-year-old Joan Easdale was seeking rooms in Bloomsbury, and in 1937 she had published an article in the *Adelphi*. And then, surprisingly, she became a member of Bloomsbury's extended family by becoming engaged to Jim Rendel in October 1938. Lytton Strachey was his great-uncle, and his aunt was Virginia's doctor, Elinor Rendel. Joan's wedding to Jim Rendel took place in November. Two years later in 1940, she had a baby. With Virginia Woolf's acknowledgment of Joan's motherhood, the chronicle of the Easdales in her letters and diaries ceased, but the poetry lingers on (*Letters* 6:425).

The phosphorescent poems from a chocolate box flapper were published by the sedate Hogarth Press in the Living Poets series. What did the serious young Lehmann think? What did regular Hogarth readers think, for that matter? No comments survive. Joan Easdale's flapper image is preserved in two tipped-in pictures in an edition of *A Collection of Poems* (1931)—the one a formal portrait in semiprofile, head tilted with Mona Lisa smile, and the other a photo of the coquettishly posing sixteen-year-old garden nymph in a long white dress, arms bare, one high-heeled foot cocked back, smiling coyly down into an elaborate Victorian birdbath.[5] The picture leads into Joan's first poem, "Round the Room Walked the Duchess," written when she was fourteen, with the memorable first stanza: "Round the room walked the Duchess, / Looking at the perspiration gleaming / On her husband's brow." A year later Joan had composed a metaphorical tour de force on "The Hairdresser's Young Man," more remarkable even than T. S. Eliot's "young man carbuncular" in *The Waste Land*: "His eyes are walnut-shells / Swimming in paraffin-oil; / His nose is like a rose-hip / Resting on smooth putty; / . . . / His cheeks are like two warped balloons, / Limp, half full of air." These poems and others in *A Collection of Poems* are marvelously odd and so charmingly bad that one can almost understand Virginia's attraction to them.

Joan's next effort after her *Collection of Poems* was a play which Virginia Woolf rejected, agreeing with John Lehmann's judgment that it had charm and originality but lacked maturity. But the Woolfs accepted Joan's *Clemence and Clare* the next year and, with Dorothy Wellesley's blessing, published it in the Living Poets series in March 1932. At the advanced age of eighteen, however, Joan's peak was past, and nothing in the volume quite equaled the quirky originality of the earlier poems. *Clemence and Clare*, dedicated to Virginia Woolf, was a moody, moon-drenched, romantic, dime novel of a poem about the on and off and on again engagement of two lovers. The high, or low, point comes when Clare throws Clemence's ring into the pond, only to have a carp eat it and be caught later by Clemence who reclaims the ring to reengage Clare.

Seven years later in 1939, after marriage but before her baby, Joan sent the Woolfs another long narrative gothic romance, *Amber Innocent*, which they published over John Lehmann's objections.[6] Perhaps Virginia and Leonard thought Easdale's poems over the years offered relief from other more important publications, perhaps they suspended critical judgment out of a sort of paternal loyalty to their onetime ingenue, perhaps Virginia's feminist sympathies were engaged in sponsoring Joan and giving her a room of her own through publication, or perhaps they even liked the poetry. Whatever the reasons, the appearance of Joan Easdale's poems amid the Hogarth Press poetry publications from 1931 to 1939 seems very odd indeed. None of the volumes earned profits.

C. H. B. Kitchin followed his successful crime novel of 1929 with an unsuccessful complex family chronicle, *The Sensitive One* (1931), his attempt at a big, conventional novel. It lost over £23 for Hogarth in the first year but sold surprisingly well in Germany (MSR). The Curtis Brown agency reported to Leonard Woolf that the novel had sold over 2,346 copies of the Albatross Verlag edition of 1934 (HP 219). Quite different in quality and success was the other Hogarth Press novel in February 1931, John Hampson's *Saturday Night at the Greyhound*.

"We have discovered a good novelist, homosexual, a waiter, I think, in Cardiff; but he wont help—his rags will further diminish our hoard" (*Letters* 4:221). So wrote Virginia Woolf to Hugh Walpole in September 1930, convinced that the novelist's book would fail and erode their "nice heap of gold," the profits earned by Vita Sackville-West's best-selling *The*

Edwardians (1930). She need not have worried. John Hampson's *Saturday Night at the Greyhound*, published in February 1931, quickly sold out the initial printing of 1,000 copies and within six months had gone into two more impressions and sold 2,913 copies (MSR). Its popularity continued into a Penquin edition published by Allen Lane in 1937 and a Century Library edition by Spottiswoode in 1950.

The success of *Saturday Night at the Greyhound* was no less remarkable than the life story of its author. John Hampson Simpson, no longer a Cardiff waiter, had found employment and hospitality in the home of the prosperous Wilson family at Four Ashes, Warwickshire, where he served as nurse-companion to the son, Ronald Wilson, apparently a victim of Down's syndrome.[7] The Wilsons treated Hampson as a favorite son and extended their generosity to his visiting friends who soon included writers Forrest Reid, William Plomer, E. M. Forster, and Walter Allen. Self-educated and barely self-supported, Hampson had drifted through a number of kitchen, pub, and hotel jobs, had served a sentence in Wormwood Scrubs for book theft, and thus by hook or by crook had managed to survive until the Wilsons found him around 1925. Fear of his prison record or unhappy family memories may have led him to use Hampson as his pen name rather than his surname, Simpson.

An obsessive reader and a seriously committed writer, Hampson lived through his books and his circle of writing friends. Virginia Woolf described him in a 1931 letter as "most curious—ravaged, exhausted . . . —but so shy its difficult to catch him" (*Letters* 4:347). Over the years he generously supported young writers like Leslie Halward and Walter Allen, forming with them the Birmingham Group of working-class writers.

Hampson dedicated *Saturday Night at the Greyhound* to Forrest Reid, the Ulster novelist and longtime friend of E. M. Forster, but it was probably William Plomer who suggested the Woolfs and the Hogarth Press as a publisher after several others had rejected his manuscripts. Hampson seems to have sent three manuscripts to the Woolfs to read, and Leonard, with his usual acumen, saw that the second one, *Saturday Night*, would be better as a starter than the other longer novel, *O Providence*, which the Woolfs both thought was "much the better book" (HP 153). They would publish it the next year. They rejected the first manuscript, a novel about homosexuals, "Go Seek a Stranger."

The chief attraction of *Saturday Night at the Greyhound* was the convincingly realistic depiction of life behind the scenes of a village inn in the industrial midlands. It was an uncharted literary landscape, and Hampson handled plot, characterization, and local color skillfully in depicting the ruination of the Greyhound's drunken owner Fred Flack, who gambles away the night's profit and brings about the closing of the inn.

When William Plomer wrote to the Woolfs that he liked the advance copy of *Saturday Night at the Greyhound*, Virginia replied with pleasure, adding that "I still think his first purely sodomitic novel was best" (*Letters* 4:270). The Woolfs published *O Providence* next, which they also preferred to *Saturday Night*, but only after Hampson had rewritten parts of it at Leonard Woolf's suggestion. In spite of the Woolf's judgment, *O Providence* did not match the popularity of *Saturday Night at the Greyhound* and was not reprinted. It started well, however, selling 1,111 copies in the first six months, but only a few after that (MSR).

After his first two novels, John Hampson never repeated his original success with Hogarth Press. Although he submitted his next two novels to the Woolfs, they were rejected. Virginia Woolf recorded in January 1933, "Hampson's new novel is so bad we are going to advise against publishing it," and later in October, apparently after a revision, she noted that she had "Hampson to read" (*Diary* 4:142, 186). The Autumn Book Supplement to the *New Statesman and Nation* on October 14, 1933, announcing forthcoming books, listed Hampson's "Foreign English" to be published by the Hogarth Press. It was not published, however, and became one of the Hogarth ghosts. Hampson published his next novel, *Strip Jack Naked*, with Heinemann in 1934.

No contrast could be greater than to juxtapose Joan Easdale's first volume of poetry with the poetic prose of Rilke's *Notebook of Malte Laurids Brigge*, released simultaneously in February 1931. With the publication of John Linton's translation of Rilke, the Hogarth Press issued the first translation in England of Rilke's prose masterpiece, one of the most influential of modern texts, and began what would be a ten-year commitment to the translations of Germany's greatest modern poet. No wonder that John Lehmann, present for the birth of the first Rilke translations in England, should, like so many young poets of his generation, be inspired by Rilke's *Brigge*. He spent his first autumn after leaving the press in 1932 in

Vienna, he wrote, "trying to learn to be the poet that Rilke had ideally imagined."[8]

When Rilke died in 1926, only a handful of his poems had been published in English. The most active early translator of Rilke was B. J. Morse, whose translations of *Ten Poems*, *Two Duino Elegies*, and *The Story of the Love and Death of Cornet Christopher Rilke* appeared in Trieste and Osnabrück in 1926–27. At his death Rilke was a coterie interest in England and America, but his admirers lacked adequate translations. In Germany there was no single authoritative text until the Insel-Verlag of Leipzig published the six-volume *Collected Poetry* from 1930 to 1934. The availability of these excellent texts prompted the English translations of the Hogarth Press.

John Linton wrote to Leonard Woolf in November 1929 explaining that he had obtained from the Insel-Verlag the option for a translation of *The Notebook*, a work he described as extraordinary, autobiographical, even pathological, but the work of a great lyric poet (HP 386). Linton added that the American publisher W. W. Norton had accepted his translation and was allowing him to secure an English publisher. An agreement was reached, a translation was settled on, and Leonard Woolf purchased sheets from W. W. Norton. The Hogarth Press then printed its own title page and bound the sheets. It was a procedure first adopted by Woolf the year before in 1928 when he purchased sheets, through the Curtis Brown agency, of Robinson Jeffers's *Roan Stallion, Tamar, and Other Poems*.

After questioning Linton closely about the accuracy of some of his translations, only the title of the book remained a difficulty for the painstaking and stubborn Woolf. Elling Aannestad, associate editor of W. W. Norton, had written to Woolf in January 1930 remarking that Linton's proposed title, *The Commonplace Book of Malte Laurids Brigge*, would not sell and wondering what title would do justice to such an unusual book (HP 386). He proposed instead *The Inner Life of M. L. B.*, which Woolf at first rejected. John Linton declared his preference for "Common-place" and rejected "private, personal, notes, papers, jottings, journal, etc." As alternatives, Linton offered "The Rebirth, New Birth, New Life, Hidden Life, Quest, Self-Unveiling, Inward Vision."

Leonard Woolf finally agreed to the Norton title, *The Inner Life*, as the best of the proposals but insisted that on the Hogarth Press title page it would appear as *The Inner Life or The Notebook of Malte Laurids Brigge*. Eventually, Woolf's preferred title, *The Notebook*, prevailed on the English edition. It was closest to the German *Die Aufzeichnungen* (literally the notes or jottings) and to the French translation by Maurice Betz entitled *Les Cahiers* (1926). The Hogarth Press title was always the singular *Notebook*. W. W. Norton finally dropped the "Inner Life" but published the American edition as *The Journal of My Other Self*, a radical departure from Rilke's title. When a new American translation by H. D. Herter Norton was published in 1949, the title became the now familiar plural *The Notebooks*.

In May the Woolfs published Vita Sackville-West's next novel, *All Passion Spent*, issued almost to the day one year after *The Edwardians*, and they immediately had another best-seller on their hands. It was to prove Sackville-West's finest novel. For the first time Sackville-West abandoned her usual romantic plot, her dashing, curiously adolescent heroes, and her great house, to focus on the last years of old Lady Slane, widowed at eighty-eight. Determined to live her own way after years of submission to the unconscious tyranny of her diplomat husband and greedy, over-controlling children, Lady Slane simply does the unexpected. She sells her town house, gives many of her possessions to her grasping children and grandchildren, and rents an unprepossessing house in Hampstead.

What makes *All Passion Spent* especially interesting is how Sackville-West reveals character through the workings of Lady Slane's mind. Musing through the long afternoons, the old lady reviews her life in a series of internal monologues. She comes, most poignantly, to know herself in her many roles—the young girl, the aspiring artist, the increasingly circumscribed, frustrated, and bored diplomat's wife, the mother whose functions become her identity. As she dies, Lady Slane defies conventions once more and supports her rebellious great-granddaughter Deborah, an aspiring artist set on a career in music after breaking off a socially acceptable engagement. *All Passion Spent* suggests the inspiration of Virginia Woolf in its subjective narrative technique and in its feminist theme. Virginia liked *All Passion Spent* "a great deal better than the Edwardians," she wrote to Margaret Llewelyn Davies shortly after publication (*Letters* 4:341). The reading public liked it also, generating sales of over

14,000 copies in the first six months and over 1,000 copies the next six months (MSR).

Vita Sackville-West and her husband Harold Nicolson purchased Sissinghurst Castle in May 1930 at the time she began to reap the considerable rewards of *The Edwardians*, published that month, and plunged into the enormous job of salvaging the half-ruined buildings and laying out what would become a world-famous garden in Kent. Vita signaled her immersion into the past history of Sissinghurst and her total identification with the Tudor buildings by immediately writing an eighty-six-line poem, "Sissinghurst," dedicated in epistolary fashion to Virginia: "Sissinghurst, Thursday, To V. W." It was her acknowledgment of Virginia's *Orlando*, perhaps, but there are no allusions to Virginia, only meditations on time, history, and rural cycles.

Virginia liked it immediately when she saw it in typescript in November 1930 and asked to publish it at the press. She thought it "a nice, good poem," she wrote to Vita, and praised its "suavity and ease . . . its timelessness and shade" (*Letters* 4:256). Leonard and Virginia began to hand set and print the poem in May 1931, five and a half months after Virginia had first seen it (HP 426). Leonard thought that the dedication to Virginia should be left off the title page, Vita agreed, and the printing proceeded. Five hundred numbered copies were printed and then autographed by Vita, who after laboring to sign the numbered sheets and five extras, wrote to Leonard that she never wanted to see her name again. The beautifully printed poem sold for five shillings when released in July. It was one of the last three volumes of poetry the Woolfs would ever print by hand.

The best poetry for the year at the Hogarth Press was not Vita's *Sissinghurst*, however, but Cecil Day-Lewis's second press volume, *From Feathers to Iron*. Over a seven-year period from 1929 to 1936, Day-Lewis would publish six volumes of poetry and a pamphlet at Hogarth, and then a volume of selected poems in 1940. He became one of the most published of the Hogarth poets, and one of the most distinguished.

C. Day-Lewis had published two slender volumes of traditional verse with a slightly Georgian pastoral lyricism (*Beechen Vigil*, 1925, and *Country Comets*, 1928), had coedited *Oxford Poetry 1927* with W. H. Auden, had begun schoolmastering at Larchfield School, and had recently married when he sent his long *Transitional Poem* to Leonard Woolf in early 1929. Faber & Faber had rejected it, and so Day-Lewis became "deliriously . . . happy," he recalled, when Leonard Woolf accepted the poem for the Hogarth Press.[9] Woolf had written in March that he liked the poem, adding, "It is a remarkable piece of work, though I do not think it will have what publishers call 'a wide appeal'" (HP 253). Dorothy Wellesley had agreed to accept it, and so Leonard published the seventy-one-page poem in the Living Poets series in October 1929, issuing it in 400 copies.

Although Woolf was right about *Transitional Poem* and its appeal (it sold only ninety-seven copies in the first six months [MSR]), what he could not know at the time was that it was a breakthrough poem for Day-Lewis and the poets of the 1930s who were to become the "Auden Group." The poem was transitional in several ways, tracing Day-Lewis's personal and private development into maturity, while debating the eternal antinomies of thought and action, intellect and imagination, love and lust, religious faith and scientific fact. Among these traditional subjects for a young poet, as Samuel Hynes has pointed out, there was the problem of private experience in conflict with public experience, the continuing challenge for the thirties writers.[10] Amusingly, Day-Lewis's headmaster at Cheltenham Junior School, where he was teaching when the poem appeared, thought the verses excessively sexual and embarrassing, too private for public consumption.[11]

Although the versification, much of the imagery, and the subjects of *Transitional Poem* remained conventional, Day-Lewis began to develop the diction and imagery that would become the standards for other young poets of the day. There was the cryptic presence of Rex Warner ("the hawk-faced man") and W. H. Auden ("the tow-haired poet," "thought's companion").[12] *Transitional Poem* began the mythology of the group.

Day-Lewis's next long sequence poem, *From Feathers to Iron* (1931), his second for Hogarth, traced in twenty-nine sections and an epilogue the experiences of a young father through the gestation and birth of his first son. *Transitional Poem* had been dedicated to Rex Warner. *From Feathers to Iron* was dedicated appropriately "To the Mother," to Day-Lewis's wife May whose childbearing and baby are paralleled to the cycle of the seasons and the rural landscape. In spite of the private subject matter, the poem seemed to Michael Roberts, spokesman for the 1930s, to be a landmark achievement on the order of *Leaves of Grass* or *The Waste Land* because its modern images and metaphors communicated a sense of participation in the contemporary social life.[13] Day-Lewis began his poem with epigraphs from Auden and Keats and concluded with an epilogue "Letter to W. H. Auden," employing in between the images of rails, power lines, engines, dynamite, mines, mountains, and frontier that were so much a part of Auden's northern and industrial landscapes. The public settings for private experience, rather than political content, characterized the early thirties modernism of Day-Lewis's poem.

When he sent *From Feathers to Iron* to the Hogarth Press, Day-Lewis corresponded with John Lehmann, who addressed him as Mr. Lewis. Only later would John and Cecil come to a first-name basis, the Oxford Day-Lewis being three years older than the Cambridge Lehmann. Acting for the press in July 1931, Lehmann offered Day-Lewis publication in the Living Poets series and 10 percent royalty on all copies sold (HP 246). Day-Lewis accepted the offer on July 21, but he wanted to wait until the child had been born to complete the sequence with a twenty-ninth poem. Lehmann gave him a deadline of August 8 for the last poem. Sean Day-Lewis (expected on July 28) cooperated by being born on August 3, and the poet-father completed the sequence with a twenty-ninth poem which celebrated, "Come out in the sun, for a man is born today!" The son so born, making his first deadline, fulfilled his advance billing by becoming a writer and the skilled biographer of his father.[14] *From Feathers to Iron* appeared in September 1931 in 400 copies, but it fared better than *Transitional Poem*. Leonard Woolf had a second impression of 200 copies printed ten months later.

By September 1931 John Lehmann had seven months' experience as manager under his belt, and as with Day-Lewis's book, he had begun to make decisions and issue contracts, albeit with Leonard Woolf at his shoulder. He saw his own volume of poems, *A Garden Revisited and Other Poems*, into print and supervised the publication of the novel *Sado*, William Plomer's sixth press book and his second novel.

The peripatetic Plomer by this time had settled in England after a trans-Siberian trip from Japan and had dined with the Woolfs and spent a weekend at Monks House, quickly becoming a fringe member of Bloomsbury. Summing him up after the weekend visit, Virginia Woolf described Plomer as "a compressed inarticulate young man, thickly coated with a universal manner fit for all weather & people: tells a nice dry prim story; but has the wild eyes which I once noted in Tom [Eliot], & take to be the true index of what goes on within" (*Diary* 3:242). For the young Plomer, his growing friendship with the Woolfs and the evenings at Tavistock Square and weekends at Monks House where he met the luminaries of Bloomsbury proved to be as important to him as any experience in his life. Moreover, Leonard Woolf assisted Plomer by giving him books to review in the *Nation and Athenaeum*.

When Plomer published *Sado* with the press in 1931, nearly two years after the stories of *Paper Houses*, he returned to Japanese subject matter. The unusual lapsed time between volumes of fiction for the ever-productive Plomer can be explained partly by his travels and the task of settling into English life and partly by the sensitive subject matter of the novel. An intimate and revealing account of an Englishman's homoerotic relationship with a Japanese college student, *Sado* was Plomer's most obviously personal writing to date. It was based on his relationship with Morito Fukuzawa, the model for Sado. As Virginia noted in early February 1931, "William P. [Plomer] talked more of his new novel, the Autobiography or Experiences? of an Emigrant the other night than L. has talked of his books all his life" (*Diary* 4:8).

The first version of *Sado* ran to some 170,000 words, as Plomer wrote to Woolf in February, but he soon boiled it down to half that length (HP 349). He sent the revised typescript to the Woolfs two months later just as they returned to London after driving through western France for two weeks on their annual outing. Refreshed from their trip, the Woolfs read Plomer's novel immediately, Leonard writing to him five days later on Friday that both he and Virginia liked the book very much. They were struck by Plomer's writing and his psychological insights, finding the theme "extraordinarily interesting" and the prose less uneven than his previous writing, with "fewer, if any, air pockets" (HP 349). With the publication of *Sado*, Plomer reached maturity as a writer. Leonard had over 1,500 copies of the novel printed and issued with a handsomely stylized dust jacket in white and blue designed by John Armstrong. In spite of its promising send-off, *Sado* disappointed by selling only 837 copies the first six months and by going in the red over £64 in the first year (MSR).

In October the Woolfs published the translation of Rilke's *Duineser Elegien: Elegies from the Castle of Duino* by Vita Sackville-West and her cousin Edward Sackville-West which had been beautifully and elaborately printed for them by Count Harry Kessler at his Cranach Press. It was the Woolf's only excursion into fine printing and their most expensive product, the 134-page book selling for three guineas, but they actually had little to do with its production and ran no financial risk in the arrangement with Kessler and the Sackville-Wests.

After a publishing year of such highs as Rilke's *Notebook of Malte Laurids Brigge*, Day-Lewis's *From Feathers to Iron*, and the heady sales of Hampson's *Saturday Night at the Greyhound* and Sackville-West's *All Passion Spent*, it was appropriate that the Woolfs closed out the autumn season with two of their most important works: Virginia's novel *The Waves* and Leonard's massive political-historical study *After the Deluge*. If Leonard was disappointed with the reviews of his opus, eleven years in the making, and depressed by slow sales, Virginia was surprised by favorable reviews and solid sales of her most difficult novel.

The genesis of Virginia Woolf's seventh novel, *The Waves* (originally titled "The Moths"), probably occurred in September 1926 when she was finishing *To the Lighthouse*. On September 28 she recorded a mystical vision, exciting and frightening, of solitude in the face of the universe ("one sees a fin passing far out") (*Diary* 3:113). The idea then took impetus from Vanessa's description in May 1927 of capturing a huge moth one night at Cassis, and Virginia first recorded it in June 1927 when she mentioned a "play-poem idea" to be called "the Moths" involving a continuous flow of consciousness and description (ibid., 139). Through the labyrinths of her mind, the ideas grew in time until she began to write on July 2, 1929.

She finished the first version of the novel on April 29, 1930, and struggled through an extensive rewriting during an emotionally and physically exhausting summer and autumn. Not until February 7, 1931, could she record the glorious moment in which she had completed the second version: "I wrote the words O Death fifteen minutes ago, having reeled across the last ten pages with some moments of such intensity &

intoxication that I seemed only to stumble after my own voice, or almost, after some sort of speaker (as when I was mad)" (ibid., 4:10). She added, "I mean that I have netted that fin in the waste of waters which appeared to me over the marshes out of my window at Rodmell when I was coming to an end of To the Lighthouse."

Then came her usual grinding period of retyping and final polishing before the typescript was ready for Leonard to read. She recorded the end of her revision on July 17, 1931, noting that "for the 18th time" she had copied out the opening sentences (Diary 4:35). She gave it to Leonard the next day. Leonard read the typescript rapidly and reported two days later on Sunday morning his judgment that in spite of an extremely difficult first 100 pages, the novel was "the best of your books" (ibid., 36). He worried, however, about the average reader's ability to follow the text. He had praised it, nevertheless, and Virginia was so relieved by Leonard's words that she plunged off jubilantly for a walk in the rain.

Virginia Woolf's manner of writing, rewriting, and editing the text of a novel for publication seldom varied during her life and distinguished her as one of the most careful stylists among modern writers. Her diary is full of self-admonitions about her writing. She was her own severest critic and kept a cold eye cocked at what she saw as her weaknesses. Whether or not she actually rewrote the opening of The Waves eighteen times, there is evidence for at least six extensive rewrites. The labors to refine her fleeting vision into The Waves, her attempts to net the fin in the water, can be traced through the skillful editing of J. W. Graham who has meticulously reproduced the two existing holograph copies of the novel.[15] Woolf's way with The Waves suggests, by extension, the way she wrote her other novels.

Customarily, Virginia Woolf composed in longhand, writing in ink with an old-fashioned straight pen on the right-hand page of a manuscript book bound for her by the press. She reworked each page as she went, writing for two hours or more in the mornings. In the afternoons she would type up the morning's work, usually making only minor corrections or changes. When she had completed the first draft of the novel, represented by a holograph and a slightly edited typescript, she would then retype the book from the beginning, making whatever revisions she felt necessary, sometimes scrapping whole sections and rewriting them in markedly different ways. The final shaping of the book took place in this stage. The resulting typescript, probably bearing the marks of further revisions in ink, was given to Leonard for his critical reading. After this, Virginia would sometimes, as she did with *The Waves*, have a press secretary retype the text into a copy which she corrected for errors before sending it to R. & R. Clark to be set and printed. At some point either after the proofs were corrected or after each book was published, Virginia would destroy her typescripts, saving only the holograph copy, probably feeling, as Graham has argued, that it best represented her initial creative impulses and so was important to keep as a record of her artistic struggles. *The Waves*, however, is unique among her novels because she completely rewrote it from scratch, starting over with a new holograph version and resulting typescript. The two existing holographs, edited by Graham, total 399 and 347 pages respectively.

A carbon copy of the final typescript of *The Waves* was sent off to R. & R. Clark in Edinburgh after a heart-stopping period when the master copy seemed lost. The managing director of R. & R. Clark, with the kind of attention to detail that endeared him to the Woolfs, soon wrote back to Leonard in July 1931 explaining that while he had allowed a half-inch space in the seven places indicated in the text by their directions to "leave larger space," he believed there were other places where there were distinct breaks in the narrative, perhaps requiring two kinds of space (HP 575). He sought clarification before putting the text into page proofs. Leonard, after going over the manuscript with Virginia, replied on July 27: "The book is not divided into chapters but is in nine sections with short interludes between each. We have arranged it so that each interlude and each section is to begin a new page and also, as you will see, that the interludes are to be printed in italics. In the cases where we have merely marked 'leave larger space,' it will be correct if you leave half an inch space" (HP 575). So the unusual book was set, the page proofs were sent to Virginia, who corrected them quickly (August 10–17) with few changes, and then the volume was published on October 8, 1931, in time for the autumn book season.

Advance copies of *The Waves* brought the usual mixed reactions, more pronounced this time because of the undeniably difficult style of the novel. Virginia Woolf gloomed over Hugh Walpole's reaction (he thought it "unreal" and couldn't finish it), was disappointed but not surprised that Dorothy Wellesley and Vita Sackville-West could neither like it nor grasp its meaning, was "flushed and flooded" with pleasure by John Lehmann's enthusiastic praise, and was pleased that Harold Nicolson thought it a masterpiece (*Diary* 4:43–48). The reviews, when they came, were unexpectedly sympathetic and supportive. The *TLS* reviewer in October 1931, for example, found *The Waves* "a piece of subtle, penetrating magic," a poemlike novel, with six characters whose "secret individuality" was effectively dramatized.[16] Odd, thought Virginia, that the "dear old Lit. Sup." should praise her characters "when I meant to have none" (*Diary* 4:47).

Arnold Bennett, Virginia Woolf's old duelist over characterization, did not live to see the ultimate development of her method in *The Waves*. He had died in March, but Frank Swinnerton in the October 3, 1931, *Evening News* carried on the fight for the opposition, admiring the beautiful poetic style but finding the characters bloodless, lifeless, and the book "not very interesting to read."[17] E. M. Forster's letter, when it came over a month after publication, filled her with more pleasure than any other she received. Forster wrote that he had "the sort of excitement over it which comes from believing that one's encountered a classic" (*Diary* 4:52).

Initial sales of *The Waves*, like the reviews, were remarkably good. It sold nearly 5,000 copies in the first week, requiring an early reprint; but then by October 17, as Woolf noted, sales had fallen to 50 or so copies a day. "What has happened," she wrote, "is that the library readers cant get through it & are sending their copies back" (*Diary* 4:49). They had expected, perhaps, another *Orlando* or *To the Lighthouse*. Nevertheless, two-and-a-half months later on January 1, 1932, Woolf noted that *The Waves* had sold 9,650 copies (ibid., 61). The monthly sales (Reading) account book confirms the figure, recording sales at the end of the first six months as 10,117 volumes but only 264 volumes sold in the next six months.

When John Lehmann began work in January 1931, Virginia Woolf was finishing her revision of *The Waves*, so that he assisted with the publication in October of one of her most important novels. But Lehmann's most significant achievement at the press was to bring together the young poets of his generation in the revolutionary anthology *New Signatures*

(1932) under the editorship of Michael Roberts. It was the first time that W. H. Auden, Stephen Spender, and C. Day-Lewis, charter members of the "Auden Generation," appeared together in print. The poems in *New Signatures* vigorously announced the arrival of a second generation of modernist poets on the Hogarth list. Thanks to Lehmann, the press was once more, if briefly, on the leading edge of modern poetry, a position not enjoyed since the Woolfs had hand printed Eliot's *Waste Land* in 1923. Although he would not be present to work it through the press, Lehmann helped prepare for a second volume after *New Signatures*, a book combining prose and poetry of a more avowedly leftist bent, *New Country* (1933).

"We plunged into talk about modern poetry at once, and I discovered that he had read all my contemporaries, and what was more had an idea that they belonged together more closely, in spite of the wide apparent differences, than I . . . had detected." [18] John Lehmann thus recalled his first meeting in the autumn of 1931 with Michael Roberts, to project an anthology of young poets. From the first, the publication evolved in Lehmann's mind as a significant substitute for another yearbook of Cambridge poetry, while for the more politicized Roberts it offered the chance to unite the best of Cambridge and Oxford in common cause against the poetry of the neo-Georgians and the first-generation modernists. Roberts and Lehmann soon agreed on which poets to include, and Lehmann sold the idea to Leonard and Virginia Woolf. Dorothy Wellesley approved in turn, so the anthology could appear in the Living Poets series. Only Julian Bell grumbled about appearing as a member of any group which included the Oxford poets Auden, Spender, and Day-Lewis.

The nine poets contributed forty-three poems, and Michael Roberts wrote a preface. The poets, arranged by Roberts in alphabetical order, were W. H. Auden (Oxford), Julian Bell (Cambridge), C. Day-Lewis (Oxford), Richard Eberhardt (an American at Cambridge), William Empson (Cambridge), John Lehmann (Cambridge), William Plomer (no university), Stephen Spender (Oxford), and A. S. J. Tessimond (no university). Auden and Spender had published in the Oxford magazines and Blackwell's annual anthologies, and each had published a volume of privately printed poems. Bell, Eberhardt, Empson, and Lehmann had published in the Cambridge magazines and in the Hogarth Press *Cambridge*

Poetry 1929; Bell and Lehmann had published in the 1930 edition. Plomer and Day-Lewis were Hogarth Press poets with two volumes apiece; Lehmann's first volume at the press was out; and Day-Lewis's third volume would soon follow. Only Tessimond was something of an outsider. A copywriter for a London advertising agency, he was a friend of Lehmann's and had published poems in the *Listener*, the *Adelphi*, and *This Quarter*.

New Signatures: Poems by Several Hands created a stir when it appeared in February 1932; but like much else about the thirties generation, time and nostalgia have made it seem more programmatic in retrospect than it was. John Lehmann, more than thirty years later, thought that "the little book was like a searchlight suddenly switched on to reveal that, without anyone noticing it, a group of skirmishers had been creeping up in a concerted movement of attack."[19] Stephen Spender, with *New Country* also in mind, thought the anthologies "revealed the existence of a new, for the most part socially conscious, group of young writers" who wrote about revolutionary change and the end of the old social order.[20] And Leonard Woolf called the book "that generation's manifesto" (*Downhill* 174).

The group concept as well as the manifesto came from Michael Roberts, whose preface claimed more unanimity and purpose among the poets than they could rightly muster. F. R. Leavis, redoubtable critic of the thirties poets, was the first to challenge the solidity of the enterprise. Scrutinizing the volume in 1933, he commented dryly on "the complete discrepancy between the preface (richly illustrative of the procreant wish) and the following contents, between sales-talk and goods."[21] He thought Roberts's dubious achievement was "to see any community among so heterogeneous an array of versifiers." Nevertheless, Roberts had brought together for the first time in one volume some of the best young poets of the 1930s and attempted to provide a context and rationale for their work.

The poems offered by the nine poets did not all match the portentous preface; nevertheless, they communicated an energy and contemporaneity missing in much of the dull traditional poetry of the time. The poems of Auden, Day-Lewis, and Spender were the most obviously political and in their exuberantly revolutionary ardor captured the attention of readers and gave *New Signatures* its reputation. If the work of these three poets was what Roberts had in mind when he formulated his group theory, the poems of Lehmann, Bell, Empson, Eberhart, and Plomer counterpointed with more traditionally personal and psychological themes. They were about love, sexual passion, and the struggle to unify the divided sensibility. In spite of divergent themes and styles, the poetry of *New Signatures* made a remarkable and unique collection. It gained an immediate audience for the talents of a new generation. Issued in 600 copies in February 1932, *New Signatures* sold 906 copies the first six months and a total of 1,143 for the year (MSR), rather remarkable for a volume of poetry. It was reprinted in March 1932 and, as it kept up a steady sales, again in 1934 and 1935.

John Lehmann, in addition to *New Signatures*, also brought Christopher Isherwood to the attention of the Woolfs and helped publish his second novel, *The Memorial*. Second novels are hard to write and hard to publish, and their rejections are more painful than those of the first novel. "Christopher's self-confidence was shaken," wrote Isherwood about himself, remembering Jonathan Cape's rejection of *The Memorial*.[22] Cape had published Isherwood's first novel, *All the Conspirators* (1928), and knew that in rejecting his second they risked losing him if he connected with another publisher. Lose him they did. Isherwood became one of the Woolf's most important authors when the Hogarth Press published *The Memorial* in 1932. John Lehmann officiated at the connection, which would last until 1940 and would result in the three Berlin books and Isherwood's encoded autobiography, *Lions and Shadows* (1938).

The way from Cape to Hogarth illustrates the Auden generation at work as it related to Bloomsbury. Isherwood had rewritten *The Memorial* several times, suffered Cape's rejection, enlisted the aid of the Curtis Brown agency, which itself struck out three times (Davies, Secker, and Duckworth rejected it), then gave it to his friend Stephen Spender, who took the manuscript to his friend John Lehmann at the Hogarth Press. Spender praised, Lehmann read, and the Woolfs were persuaded. Not, however, before the cautious Leonard Woolf obtained a copy of *All the Conspirators* to compare with *The Memorial*, and the nervous Isherwood asked Spender to encourage Lehmann and the Woolfs to disregard its faults.[23] John Lehmann wrote the acceptance letter to David Higham of Curtis Brown on September 1, 1931, and told Spender, who in turn told

Isherwood's mother Kathleen the next day so she could telegraph the good news to Isherwood in Berlin. The book was published in February 1932 (HP 196).

Not until August 1932 would Isherwood finally meet Lehmann, in his last month at the press, tightening the network of Auden-Spender-Isherwood-Day-Lewis-Lehmann, the *New Signatures-New Country* writers, through personal meetings. When Lehmann subsequently joined Isherwood in Berlin, he began to plan what would become his periodical *New Writing*, with a principal role for Isherwood.

Reviews of *The Memorial* were mixed, noticing the absence of plot but praising the subtlety of characterization. The novel failed to sell; only 328 copies were bought in the first six months, incurring a loss of £71.4.9 the first year (MSR). Isherwood, as he explained later in *Lions and Shadows*, had set out to write "an epic disguised as a drawing-room comedy." [24] It's no wonder the hybrid did not thrive, but at least the novel broke ground with the Woolfs, and Isherwood's next novel three years later would introduce his memorable cast of Berlin characters and be a critical and commercial success for the author and the Hogarth Press.

William Plomer published twice again with the press in 1932, one of his best collections of poems, *The Fivefold Screen*, and an enormously popular novel, *The Case Is Altered*. Plomer grouped the thirty-four poems in five sections like the screen of his title, turning back for subject matter to his life in South Africa and his travels in Greece, Russia, and Europe. *The Case Is Altered* became a popular success through Plomer's blending of penetrating character studies with a sensational crime of passion. When Leonard Woolf wrote to Plomer accepting the manuscript of the novel in February 1932, he reported that both he and Virginia thought the novel "extremely good," in parts even "brilliant" (HP 340). They especially admired Plomer's characterizations and his description of the murder.

Based on macabre and all-too-real events in his own rooming house in Bayswater, Plomer's novel depicts the mad and eventually murderous jealousy of Mr. Fernandez for his wife Beryl, the pretty, lively young landlady of the establishment. Plomer noted in his autobiography his fortunate weekend absence, which saved him from being a second victim of the husband's razor. [25] Although the crazed butchery of Beryl Fernandez by her husband in front of their small child is the shocking climax of the novel, it does not constitute the main interest in the book. Plomer's first English novel explores in depth the traditional subject of a respectable rooming house on its way down, but the most intense aspect of the novel is the thinly disguised homosexual relationship that develops between the Plomer-like hero, Eric Alston, and Willie Pascall, the extroverted, working-class brother of Alston's girlfriend Amy. It was Plomer's most overt statement of his sexual identity in fiction and went beyond the lyrical eroticism of *Sado*.

After arranging minor editorial changes in the manuscript with Plomer, Leonard Woolf turned over the production details of *The Case Is Altered* to John Lehmann. Lehmann steered the novel past an objection to the title by the publishing firm of Benn, which had used it in a ninepenny series, and placed a printing order for 1,500 copies with R. & R. Clark (HP 340). When Rupert Hart-Davis notified the Hogarth Press that the Book Society had selected the novel for the July choice, Lehmann negotiated for the press, agreeing to send 8,500 copies to the distributor Hazell Watson by June 30, 1932, in time for the July publication date (HP 340). The Book Society's selection ensured the success of Plomer's novel, and Lehmann placed a reprint order for 12,000 copies with R. & R. Clark in May upon receipt of the final arrangements from Davis. The novel sold 11,308 copies in the first six months (compared to 837 copies of *Sado*) and earned £796 the first year (MSR). *The Case Is Altered* dramatically changed Plomer's financial condition and made him, with Vita Sackville-West, one of the most popular Hogarth Press authors in the early 1930s.

The Case Is Altered was Plomer's eighth and last book published by Leonard and Virginia Woolf. Shortly thereafter, in 1933, Plomer took his next collection of short stories to Jonathan Cape; and upon the death of Edward Garnett in 1937, he accepted the position of Garnett's successor as reader and literary adviser to Cape. The remainder of his active literary career was linked with Cape, which published all his new work—four volumes of fiction, four collections of poetry, and his two-volume autobiography. The exception to this arrangement was one volume of *Selected Poems* published by the Hogarth Press under the aegis of John Lehmann in 1940.

William Plomer's career with the Hogarth Press and after illustrates the happy success of an energetic, gregarious, talented man of letters. His move from the Hogarth Press to Jonathan Cape was acceptable to both parties, and although Leonard was not happy to lose a best-selling author, the Woolfs remained close friends with him. The six years he had spent as one of the Woolf's authors had seen him rise from the obscurity of Zululand to the visibility of the London publishing establishment and a subsequent career as a prominent, well-liked man of letters.

Almost immediately after the publication of Lady Slane's swan song in *All Passion Spent*, Vita Sackville-West was at work on her third novel in three years. The years 1930–34 were among the busiest in Sackville-West's writing career, stabilized by the acquisition of Sissinghurst Castle and by Harold Nicolson's resignation from the Foreign Office. The uncertainties of Nicolson's journalistic and political future, however, and their need to support themselves and their two sons largely from their writing income required long hours at the typewriter. Unfortunately, the pressures on Sackville-West to publish did not result in better fiction.

"Old Vita shaggy & stiff, writing another novel; but as careless about it all as ever" (*Diary* 4:39). So Virginia Woolf saw Vita in mid-August 1931, as she composed *Family History*. Less than a year later it was finished, Vita delivering the manuscript in June 1932 and Virginia recording that the book was "said to be bad" (ibid., 112). Although partly a sequel to *The Edwardians* (two of the characters are seen thirty years later), *Family History* is bereft of the rich social fabric of the earlier novel and often dull. The book is not a Galsworthian family saga in spite of the title. Rather, it seems designed to please readers of lending-library romances, focusing on the doomed love affair of the beautiful widow Evelyn Jarrold, forty years old (Vita's age), and the dashing twenty-five-year old Miles Vane-Merrick. He lives splendidly alone in a ruined castle in Kent, the spitting image of Sissinghurst shortly after the Nicolsons bought it.

To the uncertainties of characterization and plot in *Family History*, Vita Sackville-West added the peculiar burden of eccentric orthography. She explained in a preface that she had "spelt the word 'that' in two different ways: either with one 't' or with two, in order to differentiate between the conjunction and the demonstrative adjective and demonstrative or relative pronoun."[26] She admitted that such an innovation might irritate readers, but her concern was for clarity. One wonders what Sackville-West's romance readers made of the double *t*s, not to mention the Scottish typesetters at R. & R. Clark. Strange that Sackville-West should have succumbed to a reformer's zeal in such a novel, and stranger still that Leonard Woolf should have permitted the intrusive spelling.

Nevertheless, advance sales of 6,000 copies before publication on October 13, 1932, were excellent. If not the success of *All Passion Spent*, *Family History* nevertheless made money. "Oh Lord what it is to publish a best seller," wrote Virginia to Vita, her fingers sore from tying up parcels of books. "But its been great fun" (*Letters* 5:110).

Through 1932, with John Lehmann's help, the Woolfs had published their first of Christopher Isherwood's novels (*The Memorial*), their last of William Plomer's (*The Case Is Altered*), a big novel by Vita Sackville-West (*Family History*), and two more novels by authors with Cambridge connections, Bonamy Dobrée's *St. Martin's Summer* (1932) and Julia Strachey's *Cheerful Weather for the Wedding* (1932). Bonamy Dobrée's novel sank out of sight, but Julia Strachey's brisk little book has become a minor classic. It proved to be a good year for Hogarth Press fiction, and typically diverse. The novels share little in the way of style and content, although their authors enjoyed varying degrees of intimacy with the Woolfs and Bloomsbury.

Julia Strachey, the niece of Lytton, seems to have inherited his satirical eye and judicious style while belonging to an entirely different generation. *Cheerful Weather for the Wedding*, a novella in length, chronicles the few hours but intensely comic and multifarious events leading to Dolly Thatcham's marriage to the Honorable Owen Bigham. Much of Strachey's broad humor is based on solid precedents and situations. What saves this engaging comedy of manners from rollicking cliché is the astringent satire. Clear-eyed Dolly, a modern girl surely of the Cambridge mold, regrets having to marry the dully respectable Bigham (a diplomat to South America) and wishes that Joseph (her rejected suitor) would take her away. But Joseph, an intense, woolly-headed anthropologist, is too slow to comprehend what Dolly has in mind. In the meantime, Dolly tipples rum in her room as consolation and spills ink on her dress.

Cheerful Weather for the Wedding failed to generate very serious reviews when it appeared, either being passed over completely or treated to a brief paragraph in the October 20 issue of the *TLS* where the chief point was about the comic quarrel between Dolly's young brothers over green socks. Leonard Woolf fumed, writing to Julia Strachey that the reviewers had been stupid and that he had never known them "to deal so idiotically with a book" (HP 473). He enlisted David ("Bunny") Garnett to write a more balanced review in the November 4 issue of the *Spectator*; Garnett praised Strachey's rich humor and hailed her as a new and important talent. Moreover, Garnett's father, Edward, used his connections with the Viking Press to get them to pick up the American rights. Bunny Garnett then wrote another favorable review for the American edition in the February 11, 1933, issue of the *Saturday Review of Literature*. Duncan Grant designed the dust jacket for the novel. So the Cambridge-Bloomsbury network once went into action to advance the work of one of its own.

Julia Strachey's cheerful satire, however, eventually outgrew its early dependence on Bloomsbury patronage. After losing £11.6.8 in its first year of sales, the novel earned a modest profit of over £14.4.6 the next year and gradually gained a measure of popularity (MSR). In 1950 John Lehmann reprinted it in the Holiday Library for his own publishing house and put it into a second printing a year later. Strachey's only other novel, *The Man on the Pier*, was also published by Lehmann in 1951; more recently, Penguin has republished the two short novels together in one volume as a Modern Classic, changing the title of the second novel to *An Integrated Man*.

In addition to presiding over the creation of *New Signatures* and the discovery of Christopher Isherwood, John Lehmann during his first stint at Tavistock Square also could claim credit for suggesting a new Hogarth series, the seventh one begun by Leonard and Virginia Woolf. "The Hogarth Letters series," wrote Lehmann, "was one of the 'swarm of new ideas' that the three of us planned so eagerly in the first few weeks of my apprenticeship: little booklets in paper covers of six or seven thousand words in length, on all topics of the day." [27] The daily topics for Leonard and for writers of Lehmann's generation in the early 1930s were often political. As Hermione Lee has observed, "the public *Hogarth Letters* were from the first as much involved with the politics of the moment as with the future of English culture." [28] The first three letter writers in 1931, however, were E. M. Forster, Viscount Cecil, and Rosamond Lehmann, the novelist sister of John. The next year, the press published eight more Letters, but the most important of them, directly stimulated by Lehmann, was Virginia Woolf's *Letter to a Young Poet*. Lehmann, the young poet addressed, was off to Germany when the booklet appeared in July 1932.

Virginia Woolf, busy writing her lighthearted, lightweight biography of Elizabeth Barrett and Robert Browning's cocker spaniel Flush, had no novel ready for the press in 1932, but she assembled another collection of her essays as *The Common Reader: Second Series* and published the book in October. Before that, however, she had written and published in the summer *A Letter to a Young Poet*, a breezy epistle to John Lehmann and his generation, setting out her disenchantment with what she saw as the paralyzing self-absorption of the young poets and their unassimilated gritty modern subject matter of bicycles, buses, and cabbages.

John Lehmann had invited Virginia in September 1931 to contribute a "letter" on modern poetry to the new Hogarth Letters series. She had responded enthusiastically: "I think your idea of a Letter most brilliant—To a Young Poet? because I'm seething with immature and ill considered and wild and annoying ideas about prose and poetry. [She was writing *The Waves*.] So lend me your name . . . and then I'll pour forth all I can think of about you young, and we old, and novels—how damned they are—and poetry, how dead. But I must take a look into the subject . . . I must read Auden, whom I've not read, and Spender" (*Letters* 4:381). She proposed that he reply with a letter to an old novelist and that they should get Auden, Spender, and Day-Lewis to join the epistolary debate. Nothing came of the half-serious proposal to engage the Auden group in the project. In the meantime, the Lehmann-Roberts *New Signatures* volume had been published in February 1933, so that Virginia's letter in July critiqued that publication. Lehmann did not respond in print to Virginia with his own "letter," but he had some pointed commentary to make in private letters to the "old novelist," disputing her interpretation of his generation of poets. Only Peter Quennell, of the right age but of the wrong movement, offered a rejoinder in his *Letter to Mrs. Virginia Woolf* published by the press in October 1932. He missed most of the key points.

Through John Lehmann's first twelve months at the press, the Woolfs and he were delighted with each other. "Volumes pour hourly, daily, into the Press," Virginia Woolf wrote to Dadie Rylands in November 1931, "and there dear John, whom I love, sits like Prince Consort on the Albert Memorial, which seems to imply that I'm Queen Victoria. But I'm not, am I?" (*Letters* 4:403). By January 1932 Lehmann was laboring "nervously," Woolf recorded; he felt jaded and wanted a week off (*Diary* 4:63). He also wanted to be a manager and not a partner. And by February 1932, one month after his first anniversary at the press, Virginia Woolf noted that Lehmann was "fractious & irritable" (ibid. 78). In May, Virginia thought that Lehmann had an odd mixture of "emotionalism & grasping." He was "hard as nails, & then quivering" (ibid., 102). Lehmann, in turn, found Leonard Woolf getting on his nerves with his "emotional attitude towards the Press" and with his "repeated invasions of the office, anxious examinations of work being done, nagging tirades and unnecessary alarms and impatience."[29]

Leonard Woolf and John Lehmann attempted to negotiate a new arrangement which would go into effect when the original eighteen-month agreement ended. Lehmann expressed his frustration over the time-consuming hours at the press when he wanted more time for his own writing. His first proposal to Leonard would have cut nearly an hour off his daily stint (finishing the day at 4:15 P.M.), would have increased his vacation to eight weeks and his salary by £50 per year (to £300 in addition to the 10 percent of the profits), and would have provided him with the studio-storeroom Virginia used for his own writing.[30] Leonard wrote in May 1932 that he could agree to the new hours and the salary and might "sacrifice Virginia and give you the studio," but he could not agree to the long vacation. Moreover, he thought any such arrangement would only be temporary. "The whole thing has been a considerable shock or surprise to me," Leonard concluded, "to find I had completely misunderstood your attitude toward the work, etc."

A month later, in June, they worked out a radical new contract to go into effect on September 1, 1932. John Lehmann would work not more than two hours a day at the press. His duties would be "managerial, general supervision, and book production," together with the preparation of advertisements, the preliminary reading of manuscripts, and the ongoing search for "promising authors."[31] For these services, nearly the entire range of a publisher's work crammed somehow into two hours a day, Lehmann was to receive 10 percent of the press profits paid as a monthly advance of £16.13.4, or a minimum of £200 per year.

At the last minute, without warning or a word spoken to Leonard, Lehmann decided against accepting the agreement, wrote a farewell letter, and decamped, terminating his contract on August 31, 1932. Prince Albert left, and the Woolfs were not amused. "L. says he will send no answer," Virginia noted. "What could one say indeed? What a blessing! That egotistical young man with all his jealousies & vanities & ambitions, his weakness & changeableness is no loss" (*Diary* 4:123). To Rosamond Lehmann, who knew nothing of the break, Leonard wrote that her brother's behavior seemed "so either outrageous or childish" that he had decided to have nothing more to do with him.[32]

But for all the tensions his presence had engendered, Lehmann had been a valuable manager of the press, energizing the Woolfs, helping to expand the offerings back up to thirty-five volumes in 1931, and thirty-six in 1932, nearly equaling the production levels of 1927–28, and bringing in the exciting new writers of the 1930s. He would be missed. Not again in Virginia Woolf's lifetime would the press be so active and exciting.

Eight months after leaving, John Lehmann coolly wrote to Leonard Woolf in April 1933 asking for his 10 percent of the profits due him when he quit. The request provided Leonard with the opportunity to express his outrage in fine fashion and to give revealing data on the press accounts in passing. At first, wrote Leonard, he had decided that Lehmann had no legal right to share in the profits because of the suddenness of his departure. He added: "Your behavior was extremely inconsiderate, childish, and contemptible, but that in itself is a reason why I should now feel a strong distaste to entering into a controversy with you on the subject of money, especially since that you should behave badly to us was not unexpected and I cannot therefore pretend that my annoyance was anything more than temporary."[33] After this convoluted but satisfying exposition, Leonard agreed to send him his share. Three days later he had worked it out at the rate of five-twelfths of 10 percent and dispatched a check for £73.12.4 to Lehmann. The gross profits had been £3,627.12.11, Leonard wrote to Lehmann, and the losses had been £766.5.6½.[34] After salaries, rent, and other expenses were deducted, and the bonuses of £60 the press had paid to the employees, the profit was £1,766.16.5. It was on this amount that Leonard calculated Lehmann's share. The final profit for the press, deducting Lehmann's check, totaled £1,693.4.1.

The award of bonus money and the size of the net profit testify to the financial success of the press in 1932. It had also been a remarkably successful year for Virginia Woolf, who earned £2,531 from her books, giving the Woolfs a combined net income of over £4,000 (*Downhill* 142). Not again would they personally earn as much before the Second World War. After 1933, another good year, the Hogarth Press final profits would drop each year, reaching a low point of £81.5 after bonuses in 1936 and then soaring to a record high of £2,442.18.5 after bonuses in 1937. (See Appendix B.)

After Lehmann left, the press eased into the economic depression and leftist politics of the 1930s, sliding off to an average of twenty-one titles a year, meticulously if sometimes hectically managed by Leonard Woolf and a series of women office managers. Lehmann's position would be unfilled until he himself returned to the press in 1938. Friendly relations were restored in 1935, however, after Lehmann wrote Virginia Woolf a flattering and penetrating analysis of *The Waves*, and they had him to a "reconciliation" dinner in August (*Diary* 4:333).

CHAPTER SIX

★

PAMPHLETS AND POLITICS

C iting his credentials to judge the quality of political and historical writing, Leonard Woolf described himself as "a civil servant, an editor of journals dealing with the theory and practice of politics, and a publisher who specialized to some extent in the publication of political books" (*Downhill* 221). That Leonard Woolf and the Hogarth Press specialized in publications on political subjects may surprise some admirers of literary Bloomsbury, but Duncan Wilson's political biography of Woolf and Frederic Spotts's edition of his letters should lay to rest any misconceptions about the narrowness of Woolf's life. The political nature of the Hogarth Press, however, remains less well documented.

Undoubtedly the novels of Virginia Woolf gave the press its most important identity. The array of published poetry, fiction, and translation further added to its luster. But the range and importance of press publications extend beyond the fields of literature, art, and biography associated primarily with Virginia into the worldly affairs associated with Leonard. Such a dichotomy is oversimple, of course. Leonard was a successful novelist, short-story writer, and literary editor with proven experience. Virginia, although characteristically not interested in party politics, involved herself in the Co-operative movement, lectured to groups of working-class men and women, and directly entered the arena of gender politics with her two books *A Room of One's Own* and *Three Guineas*. The development of the Hogarth Press into areas quite distinct from the literary or cultural, however, is attributable solely to Leonard Woolf, underscores his political and social interests, and marks the press in this respect as more his creation than Virginia's.

Numbers are revealing. For the first six years of its existence (1917–23), the Hogarth Press published works of literature almost exclusively—a few volumes annually of poetry, fiction, memoirs, letters, or translations. In 1924, however, as the Woolfs expanded and diversified the press offerings and began publishing Freud and the International Psycho-Analytical Library, Leonard published Norman Leys's *Kenya*. To that first volume on British colonialism, Woolf gradually added more political volumes each year, so that by the late 1920s and early 1930s they totaled from one-fifth to one-fourth of the annual press output. From 1933 to 1936, in the heart of the politicized thirties, the number of books of poetry and prose dropped, total press output leveled off at between twenty-one and twenty-four volumes per year, and the political books outnumbered the literary.

Names, when added to the numbers, suggest the range and importance of the Hogarth publications in Leonard Woolf's area of interest. Among the writers enlisted by Woolf were such well-known figures as John Maynard Keynes, H. G. Wells, Harold Laski, G. D. H. Cole, Philip Noel-Baker, Maurice Dobb, Kingsley Martin, Arthur Ponsonby, and H. N. Brailsford. Woolf offered these writers, most of them well established at the time, the opportunity to publish monographs on specialized topics not easily placed with their regular publishers. He accommodated them through his series of inexpensive pamphlets and books titled the Hogarth Essays, the Hogarth Lectures, the Day to Day Pamphlets, the Hogarth Letters, and the World-Makers and World-Shakers. Many of Woolf's own political works were published by the press in these pamphlets as well as in hardcover books, including the three volumes of his magnus opus on communal psychology and politics, *After the Deluge*. Woolf's writing, his career in politics with the Fabian Society and the Labour party, and his editorship of the *Political Quarterly* (1931–59), all contributed to his direction of the Hogarth Press as it expanded into international and domestic affairs.

Leonard Woolf served the Labour party as secretary of two important advisory committees from their beginnings: the Committee on International Questions (1918) and the Committee on Imperial Questions (1924). The first committee concerned itself with political and economic cooperation among world nations and with the League of Nations as it developed. It also advised the party on various disarmament proposals and the growing peace movement in the 1920s and 1930s. The second committee originated during the brief life of the first Labour government when, as Duncan Wilson observed, Labour recognized "its new imperial responsibilities as a party of government."[1] The committee was charged with informing Labour of the economic and political exploitation of imperial territories. Leonard Woolf devoted most of his political efforts from 1924 to the outbreak of the Second World War to matters of imperialism, and especially to Africa, for which he had been designated the committee's expert.

During these fifteen years the Hogarth Press publications on political subjects emphasized either international affairs (League of Nations, Soviet Russia, ideologies of socialism and communism, disarmament, and peace) or imperialism, especially the exploitation of Africa and its struggles toward home rule. Norman Leys wrote the first political book published by the Hogarth Press, his anti-imperialist *Kenya* (1924). Coincidentally, he also wrote the last political book published by the press during the period of this study, *The Colour Bar in Africa* (1941).

"Then we had Dr. Leys to lunch on Wednesday," Virginia Woolf noted on November 30, 1918, and added, "He has spent 17 years in East Africa, & being a very sterling direct Scotchman has a terrible tale to tell about the natives" (*Diary* 1:222). Dr. Norman Leys had served two years in Portuguese East Africa before entering the British colonial medical service in 1904 and being posted to Nyasaland. For the next fifteen years he served as a public health officer in Nyasaland and in British East Africa before tuberculosis invalided him back to England in the summer of 1918. Before settling into a country medical practice at Brailsford near Derby in December, Leys spent a week in London talking to influential people about imperialism in Africa and consequently lunched with the Woolfs.

The meeting developed into a long association between Leonard Woolf and Norman Leys, as the former colonial doctor and socialist began what amounted to a second career as an anti-imperialist activist. He carried on the fight largely through the mail, especially in an extensive correspondence with the influential J. H. Oldham, secretary of the International Missionary Council.[2] Leys later served with Woolf on Labour's Advisory Committee on Imperial Questions and turned his "terrible tale" about the natives into three books published by the Hogarth Press.

In nearly his last official act as medical officer in Nyasaland, Norman Leys on February 7, 1918, wrote a long, detailed, and closely argued letter to the Colonial Office setting forth his penetrating insights into what he saw as the disastrous and muddled administration of East Africa. As the historian John Cell has noted, "Nearly all the ideas Norman Leys ever had about the colonial situation in Kenya are contained in his unpublished letter of 1918."[3] They remained virtually unaltered although expanded in his three books. The first book that he brought to Leonard Woolf in 1924, after six years' retirement at Brailsford, had grown out of his entire experience in East Africa and was over twenty years in the making.

Leys had tried to place the book with Allen & Unwin, but the publisher had asked Leys for a £350 subsidy. Leonard Woolf, writing to Leys in July 1924, thought the subsidy too high, rebutted Unwin's several options, and offered to publish the book at the Hogarth Press (HP 255). Woolf proposed printing 1,100 copies, charging the author only costs, and accounting to Leys for two-thirds of the published price plus a commission of 10 percent. Leys was delighted with the offer and surprised that Hogarth would be interested. He had the idea, he wrote to Woolf the next day, that "the publishing firm you have some connection with publishes only the kind of book that corresponds with olives and artichokes in diet" (HP 255). In late July, Leys accepted the offer of publication, and Woolf sent the manuscript off immediately to R. & R. Clark in Edinburgh. It was published in October, only three months later.

Norman Leys's *Kenya* (1924) vividly depicted the colonial government's disastrous land policies, its exploitation of native labor, its relocation of tribes, and its failure to provide minimal educational and training programs to the Africans. Leys surveyed the growing schism between archconservative white colonists, determined to maintain racial separation, and the more tolerant home government. He detailed the local abuse of authority and the occasionally cruel punitive measures taken against the tribes. In one bold gesture Leys unmasked the entire range of imperial sins both of omission and of commission which had begun to trouble deeply the conscience of the nation. His timing seemed perfect.

Leys's book, aimed at stirring Parliament into corrective action, went to press with Ramsay MacDonald's first Labour government in power and the Advisory Committee on Imperial Questions gearing up. Unfortunately for the anti-imperialists and socialist reformers, however, the MacDonald government, never decisive, waned and died in November 1924, a nine months' wonder of ineffectiveness. The book was published in October, just before the Labour government collapsed, but the open struggle against imperial exploitation in the African colonies, once begun, continued unabated. Soon there was a flurry of backstage maneuvering on the issue. By May 1925 Virginia Woolf protested with mock seriousness to Lady Cecil that their new house in Tavistock Square had become "a mere ante room to the House of Lords" where "Leonard has been caballing about Kenya day and night, and I have several times been shut out of his study while the great discoursed" (*Letters* 6:507). She added that one of their authors and caballers was "a fiery and intractable Scotchman called Norman Leys . . . a perfect Saint and martyr, but not altogether easy company in the house."

Kenya proved an instant success, helped by the controversial nature of its thesis and by the sharpness and anecdotal richness of the writing. E. M. Forster, always keen on anti-imperialist books, responded to Leys's chronicle of Kenya with his usual irony and wit in a letter to Leonard Woolf on December 31, 1924, a month after publication: "*Kenya* enthralled me, and up to the birth of Christianity I thought it a very great book. That unfortunate incident cast a shadow which was in no ways lightened by the death of Islam. Also he thinks one oughtn't to fuck. These reservations apart, I was delighted, that is to say deeply depressed" (LWP). Woolf must have laughed, and told Forster so, because in a following letter on January 2, Forster replied that "I would gladly make you laugh again, but one cannot write the word f—— every time, and I am sure that was the reason" (LWP).

Whether or not the readers of *Kenya* were similarly delighted and depressed, they bought the four-hundred-page book at 15s. a copy. The original 1,000 copies soon sold out, and Woolf put it into a second impression in 1925. In 1926 Woolf issued the book in a third, cheap edition selling for 4s.6d. (*Checklist* 27). It was the first time Woolf had put a Hogarth Press book into a cheap edition. Controversy may have helped the sales in 1926, for Leys's charge that Lord Delamere's land schemes among the Masai had involved the use of dummy applications to gain over 100,000 acres of rich land created a flurry in the press and a threat of a lawsuit. Woolf cautioned Leys to keep cool and avoid a ruinous countersuit, and eventually the furor subsided (HP 255). In 1944, Leys, old and ill, revived memories in a letter to Woolf. "I feel so grateful to the Hogarth Press," he wrote, "that I should like to make a votive offering of some sort before I die. Isn't it astonishing how 'Kenya' goes on selling after more than twenty years?" (LWP).

Leonard Woolf published *Kenya* in October 1924 and the same month began the Hogarth Essays, his first series, with three diverse works by Virginia (*Mr. Bennett and Mrs. Brown*), Roger Fry (*The Artist and Psycho-Analysis*), and Theodora Bosanquet (*Henry James at Work*). The next month he published T. S. Eliot's *Homage to John Dryden*. These short, argumentative works were congenial to the pamphlet-and-report writing Woolf, although he would wait for the next batch of Essays in July 1925 before contributing *Fear and Politics: A Debate at the Zoo*, his own first political publication for the Hogarth Press. At the same time, Woolf engaged John Maynard Keynes, another Bloomsbury friend, to publish in the pamphlet series.

John Maynard Keynes, the most intellectually gifted of the Bloomsbury men, was both a group insider and an outsider. Although he continually returned to the physical and spiritual centers of Bloomsbury to replenish his senses with the art, literature, and conversation of old friends, Keynes moved comfortably in a world of power and wealth, in spheres of influence in economics, finance, politics, and international affairs remote from Lytton Strachey, Duncan Grant, the Bells, and Virginia Woolf. But these spheres were not remote from Leonard Woolf. The two men, the most worldly members of Bloomsbury, shared many extra-Bloomsbury interests and activities. They diverged somewhat politically—Woolf an individualistic socialist and Labour party adviser, Keynes an unorthodox Liberal and capitalist—but they had similarly active careers in literary and political journalism. And they came together in the Hogarth Press, Woolf publishing three of Keynes's shorter works in 1925–26.

By the mid-1920s Maynard Keynes was an established figure of considerable influence. His early book *Indian Currency and Finance* (1913) achieved respectful praise in specialist circles, but *The Economic Consequences of the Peace* (1919) made him a public figure overnight and something of a best-selling author. Virginia Woolf noted that the book had sold 15,000 copies in less than two months, an astonishing feat for a polemic on war reparations (*Diary* 2:18).

Writing a book a year and pouring out articles for the *Manchester Guardian*, the *Nation*, and other papers, Keynes soon consolidated his position as the chief economic spokesman of his day. Major books rolled out in a seemingly effortless procession: *A Treatise on Probability* (1921), *A Revision of the Treaty* (1922), *A Tract on Monetary Reform* (1923). He became a publisher and director of the *Nation and Athenaeum* in 1923 and the first bursar of King's College, Cambridge, in 1924. Keynes next engaged in several controversies over monetary policy, the gold standard, and unemployment, married the Russian ballerina Lydia Lopokova, took a honeymoon in Russia, and lectured at two universities on how to reform the old Liberal attitude to laissez-faire. The Hogarth Press published the written results of these activities.

Keynes's first Hogarth Press publication came about in July 1925 when he wrote three articles for the *Evening Standard* titled "Unemployment and Monetary Policy." They addressed the growing crisis of inflation, a 10 percent reduction in wages and purchasing power, and an alarming imbalance in export prices on the international market. Keynes thought the government's precipitous and misinformed return to the gold standard had caused the crisis. He placed some of the blame on Winston Churchill as chancellor of the exchequer but even more on his expert advisers.

Keynes expanded his three articles by adding two chapters ("What Misled Mr. Churchill" and "The Case of the Coal Industry") and published them the same month in a Hogarth Press pamphlet with the irreverent and attention-getting title *The Economic Consequences of Mr. Churchill* (1925). Readers of Keynes could find in his pamphlet the same heady mixture of tough-minded economic analysis and skillful writing, data and rhetoric, seriousness and wit that marked all his journalism. A month after the July publication, Leonard Woolf reported to Keynes sales of over 3,000 copies and later, at the six-month mark in February 1926, a total of 7,100 copies sold outright (HP 210).

Less disputatious than his Hogarth pamphlet on Churchill and gold, Keynes's next press publication, four months later, grew out of his trip to

Russia in August 1925 after his marriage to Lydia Lopokova. Keynes visited Leningrad in the guise of Cambridge's representative to the bicentenary celebration of the Academy of Sciences, but he also went honeymooning to visit Lopokova's family. His pamphlet *A Short View of Russia* (1925) has none of the characteristics of travel writing. Instead, it explored three interrelated political and economic problems stated as the chapter titles: "What Is the Communist Faith?"; "The Economics of Soviet Russia"; and "Communism's Power to Survive." Keynes provided a penetrating look at the fanaticism of the new Soviet "religion" and inherent dangers of the economic system. He found much to dislike in Soviet Russia.

A Short View of Russia failed to sell very well at the start. Issued by Woolf in December 1925 as number thirteen in the two-year-old Hogarth Essays series, Keynes's pamphlet had sold only 700 copies by the end of February 1926 (HP 210). Perhaps his largely negative view of Soviet Russia told enthusiasts what they did not want to hear. Or perhaps if Keynes had provided a more intimate and personal glimpse of Russia to add to his cool analysis of seeing Red, the pamphlet might have ended in the black. By the end of the first six months, *A Short View of Russia* had sold 1,025 copies (MSR). For all that Keynes left out—stories of spies and peasants, a show of Cezanne and Matisse, champagne and banquets, processions of Communists in top hats, and the "two fanatical watch dogs with square faces" who guarded Maynard and Lydia—one can read Virginia Woolf's diary entry where she recorded his detailed impressions upon his return (*Diary* 3:43–44). He was wearing a Tolstoyan peasant blouse and black astrakhan hat.

The third and last work of Keynes's published by the Hogarth Press appeared in July 1926 as *The End of Laissez-Faire*. Keynes had written and delivered it as the Sidney Ball Lecture at Oxford in November 1924. He had offered it to Leonard Woolf as a pamphlet before going off to Russia with Lopokova in August 1925, and Woolf had accepted it (HP 211). Keynes delayed publication, however; he rewrote it and delivered it a second time at the University of Berlin in June 1926 before sending it to the Hogarth Press. With it he sent detailed suggestions on its design and marketing, perhaps stung by the comparatively slow sales of *A Short View of Russia*. He advised Woolf to make it a booklet with a larger page size than a pamphlet and to allot a substantial advertising budget. Woolf, not a publisher to take advice gracefully from an author, nevertheless acceded to Keynes's requests (HP 211). Whether it was the additional advertising and page size or the contents, Keynes's booklet sold 3,761 copies in the first six months (MSR).

Keynes later reprinted his three Hogarth Press pamphlets in his collection *Essays in Persuasion* (1931). Macmillan, from first to last, published all of Keynes's books in England, as did Harcourt Brace in America. Leonard Woolf and the Hogarth Press could not hope to publish Keynes's books, but the shorter works were different. It is a mark of Woolf's relationship with Keynes that on the rare occasion when Keynes published in pamphlet form, he turned to the Hogarth Press. The three press publications are among the best of Keynes's separately published shorter writings.

The peace movement and the League of Nations both expressed humanity's deepest hope in the 1920s that the savagery and oppression of war could be avoided, perhaps permanently erased, through rational discourse, international arbitration, and the application of law. It was a rationalist's credo and one in which Leonard Woolf believed deeply. As a political journalist, Woolf knew that if peace and the league were to flourish, then public opinion must be cultivated, and citizens must be educated to understand the developments in international government. Leonard Woolf's long commitment to education and his political ideology came together in fostering a series of Hogarth Press pamphlets that illustrate more clearly than any other publications how the press functioned as the educational arm of Bloomsbury.

Kathleen Innes, secretary of the Peace Committee of the Society of Friends (later sponsors of the Merttens Lectures) approached Woolf in October 1924 with a manuscript on the League of Nations intended for schoolchildren. He suggested that she appeal to both the League of Nations Union and the Society of Friends for a guaranteed number of purchased copies and subsequent distribution. After considerable negotiations, the Friends agreed to purchase £10 worth of pamphlets and to distribute them. With such minimal support, Woolf published *The Story of the League of Nations, Told for Young People* in April 1925.

Woolf also saw the market potential of the schools, and by May 11 he had managed to place *The Story of the League* on the London County Council's requisition list. A carefully screened list of publications recommended by the council as appropriate for schools, it provided a foot in the door for publishers who then advertised their wares discreetly in the professional journals. Innes's sixty-page pamphlet soon became part of the curriculum of several schools. Sales soared in the autumn, when schools reconvened, and the original printing of 1,000 copies had to be resupplied with a second impression of 1,500 copies in October. Eventually it went through at least five impressions (*Checklist* 33). By producing an attractive and informative pamphlet, by keeping the price low for students (at 1s.6d.), and by aiming at a specific market with large sales potential, Woolf achieved a solid success on the business side, while scoring a breakthrough for the press on the educational side. *The Story of the League* sold well for many years and in 1933 was still going at the rate of 300 copies a year (HP 193).

After the success of her first pamphlet, Kathleen Innes produced four more with the Hogarth Press, initially at the rate of one per year. Each pamphlet was written for a particular age group of schoolchildren and provided an introduction to the complex machinery of the League of Nations and its relation to international problems. The pattern of distribution and marketing that Woolf had established with the first pamphlet was followed for each, but none of the subsequent pamphlets enjoyed the popularity of the first, although their sales justified their publication. So Kathleen Innes published *How the League of Nations Works, Told for Young People* (1926), *The League of Nations and the World's Workers: An Introduction to the Work of the International Labour Organization* (1927), *The Reign of Law: A Short and Simple Introduction to the Work of the Permanent Court of International Justice* (1929), and then after a lapse of six years, *The League of Nations: The Complete Story Told for Young People* (1936). They were short pamphlets with long titles, but through them Bloomsbury and the Hogarth Press entered hundreds of English schoolrooms.

Leonard Woolf, like other members of Bloomsbury, was opposed to war, but he did not join such pacifist groups as the No-Conscription Fellowship, the No More War movement, or the Peace Pledge Union, although he became a member in 1915 of the Union of Democratic Control. Nevertheless, Woolf's deep-seated hatred of all forms of international or national aggression, militarism, and abusive authority led him to share many of the objectives of such organizations, especially the compelling need for disarmament and for the machinery of international arbitration. As he did in African affairs and in educational efforts for the League of Nations, Woolf used the Hogarth Press to publish works supportive of disarmament and peace at strategic times.

There were several such times between the world wars when nations, in league or not, sat down in Washington, London, Geneva, and elsewhere to hammer out disarmament agreements. Among the agreements, the Lucarno Pact (October 1925) resolved borders and promised peace. One of the last protocols of the Lucarno Pact called for support of the League of Nations Article 8 in an effort to hasten disarmament. On the strength of this statement and the immediate possibility of another disarmament conference, Philip Noel-Baker wrote what became one of the most extensive, detailed, and influential books on the subject between the wars: *Disarmament* (1926). When his arrangements with the publisher Ernest Benn fell through in March after the book was in proofs, Noel-Baker took it to his friend Leonard Woolf, who promptly arranged its publication at the Hogarth Press (HP 318). The 352-page work appeared in April.

Philip Noel-Baker, formerly a fellow of King's College, Cambridge, and at the time a professor of international relations at the University of London, was one of the remarkable academician-politicians who served the Fabians and the Labour party so well. Noel-Baker moved through a series of minor posts at important places such as the Paris Peace Conference and the League of Nations. He served with Leonard Woolf on Labour's international affairs advisory committee. In 1929 he gained a seat in Parliament as a Labour M.P., and with one brief lapse in the middle 1930s, he remained in Parliament until the 1950s. Noel-Baker received the Nobel Peace Prize in 1959.

Noel-Baker's book treated the international problem of disarmament in a detailed and systematic manner, from early chapters on definitions, reasons for disarmament, and methods of preparing for a treaty to chapters on every aspect of land, sea, and air disarmament. Naval disarmament, to avoid a battleship race, had been of paramount importance from the time of the Washington conference in 1921–22, and Noel-Baker gave complete attention to the controversies over ratios, tonnage restrictions, and replacements. But he also wrote chapters on aerial disarmament and on the control and prohibition of chemical warfare. Additional chapters on the importance of demilitarized and neutralized zones, on the need to monitor and control the private manufacturing and trafficking in military weapons, and the importance of on-site investigation and mutual control underscore the farsighted, even prophetic, nature of the book.

At the end of his book Noel-Baker recognized the extreme patience and willingness to compromise needed to achieve world peace through arms control. He called on his own government to take the next step with large reductions and to make specific proposals for a new conference. He was to be disappointed in both prospects. When the next conference came in 1927, the Americans under President Coolidge, not the British, sponsored it, and the British delegation, with those of the other world powers, found much with which to disagree. The conference adjourned without reaching an agreement. Noel-Baker examined the tangled results, extracted what good he could find, and pointed to lessons learned for future negotiations. He published his findings in a second Hogarth Press pamphlet, *Disarmament and the Coolidge Conference* (November 1927).

In the next five years the Hogarth Press published three more short works on disarmament: H. Wilson Harris's monograph *Arms and Arbitration* (1928), Viscount Cecil's *Letter to a M.P. on Disarmament* (1931), and Arthur Ponsonby's pamphlet *Disarmament: A Discussion* (1932). All three carried on the process of education and debate aimed at the general public and their representatives in Parliament. Viscount Cecil and Arthur Ponsonby were figures to be reckoned with in the 1930s, with extensive experience in Parliament and in government. Both were longtime friends and associates of Leonard Woolf. In 1914 Ponsonby had been one of the three founders of the Union of Democratic Control which aimed at revamping British foreign policy and placed emphasis on disarmament and arms control. By 1932 Ponsonby had been elevated to the peerage by the second Labour government.

Ponsonby's Hogarth Press pamphlet, published in November 1932, espoused his increasingly extreme pacifism. He argued for complete disarmament, naively placing his faith in the moral strength of the defenseless to prohibit unprovoked aggression. As a result, he was almost alone in Labour politics in opposing the Geneva Conference, which ended in bitter failure in 1934 when the Nazis insisted on arms equality for Germany. The Second World War was on the way.

In addition to the Hogarth Press books and pamphlets on disarmament, Leonard Woolf published several works on international arbitration and world peace by such Labour party figures as Will Arnold-Forster, an old Bloomsbury friend (*The Victory of Reason: A Pamphlet on Arbitration*, 1926), and H. N. Brailsford, one of the chief socialist writers and thinkers of the day (*If We Want Peace*, 1932). And seven antiwar publications came to the Hogarth Press from the Peace Committee of the Society of Friends. In 1927 the Peace Committee established an annual Merttens Lecture on War and Peace, funded by Frederick Merttens of Rugby. The committee secretary, Kathleen Innes, herself a Hogarth Press author, arranged with Leonard Woolf to publish the lectures under partial subsidy. Consequently, the Hogarth Press published the Merttens Lectures in 1927, 1928, 1929, and 1930 and, after a lapse of three years, again in 1934, 1935, and 1936. The last three lectures were issued in the Day to Day Pamphlets series.

Some of the Merttens lecturers remain little known today, but there are two exceptions, G. P. Gooch and Sir Arthur Salter. Gooch, who gave the Merttens Lecture in 1935 (*Politics and Morals*), was a distinguished writer and editor, another Trinity College man long known to Woolf. He became a noted scholar and historian of modern Europe and joint editor of the *Cambridge History of British Foreign Policy*. He was serving as president of the National Peace Council when he delivered his Merttens Lecture. Sir Arthur Salter, the last Merttens lecturer published by the press (*Economic Policies and Peace*, 1936), had served many years with the British delegation to the League of Nations as an expert in transportation, economics, and finance, was a member of the Economic Advisory Council, and would soon become a M.P. for Oxford University. He contributed frequently to the *Political Quarterly*.

In 1936, with the last of the Merttens lectures, the Hogarth Press published a final antiwar pamphlet. *The Roots of War: A Pamphlet on War and Social Order* was written by eight members of the Friends Anti-War Group and the No More War movement and edited by J. W. Strange.

H. G. Wells, another famous lecturer-writer committed to world unity and peace, moved in circles familiar to Leonard Woolf and became a Hogarth author. "Yesterday Wells asked us to publish a pamphlet for him," Virginia Woolf noted on February 12, 1927; "this is a great rise in the world for us" (*Diary* 3:128). H. G. Wells would be a Hogarth Press author until 1936, publishing three of his pamphlets and reprinting a revised edition of one of his nonfiction books. The Woolfs had known Wells since 1918 when Leonard began working with him on various Fabian Society and League of Nations projects. At the time Virginia thought him "a slab of a man formidable for his mass, but otherwise the pattern of a professional cricketer" when she first saw him at a hotly debated League of Nations Society meeting (ibid., 1:157). Leonard soon serialized Wells's *Undying Fire* in the *International Review* (1919) he was then editing. Socialism and an interest in world affairs drew the men together, and the Woolfs developed an affectionate admiration for the energetic, pugnacious, and optimistic Wells.

Manning the barricades always, H. G. Wells prided himself on being a journalist and controversialist, not an artist. And it was as a lecturer that he approached the Hogarth Press, through his wife Catherine, to publish a pamphlet for him. Her husband would be delivering an address at the Sorbonne on March 15, 1927, she wrote to Leonard Woolf in February, and he wanted to preserve the copyright by publishing it as a booklet by that date (HP 518). Woolf was delighted, Wells delivered the manuscript, and the Hogarth Press published it in March as *Democracy under Revision* (1927).

Wells's two other pamphlets published by Hogarth (*The Common Sense of World Peace*, 1929, and *The Idea of a World Encyclopedia*, 1936), followed the same pattern: publication of a formal address to establish the copyright and earn royalties. The practice of publishing speeches was common enough. Keynes's *End of Laissez-Faire* was a speech-pamphlet, but Wells seems to have had a stronger sense than many writers of the value of his writing as property, as a material possession from which to expect income. He alone among Hogarth Press pamphlet writers emphasized the importance of the copyright.

All three pamphlets, while covering a broad variety of topics, were essentially variations and restatements of his utopian political vision first announced in *A Modern Utopia* (1905), where mankind, not the individual, mattered most. In *Democracy under Revision* (1927) Wells criticized the conflicts in modern democracy between powerful business monopolies and the democratic ideal of equality. He believed that democracy must be revised so as to lead to social and political world unity. The pamphlet sold 1,322 copies in the first six months (MSR).

The message is much the same in *The Common Sense of World Peace* (1929), published by the Hogarth Press and first delivered as an address to the Reichstag in Berlin on April 15, 1929. Wells saw the dangers to world peace as the fierce competition of sovereign states fired by nationalism and patriotism. Foreseeing the possibility of new cycles of wars, Wells passionately exhorted his German audience to abandon national self-interest on behalf of a federal world state. The Nazis in the audience already had a different world state in mind. Wells's common sense sold less well than his revised democracy: 1,067 copies the first six months (MSR).

After his pamphlets Wells brought a book to the Hogarth Press in 1929. *The Open Conspiracy* had been published originally by Gollancz in 1928. That firm's two-year rights to publication were running out, and Wells wanted to revise it and reissue it with Hogarth. As Wells explained in his preface, he had been so dissatisfied with his original version that he determined almost immediately to rewrite it within two years and had made constant marginal notes to guide him in the revision.

Leonard Woolf agreed to Wells's proposal, had the book completely reset to accommodate the revisions, and published it in February 1930 in a limited edition of 1,500 copies (HP 520). Wells's subtitle told all: "A Second Version of this faith of a modern man made more explicit and plain." The "faith" Wells advocated would be the new religion of a world state brought about by an "open conspiracy." The conspiracy was to be the "declared intention of establishing a world order out of the present patchwork of particularist governments."[4] In the process militarism, private profit-seeking, and monopolies were to be eliminated. Here was the most complete statement of Wells's utopian scheme since his first book-length treatment of the subject twenty-five years earlier.

While H. G. Wells was criticizing the shortcomings of modern democracy, Leonard Woolf was *Hunting the Highbrow* (1927) in his second sprightly Hogarth pamphlet. He then returned to the subject of Africa for his first press book, *Imperialism and Civilization* (1928). Woolf had published two earlier books, *Empire and Commerce in Africa* (1919) and *Economic Imperialism* (1920), with Allen & Unwin. He now broadened these earlier studies to include a discussion of pre-nineteenth-century conflicts and to conclude with an idealistic defense of the League of Nations, an organization through which a "synthesis of civilizations" might be achieved and imperialism, with its attendant evils, ended. Although he had focused relentlessly on the economic causes of imperialism in his first two books, Woolf now admitted cultural, religious, and racial motives to imperialistic exploitation. Norman Leys's *Kenya* (1924) may have contributed to his new understanding.

Leonard Woolf's *Imperialism and Civilization* (1928) touched on Africa as it dealt with the larger issue of worldwide colonial exploitation. But Lord Olivier's *Anatomy of African Misery* (1927) and *White Capital and Coloured Labour* (1929, a new edition of his 1906 Fabian tract), as well as C. R. Buxton's *Race Problem in Africa* (1931), focused on issues familiar to readers of Leys. Olivier would publish four works with the Hogarth Press.

Sydney Olivier had been one of the original "Big Four" in the Fabian Society, with George Bernard Shaw, Sidney Webb, and Graham Wallas; but unlike Webb, who soon devoted full time to the society, Olivier remained in the Colonial Office, being posted to a number of increasingly important positions in the Caribbean and finally becoming governor of Jamaica in 1907 for six years. He retired from public life after the First World War, only to be summoned by Ramsay MacDonald in 1924 to be given a peerage and become secretary of state for India in the first Labour government. When the government failed, Olivier retired permanently, devoting himself to his anti-imperialist writings. As a lifelong Fabian, Olivier made an unusual colonial administrator. His independent and outspoken views on racial and political issues were made tolerable to conservatives only by his outstanding administrative abilities and energetic rebuilding efforts in the islands.

Virginia Woolf had known the four Olivier daughters before her marriage to Leonard as members of a slightly younger Cambridge group she called the "Neo-Pagans." Brynhild Olivier was often seen with Rupert Brooke. Anne Olivier, Brynhild's daughter by her first husband, Hugh

Popham, later married Virginia's nephew Quentin Bell to link the two families. Leonard for his part knew Sydney Olivier, as he did all of the early Fabians, from years of work with the society and its research bureau.

Lord Olivier's first book for the Woolfs, *The Anatomy of African Misery* (1927), grew out of a lecture given in 1926 to the Union of Democratic Control Summer School reflecting his sympathetic concern for the racial unrest in South Africa. The union, founded in 1914, supported the League of Nations and opposed imperialism. Leonard Woolf admired the lecture and encouraged Olivier to expand it into a 20,000-word booklet (HP 323). Eventually *The Anatomy* grew into a full-scale work and was published in March. In May the press published Olivier's short story *The Empire Builder* (1927) as the first of its new Stories series. For all of his many talents, Olivier was no short-story writer; and although Woolf admired it, the story failed and with it the new series.

Olivier's third Hogarth Press publication was a complete revision of an earlier essay written in 1906 and published by the Independent Labour party. Olivier expanded the essay into a 100,000-word book, *White Capital and Coloured Labour* (1929), retaining the original title in spite of Woolf's concerns about confusing the book with the earlier article. Lord Olivier's best-selling work for the Hogarth Press, however, was also his last, an incisive and deflationary account of Governor Eyre's disastrous rule of Jamaica and his brutal suppression of the 1865 rebellion, *The Myth of Governor Eyre* (1933). Woolf thought the book extremely interesting and the facts amazing, but the manuscript overlong (HP 325). The correspondence between Woolf and Olivier over three months reveals Woolf's skill and patience as an editor, suggesting to Olivier several specific cuts and a title change.

Leonard Woolf turned the corner into the new decade of the 1930s by bringing in John Lehmann as manager for the press and by publishing his most important work under his own imprint, *After the Deluge*, vol. 1 (1931). It followed *Imperialism and Civilization* by three years, but in effect it had been in the works for eleven years. After completing his book on economic imperialism in 1920, Woolf had set out to investigate the 125-year period of history before the First World War as a means of understanding the dynamics of world events. Admitting in his autobiography that he was no sociologist, psychologist, or historian, Woolf recalled that he had wanted to do what "the professionals had left undone." That is, he intended to study the period from 1789 (the "deluge" of the French Revolution) to 1914 and "to try to discover what the relation between the communal beliefs and desires regarding liberty, equality, and fraternity and communal action had been during those years, i.e., what, if any, had been the effect of those communal beliefs and desires not merely upon war and peace but upon historical events generally" (*Downhill* 203).

Woolf subtitled his book *A Study of Communal Psychology*. In spite of its subtitle, *After the Deluge* owed less to social psychology, by 1930 a well-established discipline anticipated by Woolf's old Fabian friend Graham Wallas, than it owed to more traditional methods of intellectual, social, and political history. From the beginning Woolf ambitiously planned a multivolume treatment of his subject. He continued with a second volume, *After the Deluge II* (1939), and completed it years later with a third volume, *Principia Politica* (1953). Looking back at the fate of his three-volume work in his autobiography, Leonard Woolf considered that the nearly 1,000 pages and 300,000 words of these books had been "to all intents and purposes . . . a complete failure" (*Downhill* 196). Their critical reception had been "fairly deep, though not very prolonged." The reviews of the first volume in 1931 by socialist colleagues were almost entirely praiseful. Harold Laski, especially, thought Woolf's volume "a remarkable beginning to what promises to be a book of the first importance."[5] All this was dashed for Woolf, however, by a half-column review in the *Times Literary Supplement*.

The conservative reviewer in the *TLS* offered tepid praise for Woolf's skill with ideas, but thought him "too rigidly logical," and complained that when Woolf digressed on the General Strike, "the book tails away into cheapness."[6] Such comments plunged Leonard into despair, indicating a vulnerability to criticism not usually revealed in his otherwise stoical, skeptical nature. Virginia, for once, found herself in the role of comforter and defender, devoting six hours of counterargument to help Leonard overcome his "curious pessimistic temper" (*Dairy* 4:51).

Leonard's depression did not last long, however, helped by initial sales. His original pessimistic prediction that the book would not sell 500 copies in six months did not come true; sales were modest, but they approached the 500 mark on January 1, 1932, less than three months after publication, and reached 604 copies sold in the first six months (MSR). In contrast, however, Virginia's "difficult" novel *The Waves*, published simultaneously, had sold 9,650 copies by January 1.

The early 1930s were years of intense and satisfying activity for both Virginia and Leonard Woolf, marked by the publication of two of their most important works and by a resurgence in the Hogarth Press operations after a couple of slack years. As the press flourished, so did Leonard Woolf's career as a political journalist and editor. He helped establish the *Political Quarterly* in January 1930, becoming coeditor with W. A. Robson in 1931 when Kingsley Martin left to become editor of the *New Statesman*. The *Political Quarterly* became one of the most prestigious publications of its kind in the interwar years, and Woolf did much to make it so. For about five years after the start of the quarterly, Woolf was involved with editorial work and publications with other publishers, and he did not publish again with his own press until 1935.

During the 1930s the Hogarth Press published four more books on Africa, including Norman Leys's *Last Chance in Kenya* (1931). In 1929 Ramsay MacDonald had formed the second, more promising Labour government, and the anti-imperialists stirred into action once more. Fabian leader Sidney Webb became Lord Passfield and sat in MacDonald's cabinet as secretary of state for colonial affairs. As a member of a select committee on Kenya, Passfield surprisingly refused to receive testimony from a Kikuyu delegation on the abuses of white supremacy. Norman Leys, ever alert, fired off his second blast through the Hogarth Press (1931).

John Cell, in commenting on the events and the book, has noted that Leys's *Last Chance in Kenya* was mostly propaganda, more of a disillusioned attack on Lord Passfield and Labour for their neglect of a great cause than an informative, well-designed work.[7] Leonard Woolf had worried over the book's title, length, and quality of the writing and advised many changes. Leys tried out several titles such as "The Road Forks in Kenya," "The Turning Point in Kenya," and the least attractive "Second Thoughts in Kenya," all rejected by Woolf, before he finally thought of "Last Chance" (HP 257). Imaginative titles were not the forte of the serious, literal Leys. Eventually the text was pruned down to acceptable size and published in December 1931. It sold less well than *Kenya* and appeared too late to have much influence as the Labour government collapsed in the summer.

Two of the other press books about South Africa were by white writers—Leonard Barnes's *New Boer War* (1932) and W. G. Ballinger's *Race and Economics in South Africa* (1934)—but the fourth book was an interesting testimony from a black African, Parmenas Mockerie: *An African Speaks for His People* (1934). Dr. Lionel Penrose, a colleague of Norman Leys, brought the book to Woolf as an important anti-imperialist statement and the first book in English by a Kikuyu. Mockerie, not surprisingly, was a protégé of Leys. Woolf thought the typescript disappointing, rather obvious and European in its points, but agreed to publish it (HP 285). Penrose acknowledged that the book's chief value lay in its "pure propaganda." Julian Huxley, then a professor at King's College, London, wrote an appreciative foreword, and the long pamphlet appeared in February 1934, the same time as Laurens van der Post's South African novel, *In a Province*. They were the last press books on Africa in the 1930s.

The height of Hogarth Press activity in the area of African imperial affairs (1929–31) coincided with the anti-imperialists' hopes for pervasive changes through the offices of MacDonald's second Labour government. The hopes evaporated when the East Africa Report of the Joint Committee of the Lords and Commons, released in November 1932 after the government had dissolved, failed to be implemented. After 1932 there was less interest and activity in African affairs, partly because attitudes and conditions improved slightly and partly because of more pressing international problems.

In addition to the publications on African affairs in the late 1920s and early 1930s, the Hogarth Press published a few interesting books and pamphlets on other areas of international concern. There were two books on Palestine with a Zionist slant by Horace Samuel—his amusing and anecdotal *Unholy Memories of the Holy Land* (1930) and his sharply critical pamphlet *Beneath the Whitewash: A Critical Analysis of the Report of the Commission on the Palestine Disturbances of August, 1929* (1930).[8] There were no other press publications on this explosively unstable area although further Arab violence against the Jewish settlers broke out in 1936 and a royal commission in 1937 proposed a controversial tripartite division of the area into Arab and Jewish states, plus a third international zone supervised by the British. The commission's recommendations were not accepted, and English concerns, including Leonard Woolf's and his press, were quickly focused on European conflicts of more immediacy than the Middle East.

The Hogarth Press published three books on conditions in India: Edward Thompson's *Other Side of the Medal* (1925), Graham Pole's *India in Transition* (1932), and K. M. Panikhar's *Caste and Democracy* (1933). All three were critical of government policies and sympathetic to Indian self-governance. Pole's book appeared the year after Gandhi's celebrated three-month visit to England in the autumn of 1931 to attend the Round Table Conference. Major Pole was vice-chairman and honorary secretary of the British Committee on Indian and Burman Affairs, an organization devoted to self-government and dominion status. There were other Hogarth Press books on China (1927), Spain (the Spanish Constitution of 1933), Ireland (Ulster in 1931), the West Indies (1933), and Germany (1934, 1939, 1940), but surprisingly few when measured against the developments in these and other European countries in the 1930s. There were, however, a number of important press publications on Soviet Russia and communism.

When Lincoln Steffens returned from Russia in 1919 and reported to Bernard Baruch that "I have been over into the future and it works," he spoke prophetically for a horde of idealistic, hopeful time-travelers to Soviet Russia in the 1920s and 1930s, each eager to praise the future and criticize the present or past. A few went in the early period, Bertrand Russell and H. N. Brailsford in 1920, for example. Beatrice Webb suggested that Leonard Woolf go in 1922, but he declined, probably because of Virginia Woolf's troubling ill health through most of the year.[9] The few became many only after 1924 when the first Labour government gave diplomatic recognition to the USSR and the Soviets began to woo Western travelers, especially labor delegations. In 1924 the British Trades Union Congress sent a representation to Russia, one of the first to go, and the British Society for Cultural Relations was established with E. M. Forster, H. T. Hobhouse, Julian Huxley, Maynard Keynes, and H. G. Wells as directors.

From 1924 until 1936 the Soviets encouraged, planned, and controlled the itineraries of Western travelers to its closed society to gain propaganda and political advantage.[10] The stream of visitors to Russia became a flood in the early 1930s, the international economic depression making Soviet achievements seem especially glittering, when there were almost more engineers, businessmen, doctors, scientists, workers, writers, photojournalists, and intellectuals knocking about Russia than at home. Among those of note who returned to write about their trip were Maynard Keynes (1925, with a Hogarth Press pamphlet), Aneurin Bevan, John Strachey, George Strauss (1931, with a Hogarth pamphlet), and Harold Laski (1934, with a press pamphlet). Only a few of the enthusiasts returned as skeptics, Keynes, Malcolm Muggeridge, Edmund Wilson, and André Gide most notably, but they too found many people, some places, and a few institutions to be praiseworthy. In 1936 the Stalinist purge trials began; and suddenly for many Communist sympathizers, the god began to fail.

Between 1924 and the late 1930s, the Hogarth Press published eight pamphlets on Russia, communism, and Marxism, all but one of them growing out of visits to the USSR. With the exception of Maynard Keynes's pamphlet, the publications presented Soviet life, institutions, and political ideology in favorable terms, part of a larger effort by British leftists to explain and disseminate Russian ideas. The motives, supported by Woolf, were political and educational, to set the record straight, to provide an insider's considered judgment. They were issued as Day to Day Pamphlets.

The first of these pamphlets, the beginning number of the Day to Day series, was Maurice Dobb's *Russia To-Day and To-Morrow* (1930). Reporting on his second trip to Russia in 1929, Dobb provided in six chapters a perceptive, generally approving, but not uncritical survey of Soviet Russian history, politics, economics, industrial development, and cultural revolution. His visit came just after the relaxed and stimulating New Economic Policy period (1921–28) had been controverted by the Five Year Plan and the Russian Association of Proletarian Writers. While Dobb recognized the increasing pressure for conformity to Marxist ideology, he still reported finding tolerance for experimentation in the arts.

A year later the Hogarth Press published an even shorter view of Russia than that of Keynes or Dobb, *What We Saw* (1931), in twenty-three pages by three sight-seeing Labour members of Parliament, Aneurin Bevan, John Strachey, and George Strauss. In their introduction they made clear their intention to present an "anti-dote" to the misleading impressions of many visitors and to help the reader appreciate the Russian situation. They claimed no specialized knowledge beyond their trades as miner (Bevan), metal merchant (Strauss), and journalist (Strachey). The traveling M. P.'s, on what became an obligatory itinerary for Russian visitors, conducted their readers through a brisk and enthusiastic tour of hydroelectric dams, ship canals, heavy machinery plants, coal mines, tractor factories, and state and collective farms.

Occasionally the trio found fault. Down in the mine with Bevan they reported a safety factor below British standards, miners with inferior skills, and an overly optimistic two years' projected output. They also recognized that the economic revolution had "been bought at a terrible price" for thousands of alienated peasants. But, they concluded, the changes in industry, agriculture, and culture were so valuable and extensive that they must survive and develop. The challenge for Britain, they saw, was to mobilize industry and business to enter "the greatest, new market in the world," a market already dominated by American and German business interests.[11]

Traveler's tales of Soviet Russia continued in one other Hogarth Press Day to Day Pamphlet, C. M. Lloyd's *Russian Notes* (1930), but the press also published two informative specialists' reports—R. D. Charques's *Soviet Education* (1932) and Harold Laski's *Law and Justice in Soviet Russia* (1935)—and two political tracts on communism, Maurice Dobb's *On Marxism To-Day* (1932) and R. Palme Dutt's *Political and Social Doctrine of Communism* (1938).

"Education in a Communist country is necessarily education in Communism," wrote Charques, "and this truism is the driving force of the Soviet educational machine."[12] Keeping Soviet political theory and ideology always before him, Charques proceeded to a thoughtful and probing examination of the Russian educational system from preschool, through primary schools, which were "polytechnic" in nature, to vocational training in factory schools, and, finally, to the higher technical institutes at the university level. He admired the Russians' successful onslaught against illiteracy and applauded many of the Soviet innovations in education. At the end of his pamphlet, Charques raised important questions about the lack of freedom and variety within the system and the dangers of a political doctrine being the ultimate measure of education and cultural development.

When Harold Laski died, according to Kingsley Martin, an Oxford don summed up the 1930s as "the Age of Laski" because of his immense influence during a time of great political turmoil. Martin added that "Laski was a scholar and political philosopher; he was a politician, orator, and journalist; he was, above all a teacher and a friend."[13] His friendships were legendary. Within English political circles he seems to have known everyone; he was a moving force in leftist politics from the Fabians and the Labour party to the Marxists where he eventually made his home. Leonard Woolf had known and worked with Harold Laski for years and had published his pamphlet on *The Crisis and the Constitution: 1931 and After* (1932) in the Day to Day series. In 1934 Laski gave a series of lectures in Moscow critical of democracy and drawn largely from his book *Democracy in Crisis* (1933). He thereby drew down on his head at home the ire of conservatives who attacked him roundly in the press and in Parliament. Shaw and Keynes defended him. While he lectured and the fires raged in England, Laski studied Russian politics and law, assembling material that would lead to his next Hogarth Press Day to Day Pamphlet, *Law and Justice in Soviet Russia* (1935).

Not surprisingly, given his ideological enthusiasm for communism, Laski's examination of the legal and political machinery of Soviet justice proved it generally superior to Western jurisprudence. The Soviet legal system had not yet passed beyond the experimental stage, Laski observed, and it lacked "settled form, dignity, procedural rigor" when compared to English law; but he believed there were "many features in which it brings law more substantially into relation with justice than anything the Common Law System has so far been able to attain."[14] He then provided a detailed description of all aspects of the system from the preparation, qualification, and selection of lawyers and judges to the conduct of pretrial examinations, trial procedure, and the penal system.

Aglow with the noble examples of Soviet justice, Laski rarely expressed uneasiness at the selection of lawyers, the behavior of judges, or the use of evidence. He saw only virtues in the pretrial police examinations and the simplified or nonexistent procedures for the conduct of trials, the absence of juries, and the partisan participation of the judges. Nor was he disturbed by the avowed political nature of the procurator's duties in ensuring that the system of law meted out justice measured by Communist ideology.

Whenever Laski's evidence in Russia became problematical, he could fall back on such examples as the Sacco and Vanzetti case to point up outrages in the Anglo-American system. If Laski idealized and believed in almost everything he saw in Russia, he was not alone. He was in Russia in 1934, before the second federal Constitution of 1936 engineered by Stalin and before the blood-drenched purges and "open" trials of the "wreckers" and "defectors" (1936–38). Laski's *Law and Justice in Soviet Russia*, an interesting and far-ranging study aimed at the general reader of the Hogarth series, documented the Russian practices and the Western approval at the time. It was not the first such examination of the Soviet legal and judicial system, but it had the advantages of thoroughness, vivid detail, and immediacy.

Five months before Charques's pamphlet on Soviet education, Leonard Woolf published Maurice Dobb's *On Marxism To-Day* (1932) as if to provide the historical and ideological basis for the applied Marxism observed by Charques. This pamphlet, Dobb's second in the series, was worked up from lectures at Cambridge where he was lecturer in economics and director of economic studies at Trinity College. It appealed to Woolf, who thought that a study of Marxism as applied to contemporary practical and intellectual issues was badly needed by socialists (HP 68). A thoroughgoing Marxist, Dobb concluded that socialism seemed "emphatically to have no future as an historical force" unless informed by historical materialism.[15]

J. A. Hobson, with H. N. Brailsford one of the founders of the Union of Democratic Control and an important thinker and writer in Fabian and Labour circles, explored a slightly different path to English socialism in another Day to Day Pamphlet that same year, *From Capitalism to Socialism* (1932). Consequently, by 1932, when Auden's generation of young poets and writers were beginning to discover the possibilities of leftist politics, Woolf with his press already had published a series of pamphlets of substance and importance on Marxist and socialist ideology and on aspects of Soviet culture, education, economic development, and politics.

On the opposite side of the political spectrum from Maurice Dobb's pamphlet on Marxism, Mussolini's *Enciclopedia Italiana* article "The Political and Social Doctrine of Fascism" made a surprising Hogarth Press publication. Mussolini's tract on fascism came to Leonard Woolf through the translator Jane Soames. After reading it in May 1933, Woolf decided it would be more appropriate first as an article in the *Political Quarterly*. A vociferous critic of authoritarian regimes, Woolf detested nazism and fascism, but it was characteristic of his editorial astuteness to see the usefulness of publishing Mussolini's tract. After running it in the July–September 1933 issue of *Political Quarterly,* Woolf published it as a twenty-six-page pamphlet in the Hogarth Press series of Day to Day Pamphlets in October 1933. An editorial note explained: "This is an authorized translation of an article contributed by the Duce in 1932 to the fourteenth volume of *Enciclopedia Italiana*. It is the only statement by Mussolini of the philosophic basis of Fascism."

The success of the Hogarth Press translation was considerable, attributable to the importance of Italian fascism in the 1930s, the uniqueness of the statement by Mussolini, and the brisk, clear, self-confident prose of the document. Mussolini's experience as a journalist shows in every sentence. The original 1,500 copies sold quickly, a reprint of 1,200 copies followed, and eventually the pamphlet went through four impressions before being reset in 1940. It was adopted in January 1935 by the Carnegie Endowment for International Peace (directed by Nicolas Murray Butler) for inclusion in its monthly periodical *International Conciliation*, and it was frequently requested for inclusion in textbooks and anthologies (HP 297).

In his own next two Hogarth Press books after the disappointments of *After the Deluge* (1931), Leonard Woolf published what he thought about Mussolini and his Fascist ambitions in *Quack, Quack!* (1935) and *The League and Abyssinia* (1936). The title of *Quack, Quack!* suggests the barnyard sounds of the orating Hitler and Mussolini. With devastating effect, Woolf matched photographs of the eye-bulging Hawaiian war god Kukailimoku to those of the gesticulating bellicose dictators. Woolf's two-hundred-page attack on fascism concentrated on the savage quackery of modern totalitarianism but also discussed the intellectual sources he found in Carlyle, Nietzsche, and Spengler. Woolf's list of heroes who battled against the totalitarians for the light of civilization began with Erasmus and Montaigne and included Thomas More, Giordano Bruno, Spinoza, Descartes, Voltaire, Rousseau, Kant, and Goethe.

To these, Woolf added the Jews in an appendix titled "A Note on Anti-Semitism." The Jews had suffered and struggled, wrote Woolf, for a civilization of "law, order, reason, and humanity." Here, he explored for the first time in his writings the particular glory and the terrible victimization of his own race. The year 1935 was a time to stand up and be counted, but it was also before the full horror of the holocaust. Leonard Woolf, remote from the grim and escalating realities in Germany, concluded his book with painful observation: "The Jew may indeed feel that perhaps after all, as a civilized man, a man into whose mind the lessons of civilization have been burnt by bitter experience, he is an appropriate victim when unfortunate people in the state of mind of the German Nazis are searching for a scapegoat." [16]

Five months after Leonard Woolf published *Quack, Quack!*, Italy invaded Abyssinia (or Ethiopia). Incensed by the vacillation of England's foreign policy and the increasing impotence of the League of Nations to stem Italy's military aggression, Woolf wrote a carefully conceived article for the *Political Quarterly*'s January–March issue of 1936, "Meditation on Abyssinia." He then expanded the article by about a third, toned down some of the rhetoric, and concluded with a section on the "Socialist Position" in which he reaffirmed his belief in the league in spite of its failure in the Ethiopian war and its rejection by his more orthodox and militant socialist colleagues. He published the rewritten essay as a Hogarth Day to Day Pamphlet, *The League and Abyssinia*, in March 1936. Addis Ababa fell to the Fascists in early May.

Leonard Woolf's pamphlet provides an excellent example of the way he developed his ideas and used the *Political Quarterly* and the Hogarth Press to disseminate those ideas to a broader public. The combined editorships gave Woolf an authority not often duplicated among political writers. Almost all of his writing began with the topicality of journalism, in this case the Italian invasion of Ethiopia, and then moved backward in history and forward to the future as Woolf argued his point and meditated on the philosophical or psychological aspects of the event.

Six months after the Italian conquest of Abyssinia, H. G. Wells delivered an address to the Royal Institution on November 20, 1936, and again requested that the Hogarth Press publish it as a pamphlet to preserve his copyright. Woolf obliged and issued *The Idea of a World Encyclopedia* (1936) as another of the Day to Day Pamphlets (HP 519). Less optimistic in tone than he was in his other press publications, Wells seemed tempered by the grim realities of the 1930s as he advocated, not the world state, but a preliminary vehicle for conditioning men's minds in preparation for global unity. The encyclopedia he envisioned, far beyond the limited services of a *Britannica*, would be "a concentration, a clarification and a synthesis" of all knowledge so as to become "the mental background of every intelligent man in the world," and "undogmatic Bible to a world culture."[17] Wells's speech-pamphlet, written when he was seventy, served education and the cause of world peace even as it became futile.

Although the Hogarth Press publications from the mid-1920s through the 1930s reflected Leonard Woolf's special interest in international affairs, imperialism, the League of Nations, disarmament, and peace, there were many publications which dealt with matters at home in England. From Maynard Keynes's *Economic Consequences of Mr. Churchill* (1925) to L. B. Pekin's *Coeducation* (1939), the Hogarth Press published over fifty books and pamphlets on domestic social and economic problems, including works in two areas of special interest, education and feminism. Bloomsbury was well represented by Keynes's two pamphlets (1925, 1926), by Leonard Woolf's *Fear and Politics: A Debate at the Zoo* (1925) and *Hunting the Highbrow* (1927), and by Virginia Woolf's *Room of One's Own* (1929) and *Three Guineas* (1938).

In addition, there were political books such as J. A. Hobson's *Notes on Law and Order* (1926), Kingsley Martin's *British Public and the General Strike* (1926), Laski's *Crisis and the Constitution* (1932), G. T. Garratt's *Mugwumps and the Labour Party* (1932), and A. L. Rowse's *Question of the House of Lords* (1934). There were books which examined aspects of culture and society such as the published results of a *Nation and Athenaeum* questionnaire edited by R. B. Braithwaite in *The State of Religious Belief* (1927), or G. D. H. Cole's *Politics and Literature* (1929) and his wife Margaret Cole's *Books and People* (1938), or Raymond Postgate's *What to Do with the B.B.C.* (1935). But perhaps most interesting of these works on domestic affairs were the publications on industrialization, labor, and economics.

The coal miners' problems with the government, as Keynes had anticipated in his press pamphlet on Mr. Churchill, led to their walkout which fostered the General Strike of 1926. Several Hogarth Press publications during the depression years studied this industry and other labor problems. *Coal: A Challenge to the National Conscience* (1927), edited by Alan Porter with six other contributors, examined the immediate crisis. Later works such as B. Bowker's *Lancashire under the Hammer* (1928), C. E.M. Joad's *Horrors of the Countryside* (1931), and Thomas Sharp's *Derelict Area: A Study of the South-West Durham Coalfield* (1935) focused on specific problem areas of industrialization.

Moving testimony about the plight of workers was offered by R. M. Fox in three remarkable books dealing with the cost of industrialization in human terms: *The Triumphant Machine* (1928), *Drifting Men* (1930), and his autobiography *Smoky Crusade* (1937). Fox's personal crusade had taken him from the gritty experience of machine operator to the Co-operative movement and into early labor agitation and unionism. His activism then led him into socialism and war resistance (he served prison terms as an objector) and later to Ruskin College, Oxford, and a writing career. His vividly written books published by Hogarth document the victory of the human mind and spirit over the crushing power of industrialization. Fox, not the machine, triumphed.

Two books addressed problems of the worker directly at the height of the depression: Rupert Trouton's *Unemployment: Its Causes and Remedies* (1931) and *A Worker's Point of View: A Symposium* (1933), which grew out of a series of articles by workingmen in the *Human Factor*, the journal of the National Institute of Industrial Psychology.

Several press publications studied such broad economic areas as *Financial Democracy* (1933) by Margaret Miller and Douglas Campbell and W. R. Lester's *Poverty and Plenty: The True National Dividend* (1935), but others examined such specific economic problems as *The Worker and Wage Incentives: The Bedaux and Other Systems* (1934) by W. F. Watson, *Land-Value Rating* (1936) by F. C. R. Douglas, and *The Bankers of London* (1938) by Percy Arnold. And for the Hogarth Press readers who wanted to do business with those London bankers and brokers, Leonard Woolf offered them *Adventures in Investing* (1936) by "Securitas" (C. P. Thompson, financial editor of *Time and Tide*).

When Leonard Woolf campaigned as a Labour candidate to Parliament for the University Constituency in 1922, he made education his priority, second only to foreign policy because of the pressing need for a restoration of peaceful international relations. Educational reform in 1922 was Woolf's most important domestic issue and a subject close to his heart throughout his career in writing, publishing, and politics. In 1922 Woolf called for "complete equality of opportunity" in education from elementary schools through the university, an "adequate staff of trained and certified teachers" at every educational level, and improved pay with a minimum-wage scale.[18] The same issues, often from a socialist viewpoint, were treated frequently in the nine books on education published by the press.

Mark Starr's *Lies and Hate in Education* (1929) was a lively, informative, and salutary examination of the distortions and misinformation that he saw communicated to schoolchildren. Not surprisingly, leftist Starr found most of the lies, whether by inference, cover-up, or silence, to be manipulation of the truth in support of nationalism or imperialism and the class system. The BBC's educational programs in 1927–28 strengthened the ideology of colonialism, thought Starr, and so did the Imperial Educational Conference of 1927. Bertrand Russell, one of Starr's heroes, is quoted as saying that civics classes were "teaching the young to die in battle for capitalist dividends."[19] The picture was no better when Starr looked at France, Germany, Austria, Hungary, Italy, and Japan, and sometimes worse. Only when Starr gazed at Russia did he find uplifting examples of schools, text, and teachers. Having criticized the Boy and Girl Scouts of England, he approved the Soviet Young Pioneers and the Young Communist League with no apparent irony.

Other Hogarth Press books on education treated specific aspects of the school system, the curriculum, and its teachers, exposing weaknesses and proposing reforms. Majorie Wise critically examined *English Village Schools* (1931), for example, and Arthur Calder-Marshall exposed social conditioning and class bias in *Challenge to Schools: A Pamphlet on Public School Education* (1934). The most complete analysis of secondary education in England, however, was provided by L. B. Pekin (pseudonym for

Reginald Snell) in two books, *Public Schools: Their Failure and Their Reform* (1932) and its companion volume *Progressive Schools: Their Principles and Practice* (1934). Pekin then wrote two Hogarth pamphlets expanding on subjects he had introduced in his books: *The Military Training of Youth: An Enquiry into the Aims and Effects of the O. T. C.* (1937) and *Coeducation* (1939). As the titles of his books and pamphlets suggest, Pekin was an innovative educator, highly critical of public schools (the British private boarding school) and in favor of progressive educational reform, including the efforts to broaden the curriculum with more science and mathematics and to introduce sex education and manual training. He strongly opposed the Officers Training Corps and supported coeducation enthusiastically. The newly formed pacifist organization the Peace Pledge Union (with luminaries Canon Dick Sheppard, Julian Huxley, Rose Macaulay, Arthur Ponsonby, Bertrand Russell, and Vera Brittain among the early sponsors) was so impressed by Pekin's OTC pamphlet that it ordered several hundred copies from Leonard Woolf for distribution to its members (HP 335).

Mary Birkinshaw, under the auspices of the National Institute of Industrial Psychology (which had supported the Hogarth Press pamphlet on the workers' symposium in 1933), conducted an occupational analysis of 3,370 women secondary-school teachers to form a profile of the contented, successful teacher. The Hogarth Press published the results as *The Successful Teacher* (1935). Birkinshaw's book, with enclosed questionnaires, thirty data-packed tables, and a summary at the end, was inelegant in style but full of useful information and refreshingly devoid of jargon.

The Successful Teacher coincided with Leonard Woolf's editorial concerns in the *Political Quarterly*. He approved of statistical tables and surveys and saw that each issue of the *Political Quarterly* contained data on some social or political aspect of English life. His innovative use of such documentation permitted readers to form their own conclusions. Over the years he had writers prepare statistics on alcoholism, marriage and divorce, crime, unemployment, the professions, police courts, the universities, women's occupations, and public education.

Among the Hogarth publications on education, *Education Today and Tomorrow* (1939), by W. H. Auden and T. C. Worsley, is something of a curiosity. Written by a poet and a journalist in an undifferentiated collaboration, the pamphlet represented an unusual sortie into educational writing by the poet. Auden was not unfamiliar with the subject, however. Once the disciple of the educational reformer Homer Lane, Auden had become an unorthodox but enthusiastic schoolmaster first at Larchfield Academy and then at the Downs School, where he was known affectionately by his students as "Uncle Wiz." He had also written sporadically on education. During the five years Auden schoolmastered (1930–35), he contributed an article on writing to a outline text for schoolchildren (1932); reviewed books on education for *Scrutiny* (1932), *New Statesman and Nation* (1932, 1935), and *Criterion* (1933); and contributed an article on the subject of honor to Graham Greene's *Old School* (1934).[20] These activities hardly made him an expert on the subject, however.

As Auden wrote to his friend Mrs. Dodds at the time, "I am sorry Nature no more intended me to write about Education than it intended Louis [MacNeice] to review, but livings must be earned."[21] T. C. Worsley, writing to Auden's bibliographer, declared that the pamphlet originated in a request from the left-wing journal *Fact* for Auden to write an article on education. He chose Worsley as collaborator, but the resulting pamphlet proved "far too factual for *Fact*." Then, added Worsley, Auden's friend John Lehmann, having just become Leonard Woolf's partner, "snapped it up for that series of theirs" (the Day to Day Pamphlets).[22]

How much of *Education Today and Tomorrow* was Auden's contribution is difficult to assess. Auden's biographer has determined that Worsley wrote most of the first section, "Fact," and the last section, "Suggestion," and that Auden wrote the middle section, "Theory," a brief historical survey of educational theory from the Middle Ages to the present.[23] Certainly the "Theory" section seems Audenesque with a sometimes racy touch in the midst of otherwise sober prose (Dr. Norwood deceiving himself "with a lot of gas about Service") and with an attack on D. H. Lawrence's reactionary and Fascist-adopted educational ideas. But Auden also may have contributed to the many liberal and common-sense recommendations to be found in "Suggestion."

The approach to education taken by Auden and Worsley was clearly and enthusiastically leftist throughout, appropriate to their political stance in 1938 and to their intended publisher, *Fact*. It also suited their eventual publisher, the Hogarth Press. Having had his say about English education, Auden, with Isherwood, decamped for the United States in January 1939, missing the pamphlet's publication in March. By that time Auden was having another brief fling at schoolmastering at St. Mark's School in Massachusetts with Richard Eberhart. Writing back to Worsley, Auden commented that American education was poor: "No one does any work or learns *anything.*"[24]

Leonard and Virginia shared an intense commitment to feminist causes. Virginia's feminism, growing steadily throughout her life and present covertly in her novels, culminated in her radical feminist polemic *Three Guineas* (1938). Her feminism has been thoroughly documented and analyzed by recent feminist scholars. Leonard's support of feminism can be seen in his extensive activities with the Women's Co-operative Guild beginning in 1912 and in his ideological and political identification with socialism and the Labour party. The women's suffrage movement had been championed from the 1890s by the Independent Labour party and by many socialists. The alliance of Labour, socialism, and feminism, as Olive Banks has shown in her study of feminism, continued in England after "the Vote" was gained in 1918 into the 1920s and 1930s with mutual commitment to disarmament, the peace movement, and welfare legislation.[25] The eleven Hogarth Press publications on women, therefore, grew naturally out of the Woolfs' concern with the status of women and existed compatibly with works on disarmament, peace, socialism, and education.

The testimony of women's lives in a male-dominated culture as recorded in reminiscences, letters, autobiography, or biography constitutes one form of feminism. The memoirs of Viola Tree (*Castles in the Air: The Story of My Singing Days*, 1926) and Elizabeth Robins (*Ibsen and the Actress*, 1928) were less obviously feminist, however, than G. S. Dutt's biography of his wife Saroj Nalini, the founder of the Women's Institute movement in India (*A Woman of India*, 1929). Nor was Jane Harrison's richly anecdotal and name-dropping *Reminiscences of a Student's Life* (1925) overtly feminist, but present throughout her short book ran the recurring awareness of a woman scholar's struggle to win her place in the masculine world of teaching and scholarship. Leonard Woolf serialized Harrison's cheerful and humorous remembrances in the November and December 1924 issues of the *Nation and Athenaeum* before Hogarth publication. The longtime Newnham College scholar of Greek and classical archaeology was an admired friend of the Woolfs.

More obviously feminist were the pamphlets by Willa Muir, distinguished translator of German literature, married to the poet Edwin Muir, and by Viscountess Rhondda. They differed markedly in their attitudes. Willa Muir in *Women: An Inquiry* (1925) announced her intention "to find a conception of womanhood as something essentially different from manhood" and to explain why women had been dominated by men.[26] With Freud and Jung hovering in the background, Muir emphasized the conscious life of men, their rationality, and their skills in ordering and forming social systems in contrast to the unconscious life of women, their instincts, emotions and intuitions, and their attachment to life. Willa Muir did not seek equal rights for women. She offered no program, merely the idealistic notion of a self-created new morality; but in so doing, Muir seems to have been partly aligned with the "new feminism" emerging in the 1920s, which, as Olive Banks described it, took into account "women's special needs and aspirations."[27]

Viscountess Rhondda, one of the great suffragists before 1918 and a prominent activist for women's rights in the 1920s after partial suffrage was won (full adult voting rights for women were not achieved in England until 1928), represented a traditional, political aspect of feminism. In the middle and late 1920s the differing aims of the equal-rights feminists and those of the "new" feminists like Eleanor Rathbone who sought special allowances and protections leading to family welfare clashed in debate and organizational splits. Viscountess Rhondda, conservative in politics and committed to legislation gaining legal equality for women, would oppose the feminist move to welfare and socialism. She published the weekly *Time and Tide* and wrote articles on women for it which she signed "Candida." Leonard Woolf approached her with an offer to publish several of her feminist articles reshaped into an essay; she accepted his offer but not his suggested title of "The Slavery of Leisured Women" (HP 375).

Her short Hogarth Press pamphlet, *Leisured Women*, when published in 1928, attacked what she saw as the threat to society of upper-middle-class women. Poorly educated, motivated only by frivolous social aspirations, they lavished their husband's income on dresses and jewelry.

Such young women threatened the health of society, she thought. The women needed full citizenship with both the responsibility to lead productive, meaningful lives and the right of access to the means of production in business and industry. The law, wrote Viscountess Rhondda, should not protect women "in ways in which it does not protect men."[28]

Two of the more memorable Hogarth Press feminist publications provided firsthand testimony of the changes in women's lives won through the long struggle for equal rights on the one hand and for special opportunities and protections on the other. They document social history by the raw and moving experience of human lives, persuasive of the importance of the feminist movement beyond rhetoric and generalities. The success of the suffrage movement and the dramatic impact of the Women's Co-operative Guild reverberate in the two books, almost companion volumes, covering between them the experience of British women from the 1850s to the mid-1930s, from farm, mining, and factory women to members of Parliament. Both books were Bloomsbury books in a sense, edited by close friends and associates of the Woolfs—Margaret Llewelyn Davies and Ray Strachey.

Life As We Have Known It (1931), edited by Margaret Llewelyn Davies, with an "Introductory Letter" by Virginia Woolf, presented the autobiographical sketches of five remarkable guildswomen, a brief profile of the guild office clerk by Davies, and shorter excerpts from the letters of twenty-one other women. These were plain tales of endurance and courage by survivors, women whose iron resolve, luck, and buoyant spirits carried them through to the Women's Co-operative Guild, which gradually and miraculously developed their potentials. Many of the stories told of abuse, exploitation, poverty, and fear. But the horror of the stories was transcended by the intelligence and expanding spirits of their authors as the sisterhood of the guild aided them economically and politically and began to satisfy their hunger for knowledge and culture.

Virginia Woolf's long "Introductory Letter" to Margaret Llewelyn Davies counterpointed the testimony of the guildswomen in a curious way. At once a polished, highly sophisticated, and self-conscious bit of prose in the style of *A Room of One's Own*, it was also an unsettling admission of her failure to understand the women's lives or their guild. Neither letter nor conventional introduction, Woolf's piece contained crosscurrents of good intentions, self-revelations, and muted frustrations. She had first published it in the *Yale Review* in September 1930 as "Memories of a Working Women's Guild." She intended to rewrite it for the Hogarth Press, she reassured Davies, "so that it won't be the same thing" (*Letters* 4:192); but Woolf left most of her text from the *Yale Review* untouched, making several minor changes (substituting actual places and names for her original fictitious ones) and revamping her tone to a more sympathetic one.[29]

In her "Introductory Letter" Virginia Woolf approached the contents of *Life As We Have Known It* obliquely. Recreating her experiences at a guild convention in 1913 with all the vivid and anecdotal power of her fiction, Woolf candidly admitted to her own puzzlement, irritation, and boredom after hours of women's speeches. "It had been a revelation and a disillusionment," she wrote.[30] The women had talked facts about baths and money; but her mind flew free of the facts, and she had baths and money. She could not know the world of the women and their guild, only offer an "aesthetic sympathy" of eye and imagination. She remained an outsider. The written record of the women's lives, however, helped Woolf to gain entrance into a world beyond her ken.

The women's writing was not literature, the book not a book, Woolf claimed, but she responded emotionally and aesthetically to the simple power of their writing. She responded to them as women writers struggling to shape their experience verbally in a world without the masculine advantages of a private room and unearned income. They wrote, she noted, "in kitchens, at odds and ends of leisure, in the midst of distractions and obstacles." When she thought of them as plain, hardworking, disadvantaged women engaging in feminist politics, she tinged her sympathy with condescension and never forgot that "it is much better to be a lady."[31] Only by imagining them wrestling with words could she feel the bond of sisterhood. "You'll never like my books," Virginia Woolf had written to Davies in 1919, "but then shall I ever understand your Guild? Probably not" (*Letters* 2:399).

The other Bloomsbury feminist book, *Our Freedom and Its Results* (1936), by five distinguished women and edited by Ray Strachey, presented the upper end of the social and political spectrum of the feminist movement. Each of the women, expert in their fields, addressed the developments and changes in five crucial areas of public and private life since the first suffrage bill of 1918. Eleanor Rathbone, member of Parliament and president of the National Council of Societies for Equal Citizenship, addressed the changes in public life; Dr. Erna Reiss, a barrister and member of Lincoln's Inn, discussed the law; Ray Strachey wrote about changes in employment; Alison Neilans, secretary of the Association for Moral and Social Hygiene, examined "sex morality"; and Mary Agnes ("Molly") Hamilton, socialist friend of Leonard Woolf, a former Labour M.P., and a governor of the BBC, wrote about changes in social life. Hamilton had written an article on "Women in Politics" for Leonard's *Political Quarterly* in the January-March 1932 issue. The writers shaped their essays to provide a historical summary of the subject before enfranchisement, followed by a detailed analysis of developments after 1918 and a prediction of future changes. The documentation and coverage were thorough, the tone objective and professional. Although the authors soberly celebrated the gains of women, they saw clearly how much remained to be done.

Ray Strachey was the right woman to conceive the project, enlist the aid of the contributors, and put the book together. Married to Lytton Strachey's older brother Oliver and the elder sister of Karin Stephen (who had married Virginia Woolf's brother Adrian), she had been an active feminist and writer since her days at Newnham College. She had helped Millicent Garrett Fawcett establish the London and National Society for Women's Service in 1919 and edited the society's periodical, *Woman's Leader* (1920–23). As a writer on feminist subjects, Strachey had ranged far with considerable success. She had two women's biographies to her credit—of the American feminist Frances Willard (1916) and of Millicent Garrett Fawcett (1931)—and an important history of English feminism, *The Cause: A Short History of the Women's Movement in Great Britain* (1928). For Leonard Woolf's *Political Quarterly* in the October–December 1934 issue, Strachey had compiled a census "Occupations for Women"; she then turned her research into a book, *Careers and Openings for Women* (1935). So it was that Strachey's Hogarth Press book, *Our Freedom and Its Results,* complemented *The Cause* and her other feminist works, serving as sequel to her history and bringing it up to 1936.

When Ray Strachey first proposed the book to Leonard Woolf in

December 1935, he thought it best if she wrote it alone, but since that might delay the project for several years he agreed to her plan for an "omnibus" work by several writers. He suggested a 75,000-word book with an advance of £75 to be divided among them (HP 475). Not worth her while, replied the strong-minded Strachey, who wanted a £100 advance to cover the writers of the five 15,000-word-chapters—£10 for each of the "easy" sections on politics and law, £25 for each of the difficult sections on morality and general social effects, and to herself, £15 for her section on employment and £15 for editing the volume. She suggested Rathbone, Reiss, and Neilans for their sections but was uncertain about someone for the social section. Woolf conceded the £100 advance to her, and after extensive negotiations they agreed on Molly Hamilton as the fifth contributor.

Throughout the planning, writing, and editing of *Our Freedom,* all correspondence was between Strachey and Leonard Woolf; Virginia Woolf did not involve herself in the project. One month before publication she had not read it, as she wrote to Elizabeth Robins, but hoped when it appeared that it would be "worth reading" (*Letters* 6:74). Worth reading it was, and is today, but it is unclear whether Virginia Woolf ever read it.

Aside from her dislike of committee politics, masculine or feminine, Virginia Woolf thought that too much attention to causes had a deleterious effect on women, eroding their charm and coarsening them. In 1918 she thought Ray Strachey had lost her femininity from "perpetual testifying to the right" (*Diary* 1:155). One year later, in a letter to Vanessa Bell, Woolf despaired over Strachey, who had become "floppy, fat, untidy, clumsy" and was so thoroughly absorbed in her role of "public woman" that she made "fewer concessions than ever to brilliancy, charm, politeness, wit, art, manners, literature and so forth" (*Letters* 2:357). Strachey talked about the future of women, "but, my God," declared Woolf, "if *thats* the future whats the point in it?" Virginia Woolf's snobbery of status and style allowed her to admire the grande dame Margaret Llewelyn Davies but not the untidy Ray Strachey.

How different Virginia Woolf's feminism was from that of Margaret Llewelyn Davies, the guildswomen, Viscountess Rhondda, Molly Hamilton, Ray and Philippa Strachey, and all the other feminists Woolf knew can be seen in the two nonfiction feminist works she published with the Hogarth Press: *A Room of One's Own* (1929) and *Three Guineas* (1938).

There was more fiction than fact in Woolf's most famous and beloved feminist polemic, *A Room of One's Own*. The occasion was an address to the young women of Newnham and Girton colleges on the subject of women and fiction, which she subsequently rewrote into the expanded form of the published book. Woolf's form followed function. She created clever and pointed fictions before their eyes, inventing, among others, Shakespeare's thwarted sister Judith and the young modern novelist Mary Carmichael. There were few facts partly because she presumed to dislike them and partly because the works on women containing the facts (all erroneous) had been written by men. Woolf chose not to recognize the existence of useful, accurate, and understanding accounts of women by women. Nor did she mention directly the achievements of such women as Fawcett or Strachey or Davies. Strachey's *Cause* was a year old when Woolf created her story of her own room and an inheritance of £500 per year, yet there is only a brief quotation from it, identified in a footnote. Facts aside, the wit and irony of her writing, her satirical exposure of patriarchal attitudes, her leaps of intuitive understanding, her subjective experience made the book memorable and influential.

In 1931, seven months after the publication of *Life As We Have Known It,* Woolf protested to Davies, "I cant conceive how you politicians can go on being political" (*Letters* 4:392). All summer long the men had talked politics until she "finally felt it so completely silly, futile, petty, personal and unreal—all this about money—that I retired to my room and read poetry in a rage." The political world of Margaret Llewelyn Davies and Ray Strachey, like that of Leonard Woolf, with all its talk about baths and money, committees and constituencies, seemed absurd and vexatious to Virginia Woolf throughout her life. She never wished to play a role in those worlds and found them largely incomprehensible.

All the more interesting, therefore, when Woolf deliberately approached those worlds in her most aggressively feminist book, *Three Guineas* (1938). Brenda Silver's extensive work on Virginia Woolf's reading notebooks and scrapbooks and her analysis of *Three Guineas* have made clear how much labor went into Woolf's gathering of facts: twelve volumes of notes, including three scrapbooks compiled between 1931 and 1937.[32] In the power, anger, wit, and satire of her attack on repressive masculine institutions, Woolf chose not to write in the discourse of a traditional historian, sociologist, politician, suffragist, or guildswoman. She developed her arguments, cited her examples, digressed through provocative and unorthodox footnotes, to flail the misogyny and militarism of the patriarchal establishment with all the craft of the essayist and novelist. If she took little notice of feminist history or the sociopolitical status of women in the 1930s as documented by Strachey and others, her book proved so welcome an offensive against enduring male sexist attitudes that her sisters in the trenches overlooked her lapses. They gleefully applauded her achievement. Even Viscountess Rhondda, a feminist of a different persuasion, wrote in appreciation. Vita Sackville-West expressed reservations privately and angered Virginia, but only Queenie Leavis publicly quarreled with Woolf's position, drawing a sharp put-down ("old strumpets").

Taken together, *A Room of One's Own* and *Three Guineas* are unquestionably the most widely read and well remembered of the feminist publications issued by the Hogarth Press. They have had an effect on the rhetoric and strategies of feminism far greater than any of the other pamphlets or books the press published, and they remain today powerful molders of opinion.

Shaping attitudes, educating readers to the evils of imperialism or the needs for political and social reforms at home, Leonard Woolf's Hogarth Press publications in the late 1930s turned increasingly to ideologies. From the remarkable success in 1933 of Mussolini's pamphlet on the political and social aspects of fascism, Leonard Woolf saw that there might be a market for a Communist statement comparable to Mussolini's, and in February 1937 he proposed the idea to John Strachey. After his brief stint as a M. P. in the second Labour government and his trip to Russia with Bevan and Strauss, Strachey had returned to writing and editing. Strachey, to Woolf's regret, declined the offer due to his work with the Left Book Club, but he suggested R. Palme Dutt.

Leonard Woolf, however, approached Maurice Dobb. When Dobb also declined, Woolf finally turned to Dutt, who accepted the proposal in March 1938 (HP 75). Woolf's pamphlet in search of an author had taken twelve months and would take another seven months to materialize as *The Political and Social Doctrine of Communism* (1938). The entire nineteen-month process from his original concept to publication illustrates the careful, patient side of Woolf as a socialist publisher and educator. Dutt's pamphlet, a ringing polemic in favor of dialectical materialism and the dictatorship of the proletariat, said little about conditions in Soviet Russia (conveniently avoiding the purge trials) but a great deal about the worldwide threat of fascism. In this regard, Dutt responded more to immediate international politics than the other Hogarth pamphleteers. His publication called to arms all Popular Fronts to gird for the coming war with the Fascists.

Leonard Woolf's year-and-a-half long effort to publish the doctrine of communism was only a skirmish compared to his four-year struggle to publish a full-length history of socialism, a subject nearer his heart. Originally Woolf proposed the topic with detailed suggestions to Maurice Dobb in April 1935 (HP 68). Dobb declined, and so did Frank Hardie. Finally he approached Sally Graves, who accepted and signed the Hogarth contract in February 1936. Graves, a recent graduate of Somerville College, Oxford, was the niece of poet Robert Graves and a close friend of Anastasia Anrep, daughter of the Woolfs' friend Helen Anrep. A year later, still without a manuscript, Woolf encouraged Graves (recently become Mrs. Chilvers) to speed up lest Gollancz beat them to the book (HP 135). When the first manuscript finally arrived in August 1938, Woolf found it extremely good and "full of meat," but at his back he could hear his old colleague H. N. Brailsford with Gollancz hurrying near, and he exhorted Graves to rush on with her writing. When the Hogarth Press published Graves's *History of Socialism* in early 1939, it won the day. Brailsford and company did not compete.

The history Sally Graves wrote surveyed the origins and development of socialism from the early nineteenth-century English roots, through the growth of French, Marxist, German, and Russian socialism, to the evolution of the English Labour party, the effects of the First World War, and the subsequent rise of international socialism and Soviet communism. Her final chapter, "The Crisis in Socialism, 1919–39," quickly covered the interwar years and concluded with a brief proposal for British socialists and Labour party members to strengthen their resistance to fascism and capitalism in preparation for the effects of approaching war. As a historical survey of international socialism, Graves's book is solid; as a survey of English socialism, it is less useful. Graves avoided mention of the sectarian disputes within Labour and the Fabians (she cited the Webbs only in the early history and never G. D. H. Cole), thereby omitting much of importance in English socialism between the wars.

Of all the old-line Fabian and socialist writers, G. D. H. Cole was less to Leonard Woolf's liking than the others. He thought Cole and his wife Margaret had been ruthless and arrogant toward the Webbs early in their careers. Nevertheless, Woolf frequently worked with Cole on the Fabian Research Committee, shared some of Cole's disaffections with the Webbs in the early 1920s, and helped him and others reconstitute the Fabians around 1930. Woolf printed ten of Cole's articles in the *Political Quarterly* from 1931 to 1941 and published a book and a pamphlet by him with the Hogarth Press. Aside from the astringent, electrical quality of Cole's self-confident ambition in the early years, which Woolf disliked, there was an ideological difference between Woolf and the tireless advocate of guild socialism. Once Cole largely abandoned his insistence on guild socialism, the two men worked together harmoniously on Cole's articles for the *Political Quarterly*.

The turn to a more cooperative relationship seems to have been marked by Woolf's proposal to Cole in June 1928 that he write a book for the press on political literature (HP 58). Not often did Woolf propose a book to a prospective author, the few expectations being to those writers he held in esteem on subjects he deemed immediately important. Cole's book, especially planned for the new Hogarth Lectures series, can be seen as part of the educational and cultural thrust of the press as Woolf expanded its offerings in the late 1920s. Cole agreed to Woolf's proposal and wrote the book, a systematic examination of political literature from Hooker and Bacon to Russell and Shaw, during the autumn and winter. The Hogarth Press published it as *Politics and Literature* in October 1929.

G. D. H. Cole's second work for the Hogarth Press, a long pamphlet on *The Machinery of Socialist Planning* (1938), was written, he explained in a headnote to the volume, "for consideration by the Planning Section of the New Fabian Research Bureau." It grew out of committee meetings, represented his opinion, but did not commit the research bureau to his proposals. Here again one can see the usefulness of Woolf's Hogarth Press to writers of his general persuasion. With Woolf's press, Cole was able to make public the plans and proposals he favored that might not have emerged from the policy squabbles of the bureau.

The Machinery of Socialist Planning in 1938 looked forward to a time when the next socialist government would come to power and begin the long process of socialization. Cole's thorough and pragmatic pamphlet provided a blueprint for the way a socialist government might go about putting its new house in order. Cole's deep pessimism in the late 1930s conditioned his careful approach to planning the slow transition to socialism. Alarmed by international events and nearly as gloomy as Woolf, Cole feared the chaotic destruction of all he valued most. From a relatively unimportant pamphlet such as this, Cole's quality of mind, temper, and political astuteness can be seen clearly, qualities that have made him a central figure in the twentieth-century history of British socialism.

"Leonard is working hard at a second vol, of the Deluge; it should be out next autumn," wrote Virginia to Margaret Llewelyn Davies in November 1938. "Also," she added, "he is writing a book on Civilization for Gollancz, the Left Book Club; and has finished a play" (*Letters* 6:305). All three works, in their different ways, depict the breakdown of civilized values and the onrush of savage violence. They can serve as companion volumes, reflecting the deep gloom and pessimism that infected the Woolfs and many of their Hogarth Press authors in the last two years of the thirties. Leonard Woolf wrote them in the shadow of the approaching war, publishing his play, *The Hotel,* in the spring of 1939 and his two other books, *After the Deluge II* in September and *Barbarians at the Gate* in October 1939 (for the Left Book Club), shortly after Europe fell apart into war.

For all his skill as a short-story writer, novelist, and essayist, Leonard Woolf was no dramatist. He admitted in his introduction to *The Hotel* that he had never written a play before but had long wanted to write one. A short three-act play, *The Hotel* suffers from creeping allegory and creaking plot. The once opulent and civilized "Adriatic Hotel du Paradis," like the condition of Europe, has deteriorated into the seedy, bedbug-infested "Grand Hotel de l'Universe et du Commerce." It has become the stage for power struggles among Nazi, Fascist, and Russian Communist agents. Woolf's wit lightens the otherwise earnest maneuvering, but in the end the hotel and its denizens go down to darkness, the boiler room blown up, the clock smashed, the ceiling collapsed, and the proprietor abandoning the hotel to the bedbugs.

The Hotel impressed Maynard Keynes when Leonard read it to him in October 1938, according to Virginia (*Letters* 6:287), and Stephen Spender and Christopher Isherwood recommended it to Rupert Doone for the Group Theater, but *The Hotel* never opened its revolving door on the stage. In spite of his failure to have the play produced, Leonard's efforts in an uncongenial genre may have prompted Virginia's use of a play in *Between the Acts*. She began writing the novel in April 1938, gradually developing Miss La Trobe's pageant of English history and character, which plays out against the background of ancient Pointz Hall (a form of the Hotel du Paradis), as war threatens across the Channel.

Leonard Woolf's second Hogarth Press book in 1939, *After the Deluge II*, continued his grand study by concentrating on the English Reform Act of 1832 and the French Revolution of 1830. His long section on the interactions of French politics and the middle class leading to the July Revolution in France shows Woolf at his best in narrating a historical account of great complexity. Writing to Ethel Smyth on September 26, 1939, Virginia commented that she and Leonard had "decided to go on publishing [in spite of the outbreak of war], brought out all our books yesterday—L's 2nd volume: a masterly work. Pray God some one will buy it" (*Letters* 6:359). Not many did, and reviews of the book were few; scholarly concern for the events of the 1830s must have seemed irrelevant in the midst of those of 1939. The *TLS*, however, gave it a long review and thought it had "that stimulating quality which is achieved when abstract thought is most closely interwoven with accurate analysis of fact." [33] *After the Deluge II* was Woolf's last Hogarth Press book for fourteen years. In 1953 he published the third and final volume in his study, changing the title from *Deluge* to *Principia Politica* at the suggestion of Maynard Keynes.

As a Hogarth Press author, Leonard Woolf contributed nineteen books and pamphlets over a period of more than fifty years. During the years covered by this history of the press, he published eleven works, all but four of which (*Two Stories, Stories of the East, The Debate at the Zoo, and Hotel*) were expository. Unlike Virginia, who with her books became solely a Hogarth Press author, Leonard published works with several other publishers. His Hogarth Press books and pamphlets were not the only fruits of his writing career but perhaps were the best part.

CHAPTER SEVEN

★

THE THIRTIES, 1933–37

I
n January 1932, when the jaded John Lehmann sought a week off and declared his preference for being a manager, not a partner, Virginia Woolf apostrophized "the dear old Press to which I owe so much labor . . . & fun—oh yes, a great deal of variety & oddity, life on tap down here whenever it flags upstairs" (*Diary* 4:63). Life belowstairs was animated by Lehmann and by three young clerk-typists, Peggy Belsher, Molly Cashin, and Peggy Walton. Virginia Woolf's enthusiasm would wane with Lehmann's departure and the resulting increased workload. As she had three years earlier in October 1930, Virginia suddenly determined in October 1933 "to stop the career of the Hogarth Press; to revert to Richmond days" (ibid., 185). She was tired of "drudging & sweating" and curtailing their travel plans. "But to me," she continued in her diary, "the press has lost its spring & balance, & could regain it if it now made a constriction to the old ideals." And in December 1935, on what appears to have been almost a regular two-to-three-year cycle of discontent, Virginia was out walking with Leonard and agreed with him to "decide on a date & stop it." "Yes," she added in her diary, "I want to be free to travel . . . free of MSS" (ibid., 356). Perhaps they could find an "intelligent youth" to run the press for them, she thought.

No ideal youth was forthcoming, and they "drifted on," Leonard Woolf observed in his autobiography, "as one does, when something which one has oneself started in life without much thought of the future or of the consequences takes control of one" (*Downhill* 176–77). Allowing the press to drift into the 1930s, the Woolfs hired a series of women managers and clerk-typists. Even before Lehmann left, Leonard considered Hilda Matheson as his replacement in May 1932. She had been the first director of talks at the BBC and was an intimate friend of both Vita Sackville-West and Dorothy Wellesley. She had planned and edited with Wellesley the *Broadcast Anthology of Modern Poetry* (1930). After a week's deliberation she wrote to decline his offer, saying that she had vowed not to take a full-time job in London after her recent departure from the BBC (LWP).

Scott Johnson was eventually hired as manager in January 1933, but she left in February and was replaced by Margaret West in early March. She remained for four years, until her death by pneumonia in January 1937. Margaret West became well known and well liked at the press, the best manager of all, thought Virginia. Leonard offered her a starting salary of £250 for the first year, to be raised to £300 the second. As Leonard wrote on February 10, 1933, to West, "the point really is that the Press, run on my lines, ought not to be able to reach the point when it can normally pay £300, and with a little luck and more efficient management, including greater attention to the sales side, it might easily go still further ahead on the same lines" (LWP). But, he emphasized, he did not want to be in the position of publishing books merely because "they were paying propositions." The press at this time was producing a final profit of less than £1,000 per year. (See Appendix B.)

Shortly after the arrival of Miss West, Julian Bell suggested Kathleen Raine to the Woolfs as a possible assistant. Bell was struggling to write a second dissertation in hopes of a fellowship at King's and had met the Girton College graduate. He considered her "penniless" and in need of a job. Virginia Woolf interviewed the future distinguished poet and scholar of Blake and Yeats, finding her, as she wrote to Quentin Bell, "the size of a robin" with "the mind of a lovely snowball" but unsuitable for the press (*Letters* 5:245). One wonders how Raine would have survived in the hothouse basement world of Tavistock Square.

In 1933 the press published twenty titles, down dramatically from the near record number of thirty-six published the year before. As the numbers dropped, so did the books of poetry and prose. At times in the thirties the press published only a volume or two of poetry or prose, as meager a yearly offering in these genres as the early 1920s when the Woolfs had handprinted most of the books themselves. (See Appendix A.)

But if the thirties were marked by a dip in imaginative literature published by the press, it was the period when Leonard Woolf's political interest provided almost a new identity for Hogarth. The press soon issued an average of eight titles a year on a variety of political and social subjects. Some of the works of literature, however, outshone the many pamphlets and monographs. In March 1933, for example, the Woolfs began their first publishing season of the new year without Lehmann by issuing a translation of Ivan Bunin, a volume of poetry by C. Day-Lewis, and a second Michael Roberts anthology.

Eleven years after publishing Ivan Bunin's *Gentleman from San Francisco and Other Stories*, the Hogarth Press published *The Well of Days* in March 1933 and thereby contributed to Bunin's growing international reputation. The Hogarth Press publication was timely; Bunin was awarded the Nobel Prize seven months later on November 9, the first Russian writer to be so honored. In America, Alfred Knopf had become Bunin's primary publisher with the Guerney translation of *The Gentleman and Other Stories* (1927, reprinted 1933). Holt and Liveright had also produced Bunin books in America. As Bunin stated in a *New York Times* interview after hearing of the Nobel committee's decision, "I owe it partly to American friends who have interested themselves in my work."[1] With Knopf in America and Hogarth in England, there was a strong Anglo-American publishing interest in Bunin, working cooperatively.

The Well of Days, the first and longest section of Bunin's autobiographical novel *The Life of Arseniev: The Well of Days*, was serialized by Bunin beginning in 1928 in the Russian-language periodical *Sovremenye Zapiski* published in Paris. It finally appeared in a French translation as a volume in 1930. Shortly thereafter, in November 1931, with the alertness and instinctive feel for important contemporary writing that characterized his editorial and publishing career, John Lehmann opened correspondence with Bunin to arrange for an English translation of *The Well of Days*. Lehmann was only in his second month as manager of Hogarth Press but already was scouring about for interesting manuscripts.

"Nous avons lu La Source des jours avec beaucoup de plaisir," wrote Lehmann (HP 40). He continued, "Nous le trouvons un livre très interesant et très charmant, et nous sommes disposés a publier un traduction anglaise." Bunin replied immediately that he was interested, agreeing that

a skilled translator was needed for his book "parce que c'est un poeme."
He recommended as cotranslators Hamish Miles, the English critic and
translator, and M. G. Struve, the Russian writer. Quickly agreeing to
Bunin's request, Miles and Struve produced a translation which the
Bunin expert Serge Kryzytski has termed a "very carefully and artistically"
rendered English version of *The Well of Days*.[2] Although sales started
slowly, with only 643 copies sold in the first six months, Bunin's Nobel
Prize primed the pump, and Woolf had a second impression printed after
most of the original 1,200 copies had been sold (MSR).

In 1935 the Hogarth Press published its last Bunin book, a collection
of ten short stories entitled *Grammar of Love* containing "Sunstroke,"
often considered one of the best of his short erotic tales. Leonard Woolf
obtained the volume, translated by J. Cournos, from the American publisher Smith-Haas. In the absence of Lehmann, Woolf corresponded with
Marc Slonim, then Bunin's agent in Paris, and directly with Bunin, writing in French. During a thirteen-year period from 1922 to 1935, the press
had introduced and fostered the work of Bunin in England, publishing
in the process some of Bunin's best work, including his undisputed classic, "The Gentleman from San Francisco." Leonard Woolf had justifiable
pride in this achievement.

Michael Roberts's first collection, *New Signatures* (1932), in the Living Poets series, had introduced W. H. Auden, Stephen Spender, and
other young poets to a wider audience and distinguished itself as a result.
But Dorothy Wellesley found the poetry of such poets uncongenial, and
New Signatures marked the end of her participation in the series. She did
not like the poetry of Louis MacNeice, the one important thirties poet
missing from the series. As early as March 1928, Dorothy and Leonard
had rejected MacNeice's poetry for the series as "sham Eliot" when Eliot
himself had passed on a manuscript of MacNeice's with approval (HP
176). Lehmann at the time, probably through the urging of his friend
Anthony Blunt with whom MacNeice corresponded, had encouraged
Leonard to persuade Dorothy that MacNeice should be included.[3]

Leonard wrote to Dorothy in July 1932 admitting he found faults in
the poems of MacNeice and Tessimond but affirming that they were
"both genuine poets of some merit, and if the series is to continue as a
home of modern poetry, they are, I think, just the sort of people who

ought to be published in it" (HP 176). He added, later, that he thought MacNeice the better poet but that both were interesting. He urged her to decide whether or not to continue the series so that he could be free to publish poetry such as MacNeice's or Tessimond's in some form if she decided to end the series. He thought they should publish a volume by the autumn season because "there is a special sale . . . of poetry at Christmas,—even poets have to give Christmas presents, and tend to give their own volumes to their friends" (HP 176).

The result of several letters was that they skipped the autumn season, Dorothy rejecting MacNeice, Tessimond, and Day-Lewis's *Magnetic Mountain*. Finally, with some displeasure at Leonard's insistence that she make up her mind about continuing, Dorothy Wellesley decided in January 1933 to stop paying for the series "in view of other claims and duties now coming on" and because she thought the series well established. She did not object to Leonard's continuing it without her. In her memoir *Far Have I Travelled* (1952), Wellesley remembered that she had to discontinue the series because of financial reasons after Ramsay MacDonald's Labour government came into power.[4] Whether MacDonald or MacNeice and Day-Lewis were to be blamed, Wellesley withdrew, and Leonard Woolf began the second series of the Living Poets with C. Day-Lewis's *Magnetic Mountain* in March, in time for the spring list.

Leonard Woolf enthused to an unusual degree over the manuscript of *The Magnetic Mountain* when Day-Lewis sent his third book to him in late December 1932. He thought it the best thing Day-Lewis had done and "the best long poem that [he had] read for many a long day."[5] Woolf found the poem alive with ideas that interested him, unlike most of the poems he read. He agreed to publish it, but it would take him until January to bring the vacillating Dorothy Wellesley around to a decision about the Living Poets series and Day-Lewis's book (HP 247). Once Wellesley agreed to end her support, Leonard was able to publish *The Magnetic Mountain* in March as the first book in the second series.

So certain was he of the audience for Day-Lewis's poem that Leonard Woolf did the almost unthinkable for him. He had a limited edition of *The Magnetic Mountain* printed, one hundred numbered, signed, and bound copies in rose-brown cloth printed in gilt. It sold for 7s.6d. Then he had a regular trade edition published in 500 copies and sold at the standard price of 3s.6d. (*Checklist* III). Leonard had reasonable expectations. In what was becoming more formidably self-referential than Bloomsbury, the Auden group of friends, lovers, poets, fiction writers, and sometime political propagandists wrote poems and stories to and about each other. By celebrating themselves they publicized their privateness and helped create a market for their books. The Hogarth Press, with John Lehmann's encouragement, became a part of the support system and produced and marketed their writing.

Day-Lewis's *The Magnetic Mountain,* for example, had been published in several installments before book publication in March 1933. First, Michael Roberts had included seven poems from *The Magnetic Mountain* in *New Signatures* (February 1932). Eleven months later, Geoffrey Grigson launched *New Verse,* which quickly became one of the most significant publications for new poetry during the thirties. In the first issue of January 1933, he published two poems from *The Magnetic Mountain,* poems nos. 26 and 27 from part four, totaling fifty-eight lines. And simultaneously with the publication of the book in March 1933, the Hogarth Press issued Michael Roberts's second collection, *New Country,* which included four poems from *The Magnetic Mountain.* Thirteen poems out of thirty-six in the four sections of *The Magnetic Mountain,* by line count over one-third of the total poetic sequence, were published before or simultaneously with the volume. Readers of Day-Lewis were well primed for the book when it appeared. Unfortunately, the volume did not fare as well in the market as Leonard Woolf had expected. It sold a modest 356 copies in six months (MSR).

In the rhetoric and exhortation of *The Magnetic Mountain,* Day-Lewis made his most overtly political statement of the thirties in verse form, indicating a diseased and moribund society and calling the young to follow the leader over the border, across the frontier to the great mountain of leftist ideology where a new life could begin. The leader, no surprise to anyone, was W. H. Auden, addressed twice directly by Day-Lewis ("Look west, Wystan, lone flyer, birdman, my bully boy!") and evoked constantly. Such unabashed hero calling, embarrassing out of context, was part of the fervent mythologizing in the political poetry of the group. *The Magnetic Mountain* in tone, imagery, and diction is the most Audenesque of Day-Lewis's poetry. But amid the ringing calls for escape and for some unspecified revolutionary action, Day-Lewis wrote lovingly of the English landscape in terms that were his own.

In November 1933, eight months after publication of *The Magnetic Mountain,* Day-Lewis wrote to Leonard Woolf asking whether he would consider sending the volume to compete for a prize medal (HP 247). Woolf declared himself against the idea, which he thought was ridiculous, but then admitted his prejudice against all such awards and agreed to do it if Day-Lewis wished. A medal might help sell a few copies, he thought. But then Day-Lewis agreed with Woolf's reservations, and the medal attempt was dropped.

Lehmann had left the Hogarth Press in August 1932, and in his absence Michael Roberts corresponded with Leonard Woolf in late September proposing his new collection. The volume was not to be a sequel to *New Signatures,* wrote Roberts, for that work had been a gesture not to be repeated, but rather it was to be a collection "to clarify by juxtaposition of prose and verse contributions, what may be called the Spender–Day-Lewis–Auden–Isherwood attitude" (HP 396). That attitude, Roberts saw, expressed their desire as intellectuals "to fulfill our proper social function." Leonard Woolf accepted the idea for the book, provided it had unity, and they exchanged title proposals. Woolf liked "Newer Signatures"; Roberts countered with "Notes for Intellectuals," "Notes for Revolutionaries," "New Country," and "How Shall We Live?" Woolf accepted Roberts's third title, and the volume was titled *New Country: Prose and Poetry by the Authors of* New Signatures when it appeared in March 1933.

The subtitle was only partly correct. Four nonpolitical poets from the first volume were dropped (Julian Bell, Richard Eberhart, William Empson, and William Plomer), and four true believers were added (Richard Goodman, Charles Madge, Michael Roberts himself, and Rex Warner). Of the nine prose writers, three were new—G. F. Brett, T. O. Beachcroft, and Edward Upward.

Michael Roberts's preface to *New Country* struck a defiantly Marxist posture, far more political and militant then his introduction to *New Signatures.* The intervening year had intensified political interests among the young poets and writers, but Roberts seemed to march to a faster drumbeat than the writers he introduced. Speaking for his generation, Roberts embraced a Marxism modified and developed so as "to prepare the way for an English Lenin." Revolution could save their standards, he thought, and the young writers had to renounce the old capitalist system "and to live by fighting against it."[6]

The first three essays in *New Country* dealt with the ideological issues raised by Roberts but with less tub-thumping assurance. C. Day-Lewis's "Letter to a Young Revolutionary" seemed so cautiously Marxist as to be antirevolutionary, warning the young poet addressed of the manifold dangers of communism to his art. G. F. Brett surveyed science and read into its history and sociology a Marxist imperative in "Science Making Time." And Stephen Spender made clear the distinctions between artist and propagandist in "Poetry and Revolution," arguing for artistic freedom.

The eight stories that followed bore little connection ideologically with what went before, being literary pieces in spite of Roberts's denial, although they depicted working-class or lower-middle-class characters. Only the stories by Roberts and Upward at the end of the volume carried the freight of the preface. There were stories by T. O. Beachcroft ("The Half-Mile" and "A Week at the Union"), John Hampson ("The Long Shadow"), Christopher Isherwood ("An Evening at the Bay"), William Plomer ("The Child of Queen Victoria"), and Michael Roberts ("Non-Stop Variety"). Epward Upward's two slight pieces, "The Colleagues" and "Sunday," cautiously reflected the Marxism espoused in Roberts's preface, but through the self-conscious modernist technique of the interior monologue. Neurotic and paralyzed by self-doubt, the clerk-narrator of "Sunday" resembles Prufrock trying to force the moment to its crisis. Plagued by nervous diarrhea and other psychosomatic troubles, he finally resolves to accept the historical imperative and join the Party.

Upward's "Sunday" became famous. Christopher Isherwood, for one, thought it an "extraordinary short story" and remembered being "thrilled by the austerity" of Upward's tone. "Sunday" was "an intensely exciting . . . declaration that 'history'—the force of revolutionary change—is at work everywhere." Stephen Spender, for his part, devoted eight pages of his influential critical work *The Destructive Element* (1935) to a praiseful examination of Upward's stories. Not surprisingly, he found "Sunday" remarkable "because it shows that it is possible for a writer to create by going forward into a new tradition."[7]

The thirty-two poems by nine poets in *New Country,* like the prose, did not quite live up to Roberts's manifested preface. Among the more obviously political were Goodman's "The Squadrons," "It Is Too Late," and "Sorrow," along with Madge's "Letter to the Intelligentsia," with its line "Lenin would you were living at this hour / England has need of you," and Warner's "Hymn," with the famous refrain "Come then, companions. This is the spring of blood, / Heart's hey-day, movement of masses, beginning of good."[8] Day-Lewis's poems from *The Magnetic Mountain* also sounded the proper note while apostrophizing Auden as flyer and birdman.

Auden himself featured larger in *New Country* than he did in the first collection, with "Prologue," "A Happy New Year (To Gerald Heard)," "A Communist to Others," and "Poem." His rollicking satire in tetrameter seven-line stanzas to Gerald Heard showed Auden in his breeziest, most facile "Uncle Wiz" style ("In the ditch below me sulked Maynard Keynes / 'In Cambridge,' he blubbered, 'they think I have brains.' "). Of more significance, however, Auden's "Prologue" ("O Love, the interest itself in thoughtless Heaven / Make simpler daily the beating of man's heart") combined social concerns with an elevated, celebrative tone characteristic of his best poetry.[9]

As Samuel Hynes has noted in his extensive analysis of *New Country,* the 256-page book reflected not only the success of the earlier *New Signatures* and the greater public recognition of the contributors but also "a revised notion of what is the appropriate form of expression for a serious young writer."[10] So the combination in the volume of poetry, essays, and fiction, given focus and a sense of unity by Robert's preface, asserted the political obligations of the group to work for revolutionary change.

The book was an important document of the times. For all its stirring effect on the contributors and their friends, however, *New Country* fell far short of *New Signatures* in sales. Only 556 copies were sold in the first six months (MSR). Nevertheless, taken together, the two anthologies developed by Michael Roberts thrust the Hogarth Press dramatically and suddenly into the forefront of literary developments in the early 1930s. The two collections spawned namesake publications of importance for the thirties—Geoffrey Grigson's little magazine *New Verse* (1933–39) and John Lehmann's *New Writing* (1936–39).

In spite of his financially cautious recruitment of Margaret West for Hogarth manager in February 1933 and his by-now-familiar claim that he did not want to publish books merely because they might be profitable, Leonard Woolf did not neglect to pump up the press income when he could. In that very month he tried to rescue the Hogarth Letters series after twelve titles by binding together eleven of the letters into a single volume with a new title page as *The Hogarth Letters*. The effort was not successful, and he terminated the series after publishing the last one in March, Rebecca West's *Letter to a Grandfather*.

A much more lucrative venture that February was the press's publication of Derrick Leon's big (653 pages) novel *Livingstones: A Novel of Contemporary Life* (1933). A good read about the fortunes of a furniture store, Leon's novel was the sort the Woolfs seldom sought to publish. Its author had worked in a furniture store in Wigmore Street and would later work at Fortnum & Mason's. He had no connections with Cambridge or Bloomsbury. However, Virginia Woolf liked him, she wrote years later, and thought his novel "very good" (*Letters* 6:448). So were its sales, and Leonard had a second impression printed in March and put it into a cheap edition in 1936 (*Checklist* 114). Years later, in 1944, the Hogarth Press reissued it in a new edition.

Lord Olivier's last Hogarth Press book, *the Myth of Governor Eyre,* did well for nonfiction when it appeared in October, but the big seller for 1933 was Virginia Woolf's *Flush,* her unblushing biography of Elizabeth Barrett Browning's dog. Selected by the Book Society for its October offering in England, and by the American Book-of-the-Month Club for its September list, *Flush* sold 14,390 copies in the first six months, outselling even *Orlando* at the outset (MSR). Vita Sackville-West's *Edwardians* (1930), the all-time Hogarth Press best-seller, had sold 26,856 copies the first six months; it must have given Virginia some uneasy pride to have approximated Vita's success with such a slight work.

Vita Sackville-West in the summer of 1933 was between books, she and Harold Nicolson concluding a three-month lecture tour of the United States, and so she was receptive to Leonard Woolf's proposed collection of her poems to be published in two small volumes, each priced at 7s.6d. (HP 413). But, she told Leonard, she would prefer one important-looking volume to the two smaller ones, estimating that such a volume would run to about 300 pages and sell for 10s.6d. Practical Vita knew her books. When published in November, the *Collected Poems,* vol. 1, contained 325 pages and sold for 10s.6d.

Although she thought the project of collected poems slightly pretentious, Vita energetically assembled them and wrote the many letters required to resolve royalty and copyright agreements. Leonard thought the manuscript "very impressive" when it reached him in August. "It will be a book which will be a real pleasure to publish" (HP 413). What Vita assembled for the only volume of her collected verse (there was no second volume) was a seven-part collection containing 100 poems arranged topically rather than chronologically. *The Land* (1926), her long prize-winning poem of rural English cycles, opened the collection and, oddly, *King's Daughter,* her Hogarth Press poem of 1929, closed it, while in between were sections titled "In England" (with "Sissinghurst" the lead poem), "Abroad," "People," "Insurrection," and "Love."

The *Collected Poems* pleased Vita Sackville-West's devoted admirers but predictably did nothing to make her more acceptable to younger poets. Nevertheless, W. B. Yeats would include "On the Lake" and "Greater Cats" in his *Oxford Book of Modern Verse* (1936), and David Cecil and Allen Tate would put "On the Lake" and "A Dream" in their influential *Modern Verse in English* (1958). Vita saw herself, as she confessed in "To Enid Bagnold" in the *Collected Poems,* "A damned out-moded poet." The ways of "Sissinghurst" or "On the lake," for all their lyricism, were not the new ways of Auden, Spender, and Day-Lewis recently anthologized for the Hogarth Press. Vita's collection appeared seven months after *New Country.*

In October 1933 the Woolfs published what is undoubtedly the strangest and most exotic of the press translations: C. P. Sanger's version of Imre Madách's nineteenth-century Hungarian verse drama *The Tragedy of Man* (1933). It was in reality a memorial volume for Sanger, an old Cambridge friend of Leonard's who had died in 1930. An editorial note to the Hogarth Press volume indicates that Sanger's translation had been made "many years before he died."

Leonard Woolf had known and admired Sanger from Cambridge days when he used to join G. E. Moore and other Apostles for Moore's annual "reading parties" during the Easter vacation. Sanger was nine years older than Woolf, a contemporary of Bertrand Russell, and an established barrister. He also had written a still consulted analysis of *Wuthering Heights* (*The Structure of Wuthering Heights*) published by the Hogarth Press in 1926. Woolf fondly remembered him in his autobiography as a "gnomelike man with the brightest eyes I have ever seen and the character of a saint, but he was a very amusing, ribald, completely sceptical saint with a first-class mind and an extremely witty tongue, a mixture which I never came across in any other human being" (*Sowing* 201).

Imre Madách died in 1864 at the age of forty-one, only three years after *The Tragedy of Man* was published. His long verse play created considerable controversy at the time, but from its first production in the National Theater of Budapest in 1883, *The Tragedy of Man* has been remarkably popular, having a thousand performances in the Hungarian National Theater up to 1963. It became a national classic and was required reading in the public schools.

The Hungarian text, according to experts, is craggy with awkward locutions, irregular versifications, and puzzling ambiguities, yet in spite of its problems and the occasional melodrama of its plot, *The Tragedy of Man* mounts to such a momentum and an emotional intensity that it triumphs over all criticism, at least for Hungarian readers. The difficulties of text and content must be daunting to a translator. C. P. Sanger seems to have overcome many of them, if his Hogarth Press translation is compared to the only previous English translation, made in 1908 by William Loew, which is full of ponderous Victorian rhetoric. Since Sanger's, there have been a few other English translations, but the Hogarth Press version made Madách's classic available to those readers in England who, like Sanger, were attracted to the desperately uncertain contest between cynical Lucifer and questing Adam, man's noble progenitor, searching for an enduring brotherhood of man. Leonard Woolf may have felt the same attraction to *The Tragedy of Man* as Sanger and seen in the cosmic drama some aspects of the Cambridge Apostles' creed.

Freud, after an absence of three years from the International Psycho-Analytical Library, helped close out the Woolfs' fall season of 1933 with his *New Introductory Lectures on Psycho-Analysis,* published in November. Alarmed by the low finances of his Internationaler Psychoanalytischer Verlag, Freud hoped to generate sales with his new lectures. The Hogarth

Press, as always with Freud's own works, benefited from his success as an author.

As they had in 1933 with a translation of Ivan Bunin, the Woolfs began their publishing year in 1934 with a major translation, this time of Rilke. They had published a translation of Rilke's *Notebook of Malte Laurids Brigge* in 1930 and *Duineser Elegien* in 1931. The beautiful but flawed translation of the elegies by Vita and Edward Sackville-West, printed so elegantly by Count Harry Kessler, had been roundly attacked by several Rilke scholars as inexact and misleading. This time, the Hogarth Press translator was a scholar, and over a five-year period at the rate of nearly a volume a year, he would bring virtually all of Rilke's poetry to the press in translation.

In the early summer of 1933, J. B. Leishman, a professor of German at University College, Southhampton, sent a selection of Rilke's poems to Leonard Woolf. Impressed by the quality and thoroughness of the translations, Woolf agreed to publish them after Leishman had obtained publishing rights from the Insel-Verlag, although, as Woolf explained to Leishman, his experience with publishing Rilke and poetry in general led him to expect publication at a loss (HP 387). Woolf proposed, accordingly, 10 percent royalties on the first 1,000 copies sold, to be shared between Leishman and Insel-Verlag, and 20 percent royalties to be shared on all subsequent copies.

Leishman selected poems from Rilke's *Die frühen Gedichte* (*Early Poems*), *Das Buch der Bilder* (*The Book of Images*), *Neue Gedichte* (*New Poems*), and *Letzte Gedichte und Fragmentarisches* (*Last Poems and Fragments*). Although the English translations were printed without the German text, Leishman provided German titles and cross-references to the authoritative *Gesammelte Werke* (*Collected Works*). *Poems* was published in February 1934 in an edition of 1,000 copies, and not reprinted until 1939. The most notable aspects of the publication were a small drama over Leonard Woolf's reluctance to do business with Nazi Germany and an amusing contretemps with Stephen Spender over translation rights.

As the moment approached for Leonard Woolf to sign the agreement for translation rights with the Insel-Verlag, he felt "great repugnance to do so," he wrote to Leishman on August 27, 1933. "The more I think about the recent situation in Germany," he said, "the more barbarous does the behaviour of the Government seem to me, and I feel that I do not want to have any personal or business relations with those who support or tolerate it."[11] Appealing to Leishman's generosity, Woolf asked to be released from his contractual obligation. Leishman responded eloquently, defending the greatness of Rilke and German culture. Leishman expressed the hope that Woolf would reconsider in the light of the cultural opportunity of publishing so great a poet, thereby establishing "one of those conversions by which nationalism passes into internationalism and hatred into sympathy and pity" (HP 387).

Leonard Woolf was not convinced. "It seems to me," he responded in September 1933, "that the only way of showing people in Germany what the view of non-Germans is with regard to the barbarism—which you say yourself is desirable—is by individual action such as the kind I suggested."[12] But after discussion with others, Woolf found few who supported his view, and so reluctantly he agreed to proceed with the arrangement. Leonard Woolf's attitude, held with his customary moral intensity and supported by his understanding of international affairs, proved a lonely one. It was remarkable given the confusion and reluctance of Woolf's associates in pacifist and socialist circles to take a stand against Hitler. And not many businessmen in England, of whatever stripe, could have had Leonard's scruples in 1933 about dealing with Germany.

The brush with Stephen Spender over translation rights amusingly reveals both the publishing naïveté of Spender and Geoffrey Grigson at the time and Woolf's severity with ignorance. While Leishman was settling the contents of Rilke's *Poems* in November 1933, Spender published a translation of "Orpheus Euridice Hermes" in the October issue of *New Verse*. The poem was one to be included in Leishman's volume. Woolf investigated and learned that no translation rights had been given to Spender or to Grigson's *New Verse*. Spender wrote a "Dear Leonard and Virginia" letter in November 1933 apologizing and explaining his action. Woolf's reply on November 23, quick and to the point, gave Spender a primer on contracts. The publishing rights were a form of property, he explained, belonging to Rilke's heirs and the Insel-Verlag; he expected to lose between £25 and £50 on the Leishman translation "as there is no public of any size for Rilke's poems in English"; there was clearly no room for two translations, so that it was impossible to agree to other translations appearing in English (HP 387). When a chastened Grigson wrote to the Hogarth Press in apology, claiming ignorance, the manager, Miss West, reminded him tartly that an editor ought to know about translation rights.

Stephen Spender in the early thirties was known and well liked by the Woolfs. After publication, Spender's review of Leishman's translation of *Poems* in the March 1934 *Bookman* was "particularly generous," Leonard thought, in view of his own interest in the translations. Leishman agreed, praised Spender as a good poet, and began to think of collaborating with him on a future Rilke translation. Thus were sown the seeds of their thorny collaboration on the *Duino Elegies* published by Hogarth in 1939.

Between the publication of his first Hogarth Press translation of Rilke's *Poems* (1934) and his work with Spender on the *Elegies,* Leishman translated and published three more volumes of Rilke's poetry with the Hogarth Press: *Requiem and Other Poems* (1935), *Sonnets to Orpheus* (1936), and *Later Poems* (1938). There were a few problems connected with these volumes aside from Woolf's cautious acceptance of each translation, worried as he was about the modest sales and the almost annual offerings of Leishman.

The American rights were a clear disappointment. Although W. W. Norton had published John Linton's translation of *The Notebook of Malte Laurids Brigge,* Norton rejected the Leishman translation of *Poems* (as did Houghton Mifflin and Coward McCann) and *Requiem.* When Mrs. Norton read the proofs of *Requiem,* she carefully compared Leishman's translations with the German originals and consulted a Rilke scholar at Princeton. They both agreed, as W. W. Norton wrote to Hogarth in April 1935, that Leishman's translation was an improvement over the previous translations, but they could not publish it because they found his work uneven (HP 389).

Rejection became a familiar pattern. Knight Publications did not respond, and Vanguard rejected *Requiem.* So it was that the Hogarth Press was the sole publisher of Rilke translations in England and America between 1932 and 1938. Mrs. Norton published her own *Translations from the Poetry of Rainer Maria Rilke* in 1938. Her selections precluded any interest by W. W. Norton in Leishman's translation of *Later Poems* in the same year.

Laurens van der Post, compatriot of William Plomer, brought his first novel, *In a Province,* to the Woolfs in 1934 and began what would be nearly a career-long relationship with the press. Three years younger than William Plomer, three years older than Stephen Spender, almost the same age as Auden, Laurens van der Post might have become either a member of the thirties generation of Auden-Spender-Isherwood or one of the fringe members of Bloomsbury like his fellow countryman Plomer. *In a Province* (1934) owed something of its content to Plomer and something of its political consciousness to Auden and Spender, but van der Post went his own way as a South African journalist, war hero with the British army, prisoner of war under the Japanese, and later as an agent for the British government and the Colonial Development Corporation in Africa. His career as a prolific writer—novels, journalism, travel books, lectures, film scripts—blossomed only after 1951 when he published the internationally successful *Venture to the Interior,* his meditative and richly observant report of an agricultural mission to Nyasaland, and his mythic rendering of the Bushmen's culture in *The Lost World of the Kalahari* (1958).

In a Province (1934), published when van der Post was twenty-eight, combined his extensive South African experience with his journalist's knowledge of political agitation in the thirties. The two elements form an intertwined narrative thread in which deeply personal black-white relations in South Africa are worked out against a background of increasingly dangerous political and racial conflict. Stephen Spender gave a measure of fame to van der Post's novel by discussing it in his influential *The Destructive Element* (1935) along with Edward Upward's story "Sunday." Van der Post's novel merited consideration, wrote Spender, because it "has as its subject revolutionary politics, but . . . is not propagandist."[13] Spender's account of *In a Province* certified it for the 1930s canon, but failed to stimulate sales. The bookseller W. H. Smith & Son had canceled its order because Methodist Smith considered the novel sexually indecent. The press lost £14.7.2 on the book the first year, with only 642 copies sold (MSR). The subject and manner of his novel were appropriate to the politics of the times, but van der Post was more concerned with the heart than with historical imperatives. His later writing pursued different interests, but the Hogarth Press had given him his start by publishing his first novel.

Three other Hogarth Press authors returned with their wares in October 1934, John Lehmann marking his resumption of good relations with the Woolfs with a volume of poetry (*The Noise of History*), C. H. B. Kitchin with another mystery (*Crime at Christmas*), and Vita Sackville-West with a murky gothic romance.

Lehmann's second volume of poetry with the press arrived from Germany where he was witnessing the Nazis upheavals in Germany and Austria with Christopher Isherwood. *The Noise of History,* uneven though it was and denounced at home by critics from both left and right, nevertheless dramatized the struggle of a lyric poet to account for the chaos and confusion of historical events. Lehmann had created, in the words of Samuel Hynes, "a parable of political terror, privately felt," at the moment when democratic Europe lurched toward fascism.[14] Here in Lehmann's poems and prose-poems was firsthand support for Leonard Woolf's outraged protest against doing business with Germans.

When he returned to the detective story genre for *Crime at Christmas* (1934), after the disappointments of his big novel *The Sensitive One* (1931), C. H. B. Kitchin brought back his amateur sleuth Malcolm Warren but this time in cahoots with a skillful professional, Inspector Parris of Scotland Yard. *Crime at Christmas,* more complexly plotted than *Death of My Aunt* (1929), offered some of the same pleasures. Warren narrates the story, as he did in his first appearance, but in *Crime at Christmas* he is more of an observer than an actor. It is Inspector Parris who, in the style of Christie's Poirot, pulls the rabbits out of a hat in the final scene, confronting the assembled players.

Crime at Christmas (1934) proved another success for Kitchin and the Hogarth Press. Reviewers praised it, and sales soared. The first year's profit was £133.11.5 (MSR). It has endured through reprintings to join *Death of My Aunt* in Hamish Hamilton's Fingerprint series. Kitchin was not pleased, however, with Leonard Woolf's merchandising of his book and quarreled with him over distribution and advertising. Leonard, of course, defended the Hogarth record vigorously, claiming promotional success equal to any larger publisher. Kitchin argued that the Hogarth Press was an unsuitable medium for detective novels (HP 216). Leonard reluctantly let Kitchin go to Constable but asked to see the sales figures on his next book. The figures when Kitchin sent them in 1938 confirmed Leonard's claims.[15] At the time Virginia Woolf saw Kitchin unflatteringly as "little fat & white & cunning & not up to the mark. A rather conceited touchy man, I guess; has a good opinion of himself; & is slightly commonplace" (*Diary* 4:263). One ran a risk crossing pens with the Woolfs.

C. H. B. Kitchin's nine-year, five-novel association with the Hogarth Press, in spite of its unhappy conclusion, had been rewarding for both parties. Kitchin ranks with Vita Sackville-West and William Plomer as the three most published Hogarth Press novelists after Virginia Woolf, each publishing five works of fiction, although Sackville-West outsold the other two, and both she and Plomer published poetry with the press. If Kitchin is now remembered chiefly as a mystery writer, famous for *Death of My Aunt,* his other Hogarth Press novels were interesting in a highly individualistic way. Lytton Strachey, for one, preferred the three novels to the two crime stories and particularly admired *The Sensitive One,* which he had in his library.[16]

Vita Sackville-West's new novel for 1934, *The Dark Island,* would prove to be her last novel, although not her last book, for the Hogarth Press. The novel appealed to neither Harold Nicolson nor the Woolfs when they read it before publication, representing a return to the gothicism of the early novels, infused now with darker elements—sadomasochism, lesbianism, and murder. Harold Nicolson thought the novel "morbid and distressing," writing to Vita that he did not like it and ranking it last on his list of her works.[17] Leonard Woolf, strangely, praised the novel to Vita in a letter in July 1934, just after he had read the manuscript "with considerable excitement."[18] He liked the novel much better than *Family History,* he added. The same day, however, Virginia recorded Leonard's judgment of *The Dark Island* as "perilous fantastic stuff, a woman flagellated in a cave" (*Diary* 4:226). She wondered, "How much will the public stand?" Vita had come to lunch, and Virginia saw her rather mercilessly as "opulent & bold & red—tomatoe colored," with painted fingernails and lips. Seven months later Virginia would mark in her diary the end of their affair: "My friendship with Vita is over. Not with a quarrel, not with a bang, but as ripe fruit falls" (ibid., 287). She meant her love affair, not her friendship, which continued strong to the end of Virginia's life.

Rarely did Vita Sackville-West make any requests of her publisher, diffident as she was about her writing. Now she made two in connection with *The Dark Island*. The first request was that her older son Ben be allowed to design the book jacket and to supply a map of the locale. Leonard Woolf gladly agreed. Ben submitted three designs, and Leonard chose one and paid the pleased nineteen-year-old a guinea for his efforts (HP 415).

Vita's second, more important, request, a difficult one for her, was for more money. Hating to bargain with friends, Vita wrote to Leonard on June 29, 1934, reminding him of a discussion she and Harold had had the previous year with the Woolfs when they had "made it clear to you both that we had some difficulty in carrying on our life, and the education of Ben and Nigel, on what we were able to make by books or journalism" (HP 415). Ben was Oxford-bound, and seventeen-year-old Nigel was at Eton. It was a time, Nigel Nicolson has noted, when the Nicolsons "were spending at the rate of £6000 a year and were earning at the rate of £3000." [19]

Vita had rejected the siren's song of Cassell in September 1933, when it had offered her £1,000 to change publishers. She had remained loyal to Hogarth, but now in 1934 she hoped for a better contract and proposed that Leonard pay her £200 for the delivered manuscript, £200 on the date of publication, and 20 percent (not 15 percent) on the first 3,000 copies sold (HP 415). Leonard agreed immediately to all her requests, feeling, as he wrote to Vita, a "little guilty in having put the burden of suggesting them upon you." Virginia expressed herself more completely, writing to Vita that she and Leonard always thought of her as the most "perfectly disinterested and incorruptible and mild and modest and magnanimous of all our crew" (*Letters* 5:312).

The Dark Island made money for Sackville-West and the Woolfs, in spite of its perilous stuff, but not much, as if in answer to Virginia's question about the public. After her early novel *Seducers in Ecuador* (1924), *The Dark Island* was the least successful of Vita's Hogarth Press novels, both artistically and commercially, and marked the clear downswing of her talents as a novelist. The data on Vita's four major novels, taken from the press's monthly sales (Reading) account book shows dramatically her falling sales: *The Edwardians* (1930) was issued in 18,000 copies, quickly went through three more impressions totaling 14,000 more copies, sold 26,856 copies the first six months, realized a first-year profit of £1,907.2.7

and a second-year profit of £2,136.6.4: *All Passion Spent* (1931) was issued in 12,050 copies, went through two more impressions totaling 9,000 more copies, sold 14,204 copies the first six months, realized a first-year profit of £1,118.15.7: *Family History* (1932) was issued in 12,170 copies, had no subsequent impressions, sold 7,565 copies the first six months, realized a first-year profit of £336.11.2½: *The Dark Island* (1934) was issued in 10,590 copies, had no subsequent impressions, sold 6,071 copies the first six months, realized a first-year profit of £57.8.5½. The low profit margin of *The Dark Island* was partly attributable to the larger royalties paid to Sackville-West under the new contract.

As Vita Sackville-West's popularity dwindled and William Plomer changed publishers, Christopher Isherwood developed into an important and fast-selling novelist to keep the Hogarth Press fiction list alive at a crucial time when Virginia Woolf was between novels. Much had happened to Isherwood in the three-year interval between *The Memorial* and the next novel he submitted to the Hogarth Press, *Mr. Norris Changes Trains* (1935). Constantly in and out of Berlin, Isherwood began and abandoned an autobiographical book which would become *Lions and Shadows* and began an ambitious, many-sectioned epic on modern Germany, never published, to be called "The Lost."

In his private life Isherwood lived through the tumultuous days in Germany he chronicled later in his autobiography *Christopher and His Kind* (1976). Aside from his English friends and the boys from the Cozy Corner like Bubi and Otto, Isherwood met the Berliners who were to become so well known by their fictional names in his stories: Jean Ross (to become Sally Bowles), Gerald Hamilton (Arthur Norris), his landlady Frl. Thurau (Frl. Schroeder), Gisa Soloweitschik (Natalia Landauer), Wilfrid Israel (Bernhard Landauer), Willie Münzenberg (Comrade Bayer), and a host of lesser characters. With the chaotic collapse of order in Berlin in 1932 and Hitler's ruthless seizure of total power in 1933, Isherwood decamped to wander restlessly across Europe with his lover Heinz. The four years in Germany were over; the diaries, letters, memories, and preliminary fictional treatment of those years were being shaped patiently by Isherwood into his vivid fiction of the 1930s.

The first publication from the rich lode of "The Lost" became *Mr. Norris Changes Trains,* published by the Hogarth Press in March 1935. Isherwood had hoped for earlier publication, convinced in 1934 that war was imminent and might render his book meaningless.[20] The American edition, issued by W. Morrow the same year, carried the strangely inappropriate title of *The Last of Mr. Norris* (Arthur Norris's frantic evasions of pursuit by the evil Schmidt through South America and the United States never end). The anonymous reviewers for the *TLS* and the *Nation* liked the book chiefly because of its depiction of decadent Berlin, although the *Nation* reviewer regretted the absence of a good international spy plot.[21] More discerning critics, Cyril Connolly (*New Statesman and Nation*), Edwin Muir (*Listener*), and William Plomer (*Spectator*), praised Isherwood's wit, satire, originality, and psychological insights.

Leonard Woolf, thinking of his ad campaign for the novel, wrote to Hugh Walpole asking "something which as a publisher I have never asked before" (*Letters* 5:376). Learning that Walpole admired Isherwood's novel, Woolf asked him for a quotable puff for the book. Walpole agreed, and Woolf took out a full-page ad in the *New Statesman and Nation* in the March 23, 1935, issue, devoting half of the ad to *Mr. Norris Changes Trains* and featuring Walpole's praise along with quotations from the reviews by Plomer, Connolly, and Muir. Walpole placed Isherwood in the line of Baron Corvo and Norman Douglas, praised his "charming malice" and knowledge of people, and rated *Mr. Norris* as "one of the half-dozen intelligent novels of the spring."[22] Woolf seldom advertised with such expansiveness, but he knew a popular success when he saw one.

The Hogarth Press published Isherwood's novel in an edition of 1,730 copies in February, but sales were so brisk, aided by its selection by the Times Book Club, that Leonard Woolf put it into a second impression in March. His ad with Walpole's blurb was timed to keep the sales running. In the first six months, *Mr. Norris Changes Trains* sold 2,830 copies, and it earned a solid first-year profit of £241.6.5 (MSR). Additional reprintings occurred after the war in 1947 and 1952 as the novel's popularity and critical acclaim continued to grow. Isherwood achieved his first measure of fame with this book, and he appreciated both the lionizing and the income.

Following publication of Isherwood's novel, C. Day-Lewis's next volume of poetry in March 1935 brought back to Hogarth one of the Woolfs' most important writers of the thirties. After the exhilaration of

The Magnetic Mountain (1933), C. Day-Lewis had turned to a boy's adventure story, *Dick Willoughby* (1933), his first prose fiction, and to a long critical essay, *A Hope for Poetry* (1934), both published by Basil Blackwell. The story of plucky Dick amid the horrors of decaying phantoms and evil servants in Tudor England would lead Day-Lewis to write detective novels within a year. *A Hope for Poetry* set forth at length his arguments for the poetry of his generation, its indebtedness to the poetry of Gerard Manley Hopkins, Wilfred Owen, and T. S. Eliot, and its sociopolitical importance in a time of revolutionary change.

The next year, sensing the time was right, the Hogarth Press issued Day-Lewis's *Collected Poems, 1929–1933*. The volume included his three important Hogarth volumes, *Transitional Poem, From Feathers to Iron,* and *The Magnetic Mountain*. Simultaneously the press published his new book of poems, *A Time to Dance and Other Poems*. Unlike the spotty sales of his previous volumes, the new poems did well from the beginning. Leonard Woolf printed 750 copies of *A Time to Dance* and soon put the volume through three reprintings. It sold 1,100 copies in the first six months (MSR). Its success may have been due to the accessibility of the twelve short poems and the long title sequence with its narration of a nonstop heroic flight to Australia in 1920 by two Australian aviators. *A Time to Dance* consolidated the themes of Day-Lewis's *Magnetic Mountain* but showed little advance in subject.

Driven by the financial needs of his growing family, Day-Lewis turned to detective fiction, picked up the literary agent A. D. Peters, and sold his first mystery novel, *A Question of Proof* (1935), under the pseudonym of Nicholas Blake, to the publisher Collins for inclusion in its well-established Crime Club series (writer-members included Agatha Christie and Ngaio Marsh). *A Question of Proof,* with the detective Nigel Strangeways, began a long line of twenty very successful Nicholas Blake novels between 1935 and 1968.

At the time Day-Lewis wrote to Leonard Woolfe requesting a release from the Hogarth Press contract for his mysteries. Typically, Leonard agreed to release the first novel but requested the right to consider the next one (HP 251). Day-Lewis argued persuasively that he wanted his serious work published by Hogarth, but that his detective novels were not in the same line and therefore would not compete with those works.

Leonard, never one to give ground easily when his editorial rights were at risk, grumpily acceded, later admitting that he had been too severe. Leonard had gone through the same argument with C. H. B. Kitchin just one month before, but with less grace. It is evidence of Leonard Woolf's respect for Day-Lewis that he protested so little.

In 1935 Day-Lewis quit schoolmastering for full-time writing, moved toward joining the Communist party of Great Britain, and published his third Hogarth work for the year and his most polemical prose work. *Revolution in Writing* appeared in October in the press series of Day to Day Pamphlets. The essay had originated in a BBC broadcast in March, "Youth Looks Ahead," and in an article on "Revolutionaries and Poetry" published in the *Left Review*.[23] Leonard Woolf liked the idea of putting the two pieces together in a pamphlet if Day-Lewis would write a bridge passage of 1,000 words linking them (HP 249). The resulting tripartite *Revolution in Writing* (1935) posed the crucial questions facing a Marxist writer from the upper middle class bent on revolution but caught in a bourgeois culture that was slow to die. Day-Lewis's honesty and self-doubt were impressive even if his Marxist ideology was shaky. Predictably, both the left and the right, and the liberals in between, found fault with his pamphlet.

C. Day-Lewis's final Hogarth Press publication, *Noah and the Waters* (1936), seems to have been his justification for the uncertain ideology of *Revolution in Writing*. The book offered a pseudo-morality play, casting Day-Lewis as a Marxist Noah faced with the flood of the masses. In addition to the problematical allegory (the workers united are faceless floodwaters, soon to be evaporated), Day-Lewis's verse drama failed to give Noah any real conflict or choice. His acceptance of the watery revolution is fate, not dialectic. *Noah and the Waters,* unsatisfactory both as literature and as politics, was roundly criticized. But it attracted attention and sold 607 copies in six months (MSR). It represented Day-Lewis's most extreme abandonment of art for ideology. In less than two years, he would return to more traditional themes.

With the manuscript of *Noah and the Waters,* Day-Lewis announced to Leonard Woolf in December 1935 that he would leave the Hogarth Press for a publisher with a larger merchandizing operation, so he could support his family completely through his writing (HP 248). He intended to try his hand at serious novels, but his friendship with the Woolfs made it difficult to leave. "Your encouragement of my earlier work," he wrote, "has meant an enormous amount to me," and he hoped to stay in touch personally. Leonard Woolf replied that he was sorry and that Day-Lewis's departure was not unexpected.[24] And so, with good feelings on both sides, Day-Lewis and the Woolfs parted company after five volumes of poetry, a morality play, and a pamphlet. Four years later, when John Lehmann began the New Hogarth Library series, he included Day-Lewis's *Selected Poems* (1940) as the second volume in the series. For his other literary works, Day-Lewis went to Jonathan Cape, remaining with that publisher until after the war.

In the last three years before Lehmann's return in 1938, the Hogarth Press poetry list dropped off markedly to a total of only six volumes during 1935–37. Without Day-Lewis's three volumes (two in 1935, one in 1936), there would have been little to celebrate. Old Bloomsbury friend R. C. Trevelyan published *Beelzebub and Other Poems* (1935), his poetry increasingly remote from the times, and newcomer Christopher Lee published *Poems* (1937), a last volume in Leonard Woolf's moribund Living Poets second series. But at least there was the promise of better poems to come with Julian Bell's *Work for the Winter and Other Poems* (1936).

Julian Bell, exemplary second-generation Bloomsbury, revealed a most un-Bloomsburyan commitment to poetry. By the end of his second year at Cambridge in 1929, Julian Bell had formed an important literary friendship with Lehmann and had established himself as a promising young poet by publishing numerous poems in the undergraduate magazines *Cambridge Review* and *Venture*. Two of his poems had been included in the Hogarth Press anthology *Cambridge Poetry 1929* and three in *Cambridge Poetry 1930*.

As he completed his undergraduate years at King's College, Bell sent off his twenty-seven best poems not to Hogarth but to Chatto & Windus, which published them in 1930 as *Winter Movement*. Many of these poems were neo-Georgian descriptive poems. By the time Michael Roberts, with John Lehmann's assistance, was assembling the poets and poems to include in *New Signatures* (1932), Julian Bell had begun interesting himself in the eighteenth century. He espoused Pope over Keats and extolled reason, order, and clarity over neo-Romantic attitudes. Not surprisingly,

Bell had strong doubts about being included with the Oxford poets in the Roberts anthology, and he exchanged bristling letters with Lehmann over the subject. Nevertheless, *New Signatures* contained three of Bell's poems.

The next few years in Julian Bell's life after Cambridge were a mixture of idealism and boredom, misdirected energy and frustration. His thesis on Pope failed to earn him a fellowship at Cambridge, and the Woolfs rejected it for the Hogarth Press. After time in London, various romances, literary projects which he never completed, and growing restlessness, Bell won an appointment to teach English at the National University of Wuhan, China. He departed for China in August 1935 and remained a year and a half. While there, Bell assembled and dispatched to the Woolfs over thirty-three poems written during a four-year period, and the Hogarth Press published them as *Work for the Winter* in March 1936. It would be the only work of Bell's the Woolfs would publish while he was alive.

Most of the poems were traditional in tone and subject, although no longer deliberately Popean. Bell grouped his winter work into five sections, "Political Poems" (five poems), "London" (seven poems), "Love Poems" (nine poems), "Descriptions" (two poems), and "Constructions" (nine poems). He added a translation of Rimbaud's "Bateau Ivre" in collaboration with Charles Mauron. "Tranquility Recollected" was reprinted, and remains one of the best in the volume, and a new poem, "Redshanks," explored in tight couplets the contrast between the soaring, cold-eyed hawk "impartial to our human plight" and the uncertain poet below. *Work for the Winter* pleased Bloomsbury and interested John Masefield, but it sold only 102 copies in six months (MSR). At Masefield's suggestion, Leonard Woolf, in spite of his dislike of such contests, sent off a copy of the book in March to be considered for the Royal Medal for Poetry (HP 20). It failed to win. Woolf had discouraged Day-Lewis from such a competition in 1933.

After months of anxiety and indecision, Julian Bell resigned from his teaching post in China and returned home in March 1937 with plans to participate in the Spanish civil war. By April he had joined the Spanish Medical Aid group and was being trained to drive ambulances. He left England for Spain in early June, and in little over a month, on July 18,

1937, he was killed near Madrid during the battle of Brunete when his ambulance was hit by a bomb. He was twenty-nine years old.

The most active period of Hogarth Press translations had been in the early 1920s with Koteliansky's Russian translations. After that, the press continued to release two translations every year or so (excluding IPL books) from a variety of sources into the 1930s, such as Madách's *Tragedy of Man* (1933) and Mussolini's pamphlet on fascism (1933). These seldom reached the significance of the early Russian works. Exceptions were translations of Ivan Bunin (1922, 1933, 1935), Italo Svevo (1929, 1930), and Rilke (1931, 1934, 1935, 1936, 1938, 1939, 1941). As the Woolfs published the last of Bunin (his *Grammar of Love* in 1935) and continued their almost annual release of Rilke in the Leishman translations (*Requiems and Other Poems* in 1935 and *Sonnets to Orpheus* in 1936), they published an unusual novel by an early Soviet author, Yuri Olesha, and lost the opportunity to publish a book by Pushkin.

Yuri Olesha is remembered in the West as the author of one novel, the sensationally popular *Envy,* first issued in Russia in 1927 and published in English translation by the Hogarth Press in October 1936. Olesha's other writings—another novel, a long story, a collection of stories, three plays—were pale versions of his original success. His rise and fall in Russia was meteoric; his present reputation among Western critics of Soviet literature is solid and growing. Olesha's glories, past and present, are attributable to the plot and texture of *Envy* and to the insistent voice of his character Kavalerov, the rebellious antihero of the book.

Envy was immensely popular when published in Russia in 1927, generating praise for its attack on bourgeois personality and values. Dissenters, however, quickly pointed out the ambiguities and paradoxes in Olesha's richly textured novel. Babichev resembles the sausages he extols, Makarov the machine, and only the repellent Kavalerov is truly and noisily alive, embodying the conflicting values, the sordidness as well as the potential nobility of free men. Olesha was soon out of favor and out of the main stream of Soviet literature. Subsequent critics, mostly Westerners, have praised *Envy* as the outstanding Soviet novel of its period. They have found in Olesha's complex image clusters and ironic style a modernist novel more daringly experimental than the social realism of the proletarian novels soon to be in favor.

When the Woolfs published Olesha's *Envy* in 1936, they were introducing English readers to a work almost ten years old, written by an author no longer active. Even with a customary cultural lag, the delay in the appearance of an English translation of such a well-known and controversial book remains unexplained. Most of the Revolutionary and NEP-period Soviet writers were quickly translated during 1929–33. The delay is attributable perhaps to Olesha's inactivity as a writer or, as the *TLS* reviewer speculated, to the fact that "it means much more to the reading public in Russia than it can mean anywhere else, and that even in Russia its importance is not of a strictly literary nature."[25] Such an assessment no longer holds. *Envy* now merits considerable critical commentary for its literary qualities.

The Woolfs and their translator had their difficulties. Negotiations over the translation between Leonard Woolf, John Rodker acting as agent, and the translator Robert Payne (listed on the title page as "Anthony Wolfe") consumed several months. It was complicated by the control over the translation rights exercised by Preslit, the Soviet bureau responsible to authors for their Western publication. Preslit found many errors in Payne's version and eventually submitted nineteen pages of meticulous corrections in four columns—page reference, Russian text, Payne's translation, and Preslit's corrected translation. Thus Payne's "I was like a dog, whenever anyone yawns" became "I yawned like a dog." "He is a good fellow" was corrected to "He's a genius," and "Kavalerov's trembling" was expanded by Preslit into "Kavalerov's big toes were wriggling with embarrassment" (HP 327). Even with these emendations the translation remained flawed, but the Hogarth Press translation of Olesha's *Envy* made available to English readers an important Soviet novel. It remained the sole English translation until 1947. Sales, however, were disappointing, and *Envy* lost over £117 the first year (MSR).

The anecdote of the lost Pushkin is a mere footnote to the Hogarth Press history of Russian translations, but one which reveals the way manuscripts often came to the Woolfs through friends. It also reveals Leonard Woolf's intense dislike of Soviet Russia during the time he negotiated with Preslit over the translation of Olesha's *Envy*.

Recounting the story of "Jane" in his autobiography, Woolf used the tragic circumstances of a pseudonymous English wife of a Russian scientist to illustrate how the chaotic and savage authoritarianism of Stalinist Russia disrupted common lives (*Downhill* 29–33). Her husband falsely accused, arrested, and transported to a labor camp, Jane returned to London in 1936 for refuge. In 1937, the centenary year of Pushkin's death, Jane brought Leonard Woolf the translation of a short autobiographical book by Pushkin not previously available in translation. The translator, Jane's friend, remained in Russia under such perilous conditions that publication of the Pushkin in England might have endangered her. "Whether in fact to publish was a nice question," Woolf remembered, "the nicety being for her friend the thinnest partition between life and death." Woolf, enthusiastic to publish, agreed to a coded telegram exchange with the friend. If he wished to publish the Pushkin translation, Woolf would cable, "Many happy returns." If Jane's friend thought it safe to publish, she would telegram back, "Many thanks for good wishes." No reply meant that it was unsafe to publish. Woolf sent off his "happy returns" but recived no reply, and the Pushkin was never published. The Hogarth Press thereby missed an opportunity to publish another classic Russian author, and the Woolfs gained vivid personal experience of the "senseless barbarism of communist society behind the iron curtain." Harold Laski's idealistic pamphlet *Law and Justice in Soviet Russia* was only two years old.

At the time of the Olesha translation, and long after the publication of the original Tolstoy books, the Hogarth Press published in 1936 a short piece of writing by Tolstoy, uncompleted at his death. Entitled *On Socialism* by his translator Ludwig Perno, Tolstoy's writing was brought to Leonard Woolf by Roger Fry's daughter, Ruth Fry. In her prefatory note to the pamphlet, Ruth Fry explained that she had developed a friendship with Chertkov and his wife on her first visit to Moscow in 1922 and through Chertkov and Perno she had obtained Tolstoy's essay. Perno, in his "Translator's Preface," traced the origin of Tolstoy's writing to a request for a contribution to a book by young members of the Hungarian National Socialist party.

Tolstoy's essay was only marginally political, in spite of the title given by Perno, as Tolstoy used the occasion to expand on his profoundly moral and humane vision of the world. He struggled to finish the article amid an increasingly desperate and destructive family conflict, probably working on the article as late as October 27, 1910, the day before his final exodus from Yasnaya Polyana. Critical of all "superstitions" and of all ideologies not his own, Tolstoy with his customary eloquence exhorted his young Hungarian readers to study the "greatest thinkers of mankind" and so to understand "the religious basis of life." In title, if not in doctrine, Tolstoy's late-blooming Hogarth Press pamphlet fit perfectly into other press offerings in the 1930s.

Leonard Woolf published his satirical attack on the dictators, *Quack, Quack!* (1935), attended a meeting of an anti-Fascist organization, Vigilance, at Adrian Stephen's home in February 1936, and, as world affairs deteriorated, wrote and published *The League and Abyssinia* in March 1936. Italian forces conquered the capital of Abyssinia (or Ethiopia) in May. In the meantime, Horace de Vere Cole died in February, and Leonard and Virginia Woolf took a car tour of the southwest in May, including a visit to Weymouth. These seemingly unrelated personal and international events form the background to one of the oddest of Hogarth Press publications, *The Dreadnought Hoax* by Adrian Stephen published in November 1936.

Quentin Bell detailed the famous escapade in his biography of Virginia Woolf, wherein Horace Cole, Adrian Stephen, Duncan Grant, Anthony Buxton, Guy Ridley, and Virginia Stephen (two years before she married Leonard Woolf) dressed themselves as the emperor of Abyssinia (Buxton) and his court (Grant, Ridley, and Virginia), escorted by a Foreign Office official (Cole) and an interpreter (Adrian), and visited the HMS *Dreadnought* in Weymouth harbor in February 1910.[26] The Royal Navy was completely taken in by the hoaxers, extended elaborate hospitality and a tour of the mightiest and most secret ship in the navy, and reacted with predictable outrage when Cole revealed the deception to the press. The undergraduate prank, complete with disguises and Virginia's cross dressing, silly in itself, spawned an amused House of Commons inquiry and an aggressive retaliation by the Stephens' cousin William Fisher, a naval officer and flag commander aboard the *Dreadnought* at the time.

Why, after twenty-six years, Virginia's brother Adrian should have published his account of the long-forgotten affair is unclear. Hogarth Press readers must have been amused by the picture of the hoaxers in costume on the cover and by the account but puzzled by the timing. Very likely the combination of Horace Cole's death (he was the originator of the caper), the fall of Abyssinia, and Bloomsbury's passionate antiwar rejection of all forms of militarism, native or foreign, triggered Adrian's publication, although in his account he merely mentions Cole's death in passing and has only the most complimentary things to say about the naval officers who were hoaxed. But the aftermath of the hoax, wrote Quentin Bell, had left Virginia Woolf at the time with "a new sense of the brutality and silliness of men" and of "masculine violence and stupidity." The theme of such military pomposity would become an element in Virginia's novel *The Years,* which she was then writing, and a major theme in *Three Guineas,* to be published two years later in 1938. It would not be surprising to learn that Virginia was behind Adrian's decision to publish his account.[27]

After a lapse of nearly six years, Virginia Woolf finally had another novel ready for publication in 1937. Although she had envisioned greater triumphs in the hard-won style of *The Waves* (1931), her next work of fiction, *The Years* (1937), would mark an important but painful redirection of her creative energies away from the visionary lyricism of the novel-poem to the realistic fiction of social comment. Before that redirection, however, Woolf had put *The Waves* behind her and written *Flush.* She had begun to conceive the broad outlines of *The Years* before she had finished *Flush* and began to write it with a different working title ("The Pargiters") and a different focus than the final product.

To draft "The Pargiters" and develop it into *The Years,* however, proved a more difficult task for Virginia Woolf than that of any other novel. From the time she began "making up" the novel in October 1932 until she finished editing the proofs on November 30, 1936, four years elapsed, twice the time it took her to write *The Waves.* In addition, Woolf's writing was more than usually complicated by changes in conception, struggles with intractable material, much of it intensely personal, and bouts of ill health, headaches, and depression.

Virginia Woolf began writing in her manuscript book "The Pargiters: An Essay based upon a paper read to the London/National Society for Women's Service"[28] on October 11, 1932. Her speech before the society had been a direct outgrowth of *A Room of One's Own* (1929), and Woolf thought that her new work, really an extended essay, would be a sequel to that feminist monograph. By November 2, 1932, however, Woolf had begun to remodel her essay: "Its to be an Essay-Novel, called the Pargiters—& its to take in everything, sex, education, life &c.; & come, with the most powerful & agile leaps, like a chamois across precipices from 1880 to here & now" (*Diary* 4:129). *The Years,* in its final form, traces the pernicious effects on the Pargiter men and women of the Victorian and Edwardian materialistic, patriarchal society, a private world of dominant masculine egotism closely allied to a public world of repressive social rituals and militarism. It moves forward in ten sections covering the years 1880, 1891, 1907, 1908, 1910, 1911, 1913, 1914, 1917, and the "Present Day" of the 1930s.

By September 30, 1934, after two years' writing, Virginia had finished the first massive draft, 900 pages of manuscript totaling some 200,000 words by Leonard's estimate. As she noted, the writing had been "a great strain, because so many more faculties had to keep going at once" (*Diary* 4:245). There were no tears, no exaltation, at the conclusion but rather "peace & breadth." At the time she could not know the enormous effort that would be required to reshape "The Pargiters" into *The Years,* discarding hundreds of pages of manuscript along the way and eight other titles.

From November 15, 1934, to the autumn of 1935, with time out for a bout of bad headaches and nervous strain and a month's tour of Europe, Virginia Woolf worked hard at redrafting her novel. Early in September she changed the title to *The Years.* Finally on December 29, she recorded the end of the extensive rewrite, some 797 pages running roughly to 157,000 or 140,000 words. She could see that it still needed "sharpening, some bold cuts, & emphases," but the book had finally formed under her hand (*Diary* 4:360).

The labor and strain of cutting the novel, coupled with increasing periods of nervous irritability, her "fidgets," soon had Virginia despairing of ever completing the novel. Her decision to put the typescript into galley proofs before Leonard had read it, a totally unexpected and uncharacteristic step for Virginia, indicates the level of her anxiety. She wanted galley and not page proofs, noted Leonard, so that she could more easily make changes (*Downhill* 153). She may also have anticipated Leonard's disapproval of style and subject matter and so moved boldly to forestall any paralyzing criticism from him. She sent 132 pages of type-script to R. & R. Clark on March 10, 1936, and the last batch on April 8 (*Diary* 5:15, 22).

Leonard, fearing for Virginia's health, insisted she break off work on the novel at this time. They went to Monks House where Virginia spent a month mostly in bed, unable to work and not reading the proofs that had arrived. For rehabilitation, she and Leonard took a leisurely ten-day trip to Cornwall, stopping by Weymouth, the scene of the *Dreadnought* hoax. By early June she was back in London, correcting the proofs, beset by tortuous headaches and depression over the novel. The four months from June until late October were "filled with unending nightmare," as Leonard recalled (*Downhill* 153). It had been a near return for Virginia to the frightening mental state of 1913. Through it all she worked, when she could, with courage and tenacity, cutting the text drastically. Leonard had seen some of the galley proofs along the way, enough to disappoint him and to worry Virginia.

When she finally gave him the heavily edited proofs on November 1, she was convinced they were bad enough to be destroyed. "I must carry the proofs, like a dead cat, to L.," Virginia recorded, "and tell him to burn them unread" (*Diary* 5:29). She felt reconciled to losing £200 to £300 on the cost of the proofs. Over the next three days, as he read through the ten sections of the novel, Leonard reassured Virginia. She recorded his daily remarks in her diary like a medical report. Then on Thursday, November 5: "The miracle is accomplished. L. put down the last sheet about 12 last night; and could not speak. He was in tears. He says it is 'a most remarkable book'—he *likes* it better than The Waves. & has not a spark of doubt that it must be published" (ibid., 30). So the touching and sad minidrama played itself out, Virginia feeling dizzy relief "so amazing is the reversal since Tuesday morning" and Leonard feeling uneasy about his deception.

The truth was that Leonard Woolf disliked *The Years* and was led to deceive Virginia uncharacteristically because he feared an unfavorable re-sponse would lead to a serious breakdown, perhaps even to suicide. What he told Virginia, he recalled in his autobiography, was "not absolutely and completely" what he thought about it (*Downhill* 155). *The Years* was bad, but he was greatly relieved to find it not so bad as Virginia feared, and he thought "it was in many ways a remarkable book." He focused on its excessive length in his criticism to her. Later he came to think *The Years* was the worst book Virginia ever wrote.

Alternately encouraged and discouraged, clinging to Leonard's reassurance, then adrift in despair, Virginia Woolf devoted most of November 1936 to a further cutting of the galley proofs. "I wonder if anyone has ever suffered so much from a book as I have from *The Years,*" Virginia pondered, adding, "It's like a long childbirth" (*Diary* 5:31). When the pain was finally over on November 30, she had delivered her longest novel, boldly cut down from the approximately 600 pages' worth of galley proofs to what would become 469 pages of published text. She felt relieved, with no need to be unhappy with the results, "a taut, real, strenuous book," as she summed it up (ibid., 38).

Leonard, comparing the finished book with the galley proofs, noted that Virginia had "cut out bodily two enormous chunks, and there is hardly a single page on which there are not considerable rewritings or verbal alterations" (*Downhill* 156). The two chunks consist of more than ten pages deleted from the "1917" section and over twenty-five pages from a section which would have been "1921" if included. The omitted episodes present several complex and distressing experiences of Eleanor Pargiter, the most optimistic character in the novel. They are so grim, as Grace Radin has observed, that they would have deepened "the tone of the work that is already regarded as Virginia Woolf's darkest novel."[29]

Leonard Woolf and many critics of the time considered *The Years* badly flawed in characterization and structure. Recent critics, however, mostly feminist, have opened up the novel in interesting ways, making virtues of what were thought vices. Among other points, they have argued that *The Years* offers compelling evidence of Virginia Woolf's courage and genius in confronting and remaking herself as a woman in a sexist world, in focusing her frustrations to expose traditional masculine myths of marriage and sex. Such criticism and the textual studies of her revisions have made the novel seem one of the more interesting and ambitious of Woolf's books, its very ambiguities and muted anger part of its qualities. Leonard Woolf and the early male critics thought it inferior to Virginia's great modernist novels, but the average reader in 1937 had no such qualms, flocking to it with relief after the difficulties of *The Waves*.

In spite of his reservations about its literary virtues, Leonard anticipated its popularity and ordered over 18,000 copies of *The Years* for publication on March 15, 1937. Its commercial success completely
overshadowed Virginia's other novels. It sold over 13,000 copies in the
first six months (MSR). In America, Harcourt Brace printed 10,000 copies for the first edition and quickly reprinted, as *The Years* sold over
30,000 copies in six months. It became an authentic American best-seller
for 1937, ranking sixth on a list led by such heady company as Margaret
Mitchell's *Gone with the Wind* and Kenneth Roberts's *Northwest Passage*
and outranking John Steinbeck's *Of Mice and Men*.[30] One check alone
from Harcourt Brace on January 5, 1928, totaled over $5,000 (*Letters*
6:202).

With the flood of American dollars came fame and publicity. *Time*
magazine placed her picture on the cover of its April 12, 1937, issue—Man
Ray's elegant photograph taken in 1934 of a stylishly coiffed and lip-
sticked Woolf. Devoting four pages to her, *Time* reassured its audience
that "nervous readers will find *The Years* not nearly such heavy going as
their knowledge or hearsay of Virginia Woolf might lead them to expect.
Unlike some of her other books, *The Years* is not experimental. It is written 'straight.' "[31]

The same month Virginia Woolf's chronicle of the Pargiters appeared, the Hogarth Press published another family chronicle, *The Amberley Papers: The Letters and Diaries of Lord and Lady Amberley* (1937).
Bertrand Russell and his third wife Patricia edited the papers of his father,
John Russell, and his mother. The massive work, following the lives of
two eminent Victorians, resulted in a two-volume publication totaling
1,133 pages of text, each volume selling for a guinea. Both Leonard and
Virginia read the bulky original manuscript and praised it, Leonard writing to Russell that he found it fascinating as it provided "a complete
picture of the psychological history of a section of society for a period of
thirty years or so" (HP 406). Following the Woolfs' editorial suggestions,
the Russells pared the text to its present two-volume size. It fared well
commercially, went into a "cheap" edition the same year, and was reprinted by the press in 1940. Simon & Schuster reprinted the two volumes in America in 1966. It has become an important historical document
of the 1860s and 1870s.

A family chronicle of a different sort from the Russells was the next book Vita Sackville-West wrote for the Hogarth Press after *The Dark Island*. She had just written a short biography of Saint Joan for Leonard Woolf's new pamphlet series World-Makers and World-Shakers, published in 1937, when she discovered a hoard of papers and documents among her mother's possessions at Brighton about her grandmother, the Spanish dancer Pepita. Lady Sackville, Vita's mother, had died five months earlier. What Vita Sackville-West found at Brighton and subsequently in the files of the family solicitors were depositions and accounts taken in 1896 by the lawyers to establish the facts of Pepita's marriage to her Spanish husband, the dancer Juan de Oliva.

As Sackville-West described the legal expediencies of these papers in *Pepita*: "The point, in short, was the necessity of proving whether my grandmother, Pepita, had ever been married to my grandfather ["Old" Lionel, second Baron Sackville] or not. Several issues were at stake: an English peerage, and an historic inheritance [Knole]."[32] Old Lionel had fathered five children with Pepita—two sons and three daughters, including Vita's mother, Victoria. If one of the sons, Henry, could prove that Pepita had never married Juan de Oliva but had married Old Lionel, he would inherit the title and Knole. The testimony of Spanish peasants, servants, dancers, and villagers together with church documents proved that Pepita had, indeed, married Juan de Oliva and that she and Lionel had never married. Henry's suit collapsed. Victoria, in the meantime, had married her first cousin "young" Lionel Sackville-West (Vita's father), who was to inherit Knole and become the third Baron Sackville.

Vita Sackville-West, with the exciting discovery of the Pepita material, wrote immediately to Leonard Woolf proposing a family biography centered on her Spanish grandmother. She was certain, she wrote on June 19, 1936, that he would be enthralled by "the picturesque and indeed fantastic picture evoked" (HP 422). "It all sounds absolutely fascinating," Leonard responded enthusiastically, "and should make an extraordinarily good book." He wanted to know when she could deliver the manuscript. She estimated she could write the book in little over a year and have it ready by autumn 1937. Reliable as always, she delivered the completed manuscript ahead of schedule one year later, in June 1937, in time for the autumn publishing season. It was published on October 30, 1937. The biography took her approximately ten months to write.

Pepita swept the market, becoming another fast-selling book for Vita and the press. It sold nearly 15,000 copies in the first six months (MSR). Leonard Woolf had a second impression printed in October, a third impression in December, and a fourth impression in March 1938. The only sour note in a chorus of praise came from Vita's Aunt Amalia, Lady Sackville's sister, who attacked Vita in letters to the *Birmingham Post* for having "thrown mud" on Pepita's memory (*Letters* 6:191).

In America, *Pepita* was no less successful than in England. Curtis Brown, Sackville-West's literary agency, first tried serializing the book during the summer of 1937 in anticipation of an autumn publication with Doubleday, Doran. But as the New York manager of Curtis Brown reported to Sackville-West, *Pepita* was regretfully rejected by *Ladies' Home Journal, Saturday Evening Post,* and *Cosmopolitan* on the grounds that the magazines had "a great hinterland of readers who object violently to anything that they consider morally irregular, and would hold that the moral of Pepita is that the wages of sin are a jolly good time and great glory."[33] Vita and the Woolfs must have been amused, if not appalled, by the supposed moral Puritanism of America's hinterland women in 1937 and by the male editors who acted as guardian of their readers' virtue. In contrast, Doubleday, Doran had no such doubts about book publication, were excited about *Pepita,* and thought it would make a killing. It did, and was selected as the December offering for the Book-of-the-Month Club.

After the success of *Mr. Norris Changes Trains* (1935), Christopher Isherwood continued to mine the material he had assembled during his Berlin days, and he quickly linked up again with John Lehmann and the Hogarth Press. Lehmann had finally succeeded with his long-planned magazine of international scope, launching *New Writing* in the spring of 1936. He had planned the magazine with Isherwood in mind and intended to make *New Writing* hospitable to longish pieces (up to 12,000 words) not easily published in England.[34] The first issue contained Isherwood's long story "The Nowacks" (originally titled "The Kulaks"), which had been detached from his projected work "The Lost." It was an immediate success. Isherwood then submitted a draft of "Sally Bowles" to Lehmann for another issue of *New Writing,* but there were problems. Isherwood recognized the need to rewrite it and to seek approval from the original Sally, Jean Ross. Lehmann worried over the extremely long length and whether or not the printers would pass the abortion scene. In its place Lehmann published another section of the now dismantled "The Lost" in the third issue of *New Writing:* "A Berlin Diary (Autumn 1930)." It would become the opening sequence for Isherwood's novel *Goodbye to Berlin* in 1939.

After rewriting *Sally Bowles* and obtaining permission from Jean Ross, Isherwood presented it to the Hogarth Press in March 1937 for consideration through the Curtis Brown agency. Leonard Woolf accepted promptly, without blinking at the obscenity risk, but he worried over the awkward 20,000-word length and the suitable sale price (HP 195). He finally offered Isherwood a rather generous £50 advance plus the usual royalties and fixed the price for the 150-page novella at 3s.6d. In the negotiations, however, Curtis Brown balked at Woolf's insistence that Isherwood's next full-length book should come to Hogarth as part of the agreement to cover the risks the press took.

The issue opened an old wound. David Higham, the agent for Curtis Brown, recalled in his memoirs how he had argued with Leonard and Virginia Woolf in 1935 (at the time of *The Memorial*) over Isherwood's future with the press. Higham had counseled a change to a larger publisher with greater selling power. It was a red flag guaranteed to incite Woolf's ire and one he had charged at angrily before with other restless authors. Higham remembered the session in the Woolfs' Tavistock Square flat above the press offices, when Leonard sat with his back to the window "against which his splendid Old Testament prophet's profile rose in silhouette, the higher as his indignation mounted."[35] Woolf won that day in 1935 and again in 1937 over *Sally Bowles,* as the sharply worded letters flew fast and furiously.

Isherwood recalled a different source of unrest over the Hogarth Press's continuation as his publisher. He felt piqued by Virginia Woolf's failure to invite him to meet her after the success of *Mr. Norris,* and so, he wrote, "he had entered into an informal agreement with Methuen, the highest bidder," to be published by that firm when he freed himself from Hogarth.[36] He came to realize he had been childishly unprofessional. When he and Virginia met, they got on famously, Isherwood praising Virginia's novels and Virginia engaged by his charm and brightness. As she noted on February 21, 1937, nine months before the press published

Sally Bowles, "I[sherwood] rather a find: very small red cheeked nimble & vivacious" (*Diary* 5:59). He was a real novelist, she thought, and added: "Odd how few 'novelists' I know: it wd. interest me to discuss fiction with him." Unfortunately he left before they cut through the social chatter to discuss their craft as novelists. When she saw him again in November 1938, Virginia described him as "a slip of a wild boy: with quicksilver eyes" (ibid., 185). Isherwood was thirty-four at the time. In spite of Higham's arguments, Isherwood remained loyally in the Hogarth Press fold until after the Second World War and Virginia's death.

During the late 1930s the Woolfs and their press gained new authors annually, kept loyalists like Vita Sackville-West and Christopher Isherwood in spite of wooings by larger publishers, but inevitably lost a few productive writers like Plomer, Day-Lewis, and Kitchin. The press staff went through several changes of its own during these times.

With the unexpected death of Margaret West in January 1937, the press went through a staffing crisis. First, Barbara Hepworth contacted Leonard Woolf. She managed a print gallery in Baker Street after several years of running a bookshop in Dorking. Leonard Woolf hired her to travel and to be in charge of the stock, paying her £3.10 a week (LWP). She became the first salaried, full-time traveler for the press, replacing the part-time Alice Ritchie. Dorothy Lange applied for West's position as manager and was accepted, beginning in early February. She came to the press with ten years' experience in publishing, having been at Longmans Green for five years, but Woolf offered her only the salary that he had offered Margaret West four years before: £250 per year, increasing to £300 per year after six months (LWP).

Just before Dorothy Lange began work, Norah Nicholls, publicity manager at Methuen, wrote, in February 1938, applying for the position. She described herself as an experienced journalist and business person (LWP). The position was filled, of course, but Nicholls would succeed her friend Lange in May 1938, after Lange's brief one-year tenure. Nicholls would serve as Hogarth manager until 1940 when she left to do war work in civil defense. Supporting the able and experienced women managers West, Lange, and Nicholls during these years were a bevy of clerk-typists, some of whose names appear fleetingly in the Woolf diaries and letters and then vanish into obscurity: the Misses Bevan, Crabbe,

Griffiths, Perkins, and Strachan. By November 1938 there were seven clerks by Virginia Woolf's count (*Letters* 6:305). They, with the manager, were the backbone of the Hogarth Press during difficult and eventful years.

"How I loath the publishing of books," Virginia Woolf wrote to Ethel Smyth in March 1937, expressing a recurring complaint (*Letters* 6:111). It was bad enough publishing books fit only for the wastepaper basket, she said, but her real objection was to "being hooked and hauled to the surface when my natural dwelling is in the dark at the depths." She could not write if people talked to her about what she wrote. Virginia Woolf's frequent outbursts of frustration and annoyance in the past had been directed at the burden of reading too many inferior manuscripts, of having to write rejection letters to pitifully earnest and inept authors.

Now in March 1937, a new and more urgent note was sounded. The press deprived her of the quiet and privacy she needed for her writing. She felt unprotected and vulnerable, and these fears were linked directly to her growing dread of the public and of critical reaction to *The Years,* which would be published on March 15. The novel proved to be a popular and commercial success, a relief to Virginia, but the critics and Leonard were doubtful. Her feelings of vulnerability over the press and her writing continued, as she moved forward with the composition of *Three Guineas.* Virginia's uncertain health at this time, Leonard's protracted bout with an undiagnosed illness, the death of Virginia's old friend Janet Case, the tragic loss of Julian Bell in the Spanish civil war, and increasing international disorder led the Woolfs to feelings of despair and futility. They began once more to consider seriously shutting down the press. John Lehmann would change all that.

Lehmann, busy with his journalistic creation *New Writing,* moved easily in and out of Bloomsbury in 1937, gathering together a glittering array of English and European writers. He had moved his magazine from Bodley Head (when Allen Lane left to create Penguin Books) to Lawrence & Wishart, which also proved a temporary home. At the back of his mind, Lehmann recalled, was "the idea of making *New Writing* the centre of actual book publishing for the works of our generation."[37] Lehmann approached the Woolfs in the summer of 1937. A contract was worked out early in 1938, and Lehmann became Leonard Woolf's partner beginning in April 1938. The offers and counteroffers leading to the final agreement were complicated and marked by the caution and suspicion on both sides. At first Lehmann sought to raise the £6,000 necessary to buy the press outright. The market value of the press was at least that, but undoubtedly Leonard Woolf knew Lehmann could not raise such a large amount. It seems unlikely that Woolf, with his fierce attachment to the press, would have sold his entire interest to anyone.

While Lehmann considered his options, John Rodker, wealthy man of letters, translator, and private press founder (Ovid Press and Pushkin Press), approached Leonard Woolf in August 1937 with an offer to buy. He had obtained financial backing by December and requested a first option if the arrangements with Lehmann failed. He assured Leonard that the Hogarth Press imprint would not be devalued if he obtained it (LWP). His avowal did not convince Woolf. Both Rodker and Martin Secker, who also tendered an offer in December, were cold-shouldered by Leonard Woolf, who had in the meantime conceived another scheme. By October, as Virginia noted, Leonard had "developed the idea of making the young Brainies [John Lehmann, Christopher Isherwood, W. H. Auden, and Stephen Spender] take the Press as a Cooperative company" (*Diary* 5:116). The Woolfs knew and liked Spender, Isherwood, and Lehmann, so that such an arrangement would have meant that the press would be in familiar hands. "All are bubbling with discontent & ideas," added Virginia. "All want a focus; a manager: a mouthpiece: a common voice." John Lehmann would manage. But the *New Signatures–New Country–New Writing* "Brainies" were unable to find the £6,000 necessary, an outcome probably anticipated by Leonard. John Lehmann finally went it alone, offering £3,000 for a half share and a partnership in the press.

CHAPTER EIGHT

★

FREUD AND FREUDIANS

In honor of Sigmund Freud's eightieth birthday in March 1936, the German novelist Thomas Mann composed and delivered to Freud in Vienna a birthday greeting signed by 196 other writers and artists. According to Ernest Jones, Freud's biographer, the greeting praised Freud as a seer, healer, thinker, and courageous investigator into the dark and dangerous places of the soul.[1] The writers testified that they could not imagine their "mental world" without Freud's great work. Virginia Woolf was one of those who signed Mann's greeting.

Virginia Woolf, as an internationally renowned writer whose novels depicted the rich complexity of the mind, could have been expected to join the other writers in honoring Freud. Although Woolf would not have subscribed to all the terms of Mann's panegyric—could she not imagine her "mental world" without Freud?—her signature was appropriate beyond her standing as a novelist. She and Leonard Woolf had been the sole English publishers of Freud's work in translation for twelve years, ever since the Hogarth Press had contracted to publish the International Psycho-Analytic Library (IPL) in 1924. At that time Mann would have been hard-pressed to drum up a list of 196 admirers of Freud from the world of arts and letters even though the work that launched the psychoanalytic movement had been published in German since 1900 (*The Interpretation of Dreams*) and had appeared in sporadic English translations since 1910. The phenomenon of Freud's success and fame as the most distinguished exile in England at the time of his death from cancer in 1939 can be traced through a complex history. Without doubt, the Hogarth Press played a part in that history and can claim an important role in the dissemination of Freud's ideas.

By the outbreak of the First World War in 1914, Freud had published innumerable articles expounding his psychoanalytic theory and practice and several books important to his movement: *The Psychopathology of Everyday Life* (1901, 1904), *Three Essays on the Theory of Sexuality* (1905), *Totem and Taboo* (1913), and *The History of the Psycho-Analytical Movement* (1914). His followers had begun holding annual congresses in 1908 and had formed psychoanalytical societies in Vienna, Zurich, Berlin, New York, Budapest, and London.[2] Three prominent disciples had defected noisily: Alfred Adler, Wilhelm Stekel, and Carl Jung. A secret "Committee" of five members (Ernest Jones, Sandor Ferenczi, Karl Abraham, Otto Rank, and Hanns Sachs) had appointed themselves a sort of Praetorian Guard to defend and promote the interest of Freud. They awarded themselves symbolic gold rings.

After the war, the psychoanalytical movement took on fresh life and expanded dramatically. As part of the revitalization, Freud and his colleagues established the Internationaler Psychoanalytischer Verlag in 1919 with the financial assistance of the Hungarian Anton von Freund. A publishing house, the firm was to free the movement from dependence on commercial publishers and to develop operations by publishing three psychoanalytical journals (including the famous *Imago*) and the works of Freud and his circle. Directors were Freud, Ferenczi, Freund, and Rank; with the untimely death of Freund in 1920, Ernest Jones replaced him as a director. Otto Rank became managing director of the company and devoted the next five years to developing it. Theodor Reik joined him as assistant, and later the Englishman Eric Hiller worked on the English publications.[3] The early death of Freund and the unsettled financial and political affairs in Hungary and Austria after the war constantly complicated the operation of the firm, which was seldom solvent. Freud worried over its affairs, frequently labored to raise money for it, and often passed on some of his own royalties to keep it afloat.

Freud, who cherished the idea that he was especially productive in cycles of seven years, began another period of intense creativity in 1920. He published three major books in short order, *Beyond the Pleasure Principle* (1920), *Group Psychology and the Analysis of the Ego* (1921), and *The Ego and the Id* (1923). At the same time he completed the publication of his *Collected Shorter Papers* in five volumes (*Samlung kleiner Schriften zur Neurosenlehre*, 1906–22).

Meanwhile, Ernest Jones, to aid the westward development of the psychoanalytical movement after the war, had reorganized the London society into the British society in 1919 and then proposed with Otto Rank that an English branch of the Internationaler Psychoanalytischer Verlag be established in London. It would publish an English-language journal (the *International Journal of Psycho-Analysis*, established in 1920) and English translations of the firm's books. Each English translation would be printed in Czechoslovakia where the *Verlag* publications were printed and then published in London. Freud quickly saw the advantages of an English company both in spreading psychoanalysis beyond the German-speaking world and in providing funds through royalties to the firm in Vienna. Jones at first had to establish the figurehead International Psycho-Analytical Press in London to handle the company's English books because former enemy countries like Austria were prohibited from having branch offices in England.

As an important element in this publishing venture, Ernest Jones established the International Psycho-Analytical Library series, which issued in numerical sequence translations of most but not all of the Vienna firm's books. Jones used his editorial discretion in accepting titles. For example, he rejected an English translation of *A Young Girl's Diary* (1921) because it nearly caused the publisher, Unwin, to be prosecuted by the police for obscenity.[4] Soon the complicated printing arrangements with the non-English-speaking Czech printers and their lack of suitable English typefaces necessitated publishing the journal in England, first with Jonathan Cape and then with the medical publishers Bailliere, Tindall & Cox. Ernest Jones sent Eric Hiller to Vienna to assist in editing the IPL books. The first three volumes in the IPL, all published in 1921, were J. J. Putnam's *Addresses on Psycho-Analysis,* Sandor Ferenczi's *Psycho-Analysis and the War Neuroses,* and J. C. Flugel's *Psycho-Analytic Study of the Family* (which Leonard Woolf called a "publisher's dream" because it sold hundreds of copies a year for over forty years).

The next year the IPL issued two of Freud's books in translation, *Beyond the Pleasure Principle* (trans. C. J. M. Hubback) and *Group Psychology and the Analysis of the Ego* (trans. James Strachey, his first major translation). In 1923 the IPL published Ernest Jones's *Essays in Applied Psycho-Analysis,* which contained a long paper on the Madonna. Freud was concerned that Jones might risk legal action under English blasphemy laws, but no charges were filed. At the time Freud's recently translated mono-graph *Leonardo da Vinci* (his first full-scale biographical study, written in 1910) was restricted by his English publisher, Kegan, Paul & Co., to the medical profession to avoid possible police action. Then in 1924 Ernest Jones obtained Freud's permission to issue his recently published *Collected Papers* in English translation in four volumes through the IPL. And with that, the Woolfs and their Hogarth Press entered the arena of Freud-ian publication.

Acting on behalf of Ernest Jones, James Strachey approached Leon-ard Woolf in early 1924 to ask if the Hogarth Press would become the publisher for the Institute of Psycho-Analysis and the books of the IPL. Lytton Strachey's youngest brother, James, and his wife Alix had studied with Freud, had become professional analysts and translators, and now worked with Ernest Jones at the institute. The IPL proposal was dicey for the Woolfs. Not only was there the dubious business of publishing Freudian works, which might incite the suspicious public or police to legal action against "blasphemous" or "obscene" materials, but there was the real risk of financial failure. The IPL books had not been best-sellers, and only works by Freud himself seemed to have a modest chance of breaking even. Furthermore, the Hogarth Press would need to buy the rights to the previous six IPL volumes and invest capital in the four-volume Freud *Papers*. Leonard Woolf recalled one large English pub-lisher, probably Unwin, warning him against the risk, figuring Hogarth would tie up over £1,000 in capital (*Downhill* 165). In spite of the advice, Leonard went boldly ahead with the undertaking, formulating an agree-ment whereby the Hogarth Press purchased the rights to the previously published books and to Freud's *Collected Papers*. The Institute of Psycho-Analysis subsidized the *Papers* at £50 per volume. Royalties on new books were to be paid to Freud as soon as a profit was turned. In a manner of speaking, the Hogarth Press became the successor to Unwin, which had published several of the IPL volumes, a circumstance which amused Leonard, as he wrote to Stanley Unwin in August. He added that if he ended up "without loss, profit, or lawsuit," he would congratulate him-self.[5]

Once the contract had been signed, the previously printed books poured in. As Virginia Woolf wrote to Marjorie Joad in July 1924, "all the psycho-analyst books have been dumped in a fortress the size of Windsor Castle in ruins upon the floor" (*Letters* 3:119). They had invested £800 in Freud's books, Virginia wrote to Roger Fry in September, "which will sell they say because he has cancer" (ibid., 133). The piled-up volumes all carried the imprint of the International Psycho-Analytical Press, London/ Vienna, and were to be distributed by the Woolfs. With the fourth through seventh volumes in the IPL series, the Woolfs placed the Hogarth Press imprint on the dust jacket and on the green cloth binding, printed in gold, which was used throughout the series. Only with title number eight, the second volume of Freud's *Collected Papers* in 1924, did the Hogarth imprint appear on the title page jointly with the Institute of Psycho-Analysis, indicating that the volume had been printed and published entirely by the press. The institute was incorporated in 1924 to replace the Psycho-Analytical Press as the British agency through which the German firm's works would be published in English translation.

Leonard Woolf, looking back in his autobiography, saw himself in 1924 as a "fledgling inexperienced publisher" with no staff and no promotional "machine," risking all and defying the advice of the more cautious larger firms (*Downhill* 165). Although he overstated his case—the publisher of thirty-seven titles in seven years, including the Gorky, Bunin, and Dostoyevsky translations and Virginia Woolf's *Jacob's Room,* was hardly a tyro—his pride was justifiable, for the risks were real and the future was uncertain. Bloomsbury's long-standing interest in psychoanalysis and Leonard's determination to expand the press into new areas coincided with the proposal from the Institute of Psycho-Analysis. The decision to publish Freud and the volumes of the IPL was one of the major turning points in the history of the press, making it instantly a publishing house of international importance. To Leonard's delight, his risk taking was rewarded. Freud's *Collected Papers* became one of Hogarth's most successful issues.

The four volumes of Freud's *Collected Papers,* edited by Ernest Jones, represented a significant return to Freud's earliest work. Jones, in his "Editorial Preface" to the first volume, pointed out that the *Collected Papers* "constitute the real basis of Psycho-Analysis" because they were the published record of Freud's clinical investigations upon which all subsequent work was founded.[6] "It is unfortunate," added Jones, "that the

English-speaking public should for years have had access only to what may be called the super-structure of his work, the application of his psychoanalytic method to the study of dreams, sexuality, totemism, and so on, while the basis of it all remained buried in a foreign tongue," a metaphor wonderfully appropriate to the dynamics of psychoanalysis. So, he suggested, the interred experience of the past must be dug up and brought into the light of English. In the process of translating and publishing the *Collected Papers,* the past would be made accessible to the present, all explained, all forgiven. Doctors Jones and Woolf presided over the couch while the English reader watched the amazing revelations.

In his editing of the four-volume translation of Freud's *Sammlung kleiner Schriften zur Neurosenlehre,* Jones regrouped the papers with Freud's cooperation and called attention in his first preface to the dating of the writings. By arranging the papers chronologically, Jones emphasized the unfolding drama of Freud's search for truth, the way his ideas were "constantly extended and modified—under the pressure of widening and deepening experience." Freud's pioneering path, wrote Jones, "lay through a jungle hitherto completely unexplored," often requiring detours or retracings but producing nevertheless a progress measurable by "the host of workers now following in his steps."[7] Furthermore, Jones reinforced the claims that Freud's methodology was scientific by stressing his "inflexible determination" not to be sidetracked by speculations but to be guided always by "the actual material daily brought before his observation." Jones as editor thus became from the first a defender and popularizer of Freud, his bulldog, as Huxley for Darwin, dramatizing Freud's struggle for truth and attesting to the scientific rigors of the process. It was a role Jones would play consistently throughout his life, and it would culminate in his monumental biography of Freud.

The first volume of the *Collected Papers* as edited by Jones contained fourteen of Freud's "Early Papers," ranging from the famous obituary study of his great mentor "Charcot" (1893) to "My Views on the Part Played by Sexuality in the Aetiology of the Neuroses" (1905). Included were papers important to later work such as "The Aetiology of Hysteria" (1896) and "Freud's Psycho-analytic Method" (1904), a brief explanation in the third person of his developing technique.[8]

The second half of the first volume of the *Collected Papers* contained

Freud's long monograph "On the History of the Psycho-Analytic Movement" (1914), then and now one of the most interesting descriptions of the development of psychoanalysis up to the First World War, even though somewhat sanitized. The "History" had appeared at the beginning of the fourth volume of the *Sammlung kleiner Schriften,* but Jones strategically moved it to the end of the first volume of the *Collected Papers* where it provided a historical context for the preceding papers and prepared English readers for the clinical papers to follow in the next volume.

The second volume of Freud's *Collected Papers* was divided into two sections, "Clinical Papers," containing twenty-four essays written between 1906 and 1924, and "Papers on Technique," containing ten papers written between 1910 and 1919. The volume, as Jones pointed out in his preface, was the most miscellaneous of the four volumes. The "Clinical Papers" comprised a wide variety of studies growing out of Freud's private practice and only broadly "clinical" in nature. Jones grouped such papers as those on paranoia, female homosexuality, hysterical phantasies, and sexual perversion growing out of child beating, all more or less "clinical," with such papers of wider theoretical interest as those on the problem of truth in law courts, sexual enlightenment in children, the character of anal eroticism, and the neurotic mechanisms in jealousy, paranoia, and homosexuality. The "Papers on Technique" provided lessons from the master on a range of problems facing the analyst, from a paper on how to begin treatment (what to ask, how to encourage truthfulness and openness in the patient, how to use the couch, how to set fees and consulting hours) to a paper on how to cope with particularly difficult patient relationships occasioned by the "transference-love" growing out of analysis.

The chronological range of the papers in volume two was wide, covering an eighteen-year span, with the last four "Clinical Papers" piping hot from Freud's desk within months of first publication. These papers ("Neurosis and Psychosis," "The Economic Problem of Masochism," "The Passing of the Oedipus-Complex," and "The Loss of Reality in Neurosis and Psychosis") were so recent, in fact, that the last one had not yet appeared in German. Freud sent the manuscript to Jones for immediate translation and inclusion in the volume.

The four papers reflected Freud's latest ideas contained in his new book *Das Ich und Das Es* (1923) and made frequent references to that text. Jones used the German title because it had not yet been translated into English (it became *The Ego and the Id*) and advised readers that the four papers were so recondite that they should postpone their study of them until they were familiar with the book, shortly to appear in a separate translation.[9] In the four papers, Joan Riviere, the translator, followed Jones in using the German title *Das Ich und Das Es* whenever Freud referred to his book, but she translated *das Es* as "the id" and *das Über-Ich* as "the superego." Riviere explained in a footnote that *es* or "it" meant the "*impersonality* of the mind apart from its ego," and therefore the Latin *id* had been used.[10] The problem of properly rendering these terms would reappear when the book was translated.

Ernest Jones had been too optimistic. *The Ego and the Id* did not appear in the IPL series until 1927, an unfortunate gap of three years. Gradually the IPL had been narrowing the time lost between the appearance of Freud's work in German and its publication in English translation. With the notable exceptions of *An Autobiographical Study* (published in German in 1925, first translated and published in America in 1927, but not issued in the IPL until 1935) and *Inhibition, Symptom, and Anxiety* (German 1926, translated and published in America 1927, IPL 1936), Freud's works after *The Ego and the Id* were usually translated and published by the IPL and the Hogarth Press within a year of publication in German.

The previous delays in publishing Freud's works in the IPL were occasioned by Freud's casual handling of the American and English translation rights. English purchasers of the second volume of the *Collected Papers,* therefore, could have Freud's latest dictum, even if they had trouble understanding it. There must have been excited anticipation among English readers as the four volumes of the *Collected Papers* rolled off the presses. The readers could catch up with Freud through the early papers, gain a glimpse of future astonishments, and then be prepared for the separate volumes as they came fresh from the translator within months of publication by the Internationaler Psychoanalytischer Verlag. No doubt something of this unfolding drama of Freud's work spurred sales of the IPL series as Freud's reputation began to soar in the late 1920s and early 1930s.

The massive third volume of Freud's *Collected Papers* contained in over 600 pages his most famous clinical cases, five extended examples of Freudian psychoanalysis dating from 1905 to 1918. Much of Freud's reputation then and now stems from the brilliant and astounding array of revelations he produced from these cases, the magician extracting rabbits out of a series of battered hats. The experience for the beholder proved electrifying, often creating true believers on the spot. Ernest Jones remembered the deep impression Freud's analysis of the "Dora" case made on him, in spite of his inadequate German, when he first read it in the *Monatsschrift für Psychiatrie* (1905), and how he sat enthralled with others in the audience for four hours listening to Freud lecture without notes at the first Psycho-Analytical Congress in 1908 on the case of the "Rat Man."[11]

The cases in volume three began with "Fragment of an Analysis of a Case of Hysteria" (the "Dora" case, 1905), and then followed with "Analysis of a Phobia in a Five-Year-Old Boy" (the "little Hans" case, 1909), "Notes upon a Case of Obsessional Neurosis" (the "Rat Man" case, 1909), "Psycho-Analytic Notes upon an Autobiographical Account of a Case of Paranoia" (the "Dr. Schreber" case, 1911), and concluded with "From the History of an Infantile Neurosis" (the "Wolf Man" case, 1918).

James and Alix Strachey translated the five cases, the first time an entire volume of the *Collected Papers* had been turned into English by one set of translators, and the most ambitious undertaking by the Stracheys up to this time. Their efforts had extended over several years, including the 1924–25 period when Alix was in Berlin and James in London. Their interesting correspondence has been published, carefully edited by Perry Meisel and Walter Kendrick. As the Stracheys noted at the beginning of the volume, they had worked from Freud's revised text prepared for the German *Gesammelte Schriften* (Collected papers), which had begun to be published in 1924 and would run to twelve volumes when completed. It replaced the earlier *Sammlung kleiner Schriften* from which the first two volumes of the Hogarth Press's *Collected Papers* had been taken. They had also consulted Freud on difficult passages, sometimes arguing unsuccessfully with him about translations.[12]

Volume four of the *Collected Papers* concluded the series with the inclusion of two groups of writings, "Papers on Metapsychology" (eight, first published between 1911 and 1917) and "Papers on Applied Psycho-Analysis" (sixteen, published between 1908 and 1923). The first group of papers explored mental processes from Freud's newly developed "metapsychological" point of view, whereby, as Ernest Jones explained in his preface, the topographical, dynamic, and economic aspects of the processes were considered together for completeness.[13] Unlike so many of Freud's inventive and useful terms, his "metapsychology" proved awkward and unclear jargon, and he later abandoned it. But among these eight essays are five that Jones, in his biography of Freud, called "among the most profound and important of all Freud's works," written at white-hot heat within a space of six weeks in 1915.[14] He began writing the series of five with "Instincts and Their Vicissitudes" on March 15 and three weeks later had completed the second essay, "Repression." Then he took two weeks to write the most important one, and his favorite, "The Unconscious," and finished the series by writing the last two in eleven days, "Metapsychological Supplement to the Theory of Dreams" and "Mourning and Melancholia."

The loosely associated "Papers on Applied Psycho-Analysis" forming the second half of volume four gave further evidence to the reader in 1925 of Freud's broadening vision, hinting at developments to come in *The Future of an Illusion* (1925) and *Civilization and Its Discontents* (1927). Some of these essays show Freud applying psychoanalytical methods to problems in "anthropology, mythology, folklore, literature and the history of culture in general," as Jones pointed out, fields wherein such disciples as Abraham, Rank, Reik, and Róheim had been working.[15] Two of these papers were of special interest to writers and artists, Freud showing how to read a text or a texture in "The Theme of the Three Caskets" (an analysis of the casket game in *Merchant of Venice* and of Lear's fatally wrong choice among his three daughters) and in "The Moses of Michelangelo." Freud concluded that Michelangelo added new aspects to the character of Moses in his sculpture, coupling "tremendous physical power" with the "concrete expression of the highest mental achievement" possible to man.[16] Freud had written the paper in 1913 and published it anonymously in 1914, but he did not admit his authorship until 1924. His nearly lifelong fascination with Moses would culminate in the last book translated for the IPL on the eve of his death in 1939, *Moses and Monotheism*.

The four separately published volumes of Freud's *Collected Papers* earned a tidy profit for the Hogarth Press, paying Leonard Woolf for his capital risk. They sold at slightly different rates, however. The Hogarth ledger for monthly sales (Reading) records the total copies sold up to 1934 and indicates that volume two (1,061 copies) outsold volume three (1,023 copies), volume one (1,006 copies), and volume four (964 copies). (See Appendix C for yearly sales.) English buyers of Freud seemed to prefer the clinical and technical papers to the wider-ranging papers of the last volume. Taken together, the *Collected Papers* earned a sizable profit of £1,744.1.2 by 1937, according to the sales ledger. (See Appendix D.)

Freud's major work of psychoanalytic theory, *The Ego and the Id,* was published in the IPL series by the Hogarth Press in January 1927, four years after its publication in German as *Das Ich und Das Es*. The Hogarth Press published Freud's newest book in 1,500 copies, in contrast to the usual run of 1,000 copies for each volume of the *Collected Papers*. Priced at 6s., the eighty-eight-page *The Ego and the Id* had sold 1,305 copies by 1934, earning an accumulated profit of £59.7.6 by 1937. (See Appendixes C and D.)

The English title and the book's new terminology of the *Es* and the *Über-Ich* presented problems to Ernest Jones and the translator Joan Riviere (one of the institute directors and a supervisor of the *Collected Papers* translation). Freud's *das Ich* (literally "the I") had long been rendered as "the ego" in English because Freudians believed its particular usage in psychoanalytical thought differed from the connotations of "I" in English. The word had been used in the 1922 translation of *Group Psychology and the Analysis of the Ego*. The precise meaning of *das Ich* or the ego varied, however, sometimes being blurred by Freud's use of *das Selbst* (the self) in context where *das Ich* might be expected. One of the important contributions of the new book was to clarify and standardize the terminology. Freud achieved the new clarity by developing his concept of *das Es* and *das Über-Ich*. As James Strachey later explained, Freud adapted *das Es* from the writings of Georg Groddeck, who traced the term back to his teacher Ernst Schweninger, and then back to Nietzsche.[17] Coincidentally,

Groddeck's *Das Buch vom Es* (The book of the it) was published by the Internationaler Psychoanalytisher Verlag in 1923, but no English translation appeared until 1936. *Das Es* replaced Freud's earlier, ill-defined usage of "the unconscious" and "the systematic unconscious," as Strachey noted, which Freud had contrasted to the ego.

There had been some debate in 1924 over how to translate Freud's terms into English when Joan Riviere had translated his four latest "Clinical Papers" for volume two of the *Collected Papers*. Ernest Jones and Riviere had settled on "id" and "superego," but not without argument from James Strachey. James had written to Alix on October 9, 1924, reporting on his discussion with Jones: "I said I thought everyone would say 'the Yidd'. So Jones said there was no such word in English: 'There's "Yiddish," you know. And in German "Judd". But there is no such word as "Yidd" '—'Pardon, me, doctor, Yidd is a current slang word for a Jew,'— 'Ah! A slang expression. It cannot be in a very wide-spread use then.'— Simply because that l.b. [little beast] hasn't ever heard it." [18]

Now Leonard Woolf raised the question on his own when he wrote to Ernest Jones on August 9, 1926, and stated his preference for translating *Das Ich und Das Es* directly into English as *The I and the It* (HP 109). John Rickman, Jones's associate at the institute, replied on August 11 that the title was composed "of two technical expressions, and for about two years the term 'Id' has been used in the English literature to mean specifically 'das Es.' " [19] He added that "it would be seriously detrimental if the title of the book which was technical in German were not technical in English," and since "I" did not mean what the psychoanalysts meant by "ego," he believed "it would not be good policy" to adopt Woolf's suggestion. It was logical to follow the use of the Latin personal pronoun (*ego*) with the Latin demonstrative pronoun (*id*), signifying the impersonal. Jones and Rickman carried the day, and Latin won out over Woolf's English, but the issue remains controversial.

Freud's next two books, published in translation by the Hogarth Press and the institute, *The Future of an Illusion* (1928) and *Civilization and Its Discontents* (1930), took him into the fields of religion, anthropology, and sociology and away from his theories on the operation of the mind. Both books stirred controversy, but *The Future of an Illusion,* because it probed the nature of religious belief, drew the most ire from religious spokesmen. Freud was doubtful about the value of his book, according to Ernest Jones, but he wished to take advantage of religious controversy in England at the time by having it translated and published immediately.[20] He requested James Strachey, increasingly his translator of choice, but because Strachey was otherwise engaged, he settled on W. D. Robson-Scott as translator.

Civilization and Its Discontents proved less inflammatory than *The Future of an Illusion* and more acceptable to a wide audience, although sales of the two books over time were nearly equal. In it, Freud contemplated the repressive forces of society that demand restrictions on man's instinctual, sexual, aggressive, and destructive drives in the name of culture and civilization. The "fatal question" for Freud, posed at the conclusion of his book, was whether or not man's civilizing development would master the disruptions caused in society by his instinctive aggression and self-destruction.

Freud's original title in German, according to James Strachey, had been *Das Unglück in der Kultur* (Unhappiness in civilization), but he changed *Unglück* to *Unbehagen* (discomfort, malaise, or uneasiness) in the final title.[21] Writing to the translator Joan Riviere, Freud suggested "Man's Discomfort in Civilization," but she solved the problem of *Unbehagen* by settling on the now-famous *Civilization and Its Discontents*. Freud's two titles in German had emphasized a general condition by stressing the first word, "unhappiness" or "discomfort." Then his suggested English title humanized the condition by naming man as the suffering protagonist. It provided a subtle shift in emphasis. Riviere's title returned to the impersonality of Freud's original German by removing man, but it altered the emphasis to the context (civilization), not the condition (discontentedness). By whatever name, the rhetorical power and stylistic vigor of Freud, as well as the accessibility of his ideas, came through in English with considerable success, making *Civilization and Its Discontents* a widely read book, one of his most popular and commercially profitable. Priced shrewdly by Leonard Woolf at 2s.6d. more than *The Future of an Illusion,* Freud's *Civilization and Its Discontents* earned more money with fewer sales figures. (See Appendixes C and D.)

Three years elapsed before Freud's next book, *New Introductory Lectures on Psycho-Analysis* (1933). As Ernest Jones has noted, the new "lectures" were conceived primarily to earn revenue for the continually faltering Internationaler Psychoanalytischer Verlag and also to allow Freud to update several of his theories and to introduce observations on a few new subjects.[22] Freud had delivered his first twenty-eight introductory lectures to the Vienna Psychiatric Clinic fifteen years earlier. His seven new essays, although cast in the lecture form (beginning with the formal "Ladies and Gentlemen" and throughout addressed to imagined listeners), were never delivered, nor intended to be delivered. His age had absolved him from the duty of university lecturing, Freud stated in his preface to the volume, and, moreover, his cancer surgery of the mouth had rendered public speaking impossible. He took his place in the lecture room "only by an artifice of the imagination,"[23] a pretense which helped him keep his reader in mind. By sequencing the new lectures with the old (the first new lecture is numbered twenty-nine), Freud not only stressed the "dependence" of the new on the old but fostered the illusion that his audience had reassembled after a long intermission. "I have brought you together again," he began in his first lecture.

Of the seven lectures, only three provided new material. The first lecture on dreams summarized and slightly revised the old dream theory, the second discussed occultism, and the last two addressed miscellaneous topics and the need for a worldview. The three middle lectures, however, provided instruction as Freud discussed in fresh detail the dynamic interactions of the ego, superego, and id. He included a blackboard diagram, analyzed anxieties and instincts, and explored female psychosexuality. Freud's woman, suffering from narcissism, castration fear, and penis envy, struggling with a pre-Oedipus complex attachment to her mother followed by an Oedipus complex with her father, was more burdened than Freud's man with the fate of biology. He saw her as "having little sense of justice," weaker than men in her "social interest" and less able to sublimate her instincts.[24] No wonder he found her at thirty, unlike men, frightening in "her psychical rigidity" with her libido unchanging in its "final position." And no wonder that modern critics have found Freud's conclusions unjust at best, rigidly prejudiced and sexist at worst, and deplorably unchanging in their final position.

Throughout his publishing career, Freud showed little interest in copyrights, translation rights, or royalties. But the unstable financial condition of the Internationaler Psychoanalytischer Verlag in 1932 drove Freud to write the *New Introductory Lectures* partly to replenish the firm's coffers. His sudden and untypical concern with translation rights and royalties led to an interesting correspondence between Ernest Jones and Leonard Woolf which reveals the working relationships between the *Verlag*, the institute, and the Hogarth Press. It also reveals the passionate attachment to their creations of two strong-minded men, Freud for his publishing company, Woolf for his Hogarth Press.

Ernest Jones wrote to Woolf on October 4, 1932, reporting that Freud was being "rather difficult" about his new book of lectures, with "a bee in his bonnet" about a simultaneous publication in England and America.[25] Freud's bee came from being pressured by Americans who wanted greater accessibility to his works. In addition, explained Jones, Freud wanted to earn as much money as possible for the *Verlag*, and he felt he had "behaved over-generously in the past [with royalties] and that we have taken undue advantage of it." In passing, Jones asked Woolf if the press had remitted to Freud the 10 percent royalties due him on two books published in 1922 but taken over by the press in 1924: *Beyond the Pleasure Principle* and *Group Psychology*. Freud had turned the matter over to Jones and his son Martin Freud for resolution, wrote Jones, and he asked Woolf for his best offer for translation rights, including American publication. Martin Freud had taken over the directorship of the publishing company the year before in response to its financial crisis, giving up his secure banking position to aid the cause of his father and psychoanalysis.

Leonard Woolf's response to Jones's letter on October 7, in what amounted to a new introductory lecture on the problems of publishing Freud, defended the press against charges of ungenerosity by recapitulating the past history of their relationship (HP 113). Up to the publication of *Civilization and Its Discontents* (1930), wrote Woolf, no American publisher would accept Freud's books. (Woolf overstated his case, for Macmillan in New York had published A. A. Brill's translations of the early Freud books in 1913 and 1914.) When visiting American publishers were shown Freud's books in the IPL, continued Woolf, they remarked that "there was no sale for psychoanalytical books in America."[26] Just before he published *Civilization and Its Discontents*, noted Woolf, there had been "a sudden flare-up of interest in Freud," and when the book came out, the Hogarth Press received many telegrams from Americans seeking publishing rights. Hogarth then sold the rights to Harrison Smith and Jonathan Cape and paid Freud his share. Hogarth had paid Freud royalties on the two early books, *Beyond the Pleasure Principle* and *Group Psychology*, added Woolf, "though of course we were under no obligation in the matter." (Woolf had sent Freud a royalty check for over £23 in April 1931, one of the few times he wrote directly to Freud.)[27] To emphasize the initial risk undertaken by Hogarth, Woolf then repeated the now-familiar story of the large publisher who had advised him against taking on Freud's *Collected Papers* and the IPL. No American publisher at the time would publish the *Papers*.

Under the circumstances, argued Woolf, he could not agree that the press had taken advantage of Freud's generosity; but to avoid even a suggestion of ungenerosity, he proposed that Freud suit himself over the translation rights with America. There were two options: (1) assign the British and American rights to Hogarth, which would then arrange for an American publisher and "take any percentage of the royalties paid by America" that Freud would think fair, or (2) keep the American rights himself and find an American translator and publisher. If the American publisher used the Hogarth translation, they would have to pay half the costs of translation. For the British rights to the *New Introductory Lectures,* Woolf proposed the same terms he had given for *Civilization and Its Discontents,* which he felt had been "quite generous": 10 percent royalties on the first 1,000 copies sold, 12½ percent on the next 1,000 copies, and 15 percent on those over 2,000, with an advance royalty of £20. He accepted Jones's offer of a £100 subsidy from the institute, the usual arrangement.

Ernest Jones hastened to reassure Woolf that no one questioned Hogarth's treatment of Freud (HP 113). He was sending on Woolf's proposal to Martin Freud, Jones concluded, and he noted that Freud wanted to use the Hogarth Press translation in any American publication. The matter was settled. Martin Freud accepted Woolf's proposal, and W. W. Norton published the press's translation in America.

The entire transaction followed what had become a standard procedure. Jones and Freud corresponded over policy matters, and Jones worked out the arrangements directly with Woolf. Jones would then pass on Woolf's terms to the *Verlag,* which after 1931 meant to Martin Freud. Sometimes John Rickman, Jones's associate at the institute, would correspond with Woolf about details. Woolf seldom wrote to Freud, and Freud usually did not involve himself with the details of the IPL business.

In 1935 W. W. Norton took over the rights to Freud's *Autobiographical Study,* published in America by Brentano in 1927 in a volume containing another work, *The Problem of Lay Analysis,* and asked Freud to revise it for a new American edition. Freud complied and added a postscript which brought up-to-date his contribution to psychoanalysis in the ten years since the original German version had been published. The occasion of a new American edition prompted the institute to sponsor an edition in the IPL series in 1935, the first time Freud's *Autobiographical Study* had appeared in England. Translation rights for the book on *Lay Analysis* proved too complicated to unravel for the institute, however, and so the Hogarth Press could not publish it. It was the one book that got away. James Strachey had provided the original translation for Brentano's publication of the *Autobiographical Study,* and he revised it now to include Freud's postscript. Because the twelve-volume German edition of Freud's work, *Gesammelte Schriften,* had completed publication in 1934, including the *Autobiographical Study* in volume eleven, it did not contain Freud's revisions and postscript. The English and American editions of 1935 thus contained new material not seen in any German edition at the time.

In 1936, the year of Freud's eightieth birthday, the Hogarth Press and the institute resurrected another of Freud's earlier books for a new translation and first publication in England. The original *Hemmung, Symptom, und Angst* (1926) had been translated and published in America as *Inhibition, Symptom, and Anxiety* (1927) and then retranslated in a new edition in 1935 by H. A. Bunker, unbeknownst to the institute. About this time, in June 1935, James Strachey suggested to Leonard Woolf that the Hogarth Press ought to issue a translation of the book. Woolf wrote to Jones, who agreed, and since Freud had kept the translation rights in England, he could authorize Strachey to proceed (HP 112). Actually Alix Strachey, not James, provided the translation, receiving a £20 payment from Hogarth for her efforts. Her translation, employing the plural in the title, *Inhibitions, Symptoms, and Anxiety,* was published in November 1936. Only after the fact did Jones and Woolf learn to their chagrin that

Freud had previously given the translation rights in America to Bunker, so that Alix Strachey and Bunker had worked without awareness of each other's efforts. The entire institute was exasperated over Freud's casual handling of rights, drawing from Freud the meek response that he had meant no harm.

By the mid-1930s the Freud industry was booming, and American publishers were clamoring for his books. Leonard Woolf at times felt beleaguered. John Rickman proposed in November 1936 that the Hogarth Press accede to the English publisher Dent's desire to issue an anthology of Freud's work in the Everyman series. Rickman would edit it. Dent pushed hard, but Woolf pushed back, resulting in some sharply worded correspondence between Woolf, Rickman, and Martin Freud before the issue was completely settled a year later when the Hogarth Press published *A General Selection from the Works of Sigmund Freud* (1937).

At the outset, Leonard Woolf predictably rejected the Dent plan as likely to gut the IPL series. He proposed instead that Rickman write an 80,000-word exposition of Freud's "views and doctrines" (HP 110). Rickman sensibly rejected Woolf's idea, favoring the Dent anthology approach, because, as he wrote to Leonard, Freud's own words are readable, "clean," and interesting on a wide range of subjects (HP 110). Woolf was unmoved even by cleanliness. "You will, I know," he wrote back to Rickman in late December, "think me obstinate, churlish, and money-grubbing, and I daresay I am, but I cannot agree with you."[28] He was tired of large firms pouncing on profitable authors after smaller firms had risked their funds on the author's early unprofitable books. As proof, Woolf trotted out his much-used anecdote of being warned off Freud in 1924 by the large publisher prophesying doom. He would not agree to hand over Freud to Dent, the royalty from Everyman being "infinitesimal" and insufficient to counter Hogarth's lost sales. So, reluctantly, Woolf agreed to publish a Freud anthology himself if Rickman insisted.

Two months later, in March 1937, Woolf still grumbled about the project, never conceding anything easily. He thought the "potted Freud" presented grave difficulties. There were problems with clarity, with deletions, and with Freud's complexity. "There is nothing that I know read by that public [Everyman readers]," wrote Woolf, "anything like as difficult from the technical point of view of language as *The Ego and The Id*"

(HP 110). But the idea of presenting selections from Freud to a large, popular audience through an inexpensive series like Dent's Everyman finally took hold of Woolf, and by April he had made it his own. He wrote to Ernest Jones proposing a new Hogarth Press series of books to sell at 5s. for not over 80,000 words, and at 3s.6d. for 16,000 words. The new series would be called the Psycho-Analytical Epitomes, with Freud's *General Selection* the first volume. But now Jones balked, worried about the condensed Freud and the difficulty of finding enough salable authors other than Freud to keep the series going. When Woolf presented the series and anthology to Martin Freud in May, other problems arose, chiefly because Woolf proposed a 5 percent royalty on the cheaper edition.

"I am having the usual difficulty of getting Dr. Martin Freud to come to a decision," Woolf wrote to Rickman in June 1937, asking for his help (HP 110). Martin Freud responded that he worried about the risk to his father's sales of the cheap anthology and protested strongly about the 5 percent royalties. He preferred a 15 percent royalty but might accept a 10 percent royalty out of courtesy to Rickman and the Hogarth Press. Woolf replied to Rickman that he thought Freud's request for 15 percent "pretty monstrous," especially because nine-tenths of the anthology would be taken from early Freud books (before the Hogarth Press contract in 1924), from which no royalties were legally due, although he had paid them for years. Eventually Woolf's logic and tenacity won the day. Martin Freud resigned from the argument, and then Woolf, having proven his point, offered 7½ percent as a gesture of compromise. The Epitomes series was launched with a printing of over 3,000 copies of Freud's *General Selection,* published in November 1937 and selling for 5s.

Four months later, on March 11, 1938, Hitler's Nazis invaded Austria, putting an end to the Verlag Internationaler Psychoanalytischer and to Freud's long residence and psychoanalytic practice in Vienna. The Nazis had burned Freud's books in Berlin in 1933 and had closed down the Berlin Psychoanalytic Institute soon after. In 1936 the Gestapo had seized the *Verlag*'s warehouse in Leipsig where the books and periodicals were stored for distribution in Germany and Austria. In Austria the Anschluss quickly led to the seizure of the *Verlag* itself, the temporary arrest of Martin Freud and Ernest Jones, the confiscation of the Vienna Society's library, and the complete shutdown of all Viennese psychoanalytic activities. Thus began the long and difficult negotiations to extricate Freud and his family from Nazi clutches. With the aid of the American ambassador to France, William Bullitt, and President Roosevelt, Freud finally arrived safely in London in early June 1938, generously welcomed by the English. A nearly royal presence in exile, he had only fifteen months to live.

Appropriately for the time, John Rickman edited another selection of Freud's works for the fourth volume of Epitomes in 1939, entitled *Civilization, War, and Death: Selections from Three Works by Sigmund Freud*. Rickman chose passages from "Thoughts for the Time on War and Death" (1915), written during the First World War, and from *Civilization and Its Discontents* (1929, translated 1930). Rickman concluded the three-part selection with Freud's letter to Einstein, "Why War," written in September 1932 in response to a request from Einstein on behalf of the League of Nations' International Institute of Intellectual Co-operation. Ernest Jones noted in his biography that Freud thought his exchange with Einstein was "tedious and sterile," perhaps because he felt it only as a public obligation to correspond with a man he barely knew.[29]

Freud's thoughts on death were anything but tedious and included the memorable sentence, "Our own death is indeed unimaginable, and whenever we make the attempt to imagine it we can perceive that we really survive as spectators."[30] Freud concluded his essay with the translation of a Latin quotation ("Si vis vitam, para mortem") congenial to his stoicism: "If you would endure life, be prepared for death." In September 1938, three months after arriving in England, Freud had his last severe cancer operation, only to have the disease recur in February 1939 too advanced for operation. He began receiving radium treatments and prepared for death.

Freud's last book for the Hogarth Press and the institute, *Moses and Monotheism,* was translated by Katherine Jones (the wife of Ernest Jones) and produced by Hogarth in a rush to beat the author's death. Freud had completed a draft of the work in the summer of 1934, describing it in a letter to Arnold Zweig as a three-part study of Moses entitled "Moses the Man, a Historical Novel." The first part read "like an interesting novel," he thought, the second part was "laborious and lengthy," but the third part was "substantial and exacting."[31] Although it might be said of Freud what was said of William James, that he wrote psychology like a novelist, his study of Moses was no novel in spite of his original title. He did not dare publish the book, he told Zweig, because it would likely stir up the Catholic power structure in Vienna, resulting in hostile actions against the practice of psychoanalysis. Whatever Freud's reasons for keeping secret his book on Moses, he reworked the manuscript during the summer of 1936, publishing the first part, "Moses an Egyptian," in *Imago* early in 1937 and the second part, "If Moses Was an Egyptian," in a later issue of *Imago* the same year. By making Moses an Egyptian, Freud outraged many Jews and ran afoul of well-established biblical scholarship. Aside from a few admiring writers and controversialists like H. G. Wells, he found no takers of his thesis among scholars.

Only after he arrived in England could Freud contemplate rewriting the long and complex third part, "Moses, His People, and Monotheist Religion." As he explained in his "Summary and Recapitulation" to the second section of this last part, in England he "found the temptation irresistible to make the knowledge [he] had held back accessible to the world" and so reworked it "to fit it on to the two parts that had already been published."[32]

The resulting book, complicated by these delays, suppressions, rewritings, separate publications, and final stitching together, was unusually fragmented for Freud. James Strachey thought it unorthodox and eccentric in construction.[33] Ernest Jones himself admitted that the book was "rather badly strung together."[34] The repetitions and summaries can be explained, as Strachey did, by the four-year genesis of the final book and by the severe interruptions and dislocations experienced by Freud. But Strachey's explanation does not include Freud's personal difficulty in writing the book on Moses. The subject matter not only obsessed Freud for years as an intellectual puzzle but immersed him in many levels of anxiety, repression, and guilt as he struggled to account for his Jewish identity, his Oedipal relationship with his father, and his own paternalistic, authoritarian self-image. The character of Moses, as Freud saw him, was too close to his own for comfort.

Aside from the problems of writing and editing the volume, Freud had had his difficulties over publication. Originally he wanted to appeal to a large popular audience and so contemplated publishing with Cassell for a £500 advance. After Leonard Woolf dissuaded him from publishing outside the IPL series, Woolf tried to have Freud simplify his title to *Moses*. As he wrote to Freud, Woolf thought many readers would be frightened by the word *Monotheism* in the longer title.[35] But this time Freud dissuaded Woolf. *Moses and Monotheism*, Freud's last great book, was published by the Hogarth Press in March 1939.

Freud, wrote Leonard Woolf in his autobiography, "was not only a genius, but also, unlike many geniuses, an extraordinarily nice man" (*Downhill* 166). Moreover, his sons and daughter, Martin, Ernst, and Anna, had inherited Freud's "civilized temperament . . . which made every kind of relationship with him so pleasant." After fifteen years of such relationships, the Woolfs finally met Freud. On January 28, 1939, they had tea with Freud at his house in Hampstead, finding him formidable, with an aura of greatness, "courteous in a formal, old-fashioned way," yet also like "a half-extinct volcano" (ibid., 169). He was gentle, but even though ravaged by cancer, he gave the impression of great strength, of "something sombre, suppressed, reserved." To Virginia Woolf he presented a narcissus. She thought him "a screwed up shrunk very old man" but one with "immense potential . . . an old fire now flickering" (*Diary* 5:202). They exchanged pleasantries. Freud was amused by Leonard's anecdote of the bookshop thief who stole one of Freud's books and the judge who wished to sentence him to read all of them as punishment. Freud thought his books "had made him infamous, not famous." The short meeting over, the Woolfs left and never saw Freud again. But Freud sent a brief letter to Leonard three days later, gracefully regretting that his English was insufficient for him to express fully his pleasure at meeting the Woolfs (MHP). Eight months later he died.

Freud's death in September 1939 prompted Leonard Woolf to propose publishing his complete works through the Hogarth Press and the IPL. Ernest Jones agreed to consider the proposal but then mentioned the idea to Stanley Unwin, who moved aggressively to take over the project from Hogarth. Woolf, rightly alarmed by this infringement, exchanged exasperated letters with Unwin and Jones.[36] Ernest Jones apologized, and the three eventually agreed to a joint publishing venture between Hogarth Press and Allen & Unwin for the complete works. Delayed by the war, the project of a standard edition of Freud's work became the multiyear labor of James Strachey's after the war. The Hogarth Press and the IPL published the twenty-three-volume edition without Allen & Unwin.

Freud, after death, became if anything a more valuable property than when alive, and more of his work was published posthumously in the *Standard Edition* English translation than during his lifetime. Ironically, of all the Hogarth Press authors, only Virginia Woolf and Sigmund Freud have achieved this measure of greatness and continuity. They alone have been published with a regularity which defies the extinction of the grave.

Sigmund Freud's thirteen books and two Epitomes published by the Hogarth Press and the Institute of Psycho-Analysis between 1921 and 1939 dominate the IPL series, giving it luster, intellectual importance, and accessibility even to a nonspecialist audience to a greater extent than much psychoanalytic literature. The IPL was designed from the start to showcase Freud's genius, and it was carefully managed by Ernest Jones and John Rickman so that no one upstaged the master. There were fifteen titles from Freud but only twenty-two from all the others who published with the *Verlag* in Vienna. Ten of the fifteen authors published in the IPL were represented by only one title apiece, four were allowed two titles (Sandor Ferenczi, J. C. Flugel, Ernest Jones, and René Laforgue), and only one, Theodor Reik, enjoyed the distinction of three titles. These limitations partly reflected the marketplace, but there were also ideological and political factors at work.

Ernest Jones selected those IPL authors who were psychoanalytically "correct" in their writings and established members in good standing in the international movement. The authors were American, English, Austrian, German, Hungarian, and French, with more English writers than any others. J. J. Putnam (1921) was the only American. No renegade appeared in the IPL series. There were, of course, no books by the early defectors Adler, Stekel, or Jung, who had left the fold before the *Verlag* was established in 1919. Otto Rank broke with Freud in 1924 after both the publishing firm and the IPL were well under way, but he is absent from the list of authors. None of Ferenczi's later unorthodox studies saw print in the IPL. From among the currently faithful, however, there came interesting books, supplementing and supporting the pioneer work of Freud.

More volumes in the IPL by Freudians were clinical than cultural, but by only a small margin. During the first twenty years of psychoanalytic publishing by the Hogarth Press, there were eleven books plus one Epitome on clinically based psychoanalytic subjects, while there were nine books plus one Epitome on such broader subjects as literature, art, anthropology, and religion. In the first few years of the IPL, most of the books published adhered to straight clinical topics. In the 1920s books by Putnam, Ferenczi, Flugel, Karl Abraham, and Rickman characterized the series. The two most important and extensive of these were Ferenczi's *Further Contributions to the Theory and Technique of Psycho-Analysis* (1926) and Abraham's *Selected Papers* (1927) with an introductory memoir by Ernest Jones.

The Abraham volume had been planned in the autumn of 1925 as "Clinical Papers on Psycho-Analysis," but before the book could go to press, Abraham died on Christmas Day at the age of forty-eight from undiagnosed lung cancer. The book then became a memorial tribute to one of the movement's most important figures.[37] He was an early follower of Freud (they met in 1907), the first practicing Freudian psychoanalyst in Germany, an officer at several levels in the International Psycho-Analytical Association, and finally president. He became Freud's champion against Jung and a member of the "Committee." He analyzed and trained such distinguished psychoanalysts and future IPL authors as Helene Deutsch, Melanie Klein, and Theodor Reik. He analyzed Alix Strachey.

Although, as Jones commented in his introductory memoir, Abraham was not a prolific writer, his papers often presented significant contributions to the growing field of psychoanalysis. The twenty-six papers contained in the volume cover his career from 1907 to 1924 and include essays on hysterical dreams, fetishism, scoptophilia (voyeurism), ejaculatio praecox, the female castration complex, and a long monograph on the development of the libido. Abraham's *Selected Papers* (1927) thus became a companion to Freud's four-volume *Collected Papers* (1924–25). Ernest Jones's extensive and praiseful biographical essay did for Abraham what his later biography of Freud accomplished on a grander scale, not only explaining the man and his work but placing him in the pantheon of the new gods of psychoanalysis.

The 1930s produced several more works based on psychoanalytical practice such as those by Ella Freeman Sharpe (a handbook of dream analysis, 1937) and René Laforgue (clinical cases, 1938), but the three most important works were by women: Melanie Klein's *Psycho-Analysis of Children* (1932), Helene Deutsch's *Psycho-Analysis of the Neurosis* (1932), and Anna Freud's *The Ego and the Mechanism of Defence* (1937). The twenties and thirties thus saw the rise of the second generation of psychoanalysts who began to expand and extend the practice into areas only suggested by Freud and his early followers. A number of brilliant and gifted women made their appearance in international psychoanalytic circles at this time.

Melanie Klein, a Hungarian and former student of Karl Abraham, began analyzing children in the early 1920s, publishing a series of papers on her findings which gradually began to differ from orthodox Freudianism. In 1926, encouraged by Ernest Jones, she emigrated to England and soon established an extensive practice in child analysis. Her two chief contributions in theory and practice up to 1932, culminating in her landmark Hogarth Press–Institute of Psycho-Analysis book *The Psycho-Analysis of Children* (1932), were to reduce the age at which children first experience Oedipal anxieties to around two years from the previously accepted age of three or four and to base her analysis on observed children's play in which their actions could be interpreted symbolically as expressions of conflict in a method equivalent to the use of verbal free association with adults.

Melanie Klein's use of play technique in children and her early insistence on the complex but successful analysis of children (previously doubted by Freud) revolutionized child psychiatry. It also began to bring her into conflict with Freud, especially as she began to argue that the mother-child relationship was more important than Freud's classic father-child relationship. Ernest Jones, a convinced supporter of Klein, had to defend her to Freud when she began to differ openly in 1935 with Anna Freud's more traditional findings. In the late 1930s and early 1940s, Klein moved further away from orthodoxy and dropped from the fold as she developed her own concepts of manic defense mechanisms and depression and of paranoid-schizoid relationships. Her *Psycho-Analysis of Children* (1932) thus represented not only an important contribution to psychoanalysis but the end of an important phase in her career. After this book Klein's theories would no longer be acceptable to traditional Freudians. Her papers from the later years, however, would be published by the Hogarth Press in 1948 as *Contribution to Psycho-Analysis, 1921–45*.

Anna Freud's first important book in England was *The Ego and the Mechanisms of Defence* (1936, translated 1937), an announcement to the world, as it were, that she had achieved stature within the international movement in her own right. Like Melanie Klein, Anna Freud began her career by publishing a number of papers on child analysis and related subjects through the 1920s in various psychoanalytic journals. By 1925 Anna Freud had become so important to her father and the movement that she was admitted to membership in the "Committee" as a replacement for the defecting Otto Rank. Then she published two small books of lectures growing out of her experience with a Viennese camp school for children made homeless in the First World War and from her experience with a child guidance clinic: *Four Lectures on Child Analysis* (1927–29; first translated and published in America by the Nervous and Mental Disease Publishing Co. 1928) and *Four Lectures on Psychoanalysis for Teachers and Parents* (1929–30; translated and published in England in 1931 by Allen & Unwin).

Through the 1930s Anna Freud developed her reputation in child analysis, pursuing more traditional paths than Melanie Klein and working at the guidance clinic in Vienna with children up to the age of puberty. With the disastrous events of 1938–39, she was forced to move with her father to London where she helped establish and direct the Hampstead War Nurseries with Dorothy Burlingham. After the war the nurseries became the Hampstead Child Therapy Clinic, and Anna Freud's career as a child specialist assumed international importance. Her Hogarth Press–Institute of Psycho-Analysis book *The Ego and the Mechanisms of Defence* in 1937 thus helped her establish her credentials in traditional areas of psychoanalysis but barely touched on the subjects that she would develop later in her career. Ernest Jones had urged publication of the book in October 1936 because, as he explained to Leonard Woolf, Freud's daughter was "coming to the front very much" in Vienna (HP 102). Also, Jones predicted good sales from the American rights, because the American psychoanalysts thought highly of her. Anna Freud's theories were more acceptable in America than Melanie Klein's.

The nine books and one Epitome in the IPL series published by

Freudians on broad cultural subjects must have interested a general public and probably were published by the Hogarth Press and the institute not only because they were meritorious but also because they helped diversify the series and increase sales. They range from Ernest Jones's *Essays in Applied Psycho-Analysis* (1923) to Theodor Reik's *Ritual: Psycho-Analytic Studies* (1928) and René Laforgue's *Clinical Aspects of Psycho-Analysis* (1938) and from J. C. Flugel's *Psychology of Clothes* (1930) to Géza Róheim's *Riddle of the Sphinx, or Human Origins* (1934). Six of the ten volumes appeared between 1930 and 1934, a time of grave financial crisis for the Internationaler Psychoanalytischer Verlag when Freud created his *New Introductory Lectures* (1933).

Like the Hogarth Press itself, the International Psycho-Analytical Library has continued to publish interesting and important works related to psychoanalysis. When Leonard Woolf picked up the proposal by Strachey and Jones in 1924 to join with the institute of Psycho-Analysis in publishing Freud's *Collected Papers,* he calculated his risks, committed nearly £800 of hard-earned capital, and plunged into the venture. To his great relief, the IPL series succeeded. Freud's surge in popularity and importance after 1924 pulled many of the other books in the series through, and the editorial planning by Jones, Rickman, and Woolf diversified the series and kept it lively and interesting enough to ensure its solvency. (For sales and profits of the IPL series, see Appendixes C and D.)

"Better to have a good friend than a good translator," wrote Freud, who considered loyalty a prime virtue.[38] He was responding to Ernest Jones's concern over the "seriously inaccurate . . . ambiguous . . . undignified and colloquial" translations in America by A. A. Brill and his associates, at a time when Adler and Stekel were bolting the traces. Freud had given his friend Brill, an Austrian emigrant and his great champion and developer of psychoanalysis in America, the translation rights without considering Brill's adequacy as a translator. That a writer famous for the felicity of his prose style (Freud won the Goethe Prize in 1930 for his literary merit) could be so cavalier about translations troubled Jones. Freud's attitude, thought Jones, almost seemed like "indifference concerning the promulgation of his work abroad." His casualness led not only to misleading and uneven translations but to legal entanglements when the Hogarth Press and the institute launched the IPL series in England. Leonard Woolf and Ernest Jones had to remind Freud constantly of the important distinction between English and American rights. The legal problems with translation rights would continue to plague James Strachey when he set to work on the *Standard Edition* of Freud's *Complete Works* years later.

Freud, a translator himself, was competent in written English, as was his daughter Anna, who worked with Strachey on the *Standard Edition*. Unlike his treatment of American translators, Freud assisted Jones with the translations in England, providing "detailed cooperation." As Jones remarked, "We sent him question after question about slight ambiguities in his expositions, and made various suggestions concerning inner contradictions and the like." [39] The interchange, fostered by Jones, himself fluent in German and a skilled writer of English prose, resulted in IPL translations superior to the American ones. From the first, Ernest Jones as general editor of the series enlisted the aid of two formidable translators and editors, Joan Riviere and James Strachey. Between them they largely divided the translations of Freud's books and papers up to his death and the Second World War, after which Strachey began the enormous task of translating and editing the *Standard Edition*.

Joan Riviere met Freud in 1920, underwent analysis and training with him in 1922, and shortly thereafter began her career as a lay analyst in London. She made her first mark as a translator in 1917 with a careful rendering of *Introductory Lectures on Psycho-Analysis* (published by Allen & Unwin), one of Freud's most popular books, and then in 1924 she assumed the important role of supervisor and translator of the four-volume *Collected Papers* (1924–25) under Jones's general editorship. Riviere supervised a large number of English Freudians who participated in the work. Almost everyone seems to have had a crack at the papers with the interesting exception of Ernest Jones. Discounting volume three, which Alix and James Strachey translated themselves, volumes one, two, and four of the *Collected Papers* contained seventy-three papers of varying length, difficulty, and importance—from mere notes, like the two-page "A Connection between a Symbol and a Symptom" (vol. 2, trans. Douglas Bryan) to the extended seventy-two-page essay "On the History of the Psycho-Analytic Movement" (vol. 1, trans. Joan Riviere). Riviere herself translated twenty-one of the papers, most of them in the second volume, including the latest, most important of the "Clinical Papers" and all but one of the ten "Papers on Technique." She used sixteen translators for the other papers. Some of them contributed only one or two brief translations, but others did more: Douglas Bryan, Edward Glover, and C. M. J. Hubback translated four papers apiece (Bryan and Glover, with Riviere, would become directors of the institute), J. Bernays and John Rickman (later a director) five papers each, and Cecil M. Baines and E. Colburn Mayne six papers each. Alix and James Strachey translated two papers apiece and collaborated on one. In spite of the number of translators, the *Collected Papers* reads remarkably well, for Riviere smoothed out most of the stylistic differences.

After her extensive work with the *Collected Papers,* Joan Riviere translated two more of Freud's books, *The Ego and the Id* (1927) and *Civilization and Its Discontents* (1930). She had translated the last four "Clinical Papers" in the second volume of the *Papers,* which had been written in 1924, the year following the completion of *Das Ich und das Es* (1923), so that she had worked with some of Freud's most difficult theoretical writing. Although English readers of these papers had to wait three years for Riviere's translation of *The Ego and the Id* for complete understanding, they had the advantage, finally, of a clear and consistent translation of both papers and book. There would not be the same degree of continuity in the translations again until Strachey's *Standard Edition.*

From 1922 to 1939 the IPL series offered nine of Freud's books and two Epitomes. Joan Riviere translated two of the nine books, James Strachey two books (*Group Psychology and the Analysis of the Ego,* 1922, and *An Autobiographical Study,* 1935), and Alix Strachey one book (*Inhibitions, Symptoms, and Anxiety,* 1936). Only four other translators were entrusted with translating Freud's books in the series: C. M. J. Hubback (*Beyond the Pleasure Principle,* 1922), W. D. Robson-Scott (*The Future of an Illusion,* 1928), W. J. H. Sprott (*New Introductory Lectures on Psycho-Analysis,* 1933), and Katherine Jones (*Moses and Monotheism,* 1939).

Two of these translators were known to Bloomsbury. "Sebastian" Sprott was a fringe member, friend of E. M. Forster, Maynard Keynes, Lytton Strachey, and George Rylands. First a Cambridge Apostle, then a researcher in the Cambridge Psychological Laboratory, he later became a lecturer in psychology at the University of Nottingham. Leonard Woolf negotiated with him directly over the translation of Freud's *New Introductory Lectures,* offering him the standard fee of £1 per 1,000 words, with a maximum of £50 and a royalty of 2½ percent on all copies sold over 2,000.[40] Katherine Jones, the last of Freud's translators in his lifetime, was the second wife of Ernest Jones. Born in Czechoslovakia, she was raised in Vienna and educated there and in Switzerland. She had first translated Theodor Reik's *The Unknown Murderer* (1936) in the IPL series when neither James Strachey nor Joan Riviere was available.

When James Strachey received the Schlegel-Tieck translation prize in 1966 for his recently completed twenty-three volume *Standard Edition of the Complete Psychological Works of Sigmund Freud,* he was recognized as the editor-translator of Freud par excellence. "I doubt," wrote Leonard Woolf, "whether any translation into the English language of comparable size can compare with his in accuracy and brilliance of translation and in the scholarly thoroughness of its editing" (*Journey* 118). Certainly Strachey deserved the praise. His thirteen years' labor on the *Standard Edition* as translator and editor brought him international fame. Strachey, however, did not stand alone. It is worth remembering that he had the close collaboration throughout of Anna Freud, keeper of the keys and defender of the faith, and the assistance of Alix Strachey and Alan Tyson, both highly skilled translators. He also had the invaluable editorial assistance of Angela Richard, who compiled the twenty-fourth and last volume, *Indexes and Bibliographies,* after Strachey's death in 1967, an important work in itself.

So much of the *Standard Edition* derived from the IPL series of Freud's books, and so many crucial translation decisions were made during those years, that some mention of it and its chief architect seems appropriate here. James Strachey and his wife Alix (née Sargant-Florence) had prepared for their dual roles as psychoanalyst-translators early on. While they were undergoing their training analysis with Freud in 1920, Strachey noted in the *Standard Edition,* Freud "suddenly instructed us to make a translation of a paper he had recently written—'Ein Kind wird geschlagen' ['A Child Is Being Beaten']—a translation now embedded here in Volume XVII."[41] The Stracheys' command performance was first published in the *International Journal of Psycho-Analysis* (1920), then in volume two of the *Collected Papers* (1924), and finally, revised, in the *Standard Edition*.

The odyssey of this article from Freud's German to Strachey's English in the *Standard Edition* via the IPL was a trip traveled by many of the books and papers assembled in the twenty-three volumes. When Strachey and his associates began their labors in 1953, they had thirty-three years of experience behind them putting Freud into English, and they had thirteen books of Freud's already in translations approved by Freud, Jones, Riviere, and Strachey. The five important early books (*Interpretation of Dreams*, 1900; *Psychopathology of Everyday Life*, 1901; *Three Essays of the Theory of Sexuality*, 1905; *Five Lectures on Psycho Analysis*, 1910; and *Totem and Taboo*, 1912–13) had been translated by A. A. Brill or his associate H. W. Chase in America and had to be extricated from the tangle of translation rights and retranslated. So, too, *The Problem of Lay Analysis* (1926), which Ernest Jones had not been able to free from American rights. There were countless other papers, prefaces, and letters to reclaim and translate afresh, and had it not been for the thirteen IPL works which needed relatively minor face-lifting, the *Standard Edition* might have taken many additional years. As Strachey proceeded to recast the translations into one consistent style, tone, and voice, he kept in mind an imaginary model, he noted, "of the writings of some English man of science of wide education born in the middle of the nineteenth century."[42]

By Freud's death, most of the editorial and translation problems had been solved by his editors and translators in England. At the commencement of the IPL, Ernest Jones had established a "Glossary Committee" to resolve matters of technical vocabulary. In 1943 Alix Strachey had collected and disseminated the work of the committee in her publication *A New German-English Psycho-Analytical Vocabulary*, and James Strachey used it with few exceptions in the *Standard Edition*. He provided in the first volume "Notes on Some Technical Terms Whose Translation Calls for Comment," and throughout the twenty-three volumes he carefully annotated problematical usages. In any such complicated undertaking, however, there remained problems and controversial readings.

The award-winning prose of Freud in German was notable for its clarity, directness, and simplicity and for its absence of technical jargon.

Freud pressed into service a wide range of words from standard usage, building into them specialized meanings. When the Freudian vocabulary came over into English through the IPL translators, some rather homely German words inexplicably became Latin or Greek, not English. Freud's *das Ich, das Es,* and *das Über-Ich,* in spite of Leonard Woolf's preference for "the I and the It," were translated as "the ego," "the id," and "the superego." More puzzling and annoying to the lay reader, Freud's *Shau-lust* (sexual pleasure in looking, or voyeurism) turned into "scoptophilia" (in the *Collected Papers*) or "scopophilia" (in the *Standard Edition*); *Beset-zung* (occupation or filling, i.e., with psychic energy) to Freud's distress became Strachey's invented word "cathexis" (based on the Greek *catach-ein*); and *Fehleistung* (faulty function, or faulty achievement, generic for "Freudian slips") fell into "parapraxis." Plain German sometimes became good English, but with different implications. Freud's often used *die Seele* or *seelisch* (literally "the soul") or *Psyche* consistently reappeared in the IPL English as "mind" or "mental." And *der Trieb* (driving force, motive power) became the ambiguous "instinct," not "drive," as Strachey acknowledged in a lengthy defense of his translation.[43]

These and other translations have been questioned by critics, such as Darius Ornston and Bruno Bettleheim, who have seen in the "mistranslations" a deliberate policy aimed at dehumanizing Freud and at turning his highly accessible, and richly ambiguous literary language into the inflexible jargon of medical specialty.[44] During the early years of the IPL series there was in England, as in America, a perceived need to protect psychoanalysis from charges of quackery or obscenity by developing a technical vocabulary. If there were a few neologisms from classical roots unpleasant to see and hear, and if some of the cultural nuances of the original German were lost in the struggle for clarity and precision, the failures seem minor compared to the successes. The *Standard Edition* of Strachey and company has remained one of the triumphs of the translator's craft, a massive work built up from the original IPL volumes with great skill and patience. With the expiration of the copyright covering Freud's translations in 1989, a new generation of Freud's translators are champing at the bit. Whether they will succeed in replacing Strachey's monumental achievement remains to be seen.

CHAPTER NINE

★

THE PARTNERSHIP, 1938–41

L eonard Woolf, ill in bed, dictated to Virginia a contract proposal to John Lehmann early in January 1938 which became the basis for their partnership beginning in April (*Letters* 6:201). There were four points, later modified slightly: (1) For £3,000 Lehmann purchased a partnership in the press, buying Virginia's share and becoming co-owner with Leonard, who also held a share. Virginia would withdraw from management of the press. (2) Lehmann would become managing director with a salary of £500 per year before profits, and Woolf would receive £200 before profits. As managing director, Lehmann would direct the office and staff, attend the office at least three days a week, and have August and September off, as well as two three-week periods during the rest of the year. During his absence Woolf would run the business, largely from Monks House in Rodmell. (3) Each partner could veto any proposed book, except for the Woolfs' own books and pamphlets. (4) Terms of dissolution had to be developed, and the possibilities of forming a private company or an advisory board from the *New Writing* "Gang" were to be considered. An advisory board was soon formed of Auden, Spender, Isherwood, Rosamond Lehmann, and Virginia Woolf. Unstated in this detailed proposal but developed later was the agreement that the press would publish Lehmann's *New Writing*.

After further negotiations, the completion of partnership papers, and an inventory of the press stock, Lehmann finally signed the agreement with Woolf to take effect on April 1, 1938 (*Letters* 6:214, 217). The signing was marred slightly by Woolf's brusqueness, for which he later apologized. As Lehmann wrote to Virginia Woolf, "Leonard was very rugged the other day when I signed the Partnership Agreement, and to my proposal that the event be marked by a mutual health-drinking, replied that he only had cold water." [1] The contretemps was eased by Virginia's return letter, declaring herself "full of sanguininity" about the arrangement, glad to shift the press burden to Lehmann's shoulders, and offering him a "good dinner (not English) at Boulestins or some such place" in lieu of the cold-water toast (*Letters* 6:224).

When John Lehmann began work as the new partner and managing director of the press in April, two of the most important books of 1938 had just been published: Christopher Isherwood's autobiography *Lions and Shadows* and Edward Upward's *Journey to the Border,* the long-awaited socialist novel by a contributor to *New Country* and a schoolboy friend of Isherwood's. Although Lehmann had nothing to do with the production of these books, he was indirectly responsible for them, having introduced Isherwood to the Woolfs.

During Isherwood's energetic wanderings around Europe with Heinz, he began and abandoned a novel, "Paul Is Alone," and a book of autobiographical fragments, "Scenes from an Education," which was to include several episodes already published by the Hogarth Press or in *New Writing* ("Berlin Diary," "Sally Bowles," and "The Nowaks"). Gradually he began to sift out the fictionalized episodes from the autobiographical ones and to conceive the story of his life from his schooldays to his departure for Berlin in 1928. The provisional title became "The Northwest Passage." [2] In the autumn of 1937 Isherwood completed his autobiography and submitted it to Leonard Woolf.

Virginia and Leonard liked the book, but two slight problems arose. First, the title had been used recently by the popular American historical novelist Kenneth Roberts. Second, Leonard was uncertain whether to publish it as fiction or biography (HP 195). One can sympathize with his dilemma. Although the circumstances of the narration were true, the characters were given fictitious names, there were few facts, and the narration read like fiction. Isherwood resolved the title by changing it to *Lions and Shadows: An Education in the Twenties* (1938). Woolf resolved the genre by advertising it as fiction, a category more profitable to a publisher than biography. Isherwood had helped by including a note "To the Reader" which explained that "this book is not . . . in the ordinary journalistic sense of the word, an autobiography." [3] Not until much later, after

Spender's brilliant autobiography of those years, *World within World* (1951), did the identities behind the code names gradually leak out to the public: Wystan Auden had appeared as "Weston," Edward Upward as "Chalmers," Stephen Spender as "Savage." Leonard's marketing strategy, Isherwood's skillful writing, and the intriguing ambiguity of the narration made *Lions and Shadows* a success then as now. In the first three months it sold 1,699 copies (MSR).

Edward Upward, one of the contributors to *New Country* (1933), had made his fictional debut in the landmark volume edited by Michael Roberts and published by the Woolfs after the departure of John Lehmann. Upward's two stories, "The Colleagues" and "Sunday," although slight as fictions, aligned themselves with the Marxist call to action of Roberts's preface. The neurotic clerk's desire to join the Party in "Sunday" concluded the story with a note of decisiveness and austerity thrilling to Christopher Isherwood and others of the group. Upward himself had joined the CPGB in 1932.

Never a prolific writer, Upward did not publish another story until 1935, two years after *New Country,* when "The Island" appeared in an early volume of the *Left Review* (1935). The next year "The Border-Line" was published in the first volume of John Lehmann's *New Writing* (September 1936); it was to become the first chapter in his novel *Journey to the Border.* The next year he published "The Tipster" in the third volume of *New Writing* (1937) and, the year after, his novel with the Hogarth Press.

Edward Upward was naturally drawn to the Woolfs' press. Isherwood had just published *Sally Bowles* (1937), and Lehmann was beginning to work out his return to the press as a partner. The Woolfs in November 1937 agreed to publish Upward's novel, after what Isherwood, in a letter to Lehmann, called "a terrific putsch" on his part and "a wonderful dinner given by the Woolfs to the Upwards, a great success."[4]

Upward soon discovered that his working title, "The Borderline," had been used previously by Heinemann for a novel (HP 507). He suggested "On the Borderline" as a substitute and recommended changing the squire's name to "Parkin" from the original "Parkinson," which was too close to Rogerson, a family whose son he had tutored ten years earlier. Leonard Woolf agreed to the name change of Parkin but thought the title change insufficient. Upward then suggested "Journey to the Border" or "Descent from the Race-Course." Woolf chose the first, and so it became.

Journey to the Border was published in March 1938 along with Isherwood's *Lions and Shadows*. The two books serve almost as companion volumes, Upward's providing a sequel to Isherwood's. *Lions and Shadows* read like fiction, contained stories, and used invented names; *Journey to the Border* contained autobiographical details and focused on Upward's conversion to communism. Isherwood's coded autobiography of his twenties education featured Edward Upward as "Allen Chalmers," co-author with Isherwood of the nightmarish porno-fables of "Mortmere." Upward's novel *Journey to the Border* contained more than one reverberation of the Mortmere stories as well as obvious parallels to Isherwood's autobiography.

Published at a time when many Marxists had become disillusioned with the party line, *Journey to the Border* reflected an earlier attitude. It seemed anachronistic, touching the springs of nostalgia with its romantic notion of conversion and its depiction of the anguish and exhilaration of young leftists six years earlier in 1932. *Journey to the Border* preceded the flood of reminiscences and autobiographical novels that was to come in 1939 and 1940. Critics praised the novel. Virginia Woolf noted with pride: "But this reminds me that our last Leonard & Virginia season is perhaps our most brilliant: all the weeklies I think single out Isherwood, Upward, & even Libby Benedict [author of *The Refugees*] for the highest places. Yes: if there is success in this world, the Hogarth Press has I suppose won what success it could. And money this year will fairly snow us under" (*Diary* 5:130). But the Woolfs were not snowed under by money from Upward's novel. It sold only 438 copies in the first year of publication.[5]

Upward's first novel was nearly his last. He published a short story, "New Order," in Lehmann's *Penguin New Writing* in 1942, but not until 1961 did he return to serious fiction. In a reversal of most literary careers, Upward became more productive after retirement from schoolteaching than before, but his fame as a thirties writer rests firmly on the two stories and one novel issued by the Hogarth Press.

After a two-year absence, J. B. Leishman brought in his third translation of Rilke, *Later Poems* (1938), but not without problems. They developed when Leishman insisted on including an introduction and lengthy notes to the volume. Having first calculated the projected page count of *Later Poems,* Woolf judged that "the proportion of notes to poems is expanded out of all knowledge," requiring that he price the 288-page book at 10s.6d. (HP 383). This he thought too high. The 188-page *Sonnets to Orpheus* had sold for 8s.6d. He recommended omitting the notes and commentary completely. So convinced was Leishman of the vital relationship of the commentary to the text that he offered to forgo his royalty of 5 percent to have the work published as he had planned it. Believing Leishman's argument "quite wrong," Woolf grudgingly agreed to keep the commentary and notes and to publish the book at 10s.6d. Leishman hastened to assure Woolf that he would not regret his decision. Leonard Woolf had a few words to say about such well-meaning consolations: "Your certainty that I shall not regret publishing LATER POEMS with the commentary consoles me for my certainty that I shall lose fifty or sixty pounds on its publication. I notice that authors like yourself, who know much more about publishing than the publisher, always stop short at taking any risks of a financial nature. They confine themselves to certainties" (HP 383).

One of the first manuscripts John Lehmann worked with as the new managing director was Kathleen Nott's long realistic novel of Jewish East End labor and socialism in the nineteenth century, *Mile End.* Leonard Woolf, predictably, liked it, but Lehmann did not, and so Rosamond Lehmann was consulted from the advisory board. She approved, the novel was published in October, and Rosamond received a fee of three guineas for her efforts (HP 322).

Then Lehmann, appropriately, helped Virginia's *Three Guineas* through the press in June, and he played an active role in publishing the memorial volume of Julian Bell's writings, *Julian Bell: Essays, Poems, and Letters,* edited by Quentin Bell, which appeared in November. The origins of Virginia Woolf's most aggressively feminist tract can be traced to the impulse in the bathtub on January 21, 1931, when she thought of writing a sequel to *A Room of One's Own* on the sexual life of women only to have it metamorphose into *The Years.* As she pruned the more recalcitrant elements from her novel, Virginia Woolf filed away some of the material to be used later in *Three Guineas.* Consequently, the novel and the tract are companion volumes. *Three Guineas* extended the range of the novel, focusing directly on such areas of exclusive masculine dominance as the university, the church, and the law and making explicit the link between sexist authoritarianism and militarism and fascism. The book provided the arguments and supporting documents that were inappropriate for the novel.

Virginia Woolf began writing *Three Guineas* on January 28, 1937, as she awaited the March publication of *The Years*, and finished the first draft on October 12, 1937. The death of Julian Bell, killed in the Spanish civil war in July, caused upheavals within the family, and Virginia stopped writing to comfort Vanessa for over a month that summer. If Julian's death slowed Virginia's progress momentarily, it furthered her resolve to attack militarism in the book. It became her "war pamphlet," as she called it in August, written as an argument with Julian (*Letters* 6:159). She revised it during January 1938, received Leonard's reaction on February 4 (he "gravely" approved of its clear analysis but thought it not on a par with the novels), then finished her proof corrections on April 12 (*Diary* 5:127). *Three Guineas* was published on June 2, 1938. Vanessa's jacket design was admired by Leonard, who paid her five guineas for her labor (HP 571).

As Bloomsbury members gradually recovered from the tragedy of Julian Bell's death in July 1937, they began to consider a memorial volume of his work. They were prompted by T. S. Eliot's interest in publishing some of his essays at Faber & Faber, especially one on Roger Fry (*Letters* 6:154–55). After considerable discussion and family consultation, Quentin Bell agreed to edit the memorial volume. He divided the volume into two parts. Part one, introduced by a foreword by Maynard Keynes, contained a reminiscence of Julian by David Garnett, Julian's own sketchy and incomplete memoir, and selections of his letters and poems. Part two, introduced by a preface by Charles Mauron, contained Julian's three essay-letters to Roger Fry, C. Day-Lewis, and E. M. Forster, with replies by the latter two. The poems of Julian's selected by Quentin represented his development, mixing short lyrics with the best of the longer poems. Quentin chose seven poems from Julian's first volume, *Winter Movement* (1930) and another seven from his Hogarth Press volume, *Work for the Winter and Other Poems* (1936), including the title poem and Julian's "Autobiography," probably his last poem before he left England for

China. Thus Quentin presented examples of Julian's best descriptive and lyrical poems but omitted the long, argumentative poems in Popean couplets.

Virginia Woolf thought the volume successfully presented a whole picture of Julian. "Also I think it makes something rather important," she wrote to Vanessa, "and not a mere scrapbook—I mean though there are so many different people writing, they all fall into line" (*Letters* 6:300). She thought it a more solid book than the memorial volume on John Cornford, the young Cambridge poet and son of Frances Cornford who was killed like Julian, fighting in Spain.

John Lehmann had several minor disagreements with Vanessa Bell and Leonard Woolf over Bell's memorial volume, and at one point the Woolfs thought that Lehmann had returned to his mannerisms of 1931–32. As Virginia described him to Vanessa in June, with her usual flair for revealing analogies, "He's as touchy as a very old spinster whose one evening dress has a hole in the behind" (*Letters* 6:244). They had hoped that life in the interval had changed him, but they found him "still so itchy." To compound matters, the Woolfs had "very tenderly" rejected his first novel (ibid., 250). But tensions eased, and relations between Lehmann and the Woolfs remained remarkably harmonious until two years after Virginia's death, with one exception. There was a brief flare-up of misunderstanding over Lehmann's second volume of *New Writing* (new series) in January 1939.

The precise arrangements for *New Writing* had been left unspecified in the partnership contract signed in March 1938. At the time Lehmann and Woolf had not settled formally on how the biannual publication would fit into the Hogarth Press publishing operation, how profits or losses would be integrated into press accounts and salaries, and what veto power, if any, Woolf might exercise over the contents of a volume. In the meantime they worked out an informal agreement. The first volume of the new series under the Hogarth imprint appeared on schedule in November 1938 without problems. But after publication, Woolf objected to the losses incurred and attempted to veto the second volume scheduled for spring 1939.

As Lehmann described it in *Thrown to the Woolfs*, "Leonard, it soon became clear, did not like *New Writing* and wanted to clip its wings, on the ground that though the reviews were still very good it was not making money."[6] Lehmann had argued that eventually it would turn a profit, which he says it did, and that "meanwhile it should be considered as a publication which brought considerable prestige" and helped attract new writers. Woolf argued by letter in January 1939 that *New Writing* had not been part of the original agreement, that the verbal terms had looked good to him (£100 advance paid to Lehmann, 1,500 copies printed, and 500 sheets sent to the United States), but that now with the losses, he could not suspend his veto on a book published twice a year which would incur a sure loss.[7] Lehmann produced a letter from Leonard from the previous year stating that *New Writing* and the Woolfs' own books should be exempt from the veto arrangement, and Leonard finally conceded. Lehmann, however, had to take a cut in his advance.

Although the conflict over *New Writing* was resolved satisfactorily, with Lehmann publishing three volumes in the new series through 1939 and then changing the title to *Folios of New Writing* for four volumes through 1940 and 1941, the alliance between the press and the publication remained an uneasy one. It was partly a matter of strong personalities in conflict over their creations and partly a matter of the inevitable stresses and strains that occur when a book publisher undertakes to publish a periodical over which he has no editorial control and little or no veto power.

As the Woolfs and Lehmann worked to bring out Julian Bell's memorial volume, Vita Sackville-West in July 1938 proposed "a longish poem to be published by Hogarth," as she wrote to Leonard Woolf, estimating its length at fifty pages. She knew poetry did not sell but offered it to Leonard if he wanted it, "as you have been my publisher for so long" (HP 427). Leonard wanted it and, after reading *Solitude,* praised it enthusiastically, finding it "extremely moving intellectually" and her best poem to date. "Its great merit," he added, "is . . . that it talks sound common sense about the universe, which very few poets have done since Lucretius" (HP 427).

What Virginia Woolf thought about *Solitude* was slow in coming. When Leonard praised the poem to her in July, Virginia balked at reading it because Vita's criticism of her *Three Guineas* still rankled her. The two repaired the damage to their friendship through conciliatory letters, a basket of peaches, and half a bottle of Château Yquem, but Virginia never completely forgave Vita. Leonard's generous praise of *Solitude* did not improve Virginia's grouchiness.

Raymond Mortimer devoted two-and-a-half columns to his review of the poem in the *New Statesman and Nation,* praising its seriousness and nobility, while recognizing that Vita's feelings and pantheistic religious sentiments, however grandly expressed, lacked sufficient intellectual foundations.[8] No doubt Vita's expressed austerity, her deliberate withdrawal from worldly follies, her stoicism and skepticism strongly appealed to Leonard who was able to overlook her fervid calls to God. The poem broods on night and death, subjects congenial to Leonard in 1938 as he contemplated the collapse of Western civilization and wrote *Barbarians at the Gate* (1939). His enthusiasm for *Solitude* was shared by readers. Leonard had 3,000 copies printed of the fifty-six-page book, priced it at 5s., and published it in November. Sales were brisk. Within one month it had sold 1,163 copies and by the end of the first year the edition was nearly exhausted, 2,272 copies sold. Leonard put it into a second impression of 1,000 copies in December 1938.[9]

Before 1938 dragged to a close in the gloom of approaching war, the Munich crisis in October caused brief panic and a flurry of activity in the streets of London. Sandbags were suddenly heaped up, trenches dug, and citizens urged to be fitted with gas masks as some expected an imminent air attack by the Nazis. The Woolfs, Lehmann, and the staff at Hogarth, calm in the midst of noise and confusion, made vague plans to continue operations. "Mrs. Nicholls," reported Virginia Woolf to her sister, "said she should prefer to lie in the trench that was being dug in the square; Miss Perkins preferred to sit in the stock room, which she had partly prepared with mattresses etc." (*Letters* 6:276). Soon the crisis passed without event.

The number of books published by the Hogarth Press in 1938 had dropped to sixteen titles, its lowest ebb since 1923, but the Lehmann-Woolf partnership pulled the total back up to twenty-one in 1939, which was close to Leonard Woolf's ideal at the time. It was fortunate for the partners that they had expanded the production in 1939, for when paper rationing came into effect in 1940, publishers were limited to a percentage of their consumption in the 1939 season.

Although there were no best-sellers among the offering of 1939, the press published some important works, many of them directly attributable to the efforts of John Lehmann. Christopher Isherwood completed his saga of Sally Bowles and the other denizens of Germany in *Goodbye to Berlin,* and Lehmann and Spender edited an anthology, *Poems for Spain.* Both of these spring books bore witness to the events leading to the war that was about to break over Europe. Leonard Woolf's political and allegorical play *Hotel* and the second volume of his *After the Deluge* added their pessimistic statements to the desperate tenor of the times.

In January 1938 Christopher Isherwood and W. H. Auden had sailed for China where they were to report on the Sino-Japanese war (an account later published as *Journey to a War,* 1939). On their return through the United States in July 1938, they had decided to emigrate to America after closing out their affairs in England. Isherwood's *Lions and Shadows* was published in his absence, as was "The Landauers," another story from "The Lost," in the spring 1938 issue of Lehmann's *New Writing.* Before leaving for China, Isherwood had completed "The Landauers," "On Ruegen Island," and "A Berlin Diary (Winter 1932–33)" and given them to John Lehmann, who was beginning his negotiations with the Woolfs to become managing director of the press. Lehmann collected the various stories from the first Berlin diary to the last and arranged them in novel form as *Goodbye to Berlin* (1939).[10] Isherwood and Auden sailed off to the United States in January 1939, and the novel was published by the Hogarth Press under Lehmann's supervision in March.

Goodbye to Berlin, thanks in part to the audacious spirit of Sally Bowles, became another fast-selling, popular success for Isherwood and the Hogarth Press. Reviewers were generally enthusiastic, although troubled by the fragmented structure and the omnipresent narrator Christopher Isherwood who bore the author's name. Few of them saw at the time the irony, art, and control with which Isherwood had shaped his characters and assembled his episodes. Edmund Wilson, almost alone, saw *Goodbye to Berlin* in terms that would become obvious to later more observant critics. Reviewing the American edition by Random House, Wilson noted that Isherwood was a master of social observation whose eye was "accurate, lucid and cool; and it is a faculty which brings its own antidote to the hopelessness and horror he describes."[11] Isherwood's prose, added Wilson, was "a perfect medium for his purpose," allowing the reader "to look right through Isherwood and to see what he sees." Bibliophile Wilson concluded with a potshot at Random House, which, in spite of its reputation for fine editions, had "turned out for Mr. Isherwood a thing that looks like a Gideon Bible with a cheap nickel clasp on the wrong side." And there were at least four misprints.

The American readership may have been slow to appreciate *Goodbye to Berlin,* but not the British, and in December 1939 Lehmann could write to Isherwood (then in Santa Monica, California) that the novel had sold 4,000 copies and had generated considerable royalties (HP 195). From the first, the sales of Isherwood's novel had been fast-paced. By publication on March 2, 1939, prepublication sales totaled 859 copies.[12] One month later, 2,393 copies had sold, and by May 2 the original printing of 3,550 copies was nearly exhausted. Leonard Woolf immediately ordered a second impression, followed by a third impression in January 1940.

After the war, in January 1946, New Directions in America published Isherwood's two novels (*The Last of Mr. Norris,* using the American title, and *Goodbye to Berlin*) in one volume under the new title *The Berlin Stories.* American playwright John van Druten in 1951 turned the material of *Goodbye to Berlin* into a successful Broadway play, *I Am a Camera,* featuring Julie Harris as the indomitable Sally Bowles. The play became a movie in 1955, and New Directions capitalized on the popularity by reissuing *The Berlin Stories* in 1954. The 1954 reprint is interesting because of the minor but revealing stylistic changes Isherwood made to the text.[13] In 1966 Isherwood's classic was adapted once more to the stage as the musical *Cabaret* and eventually into the Academy Award–winning film by the same title in 1972; Liza Minnelli had replaced Julie Harris as Sally. Then in 1975, the Hogarth Press, which had kept in print both *Mr. Norris Changes Trains* and *Goodbye to Berlin,* bowed to the inevitable and regrouped the novels in one volume as New Directions had done twenty-nine years earlier, but now under the somewhat misleading title *The Berlin of Sally Bowles.* The Hogarth Press one-volume edition contains the original text and does not follow the emended American text.

Christopher Isherwood went on writing successfully and living happily in California while his great legacy of the 1930s, the two Berlin novels and his autobiography *Lions and Shadows,* continued to earn critical praise and substantial royalties. The Hogarth Press, through the offices of John Lehmann and Leonard Woolf, saw Isherwood's best writing into print when other publishers had rejected him. Isherwood, in turn, became for the press one of its most distinguished novelists.

The Spanish civil war began with a bang in July 1936 and ended with a whimper in March 1939, as Franco and his Nationalists took over a collapsed republic. The Lehmann-Spender anthology *Poems for Spain* (1939) thus became an elegy for a lost cause, a posthumous memorial volume, and not the stirring call to arms suggested by the title. Although the poets' war in Spain, as Stephen Spender dubbed it, produced an outpouring of verse published during the conflict in little magazines, broadsides, and established journals, the Hogarth Press volume captured the field as the only contemporary collection of Spanish war poetry in England. It remains an important document even as subsequent studies and collections have amplified its scope.

Spender wrote the introduction to the volume and then assisted Lehmann with arranging the poems. Together they selected fifty-three poems by thirty-five poets and grouped them into six categories: Action (eleven poems), Death (twelve poems), The Map (six poems), Satire (four poems), Romances (seventeen poems), and Lorca (three poems). With the English poets were seven Spanish-speaking poets: Miguel Hernández, Manuel Altolaguirre, Pablo Neruda, Antonio Agray, José Petre, Pedro Garfias, and Leopoldo Urrutia. The anthology carried a suitably international flavor.

Of greatest interest in the collection are the poems by W. H. Auden, ("Spain'), John Cornford ("Poem" and "Full Moon at Tierz"), C. Day-Lewis ("Bombers"), Louis MacNeice ("Remembering Spain"), and Stephen Spender ("At Castellon," "Regum Ultimo Ratio," "Fall of a City," and "Port Bou"). Auden's "Spain," with the powerful rhetorical refrain "but to-day the struggle," became one of the best-known poems of the war. MacNeice's haunting images of a dreary prewar Spain remembered as background to the unexpected, transforming power of the Spanish front, became part six of his *Autumn Journal*. There were no poems by John Lehmann or Julian Bell, but Cambridge was well served by John Cornford, the most promising young poet killed in Spain, dead on his twenty-first birthday in December 1936.

John Lehmann, always an instigator of projects, also began a new Hogarth series in 1939, "one of the chief aims of which," he recalled, "was to show that we could produce poetry as elegantly as any other publisher, and not merely in the rather mean, reach-me-down get-up of the " 'Living Poets.' "[14] He had obtained enough quality paper for three volumes, and so could continue the annual publication into 1942. As with the Living Poets series, Lehmann's Poets of Tomorrow would be living practitioners, but unlike many of the poets in the old series, these were to be young and promising. He saw the series as a means of encouraging and sustaining young poets at a time when they had diminished access to readers. For his first volume Lehmann chose four poets—Peter Hewett, H. B. Mallalieu, Ruthven Todd, and Robert Waller—and allowed them ten to twelve poems apiece. He prefaced each poet's section with a short biographical sketch. Lehmann had published all four of the poets in previous issues of *New Writing* and had included Mallalieu and Todd in *Poems for Spain,* so that as editor and publisher in the Bloomsbury tradition he consolidated his efforts and promoted his writers.

As the Spanish civil war raged and eventually burned itself out, but before the beginning of the great war to come in September 1939, the Hogarth Press had its own conflict going over a translation of Rilke by J. B. Leishman and Stephen Spender. It was one of the most extended, heated, and, in retrospect, amusing editorial confrontations in Hogarth Press history. As in most conflicts, the beginning was deceptively quiet. After Leonard Woolf had rejected a proposal from Robert Hull to translate the *Duino Elegies* in May 1937, Leishman suggested that a collaboration would be particularly desirable on the difficult work. He recommended either Edward Sackville-West, who Leishman thought might be glad of "atoning" for his errors in the earlier translation of the *Elegies,* or Stephen Spender. Woolf quickly resolved the matter in favor of Spender. Leishman proposed, and Spender accepted in late June. Leishman then sent Spender his translation of the first three *Elegies* in July. Soon Leishman was worried. His attempts to meet with the busy Spender failed; weeks went by with no response, and Leishman was accustomed to weekly, almost daily, correspondence over Rilke translations with Woolf or with his German colleagues. Spender's elusiveness concerned him.

By September 1937, after his long vacation from teaching at South-hampton, the disciplined Leishman had completed a first draft of the entire book; but in his attempts to meet with Spender, he had received only a note reporting Spender's recuperation from an operation. In late October, Leishman proposed abandoning the collaboration, being "dis-gusted," he wrote Woolf, with Spender's offhand manner and apparent lack of interest. And so it went through December, Leishman worrying Woolf constantly about Spender's lack of response; Spender stretched thin with writing projects, earning his own income, arranging a delega-tion of writers and artists to Spain; and Woolf mediating between them with growing exasperation. Woolf had to tell Leishman that W. W. Nor-ton in America would not accept his translation without Spender's con-tribution.[15] "I quite agree with you," Woolf wrote to Spender after one heated exchange; "the man is obviously an ass. But you had better not keep him waiting for more than a week" (HP 380).

Once the two men began exchanging drafts regularly in December 1937, their strongly held differences of opinion about translation soon threatened the project anew. Spender used an irregular meter in his trans-lation because, as he wrote to Woolf, "it seems to me that the hexameter is boring and monotonous in English and also demands too many sacri-fices in the way of distortion, verboseness and paraphrase from the trans-lator: too much is sacrificed to the metre" (HP 380). Thus Spender struggled with the same problem the Sackville-Wests had resolved by em-ploying a flexible blank verse. Spender wanted to preserve the "move-ment" of Rilke's poetry and the effect of the hexameter. He also tried to preserve Rilke's "exact imagery," and so sometimes rejected Leishman's paraphrasing. For the translator, wrote Spender, "the essential is what Rilke said, not what we think he meant."

Leishman, for his part, found Spender's principles unacceptable. He objected to almost every one of Spender's statements about translations and once again questioned the entire collaborative enterprise. "What Rilke *said* he said in German," wrote Leishman, "and *what* is often indis-tinguishable from the *how*. Therefore, the translator must often take his courage in both hands, and aim, not at a *literal* version (which would not be what Rilke said) but at an *equivalent*" (HP 380). So the lines were drawn between them: the poet argued for exactness of meaning and imagery but flexibility in verse form; the scholar argued for equivalent or paraphrased meaning and imagery but exactness in verse form.

Thirty-four years later, in 1973 at a conference on translation, Spender would return to the subject and have the last word, reaffirming his belief in the primacy of the literal meaning and the accuracy of the imagery: "I found in Leishman a tendency to have a great confidence in paraphrase. He would take a poem and paraphrase it, so that everything was altered, but nevertheless he could say that within the paraphrase it meant the same thing as Rilke meant. . . . So, often in order to retain the rhyme scheme, Leishman would shove in different images."[16]

Leonard Woolf, with increased impatience, reminded Leishman that he could not become an arbiter between the collaborators and that either they agreed to one translation or not. Spender arranged to meet with John Lehmann (soon to be a Hogarth partner) to negotiate the matter. In the meantime, he thought he might prescribe for Leishman "a very corrupt life in Central Europe" to clear up their difficulties (HP 380).

Woolf then sent Leishman a "stiff letter" insisting on one translation with Spender's collaboration and commented to Spender that "if you can send Leishman away to the corrupt life of Central Europe, that would please me more." Spender believed Leishman wanted to drop him at all costs. "He seems to have a feeling that if he sent me an examination paper on Rilke, he would plough me, and there the matter ends," he wrote to Woolf. But a few days later, Spender finally got around to meeting Leishman, almost six months after the agreement to collaborate had been reached. Much to his surprise, he found he liked Leishman. They agreed to resolve their differences, to adopt each other's criticisms, and to have the "First Elegy" ready by February and the entire volume by the autumn of 1938. Leonard Woolf replied to Spender that "I have always suspected that Leishman might be personally rather a nice stupid man. I am very glad to learn that he is, and that you will give him another trial." There followed sixteen months of reasonably harmonious collaboration until the translation was completed in March 1939.

Only one more flap occurred before publication, bringing back some of the friction of the first months of collaboration. Leishman drafted a preface wherein he suggested rather ungraciously that Spender's role had been a decidedly minor one, if indeed a collaboration at all. The affronted

Spender protested to Leishman, sending a copy to Woolf, that whereas he had always been anxious that "full justice should be done to [your] wonderful work" and while he recognized that Leishman's labor with the extensive introduction and commentary had been greater than his, nevertheless he believed that the translation had been a collaboration on somewhat equal grounds. Leonard Woolf interceded once more and drafted a statement on the collaboration to be included in a short prefatory note. Woolf noted to Leishman that W. W. Norton believed that "in view of the public Mr. Spender has in America the success of the book depends largely on there being no possibility of misunderstanding Mr. Spender's very active collaboration" (HP 380). The eventual preface, initialed by both Spender and Leishman, stated: "In undertaking this most difficult piece of work, we have tried to divise a method which should achieve, above all, unity of style. Accordingly, J. B. Leishman prepared a draft of the whole work, on the basis of which Stephen Spender prepared a second version; then, with these two versions before him, J. B. Leishman prepared the final version, which was approved by both of us."

There remained only the title. Through most of the correspondence, Rilke's great work had been generally referred to as the "Duinese Elegies." Leishman, however, preferred "Duino Elegies" because "Duinese" seemed un-English. The analogy was to Byron's *Ravenna Journal*. English does not form adjectives from names as readily as German, Leishman argued in a letter to Leonard Woolf in April 1939, and therefore the most characteristically English translation of Rilke's *Duineser Elegien* would be "Duino Elegies" (HP 380). The Sackville-Wests had avoided the issue by using the longer form *Elegies from the Castle of Duino*. Woolf agreed with Leishman, and so the title has remained *Duino Elegies* in English through most subsequent translations, of which there have been many in the more than fifty years since the Leishman-Spender version. Later translators of the *Elegies* usually have begun by declaring their indebtedness to the Leishman-Spender translation. Whatever else may be said about the achievement or influence of the Hogarth Press between the wars, its preeminence is unchallenged in the field of Rilke translations, from John Linton's *Notebook* and the now-forgotten, error-laden, but often beautiful Sackville-West *Elegies* to the landmark Leishman-Spender translation.

In spite of an ominously approaching war, John Lehmann optimistically looked for beginnings, not endings. He searched fruitfully for new authors. "The arrival of Henry Green as a Hogarth author seemed to me to start a new phase, and gave me confidence for the future."[17] So wrote John Lehmann, thinking back to 1938–39, his first year as partner in the Hogarth Press. "I felt that a new momentum was gathering," he added, "leading me to turn my gaze . . . towards the discoveries of the future." Lehmann, with his energy, enthusiasm, and sharp eye for talent, would be responsible for discovering and developing a number of writers for the press just before the Second World War. Two of the fiction writers, Henry Green and Tom Hopkinson, would become increasingly valuable writers in the late 1940s, and Green especially would come to rank as an innovative novelist of importance.

Henry Vincent Yorke, son of a wealthy industrialist, started to use "Henry Michaelis," switched to "Henry Browne," and settled on "Henry Green" as his pen name, the color and the condition pervasive in his first novel, *Blindness* (1926). Yorke he remained as his father's successful heir, managing director of H. Pontifex and Sons, manufacturers and distributors of chemical, distilling, and brewery apparatus; but Green he became for his nine novels and one autobiography. All but the first two were published by the Hogarth Press; and in critical acclaim, if not in sales, Green must be considered one of the most important novelists published by the Woolfs.

As evasive with his pen name as he was with the camera—he avoided full-face photographs, offering a profile or the back of his head only—Green created additional mysteries through his riddling texts, his reflexive symbolism, his stylistic puzzles, his enigmatic plots and characters, and his hauntingly suggestive one-word titles. He kept his two lives separate. Yorke, the wealthy international executive, husband, and father, expanded the family business while Green, the innovative stylist and symbolist, remade the novel. When he brought his third novel, *Party Going,* to the Woolfs in 1939, it had been ten years since his second novel *Living* (1929) had achieved fame among Auden's generation as the best proletarian novel of the time.

Why it took Green ten years between his second and third novels is not clear. Establishing his family and career may have absorbed his creative energies. But he also seems to have struggled with the writing over a seven-year period, as he dated *Party Going,* in Joycean fashion, "London, 1931–1938." He told John Russell that it was the hardest to write of his novels, requiring nine or ten beginnings.[18] John Lehmann remembered that Dent, his first publisher, had not been interested in the novel and that Green "had let it lie in a bottom drawer until urged to send it to me."[19] What seems likely, as Michael North has argued, is that Green began the novel around 1931 in the manner of his friend Evelyn Waugh's brilliant social satires, exemplified by *Vile Bodies* (1930), and finally evolved it with difficulty into the manner and mood of the late 1930s. It spans the decade, wrote North, "in the way it brings the subject matter and the stock imagery of the early thirties into collision with the political realities of 1939."[20]

When Lehmann accepted the manuscript of *Party Going* for the press in February 1939, Green responded with delight, noting that "as I have told you before I would rather be published by the Hogarth Press than anyone" (HP 149). After he discussed the press terms and accepted them, Green added, "As to the manuscript I never want to see it again." *Party Going* was published in September 1939 at the outbreak of the Second World War; in spite of the unpromising times, it sold well and turned a profit. Within the first year, it sold 1,285 copies.[21]

Within a month of the release of *Party Going,* Green sent the manuscript of his autobiography, which he called "Self-Portrait," to Rosamond Lehmann, a member of the Hogarth advisory committee, who approved and passed it on to her brother John. Lehmann read it over a weekend and reported back to Rosamond in early November 1939 that he enjoyed it, thought it must be published, but considered it not as good as *Party Going.* There were brilliant passages in the early part of the book, especially those about Green's private school, but Lehmann considered the later half of the book "uneven and disjointed," the style "unnecessarily clumsy at times" as if Green had rushed the writing of it (HP 149). Lehmann suggested a few alterations and a general polishing. He concluded his letter to Rosamond with a perceptive summary of Green's style: "What a merciless eye he has for human behaviour: and how unexpected and fascinating his metaphors nearly always are!"

On December 1, Lehmann wrote to Green offering Hogarth publication by spring 1941, or by Christmas 1940 if possible, to tie in with the continuing success of *Party Going*. Green responded with pleasure, agreed to the suggested alterations and polishing, but worried over too long a delay between books. "What I write is quickly forgotten," he wrote, "and to leave too long an interval would be to lose a good part of whatever small public *Party Going* may have attracted" (HP 149). Canny businessman Green then proposed a £50 compensation to be paid him by the press if "Self Portrait" had not been published by Christmas 1940 and an additional £50 if not published by May 30, 1941. He need not have worried. What he wrote was not, after all, so easily forgotten, and the press acted with dispatch. Green's autobiography was out for the Christmas list in 1940.

Before publication, however, there was some jockeying over the title. *Self Portrait,* it developed, had been recently used by Gilbert Frankau, so Green suggested to press office manager Norah Nicholls either "Henry Green by Henry Green" or "Before a War," not titles to inspire a publisher (HP 149). John Lehmann countered with three suggestions: "Pack My Bag," "Taking Stock," or "A Chance to Live." Green preferred the first, and so the eccentric autobiography became *Pack My Bag*.

What Green packed in his life's story was traditional in outline but untraditional in style. If style is the man, Green's brooding fatality, mixed with wit, and the peculiarly distancing prose (Green omitted personal names, dates, and most places) suggest a man bent on shaping his life into the same haunting patterns of mysterious ritual, inactivity, and obscure meaning characteristic of *Party Going*. But the result is oddly liberating, and Green closed his bag with praise for his father's industrial enterprise, which sprang him into the real world, and for his maturing romance, which brought him marriage. The last word of the book is "love." Henry Yorke, sustained by job and family, survived the war to write Henry Green's most important books. He began a remarkable run of four novels in the 1940s with *Caught* (1943), all published by the Hogarth Press.

Tom Hopkinson, another new author, came to the Hogarth Press from journalism; and although he would publish three novels with the press and two collections of short stories with other publishers, he established his reputation not as a novelist but as a distinguished journalist and editor. At the time that John Lehmann saw his manuscript of *The Man*

Below in 1938, Hopkinson was completing four years as an assistant editor or the *Weekly Illustrated*. In the summer of 1938 he left the *Weekly* to join the brilliant and eccentric Stefan Lorant as cofounder and assistant editor of the *Picture Post,* which made its auspicious debut in October 1938. By 1940 Hopkinson was the editor, and he steered the picture magazine to fame through the war years.

Just as Leonard Woolf used his position as literary editor of the *Nation and Athenaeum* to recruit writers for the Hogarth Press, so John Lehmann as editor of *New Writing* led some of his contributers to become Hogarth authors. Tom Hopkinson was one, having first published a story, "I Have Been Drowned," in the third volume of *New Writing*. That story and the long sailing sequence in *The Man Below* show Hopkinson's knowledge of boats, the perils of the sea, and the experience of extreme physical danger. Although its title suggests Conradian secret-sharers, *The Man Below* (1939) unfolds as a variation of the schoolboy development story in the autobiographical-fictional mode peculiar to the late 1930s and exemplified by Isherwood's *Lions and Shadows* (1938) and Green's *Pack My Bag* (1940). *The Man Below* was a promising first novel. The promise was realized in Hopkinson's later fictions, published after the war by the Hogarth Press: *Mist on the Tagus* (1946) and *Down the Long Slide* (1949).

Lehmann, in addition to his development of Henry Green and Tom Hopkinson, launched two new series in 1939: Poets of To-Morrow and Sixpenny Pamphlets. The latter series, as announced in the press flyer for spring 1939, was to provide thinking people with the means to reconsider "fundamental problems" in art, literature, taste, and morals. The first five titles began with the most famous of all, E. M. Forster's *What I Believe,* a timely reminder of humane and individualistic values in the face of the totalitarian onslaught. John Betjeman and Stephen Spender wrote for the Sixpenny series, as did Virginia Woolf, whose *Reviewing* was pamphlet number four.

Lehmann wrote to Forster in October 1938 asking permission to reprint his *London Mercury* article "Credo" in the new Hogarth Sixpenny Pamphlet series he was starting (HP 94). Forster worried about complications over the American rights, since the essay had appeared in July as "Two Cheers for Democracy" in the *Nation* as part of a series and then had been published in *I Believe,* edited by Clifton Fadiman. Among the twenty-one contributors in that book were W. H. Auden, Harold Laski, Thomas Mann, George Santayana, James Thurber, and Rebecca West. The difficulties were resolved, however; Forster signed a contract with Hogarth in late February 1939, and Sixpenny Pamphlet number one rolled off the presses in May 1939, as Forster's memorable *What I Believe*.

It may be Forster's best-known and best-loved piece of writing next to *A Passage to India*. Forster's statement of belief was one of the great declarations of sanity and humanity in a time of chaos. The Second World War erupted four months later. Among the things Forster believed in were personal relationships, the primacy of the heart, and an "aristocracy of the sensitive, the considerate and the plucky."[22]

In the summer of 1938 Forster wrote a pageant play in support of the Dorking and Leith Hill District Preservation Society. Set to music by Ralph Vaughan Williams, *England's Pleasant Land* was produced by Tom Harrison and performed at Milton Court in early July. Forster had conceived the idea for the pageant and had enjoyed working on the text with his friend Vaughan Williams. Four years earlier, Forster had tried his hand at his first village pageant play, *Pageant of Abinger*, at the insistence of Harrison, who was active with the Parish Church Preservation Fund; Vaughan Williams had provided the music and Forster the program notes and the speeches for the various narrators. The text of *England's Pleasant Land*, in contrast, was entirely Forster's work and reflected his appreciative but ironic view of local history. The action of the pageant covered a period of nearly one thousand years, and, in the words of Forster's "Recorder," the play was "about the countryside, how it was made, how it changed as the centuries passed, how today it is in peril, and maybe lost for ever."[23] The pageant was Forster's last published work for the Hogarth Press. Lehmann, faced with sudden paper rationing in March 1940, probably saw in Forster's short play an ideal way to adapt to the shortage while keeping the work of a famous Hogarth author before the public. *England's Pleasant Land* appeared in April 1940, and German bombers swarmed over that land in August.

The Hogarth Press did not loom large in E. M. Forster's life as a writer. Although Forster's work produced by the press was interesting and even memorable, the seven titles did little to extend his literary reputation. Nevertheless, the press played a lively supporting role for Forster, and he always responded positively to the requests of Leonard Woolf or John Lehmann for manuscripts. The Woolfs, in turn, provided Forster with the means to publish in pamphlet form the short, single work that could not be placed easily with his regular publisher, Edward Arnold. For the Hogarth Press, the advantages of having a few of Forster's titles on the list were obvious. The nature of the man and his writings were especially congenial to the press. The Woolfs and Lehmann, valuing Forster's stature and reliability, turned twice to him to inaugurate a new series— the Hogarth Letters and the Sixpenny Pamphlets. The twenty-year professional association between the mole and the lions was mutually rewarding, if not the stuff of fables.

In mid-August, just weeks before the outbreak of war, the Woolfs and their staff began to move to their new home and office at 37 Mecklenburgh Square. Redevelopment plans for Tavistock Square required the move, a less than happy one for the Woolfs after fifteen years in residence. The city was in a prewar crisis, and vans were hard to come by. The move was complicated by the large staff and extensive stock. By August 24, one week before Germany invaded Poland, the Woolfs finally moved their personal possessions into the upper floors of the new house. Their ground-floor tenants, the solicitors Dollman & Pritchard, moved with the Woolfs to the new location.

At the outbreak of the war in late 1939, Lehmann and Woolf planned their publishing strategy to accommodate the disruptions in the book trade and the inevitable shortages of supplies. Virginia Woolf's books were to be given top priority, followed by Freud's books and others in the IPL series.[24] Then Leonard Woolf's books and John Lehmann's *New Writing* were to be supported, followed by such thirties writers as Isherwood and Spender and the newly obtained novelists Henry Green and Tom Hopkinson. The realities of war were worse than expected, however, and severe adjustments had to be made. Woolf and Lehmann discovered that almost no new titles could be introduced if the most successful Hogarth authors were kept in print. The problem of short paper supply was exacerbated by the implementation of rationing under the government's Paper Control, which went into effect on March 3, 1940.[25] At first limiting publishers to 60 percent of their consumption during the twelve months prior to August 31, 1939, the Paper Control reduced percentages from time to time as paper supplies from Scandinavia and French North Africa were cut off by the war and enemy action at home took its toll.

According to Lehmann, the Hogarth Press was reduced to 40 percent of its 1939 consumption, which translated into something like 6 ½ tons of paper a year.[26] Lehmann noted that it required 2 ½ tons of paper to print three impressions of a posthumous collection of Virginia Woolf's essays, *Death of the Moth,* in 1942 and an additional 2 tons of paper for other Woolf reprints. Not much tonnage was left for other press books, although the psychoanalytical books of the IPL were assisted by the Moberly Pool, a special reserve supply of paper established by the Ministry of Supply and the Paper Control to protect the publication of educational, medical, scientific, and other "essential" works.[27]

The paper restrictions in the first war year of 1940 meant that the Hogarth Press published only ten titles, less than half the number in 1939. Outstanding among the ten were Virginia Woolf's *Roger Fry* and Henry Green's *Pack My Bag*. Less successful was Stephen Spender's first and only novel, *The Backward Son*. With three volumes of the well-produced Poets of To-Morrow series successfully concluded in 1940, Lehmann conceived a new series to "keep up [the press's] name for avant-garde publishing at very little cost in paper consumption."[28] The Woolfs agreed, and the New Hogarth Library began with two volumes of selected poems from the work of C. Day-Lewis and William Plomer. The fifty- to sixty-page format became a popular one, and the next year the press published four more volumes of poetry, including selections from Vita Sackville-West, Rilke, and Terence Tiller, a new discovery of Lehmann's.

About the time John Lehmann and Leonard Woolf were planning the New Hogarth Library series and putting E. M. Forster's and Henry Green's works into print, Virginia Woolf was completing *Roger Fry*. Virginia's biography of Fry, a study of the painter and art critic, had been urged on her by Fry's widow, Margery, and by Vanessa Bell after his death in 1934. It was her next book after *Three Guineas* (1938) and the last book she published with the press while alive. Leonard thought she should not have undertaken it, and when it was completed, he thought it one of her four books written against the grain. Virginia often found the research and writing both restrictive and burdensome, curtailed as she was by propriety from treating openly Fry's personal and sexual life (his passionate affair with Vanessa, for example); yet much of the work was intellectually and artistically challenging as she strove to create a critical biography of a man she had known and deeply admired since 1911. She began reading Fry's correspondence and making notes as early as October 1935, in the midst of rewriting "The Pargiters" and turning it into *The Years,* but she did not begin writing the book until April 1, 1938, about the time she was correcting page proofs for *Three Guineas.* Once more her books overlapped.

Virginia Woolf finished her draft of *Roger Fry* in early March 1940, feeling confident at last that she had "caught a good deal of that iridescent man in my oh so laborious butterfly net" (*Diary* 5:266). By her own count she had rewritten some pages ten or fifteen times. Although Leonard criticized it harshly (his criticism "was like being pecked by a very hard strong beak," she noted), both Margery Fry and Vanessa were deeply moved and full of praise for the manuscript (ibid., 271). When the book was published on July 25, 1940, Leonard remained doubtful, but the Bloomsbury critics Desmond MacCarthy and Clive Bell were praiseful (ibid., 309–10).

Mrs. Rudolph Lehmann, John's mother, was among those praising Virginia's *Roger Fry.* Virginia wrote back in late July, thanking Mrs. Lehmann and acknowledging that it was a bad time for publishing books. She was sorry for John, beginning his partnership at the press as the war came on, but was pleased that the arrangement was turning out so successfully. "Its years since Leonard has had such a free time," wrote Virginia, "and I'm sure, when the war ends, John will make a great success of it" (*Letters* 6:407).

The Hogarth Press escaped the terrible destruction of Paternoster Row on Sunday night, December 29, 1940, when incendiary bombs blasted the buildings of over twenty publishers, destroying five million volumes in stock and ravaging Stationers' Hall and the wholesaler Simpkin Marshall.[29] But the press had already been damaged from the heavy pounding of the Blitz. On Tuesday, September 10, after a night of bombing in the area, an unexploded delayed-action bomb was found in Mecklenburgh Square directly opposite the Woolfs' house. Up from the country for the day, Leonard and Virginia were not permitted to enter the house because of the police cordon, but they could see that the building was untouched except for some broken windows. Not until Saturday,

September 14, did the bomb explode, blowing out windows, tearing the front door off its hinges, damaging the roof and the ceilings, and smashing some of Virginia's china (*Journey* 62). Soon another bomb exploded at the back of the house, causing additional damage. Bookcases and books lay everywhere covered by rubble. Burst waterpipes and rain seeping through the roof puddled the floors. In the press offices in the basement, Leonard wrote, "books, files, paper, the printing-machine and the type were in a horrible grimy mess" (ibid., 63).

Salvaging what he could, Lehmann and the staff moved the press operations to the Garden City Press in Letchworth, Hertfordshire. As one of the Hogarth's chief printers at the time, the Garden City Press generously offered the sanctuary of offices in its plant. The Hogarth Press staff stayed on and migrated to Letchworth for the remaining war years. John Lehmann lived in Cambridge or London and commuted to the press offices during the week. The Woolfs remained in the relative safety of Rodmell, near Lewes, Leonard journeying up to London once a week to confer with Lehmann or, infrequently, traveling the long and difficult way by train from Lewes to Letchworth and back in one day.

In October the house at Mecklenburgh Square was damaged further by bombs in the vicinity, and the Woolfs evacuated their sodden and grimy belongings to Rodmell in three hired vans. The loads began arriving early in December, and the Woolfs stored some of the furniture in rooms rented from a neighboring farmer. Most of their possessions, however, had to be crammed into Monks House. "So I'm all black and blue with moving," Virginia Woolf wrote to Ethel Smyth, "and the house is packed like an emporium. And 4 tons of books came yesterday. And the Printing Press and all the type come tomorrow" (*Letters* 6:449).

After the destruction of Mecklenburgh Square and the removal of the press to Letchworth, John Lehmann virtually managed the operations alone, keeping Leonard Woolf informed through reports and their weekly meetings in London. Leonard Woolf's total involvement with press affairs had altered with the establishment of the partnership in 1938 and decreased after the move to Mecklenburgh Square in August 1939, as the Woolfs spent more time at Monks House than in London. By November 1940 Virginia was so out of touch with the daily operations of the press that she learned of the intended third impression of her *Roger*

Fry only through the pages of the Sunday *Times*. But Leonard's hand was never far from the controls, and he kept himself fully informed of operations. He continued to make major decisions with Lehmann throughout the war.

Virginia Woolf's struggles with Roger Fry and dropping bombs through the autumn of 1940 were paralleled by her struggles to write what would be her last novel, published after her death as *Between the Acts*. The first glimmerings of the novel-to-be had shown forth three years earlier, the summer Julian Bell was killed, as she neared completion of her first draft of *Three Guineas*. "Will another novel ever swim up?" she asked herself that August 1937. "The only hint I have towards it is that it's to be dialogue: & poetry: & prose: all quite distinct" (*Diary* 5:105). And then, two months later she noted her sudden conception of the new novel: "Its to be first the statement of the theme: then the restatement: & so on: repeating the same story: . . . until the central idea is stated" (ibid., 114). There is no mention here of what that theme would be, but she was returning to the mode of her visionary, lyrical fiction, the way of *The Waves*.

Punning and working the connotations of *pointed, poignant,* and *pointillist,* all appropriate to the novel she wrote, Woolf first named the book "Poyntzet Hall" when she began thinking seriously about it in late April 1938: "a centre: all lit. discussed in connection with real little incongruous living humour; . . . but I rejected: We substituted: to whom at the end there shall be an invocation? We . . . all life, all art, all waifs & strays—a rambling capricious but somehow unified whole—. . . . And English country; & a scenic old house—& a terrace where nursemaids walk? & people passing—& a perpetual variety & change from intensity to prose. & facts—& notes" (*Diary* 5:135). She would simplify the working title to "Pointz Hall" and drop the notes, but she developed her other ideas into the complex, radiant world of the old house with its three generations of families. Miss La Trobe's grand outdoor pageant of English history and literature played out on the terrace of Pointz Hall gathered together the entire village community as actors and audience.

Virginia Woolf wrote the novel in tandem with *Roger Fry,* allowing herself an hour or two here and there to write fiction as a relief from the efforts of sifting through piles of Fry's letters and papers. Overlapping one work with another had become her modus operandi, but never quite this way. One she wrote under the public scrutiny of husband, sister, and the subject's widow; the other she wrote privately, almost guiltily with time stolen from the public book. "Another 10 minutes," she noted. "I'm taking a frisk at *P. H.* at wh. I can only write for one hour. Like the Waves, I enjoy it intensely: head screwed up over Roger" (*Diary* 5:179). Very likely the exhilarating pleasures of "Pointz Hall" helped her over the difficult times of Fry's biography, and just as likely the richness, detail, and restless achievement of Fry's life led Virginia Woolf to texture her visionary novel with social and historical details.

She began writing both books in April 1938, finished her first draft of *Roger Fry* in March 1940, and completed her first draft of the novel on November 23, 1940. Just before that, on September 18, 1940, Virginia Woolf started a new notebook entitled "Reading at Random / Notes" which became a workbook for a projected study of English literature and social history. She did not live to complete her grand project, conceived as early as 1938, but out of it came two unpublished essays, "Anon" and "The Reader."[30] During the two months before finishing the first draft of "Pointz Hall" and throughout her revision, Woolf worked busily at reading widely in English literature and making notes in her "Reading at Random" notebook. The two projects, novel and survey of English literature, thus worked together in her mind during the last six months of her life.

Virginia Woolf felt triumphant about her "new method," as she reported for November 23. "I think its more quintessential than the others. More milk skimmed off. A richer pat, certainly fresher than that misery The Years. I've enjoyed writing almost every page" (*Diary* 5:340). She resolved to continue her scheme with future books, one book like Fry's biography, a "daily drudgery," written with one like *Between the Acts* at "moments of high pressure." In the meantime, she began to rewrite and type her novel manuscript in early January 1941, finishing on February 26 and changing the name of the novel: "Finished Pointz Hall, the Pageant: the Play—finally Between the Acts this morning" (ibid., 356).

At this point, the familiar sequence of events leading to publication—the reading by Leonard, the editing of the typescript, the transmission to R. & R. Clark—was severely interrupted. Several factors caused the disruption. Although she had been jubilant and excited over the writing of her novel, Virginia Woolf was unusually pessimistic about it after she had finished the rewriting, so much so that her mood canceled Leonard's favorable response to his reading. For the first time in their twenty-nine years of partnership in marriage and the craft of letters, they differed irreconcilably over whether to publish one of Virginia's works. Virginia's mental and emotional state had begun to deteriorate rapidly, plunging her into anxiety over a possible return of severe mental illness. The growing horror and desperation of the war and the increasing pessimism felt by the Woolfs and others in Bloomsbury over the loss of civilized values contributed to Virginia's fragmented, indecisive condition. She was not herself; her usually astute self-criticism was blanketed by the damp weight of depression and doubt. When she finished *Between the Acts* and began her debate with Leonard over publication, Virginia had only four weeks left to live before she drowned herself in the river Ouse, on March 28, 1941.

Two weeks before her suicide, Virginia and Leonard lunched with John Lehmann in London on Friday, March 14, to talk over press business. Near the end of the lunch, Leonard revealed to Lehmann that Virginia had written a new novel but that she did not believe it good enough to publish in spite of his enthusiastic conviction to the contrary. And so Lehmann became involved in the dispiriting argument against Virginia's paralyzing self-doubts. They parted with the understanding that she would take Lehmann's urgings seriously and send him the typescript of *Between the Acts* so that he could give an informed opinion. On Tuesday, March 18, Virginia seems to have written her first suicide note to Leonard. Then two days later, on Thursday, March 20, Virginia wrote to Lehmann reaffirming her judgment that her "so called novel" was "much too slight and sketchy" (*Letters* 6:482). Since Leonard disagreed with her verdict, she asked Lehmann to read the novel and give his "casting vote." "Meanwhile," she added, "dont take any steps."

Lehmann, however, had already taken steps, for which he apologized to Virginia in a return letter. Convinced that her self-doubts would soon evaporate, he had submitted an advance notice of *Between the Acts* to the *New Statesman* for inclusion in their announcements of spring and summer books.[31] The ad appeared in the March 29 issue, the day following her suicide. Shortly after writing his apologetic letter, Lehmann received the typescript of *Between the Acts* and plunged into a reading of it before going on evening Home Guard duty.

The effect on Lehmann of first looking into Virginia's *Between the Acts* was thrilling; he was deeply moved by a text that he felt had "an unparalleled imaginative power."[32] Even Virginia's eccentric typing added to the impression of the book, "as if a high-voltage electric current had been running through her fingers." His vote was for publication, which he sent in "an urgent message" to Rodmell the next morning, probably Saturday, March 22. Virginia's response (enclosed in a cover letter from Leonard, dated Thursday, March 27, and explaining her desperate condition) argued that she couldn't publish the novel, in spite of Lehmann's vote, because it was "too silly and trivial" (*Letters* 6:486). "What I will do," she wrote, "is to revise it, and see if I can pull it together and so publish it in the autumn. If published as it is, it would certainly mean a financial loss." Leonard, alarmed by her deteriorating condition and believing her on the verge of a serious breakdown, wrote to Lehmann in the cover letter that Virginia could not possibly revise the book as she intended and that they would have to postpone publication indefinitely. By the time Lehmann received the letter on Saturday, Virginia had killed herself. Leonard's next letter, breaking the news of her suicide, reached Lehmann on Monday, March 31.

There are several sad ironies in these events which help illuminate the mind of Virginia Woolf in her last days. The Hogarth Press had been developed partly in response to Virginia's deeply felt need to avoid the anxieties of supervisory editors, and yet in this very real crisis with *Between the Acts* she submitted her novel to John Lehmann's editorial judgment. Overtly, she sought agreement with her negative view of the book by allowing him a "casting vote," as if she expected him to see more clearly than Leonard how dreadful the writing was. And yet, covertly, she may have sought his encouragement and approval, for the admiring and adoring Lehmann could be counted on to be enthusiastic about any of her writing. Then, too, there is her rationalization that the book, as unrevised, would mean a financial loss. Here she seems to have appealed to the business sense of Leonard and John Lehmann, yet is unlikely that one of her books, no matter how poorly written, would have sustained a loss serious enough to have prohibited publication. Virginia's arguments, transparent and unconvincing, were products of her despair and her uncertain hold on life. They did not convince the Hogarth Press partners.

Leonard Woolf decided after Virginia's death to publish *Between the Acts* as she had written it, editing only for spelling and minor textual errors. John Lehmann supported him completely in this decision.[33] The critical success and popularity of the book give evidence that Virginia had found her way into a new fusion of form and vision after *The Years*. After her death, Leonard carefully planned for the future, husbanding her stories, essays, and letters for judiciously timed collections. Over the next seventeen years, through 1958, Leonard published eight posthumous collections of Virginia's writing, releasing a volume every two or three years on a schedule that approximated her production when alive. In this way Leonard kept Virginia's name before the public and assisted in her growing critical acclaim. Even in death, Virginia Woolf remained the most productive and profitable of the Hogarth Press writers.

Although at the time of her suicide in late March 1941 Virginia Woolf was no longer playing an active role in editorial decisions, her death affected the operation of the Hogarth Press. A vivid picture of her involvement in 1938–39 was given by Lehmann when he later wrote about being depressed because she "would no longer be there to discuss the manuscripts that came in, to gossip about the authors . . . to plan new anthologies and new series . . . and to laugh over the day-to-day alarms and excursions in our office life."[34] The staff felt deeply her loss.

Among Hogarth Press authors, none were more personally affected by Virginia Woolf's suicide than Vita Sackville-West, then in the midst of writing a new novel, *Grand Canyon*. With curious coincidence, Vita had struggled with her novel at the same time Virginia worried over *Between the Acts*, and both books appeared together in an ad after Virginia's death, although Vita's novel would not be published by Hogarth. The idea and title for *Grand Canyon* had been enthusiastically accepted by the partners Lehmann and Woolf two years earlier in December 1939. Norah Nicholls sent Vita a Hogarth Press contract for the novel in February 1940.[35] In June 1940 Vita's American publisher Doubleday-Doran paid her an advance of $5,000, and by October Lehmann was writing to ask when they could expect her manuscript. In March 1941 Lehmann placed a full-page ad in the Spring Book issue of the *New Statesman and Nation* for Vita's *Grand Canyon* and Virginia's *Between the Acts,* obviously anticipating a late spring or early summer publication.

Vita Sackville-West did not finish *Grand Canyon* until a year later in March 1942. It was her first novel in seven years, since the murky affairs of *The Dark Island.* Neither Lehmann nor Leonard Woolf liked it. Leonard, passing on the manuscript to Lehmann in early April, thought *Grand Canyon* "not a good book" and "in many ways absurd," but he hated to reject it unless Lehmann was very sure it was not good enough to publish. He found it hard to estimate sales.[36] *Grand Canyon* was a startling departure for Sackville-West from either the gothic or the Edwardian society romances familiar to her. A war novel projected into the near future, when Nazi Germany would conquer the United States, it featured a strange spirit afterlife in which dead souls inhabit the bottom of the canyon at Phantom Ranch. It was one of those places which had impressed Vita when she had visited the Grand Canyon with Harold in 1933 on their American lecture tour.

Leonard Woolf's rejection letter to Vita was, he wrote, the most unpleasant task he had ever undertaken because of his personal regard for her and because she had always treated the press "so extraordinarily well."[37] Lehmann was against publication because he thought the book "profoundly defeatest" in wartime and might give the impression that it was useless to resist the Germans or Japanese. Leonard agreed in part with Lehmann, thinking that the novel was perhaps "a dangerous book" to publish at the moment. He also saw there was "an artistic question," with the actual events of war making the attitude of the characters "slightly ridiculous." Later, Viola Garvin, a reader for Michael Joseph, although finding the book absorbing, also would object to the defeatist aspect of the novel in wartime and suggested several changes to make it more publishable.[38]

The rejection of *Grand Canyon* led to a permanent separation between Vita Sackville-West and the Hogarth Press. Modest and professional as a writer, she probably minded the rejection of her novel less than the deeply felt absence of Virginia in Hogarth Press affairs. Without Virginia, Vita no longer had any personal reason to remain with Hogarth. Furthermore, her interests developed in different directions. After *Pepita,*

Vita had turned to gardening books, of which she wrote eight, and to biography. Michael Joseph, publisher of her first two gardening books in 1939 and 1940, eventually published *Grand Canyon* in 1942 and became the publisher of her subsequent books until her death in 1962.

Of all the Hogarth Press authors, Vita Sackville-West was the most loyal and long-standing. During the seventeen years of her business association with the Woolfs, she published fourteen books of poetry, fiction, travel, and biography. Her best work artistically as well as her most commercially successful work carried the Hogarth Press imprint. In addition to the heady income of Sackville-West's best-selling books, the broad popularity of such novels as *The Edwardians* and *All Passion Spent* diversified the press list. The years of her association, 1924–41, were the years of important press development and growth. On the other side, Virginia Woolf's loving friendship, her brilliance as a writer, and her criticism as publisher stimulated Sackville-West occasionally to advance beyond the crossroads of "good poetry" and "bad novels" to write a few good books worth remembering.

After Virginia's death, the relationship between Leonard and John Lehmann changed subtly. Virginia had acted as a buffer between Leonard and the young men he had employed as assistants. With Virginia's death, the two partners were left to resolve their conflicts alone. The severe curtailment of paper supplies by 1941 also meant that the management of the press entered a new phase, and although Leonard and John Lehmann kept it alive through the war, the identity and personality of the Hogarth Press had been changed forever.

CHAPTER TEN

★

THE PUBLISHING BUSINESS

M y experience in Ceylon had taught me (I think immodestly) to be a first-class business man, but I was not prepared to become a professional publisher. The Press was therefore a mongrel in the business world" (*Downhill* 77). Leonard Woolf, here thinking back over fifty years to the beginnings of the Hogarth Press, expressed considerable self-satisfaction at his and Virginia's unorthodoxy, their printing and binding in the dining room and interviewing printers and authors in the sitting room. He kept records, he noted, in his own way, not in the manner of a chartered accountant. When challenged by the Inland Revenue, Woolf took his books to the inspector of taxes, who accepted his accounts as showing "accurately the profit or loss on each book published, the revenue and expenditure of the business, and the annual profit or loss" (ibid., 78). Woolf liked to be right, and he took pride in his role of intelligent amateur who could show up the experts. It was characteristic of his nonconformity and self-confidence that he challenged the tax inspector and persisted in his own bookkeeping system for a number of years. Later, under pressure from Inland Revenue, he had to become more conventional in his accounting.

Throughout his autobiography, Woolf delighted in depicting the Hogarth Press as something of a maverick—the early hand-printed books unsettling booksellers by their odd sizes and unusual bindings, the plunge into Freud and the IPL defying professional advice, the operation intended to please him and Virginia only and not to make money, the rejection of friendly merger offers in order to remain independent and small. At the same time, he often enjoyed being the seasoned professional who had achieved success merely by using his brains, discounting the need for assets or previous experience. Publishing, he maintained, could be mastered by any intelligent person who took the trouble to be a good businessman and who would limit his operations, resisting the temptation to expand.

In Ceylon, Woolf had been head of a district for two years. He had been responsible for managing an office with several assistants and for keeping the accounts of revenues and expenditures. For this he had passed an examination in accounts. He had been placed in charge of a "fair-sized industry," he wrote—the manufacture, sale, and distribution of salt under a government monopoly (*Downhill* 125). Up to a point, Woolf had enjoyed the demanding job, later finding the Hogarth Press operation "child's play" in comparison. But being an efficient and tireless colonial administrator was not the same thing as being an entrepreneurial businessman, and in spite of Woolf's claims to the contrary, his approach to publishing was not characteristically businesslike.

By way of contrast, Jonathan Cape, after almost twenty years of experience in publishing, most of it as manager at Duckworth, started his own publishing house in partnership with G. Wren Howard in 1920. He had capital and assets of £12,000 (£5,000 in licenses and stock from his previous reprint company), one secretary-manager, and, soon, the services of the remarkable reader-adviser Edward Garnett. Within two years Cape had a staff of eight, including travelers and a book packer; he issued over eighty titles a year (one was the best-seller *Babbitt*), and he had developed connections with American writers and publishers through a yearly trip to the United States.[1] Jonathan Cape and Wren Howard expanded judiciously and maintained quality. They created an excellent publishing house with a list similar to that of Chatto & Windus and congenial to Hogarth Press, as their subsequent merger indicated. An enterprising businessman like Cape took calculated risks. He expanded, diversified, and kept ahead of his field. He employed experienced people and delegated authority. It can be argued that Leonard Woolf did these things rarely, if at all, and that the particular nature of the Hogarth Press resulted from the fact that Woolf was not a better businessman.

The press marched to its own drumbeat. It came into being, flourished, and changed against the odds, surviving when other small publishers collapsed. The Hogarth Press, unique among publishers, began as a recreation and became a business. It started with a handpress operated by two amateurs who had little interest in fine printing, book design, or typography. It evolved into a small publishing house within three to four years, but without working capital. It had only one modestly paid assistant (Ralph Partridge). In the peak years of 1927 and 1928 when the press published thirty-eight and thirty-six titles, the staff consisted of a manager-secretary (Mrs. Cartwright), a secretary (Peggy Belsher), and a sixteen-year-old apprentice (Richard Kennedy). Not until 1938 did the press have a salaried traveler (Barbara Hepworth) and a partner who invested capital in the business (John Lehmann). Leonard and Virginia Woolf, as full-time literary and political journalists and creative writers but part-time publishers, stand alone as originators and developers of a publishing house. Writers may find a home in publishing as readers or as directors (T. S. Eliot in Faber & Faber, C. Day-Lewis in Chatto & Windus, William Plomer in Jonathan Cape), and career publishers may write an occasional book (Arthur Waugh of Chapman & Hall, Stanley Unwin of Allen & Unwin, Geoffrey Faber of Faber & Faber, Ian Parsons of Chatto & Windus, Bennett Cerf of Random House), but the Woolfs were unique in so thoroughly combining the two endeavors. Interestingly, only John Lehmann as writer, editor, journalist, and publisher approached the Woolfs' achievement, but unlike them, he did not develop his two careers simultaneously.

Two documents of the mid-1930s help characterize Leonard Woolf and the Hogarth Press amid the legion of publishers then active. The first is from February 1934, when Woolf wrote a letter to the editor of the *Members' Circular,* the monthly newsletter of the Publishers Association, registering his "bewilderment and astonishment" at an article critical of the Co-operative Societies' bookselling arrangements (LWP). He could see no reason for the editor's flesh to creep at the idea of working-class societies selling books to their members in the manner of book clubs. "I am a small, young, and—I must presume—extremely unsuccessful [publisher]," wrote Woolf, "because I am very dissatisfied with the sales of my books, and I ascribe the smallness of the sales partly to my own incompetence and partly to the fact that people in our country don't buy books and that there are so few places where they can buy books." He knew a country town of 11,000 with no bookshop (Lewes?); a town of 150,000 twelve miles away (Brighton?) with three bookshops, but even the largest would not stock political books, and he had been unable to buy a copy of Conrad's *Nigger of the Narcissus*. The problem, thought Woolf, was not so much with the booksellers as with "a lamentable lack of the habit of bookbuying" in England. The Co-operative Societies, therefore, should not be considered a disadvantage to booksellers.

Several aspects of Woolf's letter are ingenuous. The topic of poor book-buying habits was a hoary one in 1934, and not the issue addressed by the Publishers Association. Stanley Unwin had discussed it in a 1924 *Nation and Athenaeum* article, then in his *Truth about Publishing* (1926), and again with the other contributors to Leonard Woolf's eleven-article series on the book trade in the *Nation and Athenaeum* in 1927. The National Book Council had been established in 1925 to stimulate interest and sales in book buying. The number of booksellers and the annual sales of books had multiplied dramatically since 1925, but if the problems of book buying in provincial towns like Lewes or Brighton remained, the Co-operative Societies could have no effect on the availability of Conrad's novels or Woolf's political pamphlets. Woolf, an old champion of the Co-ops, was merely firing off a salvo in defense of a principle. The real issue was the argument over the Co-ops' allowing dividends on books in violation of the Net Book Agreement. It had nothing to do with the rights of the societies to sell books to their members at standard prices. The issue went back to 1927 and reemerged in 1934 when a large Gloucester store threatened to give dividends in competition with the local Co-op.[2] Eventually most of the Co-op Societies were forced to sign the Net Book Agreement and so maintain the integrity of book prices.

The most interesting aspect of Woolf's letter is the *faux naïveté* of the description of himself as a small, young, extremely unsuccessful, and partly incompetent publisher. The admission of incompetence from the proud and self-confident Woolf was remarkable, and the remainder of the assessment is equally suspect. Woolf at fifty-four was not young, nor was the Hogarth Press at seventeen years. Although certainly small, the press could hardly be considered unsuccessful. Woolf himself noted in his autobiography that the press "was by 1935 a successful business financially" (*Journey* 99). It generally provided the Woolfs with an income of £1,000 annually. Rather, the curious self-portrait fits one of Leonard Woolf's most cherished roles, that of the small-time, noncommercial amateur among the larger professionals, the quick-witted, self-taught David among the Goliaths. And Woolf's socialism may have caused his disenchantment with the established authority of the Publishers Association.

In February 1935, one year after his blast on behalf of the Co-ops, Woolf exchanged letters with Herbert Read about publishers and booksellers, privately voicing his frustrations with the system in the most political of terms. Read had written an article, "The Sweated Author," for the *London Mercury* proposing an authors' guild which would publish books at a higher royalty rate than regular publishers, who were concerned not with literary merit, argued Read, but only with profits from best-sellers. Woolf was skeptical of the guild concept but certain about publishers. "The curse of the capitalist system," he wrote, "is that it debauches the consumer." In a follow-up letter to Read, Woolf agreed that the book trade and the habits of the reading public, conditioned to best-sellers, needed revolutionary change. "If I had not been a socialist before," he stated, "publishing would have made me one."[3] Publisher's travelers often accomplished little but taking orders for best-sellers. "If you want to see the hopeless inefficiency and futility of the capitalist system from the inside," Woolf argued, "become a publisher." Moreover, trying to talk books intelligently with 95 percent of the booksellers (and he probably meant publishers as well) was nightmarish, Woolf wrote, like "discussing meat with a butcher who held [vegetarian G. B.] Shaw's views on meat, meat-eating and meat selling."

Socialist-publisher Leonard Woolf could be generous with contracts, and at this time with such issues on his mind he would grant a first-round 20 percent royalty to Vita Sackville-West for her new novel *Dark Island* (1934), but in spite of his criticism of the profit motive, he did not become a socialist Co-op publisher. Press profits were important to the business. True, the Woolfs and their press never pursued best-sellers, although they were delighted when Virginia, Vita, or William Plomer cracked the market with one. But the press did not share equally with its authors. Leonard could castigate large publishers in private for their greedy pursuit of best-sellers and their anti-intellectualism, but he followed most accepted publishing practices.

Throughout his career as publisher, Leonard Woolf seems to have

avoided contact with other publishers and to have remained aloof from
the various organizations of the book trade: the Society of Bookmen
(founded in 1921 by Hugh Walpole), the Publishers Association, and the
National Book Council. John Lehmann has noted Woolf's often caustic
and witty comments at the expense of members of the book trade. No
doubt the Bloomsbury sense of intellectual and cultural superiority which
set him apart from the publishing fraternity, from those dynamic shakers
and makers like Jonathan Cape or Allen Lane, brought him no affection
from the professionals. But it is worth noting that Victor Gollancz, a man
of no mean intelligence and refinement, and further left politically than
Woolf, operated as an important gadfly and social conscience to the Publishers Association, generating change. It was an important role, one
which Woolf as a social-political reformer might have played. But he took
no part in any of the many battles and movements to regulate and improve book publishing and selling during the 1920s and 1930s. He preferred to maintain his stance as amateur and outsider, free to criticize.

The second revealing document of the mid-1930s is the 1936 entry for
the Hogarth Press in the *Reference Catalogue of Current Literature*. This
trade publication contained a directory of over 650 publishers in Great
Britain. The Hogarth Press entry, following the *Catalogue*'s format, listed
five series (including the IPL psychoanalytical books), foreign agents in
Canada, Australia, New Zealand, and South Africa, and the following
subjects or types of books published: anthropology, archaeology, art,
banking, bibliography, biography, classics, education, essays, fiction, history, illustrated giftbooks, music, philosophy, poetry, politics, psychology, religion, sociology, trade, and travel. Some of these require a liberal
interpretation. Did Hogarth publish anthropology, archaeology, and bibliography—perhaps books by Freud, Róheim, and Rickman? Which of
the 377 titles published through 1935 can be considered illustrated giftbooks? Roger Fry's *Twelve Original Woodcuts* (1921) or his *Sampler of Castile* (1923), Julia Cameron's *Victorian Photographs of Famous Men and Fair
Women* (1926), or Virginia Woolf's third edition of *Kew Gardens* (1927)
decorated by Vanessa Bell? Cameron's photographs might qualify, but the
other two seem doubtful.

Businesses can be expected to put their best foot forward in such
directory entries, but it seems almost out of character for the supposedly

austere and highbrow Hogarth Press. The entry reveals the other side of Leonard Woolf, his competitive nature, his pride in the accomplishments of the press, his shrewd insistence on the solid commercial and professional nature of his publishing house with representatives in four commonwealth countries. And perhaps the entry suggests a touch of cynicism in Woolf, who could be expected to despise such puffery but, finding it useful, would play the game as skillfully as the competition. The image Leonard Woolf presented in this entry is of a large, flourishing, solid establishment with years of experience behind it, the polar opposite of the one created by his letter to the editor of the *Members' Circular* in 1934.

The genres not included in Woolf's description of the Hogarth Press by their absence help define the press. It did not publish juveniles, or medical, scientific, and technical books (the IPL books excluded), or standard reference works, or maps and directories, or cookbooks, or books on sports, nature, or dogs (*Flush* may be considered an exception of sorts), or textbooks (except for those pamphlets by Kathleen Innes on the League of Nations which came to be used in schools), or Bibles, prayer books, or religious texts. Nor did the press publish humor or cater much to popular fiction, publishing only a handful of novels, including two mysteries, that might be considered just good reads.

Characteristic of the Woolfs' generally unbending attitude toward popular culture was the exchange in 1924 recorded by Francis Meynell with Virginia Woolf over the enormously popular Nonesuch Press's *Week-End Book*. The book, with sections on poems, songs, games, food, and drink, sold over a half-million copies for Meynell's usually elegant and high-culture Nonesuch, but it drew Virginia's sharp disapproval in a wonderfully malicious review in the *TLS* in which she made it out to be the epitome of philistine silliness. Meynell reported with obvious relish that Virginia approached him at one of his large, exuberant parties, "gazed fixedly into my eyes and with a firm grip on my hand said: 'The Hogarth Press may not make any money—but at least (the grip tightened) we did not publish *The Week-End Book*.' "[4] He laughed. But in 1937 the Woolfs, presumably without blushing or laughing, published Viola Tree's book with the remarkable title: *Can I Help You? Your Manners—Menus—Amusements—Friends—Charades—Make-Ups—Travel—Calling—Children—Love Affairs*. The Nonesuch weekender looks positively starchy in comparison. Viola Tree, daughter of the actor Sir Herbert Beerbohm Tree, was an old friend and the author of an earlier press book of reminiscences (*Castles in the Air,* 1926). Publishers, even the discriminating Woolfs, can make exceptions to their general line for friends, and certainly for such a sprightly, charming, anecdotal, name-dropping book as this, with pen-and-ink illustrations by Virginia Parsons.

Some publishers also publish annuals and serials or periodicals. Academic presses do this regularly, and commercial publishing houses may undertake specialized periodicals on occasion. The Hogarth Press published the *New Writing* of John Lehmann when he became a partner in 1938, but the relationship was troublesome for Leonard Woolf and one he engaged in only because of the partnership. Twice before, however, Woolf had involved the Hogarth Press in brief publishing arrangements with periodicals, neither of them satisfactory. In 1926 he had agreed to publish *Youth,* the monthly magazine of the British Federation of Youth, edited by Theodore Besterman. Hogarth published the first six issues from March to August 1926 before the federation decided to become its own publisher (*Checklist* 45). Then in October 1930 Leonard Woolf set up a contract with H. J. Schonfield to publish a new quarterly, *The Search,* to make available in summary form the results of modern scholarship in religion, philosophy, science, literature, and art. The concept certainly appealed to Woolf, who proposed that the Hogarth Press would publish the magazine at 2s.6d. per copy, distribute all copies, list it in the press autumn and spring lists, send circulars to subscribers, and travel the magazine. In return, Schonfield and his associates would pay the press a 15 percent commission on all copies sold, with a minimum commission payment of £7.10 per quarter (*HP* 447). The arrangement soon broke down, conflicts developed between Woolf and the editors, and publication with Hogarth ceased after the first four issues of January-October 1931 (*Checklist* 99). Ironically, John Lehmann during his first stint at the press had assisted with the arrangements and had written the terminating letter. He reported to Leonard in April that "after a tussle, the *Search* account has been straightened, and an (I think!) impeccable letter sent them."[5]

Nevertheless, the Hogarth list remained essentially selective and serious, with a few outstanding examples in each genre. But if a publisher can be characterized by the books it publishes, by its rejections also shall it be known. Every publishing house must reject many more manuscripts than it publishes. In the flood of unsolicited writing, the publisher has to be both gambler and fatalist to survive. "The publisher's fallibility may be taken for granted," wrote publisher Michael Joseph in 1949, adding that if a firm could turn a profit on half of its new books, it would be doing well. He estimated the average at "two successful books out of every five." Joseph also estimated that a moderate-size publisher needing an annual profit of £10,000 could achieve it ideally by publishing twenty titles a year, each with an average profit of £500, but since such success rate would be impossible, he or she would have to publish at least fifty titles a year for a margin of error.[6] Leonard Woolf considered twenty titles a year ideal for the Hogarth Press before the war and an income of £1,000 to himself and Virginia a measure of financial success. From 1924, when the press added Freud and the IPL and Leonard diversified into politics, through 1939, just before the war and paper rationing began to affect all publishers, the Hogarth Press published an average of twenty-six titles a year, with the peak years in 1927 and 1928 (thirty-eight and thirty-six titles) and in 1931 and 1932 (thirty-five and thirty-six titles). Such figures suggest at the least that the Woolfs achieved a much higher degree of success than Joseph's average of two out of five with fifty titles a year.

There is no way of knowing the precise number of manuscripts received and rejected each year by the Woolfs to provide the average twenty-six titles. Many of the published books and pamphlets on political or social subjects were either suggested to writers by Leonard Woolf or offered by authors he knew from his journalistic or political endeavors and so accepted from the beginning. To a lesser extent, the same was true of titles published in fiction and poetry, the works of Eliot, Mansfield, Forster, Isherwood, and Sackville-West, for example. But the bulk of the manuscripts sifted by the Woolfs were unsolicited novels, and the burden of reading them fell upon Virginia Woolf. Her letters and diary provide abundant evidence of the work load and its physical and psychological demands.

"Meanwhile I read vast masses of MSS," she wrote to Vita Sackville-West in 1929. "They plague my life out, these unhappy women and men, to read their mss myself and tell them how they cd. be improved." (*Letters*

4:23). To one of them, a "woman of 40," she had to write "a letter to say nothing can make this saleable though it's wrung from her entrails and gives away every bitterness and sorrow of her life. She is half educated, deserted and lives on 15/- a week with a child" (ibid., 24). And to Quentin Bell in 1930 she wrote about reading piles of virgin manuscripts, "novels six foot thick to be read instantly or I shall be knived by cadaverous men at Bournemouth whose life depends on my verdict; and amorous typists" (ibid., 141). To Ethel Smyth in 1932 she wrote that she had "20 MSS to read for violent blood thirsty authors," and to Hugh Walpole four months later that "I read 600 mss. a year now" (ibid., 74, 115). In sympathy or out, with stark realism or witty exaggeration, Virginia Woolf responded to the manuscripts. She often bitterly resented the intrusion into her own writing time and as a result periodically proposed the demise of the press.

Virginia read the fiction and some of the poetry submitted to the press but not the social and political works. Leonard apparently read every manuscript sent to the press. Nevertheless, the number of fiction and poetry manuscripts submitted each month no doubt far exceeded the total in all other genres, so that Virginia's contribution to the press as reader was enormous. Although she must have written some letters such as the one to the 'woman of 40," none of them seem to have survived. Leonard conducted daily press correspondence. His rejection letters, according to Richard Kennedy, were less sympathetic and more direct than Virginia's: "Dear Sir, We regret we are unable to accept the enclosed MS. Yours faithfully."[7] It took the maladroit apprentice an hour to type that letter, Kennedy confessed, and he made one spelling error, which did not amuse Leonard.

Virginia's diary and letters and Leonard's correspondence contain occasional references to specific rejections. Although most were of hopelessly inept attempts by unknowns, like that of the "grocer's boy" Virginia described to Vita in 1925 ("600 pages of moonshine raptures about the violet lids of ladies and Lord Eustace in a motor car" [*Letters* 3:124]), some were of flawed works by Bloomsbury friends or by as yet unknowns whose reputations would someday be well established. Bloomsbury served its members as a mutual admiration society, but it is worth noting that they could be critical of themselves and others. Leonard Woolf, for example, decided against publishing Lytton Strachey's reviews and essays in 1919, as he wrote to Edward Marsh, because he thought them "extraordinarily poor."[8] The Woolfs also rejected Evan Morgan's novel in 1921 (he became Viscount Tredegar), Violet Dickinson's edition of her great-aunt Emily's letters in 1924, Sebastian Sprott's novel in 1925, Sturge Moore's play in 1928, Archibald MacLeish's long meditative poem on Hamlet in 1928, Brian Howard's poetry in 1929, Walter Lowenfels's poetry in 1929, Stephen Spender's novel in 1931, Julian Bell's dissertation on Pope in 1932, Logan Pearsall Smith's essay in 1935, Ethel Smyth's "dog story" *Inordinate (?) Affection* (published by Cresset Press in 1936), and John Lehmann's novel "The Boy Who Disappeared" in 1938. They rejected two of John Hampson's novels in 1933 and 1936 after publishing his first two.

Especially interesting are the rejected writers like Richard Hughes who went on to become well-known authors. The Woolfs turned down his long story "Martha" in 1921 when he was an eighteen-year-old Oxford undergraduate and thereby may have lost their chance to publish his *High Wind in Jamaica* (1929), which would become a classic. In 1924 the Woolfs rejected Dorothy Bussy's translation of Gide (probably of *La porte étroite*). They rejected Gertrude Stein's *Making of Americans* in 1925 but published her *Composition as Explanation* in 1926. At Dorothy Wellesley's insistence, Leonard Woolf agreed to reject the poetry of Louis MacNeice in 1932, the only major 1930s poet who sought publication at Hogarth and was turned down. The Woolfs also rejected Kathleen Raine's prose poems in 1936 and H. G. Wells's novel *The Camford Visitation* in 1937. Of all the Woolfs' rejections, however, none is more famous than that of James Joyce's *Ulysses* in 1918, partly as a matter of taste but mostly because it was too long and difficult for them to hand print.

The Woolfs are less exempt from criticism for another well-known blunder, eleven years later, when they rejected Ivy Compton-Burnett's third novel, *Brothers and Sisters* (1929). According to Richard Kennedy's amusing account, Leonard Woolf gave the young assistant Jack Yeats's *Sligo* and Compton-Burnett's novel to read and report on.[9] Kennedy rejected Yeats's work as too slight but gave *Brothers and Sisters* to his uncle George to read. Uncle George pronounced it a work of genius, and Kennedy passed on this verdict to Woolf in his reader's report. Woolf soon returned the two manuscripts to Kennedy, telling him to send form rejection letters to both authors and remarking scornfully of Compton-Burnett, "She can't even write." Later, when Edward Sackville-West questioned the Woolfs' rejection, Virginia replied that she agreed they should have published the novel. Their rejection "was annoying—mere slackness, I suppose," she wrote, adding that "there's something bleached about Miss Compton Burnett: like hair which had never had any colour in it" (*Letters* 4:92). Ironically, Compton-Burnett dismissed Virginia Woolf as a novelist in nearly the same spirit over thirty years later in an interview with Michael Millgate. She admired Virginia Woolf's use of words, she said, but would not call her a good novelist because she lacked bone and the ability to draw character.[10]

Most rejection letters are lost to time, but acceptance letters become part of the record. The Hogarth Press files contain many from Leonard stating that he and Virginia had read a manuscript and would be pleased to publish it. These letters reveal the best side of Leonard, his warm encouragement and his sensitive awareness of the self-doubts and vanities of young writers. A fine example is the one he wrote to beginning novelist John Graham for his *Good Merchant* in January 1934: "I am afraid that 'very great interest' is a sort of stock publishers' phrase, but it meant in this case that both my wife and I thought that there were very great merits in your novel. You see things and people for yourself and are able to convey the vision to the reader; the book has a flavour of its own; and you can make words perform their duty economically and according to your wishes not theirs. We thought (and hoped) that there were signs of immaturity and that you were young . . . [because] it naturally makes a difference, when it comes to the problem of whether one is or is not to offer to publish a book, if the book is a first attempt or if it is the work of an old gentleman."[11] They offered to publish his novel in the autumn and invited him to Monks House.

The Woolfs' judgment as publishers was good, although they were both too strongly talented, opinionated, and critical as writers themselves to be without blind spots. As publisher's readers they were not so consistent as the legendary Edward Garnett. John Lehmann, however, was another good judge of literary talent and more in tune with contemporary literature than Leonard. He provided an important seasoning to Leonard Woolf's increasingly conservative taste. After Virginia's death, he and Leonard agreed to reject Vita Sackville-West's novel *Grand Canyon* (1941); but later in their increasingly difficult partnership, Lehmann claimed that Woolf vetoed such rising stars as David Gascoyne, Terence Tiller, Saul Bellow, and Sartre.[12] Woolf also rejected Auden's selections from Tennyson. Their growing disagreements over emerging writers contributed, in Lehmann's opinion, to the final breakup of the partnership in 1946.

Rejected manuscripts, like all missed opportunities, may haunt a publisher if they prove successful in the hands of a competitor, but the real ghosts that stalk a publisher's halls at midnight are the books that were planned but never published. Somewhere, in newspaper ads, in flyers, in seasonal lists and catalogues, in announcements of forthcoming publications in the backs of books, the titles that never materialized were given a bogus existence.

J. Howard Woolmer in his *Checklist of the Hogarth Press* lists seventeen ghosts that were intended for publication between 1917 and 1945, fifteen of which were listed during the years covered by this history (*Checklist* 229–31). Several of these became published works under another title or by another publisher. The *Woodcuts* by Duncan Grant and Vanessa Bell proposed in 1917, for example, became *Original Woodcuts by Various Artists* in 1918 as an Omega Workshop book. Similarly, Raymond Mortimer's announced "Essays" (1941) became *Channel Packet* and was published by Hogarth in 1942, and Vita Sackville-West's *Grand Canyon,* after rejection by Woolf and Lehmann in 1941, was published by Michael Joseph in 1942. These works are marginal ghosts because they soon existed in the flesh.

This category, or subspecies, of ghost also fits two of Virginia Woolf's essays, robust and kicking under any label. The Hogarth Press had announced in September 1927 Virginia's "Poetry, Fiction & the Future" as a forthcoming publication in the Hogarth Essays series. She had already published it in two installments in the *New York Herald Tribune* during August 1927. It never appeared as a Hogarth Essay, but thirty-one years later Leonard included it in the collection *Granite and Rainbow* (1958) as "The Narrow Bridge of Art." The press had also announced in February 1928 Virginia's "Phases of Fiction" soon to be one of the Hogarth Lectures on Literature. She published it in three issues of the *Book-*

man in New York during April, May, and June 1929, but Leonard did not publish it under the Hogarth imprint until 1958 in *Granite and Rainbow*. In both instances, Virginia Woolf published important essays in the American market for pay better than the British could offer but planned to include them in the Hogarth series. The failure of the Woolfs to publish them as planned remains a mystery.

Four Hogarth ghosts of undeniable bloodlessness were announced as forthcoming in press series, suggesting that the marketing of a multivolume series sometimes got ahead of the production. The four ghosts were Walter de la Mare's "Atmosphere in Fiction" announced for the Essays series in 1927, Hugh Walpole's "The Historical Novel" announced in 1928 for the Lectures series in 1930, Peter Quennell's "Revolutions in Literary Method" announced in 1930 for the Lectures series in 1931, and Prince Mirsky's "Literature and Films in Soviet Russia" announced in February 1932 for the Day to Day Pamphlet series. Mirsky returned to an ominous fate in Russia sometime after June 1932 and was not seen again by the Woolfs. There are no Hogarth Press files on these projected pamphlets, indicating that they never proceeded beyond the preliminary stage. The most unusual Hogarth ghost, however, is Herbert Rosinski's "Command at Sea." It has a large press file, labeled with the alternate title "Command of the Sea." The book was announced several times and was intended for 1940, but Rosinski never completed the manuscript. He had published *The German Army* with Hogarth in 1939 and had hoped to repeat with a book on the German navy.

As for advertising, Leonard Woolf wrote, "my own belief is that books are, in general, not a commodity which, like patent medicines, cigarettes, or mustard, the consumer buys or can be induced to buy by the skill of the advertiser alone." [13] Woolf's belief, here expressed in his contribution to the *Nation and Athenaeum* series of articles on the book trade in 1927, found almost uniform support from publishers in the decades between the wars. It paid to advertise a book by a well-known author, Woolf maintained, or one that was either selling well or beginning to sell well, but it almost never paid to advertise a book that was not selling or one that had "real literary or scientific or philosophic merit for which . . . there must be a small public." Stanley Unwin had stated the same conclusion the previous year in his *Truth about Publishing* (1926), and Geoffrey Faber would reiterate it eight years later in *A Publisher Speaking* (1935). Faber ranked newspaper advertising as "one of the least effective forms of publicity," well below "word of mouth" and favorable reviews.[14] Moreover, as Unwin had explained, such advertising was costly. The gross profit from 1,500 copies sold of a new 7s.6d. novel might not exceed £250, he pointed out, and yet the publisher usually spent £50 or more to advertise it, or nearly 20 percent of his profit.[15] A six-inch single-column ad placed in the *Daily Mail* cost around £50. But advertise he must. The author expected it, usually believing that publishers never advertised enough, and the book trade expected it. To keep authors happy, to keep the firm's name before the public, and perhaps even to sell a few copies, publishers, Leonard Woolf among them, designed their ads and sent them off to the newspapers and periodicals, grumbling all the while.

When Woolf placed the first Hogarth Press advertisements in the July 1920 issues of the *Nation, Times Literary Supplement, Guardian,* and *New Statesman,* he followed the established form at the time for a six-inch, single-column ad. In the rectangular ruled space, 3 1/4 inches wide, he placed the copy in bold, heavy type. The severe announcement was functional but inelegant. The top of the ad announced "The Hogarth Press," then followed with the titles of eight works with the authors' names and prices, each set off from the other by a ruled line. The ad concluded with the name of the press and its address, Hogarth House, Richmond, at the bottom. The titles were Gorky's *Tolstoy,* E. M. Forster's *Story of the Siren,* Logan Pearsall Smith's *Stories from the Old Testament,* Hope Mirrlees's *Paris,* Katherine Mansfield's *Prelude,* J. M. Murry's *Critic in Judgment,* and Virginia Woolf's *Kew Gardens* and *The Mark on the Wall.*

The style used in the early Hogarth Press ads was visually unsophisticated, the type heavy and black, the copy cramped, the list of titles and prices assaulting and dulling the eye. The quarter-page Hogarth Press ad was virtually indistinguishable from those of other houses. The ads emphasized the author's name or the book's title and carried the publisher's name modestly at the bottom in smaller type, almost as an afterthought. Periodically, during the autumn or spring publishing seasons, a publisher might vary his usual pattern with a full-page ad such as T. Fisher Unwin's

"Announcements" or William Heinemann's "Autumn List." Few publishers in the early 1920s attempted to add any more design than an occasional ornamental border or a slight change in typography. A few might embellish their full-page ads with devices (Heinemann's windmill, Unwin's and Duckworth's ornamental initials). In all such matters, Leonard Woolf was a follower, not a leader.

By 1926 Leonard Woolf had lightened the Hogarth Press ads, reducing the number of titles to two or three and using a variety of type sizes so that the author's name or the book's title stood out clearly from the supporting copy. Woolf followed the example of the better houses by regularly including puffs from reviewers. By 1928 he had begun to run the press name at the bottom of the ad, continuing to emphasize the product, not the producer. Only a few publishers by the late 1920s had realized the advantage of a distinctive house style for their ads, selling the firm's name through design and typography. The advertising of books slowly caught up with the brand-name identification so familiar in product advertising. Leonard Woolf had neither the money nor the inclination to follow the more creative advertisers such as Victor Gollancz, Chatto & Windus, and Jonathan Cape, nor, apparently, did he have the visual sense required for ad design, but gradually the press ads improved stylistically. It is interesting that he seems never to have asked Vanessa Bell to try her hand at designing an ad layout for the press, in spite of her outstanding success with jacket designs. She had designed the wolf's-head device that the Woolfs had used on their title pages from the beginning of the press.

Suddenly in December 1928, however, Leonard Woolf and the Hogarth Press found a style of its own and instantly stepped up into the company of the Capes and Gollanczes. Leonard Woolf had the well-known American painter and designer E. McKnight Kauffer design a wolf's-head device to be used in ads. Kauffer, who had been a member of Roger Fry's Omega Workshop and achieved a measure of fame by his poster designs for the London Underground, produced a strong, nearly abstract animal head more like a wolfhound than a wolf but unmistakably bold and modern. Leonard first used the Kauffer design in a half-page ad for the pre-Christmas sale in the December 8, 1928, issue of the *Nation and Athenaeum*. If not as elegantly generous as a Chatto & Windus or a Cape ad, the Hogarth ad nevertheless communicated a new degree of stylishness, efficiency, and crisp intellectuality. From this time on, all Hogarth ads carried McKnight Kauffer's single or double wolf's-head device, becoming as instantly recognizable and distinctive as the best publishing house ads. Woolf had learned the value of advertising the producer as well as the product.

John Lehmann, given the responsibility for preparing ads during his first Hogarth Press stint in 1931–32, improved upon but did not change this ad format. His best effort was a full-page ad for the *New Statesman and Nation* Autumn Books Supplement on October 10, 1931, featuring Virginia Woolf's new novel, *The Waves*. Using the full page to advantage, Lehmann headlined Virginia's novel and arranged the titles and information on five other books in a balanced, columnar design set off by star devices. Lehmann subtly modified the basic design by inserting a single device into the ruled border at the top and the press name into the ruled border at the bottom. This new form with the inserted device would be continued by Leonard Woolf and Margaret West after Lehmann had left.

Having achieved a stylish and recognizable advertising format for his books after years of trial and error, Leonard Woolf rightly clung to it and frowned on departures. No wonder he was furious when John Rickman sent in his own ad copy for the IPL to the *New Statesman and Nation* for the Melanie Klein and Joan Riviere psychoanalytical Epitome *Love, Hate, and Reparation* in November 1937. The result, appearing in the November 13 issue, returned to the bad old days before the Kauffer device. The ad itemized the titles of all twenty-four of the Klein-Riviere lectures and buried the Hogarth name in small print at the bottom. Woolf sent Rickman a scorching letter of protest, emphasizing that "if we are to continue, the publishing must really be left to me, and the editing to you" (HP 224). Noting that the style of advertising is of "material importance" to a publisher, Woolf lectured Rickman on a publisher's rights and responsibilities and fumed that the expenditure of £7.10 on a preliminary ad for an Epitome was a "complete waste of money." Rickman got the message and never again presumed to intrude on Woolf's domain.

Leonard Woolf had several exchanges over the years with authors who assumed the press was underadvertising them. As with John Rickman, Woolf could be irate, but he could also be avuncular and instructive, calling on his experience and winning the day by force of argument. But with Lyn D. Irvine (*Ten Letter Writers,* 1932), he was arguing with a strongly opinionated young writer who had experience in journalism (she had reviewed extensively for Leonard in the *Nation and Athenaeum*) and the gift of a sharp pen. Irvine, in a series of letters exchanged in October 1932, questioned Woolf's delay in advertising until after the reviews of her book appeared and then his refusal to advertise in a paper like the *Daily Telegraph* (HP 194). She was not pacified by Woolf's citation of his experience or his admission that "I am completely skeptical as to its [advertising's] utility, and that therefore it is quite possible that I am completely inconsistent in my methods." Nor did it encourage her to have him add, "But it is a complete delusion to believe that you can sell a book by advertising it." Irvine suspected Woolf of sophistry, pointing out that he carefully placed his ads for books like hers in the serious weeklies. She thought that her book appealed to a general public and should be advertised accordingly, for a readership different from Bloomsbury (HP 194).

The exchange with Irvine highlights a recurring problem for the Woolfs and their press. With their rejection of commercialism, their uneasiness with profit making, and their highbrow intellectualism, Leonard and Virginia Woolf were uncomfortable with publications that moved outside Bloomsbury or socialist Labor circles to appeal to a popular market. Yet they sometimes found themselves with the best-sellers of Vita Sackville-West or the mysteries of C. H. B. Kitchin, or books like Irvine's which straddled the fence and required a different type of promotion than Leonard found it easy to give.

For most of the books published by the press between 1928 and 1941, the ads in the serious weeklies with the Kauffer device got the job done. At the height of the blitz in early 1941, however, John Lehmann, working from Letchworth, abandoned the wolf's-head device for something like the old full-column ads listing recent offerings. Wartime shortages of paper reduced the amount of advertising permitted in the hard-pressed weeklies. Two of these ads in the *New Statesman and Nation* are uniquely interesting. The first one, appearing March 29, 1941, the day after Virginia's suicide, carried the Hogarth Press spring and summer announcements and featured Virginia Woolf's *Between the Acts* and Vita Sackville-West's *Grand Canyon.* She had rejected her own novel, and Leonard and John Lehmann would soon reject Sackville-West's novel. The second ad, almost a month later on April 26, carried Virginia Woolf's name in capitals and listed twenty books and pamphlets of hers published by the press and available through booksellers. It was bordered by a solid black band, dramatically and eloquently memorializing the dead writer.

Advertisements had become important to the press and its authors, but there were other means of promoting books and selling the company's name that Leonard also used. Most obvious were jacket blurbs and quotations from reviews in ads. Many publishers, Woolf included, were skeptical of the value of even laudatory reviews in selling books, but like ads, they formed a necessary part of the transaction. Both Leonard and Virginia Woolf had some edge over other publishers in this matter because they were well-established and prominent reviewers and literary journalists themselves, knew well the other members of the tribe, and so could hope for respectful attention to their publications. Leonard had the extreme advantage of being the literary editor of the *Nation and Athenaeum* from 1923 to 1930, crucial years for the development of the press, when he could oversee the selection of perceptive and sympathetic reviewers for the Hogarth books.

Another means of promotion was the listing of other press books by the same author or in the same series either in the front or back of a new book. And, perhaps most interesting of all, were the flyers or circulars, special and seasonal announcements of new books, and the catalogues that were distributed to booksellers, reviewers, and individual buyers. The Hogarth Press seasonal announcements began in 1923, and catalogues with complete listings in 1927. The most attractive of all is the catalogue of 1939 with Vanessa Bell's bold blue and yellow cover design. Its forty-one pages documented the achievement of the press through the summer of 1939, listing 246 authors and nearly 450 titles. Swept up in the tragedy and destruction of the war and the death of Virginia Woolf, the Hogarth Press would not issue another catalogue until after the return of peace.

In book design, too, the Woolfs and their press were followers rather than leaders. According to the authority Charles Rosner, it was not until the mid-nineteenth century that dust jackets began to be designed and printed with an eye to a prospective buyer.[16] T. Fisher Unwin pioneered most effectively the use of pictorial and decoratively printed dust jackets from the 1890s into the early 1900s. Between the two World Wars, three presses distinguished themselves with jacket designs featuring new typography and calligraphy: the Curwen Press under Oliver Simon, Victor Gollancz under Stanley Morrison, and Jonathan Cape under Hans Tisdell. The jacket became an important feature of book publishing, aimed at the market and often designed by professionals. The dust jackets of the Hogarth Press, although not innovative within the industry, nevertheless established high standards for freshness and originality. Vanessa Bell's distinctive jacket designs, for example, became a recognizable feature of Virginia Woolf's novels and shaped the Hogarth Press style. Seventeen other designers employed by Leonard Woolf helped cover the press books. Of the 474 books and pamphlets published by the Woolfs between 1917 and 1941, approximately 264 were issued with dust jackets, the remainder being pamphlets or small volumes in series that had designed covers but no jackets.[17] Some of the dust jackets were unlettered tissue or wax paper see-through jackets, and others were colored paper jackets lettered in contrasting ink. The psychoanalytical books were covered with the colored jackets. There were 156 of these undecorated colored jackets and 23 others which used a cut or a reproduction from the volume but were otherwise unadorned. In contrast, Vanessa Bell and the other designers supplied 85 jackets with pictorial or geometric designs.

Appropriately, the first decorative or pictorial dust jackets the press issued were designed by the Bloomsbury easel painters Vanessa Bell, Roger Fry, and Duncan Grant. Fry designed the jacket for his own book *A Sampler of Castile* (1923), and later he designed the jacket for William Plomer's collection of stories about Japan, *Paper Houses* (1929). Grant designed the jacket for Fry's *Duncan Grant* (1924) containing twenty-four plates of his own paintings. Grant prepared both the book cover and the jacket in the best Omega Workshop style with geometrical designs. Eight years later Grant designed the jacket for Julia Strachey's *Cheerful Weather for a Wedding* (1932). Even the young Quentin Bell, from the Charleston ménage, would try his hand at a jacket with his drawing for Peter Ibbetson's *Mr. Baldwin Explains and Other Dream Interviews* (1927), a disconcertingly aggressive Baldwin rising out of the mist and confronting the viewer.

The mistress of Charleston, Vanessa Bell, however, provided the most designs—from abstract and geometrical to pictorial. Beginning with her jacket for Virginia Woolf's *Jacob's Room* (1922), the first pictorial Hogarth Press dust jacket, to her design for Virginia's posthumous *Between the Acts* (1941), Vanessa designed twenty dust jackets, sketched the first wolf's-head device, and supplied seven designs for the various Hogarth Press series and editions during the period covered by this history. She continued to design jackets for Virginia's posthumously published works.

"We think your design lovely—Our only doubts are practical," wrote Virginia when Vanessa had submitted her first design for *Jacob's Room* (*Letters* 2:543). Leonard thought the lettering was not plain enough, nor sufficiently contrasting to the cinnamon-colored design on cream stock. He asked if Vanessa could capitalize the "r" of *room* and use another color for the lettering. Vanessa's finished design suggests an interior glimpsed through a window framed by pulled-back drapes. A bowl with three widely spaced flowers seems to float above the merest hint of a table. The title, stylishly hand lettered in black with initial capitals, dominates the clear space above the bowl. Virginia's name in similar lettering appears at the bottom of the design. Vanessa had made no attempt to provide a jacket illustrative of the novel. Her design for *Jacob's Room,* impersonal and nearly abstract, a mere suggestion of a room without an occupant, nevertheless accords well with Virginia's suggestive fictional portrait of Jacob Flanders.

The booksellers, however, "almost universally condemned" Vanessa's design, remembered Leonard in his autobiography (*Downhill* 76). There was neither an attractive woman on the jacket, nor Jacob, nor even a discernible room. The design was deplorably Postimpressionist. Several buyers even laughed. Attitudes would change with time.

Vanessa's next design, for Virginia's *Common Reader* (1925), was one of her most pleasing, the brown lettering and flowers contrasting agreeably with the green vase dominating the foreground and with the geometrical bookcase in the background. An amused Virginia wrote to her sister that a reviewer had devoted a column to the design features and had stated that Virginia had tried "to live up to them by being as revolutionary and nonsensical" in her essays (*Letters* 3:182). Whether or not Virginia reflected Vanessa's art in her critical and imaginative prose, Vanessa developed her designs almost entirely free of any concern for the contents of Virginia's books. According to John Lehmann, the usual practice was to send a dummy volume to Vanessa when the page count had been determined, thus setting the book's size, and Vanessa would design the jacket without having read the text.[18]

Vanessa's jacket for *Mrs. Dalloway* (1925), for example, has a pure abstract design; *To the Lighthouse* (1927) has a misty and mysterious evocation of a lighthouse amid waves; *A Room of One's Own* (1929) has a boxy clock set in a dark arch, the hands set in a V shape; *The Waves* (1931) has a wave pattern resembling fish scales with two shadowy figures on either side in the foreground; *The Years* (1937) has a design of three overlapping circles like plates with a rose laid across upside down; and *Three Guineas* (1938), perhaps the strongest jacket design, has three checks in mauve fanned from left to right with a quill pen and blue ink bottle in lower right foreground. For the dust jacket of Virginia's *Roger Fry* (1940), the press used Vanessa's formal oil portrait of Fry at his easel.

Virginia responded to Vanessa's designs in her letters by calling them most attractive or lovely. She was seldom more specific. But what she wrote about Vanessa's style when she had seen the jacket for *To the Lighthouse* suggests as much about Vanessa's art as it does about Virginia's response to it: "Your style is unique; because so truthful; and therefore it upsets one completely" (*Letters* 3:391). Vanessa's style that so moved Virginia suggests a serene view of the world, subtly ordered and colored, often using floral patterns, and represented by strong verticals and interlinking spaces. The style effects an intriguing emotional and visual quality.

Vanessa's jacket designs, printed in soft browns, greens, and blues on cream stock, with frequent use of black for emphasis, seem to counterpoint Virginia's increasingly bold and innovative texts. Unquestionably Vanessa's designs added an important visual quality to all of Virginia's work. As Virginia wrote to Vanessa in June 1926 after viewing an exhibition of her paintings, calling her a "mistress of the brush": "I mean, people will say, What a gifted couple!" (*Letters* 3:271). The collaboration provided a link of no little emotional significance to Virginia.[19]

In addition to her cover and jacket designs for Virginia's work, Vanessa provided two separate designs for the Hogarth Essays first series (1924–26), two designs for the Hogarth Essays second series (1926–28), a design for the short-lived Hogarth Stories (1927), one for the Living Poets first series (1927–32), and the cover design for the Uniform Edition of Virginia's novels (1929). Vanessa also provided the jackets for seven titles by writers other than Virginia, including one for Edward Upward's *Journey to the Border* (1938). She was responsible for more of the Press designs than any other artist.

Among the seventeen other identifiable Hogarth Press dust jacket designers, only E. McKnight Kauffer, Richard Kennedy, Trekkie Ritchie, and John Banting designed more than two jackets. The American Kauffer had established a reputation for his boldly designed posters with hand-drawn lettering for the London Underground, commissioned by Frank Pick after the First World War. As Michael Twyman has observed, Kauffer's "strong geometric designs brought the first breath of modern European art to the general public in the 1920s."[20] He had been influenced by cubism. As a member of Roger Fry's Omega Workshop, Kauffer had important Bloomsbury contacts. When he designed his first Hogarth dust jacket in 1928 for George Rylands's *Words and Poetry,* he was a well-established professional, the only such designer ever employed by Leonard Woolf. In 1930 Kauffer designed the new wolf's-head device for the Day-to-Day Pamphlet series, subsequently used by Leonard Woolf on other series and in newspaper advertisements. Kauffer also designed jackets for Leonard's *Quack, Quack!* (1935), R. M. Fox's *Smoky Crusade* (1937), and H. T. Hopkinson's *Man Below* (1939), for which he was paid four guineas. None of these designs, however, approached the power or brilliance of his posters.

As a boy at the Hogarth, Richard Kennedy amused and exasperated Leonard Woolf, built shelves that collapsed, flirted with Miss Belsher, got his accounts wrong, had trouble typing letters, traveled the books with mixed success, and designed dust jackets for C. H. B. Kitchin's popular mystery *Death of My Aunt* (1929) and for Wilfred Benson's *Dawn on Mont Blanc* (1930).

Kennedy's realistic pictorial design for Kitchin's book features the little bottle of "Le Secret de Venus" that poisoned Aunt Catherine and shows it falling across two strong verticals. His hand-drawn letters are as crisp as an architect's. Kennedy's design for Benson's book placed the book title and author's name in a blank diamond shape which cut through heavy horizontal lines of varying widths in the background. So effective and dynamic was this bold, geometric design that Leonard Woolf used variations of it for twenty-two other titles published through 1939, mostly nonfiction. Kennedy's only other pictorial jacket design was for *Adventures in Investing* (1936). Although Kennedy's jacket designs served the press for twenty-four titles, giving him the numerical edge over Vanessa Bell in this category up to 1941, he supplied only three designs.

Alice Ritchie's first novel, *The Peacemakers* (1928), was published by the Woolfs about the time she became a part-time traveler for the press. Her sister Trekkie, a Slade art student, designed the jacket for Alice's second Hogarth Press novel, *Occupied Territory* (1930), and went on to design jackets for three more of the press's novels, including John Hampson's *Saturday Night at the Greyhound* (1931) and Vita Sackville-West's *All Passion Spent* (1931). Her design for Hampson's novel was particularly effective, showing the men of the village gathering in front of the pub. Trekkie Ritchie, a talented easel painter, later married the publisher Ian Parsons and became a close friend of Leonard Woolf.

John Banting's dissolute life both horrified and intrigued Bloomsbury. As described by Richard Shone, Banting's all-night parties must have left little time for painting, and yet he produced a number of effective jacket designs for the press.[21] He was a member of the London Group of artists and was well known to the Charleston painters. Originally influenced by the cubism of Georges Braque and Juan Gris, Banting eventually explored surrealism and displayed his work in the 1936 International Surrealist Exhibition. Banting designed nine dust jackets for the Hogarth Press, beginning in 1932 with Christopher Isherwood's *Memorial* and concluding with Henry Green's *Party Going* (1939). He also provided the design for three series: the second series of the Living Poets (1933–37), the Hogarth Letters (1931–33), and the World-Makers and Shakers (1937). His designs for the Letters and World-Makers series successfully combine surrealistic elements with forceful geometric elements.

Through the designs of Vanessa Bell, McKnight Kauffer, Richard

Kennedy, Trekkie Ritchie, and John Banting, the Hogarth Press displayed a variety of styles on its dust jackets. Nevertheless, two aspects predominated—a continuation of the Omega Workshop decorative style with geometrical emphasis in the nonpictorial jackets and a painterly quality of impressionistic, suggestive, and allusive drawings for the others. Through the dust-jacket designs of Kauffer and Banting, the Hogarth Press occasionally spoke in the accents of European modernism, but it was the Postimpressionist, Charleston style of Vanessa Bell that spoke most eloquently and pervasively for the press.

Leonard Woolf, in his lifelong obsession with details, prided himself on his bookkeeping. His somewhat unorthodox methods were first questioned by the Inland Revenue, tolerated for awhile, and then, as the press business affairs grew complicated, required to be more conventional. Woolf, stubborn in matters he had worked out for himself, grudgingly adapted to more routine methods of bookkeeping. He seems not to have employed a professional accountant during the years covered by this history. Woolf kept his own books for years and then had his office managers assist with the various cash and sales ledgers. All of the important profit and loss accounts from 1917 through 1939, however, are recorded in Woolf's spidery handwriting. He kept his finger on every penny and every shilling until John Lehmann's partnership and the dislocations of the war required other hands on the books.

The Hogarth Press accounts from 1917 to 1941 and beyond spread through many volumes, several classifications, and now two locations, the special collections at the University of Sussex and at the University of Reading. Remarkably, given the war damages to Mecklenburgh Square and the subsequent move of the press to Letchworth, all records seem to have been preserved. With the recent discovery of four books, there appear to be very few gaps in the accounts.

Leonard Woolf's first account book, with the remarkable and tangled record of his subscription scheme, is preserved at the University of Sussex. I have designated it account book (Sussex). There in a bound, columnar account book with pages numbered 88 to 190 (the previous pages contained Leonard's personal accounts for 1906–12), Woolf recorded all Hogarth Press transactions from 1917 to 1924 including the initial investment in equipment and subsequent expenses, revenues, profits, and the names and addresses of all subscribers and purchasers. Thirty-six titles are accounted for: all publications from 1917 through 1923 and those of early 1924.

The account book (Sussex) begins with nineteen neat and uncluttered pages of accounts for expenditures and revenues of *Two Stories, Prelude, Critic in Judgment, Poems* (T. S. Eliot), and *Kew Gardens* before it plunges into the thicket of deposits "A" and "B." And at once there is an almost impenetrable series of entries, deletions, transfers, corrections, and cross-hatchings as Woolf struggled to stay abreast of accounts. Each subscriber A or B was entered chronologically with address, deposit, and subsequent charges until the one or two lines allowed between names had been completely written over and the subscribers's account had to be transferred to another page farther back in the book or, worse fate, to another category.

Leonard Woolf plainly misjudged the amount of space needed to record each transaction. In spite of his vaunted experience in accounting, Woolf could not have found the record keeping easy. Only a determined perfectionist who enjoyed such details could have kept the accounts straight, and obviously no one but Woolf could have worked with the system once it was established. An alphabetical listing or a card file for each subscriber might have simplified things. The wonder is that Woolf adhered to the subscription scheme as long as he did, in spite of its burden. Every shilling and every pence of each transaction is accounted for, true to Woolf's claim, but the tax inspector must have smiled at the archaic system.

The account book (Sussex) is the single most important record of the early years of the press and, in all it idiosyncrasies, a fascinating expression of Leonard Woolf's character. It must have been in the lot of papers, books, furniture, printing press, and type relocated to Monks House after the Mecklenburgh Square bombing and finally given to the University of Sussex after Leonard's death through the generosity of Mrs. Parsons, his executor.

Some of the continuing accounts from the first book, together with new titles published in 1924–25, are carried over into a second volume, also at the University of Sussex, covering the period of January 1922 to January 1926. Two other less complete account books are at Sussex; the profits and losses of 1934–36 and the annual accounts of 1936–38. All other bookkeeping volumes are in the press repository at the University of Reading.

The next most important early record after the account book (Sussex) is the continuation of Woolf's early records in what I have designated account book (Reading). This book was thought to have been destroyed in the bombing but must have been moved to Letchworth with the other press papers (*Checklist* xii). A few years ago it turned up and was sent with three other press account books to the University of Reading. Quarter-bound in red leather with seventy-nine pages numbered in pencil, the volume contains subscriber and purchaser entries for seventeen titles, fourteen of them published between 1920 and 1922 and three carried over from the second Sussex volume. There are some sales figures included through the late 1920s.

The other account books at the University of Reading complete the record of the early Hogarth Press years and contain figures on profits and losses through 1939. After the account book (Reading), the second most important of these is a record of monthly sales from 1922 to 1939, with a summary of the press profits and losses each year from 1917 through 1939. It is bound in green boards and contains sixty-six leaves. I have designated it monthly sales (Reading). It seems likely that Leonard Woolf used this book to summarize sales from his other account books and may have worked it up around 1938 in time to calculate the value of the press for John Lehmann's oncoming partnership. The entries seem made after the fact and not currently. Woolf entered the monthly sales on the first twenty-one leaves of this book starting from the front and the profit and loss accounts on thirty-eight leaves starting from the back of the book. Thus the cost-conscious Woolf worked both ends toward the middle in his own version of double-entry bookkeeping.

A third book contains authors' accounts and balance sheets between 1926 and 1934. Bound in green boards and containing ninety leaves, it too shows Woolf's front- and back-door entries. The authors' accounts from 1926–27 and 1927–28 are entered on 43 leaves starting from the front, and the balance sheets for 1926–27 through 1933–34 are entered on 43 leaves starting from the back. I have designated it authors' accounts (Reading). And the fourth account book, bound in limp purple covers, containing

160 leaves, carries notes on printing, binding, advertising, and distribution costs for books in print in 1928–29. Only 21 leaves contain entries. I have designated it printing costs (Reading).

Leonard Woolf began with the account book (Sussex), overlapped briefly with the second Sussex book, and then continued his accounts in the account book (Reading). In 1922, as he worked out of his two primary books, he began his monthly records and profit and loss accounts in monthly sales (Reading), and then in 1926 he began his authors' accounts (Reading). All of his bookkeeping became more complicated after 1926, just before the record publishing year of 1927, when he began to move into a variety of special ledgers. He maintained summary records to the end of the 1930s in the monthly sales (Reading) book, but there is a noticeable shift to the ledgers in 1926.

The Hogarth Press ledgers in the repository at the University of Reading complete the records from the middle 1920s through the late 1940s. They are of three types: sales ledgers, cash ledgers, and authors' statement ledgers. Whereas the various account books are small (approx. 5 1/2 by 7 3/4 inches) and bound in a variety of covers, the ledgers are large (8 by 17 inches), heavy, and quarter-bound in leather or full-bound in leatherlike boards. They are professional account ledgers, uniform in size, pagination, and columnar rulings.

There are sixteen sales ledgers at Reading covering the period of this history. Four volumes are indexed alphabetically by author; two volumes contain sales for Virginia Woolf's Uniform Editions; one volume carries sales for Virginia's novels and those of Vita Sackville-West, an interesting and even symbolic union; two volumes are devoted to Freud; two to poetry; one for IPL titles other than Freud; and one volume each for Hogarth essays, lectures, novels, and pamphlets. There are ten cash ledgers, for 1933–43, and fifteen authors' statement ledgers, for 1926–42. Entries in these thirty-one ledgers (and in the sixteen additional ledgers going beyond 1943) are in hands other than Leonard Woolf's. The shift to the massive ledgers in 1926 is one more indication that Woolf began to take a more professional approach to press affairs in the mid-1920s as he expanded the annual number of titles. The change also coincides with the arrival of Mrs. Cartwright as office manager in late 1925. Perhaps she deserves credit, not Leonard, for the uniformity of the press records in the ledgers from that time on.

Leonard and Virginia Woolf hand printed their first publications and then used Richard Madley, the Omega Workshops printer, for the second edition of *Kew Gardens* (1919) and Gorky's *Tolstoi* (1920). Having thus become fledgling publishers, the Woolfs increasingly engaged commercial printers to produce their books. From 1919 to 1941 the Woolfs used over thirty different printers. Some of them the Woolfs used only once or twice for specialized work, as when they contracted with Herbert Reiach of Hammersmith to reproduce the photographs of Julia Cameron in 1926 and Vanessa Bell's decorations of the third edition of *Kew Gardens* in 1927. Leonard Woolf had learned about Reiach, the printer for the *Burlington Magazine*, through Roger Fry, and turned to this experienced firm when he wanted the best reproductions. Other printers were used more frequently. The two Edinburgh firms of R. & R. Clark and Neill & Co. and the Garden City Press of Letchworth became their most frequently employed printers, with the venerable Hazell, Watson & Viney a distant fourth. Leonard Woolf contracted with R. & R. Clark for the printing of Dostoyevsky's *Stavrogin's Confession* and Virginia Woolf's first Hogarth Press novel, *Jacob's Room*, in 1922 and thus began a long and mutually rewarding relationship with the Scottish firm.

William Maxwell, the managing director, as Woolf recalled him in his autobiography, was "a Scot of the Scots . . . a dedicated printer and a first-class business man" (*Downhill* 73). When he saw the Woolfs' "strange, unorthodox venture into publishing," added Leonard, "he became personally interested in it, and he took as much trouble over printing 1,000 copies for us as he did in later times over printing 20,000." Maxwell would visit the press in Richmond when he was in London, and he kept up his personal relationship with Hogarth through its subsequent moves to Tavistock Square and Mecklenburgh Square. As a result of Maxwell's personal and professional interest in the Woolfs, R. & R. Clark printed all of Virginia's novels, all of Leonard's most important books after 1927 including *After the Deluge,* all of Vita Sackville-West's novels, and all of the psychoanalytical books of the IPL from 1924 until October 1936 when Leonard shifted to the Garden City Press. During the seventeen-year period between 1922 and 1938, R. & R. Clark printed ninety-eight titles for the Hogarth Press.

The other Scottish printer used frequently by Leonard Woolf, Neill & Co., printed a total of 101 titles during the nine years between 1925 and

1934. At the peak of the Hogarth's productivity in 1927 and 1928, Neill & Co. became the primary printer for Woolf, printing twenty or more volumes each year. Woolf began to use the Garden City Press in 1927 with one title, and then no more than three to five times a year until 1932, another peak year of press productivity, when he had it print twenty titles. From 1932 through the war years, the Garden City Press became the chief printer for Woolf, and then the only printer after the bombing of Mecklenburgh Square. In the twelve years between 1927 and 1938, it printed 130 titles for Woolf, making it the most frequently used of all the Hogarth Press printers.

As beginning publishers, the Woolfs brought out their first books whenever they had hand printed or machined sufficient copies. They tended to publish in May or July but found other times convenient as well, paying little or no attention to the traditional publishing seasons of spring and autumn. By 1924, however, Leonard Woolf began to follow the seasons, dividing his books for that year mostly between May and October–November. With the increasing numbers of titles he published each year, Woolf began to concentrate his releases in March and October. Over the years, he published more books in October by a third than in any other month, aiming for the Christmas market. He quickly learned to avoid the dead months of January and August, although like all publishers Woolf published a few titles in every month of the year. Virginia Woolf saw seven of her major books published in October, more than in any other month: *Night and Day* (1919), *Jacob's Room* (1922), *Orlando* (1928), *A Room of One's Own* (1929), *The Waves* (1931), *The Common Reader II* (1932), and *Flush* (1933). The next most active month for her was May, when three of her important books were published: *Mrs. Dalloway* (1925), *The Common Reader I* (1925), and *To the Lighthouse* (1927).

After a book had been printed and published and as it was being reviewed and advertised, it would be presented to booksellers who had to be persuaded to stock the book for their customers. This important and delicate act of salesmanship was the work of the traveler, or publisher's representative, who made the rounds of booksellers with a bag of newly published samples, "subscribing" books or taking orders for shipments. Most English publishers between the wars employed several travelers, one or more to concentrate on the London wholesale and retail booksellers and others to travel major cities and the provinces. Stanley Unwin noted that a town traveler in London in 1926 might take a week or two weeks to make his rounds.[22] Travelers were usually salaried employees who received a commission on the orders they placed.

As might be expected by the smallness of the operation, the deliberately amateur nature of it, and Leonard Woolf's caution in money matters, the Hogarth Press made do without a regular traveler until Woolf offered Alice Ritchie the position on a part-time basis in 1928. Before that the Woolfs personally traveled their books on a sporadic basis, placing a few copies of Mansfield's *Prelude* in 1917 with the booksellers Bain, W. H. Smith, Simpkin Marshall, and Birrell & Garnett but not traveling seriously in London until May 1919. For the country, they usually combined vacation trips to Cornwall and Devon with visits to local booksellers. Only occasionally, as in April 1926 or in May 1930, did the Woolfs make a planned tour of provincial booksellers.

The results were predictably discouraging. It is hard to imagine two less likely commercial travelers than Leonard and Virginia Woolf. At the best they might interest a bookseller in an order by their presence as author-publishers, but at the worst they might appear too intellectual or refined and too impatient to cultivate a prospective client. They were not natural salesmen. Virginia Woolf's letters recorded her impressions. After traveling press books down Kensington High Street in May 1926, she reported to Vanessa that the experience, especially seeing the poor and derelict street people, "almost made me vomit with hatred of the human race" (*Letters* 3:265). To Vita Sackville-West she wrote about traveling the press books in the West Country in May 1930: "We have made about £10 today, though the booksellers are for the most part rude, ignorant, and out for lunch or tea or something" (ibid., 4:163). And again to Vita from Cornwall three days later, she noted that "our sales have diminished steadily. The booksellers are often very rude and L. almost loses his temper" (ibid., 165).

A more congenial and successful traveler may have been young Richard Kennedy who was sent out by Leonard Woolf at the tender age of seventeen or eighteen to travel the provinces. His amusing account traces his misadventures through Nottingham, Manchester, Liverpool, Edinburgh, Glasgow, Sheffield, and back to London in 1928, with the crowning achievement of an order for £100 worth of books (including *Stavrogin's Confession*) from a Sheffield librarian.[23] For Leonard Woolf to have sent such a green youth on an errand which most publishers took very seriously probably reflected his skepticism about traveling books, as well as his avuncular liking of Kennedy.

Then, in the same year, Leonard Woolf engaged Alice Ritchie, the Newnham College graduate and budding novelist, to be the press's first salaried traveler on a part-time basis. She was, recalled Woolf, "the first woman to travel for a publisher and some booksellers did not like the innovation" (*Downhill* 169). He later described her as "a good, if unconventional, commercial traveller . . . [who] on the whole . . . enjoyed taking the Hogarth Press books round the booksellers and getting orders from them" (*Journey* 173). Not until John Lehmann's arrival in 1938, however, twenty-one years after beginning the press, did Leonard Woolf employ a full-time salaried traveler, Barbara Hepworth.

When Leonard and Virginia Woolf first went the rounds to a few booksellers in 1918 with Katherine Mansfield's *Prelude* and then more systematically traveled the London bookshops a year later, they began to establish commercial relations with the men who would sell their books. One of the earliest was James Bain of King William Street, who became an A subscriber and an enthusiastic supporter of their endeavors. Then there was the "great" Mr. Wilson of Bumpus, as Leonard called him, and Lamley of South Kensington (*Downhill* 76). Within a few years the Woolfs were distributing their books to all the major London booksellers and book clubs and to a number of provincial bookshops, such as Goulden & Curry in Tunbridge Wells and the Reigate Bookshop. On the evidence of William Plomer's letters from South Africa in 1924 and Edmund Blunden's from Tokyo in 1925, the press publications had reached bookstores in distant overseas locations by the mid-1920s. Sylvia Beach's Paris bookshop Shakespeare and Company seems to have stocked selected Hogarth Press books from at least 1925 on,[24] and she may have sold copies earlier and circulated loan copies of press books. By 1929 the Woolfs had contracted with an agent in Canada (probably Longmans, Green & Co.) to distribute the press books, and by 1936 in the *Reference Catalogue of Current Literature* they were listing agents in Australia and New Zealand (Thomas Lothian) and in South Africa (Miss Radford of Modern Books).

The first contractual arrangement with an overseas publisher was with Harcourt Brace in 1921 for the American edition of Virginia Woolf's *Monday or Tuesday*. Gerald Duckworth had used George Doran for the American editions in 1920 of Virginia's first two novels, *The Voyage Out* (1915) and *Night and Day* (1919). The Woolfs might have followed this precedent, but they chose Harcourt Brace instead, possibly to sever all ties with Duckworth or perhaps because of the example of Maynard Keynes. In 1920 Keynes's English publisher, Macmillan, had turned to Harcourt Brace to publish the American edition of *The Economic Consequences of the Peace* (1919), and they retained Harcourt Brace for subsequent books. The choice by the Woolfs proved a happy one, however they arrived at it, and over the years they established personal relationships with Donald Brace, who visited England regularly. Woolf used other American publishers on occasion, when translation rights were involved (W. W. Norton published the translations of Rilke and Freud) or when Harcourt Brace declined a book. Leonard Woolf always offered the press wares to Donald Brace first. In an exchange of letters in 1929 with Livia Schmitz-Svevo over the publication of Italo Svevo's *The Hoax,* Woolf noted that he considered Harcourt Brace the best American publisher (HP 479). To this day, Harcourt Brace Jovanovich publishes most of the Hogarth Press books in America, seventy years of a successful publishing arrangement.

CHAPTER ELEVEN

★

Conclusion

A business is a work of art and the man running it—or should I not rather say making it?—is like a painter at work on a picture."[1] Geoffrey Faber, the publisher, was speaking about the business of publishing in the 1930s. The businessman-artist, Faber went on to say, "must stand back to see what is right or wrong with it. He cannot do that if he is overwhelmed with details." Was Leonard Woolf an artist at an easel, the Hogarth Press a painting in the making? Did he, with Virginia's help, produce a great artwork, or did he overwhelm himself with details and botch it? Can Faber's analogy reasonably be applied to the Hogarth Press? And how does one evaluate the success or importance of a publisher?

From one point of view, the Hogarth Press was a business and might be measured in conventional business terms of productivity, diversification, growth, and profit and loss. Yet books, as Leonard Woolf, Geoffrey Faber, Stanley Unwin, Michael Joseph, and generations of publishers have insisted, are not fairly to be compared to consumer goods. From that point of view, the Hogarth Press produced works of literary art or documents with social and historical importance and might be measured by the significance of those works. Yet canons of the great, standards of taste and relevance, are social constructs with built-in political and gender biases, inevitably changing with time. Perspective is everything, yet perilous.

Looking back in 1968, Leonard Woolf was convinced that the Hogarth Press had been a successful venture and he a good businessman because, among other things, he had determined to limit the size of his operations. He had resisted John Lehmann's "siren song about expansion" and so avoided irresponsible growth that might have led either to "the Scylla of the take-over" by a gigantic company or to "the Charybdis of bankruptcy" (*Journey* 126). A shrewd Odysseus with wax in his ears, Leonard had sailed the press safely through the straits. In contrast, the entrepreneurial John Lehmann thought that Leonard's "unalterably tight attitude toward money," his obstinacy and argumentative temperament, his authoritarian attitude toward his managers drove away talented assistants, lost promising authors, and led to "mean production and printing" and "primitive promotion and travelling." Given the helm, Lehmann probably thought he could have sailed the ship faster, that he could have expanded the press, increased profits, and improved the quality of the publications. Woolf came to think that Lehmann had no business sense, and Lehmann that Woolf had "no flair in such matters as literary and artistic taste."[2] Both were partly right; both overstated their case.

John Lehmann unquestionably had flair and excellent timing in his literary judgments, as his record with the Hogarth Press in 1931–32 and again in 1938–41 proved. His *New Writing*, in its several forms and under a variety of titles, was one of the most important and innovative publications in the 1930s and early 1940s. Yet when on his own as a publisher from 1946 to 1952, his firm, which bore his own name, failed to sustain a profit and was closed down by the controlling interests.[3] Leonard and Virginia Woolf as publishers sustained a profit, but sometimes released works of inferior quality by most canons of taste, and except for Leonard's sponsorship of publications on political, economic, or social topics, did little to seek out and develop promising writers and their works.

Leonard and Virginia Woolf began the Hogarth Press as a handprinting hobby, not to make money but also not to drain their meager resources. Leonard's subscription scheme and his eccentric and obsessive accounting methods meant from the first that the press was solvent, no mean achievement in itself. Gradually he and Virginia expanded operations, took limited risks, earned greater profits. They were lucky with Virginia's growing commercial success and with that of Freud and Sackville-West, the consistent money-makers. Leonard and Virginia came to respect the advantages of the greater income the press brought them, but Leonard as a publisher was never driven by the profit motive. He seems to have been content to cover costs, pay his assistants, and earn a modest return for his efforts. Virginia, in a 1928 diary entry, considered the "rather hostile & cautious greed" of the editor Dorothy Todd, like that of Gerald Duckworth, and thought "this money-grubbing way is not attractive" (*Diary* 3:176). She and Leonard were not concerned with making money. "L. never makes a penny; I mean—tries to," she wrote, and then concluded wistfully, "& I could almost wish we were more lavish in our ways."

Within his self-imposed limits and by his own yardstick, Leonard Woolf's management of the Hogarth Press as a business must be considered successful. His record of annual profits and losses supports his claims. From 1917 through 1938, Leonard Woolf's accounts show profits for every year, although some were so slight (£5 to £13) as to be negligible. (See Appendix B for the complete record.) Not until 1925, when Woolf expanded to twenty-eight titles, did the press earn a profit of over £70, and not until 1928 with thirty-six titles and a small backlist did the net profit reach £380. The biggest years were 1930, 1931, and 1932 when gross profits on thirty or more titles totaled over £3,000 and net profits totaled around £2,000. John Lehmann's presence from January 1931 to August 1932 no doubt affected these figures. Another big year was 1937, when only twenty new titles and a backlist produced a gross profit of over £4,000 and a net profit of over £2,400, both figures the highest in press history between 1917 and 1941. It was the year of Virginia Woolf's best-seller *The Years*.

In looking at these profit and loss figures and judging the commercial success of the Hogarth Press, it is well to remember how important a backlist is to a publisher. Michael Joseph wrote that a successful publisher needs "capital, time, sound judgment and good luck" and at least five years to begin to build a backlist of titles that go on selling year after year.[4] With such books, the production costs are reduced to a minimum and little if anything need be spent on promotion and advertising. Leonard Woolf was lucky in 1924 to inherit with the IPL publications a classic backlist book like J. C. Flugel's *Psycho-Analytic Study of the Family* (1921). It sold nearly 500 copies a year for over thirteen years. But it took Woolf and the press longer than Michael Joseph's standard five years to develop any sort of backlist because of the early years of hand printing. Only in 1922 with Virginia Woolf's *Jacob's Room* and the Russian translations can the five-year clock be said to have started. By 1927 and 1928, in addition to expanded and diversified offerings, the press could begin to benefit from its backlist, and the yearly account shows it. Obviously, Virginia Woolf's novels, first in original form and then in the Uniform Editions begun in 1929, were the most important and profitable part of the press backlist. Freud's works and the popular novels of Vita Sackville-West and William Plomer together with the more successful pamphlet series provided additional backlist profits with low production costs.

The good years of the press for profits were those when the backlist provided a steady base and one or more new titles took off in a shower of pounds and shillings. In 1925, for example, the press published the third and fourth volumes of Freud's *Collected Papers,* Virginia Woolf's *Mrs. Dalloway,* and the first *Common Reader.* In 1927 it was Woolf's *To the Lighthouse* and Freud's *The Ego and the Id,* in 1928 Woolf's *Orlando* and Freud's *Future of an Illusion,* in 1930 Sackville-West's *Edwardians* and Freud's *Civilization and Its Discontents,* in 1931 Sackville-West's *All Passion Spent* and Woolf's *Waves,* in 1932 Sackville-West's *Family History* and Plomer's *Case Is Altered,* and in 1937 Woolf's *Years.*

If the commercial success of the Hogarth Press is measured with John Lehmann's yardstick, instead of Leonard Woolf's, then Lehmann's point about growth is well taken. Expansion in the late 1920s and early 1930s led to improved profits, and in years of fewer titles, only a few best-sellers with a strong backlist kept profits from dwindling. None of the publishing houses like Jonathan Cape, Chatto & Windus, Bodley Head, Faber & Faber, or Gollancz, to name a few compatible with Hogarth, could have survived on such limited production or such small profits. Nor would they have tolerated for long the Hogarth's spartan, somewhat shabby offices and limited staff. Expansion and development under more experienced professional guidance could have made the Hogarth Press a more profitable enterprise, but the Woolfs would have hated it, and Lehmann could not have managed it alone.

Leonard Woolf did at times become overwhelmed with details, what Geoffrey Faber had warned against, and so lost the big picture. But John Lehmann in his energetic development of talent was sometimes scornful of crucial details, of expenses and profit margins, and might have made Hogarth vulnerable to takeover bids by the larger publishers. The records of the Hogarth Press suggest that when Lehmann and Woolf worked well together, Woolf holding on to Lehmann's coattails and watching the account books and Lehmann stirring up the dust with bold new enterprises, the Hogarth Press prospered financially and artistically. Unfortunately, the early years of the Woolf-Lehmann partnership, when they worked most harmoniously together, were marred by the terrible destruction and dislocation of the war and by Virginia Woolf's suicide. The history of the Hogarth Press into the 1940s might otherwise have been different than it was.

Viewed overall as a business, therefore, the Hogarth Press was as successful as Leonard Woolf wanted it to be. It had undeveloped potential. But had it become commercially as successful as its peers and competitors, the Hogarth Press might have become an institution similar to all the others, and so without its quirky and idiosyncratic qualities that make it interesting. Leonard and Virginia Woolf, with John Lehmann, put their personal stamp on the press, and they were remarkable people.

If the business side of the Hogarth Press operation is put aside, and the literary or historical aspect of the press is considered, a different sort of achievement can be measured. Here the slippery problem of quality, of canon, of changing tastes makes the evaluation of a publisher's list especially risky. Nevertheless, Virginia Woolf's nine major works of fiction and nonfiction, T. S. Eliot's two volumes of poetry, translations of Sigmund Freud's eight best-known books, and the translations of Rilke's poetry in five volumes would make the Hogarth Press an important publisher even if it had published nothing else.

If these twenty-four publications can reasonably be counted among the best books published by the Hogarth Press, what others can be considered either important to the times or of lasting artistic or intellectual significance? From Gorky's *Tolstoi* (1920) in the early years, to Christopher Isherwood's *Goodbye to Berlin* (1939), Henry Green's *Party Going* (1939), and E. M. Forster's *What I Believe* (1939) in the later years, another twenty-six or so titles of distinction can be added to those of Woolf, Eliot, Freud, and Rilke. The resulting fifty-odd volumes from the Hogarth list of 474 titles in all subjects published between 1917 and 1941 indicate the impressive achievement of the press. Not many larger presses can match the success rate of the Hogarth. It is worth mentioning that three Hogarth authors later won the Nobel Prize in literature (Ivan Bunin, T. S. Eliot, and Bertrand Russell), three won the Nobel Prize for peace (Viscount Cecil, Fridtjof Nansen, and Philip Noel-Baker), and one (John Maynard Keynes) would certainly have won a Nobel Prize in economics had he not died in 1945, twenty-four years before the prize was established. The Woolfs and their authors kept good company.

If indeed the Hogarth Press list of books and pamphlets contributed importantly to the literary and intellectual life of England between the wars, how important was the press to Bloomsbury and to the Woolfs in particular? For regular and fringe members of Bloomsbury, the answer must be qualified. At the beginning, Bloomsbury members cast an amused and tolerant glance at the ink-stained endeavors of the Woolfs. As the press grew into a small publishing house and broadened into the Russian translations and Freud, the group of relatives and friends, central or peripheral, increasingly offered their fiction, poetry, and essays to the Woolfs. The established writers like Forster, Keynes, Fry, and Strachey were already under contract to larger publishers by the time the Hogarth Press was sturdy enough to publish book-length manuscripts, and so the major Bloomsbury talents could turn to the press only for short pieces not easily published elsewhere. The press had little effect on their careers.

For the less talented or less productive, the Cambridge poet-novelist dons, for instance, the press provided encouragement and publication for work of marginal quality. For the two talented women novelists with Cambridge-Bloomsbury connections, F. M. Mayer and Julia Strachey, however, the press served as publisher for their best books. And for such peripheral members of Bloomsbury as T. S. Eliot, William Plomer, and Edwin Muir, the press played a crucial role in publishing their early poetry and fiction and gaining for them their first recognition as writers of stature.

Aside from the opportunities for publication offered by the press to Bloomsbury and its friends, it can be argued that there was a less tangible but not insignificant contribution to the group reputation made by the Hogarth Press. Bloomsbury's publishing house presented a sometimes critical or hostile public with the evidence of a successful business enterprise, worldly and far-reaching in its interests. Its largely conservative and traditional literary offerings, with the exception of T. S. Eliot's poems and

Virginia Woolf's fiction, and the seriousness of its publications in nonliterary fields offered skeptics another face of Bloomsbury in contrast to the preciously aesthetic, seemingly frivolous, or self-admiring one seen by eyes hostile to the group. By bringing Freudian psychoanalysis, socialist and labor politics, modern Russian, German, and Italian literature in translation, neo-Georgian poetry, modernist fiction and literary criticism, and the new poetry of the 1930s all together under one imprint in twenty-four years, the Woolfs and their press transcended the narrow concerns of a privileged and exclusive coterie. Especially through its pamphlet series of lectures and essays, Hogarth became the educational arm of Bloomsbury. The press, its authors, and its publications thus moved Bloomsbury to a more central position in English intellectual and political life than it had usually been accorded.

The particular importance of the press to Virginia and Leonard Woolf was substantial. From the initial frustrations and delights of hand printing—therapeutic, instructional, creative—to the more complex and time-consuming activities of publishing—reading manuscripts, preparing mailings, traveling books, interviewing authors, interacting with staff and managers—the Hogarth Press provided Virginia Woolf with physical, emotional, and mental stimulation that must have been as valuable to her as a writer as it was sometimes exhausting to her physically. In the same way that involvement in the activities of the Abbey Theatre did for W. B. Yeats, or Faber & Faber for T. S. Eliot, the press objectified Virginia Woolf's world, allowing her to keep one hand on the vigorous pulse of daily life in the basement rooms of Tavistock Square. The press kept Virginia in touch with young writers, new movements, women's affairs, politics. It strengthened the bond with her sister Vanessa by bringing Virginia's verbal art together with Vanessa's visual art in the texts, illustrations, and dust jackets of the sisters' joint press publications.

Above all, the Hogarth Press gave Virginia Woolf the inestimable prize of editorial freedom to do what she wished as a writer without the real or imagined criticism of a publisher's reader. She need never feel an unsympathetic or repressive male editor looking over her shoulder. She could experiment boldly, remaking the form and herself each time she shaped a new fiction, responsible only to herself as writer-editor-publisher. Virginia Woolf sounded that note of freedom often, but her diary entry of September 22, 1925, can serve as example. She saw that her handwriting was deteriorating from overuse in her journalism and editing, she wrote. "Yet what I owe the Hogarth Press is barely paid by the whole of my handwriting" (*Diary* 3:42). To be battened down by donnish editors like H. A. L. Fisher, for whom she had just refused to write, made her "blood run cold." She was, she added triumphantly, "the only woman in England free to write what I like." The press, beyond doubt, had given Virginia Woolf a room of her own.

For Leonard Woolf, the creation, development, and management of the press became so essential and intertwined with his life that one can't imagine him without it. All of Leonard's energy, his interests in widely diverse fields, his deep-felt needs to manage and to educate, his passion for writing and for politics, all came into focus through the press. Originally, Leonard had conceived of the press as a support and stimulus more important to Virginia than to him. As it developed and brought the two of them together in a unique collaboration of husband and wife, of themselves as writers, coeditors and business partners, the press quickly assumed a centrality in Leonard's life that he could never seriously consider abandoning. Virginia and Leonard might chafe under the burdens of the press, and Virginia might propose ending them, but Leonard always found a way to continue the operation.

For the work-compulsive Leonard Woolf, the demands of the press became essential to his well-being. If he was at times the severe, perfectionist guardian of the press, he could also be the witty, warm, friendly, and courteous editor who encouraged a wide circle of contributors to the press as well as to the *Nation and Athenaeum* and the *Political Quarterly.* Leonard found in the multifarious world of journalism, editing, and publishing the perfect arena for his talents. The press activities, even shared uncomfortably with John Lehmann, would sustain Leonard after the traumatic loss of Virginia. Only when the press was safely in the custodial care of Ian Parsons and Chatto & Windus after the breakup of the partnership could Leonard begin to relax into the garrulous pleasures of old age—travel, conversation, autobiography.

Thinking back over the twenty-three years since the dissolution of his partnership with Lehmann, Leonard Woolf in the last volume of his autobiography saw that the Hogarth Press under new management had "pursued the even tenor of its ways" even though he could "no longer go out on the high seas on the lookout for adventure and the unrecognized genius" (*Journey* 122). Odysseus was home from the seas, Scylla, Charybdis, and the Sirens far behind him. He believed that with his death, "the Hogarth Press [would] almost certainly also die as an entity," and although he would have liked to live forever, his anticipated annihilation left him with no interest in the "little odds and ends" of him—his books, his press, his garden—that might exist for a few years after his death (ibid., 123).

As to whether the creation and development of a publishing business out of nothing, as he and Virginia had done in 1917, would be possible today, Leonard typically countered the naysayers by maintaining that the advantages of talent and friends might occur again. It was not impossible to imagine a circle of young and gifted writers waiting to be published and an intellectual businessman "determined to limit his operations" (*Journey* 126). And so, both skeptic and optimist that he was, Leonard Woolf liked to think that it all might happen again. Yet the doubts persist as one looks back over the twenty-four years at the 474 titles published with such loving labor and frugality by Leonard and Virginia Woolf and at the conjunction of rare talent, time, personal necessity, and opportunity that resulted in the flourishing of the Hogarth Press from 1917 to 1941.

Leonard concluded his autobiography by quoting his favorite passage from Montaigne—"It is not the arrival, it is the journey which matters." Apt for Leonard and Virginia Woolf, apt for the Hogarth Press, the quotation rightly praises process and becoming, not completion or termination. Yet the twenty-four-year journey of the Hogarth Press, complete and seen in its entirety, seems one that may never be repeated. The arrival did matter.

APPENDIXES
NOTES
BIBLIOGRAPHY
INDEX

APPENDIX A.
Number of Hogarth Press volumes published annually by category

Year	Fiction	Poetry	Trans.	IPL	Politics & Society	Peace & Disarm.	Biog. & Letters	Lit. Crit.	Women	Education	Misc. Art & Travel	Total
1917	1											1
1918	1											1
1919	2	2										4
1920	2	1	1									4
1921	2	2	1								1	6
1922	1	2	3	2*								6
1923	1	4	3	1*			1				2	11
1924	3	4	1	1*&1	1		2	2			2	16
1925	2	9		2	5		3	6	1			28
1926	4	7			5	1	1	8			4	30
1927	9	5	2	3	9	2	1	3			4	38
1928	2	7		2	3	4	2	10	1	1	4	36
1929	6	8	2		1	3		5	2	1	2	30
1930	4	7	2	3	5	1	2	2			3	29

Year												Total
1931	7	8	2	2	8	1		2	2	1	2	35
1932	6	5		3	8	2		6		2	4	36
1933	2	2	2	1	8		2				3	20
1934	5	1	2	1	6	1	1	1		1	2	21
1935	2	3	2	1	8		3	1		2	2	24
1936	3	2	3	2	6	2	2	1	1		1	23
1937	2	1		4	2		7	1		1	2	20
1938	3	2	1	1	5		2	1			1	16
1939	3	3	1	3	3			2		2	4	21
1940	2	3			1	2					2	10
1941	1	4	1		2							8
Total	76	92	29	29	86	17	31	51	7	11	45	474
% of Total	16%	19.4%	6.1%	6.1%	18.1%	3.6%	6.5%	10.8%	1.5%	2.3%	9.5%	100%

Note: The volume count is by year of actual publication, not by date on title page where this is in error. The count does not include volumes published privately and not for sale, nor does it include periodicals.

*These four volumes of the IPL (International Psycho-Analytical Library) were issued with the Hogarth Press imprint but were not published by the press, and therefore are not included in volume counts.

APPENDIX B.
Profit and loss of all Hogarth Press volumes, 1917–38

Years	Vols. pub.	Gross profit	Losses & salaries	Net profit	Bonuses	Final profit
1917–18	2	13. 8. 8		13. 8. 8		13. 8.8
1919	4	18. 7. 7	5. 3. 5	13.14. 2		13.14.2
1920	4	127. 0. 5	58. 1. 1	68.19. 4		68.19.4
1921	6	158.14. 3	133. 8. 9	25. 5. 6		25. 5.6
1922	6	127. 5. 0	106.12. 5	20.12. 7	10. 6. 3	10. 6.4
1923	11	203.15.10	193. 8. 2	10. 7. 8	5. 0. 0	5. 7.8
1924	16	262.16. 7	257. 2. 8	5.13.11	2.16.11	3.17.0
1925	28	589.19. 1½	443.16.10	146. 2. 3½	73. 1. 2	73. 1.1½
1926	30	723.14. 7	669.16. 4½	53.18. 2½	26.19. 1½	26.19.1
1927	38	1,149. 5. 9	1,014.17. 9	134. 8. 0	70. 6. 0	64. 2.0
1928	36	1,402.16. 3½	947. 0. 3½	455.16. 0	75. 0. 0	380.16.0
1929	30	2,030. 2.10½	1,379. 8. 2½	650.14. 8	70. 0. 0	580.14.8
1930	29	3,857. 5. 9½	1,424. 1. 7	2,433. 4. 2½	60. 0. 0	2,373. 4.2½
1931	35	3,786. 2. 6	1,400.17. 1½	2,385. 5. 4½	176. 5. 3	2,209. 0.1½
1932	36	3,672.12.11	1,800.16. 6	1,826.16. 5	133.12. 4	1,693. 4.1
1933	20	2,756.12. 6	1,766.17. 3½	989.15. 2½	60. 0. 0	929.15.2½
1934	21	2,115.15. 0	1,554. 2. 0	561.13. 0	45. 0. 0	516.13.0
1935	24	2,118. 1. 6	1,464.14. 4	653. 7. 2	55. 0. 0	598. 7.2
1936	23	1,783.15.10	1,685.10.10	98. 5. 0	14. 0. 0	84. 5.0
1937	20	4,397. 6. 2	1,634. 7. 9	2,562.18. 5	120. 0. 0	2,442.18.5
1938	16	2,632. 8. 7½	1,891. 1. 1½	741. 7. 7	6. 0. 0	35. 7.7
					700. 0. 0*	

Source: Monthly sales (Reading).
*Director's salary.

APPENDIX C.
Yearly sales of IPL volumes, 1926–34

	1926	1927	1928	1929	1930	1931	1932	1933	1934
*1. J. J. Putnam *Addresses on P-A* (1921)		No data							
*2. Sandor Ferenczi *P-A and War Neuroses* (1921)		No data							
*3. J. C. Flugel *P-A Study of the Family* (1921)	133	721	1,001	1,536	1,919	2,532	3,001	3,234	3,644
†4. Freud *Beyond Pleasure Principle* (1922) 134 pp. 7s.6d		No data							681
†5. Ernest Jones *Essays in Applied P-A* (1923) 454 pp. 18s.		No data					298	325	359
†6. Freud *Group Psy. & Anal. of the Ego* (1922) 134 pp. 7s.d.		No data							703
†7. Freud *Collected Papers 1* (1924) 359 pp. 21s.	436	520	582	649	711	787	859	925	1,006

APPENDIX C.
(*continued*)

	1926	1927	1928	1929	1930	1931	1932	1933	1934
8. Freud *Collected Papers 2* (1924) 404 pp. 21s.	428	528	599	676	737	819	895	977	1,061
9. Freud *Collected Papers 3* (1925) 607 pp. 30s.	405	492	542	632	695	775	851	941	1,023
10. Freud *Collected Papers 4* (1925) 508 pp. 21s.	375	459	526	600	662	739	813	839	964
11. Sandor Ferenczi *Contrib. to Theory and Tech. of P-A* (1927) 473 pp. 28s.		312	353	383	396	411	442	470	493
12. Freud *Ego and Id* (1927) 88 pp. 6s.		504	664	719	877	980	1,081	1,118	1,305
13. Karl Abraham *Selected Papers* (1927) 527 pp. 30s.			192	246	272	304	354	388	415

14. John Rickman *Index Psychoanalyticus* (1928) 276 pp. 18s.	138	194	213	224	244	251	261
15. Freud *Future of an Illusion* (1928) 98 pp. 6s.	801	959	1,069	1,154	1,236	1,313	1,410
16. Roger Money-Kyrle *Meaning of Sacrifice* (1930) 273 pp. 18s.			92	128	156	173	178
17. Freud *Civilization & Its Discontents* (1930) 144 pp. 8s.6d.			783	964	1,048	1,132	1,230
18. J. C. Flugel *Psychology of Clothes* (1930) 257 pp. 21s.			185	438	512	580	629
19. Theodore Reik *Ritual P-A Studies* (1931) 367 pp. 21s.				108	128	142	158
20. Ernest Jones *On the Nightmare* (1931) 374 pp. 21s.				116	195	220	239

APPENDIX C.
(continued)

	1926	1927	1928	1929	1930	1931	1932	1933	1934
21. René Laforgue *Defeat of Baudelaire* (1932) 192 pp. 10s.6d.							113	128	132
22. Melanie Klein *P-A of Children* (1932) 393 pp. 18s.							199	356	468
23. Helen Deutsch *P-A of the Neuroses* (1932) 237 pp. 10s.6d.							110	209	240
24. Freud *New Intro Lectures* (1933) 240 pp. 10s.6d.								974‡	No data
25. Géza Róheim *Riddle of Sphinx* (1934) 302 pp. 18s.									110

Source: Monthly sales (Reading).

*Not published by the Hogarth Press but distributed as booklist books when the press took over the series in 1924.
†Issued with the Hogarth Press imprint but not published by the press.
‡Data for first six months only.

APPENDIX D.
Profit and Loss of IPL volumes, 1927–37

1–6. Putnam, Ferenczi, Flugel, Freud, Jones, Freud (1921–23)	£1,572. 6.11
7–10. Freud, *Collected Papers* 1–4 (1924–25)	1,744. 1. 2
11. Ferenczi, *Contributions to Theory & Technique of P-A* (1927)	156.19. 0
12. Freud, *Ego and Id* (1927)	59. 7. 6
13. Abraham, *Selected Papers* (1927)	147. 0. 7
14. Rickman, *Index Psychoanalyticus* (1928)	26.13.11
15. Freud, *Future of an Illusion* (1928)	155. 6. 6
16. Money-Kyrle, *Meaning of Sacrifice* (1930)	13. 0. 4
17. Freud, *Civilization and Its Discontents* (1930)	265. 3. 8
18. Flugel, *Psychology of Clothes* (1930)	228. 3. 1
19. Reik, *Ritual P-A Studies* (1931)	14.17. 1
20. Jones, *On the Nightmare* (1931)	27. 6. 4
21. Laforgue, *Defeat of Baudelaire* (1932)	− 33. 4. 2
22. Klein, *P-A of Children* (1932)	105.14. 4
23. Deutsch, *P-A of the Neuroses* (1932)	4.11. 2
24. Freud, *New Introductory Lectures* (1933)	177. 7. 4
25. Róheim, *Riddle of the Sphinx* (1934)	No data
26. Freud, *Autobiographical Study* (1935)	36. 3. 1
27. Reik, *Unknown Murderer* (1936)	16.12. 1
28. Freud, *Inhibitions, Symptoms, and Anxiety* (1936)	No data
29. Sharpe, *Dream Analysis* (1937)	9.13.11
Total profit	£4,727. 3.10

Source: Monthly sales (Reading).

NOTES

1. THE HANDPRESS

1. For details, see Woolmer's *Checklist.* I have differed from Woolmer by counting a book only in the year of actual publication, not the year indicated on the title page. For Woolmer's method, see ibid., xiii. For this count I have excluded the *Poems by C. N. Sidney Woolf* (1918) and other such books printed privately and not for sale.

2. John Lehmann, *Thrown to the Woolfs* (New York, 1979), 33.

3. See Roderick Cave, *The Private Press,* 2d rev. ed. (New York, 1983), 92–98.

4. George Spater, "The Monk's House Library," *Virginia Woolf Quarterly* 1 (1973): 64.

5. As described in George Holleyman, *A Catalogue of Books Taken from the Library of Leonard and Virginia Woolf* (Brighton, 1975), section 7.

6. Leslie Stephen, as quoted by Virginia Woolf in "Leslie Stephen," *Collected Essays,* 4 vols. (London, 1966–67), 4:80.

7. *Letters* 1:4. The set is in the Washington State University Library with other volumes from the Woolfs' library. This would be the second edition in ten volumes (1839) of the original seven-volume edition (1837–38).

8. *Sowing,* 202, and *Growing,* 12. There were actually seventy volumes in the set. See George Spater and Ian Parsons, *A Marriage of True Minds: An Intimate Portrait of Leonard and Virginia Woolf* (New York, 1977), 51.

9. Spater, "The Monk's House Library," 61.

10. Quentin Bell, "The Omega Revisited," *Listener* 71 (Jan. 30, 1964): 201.

11. Denys Sutton, Introduction to *Letters of Roger Fry,* 2 vols. (New York, 1972), 1:51.

12. I am indebted to the late Mr. George Spater for the opportunity to view the books in his private collection.

13. For a discussion of the Central School and other trade schools, see Cave, *Private Press,* 303–4.

14. Anthony Powell, *Messengers of Day* (New York, 1978), 62.

15. Leonard Woolf to Prof. Majl Ewing, July 13, 1957, LWP.

16. See reproduction in *Letters* 2:153.

17. *Beginning,* 237. Earlier in *Beginning* (p. 54) he recorded a profit of £6.7 in "the first year." The later figure of £7.1 net profit is also correct because it includes revenues through July 1919. For verification, see ABS, 94.

18. Lytton Strachey to Leonard Woolf, July 17, 1917, MHP.

19. For a reproduction of the print, see Spater and Parsons, *Marriage of True Minds,* 98.

20. William Rothenstein to Leonard Woolf, n.d., MHP.

21. For a complete list of hand-printed books, see *Checklist,* 221–22.

22. For a long, and moving account of what Mansfield meant to Virginia Woolf, see *Diary* 2:225–27.

23. Katherine Mansfield, *The Collected Letters of Katherine Mansfield,* ed. Vincent O'Sullivan and Margaret Scott, 2 vols. (Oxford, 1984), 1:324.

24. Ibid., 1:330–31.

25. *Checklist,* 5, lists four copies, but not the copy I saw in the late George Spater's collection.

26. Philip Woolf in the dedication page, as reprinted in Spater and Parsons, *Marriage of True Minds,* 102.

27. Mansfield, *Collected Letters,* 2:169.

28. Ibid., 203, 200.

29. Ruth Mantz, *A Critical Bibliography of Katherine Mansfield* (London, 1931; rpt. New York, 1968), 34.

30. Jack P. Dalton, "The Text of *Ulysses,*" in *New Light on Joyce from the Dublin Symposium,* ed. Fritz Senn (Bloomington, Ind., 1972), 108–9.

31. Clive Bell, "How Pleasant to Know Mr. Eliot," in *T. S. Eliot: A Symposium,* comp. Richard March and Tambimuttu (London, 1965), 15; *Beginning,* 242.

32. Leonard Woolf, *Letters of Leonard Woolf,* ed. Frederic Spotts (New York, 1989), 279.

33. T. S. Eliot to Virginia Woolf, Jan. 29, 1919, MHP; *Diary* 1:257.

34. Donald Gallup, *T. S. Eliot: A Bibliography,* rev. ed. (New York, 1969), 25.

35. *Checklist,* 5. For Fry's marbled papers, see *Diary* 1:269 and *Letters* 2:355. Eliot liked both the original patterned paper and the blue-black paper, as he wrote to Virginia Woolf; see T. S. Eliot, *The Letters of T. S. Eliot,* vol. 1, ed. Valerie Eliot (New York, 1988), 278.

36. Francis Meynell, *My Lives* (London, 1971), 155, 161.

37. I am indebted to Librarian Leila Leudeking for information on the Woolfs' collection in the Washington State University Library.

38. See Hugh Ford, *Published in Paris: American and British Writers, Printers, and Publishers in Paris, 1920–1939* (New York, 1975).

39. Nancy Cunard as quoted in Hugh Ford, ed., *Nancy Cunard: Brave Poet, Indomitable Rebel, 1896–1965* (Philadelphia, 1968), 69. For a detailed account of her press, see Nancy Cunard's *These Were the Hours: Memories of My Hours Press, Réanville and Paris, 1928–1931* (Carbondale, Ill., 1969).

40. Leonard Woolf to J. R. Windle, May 28, 1968, LWP.

41. James Moran, "The Seizin Press of Laura Riding and Robert Graves," *Black Art* 2 (1963): 34–38; Ford, *Published in Paris,* 385–403.

2. BEGINNINGS, 1917–23

1. See Louise De Salvo's *Virginia Woolf: The Impact of Childhood Sexual Abuse on her Life and Work* (Boston, 1989).

2. Powell, *Messengers of Day,* 5.

3. ABS, 113–20. Innumerable entries, cancellations, and transfers make accuracy difficult.

4. P. N. Furbank, *E. M. Forster: A Life,* 2 vols. (New York, 1978), 2:172.

5. See B. J. Kirkpatrick, *A Bibliography of E. M. Forster* (London: 1965), 108–9.

6. ABS, 143–44. Note that Leonard Woolf made an error in arithmetic between the subtotals for June 8 and June 16, 1921, recording 178 volumes sold to date when the actual figure was 188. Consequently his totals are off by ten volumes throughout, and his final count for April 1922 of 493 should be 503 volumes.

7. ABS, 152. The calculation of profit is mine based on Leonard Woolf's figures.

8. ABR shows a total of 726 copies sold between publication on March 8, 1921, and Jan. 16, 1926.

9. *Diary* 2:119; *Letters* 3:320.

10. For details of the actual camp, see *Growing,* 86–98. Woolf's story scales down the camp's size.

11. Spater and Parsons, *Marriage of True Minds,* 94.

12. E. M. Forster, *Selected Letters of E. M. Forster,* ed. Mary Lago and P. N. Furbank, 2 vols. (Cambridge, Mass., 1983), 1:135.

13. *Diary* 2:213–15; *Downhill,* 79.

14. James Whitall, *English Years* (New York, 1935), 279–81.

15. Dorothy Wellesley, *Far Have I Travelled* (London, 1952), 153.

16. *Letters of Eliot* 1:294.

17. Gallup, *Bibliography of Eliot,* 25–26.

18. Daniel H. Woodward, "Notes on the Publishing History and Text of *The Waste Land,*" *Papers of the Bibliographical Society of America* 58 (1964):260.

19. Gallup, *Bibliography of Eliot,* 30–31.

20. Robert L. Beare, "Notes on the Text of T. S. Eliot: Variants from Russell Square," *Studies in Bibliography* 9 (1957): 32.

21. Woodward, "Notes," 262.

22. *Letters of Leonard Woolf,* 364.

23. Clive Bell, *Poems* (Richmond: Hogarth Press, 1921), 5. It would seem that Virginia, not Clive, had it right about who made the offer.

24. Robert Graves, "Introductory Letter," *The Feather Bed* (Richmond: Hogarth Press, 1923), 5.

25. Richard P. Graves in his *Robert Graves: The Assault Heroic, 1895–1926* (New York, 1987), 286–87, notes that Graves wrote to Edward Marsh bitterly complaining that Hogarth could not issue a cheap edition after the first edition sold out because the Woolfs were "limited for type." ABS, 177, records sales of 235 copies plus one leather-bound copy as of March 8, 1923. At that rate of sale the edition of 250 copies might have sold out in another month. Leonard Woolf, however, had not yet adopted the policy of putting fast-selling books into cheap editions. His first would be *Kenya* by Norman Leys in 1926, two years after its publication in 1924.

3. RUSSIAN TRANSLATIONS

1. Virginia Woolf, "On Not Knowing French," *New Republic* 13 (1929): 348.

2. Royal A. Gettmann, *Turgenev in England and America* (Urbana, Ill., 1941), 9.

3. Helen Muchnic, *Dostoevsky's English Reputation (1881–1936)* (Northhampton, 1939; rpt. New York, 1969), 5–6.

4. Leonard Woolf, "Kot," *New Statesman and Nation* 49 (1955): 170. Woolf included this obituary, with minor changes, in *Beginning,* 249–53.

5. Virginia Woolf, "The Russian Point of View," *Collected Essays* 2:238.

6. Maxim Gorky, Preface to *Reminiscences of Leo Nicolayevitch Tolstoi,* trans. S. S. Koteliansky and Leonard Woolf (Richmond: Hogarth Press, 1920).

7. Helen Muchnic, *From Gorky to Pasternak: Six Writers in Soviet Russia* (New York, 1961), 3.

8. Gorky, *Reminiscences of Tolstoi,* section 32.

9. S. S. Koteliansky and Leonard Woolf, Translators' Note to *The Autobiography of Countess Sophie Tolstoy,* trans. Koteliansky and Woolf (Richmond: Hogarth Press, 1922), 6.

10. The Woolfs spelled the name "Goldenveizer," but I have conformed to modern spelling.

11. D. H. Lawrence, *The Quest for Rananim: D. H. Lawrence's Letters to S. S. Koteliansky, 1914 to 1930,* ed. George J. Zytaruk (Montreal, 1970), 221, 224.

12. Ibid., 231, 232.

13. Ibid., 244.

14. Ivan Bunin, "Gentleman," *Dial* 72 (1922): 52.

15. G. M. Hyde in *D. H. Lawrence and the Art of Translation* (Totowa, N.J., 1981), 74, suggests that Lawrence continued to refine his translation of Bunin after publication in the *Dial,* but Lawrence's rapid traveling and the absence of any reference in the letters would make it unlikely. It seems more likely that Leonard Woolf silently edited the passage.

16. Maxim Gorky, "Reminiscences of Leonid Andreyev," in Gorky, *Reminiscences* (New York: Dover Publications, 1946), 137.

17. Marc Slonim, *Modern Russian Literature: From Chekhov to the Present* (New York, 1953), 179.

18. Leonid Andreyev, *The Dark,* trans. L. A. Magnus and K. Walter (Richmond: Hogarth Press, 1922), 28. The English translation cited by Slonim (p. 179) reads: "How do you dare to be good when I am bad?" The use of "good" more accurately suggests moral significance than the "fine" used by Magnus and Walter.

19. Muchnic, *Dostoevsky's English Reputation,* 111.

20. Virginia Woolf and S. S. Koteliansky, Translators' Note to *Stavrogin's Confession* (London, 1922; rpt. New York: Haskell House Publishers, 1972), 5.

21. Ibid., 9.

22. N. Strakhov as quoted in "A Few Extracts from Letters," trans. S. S. Koteliansky, *Criterion* 3 (1925): 167.

23. *Saturday Review* 134 (1922): 792.

4. MATURITY, 1924–30

1. Quentin Bell, *Virginia Woolf: A Biography*, 2 vols. (New York, 1972), 2: 102.

2. Stanley Unwin, *The Truth about Publishing* (London, 1926), 112–13.

3. Vita Sackville-West, *The Letters of Vita Sackville-West to Virginia Woolf*, ed. Louise DeSalvo and Mitchell Leaska (New York, 1985), 165.

4. Edwin Muir, "Varieties of Realisms," *Nation and Athenaeum*, Nov. 22, 1924, p. 302.

5. John Crowe Ransom to Robert Graves, July 11, 1922, in *Selected Letters of John Crowe Ransom*, ed. Thomas D. Young and George Core (Baton Rouge, La., 1985), 110–12.

6. Ibid., 124.

7. Ransom had tried valiantly to persuade Graves to use one of seven variations in English or Latin of the title of his oak poem ("Quercus Prisca" or "Old Oak"), including his preferred "Vaunting Oak," as the book's title, but Graves stubbornly maintained his editorial decision to use *Grace after Meat*. Ransom, long outgrown his youthful manner, thought the poem "Grace" an artistic offense, but he finally deferred to Graves's judgment. For the correspondence, see Ransom's *Selected Letters*.

8. Unwin, *Truth about Publishing*, 334.

9. Leonard Woolf as quoted in Hugh Ford's *Nancy Cunard*, 58–59.

10. T. S. Eliot, Preface to Edwin Muir, *Collected Poems* (New York, 1965).

11. Conrad Aiken, Preface to Notes to "The Divine Pilgrim," in *Collected Poems*, 2d ed. (New York, 1970), 1016.

12. See F. W. and F. C. Bonnell, *Conrad Aiken: A Bibliography (1902–1978)* (San Marino, Calif.: 1982).

13. Edith Sitwell, *Poetry and Criticism* (London: Hogarth Press, 1925), 18.

14. Ibid., 23.

15. Edith Sitwell as quoted in Donald Gallup, ed., *The Flowers of Friendship: Letters Written to Gertrude Stein* (New York: 1953), 185.

16. Gertrude Stein, *The Autobiography of Alice B. Toklas* (New York, 1960), 232. See also Edward Burns, ed., *The Letters of Gertrude Stein and Carl Van Vechten, 1913–1946*, 1 (New York, 1986): 129–30.

17. Leonard Woolf as quoted in Gallup, *Flowers of Friendship*, 193.

18. HP 351. See *Letters of Leonard Woolf*, 291.

19. William Plomer, *The Autobiography of William Plomer* (New York, 1976), 167.

20. Laurens van der Post, Introduction to *Turbott Wolfe*, by William Plomer (London, 1926; rpt. Oxford, 1985), 28, 33, 53.

21. Keynes, *Nation and Athenaeum* 40 (1927): 788.

22. Woolf, ibid., 849.

23. Edwin Muir, *Selected Letters of Edwin Muir*, ed. P. H. Butler (London, 1974), 58.

24. *Letters of Leonard Woolf*, 296.

25. See Thomas Heacox, "Proust and Bloomsbury," *Virginia Woolf Miscellany*, no. 17 (1981): 2.

26. Authors' statement ledger, 1928–29 (Reading), 327–28.

27. S. S. Alberts, *A Bibliography of the Works of Robinson Jeffers* (1933; rpt. New York: Burt Franklin, 1968), 22. I am endebted to Alberts throughout for information on Jeffers's publications.

28. Woolf to Jeffers, Oct. 3, 1929, Woolf papers, Harry Ransom Humanities Research Center, Univ. of Texas–Austin (hereafter cited as HRHRC).

29. Ibid., and in *Letters of Leonard Woolf,* 301.

30. Humbert Wolfe as quoted by Melba Bennett, *The Stone Mason of Tor House: The Life and Work of Robinson Jeffers* (Los Angeles, 1966), 133.

31. Lehmann to Woolf, Sept. 28, 1938, Lehmann Collection, HRHRC.

32. See Charles Beecher Hogan, *A Bibliography of Edwin Arlington Robinson* (New Haven, 1936).

33. Ellsworth Barnard, " 'Of This or That Estate': Robinson's Literary Reputation," in *Edwin Arlington Robinson Centenary Essays,* ed. Barnard (Athens, Ga., 1969), 4.

34. James Thornton, "Sorts of Poets," *Nation and Athenaeum* 47 (1930): 325.

35. See B. J. Kirkpatrick, *A Bibliography of Virginia Woolf,* 3d ed. (Oxford, 1980), 4–5.

36. David Higham, *Literary Gent* (New York, 1978), 145.

37. HP 416, and in *Letters of Leonard Woolf,* 302.

38. Leonard Woolf, "Detective Stories," *New Statesman and Nation* 40 (1927): 727.

39. C. H. B. Kitchin as quoted by Michael Holroyd in *Lytton Strachey: A Critical Biography,* 2 vols. (New York, 1967–68), 2: 468.

40. Jacques Barzun and Wendell H. Taylor, *A Catalogue of Crime* (New York, 1971), 266–67.

41. See Richard Ellmann's *James Joyce,* rev. ed. (New York, 1982), and P. N. Furbank, *Italo Svevo: The Man and the Writer* (Berkeley, Calif., 1966).

42. Brian Moloney, *Italo Svevo: A Critical Introduction* (Edinburgh, 1974), 130.

43. Michael Spencer Howard, *Jonathan Cape, Publisher* (London, 1971), 53–54.

44. Bell, *Virginia Woolf,* 2: 130; Spater and Parsons, *Marriage of True Minds,* 108.

45. Leonard Woolf in *Downhill,* 142, records Virginia's income in 1930 as £1,617 and the press income as £530. The press income was actually £580.14.8 as recorded in MSR. For the complete press profit account, see Appendix B. The ABS shows the original press with type cost £19.5.5, to which the Woolfs added 18s. of titling type and £11.6 worth of 12 pt. type.

5. JOHN LEHMANN, 1931–32

1. Lehmann, *Thrown to the Woolfs,* 6; *Letters of Leonard Woolf,* 303.

2. Julian Bell as quoted by Lehmann in *Thrown to the Woolfs,* 7.

3. For these and the following contractual arrangements, see the Lehmann Collection, HRHRC.

4. [Gladys Easdale], *Middle Age, 1885–1932* (London, 1935), 292–93; *Diary* 4: 345.

5. A copy of this edition is in the Louis R. Wilson Collection, Univ. of North Carolina Library, Chapel Hill.

6. Lehmann, *Thrown to the Woolfs*, 134.

7. For information on Hampson, I am indebted to Walter Allen's *As I Walked down New Grub Street: Memories of a Writing Life* (Chicago, 1981), 58–63.

8. John Lehmann, *In My Own Time: Memories of a Literary Life* (Boston, 1969), 134.

9. Cecil Day-Lewis, *The Buried Day* (London, 1960), 192.

10. Samuel Hynes, *The Auden Generation: Literature and Politics in England in the 1930s* (London, 1976), 42–46.

11. Day-Lewis, *Buried Day*, 197.

12. Cecil Day-Lewis, "Transitional Poem," in *Collected Poems* (London, 1954), 20–21.

13. Review by Michael Roberts (*Poetry Review*, Jan–Feb. 1932) as quoted in Hynes, *Auden Generation* 73–74.

14. Sean Day-Lewis, *C. Day-Lewis: An English Literary Life* (London, 1980).

15. J. W. Graham, *Virginia Woolf*, The Waves: *The Two Holograph Drafts Transcribed and Edited* 1976), 13–19; Graham, "Editing a Manuscript: Virginia Woolf's *The Waves*," in *Editing Twentieth Century Texts*, ed. Frances G. Halpenny (Toronto, 1972), 77–92.

16. *TLS* review reprinted in Robin Majumbar and Allen McLaurin, eds., *Virginia Woolf: The Critical Heritage*, (London, 1975), 263–65.

17. Frank Swinnerton reprinted in ibid., 267.

18. Lehmann, *In My Own Time*, 114.

19. Ibid., 121.

20. Stephen Spender, *World within World* (London, 1951), 138.

21. F. R. Leavis, "This Poetical Renascence," *Scrutiny* 2 (1933): 67.

22. Christopher Isherwood, *Christopher and His Kind, 1929–1939* (New York, 1976), 80.

23. Ibid., 83.

24. Christopher Isherwood, *Lions and Shadows* (Norfolk, Conn., 1947), 296–97.

25. Plomer, *Autobiography*, 241–43. For Plomer's blood and guts account of the murder at a dinner party, see Virginia Woolf's *Diary* 3: 268. A note gives the detail of the subsequent trail. See also, Peter F. Alexander's *William Plomer: A Biography* (New York, 1989), 162.

26. Vita Sackville-West, *Family History* (London: Hogarth Press, 1932), viii.

27. Lehmann, *Thrown to the Woolfs*, 29.

28. Hermione Lee, Introduction to *The Hogarth Letters* (Athens, Ga., 1986), vii.

29. Lehmann, *Thrown to the Woolfs*, 33.

30. Lehmann's proposal was summarized in Woolf's letter of May 20, 1932, Lehmann Collection, HRHRC.

31. Woolf to Lehmann, June 24, 1932, ibid.

32. *Letters of Leonard Woolf*, 311.

33. Woolf to Lehmann, April 25, 1933, Lehmann Collection, HRHRC.

34. Woolf to Lehmann, April 28, 1933, ibid.

6. PAMPHLETS AND POLITICS

1. Duncan Wilson, *Leonard Woolf: A Political Biography* (London, 1978), 161.

2. John W. Cell, ed., *By Kenya Possessed: The Correspondence of Norman Leys and J. H. Oldham, 1918–1926* (Chicago, 1976). I am indebted to Cell for information on Leys.

3. Ibid., 24.

4. H. G. Wells, *The Open Conspiracy* (London: Hogarth Press, 1929), 87.

5. Harold Laski, "The Modern World," *New Statesman and Nation* 2 (1931): 484–85.

6. *TLS* 30 (1931): 811.

7. Cell, *By Kenya Possessed,* 34–35.

8. Horace Samuel had been a lawyer and judge in Palestine from 1918 to 1928 and a member of the Council of English Zionist Federation. Leonard Woolf thought his *Unholy Memories* was extremely amusing but subject to libel; he had Samuel revise the book. See HP 431, 432.

9. Wilson, *Leonard Woolf,* 157–58.

10. See Sylvia R. Margulies, *The Pilgrimage to Russia: The Soviet Union and the Treatment of Foreigners, 1924–37* (Madison, Wis., 1968).

11. Aneurin Bevan, E. J. Strachey, and George Strauss, *What We Saw in Russia* (London: Hogarth Press, 1931), 13, 19, 28–29.

12. R. D. Charques, *Soviet Education: Some Aspects of Cultural Revolution* (London: Hogarth Press, 1932), 10.

13. Kingsley Martin, *Harold Laski (1893–1950): A Biographical Memoire* (London, 1953), 257.

14. Harold Laski, *Law and Justice in Soviet Russia,* reprinted in *The Danger of Being a Gentleman and Other Essays* (New York, 1940), 63.

15. Maurice Dobb, *On Marxism To-Day* (London: Hogarth Press, 1932), 45.

16. Leonard Woolf, *Quack, Quack!* (London: Hogarth Press, 1935), 199, 201.

17. H. G. Wells, *The Idea of a World Encyclopedia* (London: Hogarth Press, 1936), 19, 20, 32.

18. Woolf as quoted in Wilson, *Leonard Woolf,* 132.

19. Russell as quoted in Mark Starr, *Lies and Hate in Education* (London: Hogarth Press, 1929), 6.

20. B. C. Bloomfield and Edward Mendelson, eds., *W. H. Auden: A Bibliography, 1924–1969,* 2d ed. (Charlottesville, 1972), entries B6, B9, C24, C25, C30, C70.

21. Auden as quoted by Humphrey Carpenter in *W. H. Auden: A Biography* (Boston: 1981), 247.

22. Worsley as quoted in Bloomfield and Mendelson, *Auden Bibliography,* 37.

23. Carpenter, *Auden,* 247.

24. Auden as quoted in ibid., 265.

25. Olive Banks, *Faces of Feminism: A Study of Feminism as a Social Movement* (New York, 1981), 123, 157, 165.

26. Willa Muir, *Women: An Inquiry* (London: Hogarth Press, 1925), 7–8.

27. Banks, *Faces of Feminism,* 167.

28. Viscountess Rhondda, *Leisured Women* (London: Hogarth Press, 1928), 59.

29. For an interesting analysis of Woolf's changes, see Jane Marcus, *Art and Anger: Reading like a Woman* (Columbus, Ohio, 1988), 117–19. Marcus argues that "while Woolf remains as scrupulous as ever in the new essay [her revision of the *Yale Review* article for the Hogarth Press book], the cynicism is gone. She has become both more politically committed to the cooperative cause and more artistically Woolfian" (p. 119). Woolf's artistry is obvious; her political commitment seems less convincing to me.

30. Virginia Woolf, "Introductory Letter," *Life as We Have Known It,* ed. Margaret Llewelyn Davies (London: Hogarth Press, 1931), xxv.

31. Ibid., xxxix, xxvi.

32. Brenda R. Silver, *Virginia Woolf's Reading Notebooks* (Princeton, N.J., 1983), and "*Three Guineas* Before and After," in *Virginia Woolf: A Feminist Slant,* ed. Jane Marcus (Lincoln, Nebr., 1983), 254–76.

33. *TLS* 88 (1939): 606.

7. THE THIRTIES, 1933–37

1. Ivan Bunin, *New York Times,* Nov. 10, 1933, p. 23.

2. Serge Kryzytski, *The Works of Ivan Bunin* (The Hague, 1971), 15.

3. See letters from MacNeice to Anthony Blunt (especially May 7 and Nov. 15, 1932, and April 3, 1933), Blunt Collection, King's College Library, Cambridge University.

4. Wellesley, *Far Have I Travelled,* 155.

5. *Letters of Leonard Woolf,* 314.

6. Michael Roberts, Preface to *New Country,* ed. Roberts (London: Hogarth Press, 1933), 11, 13.

7. Isherwood, *Christopher and His Kind,* 98–100; Stephen Spender, *The Destructive Element* (London, 1935), 242–43.

8. Charles Madge, "Letter to the Intelligentsia," *New Country,* 232; Rex Warner, "Hymn," ibid., 254.

9. Auden, "A Happy Year," and "Prologue," ibid., 202, 193.

10. Hynes, *Auden Generation,* 102.

11. HP 387, and in *Letters of Leonard Woolf,* 316.

12. HP 387, and in *Letters of Leonard Woolf,* 319.

13. Spender, *Destructive Element,* 250–51.

14. Hynes, *Auden Generation,* 144.

15. Kitchin to Woolf, May 18, 1938, LWP reported sales of his book (probably *Olive E.,* 1937) for the first ten months as 1,204 copies. The MSR shows sales for *Crime at Christmas* of 2,166 copies in the first six months.

16. Holroyd, *Lytton Strachey,* 2:468.

17. Harold Nicolson, *Diaries and Letters, 1930–1939,* ed. Nigel Nicolson (London, 1966), 175, 185–86.

18. HP 415, and in *Letters of Leonard Woolf,* 322.

19. Nigel Nicolson in Harold Nicolson's *Diaries,* 147.

20. Isherwood to William Plomer as quoted in Brian Finney, *Christopher Isherwood: A Critical Biography* (New York, 1979), 108.

21. For reviews, see Robert W. Funk, *Christopher Isherwood: A Reference Guide* (Boston, 1979), 3–6.

22. Walpole, *Nation and Athenaeum* 9 (1935): 427.

23. Day-Lewis, *C. Day-Lewis*, 91.

24. HP 248, and in *Letters of Leonard Woolf*, 328.

25. *TLS* 35 (1936): 859.

26. Bell, *Virginia Woolf* 1: 157–61.

27. Virginia wrote to Ethel Smyth in March 1936 about Horace de Vere Cole's death and her planned trip to Weymouth "to see the shore where I played my joke on the Dreadnought" (*Letters* 6:17). And in July 1940 she wrote to Smyth again about lecturing to the Women's Institute about the hoax, which made the women laugh (ibid., 6: 407).

28. Virginia Woolf as quoted by Mitchell Leaska, *The Novels of Virginia Woolf: From Beginnings to End* (New York, 1977), 192.

29. Grace Radin, *Virginia Woolf's* The Years: *The Evolution of a Novel* (Knoxville, 1981), 81.

30. Alice Payne Hackett, *70 Year of Best Sellers, 1895–1965* (New York, 1967), 155.

31. *Time* 29 (April 12, 1937): 93.

32. Vita Sackville-West, *Pepita* (Garden City, N.Y.: Doubleday, Doran, 1937), 5.

33. Curtis Brown Agency to Sackville-West, June 16, 1937, in possession of Nigel Nicolson.

34. John Lehmann, "Two of the Conspirators," *Twentieth Century Literature* 22 (1976): 271–73.

35. Higham, *Literary Gent*, 143.

36. Isherwood, *Christopher and His Kind*, 237.

37. Lehmann, *Thrown to the Woolfs*, 57.

8. FREUD AND FREUDIANS

1. Ernest Jones, *The Life and Work of Sigmund Freud*, 3 vols. (New York, 1955–57), 3: 206. Peter Gay in *Freud: A Life for Our Time* (New York, 1988), 612, writes that Stefan Zweig was coauthor of the letter with Mann and that there were 191 signatures of writers and artists. James H. Huston, Chief of the Manuscript Division of the Library of Congress, has kindly had his staff verify the presence of Virginia Woolf's signature on the birthday greeting, a copy of which is in the Freud Papers (letter to the author August 16, 1990).

2. For a chronology of Freud and his followers, see Jones's *Freud* 2: 459–60, 3: xv-xvi.

3. Ibid., 3: 30–31.

4. Ibid., 36.

5. *Letters of Leonard Woolf*, 287.

6. Ernest Jones, "Editorial Preface" to Sigmund Freud, *Collected Papers* 1 (London: Hogarth Press, 1924): 3.

7. Ibid., 3, 4.

8. Two of these papers, "The Aetiology of Hysteria" (1896) and "My Views on the Part Played by Sexuality in the Aetiology of the Neuroses" (1905), constitute part of the battlefield in the recent skirmish over Freud's professional integrity and courage. The first paper traced hysteria and obsessional neuroses to childhood sexual abuse. The second paper reinterpreted the evidence as seduction phantasy and hysterical imaginings related to sexual repression. From this came Freud's interpretation that an imagined event could produce the psychological equivalent to an actual event and, consequently, Freud's development of dream theory and the Oedipus complex. Jeffrey Masson (in *The Assault on Truth: Freud's Suppression of the Seduction Theory* [New York 1984]), citing these papers and Freud's letters to Wilhelm Fliess, argues that Freud suppressed his evidence of child seduction for a more socially acceptable theory; the result, he argues, has had grave consequences for the treatment of children's sexual trauma. An array of Freudian and non-Freudian psychiatrists have argued against these charges.

9. Jones, Preface to Freud, *Collected Papers* 2 (London: Hogarth Press, 1924): 7.

10. Joan Riviere, note to her translation of Freud's "Neurosis and Psychosis," ibid., 250.

11. Ernest Jones, *Free Associations: Memories of a Psycho-Analyst* (New York, 1959), 159–60, 166.

12. James and Alix Strachey, *Bloomsbury/Freud: The Letters of James and Alix Strachey, 1924–25,* ed. Perry Meisel and Walter Kendrick (New York, 1985), 48.

13. Jones, Preface to Freud, *Collected Papers* 4 (London: Hogarth Press, 1925): 7.

14. Jones, *Freud* 2:185.

15. Jones, Preface to Freud, *Collected Papers* 4:7.

16. Freud, "The Moses of Michelangelo," ibid., 283.

17. James Strachey, "Editor's Introduction," *The Ego and the Id,* vol. 19 of *The Standard Edition of the Complete Psychological Works of Sigmund Freud* (London, 1961), 7.

18. James and Alix Strachey, *Letters,* 83.

19. HP 109. Perry Meisel and Walter Kendrick, in their edition of James and Alix Strachey's *Letters* (p. 307) state that Rickman proposed a literal English translation of the title and that Leonard Woolf subsequently agreed, but with reservations. However, Rickman's letter of Aug. 11, 1926, in HP 109, according to my reading, does not contain their quotation; it was Leonard Woolf who proposed the literal translation.

20. Jones, *Freud* 3: 138. Jones wrote that the bishop of Birmingham had stirred up a controversy over Freud's "exposition of the anthropological origin of the belief in transubstantiation."

21. James Strachey, Introduction to Sigmund Freud, *Civilization and Its Discontents* (New York, 1962), 5.

22. Jones, *Freud* 3: 174.

23. Freud, Preface to *New Introductory Lectures,* vol. 22 in *Standard Edition* (London, 1964), 5.

24. Freud, "Lecture XXXIII," ibid., 134–35.

25. HP 113, and in *Letters of Leonard Woolf,* 311–12.

26. HP 113, and in *Letters of Leonard Woolf,* 312–13.

27. *Letters of Leonard Woolf,* 304. Woolf explained to Freud that the press had now "repaid the original cost" of the stock of the first six IPL volumes obtained in 1924 and could now pay him royalties as the press was making a profit.

28. *Letters of Leonard Woolf,* 328.

29. Freud as quoted in Jones, Freud 3: 175.

30. Freud, *Civilization, War, and Death* (London: Hogarth Press, 1939), 15.

31. Sigmund Freud, *Letters of Sigmund Freud,* ed. Ernst L. Freud, trans. Tania and James Stern (New York, 1960), 421.

32. Freud, *Moses and Monotheism,* vol. 23 in *Standard Edition* (London, 1964), 103.

33. Strachey, "Editor's Note," ibid., 4.

34. Jones as quoted in *Letters of Leonard Woolf,* 335.

35. *Letters of Leonard Woolf,* 333–34.

36. Ibid., 338–40.

37. See correspondence between Leonard Woolf, Ernest Jones, and R. & R. Clark in HP 1.

38. Freud as quoted in Jones, *Free Associations,* 232.

39. Jones, *Freud* 3: 37.

40. Leonard Woolf to W. J. H. Sprott, Jan. 7, 1933, Sprott Papers, King's College Library, Cambridge.

41. James Strachey, "General Preface," to the *Standard Edition* in vol. 1, *Pre-Psycho-Analytic Publications* (London, 1961), xxi.

42. Ibid., xix.

43. Strachey, "Notes on Some Technical Terms," ibid., xxiv-vi.

44. Bruno Bettleheim, *Freud and Man's Soul* (New York, 1983), 86–91, 103–7. For recent criticism of the Strachey translations, see essays by Malcolm Pines, Riccardo Steiner, Darius Ornston, Alex Holder, and Helmut Junker in Edward Timms and Naomi Segal, eds., *Freud in Exile: Psychoanalysis and Its Vicissitudes* (New Haven, 1988), 177–219.

9. THE PARTNERSHIP, 1938–41

1. Lehmann, *Thrown to the Woolfs,* 59.

2. Isherwood, *Christopher and His Kind,* 257.

3. Isherwood, *Lions and Shadows,* [7].

4. Isherwood as quoted by Lehmann in *Thrown to the Woolfs,* 62.

5. Sales ledger: "Hogarth Novels (Pre-1945)," University of Reading.

6. Lehmann, *Thrown to the Woolfs,* 73.

7. Woolf letter to Lehmann in the Lehmann Collection, HRHRC.

8. Raymond Mortimer, "A Serious Poem," *New Statesman and Nation* 16 (1938): 696.

9. Sales ledger: "Poetry (Pre-1945)," University of Reading.

10. Lehmann, "Two of the Conspirators," 275.

11. Edmund Wilson, "Isherwood's Lucid Eye," *New Republic* 99 (1939): 51.

12. Sales ledger: "Hogarth Novels (Pre-1945)," University of Reading.

13. See Douglas Haynes, "Christopher Isherwood's Revision of *The Berlin Stories*," *Papers of the Bibliographical Society of America* 73, no. 2 (1979): 264–65.

14. Lehmann, *Thrown to the Woolfs*, 89.

15. *Letters of Leonard Woolf*, 331.

16. Stephen Spender, "The Importance of Meaning," *Translation* 1 (1973): 36.

17. Lehmann, *Thrown to the Woolfs*, 76.

18. John Russell, "There It Is," *Kenyon Review* 26 (1964): 443.

19. Lehmann, *Thrown to the Woolfs*, 76.

20. Michael North, *Henry Green and the Writing of His Generation* (Charlottesville, 1984), 80.

21. Sales ledger: "Hogarth Novels (Pre-1945)," University of Reading.

22. E. M. Forster, "What I Believe," In *Two Cheers for Democracy*, ed. Oliver Stallybrass (London: Edward Arnold, 1972), 70.

23. E. M. Forster, *England's Pleasant Land* (London: Hogarth Press, 1940), 17.

24. Lehmann, *Thrown to the Woolfs*, 87–88.

25. See R. J. L. Kingsford, *The Publishers Association, 1896–1946* (Cambridge, 1970), 161–62, 165–67, 171.

26. Lehmann, *Thrown to the Woolfs*, 85–86. Kingsford, *Publishers Association*, 162, estimates that one ton of paper is required for 3,000 copies of a 250-page book.

27. Kingsford, *Publishers Association*, 172–75.

28. Lehmann, *Thrown to the Woolfs*, 89.

29. Kingsford, *Publishers Association*, 167–68.

30. See Brenda Silver, " 'Anon' and 'The Reader': Virginia Woolf's Last Essays," *Twentieth Century Literature* 25 (1979): 356–65.

31. Lehmann, *Thrown to the Woolfs*, 100.

32. Ibid., 101.

33. Ibid., 102.

34. Ibid., 105.

35. The contract and other correspondence between Vita and the Hogarth Press are in the possession of Nigel Nicolson. I am indebted to him for use of this material.

36. Woolf, *Letters of Leonard Woolf*, 341.

37. Woolf to Sackville-West, April 15, 1942, in possession of Nigel Nicolson.

38. Garvin to Sackville-West, July 7, [n.d.], in possession of Nigel Nicolson.

10. THE PUBLISHING BUSINESS

1. Howard, *Jonathan Cape, Publisher*, 21–22, 25, 71, 59–60.

2. Kingsford, *Publishers Association*, 153.

3. *Letters of Leonard Woolf*, 323–24 and note.

4. Meynell, *My Lives*, 189.

5. Lehmann to Woolf, April 17, 1931, Lehmann Collection, HRHRC.

6. Michael Joseph, *The Adventure of Publishing* (London, 1949), 15, 23.

7. Richard Kennedy, *A Boy at the Hogarth Press* (London, 1972), 13.

8. *Letters of Leonard Woolf*, 280.

9. Kennedy, *Boy at the Hogarth Press*, 68–69.

10. Michael Millgate, "Interview with Miss Compton-Burnett," in *The Art of I. Compton-Burnett: A Collection of Critical Essays*, ed. Charles Burkhart (London, 1972), 39.

11. HP 131, and in *Letters of Leonard Woolf*, 320.

12. Lehmann, *Thrown to the Woolfs*, 132–40.

13. Leonard Woolf, "On Advertising Books," *Nation and Athenaeum* 40 (1927): 849.

14. Geoffrey Faber, *A Publisher Speaking* (Boston, 1935), 129.

15. Unwin, *Truth about Publishing*, 270–71.

16. Charles Rosner, *The Growth of the Book-Jacket* (Cambridge, Mass., 1954), vii-viii, xxii.

17. I am indebted to the detailed descriptions of dust jackets provided in Woolmer's *Checklist*, but the totals are mine. In some cases Woolmer could not verify the existence of a dust jacket, so my totals are not complete. The *Checklist* contains photographs of many of the dust jackets.

18. Lehmann, *Thrown to the Woolfs*, 26–27.

19. For an extended analysis of Vanessa's dust jackets and her artistic relationship to Virginia, see Diane Filby Gillespie's *The Sisters' Arts: The Writing and Painting of Virginia Woolf and Vanessa Bell* (Syracuse, N.Y., 1988), esp. 242–66.

20. Michael Twyman, *Printing, 1770–1970: An Illustrated History of Its Development and Uses in England* (London, 1970), 107.

21. Richard Shone, *Bloomsbury Portraits: Vanessa Bell, Duncan Grant, and Their Circle* (Oxford, 1976), 222.

22. Unwin, *Truth About Publishing*, 177.

23. Kennedy, *Boy at the Hogarth Press*, 54–60.

24. George Spater's private collection contained a copy of Theodora Bosanquet's *Henry James at Work* (1924), one of the Hogarth Essays, with a Shakespeare & Co. label stuck in the back and a 1925 date inscribed by the purchaser. Michael S. Reynolds in his detailed inventory, *Hemingway's Reading, 1910–1940* (Princeton, N.J., 1981), lists the following Hogarth Press books Hemingway purchased or borrowed through Beach's bookshop: Gertrude Stein's *Composition as Explanation* (1926); Virginia Woolf's *Common Reader* (1924), *Common Reader II* (1932), *Flush* (1933), *Jacob's Room* (1922), *To the Lighthouse* (1927) (all obtained by Hemingway in 1934); and Christopher Isherwood's *Lions and Shadows* (1938).

11. CONCLUSION

1. Faber, *A Publisher Speaking*, 66.

2. Lehmann, *Thrown to the Woolfs*, 154, 155.

3. Lehmann, *In My Own Time*, 504–11.

4. Joseph, *Adventure of Publishing*, 35.

SELECTED BIBLIOGRAPHY

Aiken, Conrad. *The Charnel Rose; Senlin: A Biography.* 1927; rpt. New York: Haskell House, 1971.
——. *Collected Criticism.* Introd. Rufus A. Blanshard. New York: Oxford Univ. Press, 1968.
——. *Collected Poems.* 2d ed. New York: Oxford Univ. Press, 1970.
——. *Selected Letters of Conrad Aiken.* Ed. Joseph Killorin. New Haven: Yale Univ. Press, 1978.
——. *Ushant: An Essay.* New York: Duell, Sloan and Pearce, 1952.
Alberts, S. S. *A Bibliography of the Works of Robinson Jeffers.* New York, 1933; rpt. New York: Burt Franklin, 1968.
Alexander, Peter F. *William Plomer: A Biography.* New York: Oxford Univ. Press, 1989.
Alexandrova, Vera. *A History of Soviet Literature.* Trans. Mirra Ginsberg. Garden City, N.Y.: Doubleday, 1963.
Allen, Walter. *As I Walked down New Grub Street: Memories of a Writing Life.* Chicago: Univ. of Chicago Press, 1981.
Alpers, Antony. *The Life of Katherine Mansfield.* New York: Viking, 1980.
Anan, Noel G. *Leslie Stephen.* London: MacGibbon & Kee, 1951.
Andreyev, Leonid. *Visions: Stories and Photographs.* Ed. Olga Andreyev Carlisle. New York: Harcourt Brace Jovanovich, 1987.
Arnold, Matthew. "Count Leo Tolstoi." In *The Last Word.* Vol. 2 of *The Complete Prose Works of Matthew Arnold.* Ed. R. H. Super. Ann Arbor: Univ. of Michigan Press, 1977, pp. 282–304.
Auden, W. H. "Private Pleasure." *Scrutiny* 1 (1932): 191–94.
——. "Rilke in English." *New Republic* 100 (1939): 135–36.
Banks, Olive. *Faces of Feminism: A Study of Feminism as a Social Movement.* New York: St. Martin's Press, 1981.
Barnard, Ellsworth. " 'Of This or That Estate': Robinson's Literary Reputation." In *Edwin Arlington Robinson Centenary Essays.* Ed. Ellsworth Barnard. Athens: Univ. of Georgia Press, 1969, pp. 1–14.
Barzun, Jacques, and Wendell H. Taylor. *A Catalogue of Crime.* New York: Harper & Row, 1971.
Bassoff, Bruce. *Toward Loving: The Poetics of the Novel and the Practice of Henry Green.* Columbia: Univ. of South Carolina Press, 1975.

Beare, Robert L. "Notes on the Text of T. S. Eliot: Variants from Russell Square." *Studies in Bibliography* 9 (1957): 21–49.

Bell, Clive. "How Pleasant to Know Mr. Eliot." In *T. S. Eliot: A Symposium*. Comp. Richard March and Tambimuttu. London: Frank & Cass Co., 1965, pp. 15–19.

Bell, Quentin. "The Omega Revisited." *Listener* 71 (1964): 200–201.

——. *Virginia Woolf: A Biography*. 2 vols. New York: Harcourt Brace Jovanovich, 1972.

Bennett, Melba. *The Stone Mason of Tor House: The Life and Work of Robinson Jeffers*. Los Angeles: Ward Ritchie, 1966.

Bettleheim, Bruno. *Freud and Man's Soul*. New York: A. A. Knopf, 1983.

Bevan, Aneurin, E. J. Strachey, and George Strauss. *What We Saw in Russia*. London: Hogarth Press, 1931.

Black, Naomi. "Virginia Woolf and the Women's Movement." *Virginia Woolf: A Feminist Slant*. Ed. Jane Marcus. Lincoln: Univ. of Nebraska Press, 1983, pp. 180–97.

Blanshard, Rufus A. "Checklist of Conrad Aiken's Critical Writing." In *Collected Criticism of Conrad Aiken*. New York: Oxford Univ. Press, 1968, pp. 395–408.

——. "Pilgrim's Progress: Conrad Aiken's Poetry." *Texas Quarterly* 1 (1958): 135–48.

Bloomfield, B. C., and Edward Mendelson. *W. H. Auden: A Bibliography, 1924–1969*. 2d ed. Charlottesville: Univ. Press of Virginia, 1972.

Bonnell F. W., and F. C. Bonnell. *Conrad Aiken: A Bibliography*. San Marino, Calif.: Huntington Library, 1982.

Boswell, Jeanetta. *Robinson Jeffers and the Critics, 1912–1983: A Bibliography of Secondary Sources with Selective Annotations*. Metuchen, N.J.: Scarecrow Press, 1986.

Brower, Reuben. "The Novel as Poem: Virginia Woolf, Exploring a Critical Metaphor." In *The Interpretation of Narrative: Theory and Practice*. Ed. Morton W. Bloomfield. Cambridge: Harvard Univ. Press, 1970, pp. 229–47.

Bunin, Ivan. "The Nobel Days." In *Memories and Portraits*. Trans. Vera Traill and Robin Chancellor. 1951; rpt. New York: Greenwood Press, 1968, pp. 207–17.

Burns, Edward. *The Letters of Gertrude Stein and Carl Van Vechten, 1913–1946*. Vol. 1. New York: Columbia Univ. Press, 1986.

Carpenter, Humphrey. *W. H. Auden: A Biography*. Boston: Houghton Mifflin, 1981.

Carswell, John. *Lives and Letters, 1906–1957*. New York: New Directions, 1978

Cave, Roderick. *The Private Press*. 2d ed. rev. New York: R. R. Bowker, 1983.

Ceadel, Martin. *Pacifism in Britain, 1914–1945: The Defining of a Faith*. Oxford: Clarendon Press, 1980.

Cell, John W., ed. *By Kenya Possessed: The Correspondence of Norman Leys and J. H. Oldham, 1918–1926*. Chicago: Univ. of Chicago Press, 1976.

Charques, R. D. *Soviet Education: Some Aspects of Cultural Revolution*. London: Hogarth Press, 1932.

Clair, Colin. *A Chronology of Printing*. New York: Frederick Praeger, 1969.

Cockerell, Douglas. *Bookbinding and the Care of Books: A Handbook for Amateurs, Bookbinders, and Librarians*. New York: D. Appleton, 1902.

Cole, Margaret. *The Life of G. D. H. Cole*. New York: Macmillan–St. Martin's Press, 1971.

——. *The Story of Fabian Socialism*. Stanford: Stanford Univ. Press, 1961.

Colin, Andrew G. "Ivan Bunin in Retrospect." *Slavonic and East European Review* 34 (1955): 156–73.

Comerford, Mollie J. "Rilke in English, 1946 to 1966." *Germanic Review* 42 (1967): 301–9.

Compton, F. E. "Subscription Books." In *Bowker Lectures on Book Publishing*. New York: R. R. Bowker, 1957, pp. 56–78.

Cunard, Nancy. *These Were the Hours: Memories of My Hours Press, Réanville and Paris, 1928–1931*. Carbondale: Southern Illinois Univ. Press, 1969.

Dalton, Jack P. "The Text of *Ulysses*." In *New Light on Joyce from the Dublin Symposium*. Ed. Fritz Senn. Bloomington: Indiana Univ. Press, 1972, pp. 99–119.

Darroch, Sandra Jobson. *Ottoline: The Life of Lady Ottoline Morrell*. New York: Coward, McCann, & Geoghegan, 1975.

Das, G. K., and John Beer. *E. M. Forster: A Human Exploration*. New York: New York Univ. Press, 1979.

Day-Lewis, Cecil. *The Buried Day*. London: Chatto & Windus, 1960.

——. *Collected Poems, 1954*. London: Jonathan Cape, 1954.

Day-Lewis, Sean. *C. Day-Lewis: An English Literary Life*. London: Weidenfeld and Nicolson, 1980.

Deane, Herbert A. *The Political Ideas of Harold J. Laski*. 1954; rpt. Hamden, Conn.: Shoe String Press, 1972.

De la Mare, Richard. *A Publisher on Book Production*. London: J. M. Dent, 1936.

Dent, Hugh R. *The House of Dent, 1888–1938*. London: J. M. Dent, 1938.

DeSalvo, Louise A. *Virginia Woolf: The Impact of Childhood Sexual Abuse on Her Life and Work*. Boston: Beacon Press, 1989.

——. *Virginia Woolf's First Voyage: A Novel in the Making*. Totowa, N.J.: Rowman and Littlefield, 1980.

Dobb, Maurice. *On Marxism To-Day*. London: Hogarth Press, 1932.

Dupuy, Trevor N., and Gay M. Hammerman, eds. *A Documentary History of Arms Control and Disarmament*. New York: R. R. Bowker, 1973.

[Easdale, Gladys]. *Middle Ages, 1885–1932*. London: Constable, 1935.

Eliot, T. S. Preface to *Collected Poems*. By Edwin Muir. New York: Oxford Univ. Press, 1965.

——. *The Letters of T. S. Eliot*. Vol. 1. Ed. Valerie Eliot. New York: Harcourt Brace Jovanovich, 1988.

Ellmann, Richard. *James Joyce*. Rev. ed. New York: Oxford Univ. Press, 1982.

Ettlinger, Amrei, and Joan M. Gladstone. *Russian Literature, Theatre, and Art: A Bibliography of Works in English, Published 1900–1945*. 1945; rpt. Port Washington: Kennikat Press, 1971.

Faber, Geoffrey. *A Publisher Speaking*. Boston: Houghton Mifflin, 1935.

Fadiman, Clifton, ed. *I Believe: The Personal Philosophies of Certain Eminent Men and Women of Our Time*. New York: Simon and Schuster, 1939.

Fifoot, Richard. *A Bibliography of Edith, Osbert, and Sacheverell Sitwell*. 2d ed. rev. London: Rupert Hart-Davis, 1971.

Finney, Brian. *Christopher Isherwood: A Critical Biography*. New York: Oxford Univ. Press, 1979.

——. "Laily, Mortmere, and All That." *Twentieth Century Literature* 22 (1976): 286–302.

Ford, Hugh, ed. *Published in Paris: American and British Writers, Printers, and Publishers in Paris, 1920–1939*. New York: Macmillan, 1975.

——. *Nancy Cunard: Brave Poet, Indomitable Rebel, 1896–1965*. Philadelphia: Chilton Book Co., 1968.

Forster, E. M. *Commonplace Book*. London: Scolar Press, 1978.

——. *Selected Letters of E. M. Forster*. Ed. Mary Lago and P. N. Furbank. 2 vols. Cambridge: Belknap Press, 1983.

Franklin, Colin. *The Private Press*. Chester Springs, Pa.: Dufour Editions, 1969.

Freud, Sigmund. *Letters of Sigmund Freud*. Ed Ernest L. Freud. Trans. Tania and James Stern. New York: Basic Books, 1960.

——. *The Standard Edition of the Complete Psychological Works of Sigmund Freud*. 23 vols. Ed and trans. James Strachey. London: Hogarth Press, 1961–64.

Fry, Roger. *Letters of Roger Fry*. Ed. Denys Sutton. 2 vols. New York: Random House, 1972.

Funk, Robert W. *Christopher Isherwood: A Reference Guide*. Boston: G. K. Hall, 1979.

Furbank, P. N. *E. M. Forster: A Life*. 2 vols. New York: Harcourt Brace Jovanovich, 1978.

——. "Forster and 'Bloomsbury' Prose." In *E. M. Forster: A Human Exploration*. Ed. G. K. Das and John Beer. New York: New York Univ. Press, 1979, pp. 161–66.

——. *Italo Svevo: The Man and the Writer*. Berkeley: Univ. of California Press, 1966.

Gallup, Donald. *A Bibliography of T. S. Eliot*. Rev. ed. New York: Harcourt Brace & World, 1969.

——, ed. *The Flowers of Friendship: Letters Written to Gertrude Stein*. New York: Alfred Knopf, 1953.

Gardner, Philip, ed. *E. M. Forster: The Critical Heritage*. London: Routledge & Kegan Paul, 1973.

Garnett, David. *The Flowers of the Forest*. New York: Harcourt Brace, 1956.

——. *The Golden Echo*. New York: Harcourt Brace, 1954.

Gay, Peter. *Freud: A Life for Our Time*. New York: W. W. Norton, 1988.

Gettmann, Royal A. *Turgenev in England and America*. Urbana: Univ. of Illinois Press, 1941.

Gillespie, Diane Filby. *The Sisters' Arts: The Writing and Painting of Virginia Woolf and Vanessa Bell*. Syracuse: Syracuse Univ. Press, 1988.

Glendinning, Victoria. *Edith Sitwell: A Unicorn among Lions*. New York: Alfred Knopf, 1981.

——. *Vita: The Life of V. Sackville-West*. New York: Alfred A. Knopf, 1983.

Goldstein, Jan Ellen. "The Woolfs' Response to Freud: Water Spiders, Singing Canaries, and the Second Apple." In *Literature and Psychoanalysis*. Ed. Edith Kurzweil and William Phillips. New York: Columbia Univ. Press, 1983, pp. 232–55.

Gordon, Lyndall. *Eliot's Early Years*. New York: Oxford Univ. Press, 1977.

Gorky, Maxim. *Reminiscences*. New York: Dover Publications, 1946.

Graham, John W. "Editing a Manuscript: Virginia Woolf's *The Waves*." In *Editing Twentieth Century Texts*. Ed. Frances G. Halpenny. Toronto: Univ. of Toronto Press, 1972, pp. 77–92.

——. *Virginia Woolf's* The Waves: *The Two Holograph Drafts Transcribed and Edited.* Toronto: Univ. of Toronto Press, 1976.

Grant, Joy. *Harold Monro and the Poetry Bookshop.* Berkeley: Univ. of California Press, 1967.

Grant, Michael. *T. S. Eliot: The Critical Heritage.* Vol. 1. London: Routledge & Kegan Paul, 1982.

Graves, Richard Perceval. *Robert Graves: The Assault Heroic, 1895–1926.* New York: Viking, 1987.

Graves, Robert. *In Broken Images: Selected Letters of Robert Graves, 1914–1946.* Ed. Paul O'Prey. London: Hutchinson, 1982.

Greenhood, David, and Helen Gentry. *Chronology of Books and Printing.* Rev. ed. New York: Macmillan, 1936.

Hackett, Alice Payne. *70 Years of Best Sellers, 1895–1965.* New York: R. R. Bowker, 1967.

Handley-Taylor, Geoffrey, and Timothy D'Arch Smith. *Cecil Day-Lewis: A Bibliography.* London: St. James Press, 1968.

Harkins, William E. "The Theme of Sterility in Olesha's *Envy.*" In *Major Soviet Writers.* Ed. Edward J. Brown. New York: Oxford Univ. Press, 1973, pp. 280–94.

Harris, Catherine Kirk. *Conrad Aiken: Critical Recognition, 1914–1981: A Bibliographical Guide.* New York: Garland, 1983.

Harrod, Roy F. *The Life of John Maynard Keynes.* New York: Harcourt Brace, 1951.

Häusermann, H. W. "Herbert Read's Poetry." In *Herbert Read: An Introduction to His Work by Various Hands.* Ed. Henry Treece. 1944; rpt. Port Washington: Kennikat Press, 1969, pp. 91–107.

Haynes, Douglas. "Christopher Isherwood's Revision of *The Berlin Stories,*" *Papers of the Bibliographical Society of America* 73, no. 2 (1979): 262–65.

Heacox, Thomas. "Proust and Bloomsbury." *Virginia Woolf Miscellany,* no. 17 (1981): 2.

Heilbrun, Carolyn G. "Virginia Woolf in Her Fifties." *Twentieth Century Literature* 27 (1981): 16–33.

Hewison, Robert. *Under Siege: Literary Life in London, 1939–1945.* New York: Oxford Univ. Press, 1977.

Higginson, Fred H. *A Bibliography of the Works of Robert Graves.* Hamden, Conn.: Shoe String Press, 1966.

Higham, David. *Literary Gent.* New York: Coward, McCann & Geoghegan, 1978.

Hoffman, Frederick J. *Conrad Aiken.* New York: Twayne Publishers, 1962.

Hoffman, Michael J., ed. *Critical Essays on Gertrude Stein.* Boston: G. K. Hall, 1986.

Hogan, Charles Beecher. *A Bibliography of Edwin Arlington Robinson.* New Haven: Yale Univ. Press, 1936.

Holleyman, George. *A Catalogue of Books Taken from the Library of Leonard and Virginia Woolf.* Brighton: Holleyman and Treacher, 1975.

Holroyd, Michael. *Lytton Strachey: A Critical Biography.* 2 vols. New York: Holt, Rinehart and Winston, 1967–68.

Howard, Michael Spencer. *Jonathan Cape, Publisher.* London: Jonathan Cape, 1971.

Howarth, Patrick. *Squire: "Most Generous of Men."* London: Hutchinson, 1963.

Huberman, Elizabeth. *The Poetry of Edwin Muir.* New York: Oxford Univ. Press, 1971.

Hyde, G. M. *D. H. Lawrence and the Art of Translation*. Totowa, N.J.: Barnes & Noble, 1981.

Hynes, Samuel. *The Auden Generation: Literature and Politics in England in the 1930s*. London: Bodley Head, 1976.

——. "The Whole Contention between Mr. Bennett and Mrs. Woolf." In *Edwardian Occasions*. New York: Oxford Univ. Press, 1972, pp. 24–38.

Isherwood, Christopher. *Christopher and His Kind, 1929–1939*. New York: Farrar, Straus, Giroux, 1976.

——. *Exhumations: Stories, Articles, Verses*. New York: Simon and Schuster, 1966.

——. *Lions and Shadows*. Norfolk, Conn.: New Directions, 1947.

Jackson, Holbrook. *The Printing of Books*. New York: Charles Scribner, 1939.

Jefferson, George. *Edward Garnett: A Life in Literature*. London: Jonathan Cape, 1982.

Johnstone, Richard. *The Will to Believe: Novelists of the Nineteen-Thirties*. Oxford: Oxford Univ. Press, 1982.

Jones, Ernest. *Free Associations: Memories of a Psycho-Analyst*. New York: Basic Books, 1959.

——. *The Life and Work of Sigmund Freud*. 3 vols. New York: Basic Books, 1955–57.

Joseph, Michael. *The Adventure of Publishing*. London: Allan Wingate, 1949.

Kaun, Alexander. *Maxim Gorky and His Russia*. New York: Jonathan Cape, 1931.

Keefe, H. J. *A Century in Print: The Story of Hazell's, 1839–1939*. London: Hazell Watson & Viney, 1939.

Kennedy, Richard. *A Boy at the Hogarth Press*. London: Heinemann, 1972.

Kessler, Harry. *In the Twenties: The Diaries of Harry Kessler (1918–1937)*. Intro. Otto Friedrich and trans. Charles Kessler. New York: Holt, Rinehart & Winston, 1971.

Keynes, John Maynard. "Are Books Too Dear?" *Nation and Athenaeum* 40 (1927): 788.

——. *The Collected Writings of John Maynard Keynes*. 25 vols. London: Macmillan–Cambridge Univ. Press, 1971–78.

Kingsford, R. J. L. *The Publishers Association, 1896–1946*. Cambridge: Cambridge Univ. Press, 1970.

Kirkpatrick, B. J. *A Bibliography of E. M. Forster*. London: Rupert Hart-Davis, 1965.

——. *A Bibliography of Virginia Woolf*. 3d ed. Oxford: Clarendon Press, 1980.

Kryzytski, Serge. *The Works of Ivan Bunin*. The Hague: Mouton, 1971.

Kulkarni, H. B. *Stephen Spender: Works and Criticism, an Annotated Bibliography*. New York: Garland, 1976.

Laski, Harold J. *The Danger of Being a Gentleman and Other Essays*. New York: Viking, 1940.

Lawrence, D. H. *The Quest for Rananim: D. H. Lawrence's Letters to S. S. Koteliansky, 1914 to 1930*. Ed. George J. Zytaruk. Montreal: McGill-Queen's Univ. Press, 1970.

Lea, F. A. *The Life of John Middleton Murry*. London: Methuen, 1959.

Leaska, Mitchell. *The Novels of Virginia Woolf: From Beginnings to End*. New York: John Jay Press, 1977.

Leavis, F. R. "This Poetical Renascence." *Scrutiny* 2 (1933): 65–76.

Lee, Hermione. Introduction to *The Hogarth Letters*. Athens: Univ. of Georgia Press, 1986.

——. *The Novels of Virginia Woolf*. New York: Holmes and Meier, 1977.

Lehmann, John. *In My Own Time: Memoirs of a Literary Life*. Boston: Little, Brown, 1969.

——. *Thrown to the Woolfs*. New York: Holt, Rinehart and Winston, 1979.

——. "Two of the Conspirators." *Twentieth Century Literature* 22 (1976): 264–75.

Lewanski, Richard, comp. *The Slavic Literatures*. Vol. 2 of *The Literature of the World in Translation*. New York: New York Public Library, 1967.

Lotze, Dieter. *Imre Madách*. Boston: Twayne, 1981.

Ludeking, Leila M. "Bibliography of Works by Leonard Sidney Woolf (1880–1969)." *Virginia Woolf Quarterly* 1 (1972): 120–40.

Maguire, Robert A. *Red Virgin Soil: Soviet Literature in the 1920s*. Princeton, N.J.: Princeton Univ. Press, 1968.

Maitland, Frederic W. *The Life and Letters of Leslie Stephen*. London, 1906; rpt. Detroit: Gale Research, 1968.

Majumber, Robin, and Allen McLaurin, eds. *Virginia Woolf: The Critical Heritage*. London: Routledge & Kegan Paul, 1975.

Mansfield, Katherine. *The Collected Letters of Katherine Mansfield*. Ed. Vincent O'Sullivan and Margaret Scott. 2 vols. Oxford: Clarendon Press, 1984–87.

Mantz, Ruth. *A Critical Bibliography of Katherine Mansfield*. London, 1931; rpt. New York: Burt Franklin, 1968.

Marcus, Jane. *Art and Anger: Reading like a Woman*. Columbus; Ohio State Univ. Press, 1988.

——. "Virginia Woolf and Her Violin: Mothering, Madness, and Music." In *Mothering the Mind*. Ed. Ruth Perry and Martine Watson Brownley. New York: Holmes & Meier, 1984, pp. 180–201.

——, ed. *Virginia Woolf: A Feminist Slant*. Lincoln: Univ. of Nebraska Press, 1983.

Margulies, Sylvia R. *The Pilgrimage to Russia: The Soviet Union and the Treatment of Foreigners, 1924–37*. Madison: Univ. of Wisconsin Press, 1968.

Mark, Thomas R. "Mádach Revisited: Toward a New Translation of the *Tragedy of Man*." *Canadian-American Review of Hungarian Studies* 4 (1977): 145–54.

Martin, Jay. *Conrad Aiken: A Life of His Art*. Princeton, N.J.: Princeton Univ. Press, 1962.

Martin, Kingsley. *Harold Laski (1893–1950): A Biographical Memoire*. London: Victor Gollancz, 1953.

Mason, Eudo C. *Rilke, Europe, and the English-Speaking World*. Cambridge: Cambridge Univ. Press, 1961.

Maude, Aylmer. *The Life of Tolstoy*. 2 vols. New York: Dodd, Mead, 1910.

Mellown, E. W. *Edwin Muir*. Boston: Twayne, 1979.

Mengham, Rod. *The Idiom of Time: The Writings of Henry Green*. Cambridge: Cambridge Univ. Press, 1982.

Meynell, Francis. *My Lives*. London: Bodley Head, 1971.

Middleton, Victoria. "*The Years*: 'A Deliberate Failure.'" *Bulletin of the New York Public Library* 80 (1977): 158–71.

Miller, Liam. *The Dun Emer Press, Later the Cuala Press*. Preface by Michael B. Yeats. Dublin: Dolmen Press, 1973.

Millgate, Michael. "Interview with Miss Compton-Burnett." In *The Art of I. Compton-Burnett: A Collection of Critical Essays*. Ed. Charles Burkhart. London: Victor Gollancz, 1972, pp. 32–47.

Milstad, George H. *Duckworth & Co.: Fifty Years, 1898–1948*. London: Duckworth, 1948.

Mirsky, Prince D. S. *A History of Russian Literature, from Earliest Times to the Death of Dostoevsky*. New York: Alfred A. Knopf, 1927.

——. *The Intelligentsia of Great Britain*. Trans. Alec Brown. New York: Covici-Friede, 1935.

——. *Modern Russian Literature*. London: Oxford Univ. Press, 1925.

Moloney, Brian. *Italo Svevo: A Critical Introduction*. Edinburgh: Edinburgh Univ. Press, 1974.

Montaigne, Michel. *The Complete Works of Montaigne*. Trans. Donald M. Frame. Stanford, Calif.: Stanford Univ. Press, 1957.

Moody, A. D. *Thomas Stearnes Eliot, Poet*. Cambridge: Cambridge Univ. Press, 1979.

Moran, James. "The Seizin Press of Laura Riding and Robert Graves." *Black Art* 2 (1963): 34–38.

Morpurgo, J. E. *Allen Lane, King Penguin*. London: Hutchinson, 1979.

Muchnic, Helen. *Dostoevsky's English Reputation (1881–1936)*. Northhampton, 1938; rpt. New York: Octagon Books, 1969.

——. *From Gorky to Pasternak: Six Writers in Soviet Russia*. New York: Random House, 1961.

Muir, Edwin. *An Autobiography*. London, 1954; rpt. New York: Seabury Press, 1968.

——. *Collected Poems*. Preface by T. S. Eliot. New York: Oxford Univ. Press, 1965.

——. *Selected Letters of Edwin Muir*. Ed. P. H. Butter. London: Hogarth Press, 1974.

Muir, Willa. *Women: An Inquiry*. London: Hogarth Press, 1925.

Mumby, Frank A. *Publishing and Bookselling: A History from the Earliest Times to the Present Day*. 1930; rpt. London: Jonathan Cape, 1956.

——, and Frances H. S. Stallybrass. *From Swan Sonnenschein to George Allen & Unwin*. London: George Allen & Unwin, 1955.

Muntan, Alan, and Alan Young, eds. *Seven Writers of the English Left: A Bibliography of Literature and Politics, 1916–1980*. New York: Garland, 1981.

Nansen, Fridtjof. *Adventure and Other Papers*. London, 1927; rpt. Freeport, N.Y.: Books for Libraries Press, 1967.

Neff, Emory. *Edwin Arlington Robinson*. 1948; rpt. New York: Russell & Russell, 1968.

Nicolson, Harold. *Diaries and Letters, 1930–1939*. Ed. Nigel Nicolson. London: Collins, 1966.

Nicolson, Nigel. *Portrait of a Marriage*. New York: Atheneum, 1973.

Nilsson, Nils Åke. "Through the Wrong End of Binoculars: An Introduction to Jury Olesa." In *Major Soviet Writers*. Ed. Edward J. Brown. New York: Oxford Univ. Press, 1973, pp. 254–79.

North, Michael. *Henry Green and the Writing of His Generation*. Charlottesville: Univ. Press of Virginia, 1984.

Olesha, Yuri. *Envy*. Intro. Gleb Struve. Trans. P. Ross. London: Westhouse, 1947.

Olivier, Sydney. *Letters and Selected Writings*. Ed. Margaret Olivier, London: Allen and Unwin, 1948.

O'Shea, Edward. "Yeats as Editor: Dorothy Wellesley's *Selections*." *English Language Notes* 11 (1973): 112–18.

Österling, Anders. "The Literary Prize." H. Schück, R. Sohlman, A. Österling, et al. *Nobel, the Man and His Prizes*. Ed. the Nobel Foundation. Rev. ed. New York: Elsevier, 1962, pp.75–130.

Palmer, Herbert E. *The Collected Poems of H. E. Palmer*. London: Ernest Benn, 1933.

Partridge, Frances. *Julia: A Portrait of Julia Strachey by Herself and Frances Partridge*. Boston: Little, Brown, 1983.

Plomer, William. *At Home*. New York: Noonday Press, 1958.

——. *The Autobiography of William Plomer*. Postscript by Simon Nowell-Smith. New York: Taplinger, 1976.

——. *Collected Poems*. London: Jonathan Cape, 1973.

——. *Double Lives*. 1940; rpt. London: Jonathan Cape, 1950.

Poggioli, Renato. *The Phoenix and the Spider*. Cambridge: Harvard Univ. Press, 1957.

Poole, Roger. *The Unknown Virginia Woolf*. London: Cambridge Univ. Press, 1978.

Powell, Anthony. *Messengers of Day*. New York: Holt, Rinehart and Winston, 1978.

Radin. Grace. *Virginia Woolf's* The Years: *The Evolution of a Novel*. Knoxville: Univ. of Tennessee Press, 1981.

Ransom, John Crowe. *Selected Letters of John Crowe Ransom*. Ed. Thomas D. Young and George Core. Baton Rouge: Louisiana State Univ. Press, 1985.

Ransom, Will. *Private Presses and Their Books*. New York: R. R. Bowker, 1929.

Rathbone, Irene. "Nancy Cunard." In *Nancy Cunard: Brave Poet, Indomitable Rebel*. Ed. Hugh Ford. New York: Chilton Book Co., 1968, pp. 242–59.

Read, Herbert. *Collected Poems*. Norfolk, Conn.: New Directions, n.d.

——. "The Present State of Poetry: In England." *Kenyon Review* 1 (1939): 359–69.

Reynolds, Michael S. *Hemingway's Reading, 1910–1940*. Princeton, N.J.: Princeton Univ. Press, 1981.

Rhein, Donna E. *The Handprinted Books of Leonard and Virginia Woolf at the Hogarth Press, 1917–1932*. Ann Arbor: UMI Research Press, 1985.

Rhondda, Viscountess. *Leisured Women*. London: Hogarth Press, 1928.

Riding, Laura, and Robert Graves. *A Survey of Modernist Poetry*. London: Heinemann, 1927.

Ritzer, Walter. *Rainer Maria Rilke: Bibliographie*. Vienna: Verlag O. Kerry, 1951.

Riviere, Joan. "An Intimate Impression." *Freud as We Knew Him*. Ed. Hendrik Ruitenbeek. Detroit: Wayne State Univ. Press, 1973.

Roberts, Michael. *Critique of Poetry*. London: Jonathan Cape, 1934.

——. "Notes on English Poets." *Poetry* 39 (1932): 271–79.

Robinson, Edwin Arlington. *Edwin Arlington Robinson's Letters to Edith Brower*. Ed. Richard Brower. Cambridge: Belknap Press, 1968.

——. *Selected Letters*. Ed. Ridgley Torrence. New York: Macmillan Co., 1940.

——. *Uncollected Poems and Prose*. Ed. Richard Cary. Waterville: Colby College Press, 1975.

Rosenbaum, S. P. "The First Book of Bloomsbury." *Twentieth Century Literature* 30 (1984): 388–403.

——. *Victorian Bloomsbury*. New York: St. Martin's Press, 1987.

Rosner, Charles. *The Growth of the Book-Jacket*. Cambridge: Harvard Univ. Press, 1954.

Ross, Robert H. *The Georgian Revolt, 1910–1922: Rise and Fall of a Poetic Ideal*. Carbondale: Southern Illinois Univ. Press, 1965.

Russell, John. "There It Is." *Kenyon Review* 26 (1964): 433–65.

Sackville-West, Vita. *The Letters of Vita Sackville-West to Virginia Woolf*. Ed. Louise DeSalvo and Mitchell Leaska. New York: William Morrow, 1985.

Sawyer, Julian. *Gertrude Stein: A Bibliography*. 1940; rpt. New York: Folcroft Library Editions, 1972.

Schlapp, Otto. "Correspondence." *Times Literary Supplement* 32 (1933): 230.

Schroeder, Adolf. E. "Rainer Maria Rilke in America: A Bibliography, 1926–1951." *Monatshefte* 44 (1952): 27–38.

Segal, Hanna. *Introduction to the Work of Melanie Klein*. London: Hogarth Press, 1973.

Shone, Richard. *Bloomsbury Portraits: Vanessa Bell, Duncan Grant, and Their Circle*. Oxford: Phaidon Press, 1976.

Silver, Brenda R. " 'Anon' and 'The Reader': Virginia Woolf's Last Essays." *Twentieth Century Literature* 25 (1979): 356–441.

——. "*Three Guineas* Before and After: Further Answers to Correspondents." In *Virginia Woolf: A Feminist Slant*. Ed. Jane Marcus. Lincoln: Univ. of Nebraska Press, 1983, pp. 254–76.

——, ed. *Virginia Woolf's Reading Notebooks*. Princeton, N.J.: Princeton Univ. Press, 1983.

Sitwell, Edith. "Miss Stein's Stories." *Nation and Athenaeum* 33 (1923): 492; rpt. in *Critical Essays on Gertrude Stein*. Ed. Michael J. Hoffman. Boston: G. K. Hall & Co., 1986.

——. *Poetry and Criticism*. London: Hogarth Press, 1925.

Skelton, Robin, ed. *Herbert Read: A Memorial Symposium*. London: Methuen, 1969.

Slonim, Marc. *Modern Russian Literature: From Chekhov to the Present*. New York: Oxford Univ. Press, 1953.

Southern, Terry. "Henry Green." *Paris Review,* Summer 1958, pp. 61–77.

Spater, George. "The Monks House Library." *Virginia Woolf Quarterly* 1 (1973) 60–65.

——, and Ian Parsons. *A Marriage of True Minds: An Intimate Portrait of Leonard and Virginia Woolf*. New York: Harcourt Brace Jovanovich, 1977.

Spender, Stephen. *The Destructive Element*. London: Jonathan Cape, 1935.

——. "The Importance of Meaning." *Translation* 1 (1973) 32–37.

——. *Letters to Christopher*. Ed. Lee Bartlett. Santa Barbara, Calif.: Black Sparrow Press, 1980.

——. *The Thirties and After: Poetry, Politics, and People, 1933–1970*. New York: Random House, 1978.

——. *World within World*. London: Hamish Hamilton, 1951.

Sprigge, Elizabeth. *Gertrude Stein: Her Life and Work*. New York: Harper & Brothers, 1957.

Stansky, Peter, and William Abrahams. *Journey to the Frontier: Two Roads to the Spanish Civil War*. Boston: Little, Brown, 1966.

Starr, Mark. *Lies and Hate in Education*. London: Hogarth Press, 1929.

Stein, Gertrude. *The Autobiography of Alice B. Toklas*. New York: Vintage Books, 1960.

Stephen, Leslie. *Men, Books, and Mountains: Essays by Leslie Stephen*. Comp. S. O. A. Ullmann. Minneapolis: Univ. of Minnesota Press, 1956.

Stevens, Michael. *V. Sackville-West: A Critical Biography*. New York: Charles Scribners, 1974.

Strachey, James, and Alix Strachey. *Bloomsbury/Freud: The Letters of James and Alix Strachey, 1924–25*. Ed. Perry Meisel and Walter Kendrick. New York: Basic Books, 1985.

Strachey, Ray. *The Cause: A Short History of the Women's Movement in Great Britain*. London, 1928; rpt. Port Washington: Kennikat Press, 1969.

Struve, Gleb. "The Art of Ivan Bunin." *Slavonic and East European Review* 11 (1933): 423–36.

Sutherland, Donald. *Gertrude Stein: A Biography of Her Work*. New Haven: Yale Univ. Press, 1951.

Timms, Edward, and Naomi Segal, eds. *Freud in Exile: Psychoanalysis and Its Vicissitudes*. New Haven: Yale Univ. Press, 1988.

Treece, Henry ed. *Herbert Read: An Introduction to His Work by Various Hands*. London, 1944; rpt. Port Washington: Kennikat Press, 1969.

Troyat, Henri. *Tolstoy*. Trans. Nancy Amphoux. Garden City, N.Y.: Doubleday, 1967.

Twyman, Michael. *Printing, 1770–1970: An Illustrated History of Its Development and Uses in England*. London: Eyre & Spottiswoode, 1970.

Unwin, Stanley. *The Truth about a Publisher*. London: George Allen & Unwin, 1960.

——. *The Truth about Publishing*. London: George Allen & Unwin, 1926.

Van der Post, Laurens. Introduction to *Turbott Woolfe*, by William Plomer. London, 1926; rpt. Oxford: Oxford Univ. Press, 1985.

Wasiolek, Edward, ed. *The Notebooks of* The Possessed. Trans. Victor Terras. Chicago: Univ. of Chicago Press, 1968.

Wellesley, Dorothy. *Early Light: The Collected Poems of Dorothy Wellesley*. London: Rupert Hart-Davis, 1955.

——. *Far Have I Travelled*. London: James Barrie, 1952.

West, Anthony. *H. G. Wells: Aspects of a Life*. New York: Random House, 1984.

Wexler, Joyce Piell. *Laura Riding: Pursuit of Truth*. Athens: Ohio Univ. Press, 1979.

Whitall, James. *English Years*. New York: Harcourt, Brace, 1935.

Williams, William E. *The Penguin Story, 1935–56*. London: Penguin Books, 1956.

Wilson, Duncan. *Leonard Woolf: A Political Biography*. London: Hogarth Press, 1978.

Woodcock, George. *Herbert Read: The Stream and the Source*. London: Faber & Faber, 1972.

Woodward, Daniel H. "Notes on the Publishing History and Text of *The Waste Land*." *Papers of the Bibliographical Society of America* 58 (1964): 252–69.

Woolf, Leonard. *Barbarians at the Gate*. London: Victor Gollancz, 1939.

——. *Beginning Again: An Autobiography of the Years 1911 to 1918*. New York: Harcourt, Brace & World, 1964.

——. *Diaries in Ceylon, 1908–1911: Records of a Colonial Administrator*. Colombo: Ceylon Historical Journal, 1962.

——. *Downhill All the Way: An Autobiography of the Years 1919 to 1939*. New York: Harcourt, Brace & World, 1967.

——. *Empire and Commerce in Africa: A Study in Economic Imperialism.* London, 1919; rpt. New York: Howard Fertig, 1968.

——. *Growing: An Autobiography of the Years 1904 to 1911.* New York: Harcourt, Brace & World, 1961.

——. *The Journey Not the Arrival Matters: An Autobiography of the Years 1939 to 1969.* London: Hogarth Press, 1969.

——. "Kot." *New Stateman and Nation* 49 (1955): 170, 172.

——. *Letters of Leonard Woolf.* Ed. Frederic Spotts. New York: Harcourt Brace Jovanovich, 1989.

——. "On Advertising Books." *Nation and Athenaeum* 40 (1927): 849.

——. *Quack, Quack!* London: Hogarth Press, 1935.

——. *Sowing: An Autobiography of the Years 1880 to 1904.* London: Hogarth Press, 1960.

Woolf, Virginia. *Collected Essays.* 4 vols. London: Hogarth Press, 1966–67.

——. *Contemporary Writers.* New York: Harcourt, Brace & World, 1965.

——. *The Diary of Virginia Woolf.* Ed. Anne Olivier Bell. 4 vols. New York: Harcourt Brace Jovanovich, 1977–84.

——. "Introductory Letter." In *Life as We Have Known It.* Ed. Margaret Llewelyn Davies. London: Hogarth Press, 1931.

——. *The Letters of Virginia Woolf.* Ed Nigel Nicolson and Joanne Trautmann. 6 vols. New York: Harcourt Brace Jovanovich, 1975–80.

——. *Moments of Being: Unpublished Autobiographical Writings.* Ed. Jeanne Schulkind. New York: Harcourt Brace Jovanovich, 1976.

——. *Virginia Woolf's Reading Notebooks.* Ed. Brenda Silver. Princeton, N.J.: Princeton Univ. Press, 1983.

Woolmer, J. Howard. *A Checklist of the Hogarth Press, 1917–1946.* Revere, Pa.: Woolmer, Brotherson, 1986.

Wright, A. W. *G. D. H. Cole and Socialist Democracy.* Oxford: Clarendon Press, 1979.

Yeats, W. B. *Letters on Poetry from W. B. Yeats to Dorothy Wellesley.* London: Oxford Univ. Press, 1940.

Zoete, Beryl de. "Ettore Schmitz (Italo Svevo)." *Nation and Athenaeum* 44 (1929): 521–22.

INDEX